Applied Research Approaches to Technology, Healthcare, and Business

Darrell Norman Burrell
Marymount University, USA

A volume in the Advances in Human and Social
Aspects of Technology (AHSAT) Book Series

Published in the United States of America by
  IGI Global
  Information Science Reference (an imprint of IGI Global)
  701 E. Chocolate Avenue
  Hershey PA, USA 17033
  Tel: 717-533-8845
  Fax: 717-533-8661
  E-mail: cust@igi-global.com
  Web site: http://www.igi-global.com

Library of Congress Cataloging-in-Publication Data

Names: Burrell, Darrell, 1966- editor.
Title: Applied research approaches to technology, healthcare, and business
  / edited by: Darrell Burrell.
Description: Hershey PA : Information Science Reference, [2024] | Includes
  bibliographical references. | Summary: "The editors embark on a journey
  through the intricate intersections of technology, healthcare, and
  business, guided by the underlying philosophy that knowledge is not just
  for academia, but for application in the real world"-- Provided by
  publisher.
Identifiers: LCCN 2023040147 (print) | LCCN 2023040148 (ebook) | ISBN
  9798369316306 (hardcover) | ISBN 9798369316313 (ebook)
Subjects: LCSH: Research, Industrial--Case studies.
Classification: LCC T175 .A695 2024 (print) | LCC T175 (ebook) | DDC
  607.2--dc23/eng/20230907
LC record available at https://lccn.loc.gov/2023040147
LC ebook record available at https://lccn.loc.gov/2023040148

This book is published in the IGI Global book series Advances in Human and Social Aspects of Technology (AHSAT) (ISSN: 2328-1316; eISSN: 2328-1324)

British Cataloguing in Publication Data
A Cataloguing in Publication record for this book is available from the British Library.

All work contributed to this book is new, previously-unpublished material. The views expressed in this book are those of the authors, but not necessarily of the publisher.

For electronic access to this publication, please contact: eresources@igi-global.com.

Advances in Human and Social Aspects of Technology (AHSAT) Book Series

Mehdi Khosrow-Pour, D.B.A.
Information Resources Management Association, USA

ISSN:2328-1316
EISSN:2328-1324

MISSION

In recent years, the societal impact of technology has been noted as we become increasingly more connected and are presented with more digital tools and devices. With the popularity of digital devices such as cell phones and tablets, it is crucial to consider the implications of our digital dependence and the presence of technology in our everyday lives.

The **Advances in Human and Social Aspects of Technology (AHSAT) Book Series** seeks to explore the ways in which society and human beings have been affected by technology and how the technological revolution has changed the way we conduct our lives as well as our behavior. The AHSAT book series aims to publish the most cutting-edge research on human behavior and interaction with technology and the ways in which the digital age is changing society.

COVERAGE

- Cyber Bullying
- End-User Computing
- Public Access to ICTs
- Technology and Social Change
- Technology and Freedom of Speech
- Digital Identity
- Gender and Technology
- Human-Computer Interaction
- Technoself
- Human Rights and Digitization

IGI Global is currently accepting manuscripts for publication within this series. To submit a proposal for a volume in this series, please contact our Acquisition Editors at Acquisitions@igi-global.com or visit: http://www.igi-global.com/publish/.

Titles in this Series

For a list of additional titles in this series, please visit: www.igi-global.com/book-series

Analyzing New Forms of Social Disorders in Modern Virtual Environments
Milica Boskovic (Faculty of Diplomacy and Security, University Union Nikola Tesla, Serbia) Gordana Misev (Ministry of Mining and Energy Republic of Serbia, Serbia) and Nenad Putnik (Faculty of Security Studies, University of Belgrade, Serbia)
Information Science Reference • copyright 2023 • 284pp • H/C (ISBN: 9781668457603) • US $225.00 (our price)

Adoption and Use of Technology Tools and Services by Economically Disadvantaged Communities Implications for Growth and Sustainability
Alice S. Etim (Winston-Salem State University, USA)
Information Science Reference • copyright 2023 • 300pp • H/C (ISBN: 9781668453476) • US $225.00 (our price)

Investigating the Impact of AI on Ethics and Spirituality
Swati Chakraborty (GLA University, India & Concordia University, Canada)
Information Science Reference • copyright 2023 • 300pp • H/C (ISBN: 9781668491966) • US $225.00 (our price)

Philosophy of Artificial Intelligence and Its Place in Society
Luiz Moutinho (University of Suffolk, UK) Luís Cavique (Universidade Aberta, Portugal) and Enrique Bigné (Universitat de València, Spain)
Engineering Science Reference • copyright 2023 • 320pp • H/C (ISBN: 9781668495919) • US $215.00 (our price)

Advances in Cyberology and the Advent of the Next-Gen Information Revolution
Mohd Shahid Husain (College of Applied Sciences, University of Technology and Applied Sciences, Oman) Mohammad Faisal (Integral University, Lucknow, India) Halima Sadia (Integral University, Lucknow, India) Tasneem Ahmad (Advanced Computing Research Lab, Integral University, Lucknow, India) and Saurabh Shukla (Data Science Institute, National University of Ireland, Galway, Ireland)
Information Science Reference • copyright 2023 • 271pp • H/C (ISBN: 9781668481332) • US $215.00 (our price)

Handbook of Research on Perspectives on Society and Technology Addiction
Rengim Sine Nazlı (Bolu Abant İzzet Baysal University, Turkey) and Gülşah Sari (Aksaray University, Turkey)
Information Science Reference • copyright 2023 • 603pp • H/C (ISBN: 9781668483978) • US $270.00 (our price)

Impact of Disruptive Technologies on the Socio-Economic Development of Emerging Countries
Fredrick Japhet Mtenzi (Institute for Educational Development, The Aga Khan University, Tanzania) George S. Oreku (The Open University of Tanzania, Tanzania) and Dennis M. Lupiana (Institute of Finance Management, Tanzania)

701 East Chocolate Avenue, Hershey, PA 17033, USA
Tel: 717-533-8845 x100 • Fax: 717-533-8661
E-Mail: cust@igi-global.com • www.igi-global.com

Table of Contents

Detailed Table of Contents

    Allison Huff, College of Medicine, University of Arizona, USA
    Darrell Norman Burrell, Marymount University, USA
    Calvin Nobles, Illinois Institute of Technology, USA
    Kevin Richardson, Capitol Technology University, USA
    Jorja Brittany Wright, Capitol Technology University, USA
    Sharon L. Burton, Capitol Technology University, USA
    Angel J. Jones, University of Virginia, USA
    Delores Springs, Regent University, USA
    Marwan Omar, Illinois Institute of Technology, USA
    Kim Brown-Jackson, Capitol Technology University, USA

In the rapidly advancing landscape of biotechnology, laboratories, and healthcare research, the criticality of robust cybersecurity risk management techniques cannot be overstated. As these industries increasingly rely on interconnected technologies and digitized data for innovation and patient care, they become attractive targets for malicious cyber threats. This chapter underscores the paramount importance for biotechnology companies, laboratories, and healthcare research organizations to develop real-world and practical cybersecurity risk management techniques. By proactively addressing cybersecurity vulnerabilities, these entities can safeguard their sensitive data, protect intellectual property, ensure patient privacy, and maintain the trust of stakeholders. This chapter emphasizes the necessity of adopting effective cybersecurity strategies tailored to the specific needs of each sector, taking into account the dynamic threat landscape and the potential consequences of cyber incidents.

    Kevin Richardson, Edward Waters University, USA

By definition, sustainability means meeting personal needs without jeopardizing the ability of future generations to meet their own needs. In that context, sustainability calls for the Earth's environmental systems to be balanced while ensuring that natural resources are consumed at a rate that they are naturally replenished. Researches on sustainability and environmental racism expound on the overall impacts on blacks by showing that this group is more highly affected by pollution than the white population. Scholars note that the main issue with environmental racism is that most American citizens hold onto the belief that everybody is subject to equal opportunities. Such an approach is detrimental since the concept of environmental injustice is treated as a personal choice and not a matter of racial discrimination. The lack of a clear understanding of environmental racism undermines all efforts to fix the problem, which entails focusing on race as a notable predictor of an individual's exposure to environmental hazards.

Chapter 3

    Eugene J. Lewis, Capitol Technology University, USA
    Maria D. Baez, Capitol Technology University, USA

Nearly 1 billion emails were exposed in 1 single year affecting 20% or 1 and 5 internet users, causing cyber security warfare worldwide. Under the control theoretic approach, users can prescribe defense actions to security alerts that provide system alerts of cyber-attacks in progress when the network is compromised. This critical analytical view of the World Economic Forum statistical data surrounds the five major drivers affecting the geopolitical and economic conditions of the top 50 nations based on public motivation, government policy, education system, labor market, and population inclusivity. The statistical data illustrates how data breaches have become an ongoing business issue causing an average of $4.35 million annually per organization. Within the cyber security market spectrum, control theory can address some of the challenges associated with geopolitical and economic drivers affecting cyber security warfare by providing a framework for designing and implementing adaptive security systems.

Chapter 4

    Stacey L. Morin, Marymount University, USA

This chapter illustrates how corporations need to go beyond the D in diversity and focus on the E in equity and I for inclusion to prioritize the worker based on the alignment of critical theory. The literature search led to the discovery of critical theory, which was then used to inform a strategic intervention. Diversity is existence of variations of different characteristics in a group of people. Equity is fair treatment, access, and advancement for each person in an organization. Inclusion is an outcome to ensure those who are diverse feel and/or are welcomed. Obstacles in the way of the E and I need to be addressed if organizations truly want to create a robust DEI program for their workers. This chapter examines how scholars and senior leadership will acknowledge inequity and exclusive behavior in their organizations, bringing the awareness of the need to focus on the E and I.

Chapter 5

    Paula Anderson, PACE Consulting, USA

African American female leaders in organizations face several issues due to the intersection of their race and gender, including psychological distress, intersectional invisibility, and discrimination in their role as leaders. The purpose of this qualitative transcendental phenomenological research study was to explore the psychological distress experiences of African American female leaders who encountered intersectional invisibility at the middle management leadership level in large U.S. organizations. This study revealed several psychological distress experiences and revealed the impact their psychological distress experiences had on their health and career decisions. Three theoretical constructs, social stress theory, the model of intersectional invisibility, and role congruity theory, framed and supported this study. One central research question and three sub-questions informed the study design. Semi structured interviews with 10 African American female middle-level leaders revealed six themes.

Chapter 6
Jorja B. Wright, Capitol Technology University, USA

The planning fallacy is a specific bias pertaining to judgment errors that hamper the success cybersecurity business planning in healthcare organizations. The concepts explored include errors in human judgment, planning fallacy (cognitive bias), and how to mitigate this cognitive error. First, important concepts will be defined: cognitive bias, planning fallacy, and heuristic. Next, how cognitive biases contribute to human error in the decision-making process; third, the planning fallacy and how it pertains to both collaborative and complexity leadership theories will be analyzed. Finally, this chapter will conclude with possible implications for leaders to alleviate the consequences of the planning fallacy and provide insights for more effective approaches to business continuity planning for medical organizations.

Chapter 7
Jessica Parker, Marymount University, USA

This cybersecurity case study provides a comprehensive remediation plan for an organization that recently experienced a data breach and lacks a risk management strategy. Starting with a current state analysis, the plan includes strategies to support the new organizational behaviors, understanding and aligning company culture, supporting changes with ethical decision-making and strong leadership, and ensuring changes are maintained and reinforced. Foundation theories and models are used to support the plan: human factors, theory of constraints, the plan-do-check-act cycle, Schein's model of organizational culture, the Deal and Kennedy culture model, Lewin's change management model, nudge theory, the duty-based approach to ethical decision-making, and transformational leadership. The resulting plan ensures that the organization is able to prevent most cyberattacks and has a ready response plan for dealing with any future breaches.

Chapter 8
DeAnjelo J. L. Bradley, Capital Technology University, USA

Working well under tremendous strain for relatively short periods is a topic of great importance in firefighting. This study put firefighters through a series of stressful solo smoke dives around a dark, winding simulation track to examine how their stress reactions affected their cognitive function. Male firefighters' heart rates were recorded during a smoke-diving exercise and compared with baseline readings and maximal rates. Male firefighters were used to studying these stressors. The firefighters thought aloud as they performed the smoke-diving maneuver to demonstrate their mental acuity. This study used a content analysis review of the literature published between the years 2017 to 2021 to define the problem, outline its complexities, and find needed solutions from dispersed sources.

Chapter 9

The mystification of the term sustainability with society's desiderata, desegregate sustainability into three types: social, economic, and environmental. The triple bottom line needs to be integrated into every stratum of the business for corporate responsibility. The optimal performance ensures sustainability and brings together strategies that relate to the environment and society. This chapter serves as a road map to bring about a zero triple bottom line, thus ensuring a sustainable business ecosystem. A sustainability strategy aligns business sustainability goals with environmental and social stewardship goals. Corporations need to create a synergistic relationship with key stakeholders and the global communities regarding the biosphere. A call of duty requires that corporations/firms need go beyond product stewardship into beneficial relationships relating to the communities and the Earth. Ample opportunities and significant challenges abound for organizations globally.

Chapter 10

The evolution of technology has brought about a transformation in the delivery and utilization of financial services. Companies have leveraged technology to create value in the digital realm, presenting innovative opportunities that prioritize customer-centric approaches. Despite the numerous benefits of e-banking, the user experience during authentication has had an impact on its adoption in developing economies. Hence, this study investigated the authentication experience of users in the realm of e-banking using Nigeria as a case study. The research used five constructs of UTAUT2 to analyze this phenomenon.

Chapter 11

More than half the population today lives in urban areas. The UN predicts with 80% confidence that the global population will get to between 9.6 billion and 12.3 billion people within the 21st century. Population increase leads to more people in the city. More people in the city translates to new challenges that need addressing. When addressing the new challenges, cities evolve by improving the efficiency of services. Eventually, cities change in both structure and composition. In helping show how the cities have changed, the authors utilized the industrial revolution theory which occurred in stages from the first industrial revolution to Industry 5.0. Just like the industrial revolution, cities evolve in stages with the latter stage using the success of the former stage as building blocks. Smart cities which are characterized by progressive city plans and state-of-the-art infrastructure act as a building block for cognitive cities which are characterized by the ability to have connectivity, and common data architecture for people to share and drive innovation.

Leadership development and clinical counseling supervision have an established position in the literature. Counseling leadership development has been researched by Chang et al. and Peters et al. while clinical counseling supervision has been explored by Bernard and Goodyear and Elswick et al. This study defined leadership as a biodirectional social influence process that features a supervisor questing for willing involvement of supervisees to realize organizational objectives while also demonstrating managerial leadership in the organization's structure. Research has focused on the convergence of these disciplines. However, a 20-year metastudy of publication characteristics in Counselor Education and Supervision found no direct category featuring on organizational leadership or business topics. This qualitative phenomenological study explored the clinical healthcare leadership development experiences of eight clinical counseling supervisors.

Chapter 13

The healthcare industry is one of the industries that has undergone a substantial digital transformation. The paperwork initially used by hospitals has been changed to cloud services, smart devices, and the introduction of the internet of medical things (IoMT). Electronic health records have improved healthcare quality, among other factors. The increased cyber security in the healthcare system and workers' limited knowledge of cyber security has been attributed to workers' negligence. The inability to secure healthcare information and data has intense implications for the healthcare organization. These threats may be limited through ethical decision-making models and organizational culture models. The leadership theory, decision-making model, strategy model theory, change managerial theory, and desired state of the organizational culture are some of the methodologies that can be used in securing cyber threats. The topic concerning the various methods of protecting healthcare information from cyberbullies is important because it protects all data categories from damage and theft.

This case study begins with a company purchase card audit that brought years of unethical purchasing practices to light. The author discusses how the purchases impacted organizational culture, leadership, and employee well-being. Risk management policies are examined to determine the best methods to reduce employee fallout impacting the organization. Change management, organizational culture, and leadership theories are analyzed to mitigate the negative impact unethical leadership has on the overall health of an organization.

Chapter 15

The modern public sector confronts myriad crises, which demand sound decision-making in turbulent systems. More and more contemporary problems reveal long-held systemic injustices, inequity, and the inadequacy of public policies to create genuine social change. Still, modern society considers pluralism and diversity as unimpressive and toxic. Public administration must prioritize the ethnic mosaic to contribute to practical and effective global policymaking. Transformational leadership proposes a cultural metamorphosis focusing on approach and values to achieve institutional effectiveness. This framework is relevant to contemporary public leadership as it concentrates on moral and ethical markers, dynamism in the global economy, culture as the backdrop of change, innovation through ingenuity and intellectual motivation, and optimal performance through public service inspiration. This chapter explores the potential of transformational leadership to promote diversity in the public room and build a just and impactful society.

Chapter 16

Executive leadership coaching can have significant benefits for police officers and law enforcement agencies in addressing critical issues such as race relations, misconduct, and professionalism. Leadership coaches can help police officers develop a deeper understanding of their own biases and improve their cultural competence. This increased self-awareness enables leaders to foster a more inclusive and respectful work environment, promoting better relationships between officers and diverse communities. Additionally, coaching can help officers enhance their decision-making skills, encouraging them to implement fair and just policies that prioritize accountability and transparency. Ultimately, executive leadership coaching empowers police officers and their superiors to create a more equitable and trustworthy law enforcement system, benefiting both the officers and the communities they serve. This chapter uses theories and research from the literature to argue for the viability of the deployment of executive coaching as a tool to develop better police leaders at every level.

Chapter 17

Researchers theorize that smart cities are a new concept aligned with the idea of sustainability. In understanding the significance of smart cities in enhanced sustainability, scholars purport that they are towns typified by residents' ability to securely gather, manage, and disseminate information that relates to their daily endeavors ubiquitously and sustainably. The bigger picture about smart cities is that they are linked to the Industry 5.0 theme, which is associated with personalization or adding a human touch to technological collaboration. The concept of Industry 5.0 begs the question of whether African Americans and other People of Color are indeed humans. If they are humans, for sustainability, smart cities need to treat them as humans by providing the needed infrastructure such as charging stations to allow for development in Black and People of Color-dominated neighborhoods. As a result, the concept of personalization in smart cities can be understood from the perspective of incorporating electric vehicles.

*José G. Vargas-Hernandez, Postgraduate and Research Division, Tecnológico Suoerior de
Jalisco Mario Molina Pasquel y Henríquez, Unidad Académica Zapopan, Mexico
Omar C. Vargas-González, Tecnológico Nacional de México, Ciudad Guzmán, Mexico*

This chapter begins the analysis from the assumption that the study of anthropological disciplines applied to organizations is leading to influence the organizational socio-intercultural manifestations and expressions of the anthropology in organizations. The method employed is the analytic-descriptive inducing to the reflection on the main issues related to the theoretical and empirical literature review on the topic. The study concludes that organizational socio-interculture has been influenced by both the ethnographic and quantitative methodology used by the organizational anthropology.

*Sharon L. Burton, Capitol Technology University, USA
Yoshino W. White, Florida State University, USA*

Online education is continuously evolving to enhance learning and reduce costs. In today's fast-paced world, technology is a driving force in education and business, making it crucial to understand the cost-saving benefits and efficiencies of e-learning. This requires careful planning and investment, similar to online business enterprises. Historical data can inform future strategies, but new information and process improvements are necessary to remain competitive. Aligning training with business objectives and evaluating business results are critical for success. Investing in online training benefits both learners and training professionals. Organizational learning capabilities can be tied to business values, and practitioners can learn about the key components needed to calculate ROI in a technology-driven 21st century. This chapter explores the importance of aligning ROI with training, business objectives, evaluating business results, and investing in online training.

Amalisha Sabie Aridi, Capitol Technology University, USA

The Apex Restaurant Group recently went public with several allegations of sexual misconduct against the founder and other executives. The result of the allegations includes a class action complaint lodged by 25 women working within the organization. The whole senior leadership, which was all men, has been replaced by a management team of all women. An organizational development management consultant has been brought in to investigate and recommend viable solutions. This chapter explores the utility of intervention action research to find real-world solutions through the deployment of a consultant.

Chapter 21

The presence of non-reputable journals and low-quality research publications has imposed the development of a machine learning-based system to facilitate the swift and accurate identification of reputable sources. Using Python libraries, such as Pandas and Scikit-learn, this research analyzed data from the Kaggle database collection to create a supervised learning model. The logistic regression classification algorithm was implemented as the basis of this model, while performance metrics were calculated using accuracy, precision, recall, and F1-scores. The results of this study demonstrate an accuracy of 0.9600 for the training data, an accuracy of 0.9433 for the testing data, and a k-5 score accuracy of 0.94. These findings indicate the effectiveness and reliability of the proposed system in recognizing reputable and non-reputable journals. By streamlining the literature review process, this machine learning-based approach can significantly improve students' ability to identify high-quality sources for their academic endeavors.

Chapter 22

According to researchers, environmental, social, and governance (ESG) has been discussed extensively, specifically as a socially responsible investment. Regardless of this exploration, researchers have failed to critically examine the concept of ESG integration and how it impacts the transformation of business models from conventional to more sustainable ones. The chapter utilized a meta-analysis to critically examine previous research findings. The data collection method involved analyzing qualitative and quantitative research that allowed deriving generalized conclusions about ESG and building sustainable business models based on the existing literature. ESG integration benefits the pertinent firms. The advantages are apparent with the study showing that ESG integration results in positive returns on equity and assets. Organizations with strong ESG performance are ranked as best-performing firms and have a lower cost of debt. This benefit means that firms should focus on ESG integration and building new business models resulting in improved financial performance.

Chapter 23

Strategic changes and policy implementation have a significant impact on health and health-related issues. The motivation of this study is to evaluate the opinions of specialist physicians towards city hospitals, which is a new and controversial policy action, and to analyze the findings obtained from these opinions by using various classification and machine learning methods. In order to evaluate their views on city hospitals, specialist physicians were divided into three groups using hierarchical clustering method in terms of health service quality and efficiency, coordination of care components, interdisciplinary care teams, and integration of health services dimensions. The differences between these groups were found to be statistically significant in terms of four dimensions (p < 0.0001). Naïve Bayes (AUC=0.896, F1=0.757), one of the machine learning techniques used to predict clusters obtained from four dimensions obtained from the evaluations of specialist physicians, was found to be the best predictor of four-dimensional classroom evaluations.

Preface

Welcome to *Applied Research Approaches to Technology, Healthcare, and Business*. In this edited reference book, we embark on a journey through the intricate intersections of technology, healthcare, and business, guided by the underlying philosophy that knowledge is not just for academia, but for application in the real world. As editor, I am honored to present this compilation of diverse perspectives that delve into the heart of contemporary challenges and innovative solutions across these vital domains.

Vernā Myers, the distinguished diversity expert, eloquently stated, "Diversity is being invited to the party; inclusion is being asked to dance." These words encapsulate the essence of the multifaceted issues we explore. Our world is facing a confluence of transformative events, from paradigm-shifting workplace cultures to technological advancements that promise both empowerment and peril. The complexities of inclusion, equity, and organizational efficiency reverberate across sectors, including Healthcare, Education, Business, and Technology.

The zeitgeist demands transformation in the fabric of our workplaces and norms. At the forefront of this evolution stand organizational development and process improvement, driving the pursuit of psychological safety, inclusive cultures, and technological innovations. Organizational Development, often abbreviated as OD, serves as a linchpin in this endeavor, refining existing processes, proposing solutions to intricate problems, and fostering cultural metamorphosis. The book's pages reflect the rich tapestry of improvement that different organizations seek, guided by the ever-evolving ideals of equity, inclusivity, collaboration, effectiveness, and efficiency.

Taking an interdisciplinary and systems-oriented approach, this book delves into the tangible impact of complex challenges and offers practical solutions in Healthcare, Education, Business, and Technology. We invite readers to explore a myriad of innovative ideas and strategies that address dynamics, processes, and interactions that can undermine organizations, harm individuals, and perpetuate exclusion.

The book's core aspiration is to equip readers with tangible solutions recommended by scholars, designed to rectify vulnerabilities and uplift communities. With a focus on real-world application, we aim to make organizations and communities more effective, strategic, equitable, caring, and productive.

CHAPTER OVERVIEW

Chapter 1: In the ever-evolving landscape of biotechnology, laboratories, and healthcare research, the necessity of robust cybersecurity risk management techniques is paramount. This chapter emphasizes the need for biotechnology companies, laboratories, and healthcare research organizations to proactively develop practical and effective cybersecurity strategies. By doing so, these entities can protect sensitive data, intellectual property, patient privacy, and stakeholder trust, safeguarding their operations against the dynamic threat landscape of cyber incidents.

Chapter 2: Sustainability, often misconstrued as a general concept, is analyzed in its various dimensions: social, economic, and environmental. Focusing on environmental racism, this chapter highlights the disproportionate impact of pollution on minority communities. It exposes the challenge of addressing environmental racism within the context of perceived equal opportunities, urging a shift toward recognizing environmental injustice as a matter of racial discrimination.

Chapter 3: The prevalence of cyber threats and data breaches underscores the importance of effective cybersecurity strategies. This chapter delves into the control theoretic approach and its potential to address the challenges posed by cyber warfare and data breaches. Statistical data on cyber incidents and their economic impact are examined, revealing the significance of implementing adaptive security systems in response to geopolitical and economic drivers.

Chapter 4: Beyond mere diversity lies the need for equity and inclusion in corporate environments. Drawing from critical theory, this chapter emphasizes the importance of focusing on equity and inclusion alongside diversity. It explores how acknowledging and addressing inequity and exclusion are vital for organizations to establish robust diversity, equity, and inclusion (DEI) programs.

Chapter 5: African American female leaders face unique challenges due to the intersection of their race and gender. This chapter presents a qualitative study that explores the psychological distress experienced by African American female leaders in middle management positions. It delves into the impact of intersectional invisibility on their health and career decisions, utilizing theoretical constructs to frame and support the research.

Chapter 6: The planning fallacy, a cognitive bias affecting decision-making, can hinder effective cybersecurity business planning in healthcare organizations. This chapter delves into the planning fallacy's implications, connecting it to collaborative and complexity leadership theories. It concludes with insights to alleviate the consequences of the planning fallacy and enhance business continuity planning in medical organizations.

Chapter 7: A comprehensive remediation plan for a recent data breach is outlined in this chapter. The plan utilizes foundation theories and models to support strategies that foster new organizational behaviors, ethical decision-making, and strong leadership. By aligning with organizational culture and change management models, the plan aims to prevent cyberattacks and ensure a resilient response to future breaches.

Chapter 8: Stress reactions' impact on cognitive function is explored in the context of firefighting. This chapter investigates how stress affects male firefighters' heart rates and cognitive performance during smoke-diving exercises. The study's findings shed light on the cognitive aspects of firefighting under stress, adding insights to the existing literature.

Chapter 9: Sustainability is dissected into social, economic, and environmental dimensions, aligning with the concept of the triple bottom line. The chapter discusses the importance of integrating sustainability goals with environmental and social stewardship, stressing the need for corporations to create beneficial relationships with communities and the environment.

Chapter 10: E-banking adoption in developing economies is analyzed through the lens of the user authentication experience. This chapter employs the UTAUT2 constructs to examine the factors influencing users' acceptance of e-banking in Nigeria. By understanding these factors, it aims to enhance the adoption of e-banking and improve customer experience.

Chapter 11: The transformation of cities in response to population growth is paralleled with the stages of industrial revolution. This chapter explores how smart cities pave the way for cognitive cities, driven by connectivity and innovation. It underscores the importance of addressing urban challenges and utilizing technology to create sustainable urban environments.

Chapter 12: Leadership development and clinical counseling supervision intersect in this chapter. It examines how leadership development in clinical counseling supervisors can positively impact their role. By aligning theoretical constructs and exploring this convergence, the chapter sheds light on the potential benefits of leadership development in clinical settings.

Chapter 13: The integration of cybersecurity in the healthcare industry is crucial to protect sensitive information from cyber threats. This chapter explores the impact of workers' limited knowledge of cybersecurity on healthcare security. It emphasizes the need for ethical decision-making models and organizational culture to mitigate cyber threats, ensuring the protection of healthcare data.

Chapter 14: Organizational ethics and leadership face scrutiny in the aftermath of sexual misconduct allegations within a company. This chapter investigates the impact of unethical leadership on organizational culture and employee well-being. It aims to provide insights into addressing and mitigating the negative effects of such incidents.

Chapter 15: Transformational leadership's potential to promote diversity and justice in the public sector is explored. This chapter examines the role of transformational leadership in fostering institutional effectiveness and achieving ethical and impactful societal change.

Chapter 16: Executive leadership coaching is presented as a tool to address critical issues in law enforcement, such as race relations and misconduct. The chapter discusses how coaching can enhance police officers' cultural competence, decision-making skills, and ability to create inclusive work environments.

Chapter 17: Machine learning-based systems can aid in identifying reputable research sources. This chapter outlines a supervised learning model to distinguish between reputable and non-reputable journals. The proposed system streamlines the literature review process and improves the quality of academic research.

Chapter 18: The transformation of conventional business models into sustainable ones is influenced by ESG integration. This chapter critically analyzes previous research findings to showcase how ESG integration leads to positive returns on equity and assets. It highlights the financial benefits for organizations that prioritize ESG integration.

Chapter 19: Online education's impact on learning and cost reduction is explored in this chapter. It underscores the importance of aligning training with business objectives, evaluating business results, and investing in online training. By doing so, organizations can enhance both learners' experiences and training professionals' effectiveness.

Chapter 20: Organizational intervention action research is employed to address allegations of sexual misconduct within the Apex Restaurant Group. This chapter explores the role of a management consultant in investigating and recommending viable solutions to real-world challenges faced by the organization.

Chapter 21: A machine learning-based approach is proposed to identify reputable research journals. The chapter presents a logistic regression classification algorithm to distinguish between reputable and non-reputable journals. This approach aims to streamline the identification of high-quality sources for academic research.

Chapter 22: The concept of ESG integration's impact on transforming conventional business models is explored in this chapter. It critically examines the benefits of ESG integration for organizations' financial performance, highlighting its positive effects on returns, rankings, and cost of debt.

Chapter 23: The opinions of specialist physicians toward city hospitals and their impact on health-related issues are analyzed using classification and machine learning methods. This chapter examines different groups of specialist physicians' views on city hospitals, revealing statistically significant differences among them.

These diverse chapters collectively contribute to the interdisciplinary exploration of complex issues in technology, healthcare, and business, offering insights and solutions that bridge theory and practice.

The intended audience is vast and diverse, including university faculty, professionals, doctoral students, management consultants, corporate leaders, researchers, diversity and inclusion professionals, and policy makers. The topics covered reflect the breadth of modern challenges, ranging from technological biases to workplace conflicts, and from healthcare leadership to social determinants of health.

The diverse and pioneering topics covered in this book emerge as guideposts, illuminating the paths to a future where innovation, understanding, and collaboration converge to address the most pressing issues of our time. As editor, I extend my gratitude to all contributors for their invaluable insights, and I invite readers to delve into the research that melds the theoretical and the practical, elevating knowledge into transformative action.

Darrell Norman Burrell
Marymount University, USA

Chapter 1
Management Practices for Mitigating Cybersecurity Threats to Biotechnology Companies, Laboratories, and Healthcare Research Organizations

Allison Huff
iD https://orcid.org/0000-0001-6102-8013
College of Medicine, University of Arizona, USA

Sharon L. Burton
iD https://orcid.org/0000-0003-1653-9783
Capitol Technology University, USA

Darrell Norman Burrell
iD https://orcid.org/0000-0002-4675-9544
Marymount University, USA

Angel J. Jones
iD https://orcid.org/0009-0007-9740-6611
University of Virginia, USA

Calvin Nobles
iD https://orcid.org/0000-0003-4002-1108
Illinois Institute of Technology, USA

Delores Springs
iD https://orcid.org/0000-0003-0940-1225
Regent University, USA

Kevin Richardson
iD https://orcid.org/0009-0002-3212-8669
Capitol Technology University, USA

Marwan Omar
Illinois Institute of Technology, USA

Jorja Brittany Wright
iD https://orcid.org/0000-0002-7028-995X
Capitol Technology University, USA

Kim Brown-Jackson
iD https://orcid.org/0000-0001-9231-2076
Capitol Technology University, USA

DOI: 10.4018/979-8-3693-1630-6.ch001

ABSTRACT

In the rapidly advancing landscape of biotechnology, laboratories, and healthcare research, the criticality of robust cybersecurity risk management techniques cannot be overstated. As these industries increasingly rely on interconnected technologies and digitized data for innovation and patient care, they become attractive targets for malicious cyber threats. This chapter underscores the paramount importance for biotechnology companies, laboratories, and healthcare research organizations to develop real-world and practical cybersecurity risk management techniques. By proactively addressing cybersecurity vulnerabilities, these entities can safeguard their sensitive data, protect intellectual property, ensure patient privacy, and maintain the trust of stakeholders. This chapter emphasizes the necessity of adopting effective cybersecurity strategies tailored to the specific needs of each sector, taking into account the dynamic threat landscape and the potential consequences of cyber incidents.

INTRODUCTION AND BACKGROUND

The landscape of cybersecurity threats is ever-evolving, and with the rapid digitization and integration of technology across diverse industries, laboratories, and healthcare research organizations have become prime targets for malicious actors seeking to exploit vulnerabilities (Luh & Yen, 2020; Lam, & Wong, 2021).The emerging cybersecurity risks in these critical sectors pose profound challenges to data integrity, intellectual property protection, and the safety and well-being of patients and researchers alike (Luh & Yen, 2020; Lam, & Wong, 2021).

This introduction highlights the burgeoning threats faced by the science, laboratory, and healthcare research communities, emphasizing the urgent need for comprehensive measures to safeguard their digital assets and ensure the continuity of groundbreaking research and essential medical services (Luh & Yen, 2020; Lam, & Wong, 2021).

The convergence of advanced technologies, including internet-connected devices, big data analytics, and cloud computing, has revolutionized the way scientific experiments are conducted, laboratory workflows managed, and healthcare services delivered (Luh & Yen, 2020; Lam, & Wong, 2021). However, this digital transformation has simultaneously exposed these domains to a myriad of cybersecurity threats that exploit technological complexities and human vulnerabilities (Luh & Yen, 2020; Lam, & Wong, 2021).

In science, researchers are at the forefront of innovation, working relentlessly to unravel the mysteries of the universe and develop solutions to pressing global challenges (Luh & Yen, 2020; Lam, & Wong, 2021)Yet, their valuable research data and intellectual property are at risk of theft, tampering, or destruction by cyber adversaries (Luh & Yen, 2020; Lam, & Wong, 2021).

From academic institutions to private research laboratories, the potential consequences of cyber incidents on scientific progress and knowledge dissemination are profound, warranting an in-depth analysis of emerging threats and vulnerabilities (Luh & Yen, 2020; Lam, & Wong, 2021). Laboratories, as the epicenters of experimentation and discovery, heavily rely on data-driven processes and interconnected instruments (Luh & Yen, 2020; Lam, & Wong, 2021)

This interconnectedness, while enhancing productivity and collaboration, also introduces critical security gaps that could be exploited by malicious hackers (Luh & Yen, 2020; Lam, & Wong, 2021)

Cybersecurity risks in laboratories encompass data breaches, supply chain attacks on equipment and software, and the unauthorized manipulation of experimental outcomes, jeopardizing the reliability of scientific findings(Luh & Yen, 2020; Lam, & Wong, 2021).In healthcare research, the digitization of patient records, medical imaging, and genomic data has ushered in a new era of precision medicine and improved healthcare outcomes (Luh & Yen, 2020; Lam, & Wong, 2021).

However, with sensitive medical information now stored and transmitted electronically, the healthcare sector faces unprecedented challenges in protecting patient privacy and ensuring the confidentiality and integrity of medical data (Luh & Yen, 2020; Lam, & Wong, 2021). Cyber threats such as ransomware attacks on hospitals, data breaches compromising patient information, and the disruption of medical research are just a few of the emerging risks that demand urgent attention (Luh & Yen, 2020; Lam, & Wong, 2021).

This introduction sets the stage for a comprehensive exploration of the emerging cybersecurity risks in science, laboratories, and healthcare research (Luh & Yen, 2020; Lam, & Wong, 2021). By critically analyzing the ever-evolving threat landscape and understanding the unique vulnerabilities in each domain, this study aims to propose proactive and resilient cybersecurity strategies tailored to the specific needs of these sectors (Luh & Yen, 2020; Lam, & Wong, 2021). Mitigating these emerging risks and fortifying the defenses of scientific, laboratory, and healthcare research institutions is not only imperative for preserving the integrity of their work but also essential for safeguarding public health, scientific advancement, and the greater good of society (Luh & Yen, 2020; Lam, & Wong, 2021).

Cybersecurity risk management is essential for contemporary businesses due to cyberthreats (Ganin et al., 2020). Data breaches, ransomware attacks, and insider threats affect organizations of all sizes and sectors (Spremić & Šimunic, 2018). An organization's reputation, customer trust, and legal liabilities can suffer from a poor cybersecurity culture (Ponemon Institute, 2020). A strong cybersecurity culture protects sensitive data and assets, corporate culture, employee morale, and operations (Kalhoro et al., 2021). Poor cybersecurity culture led to a breach. The breach has affected the company's reputation, lost customer trust, and caused legal concerns. The company has no risk management plan or strategy, and its culture has to change. Employee morale has dropped, causing disengagement, anxiety, and job dissatisfaction. If these vulnerabilities are not addressed, the firm will remain vulnerable to cybersecurity breaches, legal liability, and consumer distrust. Employee turnover, productivity, and workplace conflicts will continue due to the negative effect. A positive cybersecurity culture requires policies, training, and senior leadership's support. Access restrictions, data protection, incident response, and risk management should be addressed in organizational cybersecurity policies. All employees should receive cybersecurity training that includes password protection, phishing awareness, and strategies for social engineering. Senior leadership support is essential for establishing a basic cybersecurity culture because leaders must prioritize cybersecurity and demonstrate their commitment by providing the necessary resources and financing for cybersecurity initiatives (Reegård et al., 2019).

Problem Statement

Laboratories, biotechnology companies, and pharmaceutical companies have increasingly become prime targets for sophisticated threat actors, facing relentless and strategic cyberattacks. Recent data reveals that in 2021, an alarming 98% of pharmaceutical companies encountered security intrusions, underscoring the gravity of the cyber threat landscape within the industry. Equally concerning is the staggering statistic that over 20% of businesses, including laboratories, biotechnology companies, and pharmaceutical companies, suffered the loss of vital business-critical data and valuable intellectual property in the span of a single year. These figures illustrate the urgent need for comprehensive and robust cybersecurity measures to safeguard sensitive information, protect intellectual assets, and ensure the continuity of critical operations in this highly targeted and vulnerable sector.

Organizations with weak cybersecurity cultures and risk management procedures are more likely to experience cybersecurity breaches (Ulven & Wangen, 2021). In order to deal with these issues, we have assigned employees to a team of risk management specialists who will evaluate our cybersecurity practices, identify gaps and weaknesses, and build and execute a thorough risk management strategy. Cybersecurity risk management necessitates an interdisciplinary approach that draws on both technical and cultural approaches (Alahmari & Duncan, 2020). By utilizing these models, organizations can effectively prevent and handle cybersecurity incidents while promoting a culture of security and resilience.

Strategy Models

Assessing an organization's cybersecurity culture is crucial to developing a robust and effective cybersecurity strategy. One approach is to conduct a need-gap analysis, which involves evaluating the current state of the culture and comparing it to the desired state to identify areas that require improvement (Uchendu et al., 2021). The analysis can pinpoint specific aspects, such as employee education, policies and procedures, and risk management strategies, in which the organization should improve. By utilizing a need-gap analysis to evaluate its cybersecurity culture, an organization can design targeted strategies to address specific areas for improvement. This approach can aid in the development of a robust and effective cybersecurity culture, which is essential in safeguarding against cyber threats and preserving the security of the organization's digital assets (Uchendu et al., 2021). For example, an analysis may reveal that employees lack sufficient training on cybersecurity best practices, increasing the risk of a breach. To address this deficiency, the organization can create and implement training programs (Georgiadou, Mouzakitis, Bounas, & Askounis, 2022). Similarly, the analysis could show that the company's current security measures are insufficient to face new types of attacks. In that case, the organization can review and revise its policies and procedures to ensure they are current and effective in mitigating risk (Georgiadou, Mouzakitis, & Askounis, 2021).

Organizational Culture Models

According to Schein, organizational culture is comprised of three levels: artifacts and behaviors, espoused values, and underlying assumptions (Schein, 2010). Schein's model of organizational culture is another useful framework for understanding cybersecurity culture within an organization. Specifically, in the context of cybersecurity culture, artifacts and behaviors refer to the observable actions and practices related to cybersecurity, such as the use of strong passwords and regular system updates (Bradley, Noble, & Hendricks, 2020). Espoused values relate to the stated beliefs and attitudes of the organization towards cybersecurity, such as the importance placed on protecting sensitive data (Tallman, Shenkar, & Wu, 2021). Underlying assumptions are the unspoken, deeply held beliefs and assumptions about cybersecurity within the organization (Bradley, Noble, & Hendricks, 2020). It is worth noting that applying Schein's model of organizational culture to cybersecurity has been successful in several organizations. For example, a case study conducted by Bradley, Noble and Hendricks (2020) demonstrated how using Schein's model helped an organization improve its cybersecurity culture. The organization had previously struggled with a lack of employee engagement and compliance with cybersecurity policies. By using Schein's model to identify and address underlying assumptions and values, the organization was able to create a more cohesive and effective cybersecurity culture. This included developing a training program that emphasized the importance of cybersecurity, providing incentives for compliance, and promoting a culture of transparency and communication around cybersecurity issues. By understanding these levels of organizational culture, managers can better identify the factors that contribute to a weak cybersecurity culture, such as a lack of leadership support or conflicting values (Alshaikh, 2020). For instance, if the espoused values within an organization prioritize productivity over security, employees may be more likely to prioritize speed and convenience over proper cybersecurity protocols (Tallman, Shenkar, & Wu, 2021). By recognizing these underlying assumptions, managers can work to shift the culture towards a stronger focus on cybersecurity. Applying Schein's model of organizational culture to cybersecurity can also help with the development of a change management plan. By identifying the underlying assumptions and values that contribute to a weak cybersecurity culture, managers can better target areas for change and develop strategies for communicating the importance of cybersecurity throughout the organization (Bradley, Noble, & Hendricks, 2020). This can include developing training programs, providing incentives for compliance, and regularly reviewing and updating cybersecurity policies.

Change Management Models

Change Management Models: Lewin's change management model is another useful tool for managing the changes required to improve a company's cybersecurity culture (Cameron & Green, 2019). Developed by Kurt Lewin in the 1940s, this model remains relevant and widely used in various industries today (Desmond & Wilson, 2019). To improve a company's cybersecurity culture, Lewin's change management model consists of three stages: unfreezing, changing, and refreezing. In the unfreezing stage, managers must create a sense of urgency and motivate employees to change their behavior (Ryttare, 2019). This can be done using a variety of methods, including education and training on the significance of cybersecurity and highlighting the consequences of a breach. Once a sense of urgency is created, the next stage involves implementing the changes required to improve the company's cybersecurity culture. This could involve developing new policies and procedures, implementing new technologies, and enhancing employee training programs. Finally, in the refreezing stage, managers must work to sustain the changes over time and ensure that the new cybersecurity culture becomes part of the company's everyday operations (Ryttare, 2019). By using Lewin's change management model, managers can effectively plan and execute the changes required to improve their company's cybersecurity culture, which can help address the ethical issues related to the cybersecurity breach and ensure that the company is better prepared to manage future risks (Ryttare, 2019). For example, a company may use Lewin's change management model to implement new cybersecurity policies and procedures and to develop a training program that ensures all employees are educated on the importance of cybersecurity. Through this process, the company can create a culture where cybersecurity is ingrained in the company's operations and is viewed as a critical component of the company's success (Ryttare, 2019).

Ethical Decision-Making Models

Ethical decision-making is critical in the realm of cybersecurity, and one commonly used approach is the utilitarian model, which emphasizes taking actions that yield the most significant overall benefit for the most people (Manjikian, 2022). However, applying this approach to cybersecurity can be challenging since it requires balancing competing interests and values. For instance, implementing more stringent cybersecurity measures may increase costs for the organization, negatively impacting shareholders, while not taking action may result in harm to customers and damage to the organization's reputation. To navigate these ethical dilemmas, cybersecurity professionals can benefit from training in ethical decision-making and the use of ethical frameworks, such as the utilitarian approach (Loi & Christen, 2020). Moreover, organizations can establish a culture that values ethical decision-making and encourages employees to report potential breaches and other ethical concerns (Valentine & Godkin, 2019). Incorporating ethical decision-making models, such as the utilitarian approach, into cybersecurity culture can improve risk management and protect against potential breaches, contributing to the organization's competitive position in the market (Anshari et al., 2022). Particularly, a lot of notable cybersecurity incidents have highlighted the importance of ethical decision-making in this industry. The Equifax data breach of 2017 exposed personal data for millions of consumers, and the company's response was widely panned (Gressin, 2017). Similarly, the 2016 breach of the servers of the Democratic National Committee raised ethical concerns regarding the role of cybersecurity in securing democratic institutions. In both cases, ethical decision-making and the use of frameworks such as the utilitarian model could have helped prevent or mitigate the impacts of these breaches (Johns & Riles, 2016).

Leadership Models

James MacGregor Burns created the Transformational Theory of Leadership, which Bernard Bass later developed, and it focuses on the leader's capacity to inspire and motivate followers to accomplish organizational goals outside of their own self-interest (Ng, 2018).This theory emphasizes the significance of creating and implementing successful cybersecurity strategies by emphasizing the need for a healthy corporate culture that encourages employees to be creative, innovative, and work together. Transformational leaders typically exhibit four key behaviors: idealized influence, inspirational motivation, intellectual stimulation, and individualized consideration (Raziq et al., 2018). Idealized influence refers to the leader's ability to serve as a role model for ethical behavior and to engender trust and respect among followers. Inspirational motivation involves the leader's ability to inspire and motivate followers to work towards a shared vision. Intellectual stimulation involves encouraging creativity and innovation among followers, while individualized consideration involves attending to the individual needs and concerns of each follower (Raziq et al., 2018). Applying the Transformational Theory of Leadership to cybersecurity can help organizations develop a positive cybersecurity culture that encourages employees to view cybersecurity as a shared responsibility and actively contribute to its success (Choi, Lee, & Hwang, 2018). By creating a culture that values cybersecurity and encourages employees to be proactive in identifying and reporting potential threats, organizations can help prevent cybersecurity breaches before they occur (Fisher, Porod, & Peterson, 2021). Furthermore, transformational leaders can foster a culture of continuous learning and improvement, which can be critical for staying ahead of rapidly evolving cyber threats (Burrell, Aridi, & Nobles, 2018). Organizations can effectively prepare themselves to deal with cybersecurity risks if their leaders foster a culture of collaboration and knowledge sharing among their employees by providing opportunities for them to participate in ongoing cybersecurity training and share their knowledge and expertise with others in the organization (Burton, 2022).

Situation Analysis

Due to a recent cybersecurity breach caused by a weak cybersecurity culture, the firm is in a precarious position right now. Loss of customer trust, reputational damage, and significant legal liability are just some of the dire outcomes of this breach. The existing absence of a risk management plan or strategy demonstrates the need of making substantial adjustments to the company's culture. Employees have been negatively impacted by this scenario as well, experiencing disengagement, anxiety, and discontent with their jobs as a result. If these problems aren't fixed, the company is leaving itself vulnerable to other cybersecurity breaches and other problems. The result may be more legal trouble, a damaged reputation, and a drop in customer confidence. The morale of the staff will also continue to decline, leading to more turnover, decreased output, and maybe even workplace confrontations. In order to mitigate any additional harm and strengthen the company's cybersecurity culture as a whole, it is crucial that these concerns be resolved as quickly as feasible.

Needed Changes to Address the Impact on Employees

The cybersecurity breach has had a significant impact on employees, leading to disengagement, anxiety, and job dissatisfaction. More employees leaving their jobs, less work being done, and even workplace disputes are all possible outcomes of these negative consequences (Bevan, 2013). Hence, the company should take care of these problems and foster an encouraging environment that promotes employee satisfaction and productivity. To do so, a multifaceted strategy involving policies, training, and senior leadership support is necessary.

Policies

Clear policies and procedures are needed to govern cybersecurity practices within the organization. These policies should be frequently reviewed and revised to ensure their continued efficacy and relevance. The policies should cover areas such as access controls, data protection, incident response, and risk management (Uchendu et al., 2021). Proper implementation and enforcement of these policies can help mitigate the harm caused by cybersecurity breaches to the organization's culture, employee morale, and overall operations.

Training

Cybersecurity training is essential for employees at all organizational levels. This training should cover topics such as password security, phishing awareness, and social engineering tactics. Additionally, specialized training should be provided for employees with specific cybersecurity responsibilities, such as IT staff or security analysts (Reegård, Blackett, & Katta, 2019). The importance of training in promoting a cybersecurity culture and reducing the risk of breaches cannot be understated, as it has been shown to contribute to enhanced employee awareness and preparedness.

Senior Leadership Support

Senior leadership support is critical for establishing a positive cybersecurity culture within the organization. Leaders should prioritize cybersecurity and demonstrate a commitment to it by providing the necessary resources and funding for cybersecurity initiatives (Burrell, Aridi, & Nobles, 2018). Strong leadership commitment can also help drive the necessary changes in operations and organizational culture to support a more secure environment.

ACTION PLAN FOR CHANGE

Step 1: Need-Gap Analysis

Conduct a thorough assessment of the organization's cybersecurity policies, procedures, and training programs to identify gaps between the current state and the desired state (National Institute of Standards and Technology, 2020). This process involves prioritizing areas for improvement based on the level of risk. By identifying and addressing these gaps, the organization can work towards improving its cybersecurity culture, employee morale, and overall operations (Ponemon Institute, 2020).

Step 2: Schein's Model of Organizational Culture

Evaluate the organization's current culture and values related to cybersecurity using Schein's Model of Organizational Culture (Schein, 2010). This model includes three levels: artifacts, espoused values, and basic assumptions. Understanding these levels can help identify any cultural barriers to implementing effective cybersecurity measures (Schein, 2010). For example, the organization may have artifacts such as posters promoting cybersecurity awareness, but the espoused values and basic assumptions may not truly prioritize security, leading to a lax approach to cybersecurity.

Step 3: Lewin's Change Management Model

Develop a comprehensive plan that includes policies and procedures, training programs, and senior leadership support initiatives. Implement a change management strategy that addresses any resistance to change and ensures buy-in from employees at all levels (Lewin, 1947). Lewin's model involves three stages: unfreezing, changing, and refreezing. In the unfreezing stage, the organization needs to recognize the need for change and create a sense of urgency. During the changing stage, new policies, procedures, and training programs are implemented. Finally, in the refreezing stage, the new changes are reinforced, and the organization's culture and operations adapt to the new cybersecurity-focused environment (Lewin, 1947).

Step 4: Utilitarian Model

Prioritize actions based on the greatest good for the greatest number of stakeholders, using the utilitarian model (Mill, 1863). Consider the costs and benefits of each action and prioritize those with the highest benefit-to-cost ratio. This approach helps ensure that the organization's resources are allocated effectively and efficiently, ultimately improving the cybersecurity culture, employee morale, and operations (Cavusoglu et al., 2005).

Step 5: Transformational Theory of Leadership

Empower employees to take ownership of the cybersecurity culture using the Transformational Theory of Leadership (Bass & Riggio, 2006). Transformational leaders inspire, motivate, and encourage employees to achieve their full potential and contribute positively to the organization's cybersecurity efforts. By fostering a sense of shared responsibility for cybersecurity, employees become more engaged, and the organization's culture and operations adapt to prioritize security (Bass & Riggio, 2006).

Step 6: Evaluation

Continuously evaluate the effectiveness of the plan and adjust it as necessary to ensure the organization's cybersecurity culture remains strong and relevant (National Institute of Standards and Technology, 2020). Collect feedback from employees and stakeholders to identify areas for improvement. Regular assessments and adjustments can help maintain a robust cybersecurity culture, ultimately benefiting employee morale and organizational operations (Ponemon Institute, 2020).

DESIRED STATE AND IMPROVEMENT ACTIVITIES

To achieve a strong cybersecurity culture, organizations need to prioritize several key activities and actions. These include conducting a thorough assessment of the organization's current cybersecurity policies, procedures, and training programs to identify any gaps between the current state and the desired state. This process is known as a need-gap analysis and involves prioritizing areas for improvement based on the level of risk (Uchendu et al., 2021). For instance, if there is no way to ensure that staff follow the guideline that they update their passwords every six months, the company leaves itself open to cyberattacks. Another important step is evaluating the organization's current culture and values related to cybersecurity using a model such as Schein's Model of Organizational Culture (Schein, 2010). This helps identify any cultural barriers to implementing effective cybersecurity measures. Once the current state has been assessed and cultural barriers identified, organizations can develop a comprehensive plan that includes policies and procedures, training programs, and senior leadership support initiatives (Bevan, 2013). A change management strategy, based on Lewin's change management model, can be used to address any resistance to change and ensure buy-in from employees at all levels. This plan should prioritize actions based on the greatest good for the greatest number of stakeholders, using a utilitarian model. Using multi-factor authentication, for example, offers a high benefit-to-cost ratio since it delivers large security advantages at a low cost. To ensure long-term success, organizations should also empower employees to take ownership of the cybersecurity culture (Leigh, 2013). This includes providing opportunities for employees to develop their skills and take on leadership roles in promoting cybersecurity awareness, using the Transformational Theory of Leadership. Continuous evaluation and improvement of the organization's cybersecurity posture is also important, using regular assessments and reviews of policies and practices (Ng, 2018).

Overall, organizations that prioritize the development of a strong cybersecurity culture through these activities and actions will be better equipped to protect themselves against cyber threats and safeguard their sensitive data and assets (Leigh, 2013).

CONCLUSION

In the realm of science, biotechnology, and healthcare, the importance of a robust cybersecurity culture and risk management plan cannot be overstated. Safeguarding sensitive data, critical assets, and overall operations is paramount to maintain the trust of customers, protect the organization's reputation, and mitigate potential legal liabilities. Regrettably, an instance of cybersecurity breach within the organization serves as a stark reminder of the consequences that arise from a poorly developed cybersecurity culture.

The aftermath of the cybersecurity breach highlights the urgent need for a multifaceted strategy that addresses the organization's policies, training programs, and the unwavering support of senior leadership. As a consultant, conducting a need-gap analysis and evaluating the organization's existing culture and values concerning cybersecurity is crucial in devising a comprehensive plan to address vulnerabilities. Drawing from Lewin's change management model, a well-structured approach can be implemented to facilitate the adoption of cybersecurity best practices across the organization.

A vital consideration in the planning process involves prioritizing actions based on the principle of the greatest good for the greatest number of stakeholders, as suggested by the utilitarian model. This ensures that efforts are channeled toward initiatives that yield maximum impact on cybersecurity resilience, encompassing protection for customer data, employee well-being, and financial stability.

To maintain a lasting and effective cybersecurity culture, empowering employees to take ownership of their roles in cybersecurity is paramount. Utilizing the Transformational Theory of Leadership, organizational leaders can inspire and foster a sense of collective responsibility among employees. Encouraging a proactive approach to cybersecurity not only strengthens the organization's defenses but also engenders a culture of vigilance and responsiveness to potential threats.

Continuous evaluation of the implemented cybersecurity plan is essential to identify areas for improvement and adapt to the ever-changing cybersecurity landscape. As threats evolve, so must the organization's defenses and preparedness measures. A proactive approach to risk management and cybersecurity culture, therefore, becomes an ongoing process that bolsters the organization's resilience against potential cyber threats.

In conclusion, science, biotechnology, and healthcare organizations must recognize the critical role of a well-developed cybersecurity culture and risk management strategy. The consequences of a cybersecurity breach can be far-reaching, impacting customer trust, reputation, and financial stability. By implementing a comprehensive plan that leverages change management principles, prioritizes actions with the greatest impact, and fosters a transformational cybersecurity culture, these organizations can mitigate risks, safeguard sensitive data, and uphold the well-being of their stakeholders. A proactive stance on cybersecurity is not only necessary to protect against breaches but also to maintain the confidence of customers, employees, and partners in the organization's ability to secure their information and preserve their overall trust.

REFERENCES

Alahmari, A., & Duncan, B. (2020, June). Cybersecurity risk management in small and medium-sized enterprises: A systematic review of recent evidence. In 2020 international conference on cyber situational awareness, data analytics and assessment (CyberSA) (pp. 1-5). IEEE.

American Psychological Association. (2022). Publication manual of the American psychological association. American Psychological Association.

Anshari, M., Syafrudin, M., Fitriyani, N. L., & Razzaq, A. (2022). Ethical Responsibility and Sustainability (ERS) Development in a Metaverse Business Model. *Sustainability (Basel)*, *14*(23), 15805. doi:10.3390u142315805

Bevan, R. (2013). *Changemaking: Tactics and resources for managing organizational change*. eBookIt. com.

Burrell, D. N., Aridi, A. S., & Nobles, C. (2018, March). The critical need for formal leadership development programs for cybersecurity and information technology professionals. In *International Conference on Cyber Warfare and Security* (pp. 82-91). Academic Conferences International Limited.

Burton, S. L. (2022). *Cybersecurity Leadership from a Telemedicine/Telehealth Knowledge and Organizational Development Examination* [Doctoral dissertation]. Capitol Technology University.

Cameron, E., & Green, M. (2019). *Making sense of change management: A complete guide to the models, tools and techniques of organizational change*. Kogan Page Publishers.

Choi, M., Lee, J., & Hwang, K. (2018). Information systems security (ISS) of E-Government for sustainability: A dual path model of ISS influenced by institutional isomorphism. *Sustainability (Basel)*, *10*(5), 1555. doi:10.3390u10051555

Desmond, J., & Wilson, F. (2019). Democracy and worker representation in the management of change: Lessons from Kurt Lewin and the Harwood studies. *Human Relations*, *72*(11), 1805–1830. doi:10.1177/0018726718812168

Fisher, R., Porod, C., & Peterson, S. (2021). Motivating employees and organizations to adopt a cyber-security-focused culture. *Journal of Organizational Psychology*, *21*(1), 114–131.

Georgiadou, A., Mouzakitis, S., & Askounis, D. (2021). Assessing mitre att&ck risk using a cyber-security culture framework. *Sensors (Basel)*, *21*(9), 3267. doi:10.339021093267 PMID:34065086

Georgiadou, A., Mouzakitis, S., Bounas, K., & Askounis, D. (2022). A cyber-security culture framework for assessing organization readiness. *Journal of Computer Information Systems*, *62*(3), 452–462. doi:10.1080/08874417.2020.1845583

Gressin, S. (2017). The equifax data breach: What to do. Federal Trade Commission.

Johns, F., & Riles, A. (2016). Beyond Bunker and Vaccine: The DNC Hack as a Conflict of Laws Issue. *The American Journal of International Law*, *110*, 347–351.

Lam, M. L., & Wong, K. (2021). Shared Cybersecurity Risk Management in the Industry of Medical Devices. *International Journal of Cyber-Physical Systems*, *3*(1), 37–56. doi:10.4018/IJCPS.2021010103

Leigh, A. (2013). *Ethical leadership: creating and sustaining an ethical business culture*. Kogan Page Publishers.

Loi, M., & Christen, M. (2020). *Ethical frameworks for cybersecurity*. Springer International Publishing. doi:10.1007/978-3-030-29053-5_4

Luh, F., & Yen, Y. (2020). Cybersecurity in science and medicine: Threats and challenges. *Trends in Biotechnology*, *38*(8), 825–828. doi:10.1016/j.tibtech.2020.02.010 PMID:32441258

Manjikian, M. (2022). *Cybersecurity ethics: An introduction*. Taylor & Francis. doi:10.4324/9781003248828

Ng, L. T. (2018). *Exploring transformational leadership and fellowship in a cultural context: The case of the Philippines*. Academic Press.

Raziq, M. M., Borini, F. M., Malik, O. F., Ahmad, M., & Shabaz, M. (2018). Leadership styles, goal clarity, and project success: Evidence from project-based organizations in Pakistan. *Leadership and Organization Development Journal*, *39*(2), 309–323. doi:10.1108/LODJ-07-2017-0212

Reegård, K., Blackett, C., & Katta, V. (2019). The concept of cybersecurity culture. In *29th European Safety and Reliability Conference* (pp. 4036-4043). 10.3850/978-981-11-2724-3_0761-cd

Ryttare, E. (2019). *Change management: A key in achieving successful cyber security: A multiple case study of organizations in Sweden*. Academic Press.

Security, I. B. M. (2021). *Cost of a data breach report 2021*. Retrieved from https://www.ibm.com/security/data-breach

Uchendu, B., Nurse, J. R., Bada, M., & Furnell, S. (2021). Developing a cyber security culture: Current practices and future needs. *Computers & Security*, *109*, 102387. doi:10.1016/j.cose.2021.102387

Ulven, J. B., & Wangen, G. (2021). A systematic review of cybersecurity risks in higher education. *Future Internet*, *13*(2), 39. doi:10.3390/fi13020039

Valentine, S., & Godkin, L. (2019). Moral intensity, ethical decision making, and whistleblowing intention. *Journal of Business Research*, *98*, 277–288. doi:10.1016/j.jbusres.2019.01.009

Whelan, S. (2023, August 23). *Tackling Cybersecurity Threats in the Biotechnology Industry*. Technology Networks. Retrieved from: https://www.technologynetworks.com/informatics/blog/tackling-cybersecurity-threats-in-the-biotechnology-industry-364979#:~:text=Pharmaceutical%20companies%20are%20now%20routinely,in%20the%20last%20year%20alone

Chapter 2
Understanding Sustainability and How It Impacts People of Color

Kevin Richardson
ⓘD https://orcid.org/0009-0002-3212-8669
Edward Waters University, USA

ABSTRACT

By definition, sustainability means meeting personal needs without jeopardizing the ability of future generations to meet their own needs. In that context, sustainability calls for the Earth's environmental systems to be balanced while ensuring that natural resources are consumed at a rate that they are naturally replenished. Researches on sustainability and environmental racism expound on the overall impacts on blacks by showing that this group is more highly affected by pollution than the white population. Scholars note that the main issue with environmental racism is that most American citizens hold onto the belief that everybody is subject to equal opportunities. Such an approach is detrimental since the concept of environmental injustice is treated as a personal choice and not a matter of racial discrimination. The lack of a clear understanding of environmental racism undermines all efforts to fix the problem, which entails focusing on race as a notable predictor of an individual's exposure to environmental hazards.

INTRODUCTION

According to the United Nations Brundtland Commission, sustainability means being able to meet personal needs without jeopardizing the ability of future generations to meet their own needs (Hajian & Kashani, 2021). In that context, sustainability calls for the earth's environmental systems to be kept in balance while ensuring that natural resources are consumed at a rate that they are naturally replenished (Viswanathan & Varghese, 2018). Though sustainability ought to be approached equally in all tenets of life, the issue of environmental racism is more likely to affect people of color than whites (Waldron, 2021). According to Benz (2017), environmental racism refers to a form of inequality that subjects blacks to more environmental hazards, such as living in polluted areas, than their white counterparts.

DOI: 10.4018/979-8-3693-1630-6.ch002

Benz (2017) notes that since the 1980s, when this term came to light following environmental protests, the concept of sustainability has continued to adversely affect people of color. Bullard (2002) elaborates this concept further by showing that environmental racism, as a concept, may be interpreted based on several meanings. The first interpretation refers to inequalities in external environmental conditions. As a consequence, the health status of people of color is likely to deteriorate more than their white counterparts (Bullard, 2022). Secondly, environmental discrimination may be understood from the perspective of ecological policies. For instance, environmental policies in the United States have contributed to the construction of hazardous enterprises in impoverished areas inhabited by people of color.

Numerous research on sustainability and environmental racism illustrates the overall impacts on blacks by showing that this group is highly affected by pollution than the white population (Nardone et al., 2020). Research findings show that the adverse impacts of sustainability on the black population are ascribed to the concept of racism, which results in environmental injustice (Wright, 2021; Collins & Grineski, 2019; Pulido, 2017). In the United States, environmental injustice means that people of color are more likely to live in polluted areas (Lee, 2019). This occurrence is intentional since most companies are deliberately located in these areas, increasing pollution rates. As a result, blacks reside in neighborhoods characterized by few health-promoting environmental amenities, such as parks, and having more environmental hazards (Boone et al., 2009). The inequality is detrimental to this population since they are exposed to racial health disparities, such as asthma and cancer, resulting from living in environmentally polluted areas.

Further research shows that communities inhabited by people of color, such as in California, are more susceptible to environmentally-related sicknesses, such as cancer, because of highly toxic air contaminants (Cushing et al., 2015). The high risk of environmentally sensitive illnesses is also attributed to the high average levels of nitrate contamination in drinking water and being close to hazardous wastewater sites (Mathewson et al, 2020). Ahmed et al. (2021) hypothesize that the concept of sustainability and its impacts on people of color may not be researched thoroughly. Therefore, researchers must conduct further analytic frameworks to help understand how this group of people is exposed to multiple environmental hazards (Schusler et al., 2020). Schusler et al. mentions that the frameworks should be used to consider the differential susceptibility to health impacts from pollution exposure. The assessment should also consider that the impacts of sustainability and the concept of environmental racism may have diverse impacts on a population, especially from an individual and community-level perspective (Schusler et al., 2020). Specifically, the evaluation should consider the age and health status of the black population in the respective neighborhoods as it will help determine the specific impacts of environmental racism on this population (Schusler et al., 2020). The approach may also factor in preexisting conditions, increasing air pollution vulnerability.

Several studies have focused on understanding the impacts of environmental pollution and sustainability impacts on the black population (Egede & Walker, 2020; Taylor, 2020; Banzhaf, Ma & Timmins, 2019). On close examination, these studies have found that poverty levels among people of color are a notable contributor to continued struggle. Downey (2006) explores this by showing that since most blacks are financially deprived, the concept of sustainability does not favor them since it hinders their access to adequate medical care and nutrition, which makes it hard for them to prevent and manage the health impacts of pollution in their neighborhoods. At the community level, the poverty levels among blacks mean they are disadvantaged, increasing their vulnerability to environmental stressors (Polasky et al., 2019). However, Byrnes (2013) notes that an overall understanding of sustainability and its impacts on people of color is shaky since the field is still in its infancy. Therefore, the findings of the different studies are hypothetical and meant to reflect the cumulative impacts of environmental pollution on the black population.

Further analysis of sustainability and its disproportionate impacts on African Americans is reflected in the push for gentrification and electric vehicles (Dlugosch, Brandt & Neumann, 2020). According to Bostic and Martin (2003), gentrification refers to repairing and rebuilding homes in economically dilapidated areas, which creates room for an influx of affluent people and displacement of previously poor residents. Primarily, the push for urbanization, in this context, should be a driving force in tackling the issue of inequality emanating from environmental injustice (Dlugosch et al., 2020). Scholarly examination affirms this by noting that modernized cities should be engines for economic growth and help pull people from poverty (Nicholls et al., 2020; Mora-Rivera & García-Mora, 2021). However, the problem with this approach is that if urbanization helps African American communities, planning and execution are mandatory since there is a high likelihood of black communities being locked into patterns of unsustainable and inequitable development (Toolis, 2021).

Similarly, electric vehicles are a notable move towards improved sustainability in black neighborhoods (Hardman et al., 2021). According to research, most people of color are more likely to use public transit than their white counterparts because they do not own cars (Momeni & Antipova, 2022). Consequently, Park and Kwan (2020), posit black people generate a disproportionately small share of environmental pollution. Regardless, they are likely to suffer disproportionately larger impacts of environmental pollution because they live in areas with high environmental pollution (Hsu & Fingerman, 2021). Bearing this in mind, researchers believe that embracing electric vehicles should be a viable solution to this environmental pollution issue (Zhao et al., 2021). The only setback to this approach is that what is most apparent about electric vehicles is that neighborhoods occupied by Blacks and Latinos are charging deserts (Hardman et al., 2021). Thus, despite electric vehicles gaining popularity in well-to-do societies, black neighborhoods are more likely to be left behind. The lack of charging stations means that African Americans are less likely to embrace electric vehicles, which exposes them to uneven vehicle pollution as they will still depend on gasoline-powered cars because they are easier to buy, though expensive to maintain and fuel (Park & Kwan, 2020).

PROBLEM STATEMENT

General Problem Statement

Environmental racism disproportionately affects people of color since they are more likely to live in neighborhoods with heavy pollution and die of environmental pollution causes. Banzhaf et al. (2019) expound on the problem further by noting that though sustainability should create a better society for everyone, environmental racism subjects people of color to disproportionate victimization by environmental hazards. Statistical evidence shows that 75% of African Americans are more likely to live in "fence-line" communities, which are associated with a heavy population (Browne, 2018).

Specific Problem Statement

Environmental racism translates to unequal access to a clean environment and environmental resources by people of color. That is, blacks are far more likely to live in areas with all sorts of pollution, such as industrial emissions and traffic. Additionally, African Americans have a higher likelihood of dying because of environmental-related illnesses.

Purpose Statement

The purpose of this qualitative research is to critically explore the concept of sustainability and how it affects people of color. In doing so, the paper will approach this issue from the perspective of how -African Americans are disproportionately affected by pollution, especially as evidenced by gentrification and the adoption of electric vehicles. Regardless of the fact that sustainability should create better societies, its impacts on the blacks should be approached by understanding the critical component concerning their living conditions. This approach identifies that blacks make up 13% of the U.S. population and a startling 68% live in areas that are within 30 miles of coal-fired plants, compared to 56% of the white population (Graves & Goodman, 2021). Data collection methods used in this research involve surveying responses from self-identified African Americans living in the United States. The survey will conduct an online interview by asking questions, such as their understanding of sustainability, environmental racism, higher vulnerability to environmental pollution, and their understanding of how sustainability was affecting black communities (Parris et al., 2020). Further, the independent variable in this survey is environmental discrimination, while the dependent variables include measures of how blacks are more vulnerable to pollution than whites, especially in regard to the adoption of electric cars and push for gentrification.

Significance of Study

The extensive effects of sustainability on societies raises the question of its impact on the people of color. Based on this question, the significance of this study is apparent in that it helps highlight the issue of environmental racism and how sustainability has not benefited blacks. Statistical evidence supports this assertion by noting that African Americans comprise 13% of the U.S. population and a startling 68% live in areas that are within 30 miles of coal-fired plants, compared to 56% of the white population (Graves & Goodman, 2021). This trend supposes that in understanding the issue of sustainability and its effect on people of color, the primary focus should be to comprehend individual-level factors, such as experiences, attitudes, and identities. A critical understanding of these factors is imperative as they reveal people's comprehension of environmental injustice.

According to research, environmental racism is still a new field, and few people have critically examined the overall issue (Toolis, 2021). Therefore, by paying attention to the necessary details concerning environmental justice, the study will contribute to a better understanding of how sustainability affects people of color by expounding on previous studies and findings about how blacks perceive environmental justice and its connection to their ethnic identity. More importantly, the study offers critical insight into how black people, even the less affected individuals by the issue of black neighborhoods' environmental harms, have become more sensitized to the issue of environmental racism. Specifically, most black people indicated that they were conscious that environmental problems in black neighborhoods were a racialized issue, which explains why they are exposed to more pollution than the white population.

Definition of Terms

This section will define terms used operationally in this study. Specifically, the section will clarify terms, which are not common knowledge, and they may include words with special meanings, acronyms, technical terminologies, and contextual terms. These terms include:

1. **Sustainability:** According to Hajian and Kashani (2021), this term refers to people's ability to meet personal needs without jeopardizing the ability of future generations to meet their own needs.
2. **Environmental Racism:** According to Benz (2017), it refers to a form of inequality that subjects blacks to more environmental hazards, such as living in polluted areas, than their white counterparts.
3. **Environmental Discrimination:** Bullard (2022) posits that the term may be understood from the perspective of ecological policies; for instance, how environmental policies in the United States have contributed to the construction of hazardous enterprises in impoverished areas inhabited by people of color.
4. **Environmental Injustice:** The term means that people of color are more likely to live in polluted areas (Lee, 2019).
5. **Gentrification:** According to Bostic and Martin (2003), gentrification refers to repairing and rebuilding homes in economically dilapidated areas, which creates room for an influx of affluent people and displacement of previously poor residents.
6. **Electric Vehicles:** Hardman et al. (2021) define electric vehicles as automobiles that use battery instead of gasoline, which qualifies them as a notable move towards improved sustainability in black neighborhoods. Zhao et al. (2021) defines them further by stating that embracing electric vehicles should be a viable solution to this environmental pollution issue.
7. **Environmental Hazards:** They refer to substances that have the potential of threatening the natural environment, which is evidenced in how 75% of African Americans are more likely to live in "fence-line" communities, which are associated with a heavy population (Browne, 2018).
8. **Environmental Fragility:** The term refers to a combination of exposures to environmental and climate health risks, which are exacerbated by system's insufficiency to absorb the shock. For instance, as Arora et al. (2018) put it, blacks need to understand how human activities jeopardize the overall efforts of environmental sustainability.
9. **Environmentally Responsible Behaviors:** According to Yue et al. (2020), the term refers to people's behaviors, which promote sustainability, particularly the utilization of natural resources.
10. **Stronger Environmental Identity:** The term refers to a sense of connection, which is vital since it allows individuals to understand environmental shifts, hence increased likelihood of focusing on environmental harms and how they impact their operations (Clayton, 2020).

Theoretical Framework

The theoretical models adopted in this study are the liberation theory and trauma theory (Wagaman et al., 2019; Onwuachi-Willig, 2021). The two have were chosen since they help to critically understand the issue of sustainability and environmental racism, particularly because they help understand and identify the impacts of environmental racism on the lives of African Americans and how sustainability can help alleviate this type of oppression. The first theory of trauma is apt for this analysis since it assists in examining how environmental racism may lead to race-based traumatic stress. Thus, its utilization will elaborate further on the significance of the environmental justice movement in mitigating racial oppression and the specific moves that can be used to eliminate this deadly and insidious form of racism (Comas-Díaz et al., 2019). According to Keeble (2021), the trauma theory can also help explore the impacts of environmental racism on the psychological health of African Americans. The bigger picture about this theory and how it aligns with environmental sustainability is apparent in that it is a broad theoretical framework, which attempts to comprehensively address the potential impacts on the afflicted communities and also include individuals' psychological blueprint and how they are affected by the natural environment (Kirkinis et al., 2021).

The liberation theory will also be utilized to reflect on factors associated with all forms of racism. Precisely, this theory will help identify environmental racism as a distinct form of institutional racism, which may be both intentional and unintentional (Neville et al., 2021; Kojola & Pellow, 2021). Thus, this theoretical framework will help focus and determine the actions necessary to confront unintentional means of environmental racism and how they are perpetuated. The bigger picture about liberation theory is that it promotes psychological liberations for the oppressed community by deconstructing the socialization processes, which perpetuate elusive forms of racism in current African American neighborhoods (Comas-Díaz et al., 2019). Precisely, the theory will help reveal the oppressive components of socialization, which entails advocating for liberation that takes place at collective levels of social action. Scholars approach this theory by noting that the practice of liberatory consciousness ought to be approached at individual and collective levels (Daystar, 2021). For this purpose, the theory is chosen to deconstruct whiteness in environmental racism and also to decentralize it.

METHODS

Data collection involved examining responses from self-identified African Americans living in the United States. The survey specifically entailed conducting online interviews. The interviews asked participants questions, such as their understanding of sustainability, environmental racism, higher vulnerability to environmental pollution, and their understanding of how sustainability was affecting black communities (Parris et al., 2020). The survey employed detailed frameworks for a comprehensive report that involved diverse sampling data, such as participants' age, gender, and geography. For a comprehensive report, the survey made sure that from the chosen population, the respondents were at least 100. The survey was successful, and the targeted number of respondents was easily achieved. The success was attributed to the fact that the survey contained brief questions and consumed roughly 20 minutes of the participants' time. Secondly, for comprehensive data, the study participants should have lived in black neighborhoods for a significant period. From this approach, the chosen participants ought to have lived in black neighborhoods for a period of roughly more than ten years. The period of stay was important as it allowed a clear understanding of how environmental racism and sustainability attempts have affected people of color regarding adequate access to medical health and nutrition and the poverty levels in these areas (Banzhaf et al., 2019).

The measures during the survey process included capturing dependent and dependent variables inherent to this topic of sustainability and how environmental racism affects people of color. For the dependent variables, the survey concentrated on the overall assessment of environmental justice. To determine the extent of environmental injustice and its impacts on the blacks, the survey used a 7-point Likert scale; 1 denoted sting disagreement while 7 signified strong agreement. The scale helped to tap into conceptual notions of procedural and distributive justice and their connection to environmental sustainability. The principal component of this analysis is that it focused on identifying the two-factor solution tied to the concepts of procedural and distributive environmental justice (Clough, 2018). The distributive environmental justice scale was used to express the degree of disproportionate environmental damage and the distribution of toxins in neighborhoods of people of color (Althor & Witt, 2020). A higher response value meant that the respondents believed that environmental harm was disproportionately distributed, with more black neighborhoods exposed to environmental pollution than whites. On the other hand, the measure of procedural environmental justice presumed that the respondents had little experience regarding community environmental issues. Based on this assumption, the scale was prescriptive and was used to examine the concept of equal treatment, people's general responsibility for environmental conservation, and decisions concerning situating polluting industries.

The other section of the methodology was a critical examination of independent variables. For this analysis, the survey used the 7-point Likert scale (Parris et al., 2021). One signified strongly disagree, and seven denoted strongly agree. The scale helped to identify the different items, precisely those about abusive treatment of the ecosystem (Parris et al., 2021). Higher values from the assessment represented a greater perception of environmental fragility. The items related to this examination included the hypothesis that humans abuse the environment, excessive exploitation of natural resources is progressing towards earth's limits, failed actions may result in ecological catastrophe, and greenhouses are dangerously affecting the environment (Pastor, 2007). The second approach in this segment included measuring environmental discrimination based on Williams' Everyday Discrimination Scale (Harnois et al., 2019). The 7-point scale had five responses ranging from never to almost every day, from 1 to 5, respectively. The questions inherent to this evaluation included whether people of color are treated differently if they receive poor services and if others act superior to them.

RESULTS

Missing data on some indicators contributed to the reduced number of respondents. As a result, the survey used interpolation to estimate values, especially missing values. Based on this approach, the assessment used seemingly unrelated regression to examine how the independent variables affected environmental procedural justice and distributive justice. The seemingly unrelated regression was vital for this assessment as it determined how dependent variables were theoretically distinct but empirically not independent. The results for SUR were interpreted similarly as the least square regression. Thus, every environmental injustice was examined based on the concepts of the attitude of environmental fragility, attitudes and experiences, and blacks' identity with the environmental and sustainability strategies.

Descriptive statistics from this survey provided detailed information about the two justice examinations. The findings indicated that they are considerably similar, construed to mean comparability between procedural environmental justice prescriptions and distributive environmental justice examinations. Based on the Likert scale, the mean for environmental fragility was 5.28, which was more than the middle point. The mean regarding experience with discrimination was 2.70, which was also slightly above the middle point of the 5-point scale. The identity measures recorded a mean of 4.60, which denoted the environmental identity and was above the middle point. The median for the black people's racial identity, their average was 3.98. The results indicated that the issue of environmental pollution was quite prevalent in the respondents' neighborhoods. Deductively, this finding was based on the conception that all data positively related to distributive environmental justice. Therefore, the impact of environmental sustainability on people of color included disproportionate sitting in an environment characterized by having higher environmental harms than other areas.

DISCUSSION

Racism and discrimination are undeniably immoral in all their manifestation. Thus, the modern-day society is obliged to fight environmental racism by considering all ethical arguments. For instance, what could have been previously a public norm may be a crime and shameful. According to Banzhaf et al. (2019), environmental racism falls under this category, and its needs addressing. The bigger picture about environmental destruction is that it affects the plant and global climate changes, but the effects may be more prevalent in a certain group (Ash & Boyce, 2018). Researchers affirm this by showing that people of color, in the United States and other parts of the world, are disproportionately subjected to extreme environmental degradation. The reason for such an occurrence is that other groups, in this case, white individuals, capitalize on the huge profits at the expense of destroying the environment, while the bigger population of colored people pay the price for such endeavors (Brulle & Pellow, 2006). Thus, the concept of environmental racism needs to be critically explored by focusing on the uneven burden of environmental hazards people of color have to deal with. The need to focus on this is based on the conception that environmental oppression is usually achieved systemically, particularly because practices and policies place low-income black communities in close proximities to polluting facilities.

A general overview of the results suggests that in understanding the issue of sustainability and its effect on people of color, the primary focus should be to comprehend individual-level factors, such as experiences, attitudes, and identities. A critical understanding of these factors is imperative as they reveal people's comprehension of environmental injustice (Malin & Ryder, 2018). The survey showed that environmental racism is still a new field, and few people have critically examined the overall issue (Clayton, 2003). However, by paying attention to the necessary details concerning environmental justice, the survey identified previous studies and findings about how blacks perceive environmental justice and its connection to their ethnic identity. More importantly, the survey offers critical insight into how black people, even the less affected individuals by the issue of black neighborhoods' environmental harms, have become more sensitized to the issue of environmental racism. Specifically, most black people indicated that they were conscious that environmental problems in black neighborhoods were a racialized issue, which explains why they are exposed to more pollution than the white population.

The empirical data from the survey support the hypothesis that though the United States is conscious of environmental sustainability, the issue of environmental injustice continues to adversely affect African American population (Wright, 2021). Further, the findings related to environmental fragility suggest that blacks' attitude about this concept is vital, especially the need to note that human activities jeopardize the overall efforts of environmental sustainability (Arora et al., 2018). The supposition is strongly associated with the examination of distributive environmental injustice and procedural environmental justice. In African American neighborhoods, the distribution of pollution and other environmental pollution should call for a better approach entailing making crucial decisions about environmental resources and hazards (Ash & Boyce, 2018). According to Agyeman et al. (2016), the results of this analysis imply that environmental racism should be addressed accordingly to help reduce environmental injustices in the future. Theoretical arguments about environmental injustice conform to this approach by showing that environmentally responsible behaviors are important and should include people's attitudes regardless of the fact that they play less important roles in the context of environmental identity (Su et al., 2020). Nonetheless, people's attitude cannot be ignored as it matters in judging environmental fairness. This survey also indicates that future research is necessary, particularly a critical examination of attitudes towards environmental fragility. Necessary actions should consider the impacts on an individual and collective level. Doing so helps understand the entire concept of environmental injustices and how to rectify them. At the individual level, research should consider behaviors necessary in environmental risk avoidance, which may include restricting outdoor activities and taking necessary precautions to avoid environmentally-sensitive health risks.

The concept of black identity is the second concept to consider in understanding sustainability, its link to environmental racism, and its impacts on people of color. Black identity is important as it increases recognition of environmental injustices disproportionately meant to adversely affect black communities. According to Jones and Rainey (2006), the significance of black identity in understanding the overall concept of sustainability is that it strongly affects the overall evaluation concerning the distribution of environmental harms and the pertinent decision-making process about environmental issues. Few studies have critically explored this topic, but those that have, have gone beyond the classification of what race entails. Regardless of this shortcoming, the study showed the connection between racial categorization and the explicit influence on judgments about environmental phenomena. The approach is vital as it illustrates the heterogeneous nature of particular racial groups, which then assists in disrupting the overall perception of the black community being monolithic. Black identity is also linked to the fact that it is consistently a strong predictor of matters related to distributive environmental justice. In Brulle and Pellow's (2006) opinion, a clear understanding of distributive environmental justice is better than experience in this scenario since the latter may affect the former but cannot interfere with procedural environmental justice.

Though not surprisingly, sustainability and its impacts on people of color are experienced at individual levels. Such an occurrence corresponds with the concept of disproportionate distribution of pollution, which is an outcome of discrimination, perhaps by government authorities and businesses (Feagin, 2013). Deductively, the differential impacts affecting experiences with discrimination may have originated from the embraced approach in the assessment process. Since distributive justice is more backward-looking, procedural environmental justice may be more viable since it focuses on the future. Therefore, adopting a procedural environmental justice approach is paramount as it suggests the specific strategy necessary for the decision-making process. With this in mind, black identity can be approached from the perspective that it is more connected to the concept of environmental justice assessment than to environmental identity (Perry et al., 2021). Besides, environmental identity greatly influences procedural environmental justice but has less effect on distributive environmental justice (Holland, 2020). This finding is important as it calls for thoroughly examining the strong and consistent nexus between procedural environmental justice and personal identity.

The bigger picture about black identity and how environmental sustainability affects this ethnic group is that individuals with a stronger environmental identity are more likely to focus on environmental harms and how they impact their operations (Clayton, 2003). The Kaufman's and Hajat's (2021) understanding of the concept of black identity shows that differential results concerning individual and environmental identity should emphasize how identity is connected to environmental justice. Based on this connection, researchers should evaluate the concept of neighborhood racial segregation and how it fundamentally shapes black people's perception of environmental racism and other forms of social injustices and inequalities (Payne-Sturges et al., 2021). Therefore, by exploring black people's experience with environmental racism, it is evident that black neighborhoods are situated to experience environmental harm more than white localities (Waldron, 2021). Black people's understanding of environmental racism, particularly in how sustainability affects them, is more likely influenced by their experience of discrimination. As a result, their basic approach to environmental injustice is shaped by the idea of what has happened to people of their community and not the prescription of what is likely to happen in the future.

According to Ding and Hwang (2020), the impacts of environmental sustainability on people of color are more apparent in terms of the push for gentrification and electric vehicles. This point of analysis shows that racial exclusion, segregation, and inequality subject African Americans to environmental pollution. For example, the concept of homeownership is something that this population holds dearly (McCabe, 2018). In particular, homeownership among blacks signifies more than financial stability or basic shelter; it is uniquely about a culture passed on from generation to generation. Therefore, sustainability through gentrification may not be that suitable for the black community. Studies affirm this by showing that the negative effect, displacement, will be felt disproportionately by African neighborhoods than in the white localities. A close examination of gentrification reveals that when it occurs, most residents from historically black neighborhoods, such as Detroit, move to even poorer non-gentrifying neighborhoods (Gibbons & Barton, 2016). On the contrary, gentrification in white neighborhoods gives the residents the chance to move to better and wealthier localities in the cities and the suburbs.

The exclusion of black communities in the push for a sustainable environment is also likely to exclude this group from embracing electric vehicles (Hardman et al., 2021). Policymakers have been pushing for the transition toward plug-in electric vehicles (PEVs) to help reduce greenhouse gas emissions and increase efficiency in energy consumption. In their opinion, Hardman et al. (2021) argue that the move may also benefit the disadvantaged and underrepresented communities. The benefits may be accrued from the fact that most black communities reside in areas close to pollution because of factories or being near high traffic (Nardone et al., 2020). Thus, displacing combustion engines with chargeable electric vehicles will benefit black communities regarding reduced pollution and financial strain on the household budget (Hsu & Fingerman, 2021). However, research shows that a disproportionately low number of electric vehicles are sold to black neighborhoods. The low rates are attributed to black neighborhoods lacking charging in their homes and neighborhoods and having a lower budget for vehicle purchases. Such factors mean that owning electric vehicles may exclude African Americans, especially because owning these automobiles is challenging, and only strong support by policymakers can change the overall situation.

CONCLUSION

In conclusion, in understanding how sustainability affects people of color, the first approach entails understanding what it entails. By definition, sustainability means being able to meet personal needs without jeopardizing the ability of future generations to meet their own needs. In that context, sustainability calls for the earth's environmental systems to be kept in balance while ensuring that natural resources are consumed at a rate that they are naturally replenished. Numerous research on sustainability and environmental racism explains on the overall impacts on blacks by showing that this group is highly affected by pollution than the white population. More blacks being affected by environmental harm than whites are known as environmental injustice, which translates to more people of color living in polluted areas. This occurrence is intentional since most companies are deliberately constructed in these areas, increasing pollution rates.

Researchers have critically explored the issue of environmental racism by showing that since most blacks are financially deprived, the concept of sustainability does not favor them since it hinders their access to adequate medical care and nutrition, which makes it hard for them to prevent and manage the health impacts of pollution in their neighborhoods. At the community level, the poverty levels among blacks mean they are disadvantaged, increasing their vulnerability to environmental stressors. The empirical data from the survey support the hypothesis that though the United States is conscious of environmental sustainability, the issue of environmental injustice continues to adversely affect African American population. Further, the findings related to environmental fragility suggest that blacks' attitude about this concept is vital, especially the need to note that human activities jeopardize the overall efforts of environmental sustainability. The supposition is strongly associated with the examination of distributive environmental injustice and procedural environmental justice.

The bigger picture about environmental sustainability and its effect on black communities is that policymakers need to be keen on approaches supposed to help this group but end up excluding them even more. Research shows that black communities have evolved from a unique set of circumstances that block them from being able to prosper. Considering the negative aspects of black communities, such as widespread discrimination, poor housing, and concentration of poverty, they need unique considerations if they are to thrive. In particular, gentrification is arguably a good move that will likely transform black neighborhoods for the better. However, its effectiveness requires that urban and regional planners are keen on ensuring that it does discriminate against blacks from thriving. In that context, homeownership among blacks should be treated so that the gentrification process does not remove them from their homes; rather, it should improve their access to safer, better, and more affordable housing. On the other hand, the issue of electric vehicles can only benefit black communities by ensuring that policymakers strongly support the overall concept. Thus, in planning for areas with charging systems, black neighborhoods need prioritization as it is the only way they can embrace this concept of a clean energy economy.

REFERENCES

Agyeman, J., Schlosberg, D., Craven, L., & Matthews, C. (2016). Trends and directions in environmental justice: From inequity to everyday life, community, and just Sustainabilities. *Annual Review of Environment and Resources*, *41*(1), 321–340. doi:10.1146/annurev-environ-110615-090052

Ahmed, U. A., Aktar, M. A., & Alam, M. M. (2021). Racial discrimination and poverty reduction for sustainable development. Encyclopedia of the UN Sustainable Development Goals, 741-750. https://doi.org/ doi:10.1007/978-3-319-95714-2_10

Althor, G., & Witt, B. (2020). A quantitative systematic review of distributive environmental justice literature: A rich history and the need for an enterprising future. *Journal of Environmental Studies and Sciences*, *10*(1), 91–103. doi:10.100713412-019-00582-9

Arora, N. K., Fatima, T., Mishra, I., Verma, M., Mishra, J., & Mishra, V. (2018). Environmental sustainability: Challenges and viable solutions. *Environmental Sustainability*, *1*(4), 309–340. doi:10.100742398-018-00038-w

Ash, M., & Boyce, J. K. (2018). Racial disparities in pollution exposure and employment at US industrial facilities. *Proceedings of the National Academy of Sciences of the United States of America*, *115*(42), 10636–10641. doi:10.1073/pnas.1721640115 PMID:30275295

Banzhaf, H. S., Ma, L., & Timmins, C. (2019). Environmental justice: Establishing causal relationships. *Annual Review of Resource Economics*, *11*(1), 377–398. doi:10.1146/annurev-resource-100518-094131

Banzhaf, S., Ma, L., & Timmins, C. (2019). Environmental justice: The economics of race, place, and pollution. *The Journal of Economic Perspectives*, *33*(1), 185–208. doi:10.1257/jep.33.1.185 PMID:30707005

Benz, T. A. (2017). Toxic cities: Neoliberalism and environmental racism in Flint and Detroit Michigan. *Critical Sociology*, *45*(1), 49–62. doi:10.1177/0896920517708339

Boone, C. G., Buckley, G. L., Grove, J. M., & Sister, C. (2009). Parks and people: An environmental justice inquiry in Baltimore, Maryland. *Annals of the Association of American Geographers*, *99*(4), 767–787. doi:10.1080/00045600903102949

Bostic, R. W., & Martin, R. W. (2003). Black home-owners as a gentrifying force? Neighbourhood dynamics in the context of minority home-ownership. *Urban Studies (Edinburgh, Scotland)*, *40*(12), 2427–2449. doi:10.1080/0042098032000136147

Brulle, R. J., & Pellow, D. N. (2006). Environmental justice: Human health and environmental inequalities. *Annual Review of Public Health*, *27*(1), 103–124. doi:10.1146/annurev.publhealth.27.021405.102124 PMID:16533111

Bullard, R. D. (2002). Confronting environmental racism in the twenty-first century. *Global Dialogue*, *4*(1), 34. https://www.proquest.com/openview/639d07e04d3cbf5beab4a8cbcb f3c406/1?pq-origsite=gscholar&cbl=55193

Byrnes, W. M. (2013). Climate justice, Hurricane Katrina, and African American environmentalism. *Journal of African American Studies*, *18*(3), 305–314. doi:10.100712111-013-9270-5

Clayton, S. (2003). Environmental identity: A conceptual and an operational definition. *Identity and the natural environment: The psychological significance of nature*, 45-65.

Clough, E. (2018). Environmental justice and fracking: A review. *Current Opinion in Environmental Science & Health*, *3*, 14–18. doi:10.1016/j.coesh.2018.02.005

Collins, T. W., & Grineski, S. E. (2019). Environmental injustice and religion: Outdoor air pollution disparities in metropolitan Salt Lake City, Utah. *Annals of the American Association of Geographers*, *109*(5), 1597–1617. doi:10.1080/24694452.2018.1546568

Cushing, L. J., Faust, J., August, L. M., Cendak, R., Wieland, W., & Alexeeff, G. (2015). Racial/Ethnic disparities in cumulative environmental health impacts in California: Evidence from a statewide environmental justice screening tool (Calenviroscreen 1.1). *ISEE Conference Abstracts*, 2015(1), 1790. 10.1289/isee.2015.2015-1790

Daystar, M. (2021). Developing a Liberatory Consciousness. *Women and Leadership Development in College: A Facilitation Resource.*

Ding, L., & Hwang, J. (2020). *Effects of gentrification on homeowners: Evidence from a natural experiment.* Working paper (Federal Reserve Bank of Philadelphia). doi:10.21799/frbp.wp

Dlugosch, O., Brandt, T., & Neumann, D. (2020). Combining analytics and simulation methods to assess the impact of shared, autonomous electric vehicles on sustainable urban mobility. *Information & Management*, 103285.

Downey, L. (2006). Environmental racial inequality in Detroit. *Social Forces*, *85*(2), 771–796. doi:10.1353of.2007.0003 PMID:21874071

Egede, L. E., & Walker, R. J. (2020). Structural racism, social risk factors, and Covid-19—A dangerous convergence for Black Americans. *The New England Journal of Medicine*, *383*(12), e77. doi:10.1056/NEJMp2023616 PMID:32706952

Feagin, J. (2013). *Systemic racism: A theory of oppression.* Routledge. doi:10.4324/9781315880938

Gibbons, J., & Barton, M. S. (2016). The association of minority self-rated health with Black versus white gentrification. *Journal of Urban Health*, *93*(6), 909–922. doi:10.100711524-016-0087-0 PMID:27761683

Graves, J. L., & Goodman, A. H. (2021). Chapter Four. Why Do Races Differ In Disease Incidence? In Racism, Not Race (pp. 82-101). Columbia University Press.

Hajian, M., & Kashani, S. J. (2021). Evolution of the concept of sustainability. From Brundtland Report to sustainable development goals. In *Sustainable Resource Management* (pp. 1–24). Elsevier. doi:10.1016/B978-0-12-824342-8.00018-3

Hardman, S., Fleming, K., Khare, E., & Ramadan, M. M. (2021). A perspective on equity in the transition to electric vehicle. *MIT Science Policy Review*, *2*, 46–54. doi:10.38105pr.e10rdoaoup

Harnois, C. E., Bastos, J. L., Campbell, M. E., & Keith, V. M. (2019). Measuring perceived mistreatment across diverse social groups: An evaluation of the Everyday Discrimination Scale. *Social Science & Medicine*, *232*, 298–306. doi:10.1016/j.socscimed.2019.05.011 PMID:31121440

Holland, B. (2020). Capabilities, well-being, and environmental justice 1. In *Environmental Justice* (pp. 64–77). Routledge. doi:10.4324/9780429029585-7

Hsu, C., & Fingerman, K. (2021). Public electric vehicle charger access disparities across race and income in California. *Transport Policy*, *100*, 59–67. doi:10.1016/j.tranpol.2020.10.003

Jones, R. E., & Rainey, S. A. (2006). Examining linkages between race, environmental concern, health, and justice in a highly polluted community of color. *Journal of Black Studies*, *36*(4), 473–496. doi:10.1177/0021934705280411

Kaufman, J. D., & Hajat, A. (2021). Confronting environmental racism. *Environmental Health Perspectives*, *129*(5), 051001. doi:10.1289/EHP9511 PMID:34014764

Keeble, A. (2021). From Trauma Theory to Systemic Violence. *The City in American Literature and Culture*, 276.

Kojola, E., & Pellow, D. N. (2021). New directions in environmental justice studies: Examining the state and violence. *Environmental Politics*, *30*(1-2), 100–118. doi:10.1080/09644016.2020.1836898

Lee, C. (2019). Toxic waste and race in the United States. In *Race and the Incidence of Environmental Hazards* (pp. 10–27). Routledge. doi:10.4324/9780429303661-2

Malin, S. A., & Ryder, S. S. (2018). Developing deeply intersectional environmental justice scholarship. *Environmental Sociology*, *4*(1), 1–7. doi:10.1080/23251042.2018.1446711

Mathewson, P. D., Evans, S., Byrnes, T., Joos, A., & Naidenko, O. V. (2020). Health and economic impact of nitrate pollution in drinking water: A Wisconsin case study. *Environmental Monitoring and Assessment*, *192*(11), 1–18. doi:10.100710661-020-08652-0 PMID:33095309

McCabe, B. J. (2018). Why buy a home? Race, ethnicity, and homeownership preferences in the United States. *Sociology of Race and Ethnicity (Thousand Oaks, Calif.)*, *4*(4), 452–472. doi:10.1177/2332649217753648

Momeni, E., & Antipova, A. (2022). A micro-level analysis of commuting and urban land using the Simpson's index and socio-demographic factors. *Applied Geography (Sevenoaks, England)*, *145*, 102755. doi:10.1016/j.apgeog.2022.102755

Mora-Rivera, J., & García-Mora, F. (2021). Internet access and poverty reduction: Evidence from rural and urban Mexico. *Telecommunications Policy*, *45*(2), 102076. doi:10.1016/j.telpol.2020.102076

Nardone, A., Rudolph, K., Morello-Frosch, R., & Casey, J. (2020). Redlines and greenspace: The relationship between historical redlining and 2010 greenspace across the United States. *ISEE Conference Abstracts,* 2020(1). 10.1289/isee.2020.virtual.P-0061

Neville, H. A., Ruedas-Gracia, N., Lee, B. A., Ogunfemi, N., Maghsoodi, A. H., Mosley, D. V., LaFromboise, T. D., & Fine, M. (2021). The public psychology for liberation training model: A call to transform the discipline. *The American Psychologist*, *76*(8), 1248–1265. doi:10.1037/amp0000887 PMID:35113591

Nicholls, E., Ely, A., Birkin, L., Basu, P., & Goulson, D. (2020). The contribution of small-scale food production in urban areas to the sustainable development goals: A review and case study. *Sustainability Science*, *15*(6), 1585–1599. doi:10.100711625-020-00792-z

Onwuachi-Willig, A. (2021). The Trauma of Awakening to Racism: Did the Tragic Killing of George Floyd Result in Cultural Trauma for Whites? *Houston Law Review*, *58*(4), 22269.

Park, Y. M., & Kwan, M. P. (2020). Understanding racial disparities in exposure to traffic-related air pollution: Considering the spatiotemporal dynamics of population distribution. *International Journal of Environmental Research and Public Health*, *17*(3), 908. doi:10.3390/ijerph17030908 PMID:32024171

Parris, C. L., Hegtvedt, K. A., & Johnson, C. (2020). Assessments of environmental injustice among Black Americans. *Social Currents*, *8*(1), 45–63. doi:10.1177/2329496520950808

Pastor, M. (2007). Environmental justice: Reflections from the United States. *Reclaiming Nature*, 351-378. doi:10.7135/UPO9781843313465.015

Payne-Sturges, D. C., Gee, G. C., & Cory-Slechta, D. A. (2021). Confronting racism in environmental health sciences: Moving the science forward for eliminating racial inequities. *Environmental Health Perspectives*, *129*(5), 055002. Advance online publication. doi:10.1289/EHP8186 PMID:33945300

Perry, M. J., Arrington, S., Freisthler, M. S., Ibe, I. N., McCray, N. L., Neumann, L. M., Tajanlangit, P., & Trejo Rosas, B. M. (2021). Pervasive structural racism in environmental epidemiology. *Environmental Health*, *20*(1), 119. Advance online publication. doi:10.118612940-021-00801-3 PMID:34784917

Polasky, S., Kling, C. L., Levin, S. A., Carpenter, S. R., Daily, G. C., Ehrlich, P. R., Heal, G. M., & Lubchenco, J. (2019). Role of economics in analyzing the environment and sustainable development. *Proceedings of the National Academy of Sciences of the United States of America*, *116*(12), 5233–5238. doi:10.1073/pnas.1901616116 PMID:30890656

Pulido, L. (2017). Rethinking environmental racism: White privilege and urban development in Southern California. In *Environment* (pp. 379–407). Routledge.

SchuslerT. M.EspedidoC. B.RiveraB. K.HernandezM.HowertonA. M.SeppK.EngelM. D.MarcosJ. ChaudharyB. (2020). Students of color speak on racial equity in environmental sustainability. https:// doi.org/ doi:10.32942/OSF.IO/NTEZC

Su, L., Hsu, M. K., & Boostrom, R. E. Jr. (2020). From recreation to responsibility: Increasing environmentally responsible behavior in tourism. *Journal of Business Research*, *109*, 557–573. doi:10.1016/j. jbusres.2018.12.055

Taylor, D. E. (2020). Mobilizing for environmental justice in communities of color: An emerging profile of people of color environmental groups. In *Ecosystem management: Adaptive strategies for natural resources organizations in the twenty-first century* (pp. 33–67). CRC Press.

Toolis, E. E. (2021). Restoring the balance between people, places, and profits: A psychosocial analysis of uneven community development and the case for placemaking processes. *Sustainability (Basel)*, *13*(13), 7256. doi:10.3390u13137256

Viswanathan, L., & Varghese, G. (2018). Greening of business: A step towards sustainability. *Journal of Public Affairs*, *18*(2), e1705. doi:10.1002/pa.1705

Wagaman, M. A., Odera, S. G., & Fraser, D. V. (2019). A pedagogical model for teaching racial justice in social work education. *Journal of Social Work Education*, *55*(2), 351–362. doi:10.1080/10437797. 2018.1513878

Waldron, I. R. (2021). *There's something in the water: Environmental racism in Indigenous & Black communities*. Fernwood Publishing.

Wright, W. J. (2021). As above, so below: Anti-Black violence as environmental racism. *Antipode*, *53*(3), 791–809. doi:10.1111/anti.12425

Zhao, J., Xi, X., Na, Q., Wang, S., Kadry, S. N., & Kumar, P. M. (2021). The technological innovation of hybrid and plug-in electric vehicles for environment carbon pollution control. *Environmental Impact Assessment Review*, *86*, 106506. doi:10.1016/j.eiar.2020.106506

Chapter 3
A Critical Analytical View of Control Theory and the Geopolitical and Economic Drivers Affecting Cyber Security Warfare

Eugene J. Lewis
ⓘD https://orcid.org/0000-0002-2956-0760
Capitol Technology University, USA

Maria D. Baez
ⓘD https://orcid.org/0000-0002-5693-3825
Capitol Technology University, USA

ABSTRACT

Nearly 1 billion emails were exposed in 1 single year affecting 20% or 1 and 5 internet users, causing cyber security warfare worldwide. Under the control theoretic approach, users can prescribe defense actions to security alerts that provide system alerts of cyber-attacks in progress when the network is compromised. This critical analytical view of the World Economic Forum statistical data surrounds the five major drivers affecting the geopolitical and economic conditions of the top 50 nations based on public motivation, government policy, education system, labor market, and population inclusivity. The statistical data illustrates how data breaches have become an ongoing business issue causing an average of $4.35 million annually per organization. Within the cyber security market spectrum, control theory can address some of the challenges associated with geopolitical and economic drivers affecting cyber security warfare by providing a framework for designing and implementing adaptive security systems.

DOI: 10.4018/979-8-3693-1630-6.ch003

A CRITICAL ANALYTICAL VIEW OF CONTROL THEORY

The concept of control theory in cyber security has multiple facets. Control theory focuses on interconnectivity with issues facing cyber security anomalies and attacks causing challenges in performance (Zhong, 2022; Han et al., 2021; Castro, De Giovannini, Sato, Hübener & Rubio, 2023). Control theory is the process of how organizations use challenges and issues to find systematic solutions to improve system infrastructure, distribution strategies, and communication channels (Ali et al., 2023). In this study, control theory is used to formulate adaptive systems to create greater efficiency and effectiveness (Han et al., 2021; Castro et al., 2023). The control factor approach assists countries and organizations with efficiency and effectiveness as cyber attackers become more knowledgeable and creative. New innovations of security are required to mitigate attacks (Han et al., 2021; Castro et al., 2023). The concept of control theory was initially proposed as an engineering quality assurance (QA) function to resolve issues and challenges in production and manufacturing. However, the concept later used in cyber security to develop new ways of determining cluster-based attacks, cascading system failures, and overall decrease data congestion (Han et al., 2021; Castro et al., 2023). Although, the basis of control theory is a quality assurance (QA) function the concept is relevant to the cyber security warfare challenges of today.

The critical analytical view of control theory is useful to organizations as interconnectivity play a significant role in quality assurance measurements. As cyber security warfare expands, so do the culprits (Ali et al., 2023). Incorrect control signals and data interruptions provide root causes in cyber security challenges (Han et al., 2021; Castro et al., 2023). Therefore, adapting a quality assurance function to assist in the fight against cyber security attacks is appropriate to the long-standing view of future developments and innovations of security (Han et al., 2021; Castro et al., 2023; Castro et al., 2023). Moreover, failures in critical infrastructure due to software developments and internet connectivity cause organizations to become extremely volatile to cyber-attacks of all kinds (Ali et al., 2023; Han). Organizations must transition failure rates, network instability, and security interfaces in assessing high demands of loss, delay, error, or other risks (Han et al., 2021; Castro et al., 2023). Control theory is the framework for how organizations develop real-time data updates that are executable as quality control measurements, protocols, and commands (Han et al., 2021; Castro et al., 2023). Control theory functions as a probe of reliable security control structures and plans to develop corrective actions to growing failures.

THE GEOPOLITICAL AND ECONOMIC DRIVERS AFFECTING CYBER SECURITY WARFARE

According to the Cybersecurity and Infrastructure Security Agency [CISA] (2022), 47% of American Adults have had their personal information exposed by cyber criminals (Chen et al., 2022). Combining control theory and understanding the geopolitical and economic drivers affecting cyber security warfare can help improve digital infrastructure security and protect against cyber-attacks (Bello et al., 2023; Cai & Zhao, 2023; Zhao et al., 2021; Han, et al., 2021). Control theory in the cyber security industry is the method in which organizations use methodology of encryption and decryption to secure networks from cyber anomalies and attacks (Bello et al., 2023; Zhao et al., 2021. According to Microsoft, nearly 80% of nation-state attackers targeted government agencies, think tanks, and other non-government entities (Watters, 2023). In addition, fraud cases increased in 2020 by nearly 70% as the quest for information proceeds (Sobers, 2022).

Data has become an expensive yet delicate resource to nations worldwide. The concept of government control or control theory further highlights a growing sentiment involving studying how systems are designed and controlled. To achieve specific goals, stability, performance, and robustness security measures must be adopted to enhance security measurements. For example, cybercrime statistics by attack type determined that phishing attacks increased by 48% in the first half of 2022, with reports of 11,395 incidents costing businesses $12.3 million (Sobers, 2022; Watters, 2023; Zhao et al., 2021).

Research suggests that up to 40% of cyber threats occur directly through supply chain channels (Watters, 2023). Cyber security warfare and control theory apply as security systems respond to changing threats (Cai & Zhao, 2023). Geopolitical and economic drivers significantly impact cyber security warfare (Chen et al., 2022; Bello et al., 2023). These drivers include political tensions between countries, economic competition, and a desire for strategic advantage. These drivers can shape how countries approach cyber security warfare (Chen et al., 2022; Huang et al., 2023). Moreover, influence the design and implementation of security systems.

Control theory suggests controlling the infrastructure of the cyber security network (Zhao et al., 2021). Control theory protects computer networks and systems from cyber-attacks (Zhao et al., 2021; Zhong, 2022). The geopolitical and economic drivers are complex and multifaceted features of controlling those mechanisms. Geopolitical drivers, such as political tensions between nations, can increase cyber-attacks through espionage or sabotage. In such scenarios, control theory detects and responds to cyber-attacks in real-time (Chen et al., 2022; Huang et al., 2023). Intrusion detection systems, firewalls, and other security protocols prevent unauthorized access to computer systems. Economic drivers, such as the growing importance of digital commerce, impact cyber security warfare as more businesses rely on digital technologies to conduct their daily activities.

The potential impact of cyber-attacks on these systems becomes increasingly significant. Control theory protocols protect cyber-attacks, such as encryption, authentication, and access control mechanisms (Zhao et al., 2021; Bello et al., 2023). In addition, other factors such as technological advancements, social and cultural norms, and legal and regulatory frameworks impact cyber security warfare. Control theory implements control mechanisms addressing these factors and mitigating the risk associated with the potential breach (Zhao et al., 2021; Bello et al., 2023). Overall, control theory plays an invaluable role in strategizing sustainability measurements (Zhong, 2022).

Problem Statement

The issue of cybersecurity has emerged as a crucial concern for nations globally as geopolitical and economic factors have begun to impact their cybersecurity infrastructure. The Council of Economic Advisers (CEA) and the National Cyber Security Centre (NCS) have identified challenges the leading 50 nations encounter in tackling the drivers mentioned above. These challenges include but are not limited to public motivation, government policy, the education system, the labor market, and population inclusivity. Nonetheless, a need for more all-encompassing research exists regarding the impact of these drivers on the cybersecurity of nations, as mentioned earlier (United Nations [UN], 2018; World Economic Forum [WEF], 2018).

Moreover, the existing literature needs to be more comprehensive in exploring the potential of control theory in mitigating the factors and enhancing cybersecurity in concerned countries (International Labour Organization [ILO], 2018; UNU, 2018). The overarching concern is to examine the impact of the five primary factors on geopolitical and economic conditions. The focal matter pertains to devising strategies for the top 50 nations, which are selected based on public motivation, government policy, education system, labor market, and population inclusivity, to tackle cybersecurity threats. The proposed approach involves leveraging control theory to enhance cybersecurity measures.

Purpose of the Study

The purpose of the study is to demonstrate how cybersecurity warfare is a growing challenge all over the world, not just in the United States. The study seeks to provide enlightenment into an ever-growing challenge and issue in the cyber security industry which is the lack of quality controls. Control theory in developing conjunctive frameworks can potentially assist organizations with quality assurance measurements to mitigate risk factors affecting the company's infrastructure with data anomalies and attacks. The purpose of the research is to assist industry and academics in developing prospective solutions of using control theory as a quality assurance measurement for adaptive security systems.

Significance of the Study

The significance of the study is an invaluable view into how cyber security managed throughout countries and businesses. The mismanagement of calculating risk through determining factors affecting the bottom-line is the significance. Furthermore, failure to enact operational and strategic plans to determine "fragility" in cyber security systems and network adaptability is a continuous challenge amongst practitioners and researchers attempting to gain understanding on future innovations.

Finding The Gap in The Research

The gap in research consists of determining the root causes of cyber security warfare. The cybersecurity statistics demonstrate that one in three homes with computers is infected with malicious software code (CISA, 2022). According to CISA (2022), 65% of Americans online received at least one online scam offer. Furthermore, worldwide consumers lost approximately $386 on average per year dealing with the effects of online criminals and the dark web (CISA, 2022). A lack of data protection, the side effects of a global pandemic, and an increase in exploit sophistication of system protocols become a significant detriment to an organization's bottom line (Cai & Zhao, 2023; Huang et al., 2023).

Cyber-attacks through hacking and system breaches have significant impacts (Sobers, 2022; Chen et al., 2022). According to World Economic Forum, 95% of cybersecurity breaches are caused by human error. Humans sometimes click on the information they deem necessary only to be a function of phishing, malware, or other adware to disrupt an organization's current operations. Therefore, current research must investigate productive ways to combat cyber security warfare issues worldwide.

Regulatory Factors Affecting Cyber Security Warfare

Cybersecurity warfare is rapidly evolving, and many regulatory factors can affect it. Cybersecurity warfare is an ever-growing concern in the modern world, and regulatory factors play a crucial role in shaping the landscape (Cai & Zhao, 2023). One of the most critical regulatory factors affecting cyber security warfare is international law, which establishes the norms and rules of conduct between nations (Huang et al., 2023). International law guides on cyber espionage, cyber terrorism, and cyber-attacks on critical infrastructure (Cai & Zhao, 2023; Huang et al., 2023). Another regulatory factor affecting cyber security warfare is domestic law, which varies by country and can impose legal obligations on individuals and organizations related to cyber security (Cai & Zhao, 2023). In some cases, governments may require certain organizations to implement specific security measures, such as encryption or regular vulnerability assessments.

Industry-specific regulations can also have an impact on cyber security warfare. For example, the financial industry is subject to strict rules regarding the protection of customer data, while the healthcare industry must comply with regulations designed to protect patient data privacy (Cai & Zhao, 2023; Huang et al., 2023). Finally, technological developments can also impact cyber security warfare. For example, emerging technologies such as artificial intelligence and quantum computing will likely have significant implications for cyber security, and regulatory frameworks must adapt to address these new challenges (Cai & Zhao, 2023; Huang et al., 2023). Overall, regulatory factors are critical in shaping the cyber security landscape. Therefore, staying current with these regulations is essential for individuals and organizations to keep safe and secure in an increasingly connected world (Table 1).

Several regulatory factors affect cyber security warfare. They are described as follows:

- **National laws and regulations**. Each country has its own rules and regulations governing cybersecurity and cyber warfare. These laws may address data protection, cybercrime, and information security issues.
- **International law:** International law also plays a role in regulating cyber warfare. The Tallinn Manual, for example, guides the application of international law to cyber operations.
- **Treaties and agreements**: Many countries have signed cyber security and cyber warfare treaties. For example, the Budapest Convention on Cybercrime is an international treaty that aims to harmonize national laws and improve cooperation among countries to combat cybercrime.
- **Industry standards and best practices**: Besides legal and regulatory requirements, industry standards and best practices can help improve cyber security (Cai & Zhao, 2023). These standards may be developed by organizations such as the International Organization for Standardization (ISO) or the National Institute of Standards and Technology (NIST).
- **Government policies**: Governments may also develop policies and guidelines to improve cyber security within their organizations or nationwide. For example, the U.S. government has developed the Cybersecurity Framework to help organizations manage and reduce cyber risk.

These regulatory factors are essential in shaping cybersecurity warfare's legal and operational landscape (Cai & Zhao, 2023). Organizations and individuals involved in cyber security must be aware of these regulations and comply to protect themselves and others from cyber threats (Cai & Zhao, 2023). Geopolitical tensions and rivalries between countries have led to cyber-attacks becoming a tool of statecraft. Nation-states are using cyber-attacks to achieve their strategic objectives, including stealing intellectual property, disrupting critical infrastructure, and conducting espionage. State-sponsored hackers target government agencies, defense contractors, and critical infrastructure providers, such as power grids and water treatment plants, to cause widespread disruption and chaos (Huang et al., 2023).

The use of cyber-attacks as a geopolitical tool is on the rise, and this trend will likely continue in the future (Cai & Zhao, 2023; Huang et al., 2023). From an economic perspective, cyber-attacks have become a lucrative business for criminal organizations (Bronk & Jones, 2022; Zhong, 2022). Cybercriminals are motivated by financial gain and constantly seek new ways to exploit vulnerabilities in computer systems

(Cai & Zhao, 2023). In addition, the rise of cryptocurrencies and the dark web has made it easier for cyber criminals to monetize their activities, as they can receive payment anonymously and avoid detection (Arianna et al., 2022).

Moreover, the increased digitalization of businesses and the broader use of cloud computing and the Internet of Things (IT) have created new attack vectors for cybercriminals (Huang et al., 2023). The need for more skilled cybersecurity professionals has also created vulnerabilities in the industry (Huang et al., 2023). As more businesses adopt digital technologies, the demand for cybersecurity professionals has outpaced supply, leading to a skills gap that cyber criminals exploit (Cai & Zhao, 2023; Huang et al., 2023). Table 1 displays the increased vulnerabilities in the cybersecurity industry from a geopolitical and economic perspective due to state-sponsored cyber-attacks, the monetization of cybercrime, the expanding attack surface of digital technologies, and the shortage of skilled cybersecurity professionals.

Table 1. Regulatory factors affecting cyber security warfare

	Factors	Rationale
1	Nation-state competition	One of the primary drivers of cybersecurity warfare is competition between nation-states. Countries seek to gain an advantage over their rivals by conducting cyber espionage, launching cyber-attacks, and stealing intellectual property.
2	Cyber security regulation	Governments around the world are increasingly implementing cybersecurity regulations that require companies to protect their data and networks from cyber threats. These regulations can have a significant impact on the cybersecurity posture of businesses and nations.
3	Economic Espionage	Cybersecurity warfare can also be driven by economic espionage, as nations seek to steal intellectual property and trade secrets from their competitors. This can give them an advantage in the global marketplace and undermine the competitiveness of their rivals.
4	State sponsored cyber attacks	State-sponsored cyber-attacks are a growing threat to national security, as governments use cyber warfare tactics to disrupt critical infrastructure, conduct espionage, and steal sensitive information.
5	Cyber crime	Cybercrime is a major driver of cybersecurity warfare, as cybercriminals seek to steal personal information, financial data, and intellectual property from individuals and organizations.
6	Cyber security technology advancements	Advances in cybersecurity technology can also drive cybersecurity warfare. As nations and companies develop new technologies to protect against cyber threats, adversaries may seek to develop new tactics to circumvent these defenses.
7	Supply chain vulnerabilities	Supply chain vulnerabilities are a growing concern in cybersecurity warfare, as attackers seek to exploit weaknesses in the technology supply chain to gain access to sensitive data and networks.

Cybersecurity warfare is a critical area heavily regulated by various laws and regulations globally. These regulatory factors ensure information systems, networks, and data safety and security against cyber-attacks (Cai & Zhao, 2023; Huang et al., 2023). For example, in the United States, the National Institute of Standards and Technology (NIST) developed cybersecurity frameworks that organizations can adopt to manage and reduce cybersecurity risk. Additionally, the Federal Information Security Management Act (FISMA) and the Health Insurance Portability and Accountability Act (HIPAA) impose stringent requirements on government agencies and healthcare organizations, respectively, to protect sensitive data.

Similarly, the European Union's General Data Protection Regulation (GDPR) enforces strict regulations on protecting personal data, including data breaches. At the same time, the Network and Information Security Directive (NIS Directive) imposes security requirements on critical infrastructure operators across the EU. In Asia, Japan has implemented the Protection of Personal Information (APPI) Act to regulate the collection, use, and handling of personal information by companies and government agencies. In addition, the International Organization for Standardization (ISO) has also established ISO 27001, a widely recognized information security management standard that systematically manages sensitive information.

Compliance with these regulatory factors is essential in ensuring organizations mitigate cyber-attacks and safeguard sensitive data (Cai & Zhao, 2023). Non-compliance with these regulations can result in significant financial and legal consequences, including hefty fines and reputational damage (Cai & Zhao, 2023; Huang et al., 2023). Overall, cybersecurity warfare's geopolitical and economic drivers are complex and interrelated, and they are likely to evolve as technology and global competition develop.

METHODOLOGY

The methodology for this research study is exploratory design. The experimental research discovers qualitative anomalies through a specific review of the research collected (Creswell, 2014; Zhao et al., 2021). Qualitative research was implemented in this investigation due to its systematic approach that guided us to understanding the lived experiences of individuals in those nations facing cyber warfare due to limitations in security measurements to improve the organizational information system (Creswell, 2014; Kingston, 2023). Control theory is a crucial tool in many fields, including cyber security warfare, where it is used to strategize, detect, and respond to cyber-attacks (Bello et al., 2023; Huang et al., 2023; Zhao et al., 2021). In the investigation of cyber security warfare, several geopolitical and economic drivers can affect the effectiveness of "state and non-state actors" employing the control theory-based approaches (Bello et al., 2023).

State Actors Versus Non-State Actors

The concept of state actors and non-state actors are sub-variables of how control theory impacts and influences geopolitical and economic drivers related to cyber security (Zhao et al., 2021). First, economic factors develop significant financial consequences as digital economies of scale, such as crypto-currency, digital real estate, and other digital forms of capital, create additional revenue streams for the consumer and nations, thus making these facets risk-based (Huang et al., 2023). Second, a resource-based view incentivizing state and non-state actors to engage in cyber-attacks further energizes the technological cyber channels' competitiveness to enhance and gather data (Bronk & Jones, 2022; Yoo, 2022). Third, the digital footprint causes a need for technological advances. Rapid technological advances, such as artificial intelligence and machine learning development, make detecting and responding to cyber-attacks more difficult (Xia & Da-Wei, 2023; Yoo, 2022; Huang).

The theoretical framework surrounding control theory approaches inhabits organizations implementing strategies to adapt and evolve constantly (Bello et al., 2023; Zhao et al., 2021). To effectively address these geopolitical and economic drivers, control theory-based approaches in cyber security warfare being adaptive and responsive (Bronk & Jones, 2022). This requires a deep understanding of the threat landscape and commitment to ongoing research and development. Additionally, collaboration and information sharing among stakeholders, including governments, private sector organizations, and academic institutions, improve the effectiveness of control theory-based approaches in cyber security warfare (Zhao et al., 2021). In Table 2, the diagram demonstrates the differentiation between both state and non-state actors.

Table 2. State actors vs. non-state actors

Unit	Accounts
State Actors	State actors are increasingly involved in cyber security warfare, using sophisticated cyber-attacks to achieve strategic objectives. These actors often have significant resources and capabilities, which can make it difficult for control theory-based approaches to keep up with their tactics.
Non-State Actors	Non-state actors, such as hacktivists, criminal groups, and terrorist organizations, can also pose significant cyber security threats. These actors may be less well-resourced than state actors, but they can still cause significant damage and disruption.

Theoretical Framework Explained

The theoretical framework for this study focuses on critical analytical view as a research method used to understand and interpret complex phenomena, such as cyber security threats and risks, based on non-numerical data (Yoo, 2022). However, this study will analyze current statistical data to discover new phenomena and experiences of nations experiencing cyber-security challenges (Yoo, 2022; Huang et al., 2023). In addition, critical analytical view will be used to identify, understand, and evaluate the effectiveness of security controls and assess the impact of potential threats and vulnerabilities.

For the investigative exploratory critical analytical view, the research will concentrate on the global nation's cyber security measurements. Table 3 validated how this qualitative research methodology involved structured research steps.

Table 3. Qualitative research methodology steps

	Steps	Rationale
1	Defining the research question	This step involves identifying the key research questions or objectives that the analysis aims to answer. For example, the research question could be "What are the key cyber security threats facing our organization, and how effective are our current security controls in mitigating these threats?"
2	Gather data	The next step involves collecting relevant data that can help answer the research questions. This could involve reviewing existing cyber security policies, procedures, and controls, conducting interviews with key stakeholders, and reviewing relevant documentation and reports.
3	Analyze the data	The collected data is then analyzed to identify patterns, themes and trends. This could involve using techniques such as content analysis, thematic analysis, and discourse analysis to identify key themes and patterns in the data.
4	Interpret the findings	Once the data has been analyzed, the findings are then interpreted to draw conclusions and make recommendations. This could involve identifying the key cyber security threats facing the organization, evaluating the effectiveness of existing security controls, and identifying areas where improvements can be made.
5	Communicate the results	The final step involves communicating the findings to relevant stakeholders, such as senior management, IT teams, and other relevant stakeholders. This could involve presenting the findings in a report, presentation, or other format, and providing recommendations for improving the organization's cyber security posture.

Overall, a critical analytical view focused on cyber security organizations better understanding their cyber security risks and threats and identifying areas where improvements can be made to better protect against cyber-attacks (Huang et al., 2023; Yoo, 2022). The theoretical framework used to model and analyze the behavior of systems is called control theory (Bello et al., 2023; Zhong, 2022). It deals with the study of systems, including their feedback loops, and aims to design controllers that can regulate the behavior of these systems. In cybersecurity warfare, control theory can be used to analyze and control the behavior of cyber systems, such as computer networks, to detect and mitigate cyber-attacks (Bello et al., 2023; Huang et al., 2023).

By modeling the behavior of these systems and designing controllers that can regulate their operation, control theory can be used to enhance the resilience of cyber systems against cyber threats. Control theory can be used to design intrusion detection systems (IDS) that can detect and respond to cyber-attacks by monitoring the behavior of a network and generating alerts when abnormal activity is detected (Bello et al., 2023; Zhong, 2022;).

Data Collection

All data collected by World Economic Forum [WEF] (2020) on cyber security. The qualitative study offers an analysis of the statistical data provided by the WEF and the impacts on global cyber security warfare. Control theory provides an informative research opportunity into the data displays of the top 50 countries with a total scale of 800 in safety and security measurements within the cyber security environment (Bello et al., 2023; WEF, 2020; Zhao et al., 2021). Based on the index, the diagram demonstrates five significant drivers affecting the geopolitical and economic communities of the top 50 nations: (a) public motivation, (b) government policy, (c) the education system, (d) the labor market, and (e) population inclusivity. These drivers are the root causes of geopolitical and economic cyber-attacks (WEF, 2020). In addition, top-ranked countries ensure commitment to cyber-risk literacy shifts to potentially more issues based on the political impacts of leadership in each nation (Huang et al., 2023; WEF, 2020). The investigative research provides insights into how countries measure cybersecurity warfare and safety.

FINDINGS AND RESULTS

The study conducted on Control Theory and the Geopolitical and Economic Drivers influencing Cyber Security Warfare through a qualitative approach revealed crucial factors influencing cybersecurity. The research findings have identified five primary determinants that impact a nation's cyber risk, encompassing geopolitical and economic aspects. The examination determined the fundamental origins of the cyber assaults resulting from said factors. Furthermore, the research evaluated the comprehensive condition of the geopolitical and economic catalysts and pinpointed the pivotal motivations that could significantly influence cybersecurity. The study's results significantly contribute to the intricate relationship between geopolitical and economic factors within cybersecurity. These insights can assist policymakers, and security professionals in devising more efficient approaches to address cyber threats.

Critical Factors Affecting Cyber Security Warfare

The findings from the qualitative research provide critical factors in the cyber warfare challenge. Control theory can also be used to design adaptive defense mechanisms that can dynamically adjust their operation based on the changing behavior of the cyber system (Bello et al., 2023). In short, control theory provides a theoretical framework for analyzing and controlling the behavior of cyber systems in the context of cybersecurity warfare (Bello et al., 2023; Chen et al., 2023; Verstraete & Zarsky, 2022). By applying control theory principles, cyber security professionals can design more robust and adaptive defenses against cyber-attacks (Bello et al., 2023).

In cyber security warfare, control theory designs and implements control mechanisms that enable defenders to detect, prevent, and respond to attacks (Yoo, 2022; Bello et al., 2023). One of the primary applications of control theory in cyber security is the design of intrusion detection systems (IDS)(Bello et al., 2023). An IDS is a software or hardware system that monitors network traffic for malicious activity and generates alerts when it detects a potential attack. Control theory is used in the design of IDS to ensure that they effectively see attacks and minimize false positives (Zhong, 2022; Bello et al., 2023). In addition, control theory also designs response mechanisms for cyber-attack attacks (Zhong, 2022; Bello et al., 2023). In the event of a successful attack, the response mechanism should be able to control the damage and limit the attacker's ability to cause further harm. Overall, geopolitical and economic factors can significantly impact cyber security warfare (Huang et al., 2023). Therefore, organizations and governments must stay informed of these drivers and proactively address them. Table 5 exhibits several geopolitical and economic drivers affecting cyber security warfare.

Table 4. Key factors affecting cyber security warfare

Factor	Determinant	Grounds
1	Geopolitical tensions	Geopolitical tensions between nations can lead to an increase in state-sponsored cyber-attacks. For example, political tensions between the United States and Russia have led to a rise in cyber espionage and cyber-attacks.
2	Economic competition	Economic competition between nations can lead to theft of intellectual property and trade secrets. Cyber espionage is often used to steal sensitive information from foreign companies to gain a competitive advantage.
3	Cybersecurity regulations	Government regulations and compliance requirements can impact the way organizations approach cyber security. For example, the General Data Protection Regulation (GDPR) in the European Union requires companies to implement strong data protection measures.
4	Cybersecurity investment	The level of investment in cyber security can impact a nation's ability to defend against cyber-attacks. Countries that invest heavily in cyber security are more likely to have stronger defenses against cyber threats.
5	Cybersecurity talent	The availability of skilled cyber security professionals can impact a nation's ability to defend against cyber-attacks. Countries with a shortage of cyber security talent may struggle to defend against sophisticated cyber threats.
6	International cooperation	International cooperation on cyber security issues can help to prevent cyber-attacks and promote cyber security best practices. Collaboration between nations can help to identify and mitigate cyber threats before they become widespread.

Critical Analytical View of the Cyber Risk by Country Using the Five Major Drivers

In Figure 1, the imagery shows the critical analytical view of how Cyber Risk Literacy and Education Index Rankings by country relate to the five significant drivers constituting the Index underpinned by key pillars related to population risk literacy and education. Also, Figure 1 displays the cyber risks using the five primary drivers of public motivation, government policy, education system, labor market, and population inclusivity as root causes of geopolitical and economic cyber-attacks (WEF, 2020).

Figure 1. Cyber risk literacy and education index rankings by country

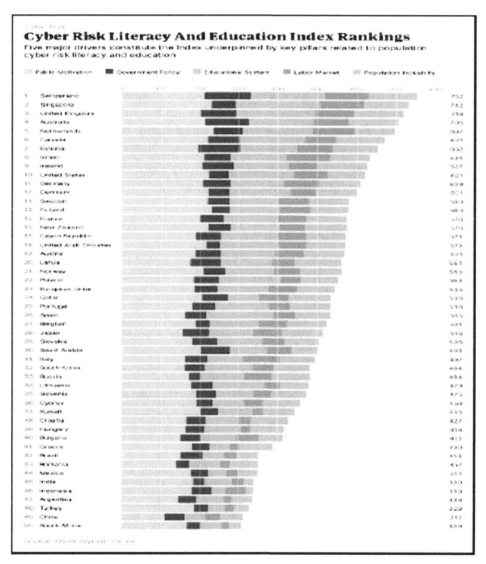

Top-ranked countries ensure commitment to cyber-risk literacy shifts to potentially more issues based on the political impacts of leadership in each nation (WEF, 2020). For example, Switzerland ranked #1 according to the index, which displays how the country's specific goals are transparency to its citizens when assessing cyber warfare. A comprehensive approach to national security by delivering consumer and organizational social responsibility is paramount to the country's growth factor (WEF, 2020). Therefore, giving Switzerland a higher marking as one of the more prosperous nations responsible for ensuring that citizens receive cyber-risk education (WEF, 2020). The nation is educating citizens in the geopolitical and economic space to limit the risk of attacks through cyber wellness (Verstraete & Zarsky, 2022).

Root Causes of Geopolitical and Economic Cyber-Attacks

Overall geopolitical and economic drivers impact cyber security warfare, and countries and businesses must develop effective strategies to protect against cyberattacks (Huang et al., 2023). Table 5 shows the root causes of geopolitical and economic cyberattacks defined by seven key variables.

Table 5. Root causes of geopolitical and economic cyber-attacks

	Roots Causes	Determinants
1	Geopolitical tensions	Political conflicts between nations can lead to cyber-attacks as a means of espionage, sabotage, or disruption. For example, tensions between the US and China have led to accusations of state-sponsored cyber-attacks.
2	Economic espionage	Economic competition can lead to cyber-attacks aimed at stealing intellectual property or trade secrets. This is particularly relevant in industries such a s technology, healthcare, and finance.
3	Cybercrime	Cyber criminals can operate across borders, making it difficult for law enforcement agencies to apprehend them. This can lead to an increase in cyber-attacks on businesses, governments, and individuals.
4	Cyber terrorism	Non-state actors such as terrorist organizations can use cyber-attacks as a means of disrupting critical infrastructure or causing chaos.
5	Cyber deterrence	Countries may use cyber warfare as a means of deterrence against potential adversaries. This can involve the development of offensive cyber capabilities or the establishment of cyber defense capabilities.
6	Cyber espionage	Governments may use cyber-attacks to gather intelligence on other countries. This can involve the use of sophisticated malware or social engineering techniques to gain access to sensitive information.
7	Globalization	The interconnectedness of the global economy has led to an increase in cross-border cyber-attacks. This is particularly relevant in industries such as finance and logistics, where disruptions can have a significant impact on the global economy.

These strategies should include investing in advanced technologies, training employees on cyber-security best practices, and collaborating with other organizations to share threat intelligence. It is also crucial to regularly update and test these strategies to ensure their effectiveness in the face of evolving cyber threats.

Overall Status of Geopolitical and Economic Drivers

For decades, governments have increased their cybersecurity budgets for national defense but have yet to invest enough to teach citizens adequate cyber skills despite our growing reliance on the internet. Unfortunately, this stance has contributed to cyberattacks becoming one of the fastest-growing crimes, costing an estimated $600 billion globally in 2017. Figure 1, Cyber Risk Literacy by Country using the Five Major Drivers (WEF, 2020), provides statistical data displaying how a small group of nations is moving in the right direction showing geographical rankings including European Union (EU), Switzerland, Singapore, United Kingdom, Australia, and the Netherlands providing widespread access to training and citizen support to reduce risk (Figure 2).

Figure 2. Digital identity safety of a nation's citizens (WEF, 2020)

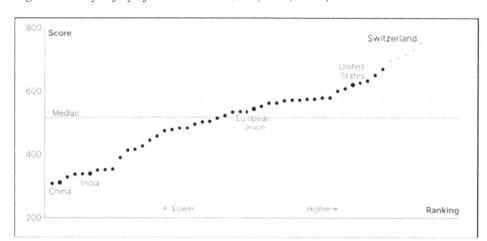

Studies show that 95% of cybersecurity issues can be traced to human error (Huang et al., 2023). Figure 2 provides scholars and researchers data related to behaviors towards cybersecurity challenges such as phishing scams and understanding how digital identity affects the improvement of cybersecurity safety for nations. Governments must improve cybersecurity using the same strategies introduced in other industries. Several geopolitical and economic drivers can affect cyber security warfare. Here are some of the key drivers (Table 6). These geopolitical and economic drivers underscore the importance of robust cybersecurity measures and proactive threat intelligence to protect against the ever-evolving cyber threat landscape (Huang et al., 2023).

Table 6. Geopolitical and economic key drivers

	Key Drivers	Argument
1	State Actors	Nation-states are increasingly engaging in cyber espionage and cyber-attacks against each other, often using cyber weapons to gain advantage over their adversaries.
2	Economic Interests	Many cyber-attacks are motivated by economic interests, such as stealing intellectual property or disrupting the operations of rival companies or countries.
3	Geopolitical Tensions	Cyber-attacks can be used as a tool of political coercion, or to gain strategic advantage in geopolitical conflicts.
4	Technological Advancements	As new technologies emerge; cyber criminals and nation-state actors are constantly adapting their tactics and techniques to take advantage of new vulnerabilities.
5	Globalization	The increasing interconnectedness of the global economy means that cyber-attacks can have far-reaching consequences, potentially disrupting critical infrastructure or causing widespread economic damage.
6	Weak Cybersecurity Practices	In many cases, cyber-attacks are made possible by weak cybersecurity practices, such as outdated software or poor network security.
7	Cybersecurity Regulations	Governments and international organizations are increasingly implementing cybersecurity regulations and standards to mitigate the risks of cyber-attacks, which can impact both businesses and nation-states.

RECOMMENDATIONS

It is advised that policymakers and security professionals adopt a multifaceted strategy to address the challenges posed by the five primary drivers of cyber risk based on the findings and outcomes of the qualitative study on Control Theory and the Geopolitical and Economic Drivers Affecting Cyber Security Warfare.

First and foremost, a thorough understanding of the geopolitical and economic forces influencing cyber risk is necessary to address the key issues affecting cybersecurity warfare. Therefore, policymakers should prioritize creating effective intelligence-gathering and analysis tools to shed light on the underlying causes of cyberattacks. It is necessary to take a comprehensive approach incorporating technical and non-technical measures to address the key issues affecting cyber security warfare. It is crucial to invest in cutting-edge cybersecurity technologies, educate cybersecurity experts, and create cybersecurity regulations suited to each nation's individual requirements.

Second, using the five main drivers in a critical analytical view of cyber risk by a nation can aid in pinpointing particular points of vulnerability and risk. Developing frameworks for information sharing and best practices to reduce cyber threats should be a top priority for policymakers' collaboration with international partners. A critical analytical view using the five main drivers should be conducted regularly to evaluate a nation's cyber risk. The political, economic, social, technological, and environmental factors that affect cybersecurity should be considered in this analysis. Based on the analysis's findings, policymakers can create targeted interventions to reduce the identified risks.

Third, it is essential to identify and address the underlying causes of geopolitical and economic cyberattacks. Consequently, it is necessary to make a concerted effort to create policies and strategies that address the fundamental geopolitical and economic problems that underpin cyberattacks. Policymakers must work to improve international cooperation and diplomatic relations to address the underlying causes of geopolitical and economic cyberattacks. To stop such attacks, it is crucial to establish moral standards and principles for responsible state behavior online.

Fourth, it is essential to continuously monitor and evaluate how geopolitical and economic drivers are faring. Regular risk assessments, trend analysis, and scenario planning are part of this to spot new risks and set resource priorities. In addition, periodic assessments of the overall status of geopolitical and economic drivers should be made to identify recent trends and potential risks. These assessments should guide policy choices and investments in cybersecurity.

Finally, the geopolitical and economic vital drivers that have the most significant effects on cybersecurity should be given priority by policymakers. This includes funding research and developing new technologies and capabilities to address unknown risks and vulnerabilities. Taking on the major forces affecting cybersecurity requires a multi-stakeholder strategy involving the public sector, private sector, civil society, and academic institutions. To create comprehensive strategies that address the complex issues of cybersecurity in a geopolitical and economic environment that is rapidly changing, cooperation is crucial. A multifaceted approach involving investments in technology, policy, and diplomacy is needed to address the conclusions and findings of the qualitative study on Control Theory and the Geopolitical and Economic Drivers Affecting Cyber Security Warfare. Policy policymakers and security experts should collaborate to address the risks identified and defend critical infrastructure, businesses, and citizens from cyber threats.

CONCLUSION

Geopolitical and economic drivers can significantly impact cyber security warfare. Understanding these drivers and their potential implications is essential for developing effective cybersecurity strategies and technologies (Huang et al., 2023). According to the Cybersecurity and Infrastructure Security Agency (CISA), 47% of American Adults have had their personal information exposed by cyber criminals (CISA, 2022). Overall, combining control theory and understanding the geopolitical and economic drivers affecting cyber security warfare can help improve digital infrastructure security and protect against cyberattacks (Yoo, 2022; Verstraete & Zarsky, 2022). It involves studying how systems can be designed and controlled to achieve specific goals, such as stability, performance, and robustness. In cyber security warfare, control theory applies the design and implementation of security systems that can adapt and respond to changing threats (Verstraete & Zarsky, 2022; Bello et al., 2023). Geopolitical and economic drivers have a significant impact on cyber security warfare.

These drivers include political tensions between countries, economic competition, and the desire for strategic advantage. These drivers can shape how countries approach cyber security warfare and influence the design and implementation of security systems. Political tensions between countries or regions can lead to an increase in cyber-attacks. For example, tensions between the US and China have led to a rise in cyber-attacks originating from China. Economic interests can also drive cyber security warfare. Countries may target other countries' critical infrastructure or intellectual property to gain a financial advantage. Military capability is another factor that can affect cyber security warfare. Countries with solid cyber capabilities may use these to attack their enemies or to defend themselves from potential attacks. Ideological differences can also be a driver of cyber security warfare. For example, groups or countries with different political or religious ideologies may use cyber-attacks to further their agendas. The increasing interconnectedness of the global economy and society has led to increased cyber-attacks. The more connected we become, the more vulnerable we are to attacks. Rapid technological advancements have made it easier for cyber attackers to exploit vulnerabilities in computer systems. At the same time, these advancements have also provided new tools and techniques for cyber defense.

Overall, these factors are complex and interconnected, and they will continue to shape the landscape of cyber security warfare in the future (Verstraete & Zarsky, 2022). Therefore, it is vital for governments and organizations to stay aware of these drivers and to take proactive steps to protect their networks and data from potential cyber-attacks (Bronk & Jones, 2022; Zhong, 2022). Control theory is also used in designing security policies and access control mechanisms to ensure that only authorized users can access sensitive information and resources (Zhong, 2022; Bello et al., 2023). Another application of control theory in cybersecurity warfare is in designing and implementing cyber defense strategies (Bello et al., 2023).

Control theory provides a framework for modeling and analyzing attackers' behavior and developing effective countermeasures to prevent or mitigate the cyber-attack impact (Bello et al., 2023; Huang et al., 2023). Control theory can also be used to develop strategies for responding to cyber-attacks in real time, such as by automatically triggering defensive measures or initiating incident response procedures (Bronk & Jones, 2022; Bello et al., 2023). Overall, control theory provides a powerful framework for enhancing the security of systems in the context of cybersecurity warfare (Zhong, 2022; Bello et al., 2023). By providing a means to detect and respond to security threats in real-time, control theory can help to prevent or mitigate the impact of cyber-attacks and protect critical infrastructure and sensitive information from malicious actors (Bronk & Jones, 2022; Huang et al., 2023). Another area of future investigation is deterrence theory and its relationship to the cyber security warfare challenge.

Deterrence theory is based on the idea that a strong defense is the best way to prevent cyberattacks and that the threat of retaliation can deter potential attackers from acting (Mastro, 2022). In cybersecurity, deterrence theory suggests that a solid defensive posture can dissuade potential attackers from targeting a system or network (Mastro, 2022). This may involve implementing firewalls, antivirus software, and other security protocols to prevent unauthorized access and protect sensitive data. In addition to defensive measures, deterrence theory also emphasizes the importance of having a credible threat of retaliation (Mastro, 2022). This means that if an attacker does breach a system or network, there must be consequences that make the risk of attack not worth the potential reward (Bronk & Jones, 2022). Overall, the deterrence theory framework suggests that a combination of solid defense and credible threats of retaliation can help to deter cyberattacks and protect against potential harm (Mastro, 2022). However, it is essential to note that this approach could be better, and other factors, such as the motivation and capabilities of attackers, must also be considered in cybersecurity warfare.

REFERENCES

Ali, N. A., Kanesan, J., Anis Salwa, M. K., Irfan, A. B., Kamangar, S., Hussien, M., & Maughal Ahmed, A. B. (2023). Training Multilayer Neural Network Based on Optimal Control Theory for Limited Computational Resources. *Mathematics*, *11*(3), 778. doi:10.3390/math11030778

Arianna, T., Kamps, J., Akartuna, E. A., Hetzel, F. J., Bennett, K., Davies, T., & Johnson, S. D. (2022). Cryptocurrencies and future financial crime. *Crime Science*, *11*(1), 1. Advance online publication. doi:10.118640163-021-00163-8 PMID:35013699

Bello, A., Jahan, S., Farid, F., & Ahamed, F. (2023). A Systemic Review of the Cybersecurity Challenges in Australian Water Infrastructure Management. *Water (Basel)*, *15*(1), 168. doi:10.3390/w15010168

Bronk, C., & Jones, N. (2023). Cyber Cases: The PICCA Framework for Documenting Geopolitically Relevant Cyber Action. *Journal of Strategic Security*, *16*(1), 72–89. doi:10.5038/1944-0472.16.1.2068

Cai, C., & Zhao, L. (2023). Information sharing and deferral option in cybersecurity investment. *PLoS One*, *18*(2), e0281314. Advance online publication. doi:10.1371/journal.pone.0281314 PMID:36745656

Castro, A., De Giovannini, U., Sato, S. A., Hübener, H., & Rubio, A. (2023). Floquet engineering with quantum optimal control theory. *New Journal of Physics*, *25*(4), 043023. doi:10.1088/1367-2630/accb05

Chen, S., Hao, M., Ding, F., Jiang, D., Dong, J., Zhang, S., Guo, Q., & Gao, C. (2023). Exploring the global geography of cybercrime and its driving forces. *Humanities & Social Sciences Communications*, *10*(1), 71. doi:10.105741599-023-01560-x PMID:36852135

Cybersecurity & Infrastructure Security Agency (CISA). (2022). *America's Cyber Defense Agency*. The Facts. https://www.cisa.gov/be-cyber-smart/facts https://connect.comptia.org/blog/cyber-security-stats-facts doi:10.1016/j.cogr.2021.05.001

Han, Y., Liu, J., Lei, Y., Liu, L., & Ye, S. (2021). The Analysis and Application of Decentralized Cyber Layer and Distributed Security Control for Interconnected Conurbation Grids under Catastrophic Cascading Failures. *2021 3rd Asia Energy and Electrical Engineering Symposium (AEEES)*, 794-799, 10.1109/AEEES51875.2021.9402955

Huang, X., Xia, Y., & Da-Wei, D. (2023). Distributed Event-Triggered Synchronization for Complex Cyber–Physical Networks under DoS Attacks. *Applied Sciences (Basel, Switzerland)*, *13*(3), 1716. doi:10.3390/app13031716

Mastro, O. S. (2022). Deterrence in the Indo-Pacific. *Asia Policy, 17*(4), 8-18. https://www.proquest.com/scholarly-journals/deterrence-indo-pacific/docview/2731215788/se-2

Sobers, R. (2022). *166 Cybersecurity Statistics and Trends*. Varonis. Inside Out Security. https://www.varonis.com/blog/cybersecurity-statistics

Verstraete, M., & Zarsky, T. (2022). Cybersecurity Spillovers. *Brigham Young University Law Review*, *47*(3), 929–999. https://www.proquest.com/scholarly-journals/cybersecurity-spillovers/docview/2677676009/se-2

Watters, A. (2023). *Top 50 Cybersecurity Statistics, Figures, and Facts. CompTIA. World Economic Forum*. Cybersecurity. After reading, writing, and arithmetic, the 4th 'r' of literacy is cyber-risk. https://www.weforum.org/agenda/2020/12/cyber-risk-cyber-security-education

Yoo, I. T. (2022). Cybersecurity Crisscrossing International Development Cooperation: Unraveling the Cyber Capacity Building of East Asian Middle Powers Amid Rising Great Power Conflicts. *Korea Observer*, *53*(3), 447–470. doi:10.29152/KOIKS.2022.53.3.447

Yuchong, L., & Qinghui, L. (2021). A comprehensive review study of cyber-attacks and cyber security; Emerging trends and recent developments. *Energy Reports*, *7*, 8176–8186. doi:10.1016/j.egyr.2021.08.126

Zhong, F. (2022). Security Control for Time-Varying Delay Systems Based on Random Switching Moving Defense Method in Cyber-Physical Environment. *Journal of Physics: Conference Series, 2381*(1), 012068. doi:10.1088/1742-6596/2381/1/012068

Zi-gang, Z., & Rong-bo, Ye. (2021). Control-theory-based security control of cyber-physical power systems under multiple cyber-attacks within a unified model framework. *Cognitive Robotics, 1*, 41–57. doi:10.1016/j.cogr.2021.05.001

Chapter 4
Going Beyond the D:
Focusing on the E and I

Stacey L. Morin

ⓘD https://orcid.org/0000-0003-2935-8332

Marymount University, USA

ABSTRACT

This chapter illustrates how corporations need to go beyond the D in diversity and focus on the E in equity and I for inclusion to prioritize the worker based on the alignment of critical theory. The literature search led to the discovery of critical theory, which was then used to inform a strategic intervention. Diversity is existence of variations of different characteristics in a group of people. Equity is fair treatment, access, and advancement for each person in an organization. Inclusion is an outcome to ensure those who are diverse feel and/or are welcomed. Obstacles in the way of the E and I need to be addressed if organizations truly want to create a robust DEI program for their workers. This chapter examines how scholars and senior leadership will acknowledge inequity and exclusive behavior in their organizations, bringing the awareness of the need to focus on the E and I.

INTRODUCTION

The purpose of this paper is to solve for the inequities and exclusive behavior in the organization. Typically, these organizations are led by white men in leadership roles (Bearden, 2018). The target audience is minorities and women who are affected most in workplace (Flynn, 2022). Organizations also suffer from lawsuits, employee turnover, etc. which is further discussed in the Literature Review section. Without a strong Diversity, Equity, and Inclusion (DEI) program that addresses all the letters and is overseen by leadership that is knowledgeable on the subject, it is impossible for organizational development. Both researchers and practitioners have strived (and struggled) to understand the concept, its effects in and on organizations, and strategies for managing such effects (Roberson, 2019). One of the major issues facing organizations is managing an increasingly diverse, inclusive, and equitable workforce. Multiple studies on workplace diversity show that there has been little to no progress. While systemic issues spanning centuries cannot be fixed by any one company, employers can put their own systems in place

DOI: 10.4018/979-8-3693-1630-6.ch004

to create equity in their work culture (Cuadra, 2022). Diversity is the range of human differences that encompasses national origin, language, race, color, disability, ethnicity, gender, age, religion, sexual orientation, gender identity, socioeconomic status, and veteran status (American Psychology Association, n.d.). Equity is fair practices and policies acknowledging structural inequalities (American Psychology Association, n.d.). Inclusion is where all employees feel a sense of belonging and respected (American Psychology Association, n.d.). A diverse workplace is the acceptance and inclusion of all employees of different backgrounds.

To address this need and keep up with the evolving business environment, researchers have focused on the study of organizational diversity, including its contexts. What is missing is a program design that emphasizes equity and inclusion. A typical organization hires a few candidates from diverse backgrounds, but they never advance nor do feel part of an inclusive environment. White men appear to have a monopoly on leadership roles; this a result of how most organizations approach leadership development (Fitzsimmons & Callan, 2020). The DEI issue is addressed utilizing a seven-step Critical Theory process. Critical Theory scholars generally call for an end to racism, sexism, and classism and the dismantling of white supremacy and patriarchy (Golash-Boza et al., 2019).

PROBLEM STATEMENT

Lack of diversity, equity, and inclusion is a form of workplace discrimination. Organizations check the diversity box by hiring a few diverse employees (gender and ethnicity), but often fall short on equity and inclusion. Research shows that diverse employees are assistants and subordinates (Bell & Hartmann, 2007). The problem is with the senior management, affecting diverse employees and or candidates in many organizations. This paper contributes to the literature addressing the needs of going beyond diversity and emphasizing equity and inclusion in the workplace and what can be done to achieve that by employing Critical Theory.

LITERATURE REVIEW

To address the role of equity and inclusion, organizations should commit to DEI in the workplace addressing all the letters. A literature search was conducted by searching for articles on Corporate Social Responsibility (CSR) in Organizations. CSR is a broad subject. The emphasis is narrowed to DEI within an organization. It is narrowed further to focus on equity and inclusion within the organization. Several theories were examined in the literature review, and critical theory was selected. This paper will concentrate on Critical Theory only. Critical Theory is one of the primary theories in DEI and integration. Critical theory gives employees more control over the outcome (Fay, 1987). White men having all the decision-making authority is not working. Google Scholar, ProQuest, Business Source Complete (EBSCO Host), and JSTOR was used for the study design for going beyond the D, and focusing on the E and I. The research intended to illustrate the relationship between all the letters of DEI and applying theory.

Numerous research has examined the connection between DEI in the organization and the demographic composition by gender and ethnicity. Table 1 illustrates the demographics of *Fortune* 500 CEOs over a 3-year period. Senior management consists of white men. Eighty-six percent of *Fortune* 500 CEOs were white men, according to data provided exclusively to SHRM (Bearden, 2018). Table 2 illustrates the demographics of *Fortune* 500 board seats over an 8-year period. To date, women and minorities are underrepresented on corporate boards and as CEOs of *Fortune* 500 companies. Development processes alone will not result in more diverse senior leadership populations. These findings present a significant challenge to proponents of leadership development approaches that fail to recognize the fields of power that determine who advance as a leader (Williams, 2018). It is the continuation of white men hiring and promoting white men. These tables tell a story: women and minorities do not have a seat at the table. The fact remains, that progress has been painfully slow making it impossible to move past the D to concentrating on the E and I. This paper will bridge the science-practitioner gap despite white men continuing to be in charge, and making it possible to go beyond the D, focusing on the E and I. Critical Theory will be addressed as a solution in a later section.

Table 1. Demographics of Fortune 500 CEOs by ethnicity/gender

Demographics	2019	2020	2021	2019%	2020%	2021%
White Men	428	431	430	85.6%	86.2%	86.0%
White Women	35	35	34	7.0%	7.0%	6.8%
Black Men	4	5	2	0.8%	1.0%	0.4%
Black Women	1	0	2	0.2%	0.0%	0.4%
Latin Men	20	16	17	4.0%	3.2%	3.4%
Latin Women	0	1	0	0.0%	0.2%	0.0%
Asian Men	10	10	10	2.0%	2.0%	2.0%
Asian Women	2	2	5	0.4%	0.4%	1.0%
Total	500	500	500	100%	100%	100%

Source: Analysis by Richard L. Zweigenhaft and G. William Domhoff (Bearden, 2018).

Table 2. Demographics of Fortune 500 board seats by race/ethnicity

Demographics	2012	2016	2018	2020	2012%	2016%	2018%	2020%
White	4757	4656	4758	4853	86.7%	85.6%	83.9%	82.5%
African American	406	428	486	510	7.4%	7.9%	8.6%	8.7%
Asian	141	167	209	270	2.6%	3.1%	3.7%	4.6%
Latin	182	188	213	240	3.3%	3.5%	3.8%	4.1%
Other	2	1	4	7	0.0%	0.0%	0.1%	0.1%
Total	5488	5440	5670	5880	100%	100%	100%	100%

Source: Analysis by Lopez et al. (2020).

There are impacts of a non-equitable and non-inclusive environment in the organization which are lawsuits, employee disengagement, lack of innovation and productivity, employee turnover, and dysfunctional teams to name a few. This is detrimental to the health of an organization.

Lawsuits: The Equal Employment Opportunity Commission (EEOC) reported that there were 61,331 charges of discrimination filed in 2021 leading to lawsuits and employers paid out roughly $484 million in settlements to discrimination victims (Equal Employment Opportunity Commission, 2021); The average workplace settlement amount is $40 thousand (Flynn, 2022).

Employee disengagement: lack of equity and inclusion, drains employees' motivation, commitment to their jobs and their engagement (Maese & LLoyd, 2021). Gallup analytics estimates the global economy loses $7 trillion a year to disengagement with the greatest burden on companies (Maese & Lloyd, 2021).

Employee innovation and productivity: 70% of employees have experienced discrimination in the workplace which has impacted their productivity, engagement, and performance (Perna, 2021). Workplace discrimination can also affect their feelings of psychological safety and belonging and their ability to do their best work (Maese & LLoyd, 2021).

Employee turnover: employees who experience lack of equity and inclusion are much more likely to actively look for another job (Maese & LLoyd, 2021). Employees spend a lot of time working and if their environment is not welcoming nor do they feel respected, there are consequences to the business and organizational culture. This level of disruption prevents the success of any enterprise (Bell & Hartmann, 2007).

There are benefits of a diverse organization with inclusive and equitable environments. A diverse workforce that feels valued, equal, and included, results in happier and healthier workers which benefits the organization. A study from Harvard Business Review found that diverse companies had a 19% higher innovation revenue than non-diverse companies (Tynes, 2022). According to Tynes (2022), 1,700 companies were surveyed within a variety of industries and company sizes, examining diversity in management positions. The outcome found was a statistically significant relationship between diversity and innovation where most diverse enterprises were more innovative and had higher revenue. Going beyond Diversity, and focusing on equity, and inclusion are important because it greatly benefits the organization. Diversity and inclusion breed productivity as the ability to learn and grow from each other is exponentially expanded.

Currently you have white men who are in leadership positions, hiring a few diverse candidates but never promoting them nor making them feel included. Critical Theory will be used to dismantle the system.

OVERVIEW

This topic is significant as the research demonstrates how vital equality and inclusion are—if not more so than diversity alone; The majority of company leadership teams are composed of white men, with a small number of white women and minority personnel serving in entry-level to administrative positions (Roberson, 2019). Although they check the box for diversity, many employees do not believe that the workplace is welcoming or egalitarian. There has been little to no change, according to numerous studies on diversity in the workplace (Bearden, 2018). Employees are impacted and an organization suffers as a result demonstrated in the prior section. We wouldn't bring varied viewpoints to the table if we were all the same. Equity and inclusiveness in a diverse work setting, makes us stronger and brings more value to the organization, outperforming non-diverse organizations. How to achieve the organizational change required to increase equal opportunities in organizations dominated by majority norms and values is much less obvious (*Shadows and Light: Diversity Management as Phantasmagoria - Christina Schwa-*

benland, Frances Tomlinson, 2015, n.d.). The next paragraph summarizes all the social movements that are calling for change and the importance of the topic.

There were several social movements taking place between the #MeToo, social media posting by the younger generation, #StopAsianHate, and Black Lives Matter. The #MeToo movement provided a platform for women to speak out about sexual advancement made by senior executives and how this caused leadership doors to either close or open for them (Ross & Bookchin, 2020). If you allowed sexual advancement, doors would open. Doors closed if you denied advancement. These executives held the keys to the kingdom of leadership. Social issues had exploded, and social justice is especially important to the younger employees. This is the same generation that grew up with social media. They have no issue posting for the entire world to see what they believe. Those conversations became front and center. The younger generation of employees anticipate businesses to uphold their commitment to social justice and other principles in relation to matters that are significant to diverse communities. Asian hate crimes increased during the COVID pandemic as a result of President Donald Trump's rhetoric (Gover et al., 2020). 2020 saw a sharp rise in DEI job ads following the death of Ahmaud Arbery, Breonna Taylor, and George Floyd (Leigh & Melwani, 2019; McCluney et al., 2017; Rosette et al., 2006). To address the DEI issue, there was a significant demand for these positions. To support their employees' eagerness to see change, many businesses pushed to fill positions rapidly. Individuals were placed in roles for which they were not supported. For the sake of checking the box, several businesses recruited chief diversity officers. Researchers, writers, and frameworks are used by experts in the DEI field to comprehend the histories, ideologies, and systems of oppressed groups (Fitzsimmons & Callan, 2020). Professionals in DEI employ the insights of the marginalized to enact systemic change while questioning their own in-grained prejudice and bias. Self-awareness is essential. The paper contributes to the body of knowledge by addressing the issues of equality and inclusion in a diverse workplace, how critical theory can be applied practically, and what can be done to achieve those goals.

CRITICAL THEORY

Critical theory is the approach to social philosophy that focuses on culture in challenging power structures. Critical diversity research has an important role in highlighting the "shadows of power" in organizations (Ahmed, 2014; Ashcraft, 2017; Holck, 2018; Holck & Muhr, 2017; Ortlieb & Sieben, 2014). Critical theory relates to concerns with the social categories used in approach to the politics of diversity in the workplace, and the emotion this creates. In the case of this paper, the power structure is senior management (white men) within a corporation. Social problems stem from social structures put in place by the white man. Critical theory perspectives are concerned with empowering human beings to transcend the constraints placed on them by race, class, and gender (Fay, 1987). Critical theory is about questioning how the organization can best offer inclusion to all individuals regardless of race, ethnicity, sex, age, religion, sexual orientation, gender identity, and socioeconomic status. It offers opportunities to everyone and encourages different perspectives. Critical theory concerns itself with the forms of authority and injustice. It aims to address oppressive beliefs and practices that have become ingrained in society. If an oppressive practice is identified, it is believed it can be corrected to reduce the impact on marginalized populations. The theory attempts to lessen the forces that cause disadvantages to certain people.

Corporations should implement a seven-step process using the foundations of critical theory to dismantle the system of white men in power. (1) Create an inclusive and equitable environment and take active steps to improve DEI in the workplace by developing a robust hiring and promotion process. Some examples are recruiting at Historical Black Colleges (HBCU); career workshops targeting veteran's, the disabled, and LGBTQ center etc. (2) Diverse employee panels participating in the hiring and promotion process. This reinforces the company's commitment to valuing and leveraging DEI to build a premier workforce. There should be clearly defined rules of the road. (3) The Chief Diversity Officer should be an Executive Committee member reporting directly to the board with a dotted line to the Chief Executive Officer and Chief Human Resources Officer. (4) Communication becoming part of the company's core values. Employees should be encouraged to speak out against discriminatory practices. (5) Create an anonymous companywide survey to offer feedback and share results. In addition to a rating system, include a section on incorporating comments. Transparency is key. (6) Engage and promote DEI activities in organizations and initiatives such as: Enterprise Resource feedback at year-end Groups, Business Unit DEI Councils, volunteer activities, community-based programs, and reverse mentorship with identified diverse talent. (7) Advance DEI learning and development through 100% completion/participation of all required DEI trainings via the system and other company designated resources. The seven-step process incorporates critical theory by transferring knowledge to marginalized groups to give them transparency and empowerment. The advantages of implementing Critical Theory benefit the marginalized employees and the organization. The marginalized employees become part of the solution and corporate performance is enhanced. According to a McKinsey research study over a several-year timeframe, racially diverse companies are 35% more likely to outperform their less diverse counterparts, while from a gender standpoint, companies with strong women representation are 25% more likely to outperform (Tynes, 2022). McKinsey's research shows a clear correlation between Gender & Ethic diversity to profitability being positive (Tynes, 2022).

DISCUSSION AND FUTURE RESEARCH

Critical theory intended to explain the relationship of the E and I in DEI. The studies were identified using Google Scholar, ProQuest, Business Source Complete (EBSCO Host), and JSTOR. The goal of the paper is to aim towards the association of all letters of DEI within an organization.

There appears to be a discrepancy between DEI programs that only focus on diversity as opposed to taking it a step further and practicing equity and inclusion. Prior studies have indicated a focus on diversity only. Management scholars often perceive organizations as race and gender-neutral structures and have neglected the organizational role in perpetuating inequalities. Moreover, definitional constraints can influence the type of research questions asked and explored in the diversity and inclusion space (Hofbauer & Podsiadlowski, 2014). The term diversity is not always clear and definitively specified (Combs et al., 2019). The definition of DEI needs to be further refined to better understand the relationship between the letters. Companies have different ideas of what DEI means, and how it is implemented. Many DEI programs are controlled by white men. Future research should be more prospective and look at the power structures while defining all the letters in DEI. Despite minimal progress toward building diverse and inclusive workplaces, challenges remain in both practical relevance and theoretical advancements (Combs et al., 2019). Future research can highlight how scholars have the opportunity to both further the understanding of DEI and bridge the science-practitioner gap.

CONCLUSION

To summarize in simple terms, there is a need to go beyond diversity, focusing on equity and inclusion, and in order to do so, a seven-step process based on Critical Theory is applied, which benefits both the employee and the organization. The research shows the impacts of employee turnover, disengagement, lack of innovation, increased cost etc. and shows the benefits of increase profits, innovation, well-being etc. The target audience are minorities and women. White men continue to be in power and applying critical theory helps to focus on equity and inclusion in the workplace. The paper strives to support scholars and practitioners to educate management on the importance of equity and inclusion in a diverse work force. The paper provides the tools to enhance DEI programs, by applying Critical Theory to the current design problem. Critical Theory addresses the inequities and exclusive behavior. It applies a seven-step process. The research addresses the need for going beyond the D and building a strong DEI practice within the organization. DEI is a company's role in taking responsibility for its activities and their impact on employees, customers, and the community. To conclude, a strong DEI program addressing the E and I, is about implementing a successful DEI program within the organization. Specifically, this paper bridges the academic/practitioner divide, as well as work across boundaries and hierarchical relationships, to engage going beyond the D, and focusing on the E and I to build a premier workforce and brings empowerment to the marginalized.

REFERENCES

Ahmed, S. (2014). Not in the Mood. *New Formations*, 82(82), 13–28. doi:10.3898/NeWF.82.01.2014

American Psychology Association. (n.d.). *Inclusive Language Guidelines*. Retrieved April 13, 2023, from https://www.apa.org/about/apa/equity-diversity-inclusion/language-guidelines

Ashcraft, K. L. (2017). 'Submission' to the rule of excellence: Ordinary affect and precarious resistance in the labor of organization and management studies. *Organization*, 24(1), 36–58. doi:10.1177/1350508416668188

Bearden, J. E. (2018). Diversity in the power elite: Ironies and unfulfilled promises. *Choice (Chicago, Ill.)*, 56(1), 134.

Bell, J. M., & Hartmann, D. (2007). Diversity in Everyday Discourse: The Cultural Ambiguities and Consequences of "Happy Talk.". *American Sociological Review*, 72(6), 895–914. doi:10.1177/000312240707200603

Combs, G. M., Milosevic, I., & Bilimoria, D. (2019). Introduction to the Special Topic Forum: Critical Discourse: Envisioning the Place and Future of Diversity and Inclusion in Organizations. *Journal of Leadership & Organizational Studies*, 26(3), 277–286. doi:10.1177/1548051819857739

Cuadra, D. (2022). Why professional development and upskilling is vital to women of color. *Employee Benefit News*. https://www.proquest.com/docview/2705282255/abstract/B207D99311A94633PQ/1

Equal Employment Opportunity Commission. (2021). *Charge Statistics (Charges filed with EEOC) FY 1997 Through FY 2021*. US EEOC. https://www.eeoc.gov/data/charge-statistics-charges-filed-eeoc-fy-1997-through-fy-2021

Fay, B. (1987). *Critical Social Science: Liberation and its Limits*. Cornell University Press.

Fitzsimmons, T. W., & Callan, V. J. (2020). The diversity gap in leadership: What are we missing in current theorizing? *The Leadership Quarterly*, *31*(4), 101347. doi:10.1016/j.leaqua.2019.101347

Flynn, J. (2022, October 31). 30+ Alarming Employment Discrimination Statistics [2023]: Recent Employment Discrimination Cases. *Zippia*. https://www.zippia.com/advice/employment-discrimination-statistics/

Golash-Boza, T., Duenas, M. D., & Xiong, C. (2019). White Supremacy, Patriarchy, and Global Capitalism in Migration Studies. *The American Behavioral Scientist*, *63*(13), 1741–1759. doi:10.1177/0002764219842624

Gover, A. R., Harper, S. B., & Langton, L. (2020). Anti-Asian Hate Crime During the COVID-19 Pandemic: Exploring the Reproduction of Inequality. *American Journal of Criminal Justice*, *45*(4), 647–667. doi:10.100712103-020-09545-1 PMID:32837171

Hofbauer, J., & Podsiadlowski, A. (2014). Envisioning "inclusive organizations" - Guest Editorial. In J. Hofbauer & A. Podsiadlowski (Eds.), *Envisioning inclusive organizations: theory-building and corporate practice, Special issue. Equality, Diversity and Inclusion: An International Journal, 33(3), 214–219.* doi:10.1108/EDI-01-2014-0008

Holck, L. (2018). Unequal by structure: Exploring the structural embeddedness of organizational diversity. *Organization*, *25*(2), 242–259. doi:10.1177/1350508417721337

Holck, L., & Muhr, S. L. (2017). Unequal solidarity? Towards a norm-critical approach to welfare logics. *Scandinavian Journal of Management*, *33*(1), 1–11. doi:10.1016/j.scaman.2016.11.001

Leigh, A., & Melwani, S. (2019). #BlackEmployeesMatter: Mega-Threats, Identity Fusion, and Enacting Positive Deviance in Organizations. *Academy of Management Review*, *44*(3), 564–591. doi:10.5465/amr.2017.0127

Lopez, E., Minkel, A., & Vergara, R. (2020). 2020 HACR Corporate Inclusion Index Index™(CII) Report. *HACR*. https://hacr.org/2020-hacr-cii-report/

Maese, E., & Lloyd, C. (2021, May 26). *Understanding the Effects of Discrimination in the Workplace*. https://www.gallup.com/workplace/349865/understanding-effects-discrimination-workplace.aspx

McCluney, C. L., Bryant, C. M., King, D. D., & Ali, A. A. (2017). Calling in Black: A dynamic model of racially traumatic events, resourcing, and safety. *Equality, Diversity and Inclusion*, *36*(8), 767–786. doi:10.1108/EDI-01-2017-0012

Ortlieb, R., & Sieben, B. (2014). The making of inclusion as structuration: Empirical evidence of a multinational company. *Equality, Diversity and Inclusion*, *33*(3), 235–248. doi:10.1108/EDI-06-2012-0052

Perna, M. C. (2021). *Workplace Discrimination And Abuse Far More Common Than We Might Think*. Forbes. https://www.forbes.com/sites/markcperna/2021/05/26/workplace-discrimination-and-abuse-far-more-common-than-we-might-think/

Roberson, Q. M. (2019). Diversity in the Workplace: A Review, Synthesis, and Future Research Agenda. *Annual Review of Organizational Psychology and Organizational Behavior*, 6(1), 69–88. doi:10.1146/annurev-orgpsych-012218-015243

Rosette, A. S., Phillips, K. W., & Leonardelli, G. J. (2006). The White Standard in Leadership Evaluations: Attributional Benefits of a White Corporate Leader. *Academy of Management Annual Meeting Proceedings*, F1–F6. 10.5465/ambpp.2006.22898280

Ross, N., & Bookchin, S. (2020). Perils of conversation: #MeToo and opportunities for peacebuilding. *Gender in Management*, 35(4), 391–404. doi:10.1108/GM-12-2019-0237

Shadows and light: Diversity management as phantasmagoria—Christina Schwabenland, Frances Tomlinson, 2015. (n.d.). Retrieved August 8, 2023, from https://journals-sagepub-com.proxymu.wrlc.org/doi/10.1177/0018726715574587

Tynes, B. (2022). *Council Post: The Importance Of Diversity And Inclusion For Today's Companies*. Forbes. https://www.forbes.com/sites/forbescommunicationscouncil/2022/03/03/the-importance-of-diversity-and-inclusion-for-todays-companies/

Williams, J. B. (2018). Accountability as a Debiasing Strategy: Testing the Effect of Racial Diversity in Employment Committees. *Iowa Law Review*, 103(4), 1593–1638.

KEY TERMS AND DEFINITIONS

Affect: Is to act on; produce a change. It is used as a verb to mean to influence someone or something.

Corporate Social Responsibility (CSR): Is the awareness that a company has on making a positive impact on environmental impacts, ethical responsibility, philanthropic, DEI, and financial responsibilities.

Critical Theory: Is the approach to social philosophy that focuses on culture in challenging power structures. It focuses on society and culture to reveal, critique, and challenge power structures.

Discrimination: Is the unfair or prejudicial treatment of people and groups based on characteristics such as race, gender, age, or sexual orientation.

Diversity: Is the range of human differences that encompasses national origin, language, race, color, disability, ethnicity, gender, age, religion, sexual orientation, gender identity, socioeconomic status, and veteran status.

Equity: Is fair practices and policies acknowledging structural inequalities. It recognizes that each person has different circumstances and allocates the exact resources and opportunities needed to reach an equal outcome.

Ethnicity: Is group identity based on culture, religion, traditions, and customs.

Gender: Is the socially constructed traits that distinguish men, women, girls, and boys. It is an identity.

Impact: Is strong influence or effect. A significant or major effect.

Inclusion: Is where all employees feel a sense of belonging and respected. Inclusive environment.

Politics: Is the science of influencing or directing policy. It is the set of activities that are associated with making decisions in groups.

Race: Is a societal categorization of individuals. It is the division of people into groups that are unique within a given society, based on similar physical or social characteristics.

Chapter 5
Exploring the Noteworthy Experiences of African American Female Mid-Level Leaders in the United States

Paula Anderson
PACE Consulting, USA

ABSTRACT

African American female leaders in organizations face several issues due to the intersection of their race and gender, including psychological distress, intersectional invisibility, and discrimination in their role as leaders. The purpose of this qualitative transcendental phenomenological research study was to explore the psychological distress experiences of African American female leaders who encountered intersectional invisibility at the middle management leadership level in large U.S. organizations. This study revealed several psychological distress experiences and revealed the impact their psychological distress experiences had on their health and career decisions. Three theoretical constructs, social stress theory, the model of intersectional invisibility, and role congruity theory, framed and supported this study. One central research question and three sub-questions informed the study design. Semi structured interviews with 10 African American female middle-level leaders revealed six themes.

1. INTRODUCTION

The research confirms that African American women face multiple issues because of the intersection of their race and gender (Dickens et al., 2019). Some of the issues include coping with higher levels of psychological distress, experiences with invisibility, and facing discrimination in their roles as leaders (Eigenberg & Park, 2015; Rossette & Livingston, 2012; Szymanski & Stewart, 2010). In general, women have reported higher levels of psychological distress (Norris & Mitchell, 2014), and women are also more likely to be diagnosed with depression and anxiety than men (Mayo Clinic, 2019). However, when you add African American (race) to women (gender), negative feelings and experiences increase. Research

DOI: 10.4018/979-8-3693-1630-6.ch005

demonstrates that while holding stress at equal levels, some groups (i.e., women, the needy, and racially underrepresented groups) still report higher psychological distress levels (Williams, 2018, Knighton et al., 2020). Studies show that racism is associated with poorer health in African American women, including general psychological distress (Chinn et al., 2021). Indicators of psychological distress are anxiety, stress, depression, and diminished self-esteem (Peteet et al., 2015). Black women are marginalized members of society who have greater exposure to chronic stressors, such as racism, violence, and poverty (Norris & Mitchell, 2014). Purdie-Vaughns and Eibach (2008) assert that people with multiple subordinate identities experience intersectional invisibility. Intersectional invisibility is the tendency to be overlooked or disregarded as a member of two underrepresented groups (Smith et al., 2018).

Past research shows evidence that there are numerous disadvantages for multiple intersectional individuals, including discrimination in the workplace and stress (Mohr & Purdie-Vaughn, 2015). Black women state that employers expect to pay them less than Black males and White females (Mohr & Purdie-Vaughn, 2015). Women of color face added forms of discrimination that White women do not. Women of color receive lower pay than White men, White women, and men of color.

2. STATEMENT OF THE PROBLEM

The problem is that we do not know how Black female mid-level leaders are experiencing psychological distress while being overlooked in large U.S. organizations. Since the mid-1970s, Black women earning bachelor's degrees have grown by 55%, and those holding master's degrees have increased 149.5% (1991-2001 from 10,700 to 26,697 degrees) (Holder et al., 2015). Black females obtaining professional and graduate degrees have risen by 219% (Holder et al., 2015). However, as more women earn professional degrees for entrance into customarily male professions, they are experiencing isolation, systemic discrimination, and exclusion from networks (Glazer-Ramo, 2001). In their report, Hewlett and Green (2015) state that 26% of Black women feel their superiors do not recognize their talents compared to 17% of White women. Sixty percent of women and men professionals of color surveyed in a 2016 report felt they pay an emotional tax at work, as they must protect themselves against racial and gender bias (Travis & Thorpe-Moscon, 2018).

3. PURPOSE OF THE STUDY

Due to their dual status as racial and gender minorities, Black female leaders encounter experiences such as invisibility, discrimination, and distress in the workplace. The purpose of this study is to understand the psychological distress experience of Black female mid-level leaders who have experienced intersectional invisibility in large American organizations.

This study will be a qualitative phenomenological research study that examines the lived experiences of Black female mid-level leaders who are experiencing psychological distress while undergoing intersectional invisibility. The data from this study will contribute to the current literature on Black female leaders. The information gathered in this study will specifically explore and understand the psychological distress of Black female mid-level leaders experiencing intersectional invisibility.

4. LITERATURE REVIEW

Black women are ascending to leadership positions in U.S. organizations (Pace, 2018; Smith et al., 2018). In their journey of climbing the corporate ladder, they experience challenges related to the intersection of their race and gender. Generally, there are not many studies focused on the experiences of Black female leaders in U.S. organizations. Of the existing research studies, the focus is on Black females and their ascension to senior leadership (Guest, 2016; Chanland & Murphy, 2018); coping strategies utilized on their ascent to senior or executive leadership (Holder et al., 2015; Ali, 2018); and their experiences once at senior and executive levels (McDowell & Carter-Francique, 2017; Smith et al., 2019). However, few studies seek to understand Black female leaders' experiences at the middle management level (mid-level).

Furthermore, there are no studies that seek to understand the psychological distress experience of Black female mid-level leaders who have undergone intersectional invisibility in the workplace. This study will be the first of its kind. To that end, the research question this study seeks to answer is, "How is psychological distress experienced by African American female mid-level leaders who have undergone intersectional invisibility in large U.S. organizations?" This chapter reviews the literature on psychological distress, intersectionality, intersectional invisibility, and Black female leaders in the workplace. Since the research is limited, the objective of this literature review is to increase the understanding of the variables mentioned above that contribute to the experiences of the Black female mid-level leader in large U.S. organizations.

The research suggests that by being both Black and female, Black females experience intersectional invisibility. They have a double minority status and are ignored in the workplace setting (Purdie-Vaughns & Eibach, 2008). Intersectional invisibility is the propensity to be overlooked or ignored as a member of two underrepresented groups (i.e., Black females) (Purdie-Vaughns & Eibach, 2008). Black women shared their feelings on invisibility, "It is our invisibility that encourages men in general and White women to talk over us and interrupt us in meetings" (Graham, 2018). Black people may feel like they are always on display, while at the same time feel alienated by the White people who are around them (Graham, 2018).

Some Black women feel and experience stress resulting from the intersection of their race and gender in the workplace. Racism and sexism are distinct stressors that contribute to increased psychosocial health risk levels among Black women and are a common psychological distress source for African Americans (Hall, 2018). Stress research has focused on individual stressors, such as chronic strain or adverse events. However, there is an increasing concern that social stressors, such as racial and gender discrimination, are embedded in larger systems of inequality (Perry et al., 2013).

According to the consulting agency Zenger Folkman, women show overall success when placed in successively higher leadership positions. They are having success in functional areas that have been customarily dominated by males (Sherwin, 2014). Zenger Folkman's study examined 16,000 leaders which included 66% of men and 33% of women. The results demonstrated women have overall leadership effectiveness over men (54.5% vs. 51.8%) (Sherwin, 2014). However, according to Eagly and Karau (2002), women leaders are not considered qualified because they do not possess the same abilities and qualities as men (Eagly & Karau, 2002). This thought process could be one reason why the number of women in an organization shrinks among senior and executive leaders (Sherwin, 2014). For a Black female leader, this carries even further repercussions. A 2012 study revealed that Black female leaders who made errors on the job were reprimanded more harshly than Black males and White female leaders. They were two levels removed from the White male leadership prototype (Rosette & Livingston, 2012). This discrimination and unfair treatment could cause Black female leaders in the workplace to experience psychological distress. This study seeks to understand psychological distress, types of distress felt, the symptoms, and how it contributes to African American women's workplace experience when undergoing intersectional invisibility as a mid-level leader. Studies have shown that Black people experience discrimination in a wide range of settings in society and that these incidents could cause significant distress (Williams & Williams-Morris, 2000). Research also suggests that being mistreated due to prejudice reduces life satisfaction, decreases positive affect, and degrades mental health (Remedios & Snyder, 2015). Individual and social stressors are linked to psychological distress and other health issues (Perry et al., 2013).

The middle management level in organizations has been studied little as well. DeChurch, Hiller, Murase, and Salas (2010) found that in the last 25 years, upper management was the focus of research in 34% of studies, lower-level management had 16% focus, and middle management only 7%. In any organization, middle management tends to have a more significant impact on company performance and tends to be the most overlooked level (Mollick, 2011). Mid-level employees are also often targeted for downsizing when a company is looking to "right-size" their organization, which means the middle management may be decreasing and must take on a more significant burden (Caughron & Mumford, 2012).

There has been a slow promotion of Black women from middle management to senior management in corporations (Pace, 2018). Even though Black women are more likely to aspire to hold a commanding position, their advancement into leadership roles has been stagnant (Pace, 2018). Only 5% of managerial and professional jobs belong to African American women (Purdie-Vaughns, 2015). Black women are at a disadvantage in bridging the familiarity gap with White men in positions of power. They are considered a "double outsider"; they are neither White nor men (McGirt, 2017). Research has shown that Black women are growing discouraged in the workplace as they continually feel overlooked, their accomplishments diminished, and encounter issues of culture, such as their hair and appearance (McGirt, 2017). In 2020, hair discrimination was still an issue. In February 2020, the state of Maryland joined California, New York, and New Jersey and passed the Crown Act. This Act aims to create a safe and respectful environment for people (Black people) to wear their natural hair without discrimination (Chandler, 2020; Sanchez, 2020).

Women of color are predicted to make up the majority of women (51.7%) by 2060, which likely means they will make up the majority of women in the United States workforce (Pace, 2018; Catalyst, 2018). They also generate $1 trillion as consumers and $361 billion in revenue as entrepreneurs, launching companies at 4x the rate of all women-owned businesses (State of Women-Owned Businesses, 2017). Due to the increase in the number and value women of color bring to the economy, they are an essential group to focus on and develop their leadership capabilities. Hunt, Prince, Dixon-Fyle, and Yee (2018) published a report titled *Delivering through Diversity*. This report shared data from their research of over 1,000 companies in 12 countries that reaffirm the global relevance of the connection between diversity and leadership of large companies and financial outperformance. They defined diversity as a higher proportion of women and ethnically/culturally diverse individuals (Hunt et al., 2018). Their research found that building a diverse leadership pipeline can benefit companies in all sectors; firms with ethnically diverse executive teams were 33% more likely to surpass their peers in profitability. Additionally, firms with executive-level gender diversity had a 21% likelihood of beating their industry competitors worldwide and are 27% more likely to have superior value creation (Hunt et al., 2018).

How Black female mid-level leaders experience psychological distress because of the intersection of their race and gender is central to this research study. This research will be a qualitative study using the phenomenological approach to gain a deeper understanding of the lived experience of Black female mid-level leaders. Previous researchers have researched intersectionality, African American female leaders, and psychological distress. However, there has not been any research that has explored all three areas in one research study, with a specific focus on these areas concerning African American female middle-level leaders and their lived experiences. This research study will address the gap in the literature.

5. REVIEW OF RESEARCH

5.1 African American Women and Psychological Distress

According to the U.S. Department of Health & Human Services (2012), African Americans are 20% more likely to report severe psychological distress compared with non-Hispanic Whites. However, the inconsistencies in mental health are even more significant because of the under-reporting and underutilization of mental health services by African Americans (Snowden, 2001). African American women are prone to experiencing stress across various social settings compared with their White counterparts. The intersection between race and gender has noticeable differences in employment opportunities (Skaggs, 2012). Multicultural feminist theories highlight the potentially harmful mental health consequences of the intersection of racism and sexism on African American women, sometimes referred to as double jeopardy (Szymanski & Stewart, 2010). Some multicultural feminist theorists have suggested that racism and sexism can have separate and direct links to African American women's psychological distress (Szymanski & Stewart, 2010).

In a quantitative study conducted by Stevens-Watkins, Perry, Pullen, Jewell, and Oser (2014), socio-contextual factors of racism and sexism intersect in African American women's lives. The intersection of racism and sexism contributes to more stressful life events and an increase in psychological distress because Black women cannot separate being an African American from being a woman (Stevens-Watkins et al., 2014). The study included 204 participants from a southeastern city in the U.S. The data analyses explored the relationships between racism, sexism, stressful events, and psychological distress. The study's findings indicated that racism and sexism have a significant influence on psychological distress; this exceeded the magnitude of the relationships between all other traumatic life events analyzed in the study (Stevens-Watkins et al., 2014). The results of this study support the existing research and theoretical concepts of intersectionality, suggesting that African American women's social location may increase their sensitivity to adverse life events and chronic stressors, often resulting in psychological distress (Stevens-Watkins et al., 2014; Greer, 2010). Being overlooked or experiencing invisibility is a form of discrimination, as we have seen in this review. As the research states, discrimination links to stress and anxiety (Lee et al., 2018).

5.2 Race-Related Stress

Past research has shown that racism and discrimination are negatively associated with physical and psychological health. Some adverse psychological outcomes related to racism are declining self-esteem, and higher psychological distress levels (Pieterse et al., 2013). Race-related stress is a distinct form of stress different from more generalized anxiety from daily life (Pieterse et al., 2013). "Race-related stress results from persistent feelings of being overlooked and mistreated and dealing with daily racism micro stressors and hassles" (Jones et al., 2007, p. 209). Scholars believe that Black women are more vulnerable to race-related stress; they are more likely to utilize passive coping strategies and tend to internalize emotions to deal with racism (Pieterse et al., 2013). Race-related stressors are more problematic for African American women, given the evidence of gender differences for depression risk (Hill & Hoggard, 2011). Previous research also shows that with the prevalence rates of depression, African American women may exceed the national average (Hill & Hoggard, 2018). African American women have a disproportionate exposure to stressors, such as racism, sexism, racialized sexism, and gendered racism, which may contribute to their elevated depression risks (Hill & Hoggard, 2018).

5.3 Intersectionality

After Crenshaw introduced the term intersectionality in 1989, it became broadly adopted because it encompasses in a single word the simultaneous experience of the multiple oppressions of Black women (Smith, 2013). Intersectionality is the study and meaning of simultaneous membership in multiple social groups (Rosette et al., 2016).

5.4 Intersectional Invisibility

Intersectional invisibility is the overall failure to fully acknowledge people with intersecting identities as members of their constituent groups (Purdie-Vaughns & Eibach, 2008). The model of intersectional invisibility is a theoretical approach to understanding multiple-stigmatized persons' treatment in an ethnocentric, androcentric, heterocentric society (Remedios & Snyder, 2018). The model of intersectional invisibility attempts to specify the unique forms of oppression experienced by those with intersecting identities. The terms used in the intersectional invisibility model are defined as *ethnocentric* (the tendency to define one's social group as the universal standard and any norms from the outgroup as a deviation from the standard); *androcentric* (the privileging of male experience and the otherizing of the female experience); *heterocentric* (looks at heterosexuality as the standard for human sexuality; homosexuality and bisexuality are considered deviant) (Purdie-Vaughns & Eibach, 2008). The model of intersectional invisibility was developed from the evidence of historical narratives, cultural representations, interest-group politics, and anti-discrimination legal frameworks (Purdie-Vaughns & Eibach, 2008).

Several themes emerged from the invisibility literature. One theme that emerged is the vital role that the intersection of race and gender plays in the negative experiences of women of color (i.e., discrimination, marginalization, and being overlooked) in the workplace. Another theme that emerged is that people of color utilize various coping strategies to counter negative experiences at work. Additionally, perceived discrimination is another theme that emerged from the literature. Perceived discrimination seems to influence how people of color experience invisibility and exclusion in the workplace setting. As stated previously in all of the cited studies, women and people of color experienced negative stressors in the workplace due to their multiple stigmatized identities, such as race and gender. Their professional capabilities were questioned, overlooked, and, in some instances, excluded as a result of discrimination (Mohr & Purdie-Vaughns, 2015).

6. METHODOLOGY

The purpose of this study was to understand the psychological distress experience of Black female mid-level leaders who have faced intersectional invisibility in large U.S. organizations. This study sought to fill the literature void by exploring these areas through a qualitative phenomenological research approach.

The approach includes semi-structured interviews with 10 participants, using open-ended questions to obtain their real lived experiences. The interviews were conducted with Black female mid-level leaders from large organizations across the United States. A sample size of this amount for this type of qualitative approach has been deemed appropriate because it looks to explore and capture data that is comprehensive and significant in the form of extended stories, personal observations, and the direct experiences of the participants (Creswell, 2007).

The 10 participants who took part in the study were all Black female middle-level managers, between 30-70 years old, had bachelor's degrees or above, experienced emotional distress at work, and encountered intersectional invisibility. The participants were from various industries and originated from different areas on the East Coast; many of the participants currently resided and worked in the Washington DC Metropolitan area. Only one of the participants presently lived and worked in the South. The limited geographic areas where the participants worked and resided was a limitation of this study. All the participants (100%) in this study held advanced degrees from master's to doctorate level (three held master's degrees, one held dual masters' degrees, one had a law degree, and five held doctorate degrees); and lastly, they all desired to be promoted in their organization. The participant demographic (Table 1) details the participants' degree level, mid-level manager title, years in mid-level management, and the industry they work(ed) in when they experienced psychological distress and encountered intersectional invisibility.

Table 1. Demographics of participants

Participant	Degree Level	Mid-Level Manager	Years In	Participant
M1	PhD	Director	17 yrs.	Higher Education-Admissions
M2	Masters	Bank Manager/Academic Specialist	19 yrs.	Banking/Public School System
M3	Masters	Director	25 ½ yrs.	Commercial Insurance/ Corporate Banking; Higher Education
M4	PhD	Chair	19 yrs.	Higher Education-Academics
M5	Dual Masters	Department Head	15 yrs.	County Government
M6	EdD	Dean of Students	15 ½ yrs.	Higher Education-Student Services
M7	EdD	Director	6 yrs.	Higher Education-Data Systems
M8	EdD	Associate Director	5 yrs.	Higher Education-Development
M9	JD	Project Leader	7 yrs.	Food Service/Hospitality
M10	Masters	Program Manager	20 yrs.	Telecommunications- Information Technology

All 10 participants experienced psychological distress at work and encountered intersectional invisibility. The themes that emerged to answer the main research question relating to the psychological distress experience are: (a) Pervasive Stress, (b) Having Self Doubt, (c) Feelings of Frustration, (d) Not Valued by Colleagues, (e) Emotionally Crushed/Hurt, and (f) Constantly Adjusting to Fit In.

Table 2. Psychological distress experience of Black female mid-level leaders

Theme	% of Participants Experienced
Pervasive Stress	100
Having Self-Doubt	90
Feelings of Frustration	70
Not Valued by Colleague	70
Emotionally Crushed/Hurt	60
Constantly Adjusting to Fit In	50

The themes that emerged from the data answered the main research question. The themes demonstrated that Black female middle-level leaders who encountered intersectional invisibility from various large U.S. organizations experienced psychological distress in varying forms such as pervasive stress, self-doubt, frustration, not feeling valued, "emotionally crushed," and constantly adjusting. The Black female leaders also reported having shared experiences in their mid-level leadership position. These experiences included being met with obstacles and roadblocks in their roles, being overlooked for promotions, not receiving credit for their accomplishments, encountering racial microaggressions, being unnoticed in meetings or having ideas credited to White colleagues, and being the only or one of few Black women in their position.

Overall, the findings of this study answered the research question and the sub questions. From the central research question, the themes that emerged were: (a) Pervasive Stress, (b) Having Self Doubt, (c) Feelings of Frustration, (d) Not Valued by Colleagues, (e) Emotionally Crushed/Hurt, and (f) Constantly Adjusting to Fit In. From the three research sub questions, 11 themes emerged. Research sub question 1a asked: How is stress experienced among African American female mid-level leaders in large U.S. organizations? The findings were: (a) Stressful Work Environment, (b) Having Psychological and Physical Ailments, and (c) Difficulty Sleeping. The findings from research sub question 1b, "How is the experience of being overlooked as an African American female mid-level leader felt in large U.S. organizations?" were: (a) Figuring out Rationale for Being Overlooked-Unsure if Overlooked due to Race or Gender or Both and (b) Ideas Ignored. Finally, Research question 1c, "What is the experience of being an African American female mid-level leader in a large U.S. organization?" produced findings of (a) Being Met with Obstacles and Roadblocks, (b) Overlooked in Promotion, (c) Not Given Credit, (d) Racial Microaggressions, (e) Unnoticed in Meetings/Ideas Credited to White colleagues, and (f) Only or One of Few Black Women in Position. The findings demonstrated the varied psychological distress experiences that Black female mid-level leaders experienced when encountering intersectional invisibility in the workplace. The research study also revealed the shared experiences Black female leaders have in large organizations' middle leadership levels.

7. RECOMMENDATIONS AND CONCLUSIONS

There are several recommendations for future practice based on the results and other findings from this research study. This study's findings resulted in six different psychological distress experiences that Black female mid-level leaders experienced when encountering intersectional invisibility. As stated, several times in this study, intersectional invisibility is a form of covert discrimination where a Black woman is overlooked due to her dual underrepresented status. As seen from the literature and the findings in this study, this form of discrimination and discrimination overall can contribute to significant emotional distress.

From this research, organizations must take a closer look at this type of pain. It was a contributing factor in 60% of the study's participants resigning from their position as middle-level leaders and going to other organizations. According to Bolden-Barnett (2017), who highlighted a 2017 Retention Report, it costs employers 33% of an employee's annual salary to hire a replacement if that person leaves; in dollar amounts, this totals to $15,000 for an employee who earns a median wage of $45,000 per year. This cost is high in dollars and productivity for companies interested in retaining their staff. The people that should take a closer look at my research findings are human resources personnel and executive and senior leadership. Human resources personnel should pay more immediate attention first as they are the people who hire, recruit, and retain their qualified diverse candidates. Second, executive and senior leaders are the ones who are part of the decisions to promote their diverse professionals to higher-level positions.

Hunt et al. (2018) highlighted a report on women in business, and firms with ethnically diverse executive teams were 33% more likely to outperform their peers in profitability. One technique firms could implement to retain their Black female middle-level leaders is diversifying their mid-level leadership positions. Organizations could help promote Black leaders by including them in mentoring programs and creating leadership development training specifically for Black and other women of color. Many of the participants in this study reported that they were often in situations where they were the only female leader of color or one of a few. This experience could contribute to distress when you look around a room, and no one looks like you. One participant mentioned that sometimes this creates tension when she notices that she is the only person of color in a room. Diversifying at this level would help with two issues. First, it would solve being "the only one" because Black women would have others like themselves in similar positions. Second, it would help diversify the pipeline to senior and executive leadership positions.

"To ensure equal possible outcomes for all individuals across the organization, equity requires that employers recognize barriers and advantages." (Heinz, 2020, p. 3). Discrimination contributes to psychological distress. From an equity perspective, organizations should provide internal and external support for Black women regarding an organization's wellness benefits. Many businesses offer Employee Assistance Programs (EAP) to increase employees' mental and physical wellness. The recommendation is that organizations take this a step further and ensure that their EAP panels are diverse, have clinicians that are people of color, and have clinicians who are well-versed in discrimination issues and race-related trauma and stress. If there is no EAP, organizations could work with or have partnerships with consulting psychologists/mental health professionals in the communities they serve who could offer similar services to the organization's diverse employees.

One of the overall feelings that the participants had in this study is that they wanted to feel valued for who they are and the contributions they brought to the workplace; additionally, Black female leaders wanted to know they belonged—this is inclusion. Organizational leaders could create an inclusive culture where Black female leaders are seen, heard, and valued to create an environment where there is psychological safety. *Psychological safety* is an environment where employees are empowered to express their ideas fully; it is a place where employees can make mistakes and trust that their colleagues will not shame them (Qosha, 2019).

This study speaks to the distress experiences of leaders in marginalized groups who are overlooked. Psychological safety could help break these patterns of discrimination and create a shift from unconscious bias to conscious inclusion (Qosha, 2019).

REFERENCES

Adu, P. (2019). *A step-by-step guide to qualitative data coding* (1st ed.). Routledge. doi:10.4324/9781351044516

Advantages and Disadvantages. (2020, April 26). *Advantages and disadvantages of qualitative research.* https://www.advantages-disadvantages.co/pros-and-cons-of-qualitative-research-benefits/

Ali, H. (2018). Coping strategies to lead and succeed as a minority woman. *Forbes.* https://www.forbes.com/sites/ellevate/2018/04/23/coping-strategies-to-lead-and-succeed-as-a-minority-woman/#583f548f3dbb

American Psychological Association. (2011, August 18). *Study finds sex differences in mental illness* [Press release]. http://www.apa.org/news/press/releases/2011/08/mental-illness

Aneshensel, C. S. (1992). Social stress: Theory and research. *Annual Review of Sociology, 18*(1), 15–38. doi:10.1146/annurev.so.18.080192.000311

Armstrong, V. (2019, July 8). *Stigma regarding mental illness among people of color.* National Council for Behavioral Health. https://www.thenationalcouncil.org/BH365/2019/07/08/stigma-regarding-mental-illness-among-people-of-color/

Baker, J., & Cangemi, J. (2016). Why are there so few women CEOs and senior leaders in corporate America? *Organization Development Journal, 34*(2), 31–43. https://tcsedsystem.idm.oclc.org/login?url=https://search-proquest-com.tcsedsystem.idm.oclc.org/docview/1791020833?accountid=34120

Belasen, A., & Belasen, A. R. (2016). Value in the middle: Cultivating middle managers in healthcare organizations. *Journal of Management Development, 35*(9), 1149–1162. doi:10.1108/JMD-12-2015-0173

Beqiri, G. (2018, March 8). Managing anxiety and stress in the workplace. *Virtual Speech.* https://virtualspeech.com/blog/managing-anxiety-stress-workplace

Berdahl, J., & Moore, C. (2006). Workplace harassment: Double jeopardy for minority women. *The Journal of Applied Psychology, 91*(2), 426–426. doi:10.1037/0021-9010.91.2.426 PMID:16551193

Berger, R. (2015). Now I see it, now I don't: Researcher's position and reflexivity in qualitative research. *Qualitative Research, 15*(2), 219–234. doi:10.1177/1468794112468475

Berman, J. (2018, March 3). When a woman or person of color becomes CEO, white men have a strange reaction. *Marketwatch.* https://www.marketwatch.com/story/when-a-woman-or-person-of-color-becomes-ceo-white-men-have-a-strange-reaction-2018-02-23

Bolden-Barnett, V. (2017, August 11). Study: Turnover costs employers $15,000 per worker. *HRDive*. https://www.hrdive.com/news/study-turnover-costs-employers-15000-per-worker/449142/

Bond, M., & Haynes, M. (2014). Workplace diversity: A social-ecological framework and policy implications. *Social Issues and Policy Review*, *8*(1), 167–201. doi:10.1111ipr.12005

Boyle, M., & Deveau, S. (2019, October 9). Bed Bath and Beyond taps target's top merchant as its new CEO. *Bloomberg*. https://www.bloomberg.com/news/articles/2019-10-09/bed-bath-beyond-names-target-s-tritton-as-its-new-ceo

Buchanan, N., & Settles, I. (2019). Managing (in)visibility and hypervisibility in the workplace. *Journal of Vocational Behavior*, *113*, 1–5. doi:10.1016/j.jvb.2018.11.001

Buchanan, T. W. (2007). Retrieval of emotional memories. *Psychological Bulletin*, *133*(5), 761–779. doi:10.1037/0033-2909.133.5.761 PMID:17723029

Bureau of Labor Statistics, U.S. Department of Labor. (2019, February 26). Black women made up 53 percent of the Black labor force in 2018 on the Internet. *The Economics Daily*. https://www.bls.gov/opub/ted/2019/black-women-made-up-53-percent-of-the-black-labor-force-in-2018.htm

Caughron, J., & Mumford, M. (2012). Embedded leadership: How do a leader's superiors impact middle-management performance. *The Leadership Quarterly*, *23*(3), 342–353. doi:10.1016/j.leaqua.2011.08.008

Chanland, D., & Murphy, W. (2018). Propelling diverse leaders to the top: A developmental network approach. *Human Resource Management*, *57*(1), 111–126. doi:10.1002/hrm.21842

Chinn, J., Martin, I., & Redmond, N. (2021). Health Equity Among Black Women in the United States. *Journal of Women's Health*, *30*(2), 212–219. doi:10.1089/jwh.2020.8868 PMID:33237831

Collins, P. H. (2015). Intersectionality's definitional dilemmas. *Annual Review of Sociology*, *41*(1), 1–20. doi:10.1146/annurev-soc-073014-112142

Cook, A., & Glass, C. (2014). Above the glass ceiling: When are women and racial/ethnic minorities promoted to CEO? *Strategic Management Journal*, *35*(7), 1080–1089. doi:10.1002mj.2161

Crenshaw, K. (2015, September 24). Why intersectionality can't wait. *The Washington Post*. https://www.washingtonpost.com/news/in-theory/wp/2015/09/24/why-intersectionality-cant-wait/

Creswell, J. (2007). *Qualitative inquiry and research design: Choosing among five approaches* (2nd ed.). Sage Publications.

Creswell, J. W. (2014). *Research design: Qualitative, quantitative, and mixed methods approaches* (4th ed.). Sage.

Davis, D. R., & Maldonado-Daniels, C. (2015). Shattering the glass ceiling: The leadership development of African American women in higher education. *Advancing Women in Leadership Journal*, *35*, 48–64. doi:10.21423/awlj-v35.a125

Deitch, E. A., Barsky, A., Butz, R. M., Chan, S., Brief, A. P., & Bradley, J. C. (2003). Subtle yet significant: The existence and impact of everyday racial discrimination in the workplace. *Human Relations*, *56*(11), 1299–1324. doi:10.1177/00187267035611002

Depression in women: Understanding the gender gap. (2019, January 29). *Mayo Clinic.* https://www.mayoclinic.org/diseases-conditions/depression/in-depth/depression/art-20047725

Dickens, D., Womack, V., & Dimes, T. (2019). Managing hypervisibility: An exploration of theory and research on identity shifting strategies in the workplace among Black women. *Journal of Vocational Behavior, 113*, 153–153. doi:10.1016/j.jvb.2018.10.008

Dickens, D.D., & Chavez, E.L. (2017). Navigating the workplace: The costs and benefits of shifting identities at work among early career U.S. Black women. *Sex Roles, 78*, 760–774. doi:10.1007/s11199-017-0844-x

Dodgson, J. E. (2019). Reflexivity in qualitative research. *Journal of Human Lactation, 35*(2), 220–222. doi:10.1177/0890334419830990 PMID:30849272

Dovidio, J. F., Gaertner, S. E., Kawakami, K., & Hodson, G. (2002). Why can't we just get along? Interpersonal biases and interracial distrust. *Cultural Diversity & Ethnic Minority Psychology, 8*(2), 88–102. doi:10.1037/1099-9809.8.2.88 PMID:11987594

Eagly, A., & Karau, S. (2002). Role congruity theory and prejudice towards female leaders. *Psychological Review, 109*(3), 573–598. doi:10.1037/0033-295X.109.3.573 PMID:12088246

Eigenberg, H., & Min Park, S. (2016). Marginalization and invisibility of women of color: A content analysis of race and gender images in introductory criminal justice and criminology texts. *Race and Justice, 6*(3), 257–279. doi:10.1177/2153368715600223

Fernandes, L., & Alsaeed, N. (2014). African Americans and workplace discrimination. *European Journal of English Language and Literature Studies, 2*(2), 56–76.

Ford, M., Cerasoli, C., Higgins, J., & Decesare, A. (2011). Relationships between psychological, physical, and behavioural health and work performance: A review and meta-analysis. *Work and Stress, 25*(3), 185–204. doi:10.1080/02678373.2011.609035

Frost, D. (2017). The benefits and challenges of health disparities and social stress frameworks for research on sexual and gender minority health. *The Journal of Social Issues, 73*(3), 462–476. doi:10.1111/josi.12226

Garcia-Retamero, R., & Lopez-Zafra, E. (2006). Prejudice against women in male-congenial environments: Perceptions of gender role congruity in leadership. *Sex Roles, 55*(1), 51–61. doi:10.100711199-006-9068-1

Glazer-Ramo, J. (2001). *Shattering the myths: Women in academe.* Johns Hopkins University Press.

Graham, C. (2018, August 29). Hypervisible, invisible: How to navigate White workplaces as a Black woman. *Career Contessa.* https://www.careercontessa.com/advice/black-woman-white-workplace/

Greer, M. (2004). Overcoming invisibility. *American Psychological Association, 35*(8). http://www.apa.org/monitor/sep04/overcoming.aspx

Greer, T. M. (2010). A structural validation of the schedule of racist events. *Measurement & Evaluation in Counseling & Development, 43*(2), 91–107. doi:10.1177/0272989X10373455

Grinnell, R. (2018, July 8). The persistence of memory: Are negative events easier to recall? *PsychCentral.* https://psychcentral.com/blog/the-persistence-of-memory-are-negative-events-easier-to-recall/

Guest, P. M. (2016). Executive mobility and minority status. *Industrial Relations, 55*(4), 604–631. doi:10.1111/irel.12153

Gumbs, A. (2018, November 26). New study proves Black women executives can't catch a break at work. *Black Enterprise.* https://www.blackenterprise.com/study-black-women-executives/

Hall, J. C. (2018). It is tough being a Black woman: Intergenerational stress and coping. *Journal of Black Studies, 49*(5), 481–501. doi:10.1177/0021934718766817

Hall, J. C., Everett, J. E., & Hamilton-Mason, J. (2012). Black women talk about workplace stress and how they cope. *Journal of Black Studies, 43*(2), 207–226. doi:10.1177/0021934711413272 PMID:22457894

Harrell, J., Hall, S., & Taliaferro, J. (2003). Physiological responses to racism and discrimination: An assessment of the evidence. *American Journal of Public Health, 93*(2), 243–248. doi:10.2105/AJPH.93.2.243 PMID:12554577

Hastwell, C. (2020, January 7). What Are employee resource groups (ERGs)? *Great Place to Work.* https://www.greatplacetowork.com/resources/blog/what-are-employee-resource-groups-ergs

Heinz, K. (2020, August 17). What does DEI mean in the workplace? *Built In.* https://builtin.com/diversity-inclusion/what-does-dei-mean-in-the-workplace#2

Hewlett, S. A., & Green, T. (2015). Black women ready to lead. *Center for Talent Innovation.* https://www.talentinnovation.org/_private/assets/BlackWomenReadyToLead_ExecSumm-CTI.pdf

Hewlett, S. A., & Wingfield, T. (2015, June 11). Qualified Black women are being held back from management. *Harvard Business Review.* https://hbr.org/2015/06/qualified-black-women-are-being-held-back-from-management

Higginbotham, E. (2004). Invited reaction: Black and White women managers: Access to opportunity. *Human Resource Development Quarterly, 15*(2), 147–152. doi:10.1002/hrdq.1095

Hilal, A. H., & Alibri, S. S. (2013). Using NVivo for data analysis in qualitative research. *International Interdisciplinary Journal of Education, 2*(2), 181–186. doi:10.12816/0002914

Hill, L., & Hoggard, L. (2018). Active coping moderates associations among race-related stress, rumination, and depressive symptoms in emerging adult African American women. *Development and Psychopathology, 30*(5), 1817–1835. doi:10.1017/S0954579418001268 PMID:30451137

Holder, A., Jackson, M., & Ponterotto, J. (2015). Racial microaggression experiences and coping strategies of Black women in corporate leadership. *Qualitative Psychology, 2*(2), 164–180. doi:10.1037/qup0000024

Hunt, V., Prince, S., Dixon-Fyle, S., & Yee, L. (2018). *Delivering through diversity.* McKinsey & Company. https://www.mckinsey.com/business-functions/organization/our-insights/delivering-through-diversity

Hunter-Gadsen, L. (2018). The troubling news about Black women in the workplace. *Forbes.* https://www.forbes.com/sites/nextavenue/2018/11/06/the-troubling-news-about-black-women-in-the-workplace/?sh=37f0896f6053

Introduction to Management: Management Types and Levels. (n.d.). *Lumens: Boundless Management.* https://courses.lumenlearning.com/boundless-management/chapter/management-levels-and-types/

Jean-Marie, G., Williams, V., & Sherman, S. (2009). Black women's leadership experiences: Examining the intersectionality of race and gender. *Advances in Developing Human Resources, 11*(5), 562–581. doi:10.1177/1523422309351836

Jefferies, K., Goldberg, L., Aston, M., & Tomblin Murphy, G. (2018). Understanding the invisibility of black nurse leaders using a black feminist poststructuralist framework. *Journal of Clinical Nursing, 27*(15-16), 3225–3234. doi:10.1111/jocn.14505 PMID:29752837

Jones, K., Sabat, I., King, E., Ahmad, A., McCausland, T., & Chen, T. (2017). Isms and schisms: A meta-analysis of the prejudice-discrimination relationship across racism, sexism, and ageism. *Journal of Organizational Behavior, 38*(7), 1076–1110. doi:10.1002/job.2187

Kessler, R., Mickelson, K., & Williams, D. (1999). The prevalence, distribution, and mental health correlates of perceived discrimination in the United States. *Journal of Health and Social Behavior, 40*(3), 208–230. doi:10.2307/2676349 PMID:10513145

Kowitt, B., & Zillman, C. (2021, January 26). New Walgreens CEO Rosalind Brewer will be the only Black woman chief executive in Fortune 500. *Fortune.* https://fortune.com/2021/01/26/walgreens-new-ceo-rosalind-roz-brewer-starbucks/

Lee, D., Peckins, M., Heinze, J., Miller, A., Assari, S., & Zimmerman, M. (2018). Psychological pathways from racial discrimination to cortisol in African American males and females. *Journal of Behavioral Medicine, 41*(2), 208–220. doi:10.100710865-017-9887-2 PMID:28942527

Lennartz, C., Proost, K., & Brebels, L. (2019). Decreasing overt discrimination increases covert discrimination: Adverse effects of equal opportunities policies. *International Journal of Selection and Assessment, 27*(2), 129–138. doi:10.1111/ijsa.12244

Lin, C.-S. (2013). Revealing the 'Essence" of things: Using phenomenology in LIS research. *Qualitative and Quantitative Methods in Libraries, 4*, 469–478.

Locatis, C., Williamson, D., Gould-Kabler, C., Zone-Smith, L., Detzler, I., Roberson, J., Maisiak, R., & Ackerman, M. (2010). Comparing in-person, video, and telephonic medical interpretation. *Journal of General Internal Medicine, 25*(4), 345–350. doi:10.100711606-009-1236-x PMID:20107916

Luxton, E. (2016). Why workplace anxiety costs us more than you think. *World Economic Forum.* https://www.weforum.org/agenda/2016/08/workplace-anxiety-costs-more-than-you-think/

Lynn, S. (2019, May 24). Meet the CEO of Bed, Bath and Beyond, she is the first Black woman to head a Fortune 500 company since Ursula Burns. *Black Enterprise.* https://www.blackenterprise.com/appointed-interim-ceo-of-bed-bath-beyond-she-is-the-first-black-woman-to-head-a-fortune-500-company-since-ursula-burns/

Maddox, T. (2013). Professional women's well-being: The role of discrimination and occupational characteristics. *Women & Health, 53*(7), 706–729. doi:10.1080/03630242.2013.822455 PMID:24093451

Magee, W., & Upenieks, L. (2017). 'Stuck in the middle with you?' Supervisory level and anger about work. *Canadian Review of Sociology, 54*(3), 309–330. doi:10.1111/cars.12152 PMID:28796459

McCluney, C., & Rabelo, V. (2018). Conditions of visibility: An intersectional examination of Black women's belongingness and distinctiveness at work. *Journal of Vocational Behavior*. Advance online publication. doi:10.1016/j.jvb.2018.09.008

McDowell, J., & Carter-Francique, A. (2017). An intersectional analysis of the workplace experiences of African American female athletic directors. *Sex Roles, 77*(5–6), 393–408. doi:10.100711199-016-0730-y

McGirt, E. (2017, September 27). The Black ceiling: Why African American women aren't making it to the top in corporate America. *Fortune.* https://www.yahoo.com/news/black-ceiling-why-african-american-103035458.html

McGlowan-Fellows, B., & Thomas, C. S. (2005). Changing roles: Corporate mentoring of Black women. *International Journal of Mental Health, 33*(4), 3–18. doi:10.1080/00207411.2004.11043387

Meyer, I., Schwartz, S., & Frost, D. (2008). Social patterning of stress and coping: Does disadvantaged social status confer more stress and fewer coping resources? *Social Science & Medicine, 67*(3), 368–379. doi:10.1016/j.socscimed.2008.03.012 PMID:18433961

Mohr, R., & Purdie-Vaughns, V. (2015). Diversity within women of color: Why experiences change felt stigma. *Sex Roles, 73*(9-10), 391–398. doi:10.100711199-015-0511-z

Moustakas, C. (1994). *Phenomenological research methods.* Sage Publications. doi:10.4135/9781412995658

Mustafa, M., Martin, L., & Hughes, M. (2016). Psychological ownership, job satisfaction and middle manager entrepreneurial behavior. *Journal of Leadership & Organizational Studies, 23*(3), 272–287. doi:10.1177/1548051815627360

Noble, H., & Smith, J. (2015). Issues of validity and reliability in qualitative research. *Evidence-Based Nursing, 18*(2), 34–35. doi:10.1136/eb-2015-102054 PMID:25653237

Norris, C., & Mitchell, F. D. (2014). Exploring the stress-support-distress process among Black women. *Journal of Black Studies, 45*(1), 3–18. doi:10.1177/0021934713517898

Offermann, L. R., Basford, T. E., Graebner, R., Jaffer, S., De Graaf, S. B., & Kaminsky, S. E. (2014). See no evil: Color blindness and perceptions of subtle racial discrimination in the workplace. *Cultural Diversity and Ethnic Minority Psychology, 20*(4), 499-507. doi:http://dx.doi.org.tcsedsystem.idm.oclc.org/10.1037/a0037237

Pace, C. (2018, August 31). How women of color get to senior management. *Harvard Business Review.* www.hbr.org/2018/08/how-women-of-color-get-to-senior-management

Perry, B., Harp, K., & Oser, C. (2013). Racial and gender discrimination in the stress process: Implications for African American women's health and well-Being. *Sociological Perspectives, 56*(1), 25–48. doi:10.1525op.2012.56.1.25 PMID:24077024

Peteet, B.J., Brown, C.M., Lige, Q.M., & Lanaway, D. A. (2015). Impostorism is associated with greater psychological distress and lower self-esteem for African American students. *Current Psychology: Research and Reviews, 34*(1), 154-163.

Pieterse, A., Carter, R., & Ray, K. (2013). Racism-related stress, general life stress, and psychological functioning among Black American women. *Journal of Multicultural Counseling and Development, 41*(1), 36–46. doi:10.1002/j.2161-1912.2013.00025.x

Purdie-Vaughns, V. (2015, April 22). Why so few black women are senior managers in 2015? *Fortune.* https://fortune.com/2015/04/22/black-women-leadership-study/

Purdie-Vaughns, V., & Eibach, R. (2008). Intersectional invisibility: The ideological sources and social consequences of non-prototypicality. *Sex Roles, 59*, 377–391. doi:10.100711199-008-9424-4

Qosha, N. (2019, November 20). Inclusive leadership: The role of psychological safety. *Training Industry.* https://trainingindustry.com/articles/leadership/inclusive-leadership-the-role-of-psychological-safety/

Quick Take: Women of Color in the United States. (2018, November 7). *Catalyst.* https://www.catalyst.org/research/women-of-color-in-the-united-states/

Rabenu, E., Yaniv, E., & Elizur, D. (2017). The relationship between psychological capital, coping with stress, well-being, and performance: Research and reviews research and reviews. *Current Psychology, 36*(4), 875-887. http://dx.doi.org.tcsedsystem.idm.oclc.org/10.1007/s12144-016-9477-4

Racial Trauma. (n.d.). *Mental Health America.* https://mhanational.org/racial-trauma

Remedios, J., & Snyder, S. (2015). How women of color detect and respond to multiple forms of prejudice. *Sex Roles, 73*(9-10), 371–383. doi:10.100711199-015-0453-5

Remedios, J., & Snyder, S. (2018). Intersectional oppression: Multiple stigmatized identities and perceptions of invisibility, discrimination, and stereotyping. *Journal of Social Sciences, 74*(2), 265–281.

Rollock, N. (2012). The invisibility of race: Intersectional reflections on the liminal space of alterity. *Race, Ethnicity and Education, 15*(1), 65–84. doi:10.1080/13613324.2012.638864

Rosette, A., & Livingston, R. (2012). Failure is not an option for Black women: Effects of organizational performance on leaders with single versus dual-subordinate identities. *Journal of Experimental Social Psychology, 48*(5), 1162–1167. doi:10.1016/j.jesp.2012.05.002

Sanchez-Hucles, J., & Davis, D. D. (2010). Women and women of color in leadership: Complexity, identity, and intersectionality. *The American Psychologist, 65*(3), 171–181. doi:10.1037/a0017459 PMID:20350016

Saunders, B., Sim, J., Kingstone, T., Baker, S., Waterfield, J., Bartlam, B., Burroughs, H., & Jinks, C. (2018). Saturation in qualitative research: Exploring its conceptualization and operationalization. *Quality & Quantity, 52*(4), 1893–1907. doi:10.100711135-017-0574-8 PMID:29937585

Seppala, E., & Cameron, K. (2015, December 1). Proof that positive work cultures are more productive. *Harvard Business Review.* https://hbr.org/2015/12/proof-that-positive-work-cultures-are-more-productive

Settles, I. H., Buchanan, N. T., & Dotson, K. (2019). Scrutinized but not recognized: (In)visibility and hypervisibility experiences of faculty of color. *Journal of Vocational Behavior, 113*, 62–74. doi:10.1016/j.jvb.2018.06.003

Sherwin, B. (2014, January 24). Why women are more effective leaders than men. *Business Insider.* https://www.businessinsider.com/study-women-are-better-leaders-2014-1

Skaggs, S. (2012). Review of 'Race gender and the labor market: Inequalities at work'. *Gender & Society, 26*(1), 123–125. doi:10.1177/0891243211423657

Smith, A., Watkins, M., Ladge, J., & Carlton, P. (2018, May 10). Interviews with 59 Black female executives explore intersectional invisibility and the strategies to overcome it. *Harvard Business Review.* https://hbr.org/2018/05/interviews-with-59-black-female-executives-explore-intersectional-invisibility-and-strategies-to-overcome-it

Smith, A. N., Watkins, M. B., Ladge, J. J., & Carlton, P. (2019). Making the invisible visible: Paradoxical effects of intersectional invisibility on the career experiences of executive Black women. *Academy of Management Journal, 62*(6), 1705–1734. doi:10.5465/amj.2017.1513

Starner, T. (2016). Why 'middle managers' are an employer's most important leaders. *HR-Dive.* https://www.hrdive.com/news/why-middle-managers-are-an-employers-most-important-leaders/425140/#:~:text=The%20impact%20of%20a%20good%20middle%20manager%20goes%20beyond%20employee%20engagement.&text=In%20fact%2C%20a%20Wharton%20School,focus%20groups%2C%E2%80%9D%20she%20says

Stevens-Watkins, D., Perry, B., Pullen, E., Jewell, J., & Oser, C. B. (2014). Examining the associations of racism, sexism, and stressful life events on psychological distress among African American women. *Cultural Diversity and Ethnic Minority Psychology, 20*(4), 561-569. http://dx.doi.org.tcsedsystem.idm.oclc.org/10.1037/a0036700

Sue, D. W., Lin, A. I., & Rivera, D. P. (2009). Racial microaggressions in the workplace: Manifestation and impact. In J. L. Chin (Ed.), Diversity in mind and in action, Vol. 2: Disparities and competence (pp. 157–172). Santa Barbara, CA: Praeger.

Szymanski, D., & Stewart, D. (2010). Racism and sexism as correlates of African American women's psychological distress. *Sex Roles, 63*(3-4), 226–238. doi:10.100711199-010-9788-0 PMID:20352053

Tan, J. (2017, December 6). For women of color, the glass ceiling is actually made of concrete. *HuffPost.* https://www.huffpost.com/entry/for-women-of-color-the-gl_b_9728056

The State of Women-Owned Businesses. (2017). *American Express.* www.ventureneer.com/wp-content/uploads/2017/11/2017-AMEX-SWOB-FINAL

Thomas, A., Hacker, J., & Hoxha, D. (2011). Gendered racial identity of Black young women. *Sex Roles, 64*(7-8), 30–42. doi:10.100711199-011-9939-y

Thomas, A., Witherspoon, K., & Speight, S. (2008). Gendered racism, psychological distress and coping styles of African American women. *Cultural Diversity & Ethnic Minority Psychology, 14*(3), 307–314. doi:10.1037/1099-9809.14.4.307 PMID:18954166

Toepoel, V. (2012). Effects of incentives in surveys. In L. Gideon (Ed.), *Handbook of survey methodology for the social sciences* (pp. 209–223). Springer. doi:10.1007/978-1-4614-3876-2_13

Travis, D. J., & Thorpe-Moscon, J. (2018) Day-to-day experiences of emotional tax among women and men of color in the workplace. *Catalyst.* https://www.catalyst.org/research/day-to-day-experiences-of-emotional-tax-among-women-and-men-of-color-in-the-workplace/

Turner, R., & Avison, W. (2003). Status variations in stress exposure: Implications for the interpretation of research on race, socioeconomic status, and gender. *Journal of Health and Social Behavior, 44*(4), 488–505. doi:10.2307/1519795 PMID:15038145

US Legal. (n.d.). *African American law and legal definition.* https://definitions.uslegal.com/a/african-americans/

Wang, J., Cheng, G., Chen, T., & Leung, K. (2019). Team creativity/innovation in culturally diverse teams: A meta-analysis. *Journal of Organizational Behavior, 40*(6), 693–708. doi:10.1002/job.2362

Warner, J., & Corley, D. (2017, May). *The women's leadership gap.* Center for American Progress. https://www.americanprogress.org/issues/women/reports/2017/05/21/432758/womens-leadership-gap/

What Is the Classification of Business Organization According to Size. (2020, April 9). *Reference.* https://www.reference.com/business-finance/classification-business-organization-according-size-f9a66b9751457c58#:~:text=With%20respect%20to%20size%2C%20business,employ%20250%20people%20or%20more

Whisenant, W., Lee, D. L., & Dees, W. (2015). Role congruity theory: Perceptions of fairness and sexism in sport management. *Public Organization Review, 15*(4), 475–485. doi:10.100711115-014-0281-z

Wilkie, D. (2018, February 2). Number of older Americans at work has grown 35 percent. *SHRM.* https://www.shrm.org/resourcesandtools/hr-topics/employee-relations/pages/older-workers-.aspx

Williams, D. R. (2018). Stress and the Mental Health of Populations of Color: Advancing Our Understanding of Race-related Stressors. *Journal of Health and Social Behavior, 59*(4), 466–485. doi:10.1177/0022146518814251 PMID:30484715

Williams, D. R., & Williams-Morris, R. (2000). Racism and mental health: The African American experience. *Ethnicity & Health, 5*(3/4), 243–268. doi:10.1080/713667453 PMID:11105267

Women of Color in the United States. (2013). *Catalyst.* https://www.catalyst.org/knowledge/African-American-women

Zamora, D. (n.d.). Anxiety at work: A career-busting condition. *WebMD.* https://www.webmd.com/anxiety-panic/features/anxiety-at-work

Chapter 6

Examining Factors That Contribute to the Planning Fallacy in Healthcare Cybersecurity Business Continuity Planning

Jorja B. Wright
https://orcid.org/0000-0002-7028-995X
Capitol Technology University, USA

ABSTRACT

The planning fallacy is a specific bias pertaining to judgment errors that hamper the success cybersecurity business planning in healthcare organizations. The concepts explored include errors in human judgment, planning fallacy (cognitive bias), and how to mitigate this cognitive error. First, important concepts will be defined: cognitive bias, planning fallacy, and heuristic. Next, how cognitive biases contribute to human error in the decision-making process; third, the planning fallacy and how it pertains to both collaborative and complexity leadership theories will be analyzed. Finally, this chapter will conclude with possible implications for leaders to alleviate the consequences of the planning fallacy and provide insights for more effective approaches to business continuity planning for medical organizations.

INTRODUCTION

In healthcare organizations Business Continuity Planning (BCP) is the process of creating preventive and recovery systems to deal with potential cyber threats to an organization or to ensure process continuity in the wake of a cyberattack. BCP's secondary goal is to ensure operational continuity before and during execution of disaster recovery. The planning entails asset and personnel protection, thus ensuring a quick recovery of operations in the event of a disaster. Briefly, the basic business continuity requirement is to keep essential functions up and running during a disaster and to recover with as little downtime as

DOI: 10.4018/979-8-3693-1630-6.ch006

possible. A business continuity plan considers various unpredictable events, such as natural disasters, fires, disease outbreaks, cyberattacks, and other external threats. The planning entails asset and personnel protection, thus ensuring a quick recovery of operations in the event of a disaster. Concisely, the basic business continuity requirement is to keep essential functions up and running during a disaster and to recover with as little downtime as possible. At a time when downtime is unacceptable for any organization, business continuity is critical to address client management, retention, and operational security. The premise of this conceptual paper is to examine how BCP can empower an organization to keep crucial functions running during downtime. This, in turn, helps the organization respond quickly to an interruption, while creating resilient operational protocols. Moreover, the COVID-19 pandemic reminded us of the importance of a comprehensive BCP within healthcare (Agarwal, 2020). A robust business continuity plan helps save money, time, and reputation/brand image. Eventually, this helps in mitigating financial risks. As with all large ventures, responding to cybersecurity attacks is extremely complex.

BACKGROUND OF THE PROBLEM

Patients now live longer and have a better quality of life due to various medical improvements. The collection, storage, and access of healthcare data have altered because of daily technological advancements. Healthcare firms must provide excellent service while remaining modern due to automation and legal requirements for enhanced backup and recovery systems (Gast, 2011).

Adoption of HIT and EHR in healthcare raises questions about the trustworthiness of automated IT systems. Medical systems that are essential cannot fail. To guarantee 99.99 percent uptime, Gartner urges all healthcare organizations to implement a formal high availability (HA) solution (Gast, 2011). High availability refers to a system (a network, a server array or cluster, etc.) that is intended to prevent service interruption by minimizing planned downtime and decreasing or managing faults (High Availability Solutions, 2022). College of Healthcare Information Management Executives (CHIME) advises placing HA first while implementing clinical automation technologies (The Association for Executives in Healthcare Applications, Data & Analytics (AEHADA) Reveals Bold New Plan for Uniting Digital Health Tech Leadership - Healthcare IT - CHIME, 2023). For example, if an organization were to implement HA, one computer serves as the production processor, and the backup computer continuously updates. The software duplicates and monitors both servers, then users can instantly switch to the backup server if the primary server malfunctions or must be repaired. Networked systems are reconnected by the backup server. When production processing resumes, users and networked systems may "failback" to the primary server (Gast, 2011; High Availability Solutions, 2022). Critical systems are organization-specific and have a direct impact on patient care, such the hospital's code paging system. Ultimately, HA solutions are a possible strategy for healthcare professional to include in BCPs to mitigate operational failures from emergency scenarios.

PROBLEM STATEMENT

The problem is healthcare organizations lack efficient BCPs resulting in a major decrease clinical, operational, and managerial processes and systems (Thorpe et al, 2016). The COVID-19 pandemic showed us how disruptions in crucial information technology (IT) functions such as medical inventory (i.e., mask, swabs, syringes) electronic healthcare record (EHRs) systems, clinical automation software for nursing personnel, automated care management workflow tools, point-of-care technology, automated medication management system, and patient case documenting software programs can cause severe consequences (Gast, 2011). Healthcare stakeholders have a strong priority on reducing costs and improving quality, but utilizing and sharing health information throughout the care continuum to achieve these goals has proven to be difficult. It is as important but perhaps more difficult to share health information for research, social service, and public health initiatives. True transformation is still a long way off without an interoperable electronic information exchange architecture that allows exchanging patient health information within the healthcare delivery system and, increasingly, outside of the healthcare delivery system (Thorpe et al, 2016). The concepts of decision making, cognitive biases, planning fallacy and human error will be discussed next.

COGNITIVE BIASES AND PLANNING FALLACY

Errors in decision making can stem from utilizing "cognitive shortcuts (i.e., heuristics)" which then leads to these cognitive biases (Buiten & Hartmann, 2013, p. 5). Cognitive biases are distorted judgments that can be attributed to the biological and evolutionary wiring of the human brain which leads to errors in rational decision-making choices (Beshears, 2015; Buiten & Hartmann, 2013; Johnson et al., 2013). Planning fallacy is a specific bias pertaining to judgment in which project completion time is grossly underestimated and overly optimistic predictions affect the success of said project (Iftekhar, 2015; Min, 2012; Sample, 2015). One crucial step to identify a possible planning fallacy bias at the beginning of any large project or venture is by asking two important questions: 1) is the problem with this collaborative effort caused by employees' (at both institutions) lack of effort? 2) Are the institutions' employees making choices that introduce "systematic errors into the decision-making process?" (Beshears, 2015, p. 5). These problems are not mutually exclusive in that they both can occur simultaneously, however, distinguishing between the problems is an effective way to approach decision-making issues. Next, heuristics and the consequences of cognitive biases will be discussed.

COGNITIVE BIASES AND HUMAN ERROR

Using reliable data and comprehensive assessment processes are a critical aspect of cybersecurity planning, decision making, and business strategy. The human brain, as efficient as it can be, still has many limitations. To expedite the decision-making process, our minds employ heuristics as a type of shortcut to reduce cognitive effort (Hilbert, 2012). Through the evolutionary process of natural selection, heuristics are the cognitive solutions to the human decision-making process (Johnson, Blumstein, & Fowler, 2013). Moreover, heuristics maximize human fitness throughout "evolutionary time in the presence of asymmetric costs of errors and the absence of certainty" (Johnson, Blumstein, & Fowler, 2013, p. 479). Due to limited time and resources, our brains use heuristics to create "approximations" and "use a representative case" instead of analyzing the specific case at hand (Hilbert, 2012, p. 5). This concept corroborates with Kahneman (2011), author of Thinking, Fast and Slow, in that intuitive thought stems from System 1 thinking; once these contextual cues are recognized, the human brain will "work whatever first comes to mind (availability)" (Hilbert, 2012, p. 5). This quick mental process does not include rational thought and is heavily influenced by our emotional and moral value system (Hilbert, 2012). System two thinking is the slower, rational thought processes that occur when we take the time to analyze situations (Kahneman, 2011).

Hence, System 1 thinking leads to profound consequences, and from an organizational standpoint these consequences can include mismanagement of resources, misappropriating funds, and conflicts amongst teammates. Rodon and Meyer (2012) support this claim by explaining how critical consequences can be for an organization when a rational decision-making process is not used. The authors explain the overall discrepancy "in the accuracy of time estimation" as it relates to "time, costs, and risks of future actions" (Rodon & Meyer, 2012, p. 108). From an emotional intelligence perspective, leaders may want to be aware of the emotional and psychological consequences cognitive biases can have on the morale of their employees. There has been some research on the emotional health of employees after the occurrence of many project failures due to cognitive biases (Iftekhar & Pannell, 2015). It is important to address these concerns because they can have a profound impact on the organization in that employees' self-image and personal motivation is hindered by repeated errors in decision making (Rodon & Meyer, 2012). Hopefully, this research can add a better understanding of the connection between decision making, consequences of cognitive biases, and human errors while providing a comprehensive theoretical framework and possible "coherent prescriptive strategies" to acknowledge, regulate, or ameliorate these irrational thought processes (Hilbert, 2012, p. 10).

Conceptual Framework

This conceptual paper focuses on healthcare cybersecurity issues for firms without effective business continuity strategies and uses prospect theory, availability heuristic, human factors, technology-centric approaches. According to prospect theory, individuals make decisions based on anticipated advantages and losses rather than absolute outcomes. This hypothesis proposes that healthcare firms may prioritize cybersecurity expenditures depending on their perceived losses from a cyber event rather than the risk of such an incident (Tversky & Kahneman, 1992). Availability heuristic theory implies that people overestimate the chance of memorable or prominent experiences. This hypothesis implies that healthcare companies may overestimate external cyber dangers and underestimate internal concerns like human error and insider threats (Manis et al., 1993). Human factors theory acknowledges that people and organizations make mistakes, and that systems and procedures must account for them. This theory says that healthcare companies must address human issues including lack of knowledge, insufficient training, and inadequate protocols and procedures that lead to cybersecurity risks (Wilson & Rutherford, 1989). These three hypotheses argue that cognitive biases, human mistakes, and ineffective business continuity strategies may make healthcare businesses vulnerable to cybersecurity assaults.

For organizations without business continuity planning and risk mitigation strategies, technology-centric ways can handle healthcare cybersecurity challenges. This entails using technology to defend healthcare systems from cyberattacks. Implement advanced security measures like firewalls, intrusion detection and prevention systems, and encryption technologies. In the case of a cyberattack, these technologies can protect sensitive healthcare data from unwanted access (Stenholm, 2019). Data analytics and machine learning algorithms can also monitor network traffic and discover security vulnerabilities (Asadzadeh, 2022). This lets healthcare institutions detect and respond to cyber-attacks before they do major damage. Implementing strong authentication and access control measures can also prevent illegal access to healthcare systems and data. This can include multi-factor authentication, role-based access to sensitive data, and strong password policies. For organizations without business continuity planning and risk mitigation strategies, technology-centric approaches may not be enough to handle healthcare cybersecurity challenges. Healthcare firms must build complete business continuity plans and risk mitigation methods that include technology-centric approaches, employee training, frequent security audits, and incident response planning (Stenholm, 2019; Asadzadeh, 2022). Healthcare businesses may safeguard their systems and data from cyber threats by taking a holistic approach to cybersecurity. To improve healthcare firms' cybersecurity and business continuity planning, this dissertation investigates these ideas and healthcare cybersecurity. Human variables, prospect theory, and availability heuristic, and technology-centric approach affect cybersecurity decision-making. Next, this paper will describe the research methodology, design and analysis used to synthesize the data.

METHODOLOGY

This conceptual paper utilized a content analysis methodology to explore the topic of Business Continuity Planning (BCP) in healthcare organizations for the purpose of mitigating cyber security risks. The aim was to identify key themes and concepts related to BCP and cyber security risks, as well as to analyze existing literature and frameworks related to these topics.

Sample Selection

The sample for this study consisted of scholarly articles, books, and reports related to BCP and cyber security risks in healthcare organizations. The articles were obtained from academic databases such as ProQuest, Ebscohost, and Google Scholar, using keywords such as "cognitive biases," "planning fallacy," "business continuity planning," "cyber security," "healthcare," and "risk management." The researcher limited the search to articles published in the last 10 years to capture the most current research on the topic. The researcher then selected a total of 43 articles to analyze for this concept paper.

Data Collection

The data collection process involved reading and analyzing the selected articles to identify key themes and concepts related to BCP and cyber security risks in healthcare organizations. Qualitative data software, NVivo, was used to code and analyze the data. The researcher used a coding scheme that was developed based on the research problem and objectives of the paper. The coding scheme consisted of six main categories: BCP, cyber security risks, healthcare organizations, risk management, mitigation strategies, and frameworks/models.

Data Analysis

The data analysis process involved reviewing the coded data to identify patterns, themes, and concepts related to BCP and cyber security risks in healthcare organizations. The analysis was conducted using a combination of inductive and deductive approaches. Inductive analysis was used to identify emerging themes and concepts that were not explicitly stated in the literature, while deductive analysis was used to examine how existing frameworks and models related to BCP and cyber security risks in healthcare organizations.

Validity and Reliability

To ensure the validity and reliability of the data analysis, the study employed multiple coders who independently coded the same set of articles. Inter-coder reliability was measured using Cohen's kappa coefficient, which indicated substantial agreement among the coders ($\kappa = 0.75$). Additionally, the study employed member checking, where the coding scheme and findings were shared with experts in the field of BCP and cyber security risks in healthcare organizations for validation.

Ethical Considerations

This study did not involve human subjects, and therefore did not require approval from an institutional review board. However, ethical considerations were considered during the data collection and analysis process, including ensuring the anonymity of the authors of the selected articles and obtaining permission to use copyrighted material. Next, the planning fallacy and how it relates to collaborative and complexity leadership theory will be discussed.

PLANNING FALLACY: HOW IT RELATES TO COLLABORATIVE LEADERSHIP AND COMPLEXITY LEADERSHIP

The consequences of the planning fallacy and overconfidence when applied to projects can be detrimental to organizations financially. Brunnermeier et al. (2016, p. 12) describe the relationship between overconfidence and optimism as "optimal" because these factors "maximize the well-being" of an individual. Moreover, the authors explain that optimism decreases as "the temporal distance to the task decreases" (Brunnermeier, Papakonstantinou, & Parker, 2016, p. 12). A commitment device in this context refers to deadlines that allow people to constrain their future actions (Brunnermeier et al., 2016). Figure 1 shows an illustration of optimal expectations and action as it relates to the planning fallacy. All constants are defined.

Figure 1.

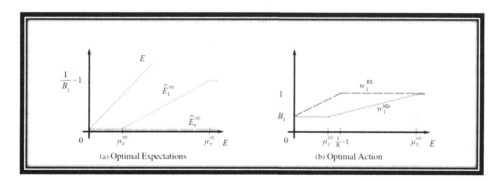

Graph (a) depicts expectation, E, as the solid black line; the yellow dashed line is optimal expectation, E_0^{ND}, when time, $t = 0$; the dotted green line is optimal expectation, E_1^{ND}, when $t = 1$. The x-axis is rational expectation, while the y-axis is arbitrary subjective beliefs as a fraction of time subtracted by one of expected total work (Brunnermeier et al., 2016). Subjective beliefs are used in this graph because they "maximize the expected present-discounted value of utility" during the decision-making process (2016, p. 2). Graph (b) depicts optimal work, ω_1^{RE}, as the dashed red line given rational expectations. The dotted blue line equals optimal work, ω_1^{ND}, given optimal beliefs without a commitment device (Brunnermeier et al., 2016). A commitment device in this context refers to deadlines that allow people to constrain their future actions (Brunnermeier et al., 2016). In the following section, the concepts of pessimism, rationality, and optimism will be presented.

PESSIMISM, RATIONALITY, AND OPTIMISM

According to Brunnermeir et al., optimism and the planning fallacy are intrinsic to an individual's psyche because both concepts stem from biases (2016). Flyvbjerg and Sunstein corroborate with that sentiment, but instead claim that pessimism is intrinsic to an individual's psyche through the Malevolent Hiding Hand (MHH) principle (2015). Under MHH, obstacles and difficulties are hidden from the decision maker (Flyvbjerg & Sunstein, 2015) especially in events that lack creativity; hence, optimism is optimal (Brunnermeier et al., 2016) and the individual is optimistic about the estimation of difficulties/costs and of creativity/benefits. For Benevolent Hiding Hand (BHH) principle, optimism applies to the estimation of difficulties/costs and pessimism to creativity/benefits. (Flyvbjerg & Sunstein, 2015). From an organizational standpoint, Flybvbjerg and Sunstein explain that with BHH employees are "tricked by their ignorance" into underestimating project difficulties and costs (2015, p. 6). Rodon and Meyer (2012) support this notion in that employees exhibit defensive pessimism (in this context) as a strategy to alleviate anxiety to achieve a project/task. Next, the effects of the planning fallacy on collaborative leadership, planning fallacy and disaster recovery will be discussed.

COLLABORATIVE LEADERSHIP, PLANNING FALLACY, AND DISASTER RECOVERY

Planning fallacy has detrimental effects on collaborative ventures because the number of relevant actors involved is greater than one. To execute large projects, timing is extremely important because it directly correlates with organizations' resources and profit. As mentioned in Nooteboom (2009), organizations that effectively exploit their resources and explore creative avenues to develop new knowledge tend to be more successful overall. Organization sustainability is tied to their bottom line; if an organization is not profitable, it will not survive in the long term. Collaborative efforts are important to improve the overall well-being of an organization because it extends an organization's dynamic capabilities. Partnerships increase the chances of an organizations success because it encourages diversity of thought and reduces fragmentation – a condition in which a social group is divisive instead of united (Conklin, 2005), and tribalism - in which people associate with other people with the same evils of thought - resulting in tribes of varying thoughts (Innes & Booher, 2010).

Brunnermeier et al. our cognitive thoughts and actions are endogenous and are formulated from our conscious and subconscious biases (2016). Which further corroborates the importance of judgment free collaborative ventures to further reduce the effects of the planning fallacy even more. For collaborative projects to be successful, the project execution process must be based on a "collective position" of inquiry that is free from judgment so that all actors and stakeholders involved feel "competent, trusted and valued" (Raelin, 2012, p. 821). The trust, social and intellectual capital gained from including stakeholders in collaborative effort are invaluable to cultivating a culture of inquiry, "knowledge creation, and resource acquisition" therefore leading to rich "interorganizational" and "intraorganizational social networks" (Raelin, 2012, p. 824).

The objective of a disaster recovery decision making planning is to make sure that a healthcare organization can answer a disaster or any emergency that affects information systems, and thus minimize the effect on business operations. Gonzalez (2004) introduces the concept of dynamic decision making (DDM), which involves sequences of numerous and interdependent decisions that occur in real-time. These decisions are constantly changing and occur in an autonomous environment (Gonzalez, 2004). Gonzalez's study shows study shows the "detrimental effects" time constraints have on decision making (2004, p. 18). Gonzalez's study explains that participants that "induce abstract relationships" as a situation unfolds over time can depart from "simple heuristics to context-based actions" (2004, p. 19). These participants may perform relatively better under time constraints, which speaks to their cognitive abilities, however, time limits are still detrimental to the decision-making process. These decisions can lead to unanticipated consequences both good and bad. Being aware of the cognitive biases in decision making can assist leaders in navigating the nonlinear causation that is typical of complexity theory. Finally, strategic foresight and its relevance to the planning fallacy will be discussed.

STRATEGIC FORESIGHT AND THE PLANNING FALLACY

A cognitive bias that seems to stem from evolutionary fitness is the planning fallacy, unrealistic optimism (Shepperd, Waters, Weinstein, & Klein, 2015) when predicting the future (Madhavan & Balasubramanian, 2016). Unrealistic optimism is when people believe a personal outcome will be successful compared to the same outcome of their peers. It differs from "dispositional optimism," which is "a personality trait representing generally positive expectations about the future" (Shepperd et al. 2015, p. 232). There are two types of unrealistic optimism: 1) "unrealistic absolute optimism," which is an invalid belief that an individual's outcome will be successful compared to other outcomes based on quantitative data from other outcomes; 2) "unrealistic comparative optimism," which refers to extremely inaccurate predictions of one's favorable personal outcomes compared to their peers' outcomes (Shepperd et al., 2015, p. 232). Though both types of optimism vary slightly, they are positively correlated in certain situations, but the differences are context specific (Shepperd et al., 2015).

Madhavan and Balasubramanian explain that with corporate strategy, strategic foresight (SF) is important because corporations are concerned with the future in that "past experiences may not be a true indicator of how the future is going to be" (2016, p. 64). Again, SF is the skill of envisioning all potential future scenarios, gaining insight, and applying that knowledge to present circumstances. Heuristics exist to streamline the process of decision-making. SF is an important sensemaking skill for leaders in this complex society because "perfect rationality" and absolute objectivity is impossible (Cossette, 2015, p. 473). Like complexity theory, predicting the future is difficult because of all the contextual dynamics at play within the environment. Planning fallacy is a major cognitive bias that affects the outcomes of organizations because it affects the success of projects. The goal of acknowledging unrealistic optimism is to be aware of strengths, weaknesses, opportunities, and threats (SWOT) that can affect projects.

Alleviating the effects of the planning fallacy is possible when leaders acknowledge the existence of cognitive biases. Rosenzweig explains that the Salience-Assessment-Weighting (SAW) model provides a framework to predict the future or forecasts the future in a "domain-general way" and offer tips for future researchers to improve "how forecasts can be led astray or improved" (2014, p. 372). The SAW model includes three important steps:

a) Salience – important dimensions that are relevant to an outcome. For example, salient factors of a problem include the five w's: who, what, where, when why. These are five questions that explicitly display obvious dimensions of a problem.

b) Assessment – the process of evaluating a dimension's utility to determine if it can be used as a "cue" in future forecasting (Rosenzweig, 2014, p. 369).

c) Weighting – the process of appropriately estimating the importance of the dimension to evaluate how it can be forecasted.

Rosenzweig explains his SAW model can be used to alleviate errors in strategic foresight because it reveals forecasting errors (Rosenzweig, 2014, p. 372). Many strategic foresight tactics are filled with trial-and-error because of the increase complexity in our society (Iftekhar & Pannell, 2015). Leaders use experience to gain knowledge of the future; this theory is explained earlier in the paper with Kahneman's definition of intuition (which is merely recognition) (2011). "Systematic learning models" are not popular when applying to real-world events (Iftekhar & Pannell, 2015), thus experiential learning through trial-and-error seems to be popular methods of learning. Managers tend to learn from past successes instead from both past and failed experiences; yet failures can be the most poignant learning experiences for leaders to gain new knowledge.

LIMITATIONS

There are some limitations within this research. First, there is limited research on this specific topic. The researcher identified scholarly articles about "planning fallacy" "BCP" or "healthcare cybersecurity" but limited research on the effects of the planning fallacy and healthcare cybersecurity continuity plans. Next, there are limitations in the methods used to collect the relevant literature. The researcher should have included search terms such as "pandemic predictions," "scenario planning" and "healthcare cybersecurity" in that information may have included more nuanced information about the topic. Finally, the researcher encountered time constraints to complete the literature review for this paper. The researcher sees there is a need for this topic to continue through a quantitative longitudinal study to fully answer the research question.

IMPLICATIONS

Business continuity planning is a crucial risk management strategy for healthcare organizations to effectively manage cybersecurity risks. This strategy involves developing a comprehensive plan that outlines how the organization will continue to operate in the event of a cyber-attack, natural disaster, or other disruptive event. Business continuity planning not only helps to ensure the continued operations of the organization but also reduces the risk of cybersecurity incidents and associated costs. However, the planning fallacy cognitive heuristic can impact the effectiveness of business continuity planning in the world of cybersecurity practice. This heuristic refers to the tendency for individuals to underestimate the time, resources, and effort required to complete a task or project. In the context of cybersecurity, this can lead to organizations underestimating the potential impact of a cyber-attack and overestimating their ability to respond and recover from such an incident.

The planning fallacy can have significant implications for healthcare organizations, as it can lead to insufficient planning and preparation for cybersecurity incidents. This can leave organizations vulnerable to cyber-attacks, which can result in significant financial losses, reputational damage, and potential harm to patients. To overcome the planning fallacy, healthcare organizations must take a proactive approach to business continuity planning and risk management. This involves conducting regular risk assessments, developing comprehensive business continuity plans, and implementing appropriate cybersecurity measures to reduce the risk of cyber-attacks. Additionally, organizations should invest in employee training and awareness programs to ensure that all staff members are aware of the potential risks of cyber-attacks and understand their role in preventing and responding to such incidents. Ultimately, while business continuity planning is a crucial cybersecurity risk management strategy, the planning fallacy cognitive heuristic can impact its effectiveness. Healthcare organizations must take a proactive approach to risk management and invest in appropriate cybersecurity measures to reduce the risk of cyber-attacks and ensure the continued operations of the organization in the event of a disruptive event.

RECOMMENDATIONS FOR FUTURE RESEARCH

Despite the existing literature on planning fallacy heuristic and BCP, there is a need for further research to identify effective strategies for mitigating planning fallacy heuristic in healthcare organizations. Some of the recommendations for future research include:

- Conducting a comparative analysis of BCP practices across different healthcare organizations to identify best practices and areas for improvement.
- Investigating the impact of involving a diverse group of stakeholders in the BCP planning process on the accuracy of timelines and resource allocation.
- Examining the role of reference class forecasting in mitigating planning fallacy heuristic in healthcare organizations.
- Investigating the impact of regular risk assessments on the accuracy of BCP planning.
- Conducting case studies to identify successful strategies for creating contingency plans for unexpected events.

Next, this conceptual review will conclude by discussing the risk assessment process, supplier and third-party risk management, and transparency amongst all stakeholders within the healthcare organization.

CONCLUSION

Organizations can no longer afford to wait until a threat is identified to start worrying about their cyber-security risk management program. A cyber-attack can cause a major business disruption across departments and severely impact day-to-day operations, both in the short and long term. For this reason, as organizations build their business continuity and disaster recovery plans, cybersecurity measures must be integrated throughout the entire process.

It is important for leaders to understand the planning the fallacy and how it affects healthcare business operations. This paper contributes to healthcare cybersecurity by highlighting a distinct perspective for cybersecurity and healthcare administrative leaders to consider when protecting patient data. By integrating cybersecurity and business continuity planning, organizations can ensure that the proper processes are being put in place and resources are allocated to help facilitate a smooth transition as they recover from an attack. To ensure that cybersecurity is being effectively blended into business continuity planning, there are several best practices to keep in mind, including business impact analysis, cyber risk assessments, supply chain management, incident response plans, and continuous monitoring.

The premise of BCP is to empower an organization to keep crucial functions running during downtime. This, in turn, helps the organization respond quickly to an interruption, while creating resilient operational protocols. A robust business continuity plan helps save money, time, and reputation/brand image. Eventually, this helps in mitigating financial risks. Disaster recovery encompasses the procedures, policies, or processes that prepare an organization's vital IT infrastructure to effectively recover from natural or human-induced disasters and ensure business continuity. It must contain scripts (instructions) which can be implemented by all cybersecurity professionals.

Effective planning, absence of fallacies is the key to recovering from a business interruption and enables you to maintain focus during the aftermath of an outage. Companies can prepare for the possibility of adverse events that interrupt their operations by developing a business impact analysis (BIA) and conducting a risk assessment (RA).

Before a business continuity plan (BCP) is created, an organization must conduct a detailed risk assessment to identify the areas of exposure and all possible threats that could potentially cause a business interruption. Types of threats that should be considered include natural, manufactured, technological, loss of utilities, and pandemic outbreaks. All possible threats should be analyzed to determine the likelihood of their occurrence and the level of impact to the organization. Consideration should also be given to what mitigation steps have been taken to lessen the likelihood of occurrence and/or impact. Threats that result in high-risk ratings should be reviewed with management to determine the need for additional mitigation strategies to lessen the possibility of the threat causing a business outage.

The risk assessment process consists of the following steps:

- **Risk Identification**: It is the process of determining risks that could potentially prevent the program, enterprise, or investment from achieving its objectives. It includes documenting and communicating the concern.

- **Risk Analysis**: Risk Analysis involves examining how project outcomes and objectives might change due to the impact of the risk event. Once the risks are identified, they are analyzed to identify the qualitative and quantitative impact of the risk on the project so that appropriate steps can be taken to mitigate them.
- **Risk Evaluation**: Risk Evaluation is the process used to compare the estimated risk against the given risk criteria to determine the significance of the risk.
- **Performing Risk Evaluation**
  - A risk evaluation can be performed in several simple steps:
  - Identify and Prioritize Assets: Consider all the diverse types of data, software applications, servers and other assets that are managed. Determine which of these is the most sensitive or would be the most damaging to the healthcare organization if compromised.
  - Locate Assets: Find and list the source of those assets. Be it desktop office computers, mobile devices, internal servers, or other connected healthcare devices and equipment.
  - Classify Assets: Categorize each asset as either public information, sensitive internal information, non-sensitive internal information, compartmentalized internal information, or regulated information.
- **Threat Modeling Exercise:** Identify and rate all the threats faced by your top-rated assets.
- **Data Finalization & Planning**: Once healthcare organization completes is cybersecurity risks threat evaluation, the planning focus starts with tackling those risks, beginning with the most critical that are established by data driven planning and assessments. Conduct a cybersecurity risk assessment.

Cybersecurity risk assessments provide healthcare organizations with a comprehensive look at its cybersecurity posture, as well as that of its third- and fourth-party vendors. When building out a business continuity plan, a cybersecurity assessment can help security teams determine not only their current level of security but also the steps that they will need to take to keep the entire network protected. A business continuity assessment should also be conducted within the specific context of an organization's business goals. In doing both things, organizations can gain a deeper understanding of their security gaps, which can be used to better inform the BCP.

Consider Supply Chain and Third-Party Risk Management

Supply chain and third-party risk management are often overlooked by organizations until it becomes an active threat to their assets or reputation. This reactive approach is no longer sufficient. As organizations increasingly work with other organizations to carry out business operations, supply chain risk management is more important than ever. Teams need to think about the impact of various cybersecurity threats throughout the entire supply chain so that additional resources and plans can be put in place to respond appropriately to said threats.

Mitigate Downtime With an Incident Response and Crisis Communication Plan

As previously mentioned, cybersecurity attacks can have a range of long-lasting damages, to an organization's legal, financial, and reputational wellbeing. To ensure that your organization can return to business as usual as quickly as possible, there needs to be an incident response plan in place. This plan should facilitate an efficient response to security incidents by clearly outlining what needs to be done and who needs to do it. When laying out this process, it is important to think about all elements of the organization's business continuity plan to help avoid redundancies and ensure that all areas are being effectively covered.

Maintain Complete Visibility and Continuously Monitor

The most effective way to proactively manage risk and mitigate business continuity concerns relating to cybersecurity is to enable both complete visibility and continuous monitoring. This allows IT security teams to have a true understanding of the organization's cyber hygiene at any given time, allowing for more confident, informed decision-making as well as ongoing compliance monitoring - which is a growing concern in many industries. Organizations should leverage solutions that provide comprehensive visibility across their entire network infrastructure, including not only vendors but the entire supply chain. The threat landscape is growing at a rapid pace, and organizations can no longer rely on point-in-time assessments to effectively portray their level of security.

The planning fallacy can hijack the process of decision-making because encompasses decision making that is not focused on use of triangulated data and constructive assessment processes. Pessimism and unrealistic optimism are cognitive biases that affect decision outcomes. As mentioned earlier, these outcomes can be significant when referring to an organization's sustainability. The planning fallacy may be an evolutionary trait within the human brain to optimize an individual's survival rate by having the individual overestimate the success of his/her decision outcomes compared to others. Overconfidence and heavy reliance on incomplete information would mean managers and corporate leaders limited their use of systematic learning models which shows failure to learn from past mistakes. Ultimately, strategic foresight is used as a method to improve the sustainability of an organization by trying to avoid mistakes and recognize environmental cues that may lead to success. Cognitive biases are a part of life, leaders can improve their thinking and organizational cultures by acknowledging the existence of heuristics and using methods, such as the SAW model, to compensate for these pitfalls. In the end, cognitive biases exist due to the increased complexity of our society.

REFERENCES

Agarwal, S., Makkar, S., & Tran, D.-T. (Eds.). (2020). *Privacy Vulnerabilities and Data Security Challenges in the IoT* (1st ed.). CRC Press. doi:10.1201/9780429322969

Asadzadeh, A., Mohammadzadeh, Z., Fathifar, Z., Jahangiri-Mirshekarlou, S., & Rezaei-Hachesu, P. (2022). A framework for information technology-based management against COVID-19 in Iran. *BMC Public Health*, 22(1), 402. doi:10.118612889-022-12781-1 PMID:35219292

Beshears, J. (2015). Leaders as Decision Architects. *Harvard Business Review*, 2–11.

Boal, K., & Schultz, P. (2007). Storytelling, time, and evolution: The role of strategic leadership in complex adaptive systems. *The Leadership Quarterly*, 18(4), 411–428. doi:10.1016/j.leaqua.2007.04.008

Brunnermeier, M., Papakonstantinou, F., & Parker, J. (2016). Optimal time-inconsistent beliefs: Misplanning, procrastination, and commitment. *Management Science*, 1-65.

Buiten, M., & Hartmann, A. (2013). Public-Private Partnerships: Cognitive Biases in the Field. In *Engineering Project Organization Conference* (pp. 1-24). EPOS.

Conklin, J. (2005). Wicked Problems & Social Complexity. In J. Conklin (Ed.), *Dialogue Mapping: Building Shared Understanding of Wicked Problems*. Wiley.

Cossette, P. (2015). Heuristics and cognitive biases in entrepreneurs: a review of the research. *Journal of the Canadian Council for Small Business & Entrepreneurship, 27*(5), 471-496. http://dx.DOI.org/10.1080/08276331.2015.1105732

Dragicevic, P. a. (2014). *Visualization-Mediated Alleviation of the Planning Fallacy. In Decisive: Workshop on Dealing with Cognitive Biases in Visualizations*. IEEE. Retrieved from http://nbn-resolving.de/urn:nbn:de:bsz:352-0-329469

Flyvbjerg, B., & Sunstein, C. (2015). The Principle of the Malevolent Hiding Hand; or the Planning Fallacy Writ Large. *SSRN*, 1–18. doi:10.2139srn.2654217

Gast, B. (2011). *The 7 critical healthcare systems IT must protect*. Healthcare IT News. Retrieved April 22, 2023, from https://www.healthcareitnews.com/news/7-critical-healthcare-systems-it-must-protect

Gerlach, K., Spreng, N., Madore, K., & Schacter, D. (2014). Future planning: Default network activity couples with frontoparietal control network and reward-processing regions during process and outcome simulations. *Social Cognitive and Affective Neuroscience, 9*(12), 1942–1951. doi:10.1093can/nsu001 PMID:24493844

Gonzalez, C. (2004). *Learning to Make Decisions in Dynamic Environments: Effects of Time Constraints and Cognitive Abilities*. Carnegie Mellon University, Department of Social and Decision Sciences. Retrieved from https://pdfs.semanticscholar.org/2ef4/2ab2c0d9fc49c0e5baeef3019979c512d217.pdf

Gross, P. (2012). *A Q methodology Analysis of Individual Perspectives of Public Decision-Making Influences of Collaborative Processes*. Scholar Works. Retrieved from https://scholarworks.waldenu.edu/dissertations/975/

Hadjichristidis, C., Summers, B., & Thomas, K. (2014). Unpacking estimates of task duration: The role of typicality and temporality. *Journal of Experimental Social Psychology, 51*, 45-50. http://dx.DOI.org/10.1016/j.jesp.2013.10.009

Heger, T., & Rohrbeck, R. (2012). Strategic foresight for collaborative exploration of new business fields. *Technological Forecasting and Social Change, 79*(5), 819–831. doi:10.1016/j.techfore.2011.11.003

High Availability Solutions | Imperva. (2022). *Learning Center*. https://www.imperva.com/learn/availability/high-availability/

Hilbert, M. (2012). Toward a Synthesis of Cognitive Biases: How Noisy Information Processing Can Bias Human Decision Making. *Psychological Bulletin, 138*(2), 211–237. doi:10.1037/a0025940 PMID:22122235

Iftekhar, M., & Pannell, D. (2015). "Biases" in Adaptive Natural Resource Management. *Conservation Letters, 8*(6), 388–396. doi:10.1111/conl.12189

Innes, J. (2016). Collaborative rationality for planning practice. *The Town Planning Review, 84*(1), 1–4. doi:10.3828/tpr.2016.1

Innes, J., & Booher, D. (2010). *Planning with complexity: An introduction to collaborative rationality for public policy.* Routledge.

Johnson, D., Blumstein, D., & Fowler, J. H. (2013). The evolution of error: error management, cognitive constraints, and adaptive decision-making biases. *Trends in Ecology & Evolution, 28*(8), 474-481. http://dx.DOI.org/10.1016/j.tree.2013.05.014

Kahneman, D. (2011). *Thinking Fast and Slow.* FSG.

Lee, C. (2011). Bounded Rationality and the emergence of simplicity amidst complexity. *Journal of Economic Surveys, 25*(3), 507–526. doi:10.1111/j.1467-6419.2010.00670.x

Luzinski, C. (2014). Identifying Leadership Competencies of the Future: Introducing the Use of Strategic Foresight. *Nurse Leader, 12*(4), 37–39. doi:10.1016/j.mnl.2014.05.009

Madhavan, S., & Balasubramanian, J. A. (2016). Planning Fallacy: A Case of Task Planning in IT Project Support Services. *Purushartha, 9*(1), 57–67.

Manis, M., Shedler, J., Jonides, J., & Nelson, T. E. (1993, September). Availability heuristic in judgments of set size and frequency of occurrence. *Journal of Personality and Social Psychology, 65*(3), 448–457. doi:10.1037/0022-3514.65.3.448

Manis, M., Shedler, J., Jonides, J., & Nelson, T. E. (1993, September). Availability heuristic in judgments of set size and frequency of occurrence. *Journal of Personality and Social Psychology, 65*(3), 448–457. doi:10.1037/0022-3514.65.3.448

Min, K., & Arkes, H. R. (2012). When Is Difficult Planning Good Planning? The Effects of Scenario-Based Planning on Optimistic Prediction Bias. *Journal of Applied Social Psychology, 42*(11), 2701–2729. doi:10.1111/j.1559-1816.2012.00958.x

Nooteboom, B. (2009). *A Cognitive Theory of the Firm.* Edward Elgar Publishing Limited. doi:10.4337/9781848447424

Parrott, L., & Stewart, W. (2012). Future landscapes: Managing within complexity. *Frontiers in Ecology and the Environment, 10*(7), 382–389. doi:10.1890/110082

Raelin, J. (2012). The manager as facilitator of dialogue. *Organization, 20*(6), 818–839. doi:10.1177/1350508412455085

Rodon, C., & Meyer, T. (2012). *Searching information on the Web and Planning Fallacy: A pilot investigation of pessimistic forecasts.* doi:10.1016/j.erap.2011.12.004

Rosenzweig, E., & Critcher, C. R. (2014). Decomposing Forecasting: The Salience-Assessment-Weighting (SAW) Model. *Current Directions in Psychological Science, 23*(5), 368–373. doi:10.1177/0963721414540300

Rouse, M. (2011). *Memorandum of understanding (MOU or MoU).* Retrieved from Whatis.com: https://whatis.techtarget.com/definition/memorandum-of-understanding-MOU-or-MoU

Sample, J. (2015). Mitigating the Planning Fallacy in Project Forecasting: An OD Perspective. *Organization Development Journal*, *33*(2), 51–66.

Shepperd, J., Waters, E., Weinstein, N., & Klein, W. (2015). A Primer on Unrealistic Optimism. *Current Directions in Psychological Science*, *24*(3), 232–237. doi:10.1177/0963721414568341 PMID:26089606

Stenholm, D., Corin Stig, D., Ivansen, L., & Bergsjö, D. (2019). A framework of practices supporting the reuse of technological knowledge. *Environment Systems & Decisions*, *39*(2), 128–145. https://DOI.org/10.1007/s10669-019-09732-4. doi:10.100710669-019-09732-4

The Association for Executives in Healthcare Applications, Data & Analytics (AEHADA) Reveals Bold New Plan for Uniting Digital Health Tech Leadership - Healthcare IT - CHIME. (2023, April 25). *Healthcare IT - CHIME*. https://chimecentral.org/the-association-for-executives-in-healthcare-applications-data-analytics-aehada-reveals-bold-new-plan-for-uniting-digital-health-tech-leadership/

Thorkildsen, A., & Ekman, M. (2013). The complexity of becoming collaborative planning and cultural heritage. *Journal of Cultural Heritage Management and Sustainable Development*, *3*(2), 148–162. doi:10.1108/JCHMSD-10-2012-0053

Thorpe, J., Gray, E., & Cartwright-Smith, L. (2016). Show Us the Data: The Critical Role Health Information Plays in Health System Transformation. *The Journal of Law, Medicine & Ethics*, *44*(4), 592–597. doi:10.1177/1073110516684800 PMID:28661247

Tversky, A., & Kahneman, D. (1992, October). Advances in prospect theory: Cumulative representation of uncertainty. *Journal of Risk and Uncertainty*, *5*(4), 297–323. doi:10.1007/BF00122574

Wilson, J. R., & Rutherford, A. (1989, December). Mental Models: Theory and Application in Human Factors. *Human Factors*, *31*(6), 617–634. doi:10.1177/001872088903100601

Chapter 7
Cybersecurity Breach Case Study

Jessica Parker
Marymount University, USA

ABSTRACT

This cybersecurity case study provides a comprehensive remediation plan for an organization that recently experienced a data breach and lacks a risk management strategy. Starting with a current state analysis, the plan includes strategies to support the new organizational behaviors, understanding and aligning company culture, supporting changes with ethical decision-making and strong leadership, and ensuring changes are maintained and reinforced. Foundation theories and models are used to support the plan: human factors, theory of constraints, the plan-do-check-act cycle, Schein's model of organizational culture, the Deal and Kennedy culture model, Lewin's change management model, nudge theory, the duty-based approach to ethical decision-making, and transformational leadership. The resulting plan ensures that the organization is able to prevent most cyberattacks and has a ready response plan for dealing with any future breaches.

INTRODUCTION

An organization experienced a cybersecurity breach and had no risk management or cybersecurity plan in place, leaving them unable to respond effectively to the breach. Threat exposure management is cited by Gartner as the number one cybersecurity trend for 2023 (Perry & Gartner, Inc., 2023). With cyberattacks increasing by 38% in 2022 (Check Point Research, 2023), the need to prevent future breaches is also on the rise. Not only are there more cyberattacks but there are also increases in adversaries, tools, and techniques used by bad actors to generate revenue (CrowdStrike, 2023). Based on the most recent World Economic Forum. Analysis of the organization's current risk management processes has identified fundamental deficiencies. As Jen Easterly, Director of the U.S. Cybersecurity and Infrastructure Security Agency, pointed out, "CEOs and boards have to own the cyber risks. We can no longer blame the CISOs" (Nash, 2023). The World Economic Forum Global Cybersecurity Outlook study found that 43% of surveyed leaders believe a cyberattack will negatively impact their organization in the next two

DOI: 10.4018/979-8-3693-1630-6.ch007

years (2023). The problem is that the organization's risk planning is deficient as it lacks both plans for addressing the current cybersecurity breach and strategies to prevent or mitigate the risks of future breaches.

LITERATURE REVIEW

To organize a comprehensive solution, *INTERNATIONAL STANDARD ISO/IEC 27001: Information technology — Security techniques — Information security management systems — Requirements* (ISO/IEC 27001: 2022) will be used as a framework aligned with the topic areas in the table of contents:

- Context of the organization - Schein's Model of Organizational Culture, Deal and Kennedy Culture Model
- Leadership - Deal and Kennedy Culture Model, Transformational Leadership
- Planning – Risk Management, Human Factors Ergonomics, Theory of Constraints
- Support - Lewin's Change Management Model, Nudge Theory, Duty-Based Approach to Ethical Decision Making
- Operation – Security Culture
- Performance evaluation – Plan-Do-Check-Act
- Improvement – Theory of Constraints, Plan-Do-Check-Act

Schein's Model of Organizational Culture

A company's culture significantly impacts organizational behaviors (Akpa et al., 2021). Given the importance of culture to the organization's effectiveness (Deal & Kennedy, 1983; Sharma & Aparicio, 2022), the team will employ *Schein's Model of Organizational Culture* as a framework to analyze the current state of the company's culture. Schein's Model will help us decipher the company's culture from a physical and social context, espoused organizational and demonstrated values, and basic assumptions (Yilmaz, 2014; Akpa et al., 2021). Using qualitative methods such as observations, analysis of rituals, and interviews (Schein, 2010), the team will gather information about the basic assumptions that determine information security risk actions and perspectives (Schlienger & Teufel, 2002; Karlsson et al., 2021). It is crucial to understand these underlying assumptions to mitigate the potential risks of anxiety and defensiveness that may occur when they are changed (Akpa et al., 2021). Additionally, leaders should model the desired culture and cybersecurity behaviors to positively influence the culture change (Schein, 2010). Given the recent breach, it is already understood that the security culture needs to change, and the following model will help support that change.

Deal and Kennedy Culture Model

In the *Deal and Kennedy Culture Model*, corporate culture can be understood by examining risk (high or low) associated with the company's activities and how quickly (fast or slow) companies – and their employees – receive feedback on the results of decisions or strategies (Deal & Kennedy, 1982). A well-developed culture is able to influence behaviors and can be recognized by the common values and norms shared among all members of the organization (Deal & Kennedy, 1982; Sinclair, 1993). To shift culture, leaders must accept and consistently demonstrate alignment with the organization's core beliefs (Deal

& Kennedy, 2000). For example, executives must demonstrate the importance of good cybersecurity behaviors and commit to enforcing policies and procedures (Sinclair, 1993; Ertan et al., 2018). In addition, the culture of the organization and each team needs to shift toward activities that protect information systems (Sharma & Aparicio, 2022). As individuals demonstrate newly learned behaviors, prompt feedback will help them develop effective self-corrective judgments (Cooper, 2000). Leaders can help guide and support team members by also applying transformational leadership skills.

Transformational Leadership

Transformational leadership focuses on "satisfying basic needs and meeting higher desires through inspiring followers to provide newer solutions and create a better workplace" (Ghasabeh et al., 2015). To guide employees through organizational change, transformational leadership leverages the techniques of influence and inspiration to identify individual needs, build a learning climate, and mobilize employee support toward organizational goals (Bass, 1999; Ghasabeh et al., 2015; Peng et al., 2021). Using transformational leadership results in an increased level of commitment, receptiveness, and preparedness to embrace change (Peng et al., 2021). By engaging team members as people rather than employees, transformational leaders build relationships based on trust and respect, fostering loyalty and admiration (Hay, 2006). These tools and techniques will be incorporated into our action plan to drive the needed organizational changes and establish a robust cybersecurity culture.

Risk Management

A foundational tool, the *risk management strategy*, "is a structured approach to addressing risks" (*10 Types of Risk Management Strategies to Follow in 2021*, 2021). Supporting the strategy is the *risk management plan* "that describes how risk management activities will be structured and performed" (Project Management Institute, 2021). A risk management plan documents the potential risks and impacts on the organization along with the action plan for each risk: mitigate, prevent, develop a contingency plan, or reject the risk (Project Management Institute, 2021; Invensis Learning, 2022). In order to be most effective, risk management planning should be collaborative, ensuring representation across functional areas and an understanding of the overall organizational environment (Decker & Galer, 2013). Transparent communication combined with fostering a disciplined approach contributes to successful risk management (Fraser & Simkins, 2010). Everyone in the organization should understand their responsibility for risk management and the owners responsible for monitoring risks and taking action when a risk becomes an issue (Decker & Galer, 2013). A best practice is to review and reassess the risk management plan frequently in order to be able to adapt to change (Mulcahy, 2003; Ganin et al., 2020; Project Management Institute, 2021). *Cybersecurity* is included within the scope of IT risks (Fadun, 2021) and "means prevention of damage to, protection of, and restoration of computers, electronic communications systems, electronic communication services, wire communication, and electronic communication, including information contained therein, to ensure its availability, integrity, authentication, confidentiality, and non-repudiation" (Bush, 2008). Cybersecurity risks need to consider not only the risks involved with the technology but also physical security and human factors risks (Ganin et al., 2020; Lee, 2021).

Human Factors Ergonomics

Human factors ergonomics (human factors) is defined as "the scientific discipline concerned with the understanding of interactions among humans and other elements of a system, and the profession that applies theory, principles, data, and methods to design in order to optimize human well-being and overall system performance" (*What Is Ergonomics (HFE)?*, n.d.). Human factors must be considered when remediating cyber risks because 95% of cybersecurity incidents can be attributed to mistakes or oversights made by individual humans (PwC Belgium, 2017; *After Reading, Writing and Arithmetic, the 4th "r" of Literacy Is Cyber-risk*, 2023). "The renewed focus on the human element continues to grow among this year's top cybersecurity trends" (Perry & Gartner, Inc., 2023). These humans decide whether to trust links in emails, assess the credibility and privacy of websites, and determine what passwords they will use (Proctor & Chen, 2015; PwC Belgium, 2017). According to Nobles (2018), "malicious actors gain access to targeted systems by exploiting human error through (a) spear phishing, (b) social engineering, (c) malware, (d) noncompliance, (e) poor policies, and (f) technology-induced vulnerabilities." These human errors can be intentional or unintentional - as individuals may not have a sufficient understanding of risks, systems, or processes (Metalidou et al., 2014; Hadlington, 2018; Yan, 2018; Ali et al., 2021). Unintentional human errors can be remediated by conducting awareness and training activities (Campean, 2019; Alsharif et al., 2022). Intentional human errors in the form of noncompliance with company policy can occur when it is more effort to comply or the individual believes there are negligible risks to noncompliance (Lawton, 1998; Yan, 2018; Rebensky et al., 2021). A perceived lack of enforcement leads to the belief that deviating from the rules is acceptable (Zhang & Bednall, 2016; Yan, 2018), although fear of negative consequences alone will not ensure compliance (Herath & Rao, 2009), improved enforcement can increase the overall level of compliance (Brown, 2018). Similarly, having a clear and sufficiently comprehensive information security policy will help address noncompliance and lack of individual awareness of roles and responsibilities (Wiafe et al., 2020; Alassaf & Alkhalifah, 2021). While investing in technology to protect against cybersecurity threats is important, technology cannot eliminate the risk of human error (Pfleeger & Caputo, 2012; Safa et al., 2015; Nobles, 2018; Jeong et al., 2019).

Theory of Constraints

Dr. Eliyahu Golratt's *Theory of Constraints (TOC)* focuses on identifying and addressing the bottlenecks in the system as the fastest way to improve processes (Theory of Constraints Institute, n.d.) by applying concepts from experimental science (Ikeziri et al., 2019). This theory can be used as a comprehensive approach to understanding how the constraints are related, and help identify the root cause of issues within the organization (Şimşit et al., 2014). The TOC has also spawned *thinking processes* (TP) that help support analyzing the constraints and solutions to address them. The *current reality tree* (CRT) is a TP used to visually represent the system's current state, including undesirable effects and root causes (Mabin et al., 2001; Gupta et al., 2010). Complementing the CRT are two TPs to help define the desired future state: the *evaporating cloud* (EC) and the *future reality tree* (FTR). The EC is used to analyze the root cause of the problem and identify a solution (Gupta et al., 2010). The FRT visually represents the future state after solution implementation and considers impacts on the organization that may need to be addressed before proceeding (Mabin et al., 2001; Gupta et al., 2010). As part of designing how to change, the *pre-requisite tree* (PRT) is used to understand obstacles and potential adverse impacts of the proposed solution and the *transition tree* (TT) details activities that need to be completed in order to address concerns identified with the PRT (Mabin et al., 2001; Gupta et al., 2010). Using these six TPs, we will be able to identify what needs to be addressed to alleviate the cybersecurity constraints, develop a plan of what needs to happen to exploit the constraints to improve results effectively, and how to effect the necessary changes in as simple a way as possible (Goldratt, 1990; Gupta et al., 2010). These activities can be repeated until the processes are sufficiently optimized (McCleskey, 2020). In addition to being planned, changes must also be managed to ensure that they are implemented successfully.

Lewin's Change Management Model

Lewin's change management model has three phases – unfreezing, changing, and refreezing (1997). In the unfreezing phase, the need for change is identified, and gaps are analyzed, selecting a solution (Lewin, 1997; Levasseur, 2001; Shirey, 2013). The change phase includes processes, plans, and communications to support the change (Lewin, 1997; Levasseur, 2001; Shirey, 2013). In the third phase, the change becomes part of the organization's standards and culture (Lewin, 1997; Levasseur, 2001; Shirey, 2013). During the change process, involve all people affected and regularly communicate about what is being changed and why (Levasseur, 2001). Employees are crucial to the proposed transformation, as they must adjust to the new standards and processes (Falch et al., 2022). Upon the completion of the change process, it will be necessary to evaluate whether the intended change has been accomplished (Hamdo, 2021). Assuming the desired change occurred, maintaining the changed behavior will be supported by our next change management theory.

Nudge Theory

Nudge Theory is a framework that preserves freedom of choice while influencing individuals in ways that encourage and enable the desired outcome (Thaler & Sunstein, 2008; Tagulao & Marques, 2022). Effective nudges work with the way people instinctively approach making simple decisions (Thaler & Sunstein, 2008; Hall-Ellis, 2015; Zimmermann & Renaud, 2021). These nudges make the desired behaviors at the moment of decision the default or the easiest option, increasing the likelihood of compliance (Thaler & Sunstein, 2008; Bock, 2015; Zimmermann & Renaud, 2021). As the nudges are designed, a feedback mechanism at key points should be incorporated to positively reinforce the behavior and to provide helpful guidance as people will make mistakes (Thaler & Sunstein, 2008; Zimmermann & Renaud, 2021). Another aspect of nudging is to make clear the relationship between the choices and beneficial outcomes, called *mapping* (Thaler & Sunstein, 2008; Zimmermann & Renaud, 2021). Nudges will include incentives to comply with policies, establishing the desired behaviors as individual and organizational norms, ensuring that the communications make the target behaviors personally relevant, and helping individuals feel good about themselves when they support the change (Thaler & Sunstein, 2008; Kankane et al., 2018). When choices are complex, organize the information in logical groupings or categories, which helps individuals to simplify the decision-making process (Thaler & Sunstein, 2008). By structuring the environment and organization in ways that make the desired behaviors instinctive and straightforward, it makes compliance easy (Thaler & Sunstein, 2008). One of the structural changes will be to frame compliance with the changes as an ethical duty, as explained in the following paragraph.

Duty-Based Approach to Ethical Decision-Making

In the *Duty-Based approach to ethical decision-making*, also known as deontology, an ethical decision conforms to the organization's moral rules (Casali, 2007). In other words, an action is determined to be ethical and correct based on the intention and principles that guide it (Ilie & Frăsineanu, 2019). In order to avoid conflicts arising from varying definitions of ethical and correct behaviors, organizations need to adopt a uniform ethical framework that is consistently applied (Casali, 2007). Individuals have the freedom to choose how they behave, and in order to be perceived as morally good, they will choose to align their behaviors with the rules of the organization (Micewski & Troy, 2007). This also connects to the ego nudge, where people behave in ways that make them feel good about themselves (Thaler & Sunstein, 2008; Kankane et al., 2018). By ensuring that individuals understand what constitutes correct behaviors from a cybersecurity perspective, the organization's security culture needs to be improved.

Security Culture

"Security culture is defined as aspects of the organizational security philosophy that directly or indirectly affects the overall security of the network" (Kraemer et al., 2009). For example, employees need to understand that unauthorized information access using their legitimately authorized credentials can be considered a cybercrime (Algarni et al., 2021). Without documented standards and training for all employees, there is a risk that a lack of awareness will cause unintentional errors that an attacker can exploit (Alsharif et al., 2022). As part of establishing a more robust security culture, existing standards for security can be leveraged: the International Standards Organization (ISO/IEC 27001:2022) as the framework, the U.S. Department of Commerce National Institute of Standards and Technology framework (*NIST Risk Management Framework*, 2023) to develop plans for addressing cybersecurity risks, the Open Worldwide Application Security Project Application Security Verification Standard (*OWASP Application Security Verification Standard 4.0.3*, 2021) for development activities, and the SANS Institute for training materials (*Security Awareness Training*, 2023) and policy templates (*Information Security Policy Templates*, n.d.). These standards will be incorporated into the overall change management and process improvement activities.

Plan-Do-Check-Act

The *plan-do-check-act* (PDCA) cycle will support the implementation of change and continuous process improvement (Schmidt et al., 2014; *INTERNATIONAL STANDARD ISO 9001*, 2015). PDCA consists of 4 steps: 1) *plan* the change that needs to be made, 2) *do* the change, testing how well it works on a small scale, 3) *check* how well the test worked, learn from the results and 4) *act* to apply what was learned to improve the process further; repeat (*INTERNATIONAL STANDARD ISO 9001*, 2015; American Society for Quality, n.d.). One of the strengths of PDCA is that employees are empowered to identify and address improvement opportunities based on learnings as changes are made (*INTERNATIONAL STANDARD ISO 9001*, 2015; Arredondo-Soto et al., 2021). From a cybersecurity perspective, the iterative nature of the PDCA cycle aids the organization so that it can adapt to the ever-changing threat landscape and continuously improve security awareness and compliance (Tatar et al., 2020; Khando et al., 2021). Not only do processes need to be changed, but the organization's culture needs to be refreshed to support these new ways of working.

CURRENT STATE

Having experienced one breach, the organization knows from experience that a cybersecurity breach can adversely affect the organization's reputation, impair security management, and cost the company money (Algarni et al., 2021). Any cyberattack of sufficient severity and impact can become a crisis for the company (Wang & Johnson, 2018). With a breach, protected data assets are accessed or shared by unauthorized individuals, costing U.S. companies an average of $9.44 million for each breach (*Cost of a Data Breach 2022*, n.d.).

This organization lacks a risk management strategy and a risk management plan. Without this, the company cannot effectively anticipate threats or respond quickly when a cybersecurity incident occurs (Cisco Secure, 2023).

The cybersecurity culture also needs to be improved so that all employees recognize how they contribute to the organization's security. No documented cybersecurity standards are in place, leaving employees uninformed about their role in protecting the organization and its data.

RECOMMENDATIONS AND IMPLEMENTATION PLAN

A multi-layered remediation plan has been developed to address the gaps identified in the organization. This remediation plan includes developing a risk management strategy and plan for cybersecurity, identifying appropriate strategies to support the new organizational behaviors, understanding and aligning company culture, supporting changes with ethical decision-making and strong leadership, and ensuring changes are maintained and reinforced. This comprehensive approach was developed using fundamental tools, theories, and models.

This process begins by developing a robust risk management strategy. This means identifying a leader and team members responsible for developing and maintaining the risk management process. This team will be responsible for risk management planning, risk identification, qualitative and quantitative risk analysis, risk response planning, and risk monitoring and control (Mulcahy, 2003). The output of this process will be a risk management plan which will identify actions the organization will take to insure, mitigate, respond to, or (occasionally) ignore the risks. The organization will follow seven steps - prepare, categorize, select, implement, assess, authorize, and monitor - to build out a plan to manage cybersecurity and risk (*NIST Risk Management Framework*, 2023). Lewin's change management model will be used to ensure that the changes outlined in the risk management plan are implemented and enforced. TOC tools will be used to identify the root causes of issues, uncover additional risks, and streamline processes. As the risk management team was hired in response to a cybersecurity breach, the poorly developed cybersecurity culture must also be addressed.

Components of a strong and effective security culture include robust and comprehensive cybersecurity policies, along with processes for monitoring and enforcement (Brumfield, 2021). Given the lack of organizational cybersecurity expertise, our team recommends implementing an internationally developed standard, the OWASP Application Security Verification (ASV) standard, which "is a list of application security requirements or tests that can be used by architects, developers, testers, security professionals, tool vendors, and consumers to define, build, test and verify secure applications" (*OWASP Application Security Verification Standard 4.0.3*, 2021). Investing in technology solutions to support effective cybersecurity is important, but investing in the people within the organization is equally important.

Complementing OWASP ASV standard, selected templates from the SANS Institute will be used to build our internal policies (*Information Security Policy Templates*, n.d.). The Duty-Based approach to ethical decision-making will be incorporated into the policies to help establish a culture of ethical cybersecurity behaviors. To support the new behaviors, the nudge theory will be used to support new behaviors that align with the new security policies. One nudge will be to provide feedback to individuals about how secure their password is when it is being created (Zimmermann & Renaud, 2021). SANS Institute training modules will be used for information security awareness training for end-users and phishing response (*Security Awareness Training*, 2023). To round out the security culture change, a human factors expert will be brought in to analyze how human-enabled errors can be reduced within the organization. Establishing these fundamentals will not address the need to change how the organization and its culture integrate with the new risk management and cybersecurity standards and activities.

To comprehensively guide the organization through these changes, this team recommends leveraging a set of checklists that complement a change management framework with seven components: clarity, management, engagement, resources, alignment, leadership, and communication (Bevan, n.d.). While it cannot guarantee success, using the checklists provides "a basis on which to assess, plan, and implement change in a systematic and integrated way" (Bevan, n.d.). As part of the change implementation process, Schein's Model of Organizational Culture and the Deal and Kennedy Culture Model will be used to identify and address cultural barriers that may hinder the adoption of new organizational behaviors. All management team members will be trained in transformational leadership so they can effectively communicate the reasons for change and support each individual team member as they navigate the change journey.

FUTURE STATE: AFTER IMPLEMENTATION

The work continues once the organizational foundation has been built with robust risk management and cybersecurity practices. Using the tools from TOC and the plan-do-check-act cycle, the organization will continue to improve practices in the areas of risk and cybersecurity management. The change management tools and techniques that aided the organization as it established the new culture can be reused as needed to support future process improvements and organizational change implementations. While these steps do not guarantee that another breach will not occur, they will ensure that the organization can respond promptly and effectively when it does.

OPPORTUNITIES FOR FUTURE RESEARCH

While the proposed approaches and models provide a solution set for creating and maintaining a robust cybersecurity culture, other tools and models could be considered and evaluated for inclusion in the future. A limitation for this case study is that it was based on a single organization and a single solution set where there was nothing in place rather than on one or more organizations where existing plans, policies, and procedures existed. Additionally, the focus here was on addressing risk management plans and cybersecurity culture, with the technology solution as a secondary consideration yet advances in artificial intelligence may lead to solutions where the technology is able to support the overall security culture more effectively and as a risk mitigation for failures in other areas.

REFERENCES

After reading, writing and arithmetic, the 4th "r" of literacy is cyber-risk. (2023, January 5). World Economic Forum. https://www.weforum.org/agenda/2020/12/cyber-risk-cyber-security-education

Akpa, V. O., Asikhia, O. U., & Nneji, N. E. (2021). Organizational Culture and Organizational Performance: A Review of Literature. *International Journal of Advances in Engineering and Management, 3*(1), 361–372. doi:10.35629/5252-0301361372

Alassaf, M., & Alkhalifah, A. (2021). Exploring the Influence of Direct and Indirect Factors on Information Security Policy Compliance: A Systematic Literature Review. *IEEE Access : Practical Innovations, Open Solutions, 9*, 162687–162705. doi:10.1109/ACCESS.2021.3132574

Algarni, A., Thayananthan, V., & Malaiya, Y. K. (2021). Quantitative Assessment of Cybersecurity Risks for Mitigating Data Breaches in Business Systems. *Applied Sciences (Basel, Switzerland), 11*(8), 3678. doi:10.3390/app11083678

Ali, R. F., Dominic, P. D. D., Ali, S. F., Rehman, M., & Sohail, A. (2021). Information Security Behavior and Information Security Policy Compliance: A Systematic Literature Review for Identifying the Transformation Process from Noncompliance to Compliance. *Applied Sciences (Basel, Switzerland), 11*(8), 3383. doi:10.3390/app11083383

Alsharif, M. G., Mishra, S., & Alshehri, M. (2022). Impact of Human Vulnerabilities on Cybersecurity. *Computer Systems Science and Engineering, 40*(3), 1153–1166. doi:10.32604/csse.2022.019938

American Society for Quality. (n.d.). *PDCA Cycle - What is the Plan-Do-Check-Act Cycle?* https://asq.org/quality-resources/pdca-cycle

Arredondo-Soto, K. C., Blanco-Fernández, J., Miranda-Ackerman, M. A., Solis-Quinteros, M. M., Realyvásquez-Vargas, A., & García-Alcaraz, J. L. (2021). A Plan-Do-Check-Act Based Process Improvement Intervention for Quality Improvement. *IEEE Access : Practical Innovations, Open Solutions, 9*, 132779–132790. doi:10.1109/ACCESS.2021.3112948

Bass, B. M. (1999). Two Decades of Research and Development in Transformational Leadership. *European Journal of Work and Organizational Psychology, 8*(1), 9–32. doi:10.1080/135943299398410

Bevan, R. (n.d.). *The Changemaking Checklists: A Toolkit for Planning, Leading, and Sustaining Change.* Changestart Press.

Bock, L. (2015). *Work Rules! Insights from Inside Google That Will Transform How You Live and Lead.* Twelve.

Brown, D. T. (2018). *Investigating Information Security Policy Characteristics: Do Quality, Enforcement and Compliance Reduce Organizational Fraud?* DigitalCommons@Kennesaw State University. https://digitalcommons.kennesaw.edu/dba_etd/40/

Bush, G. W. (2008). *National Security National Directive/Homeland Security Presidential Directive: Cybersecurity Policy* (NSPD-54/HSPD-23). The White House. https://irp.fas.org/offdocs/nspd/nspd-54.pdf

Campean, S. (2019). The Human Factor at the Center of a Cyber Security Culture. *International Journal of Information Security and Cybercrime*. doi:10.19107/IJISC.2019.01.07

Casali, G. L. (2007). A Quest for Ethical Decision Making: Searching for the Holy Grail, and Finding the Sacred Trinity in Ethical Decision-Making by Managers. *Social Responsibility Journal*, *3*(3), 50–59. doi:10.1108/17471110710835581

Check Point Research. (2023, March 16). *2023 Security Report: Cyberattacks reach an all-time high in response to geo-political conflict, and the rise of 'disruption and destruction' malware*. https://research. checkpoint.com/2023/2023-security-report-cyberattacks-reach-an-all-time-high-in-response-to-geo-political-conflict-and-the-rise-of-disruption-and-destruction-malware/

Cisco Secure. (2023). *Cisco Cybersecurity Readiness Index: Resilience in a Hybrid World*. https://www. cisco.com/c/dam/m/en_us/products/security/cybersecurity-reports/cybersecurity-readiness-index/2023/ cybersecurity-readiness-index-report.pdf

Cooper, M. (2000). Towards a model of safety culture. *Safety Science*, *36*(2), 111–136. doi:10.1016/ S0925-7535(00)00035-7

Cost of a data breach 2022. (n.d.). IBM. Retrieved April 22, 2023, from https://www.ibm.com/reports/ data-breach

CrowdStrike. (2023, February 28). *2023 Global Threat Report | CrowdStrike*. crowdstrike.com. https:// www.crowdstrike.com/global-threat-report/

Deal, T. E., & Kennedy, A. (1983). Culture: A New Look Through Old Lenses. *The Journal of Applied Behavioral Science*, *19*(4), 498–505. doi:10.1177/002188638301900411

Deal, T. E., & Kennedy, A. A. (1982). *Corporate Cultures: The Rites and Rituals of Corporate Life*. Addison Wesley.

Deal, T. E., & Kennedy, A. A. (2000). *The New Corporate Cultures: Revitalizing The Workplace After Downsizing, Mergers, And Reengineering*. Basic Books.

Decker, A., & Galer, D. (2013). *Enterprise Risk Management - Straight to the Point: An Implementation Guide Function by Function*. Createspace Independent Publishing Platform.

ErtanA.CrosslandG.HeathC.DennyD.JensenR. (2018). Everyday Cyber Security in Organisations. arXiv:2004.11768.

Fadun, S. (2021). *Cybersecurity Risk and Cybersecurity Risk Management (Cyber, Security, Risk, & Cyber Security)* [Video]. YouTube. https://www.youtube.com/watch?v=tZ7LfWinbu0

Falch, M., Olesen, H., Skouby, K. E., Tadayoni, R., & Williams, I. (2022). Cybersecurity in SMEs in the Baltic Sea Region. *International Telecommunications Society 31th European Conference 2022*.

Fraser, J. F., & Simkins, B. J. (2010). Enterprise Risk Management: An Introduction and Overview. In Enterprise Risk Management: Today's Leading Research and Best Practices for Tomorrow's Executives (1st ed.). Wiley. doi:10.1002/9781118267080.ch1

Ganin, A. A., Quach, P., Panwar, M., Collier, Z. A., Keisler, J. M., Marchese, D., & Linkov, I. (2020). Multicriteria Decision Framework for Cybersecurity Risk Assessment and Management. *Risk Analysis, 40*(1), 183–199. doi:10.1111/risa.12891 PMID:28873246

Ghasabeh, M. S., Soosay, C., & Reaiche, C. (2015). The emerging role of transformational leadership. *Journal of Developing Areas, 49*(6), 459–467. doi:10.1353/jda.2015.0090

Goldratt, E. M. (1990). *What is this Thing Called Theory of Constraints and how Should it be Implemented?* Gower Publishing Company, Limited.

Gupta, A., Bhardwaj, A., Kanda, A., & Sachdeva, A. (2010). Theory of Constraints Based Approach to Effective Change Management. *International Journal of Research, 1*(7), 40–48.

Hadlington, L. (2018). The "Human Factor" in Cybersecurity. In Advances in digital crime, forensics, and cyber terrorism book series (pp. 46–63). IGI Global. doi:10.4018/978-1-5225-4053-3.ch003

Hall-Ellis, S. D. (2015). Nudges and decision making: a winning combination. *The Bottom Line: Managing Library Finances.* doi:10.1108/BL-07-2015-0015

Hamdo, S. S. (2021). *Change Management Models: A Comparative Review* [Academic Paper]. Istanbul Okan University.

Hay, I. (2006). Transformational leadership: characteristics and criticisms. *E Journal of Organizational Learning and Leadership, 5*(2).

Herath, T. C., & Rao, H. R. (2009). Protection motivation and deterrence: A framework for security policy compliance in organisations. *European Journal of Information Systems, 18*(2), 106–125. doi:10.1057/ejis.2009.6

Ikeziri, L. M., Souza, F. G., Gupta, M. P., & De Camargo Fiorini, P. (2019). Theory of constraints: Review and bibliometric analysis. *International Journal of Production Research, 57*(15–16), 5068–5102. doi:10.1080/00207543.2018.1518602

Ilie, V., & Frăsineanu, E. (2019). Theoretical Approaches. Revisited and New Perspectives: Ethical Fundamentals in Scientific Research. *Annals of the University of Craiova, Psychology - Pedagogy, 18*(40).

Information Security Policy Templates. (n.d.). SANS Institute. Retrieved April 22, 2023, from https://www.sans.org/information-security-policy/

INTERNATIONAL STANDARD ISO 9001: Quality management systems — Requirements (ISO 9001: 2015). (2015). International Organization for Standardization.

INTERNATIONAL STANDARD ISO/IEC 27001: Information technology — Security techniques — Information security management systems — Requirements (ISO/IEC 27001: 2022). (2022). International Organization for Standardization.

Invensis Learning. (2022, October 11). *Risk Mitigation Strategies | The 5 Best Approaches of Risk Management | Invensis Learning* [Video]. YouTube. https://www.youtube.com/watch?v=pMKtWoec37c

Jeong, J., Mihelcic, J., Oliver, G., & Rudolph, C. (2019). Towards an Improved Understanding of Human Factors in Cybersecurity. *Color Imaging Conference.* 10.1109/CIC48465.2019.00047

Kankane, S., DiRusso, C., & Buckley, C. (2018). *Can We Nudge Users Toward Better Password Management?* Human Factors in Computing Systems. doi:10.1145/3170427.3188689

Karlsson, M., Karlsson, F., Åström, J., & Denk, T. (2021). The effect of perceived organizational culture on employees' information security compliance. *Information & Computer Security.* doi:10.1108/ICS-06-2021-0073

Khando, K., Gao, S., Islam, M. S., & Salman, A. (2021). Enhancing employees information security awareness in private and public organisations: A systematic literature review. *Computers & Security, 106,* 102267. doi:10.1016/j.cose.2021.102267

Kraemer, S., Carayon, P., & Clem, J. R. (2009). Human and organizational factors in computer and information security: Pathways to vulnerabilities. *Computers & Security, 28*(7), 509–520. doi:10.1016/j.cose.2009.04.006

Lawton, R. (1998). Not working to rule: Understanding procedural violations at work. *Safety Science, 28*(2), 77–95. doi:10.1016/S0925-7535(97)00073-8

Lee, I. (2021). Cybersecurity: Risk management framework and investment cost analysis. *Business Horizons, 64*(5), 659–671. doi:10.1016/j.bushor.2021.02.022

Levasseur, R. E. (2001). People Skills: Change Management Tools—Lewin's Change Model. *Interfaces, 31*(4), 71–73. doi:10.1287/inte.31.4.71.9674

Lewin, K. (1997). *Resolving social conflicts and field theory in social science.* American Psychological Association eBooks. doi:10.1037/10269-000

Mabin, V. J., Forgeson, S., & Green, L. W. (2001). Harnessing resistance: using the theory of constraints to assist change management. *Journal of European Industrial Training, 25*(2/3/4), 168–191. doi:10.1108/EUM0000000005446

McCleskey, J. A. (2020). Forty years and still evolving: The theory of constraints. *American Journal of Management, 20*(3), 65–74.

Metalidou, E., Marinagi, C., Trivellas, P., Eberhagen, N., Skourlas, C., & Giannakopoulos, G. (2014). The Human Factor of Information Security: Unintentional Damage Perspective. *Procedia: Social and Behavioral Sciences, 147,* 424–428. doi:10.1016/j.sbspro.2014.07.133

Micewski, E. R., & Troy, C. (2007). Business Ethics – Deontologically Revisited. *Journal of Business Ethics, 72*(1), 17–25. doi:10.100710551-006-9152-z

Mulcahy, R. (2003). *Risk Management: Tricks of the Trade® for Project Managers : a Course in a Book.* RMC Publications.

Nash, K. (Ed.). (2023, April 21). WSJ PRO Cybersecurity Newsletter. *Wall Street Journal.* Retrieved April 21, 2023, from http://createsend.com/t/d-035EE1F53B8C66232540EF23F30FEDED

NIST Risk Management Framework. (2023, February 23). Computer Security Division, Information Technology Laboratory, National Institute of Standards and Technology, U.S. Department of Commerce. https://csrc.nist.gov/Projects/risk-management

Nobles, C. (2018). Botching Human Factors in Cybersecurity in Business Organizations. *Holistica*, *9*(3), 71–88. doi:10.2478/hjbpa-2018-0024

OWASP Application Security Verification Standard 4.0.3. (2021, October). OWASP Foundation. https://owasp.org/www-project-application-security-verification-standard/

Peng, J., Li, M., Wang, Z., & Yuying, L. (2021). Transformational Leadership and Employees' Reactions to Organizational Change: Evidence From a Meta-Analysis. *The Journal of Applied Behavioral Science*, *57*(3), 369–397. doi:10.1177/0021886320920366

Perry, L. & Gartner, Inc. (2023, April 19). *Top Strategic Cybersecurity Trends for 2023*. Gartner. https://www.gartner.com/en/articles/top-strategic-cybersecurity-trends-for-2023

Pfleeger, S. L., & Caputo, D. D. (2012). Leveraging behavioral science to mitigate cyber security risk. *Computers & Security*, *31*(4), 597–611. doi:10.1016/j.cose.2011.12.010

Proctor, R. W., & Chen, J. M. (2015). The Role of Human Factors/Ergonomics in the Science of Security. *Human Factors*, *57*(5), 721–727. doi:10.1177/0018720815585906 PMID:25994927

Project Management Institute. (2021). *The Standard for Project Management and a Guide to the Project Management Body of Knowledge*. PMBOK Guide.

PwC Belgium. (2017). *Information Security Breaches Survey 2017 – Key takeaways*. Retrieved April 22, 2023, from https://www.pwc.be/en/documents/20170315-Information-security-breaches-survey.pdf

Rebensky, S., Carroll, M., Nakushian, A., Chaparro, M., & Prior, T. (2021). Understanding the last line of defense: human response to cybersecurity events. In *HCI for Cybersecurity, Privacy and Trust: Third International Conference, HCI-CPT 2021, Held as Part of the 23rd HCI International Conference, HCII 2021, Virtual Event, July 24–29, 2021, Proceedings*. Springer International Publishing. 10.1007/978-3-030-77392-2_23

Safa, N. S., Sookhak, M., Von Solms, R., Furnell, S., Ghani, N. A., & Herawan, T. (2015). Information security conscious care behaviour formation in organizations. *Computers & Security*, *53*, 65–78. doi:10.1016/j.cose.2015.05.012

Schein, E. H. (2010). *Organizational Culture and Leadership*. Jossey-Bass.

Schlienger, T., & Teufel, S. (2002). Information Security Culture: The Socio-Cultural Dimension in Information Security Management. In *Information Security* (pp. 191–202). https://dblp.uni-trier.de/db/conf/sec/sec2002.html#SchliengerT02

Schmidt, M. T., Elezi, F., Tommelein, I. D., & Lindemann, U. (2014). *Towards recursive plan-do-check-act cycles for continuous improvement*. Industrial Engineering and Engineering Management., doi:10.1109/IEEM.2014.7058886

Security Awareness Training. (2023, April 6). SANS Institute. https://www.sans.org/security-awareness-training/

Sharma, S., & Aparicio, E. (2022). Organizational and team culture as antecedents of protection motivation among IT employees. *Computers & Security*, *120*, 102774. doi:10.1016/j.cose.2022.102774

Shirey, M. R. (2013). Lewin's Theory of Planned Change as a Strategic Resource. *The Journal of Nursing Administration*, *43*(2), 69–72. doi:10.1097/NNA.0b013e31827f20a9 PMID:23343723

Şimşit, Z. T., Günay, N. S., & Vayvay, O. (2014). Theory of Constraints: A Literature Review. *Procedia: Social and Behavioral Sciences*, *150*, 930–936. doi:10.1016/j.sbspro.2014.09.104

Sinclair, A. (1993). Approaches to organisational culture and ethics. *Journal of Business Ethics*, *12*(1), 63–73. doi:10.1007/BF01845788

Tagulao, T. C. S., & Marques, J. L. (2022). The Application of Nudge Theory in Ensuring Change Acceptance in the Hospitality-Gaming Industry – A Case Analysis from Macau SAR, China. *2022 13th International Conference on E-business, Management and Economics*. 10.1145/3556089.3556121

Tatar, U., Gheorghe, A. V., & Keskin, O. F. (2020). *Space Infrastructures: from Risk to Resilience Governance*. IOS Press.

Thaler, R. H., & Sunstein, C. R. (2008). *Nudge: Improving Decisions about Health, Wealth, and Happiness*. Yale University Press.

Theory of Constraints Institute. (n.d.). *Theory of Constraints of Eliyahu M. Goldratt*. https://www.tocinstitute.org/theory-of-constraints.html

Types of Risk Management Strategies to Follow in 2021. (2021, February 18). AuditBoard. https://www.auditboard.com/blog/10-risk-management-strategies-2021/

Wang, P., & Johnson, C. (2018). Cybersecurity incident handling: A case study of the equifax data breach. *Issues in Information Systems*, *19*(3). Advance online publication. doi:10.48009/3_iis_2018_150-159

What Is Ergonomics (HFE)? (n.d.). The International Ergonomics Association. Retrieved April 22, 2023, from https://iea.cc/about/what-is-ergonomics/

Wiafe, I., Koranteng, F. N., Wiafe, A., Obeng, E. N., & Yaokumah, W. (2020). The role of norms in information security policy compliance. *Information and Computer Security*, *28*(5), 743–761. doi:10.1108/ICS-08-2019-0095

World Economic Forum. (2023). *Global Cybersecurity Outlook 2023*. https://www3.weforum.org/docs/WEF_Global_Security_Outlook_Report_2023.pdf

Yan, Z. (2018). *Analyzing Human Behavior in Cyberspace*. IGI Global.

Yilmaz, G. (2014). Let's Peel the Onion Together: An Application of Schein's Model of Organizational Culture. *Communication Teacher*, *28*(4), 224–228. Advance online publication. doi:10.1080/17404622.2014.939674

Zhang, Y., & Bednall, T. (2016). Antecedents of Abusive Supervision: A Meta-analytic Review. *Journal of Business Ethics*, *139*(3), 455–471. doi:10.100710551-015-2657-6

Zimmermann, V., & Renaud, K. (2021). The Nudge Puzzle. *ACM Transactions on Computer-Human Interaction*, *28*(1), 1–45. doi:10.1145/3429888

Chapter 8
Cognitive Effects on Firefighters in Oklahoma From Their Initial Start of Service Till the Present

DeAnjelo J. L. Bradley

ⓘD https://orcid.org/0000-0002-2664-8345

Capital Technology University, USA

ABSTRACT

Working well under tremendous strain for relatively short periods is a topic of great importance in fire-fighting. This study put firefighters through a series of stressful solo smoke dives around a dark, winding simulation track to examine how their stress reactions affected their cognitive function. Male firefighters' heart rates were recorded during a smoke-diving exercise and compared with baseline readings and maximal rates. Male firefighters were used to studying these stressors. The firefighters thought aloud as they performed the smoke-diving maneuver to demonstrate their mental acuity. This study used a content analysis review of the literature published between the years 2017 to 2021 to define the problem, outline its complexities, and find needed solutions from dispersed sources.

INTRODUCTION

Professional firefighters face several stressful conditions during their employment, including strenuous and constant physical demands, a hostile environment, anxiety, uncertainty, and the responsibility to save people (Klimley et al., 2018). Firefighting is psychologically and physically demanding because of the nature of the job, which includes putting out flames, handling hazardous materials, searching for victims, and performing rescues for an unpredictable period (Igboanugo et al., 2021). Firefighters are exposed to several health risks (such as burns, smoke, and falls) and unpredictability due to their duties; working in hot situations also puts strain on them physically and mentally (Barros et al., 2021). During operations involving extinguishing flames and preserving life, maintaining high levels of cognitive function and the capacity to process information is crucial (Hemmatjo et al., 2020). Firefighters must communicate quickly with their leaders and other firefighters during operations to put out flames and

DOI: 10.4018/979-8-3693-1630-6.ch008

save lives (Nowak & Łukomska, 2021). When there is a fire, they need to find their way around in the darkness, heat, and smoke to help others trapped. Although there is literature on the effects of firefighting actions and the resulting influence on physiological response, there is a shortage of studies on the impact of these tasks on information processing and work performance. Firefighters require the ability to cope with complex events and control their emotional responses to catastrophic and devastating sights. Also, they must be quick to digest information and be confident in making the right choices under pressure. Thus, it is possible for firefighters' focus, information processing, and productivity to shift during firefighting and rescue operations.

Currently, there is a lack of research on how cognitive function changes during simulated firefighting operations. Understanding how cooling methods as an intervention program affects firefighters' working memory and information processing is entirely restricted (Song et al., 2020). Based on previous findings, it is concluded that firefighters' information processing, working memory capacity, and job performance suffer due to their occupation (Stanley et al., 2018). Stanley et al. (2018) concluded that implementing body cooling techniques via practical cooling devices would enhance cognitive performance, including processing speed, working memory, and physical endurance, when performing firefighting duties while wearing protective clothing. To that end, this study's participants engaged in a series of simulated firefighting operations in a smoke-diving room before and after real-world fires to compare the effects of these tasks on firefighters' information processing, working memory capacity, and job performance. The findings are also expected to provide insight into which cooling methods have the potential to enhance data-processing capacity and physical capacity during firefighting operations.

Background

Oklahoma firefighters are tasked with more than just putting out fires; they also respond to and assist with a wide range of rescue and emergencies arising from car crashes, natural disasters, and other large-scale events. Carbon monoxide, phosgene, and extreme heat are dangers firefighters face while responding to fires. Furthermore, firefighters have high-stress levels on the job due to the mental strain of sitting around for extended periods and the chronic lack of sleep that is a consequence of working shifts (Hemmatjo et al., 2020). Research such as the one by Hemmatjo et al. (2020) have confirmed that simulated firefighting activities influence a firefighters' cognitive function. Firefighter suicide rates and mental health problems like depression and PTSD are much higher than the general population (Scott et al., 2021). The average suicide rate of first responders in the United States is 47 percent, two times higher than the general population (Scott et al., 2021). Neurocognitive performance may also be related to these risk factors in firefighters. Stress and the heat stress that comes with it may have deleterious effects on neurocognitive performance. A recent study suggests that PTSD and depression are linked to memory loss in firefighters (Armstrong et al., 2019). These mental health factors can affect the safety of firefighters and the public.

Problem Statement

Cognitive function has been shown to decrease while errors increase in firefighters when participating in simulated firefighting activities resulting in negative physical and mental consequences (Hemmatjo et al., 2020). On average, 47% of first responders, including firefighters, have had suicidal ideation in the United States because of decreased cognitive function (Scott et al., 2021). The general business problem is that simulated firefighting activities decrease cognitive function in firefighters. The specific business problem is that fire departments have not adequately addressed the needfor firefighters to retain their cognitive function while simultaneously participating in simulated firefighting activities.

Purpose of the Study

The purpose of this content analysis literature review is to explore and understand the cognitive effects on firefighters in Oklahoma during simulated firefighting activities. The targeted population are firefighters in the state of Oklahoma. The implication for positive social change is that the health of firefighters not only in the state of Oklahoma but nationally could benefit from solutions to the cognitive decline experienced during simulated firefighting activities.

Literature Review

In firefighting and rescue operations, the physical effort required significantly impacts firefighters' attention, information processing, and working memory. This effect is extended to visual and auditory states and other cognitive functions (Zare et al., 2018). These deficits may manifest as difficulties in performing one's job responsibilities. Firefighting activities induce physiological responses that reach maximum values quickly and remain high during firefighting activities (Zare et al., 2018). Firefighters may endure severe stress while doing their duties due to the intense physical exertion and psychological demands during firefighting and rescue efforts (Colquitt et al., 2018). Compared to many other occupations, firefighters are subjected to a wide range of stressors over extended periods, making their profession unique. Occupational stressors of firefighters may include night shift schedules, lack of sleep, unexpected alarm calls, strenuous physical work, exposure to smoke and other harmful substances during fire suppression, heartbreaking and tragic incidents, and victim search and rescue operations (Denkova et al., 2020).

There is a paucity of evidence regarding the impact of live-fire activities on firefighters' cognitive function; few studies have been conducted that have specifically examined cognitive function changes in replicated frequent firefighting scenarios. Multiple prior studies, such as the one by Greenlee et al. (2019) have demonstrated that modeling regular firefighting operations impact cognitive performance. Factors such as total sleep deprivation have also been found to lead to worse performance in a relatively easy-task group of firefighters (Greenlee et al., 2019). Also discovered were the effects on cognitive impairment caused by simulated firefighting operations and the increased number of mistakes made during the cognitive function test (Kujawski et al., 2018). As a result, firefighters must possess specific physical and physiological characteristics to carry out their obligations effectively and reduce the damage caused by fire suppression efforts (Kujawski et al., 2018). Specific cognitive skills are required for firefighters to communicate with command and other firefighters during firefighting operations. The ability to process information quickly and cognitively is vital, in search and rescue missions and in other stressful and threatening situations during firefighting.

Training is necessary for firefighters to attempt to prepare firefighters for the situations they encounter, such as occupational stressors and risks faced on the ground. What has been found in firefighting training is that not all training is conducted similarly. Most training involves preparing firefighters for different scenarios they may encounter, and the training is conducted in various environments. Between 2001 and 2010 a total of 108 firefighters in the United States died while performing training activities (Horn et al., 2019). Virtual reality programs to provide training for firefighters have been developed and continue to be developed to assume the role of actual training activities. A study by Jeon et al. (2019) stated that one current VR training system can convey behavioural tips, but it did not accurately reflect actual firefighters' needs and realities when they are out in the field.

In prior research, visual tests have examined cognitive abilities such as sustained attention, working memory, and information processing after participating in firefighting exercises (Langner & Eickhoff, 2017). The search for victims and the endeavor to rescue people who have become stranded in various regions of the burning building are also important in such stressful circumstances. For example, the ability to hear the victims' voices in smoky and dark environments, as well as the ability to converse with them, is required to protect and rescue their lives and property as swiftly and precisely as feasible (Langner & Eickhoff, 2017). A firefighter must have many hearing and cognitive function skills to do all these complicated things and participating in some simulated firefighting activities impair these skills.

Several recent studies have found that firefighters are a particularly high-risk group for suicide, with rates of suicidal thoughts and actions among firefighters significantly higher than those reported in the general population (Stanley et al., 2017). However, despite research demonstrating elevated levels of suicide risk among firefighters, few studies have investigated the factors that may exacerbate risk. Furthermore, my project is significant because it will help the fire service think about how to help people who are suicidal and how to prevent suicide.

Transient Symptom Depression (TSD)

Firefighters need to maintain high levels of attention for lengthy periods since even the slightest inaccuracy throughout an operation can result in catastrophic consequences. Transient symptom depression (TSD) may harm performance quality, mainly when cognitive function tests are not enjoyable and are administered over an extended period (Arbona & Schwartz, 2017). A meta-analysis revealed that the cumulative effect size of TSD influences fundamental attention and vigilance tests and that it is the largest of all cognitive domains tested (Greenlee et al., 2018). Following TSD, it has been observed that subjects do not show any substantial cognitive loss when subjected to a battery of sophisticated cognitive tests (Greenlee et al., 2018). Because of the effects of compensation, which occurs when 'participants' self-drive and motivation improve during cognitive tests following TSD, the difference between pre-and post-test is modest, and can be attributed to compensation effects (Chiang et al., 2020). The results of the study by Chiang et al. (2020) concluded that firefighters with subthreshold levels of PTSD symptoms reported higher levels of job burnout in comparison to other firefighters with fewer symptoms. As the job's complexity grows, it becomes simpler to achieve the brain's compensating response to TSD (Chiang et al., 2020). From the studies such as the ones by Greenlee et al. (2018) and Chiang et al. (2020), fire departments should consider the compensation effects of TSD when designing fire-simulated activities. A hypothesis has been proposed to account for the variation in the outcomes of sustained attention activities during TSD. This hypothesis is known as the "State Instability Hypothesis" (Hudson et al., 2020). The effects of TSD can have a significant impact on a firefighter' 's cognitive function and further research needs to be conducted on how best to address the sleep deprivation of firefighters.

TSD also has the least compensating effect when performing fundamental attention and vigilance activities (Choi, 2018). Regarding processing speed tests, the magnitude of the accuracy measures was not statistically significant in the meta-analysis, which was supported by the findings of more recent intervention-based investigations (Choi, 2018). Introducing a trade-off model may help to explain this phenomenon. When TSD hinders a subject's ability to undertake processing speed tests, the subject can "choose" the most appropriate way to deal with the irritation of the circumstance (Heydari et al., 2022). On the one hand, respondents in basic reaction time tests may seek to respond more quickly (Heydari et al., 2022). However, on the other hand, this will increase the number of mistakes or false alarms generated by the subjects due to the increased speed of response.

In many circles, sleep is considered essential in the learning process. A ' 'A firefighter's homeostatic drive for sleep, endogenous signals for wakefulness, and the compensatory effort the subject makes, significantly impacts the variability of one's attention level (Klimley, 2018). On the other hand, the variety of tasks performed by sleep is still not understood. It is critical to examine cognitive functioning in a group whose primary responsibility is to complete tasks requiring high levels of attention and rapid responses to environmental cues while maintaining high quality and making the fewest number of mistakes as reasonably possible (Kim & Yook, 2018). Furthermore, in the case of a firefighter, these tasks are done under PTSD conditions because their shifts are often 24 hours long.

The combination of firefighters' alternating 24-hour and 48-hour off-work patterns/shifts and their hazardous work surroundings puts them at risk of developing chronic sleep disturbance. In a study, the researchers investigated firefighters" physiological, cognitive, and neuromuscular performance following a structure live-fire scenario (Abrard et al., 2019). Researchers examined changes in vital signs, environmental data, and cognitive and neuromuscular performance before and after a live-fire training session in a confined setting with conditions like those found in an active structural fire (Sliter et al., 2018). There were many instances during the 30-minute sessions where highly high ambient temperatures were recorded (Abrard et al., 2019). According to the data collected after the session, the average forehead temperature climbed by 0.5 degrees Celsius, the average water body loss was 639 milliliters, and the average heart rate increased by 7.5 beats per minute (Abrard et al., 2019). Even though there was no statistically significant difference in mental calculation speed, there was a statistically significant difference in reaction time (Abrard et al., 2019). These tests showed that heat stress did not influence firefighter performance after 30 minutes of exposure to heat (Abrard et al., 2019). It appears that stress activation is beneficial following firefighting activities. A second firefighting attempt should be possible if the critical indicators stay the same.

Firefighters must engage in physical activity in their line of work, and the weather conditions significantly impact this. It is possible to suffer from heat damage at work, such as heat stroke, due to extended exposure to high temperatures. Heated work environments are associated with poor physical and mental performance, which increases the likelihood of work-related accidents (Canetti et al., 2022). However, previous studies have mostly disregarded the Impact of live-fire actions on firefighters" auditory cognitive functioning (Kujawski et al., 2018). Specifically, this study aims to determine the influence of live-fire operations on human visual and auditory cognitive capacities. Following the premise, it was hypothesized that the different types of firefighting jobs performed during live-fire exposure would impact cognitive processes, including attention and information processing skills, in firefighters wearing protective clothing (Kim et al., 2022). From the study conducted by Kim et al. (2022), it can be concluded that additional research needs to be conducted on the type of protective clothing firefighters wear that impact cognitive capacities.

Post-Traumatic Stress Disorder (PTSD) and Cognitive Functioning

Other factors can contribute to cognitive performance. Increasing efforts to reduce the number of mistakes may result in slower response times (Hemmatjo et al., 2020). PTSD has been found in most studies to negatively influence cognitive performance, mainly when the activity is prolonged and repeated (Chiang et al., 2020). Studies were conducted on various subjects, including professional drivers, house officers, and military soldiers (Stanley et al., 2018). A study of neuroimaging data found that when people are subjected to sleep deprivation, the pattern of activity during attention tests appears to be different from the pattern of activity during attention tests when they are subjected to "normal" sleep (Jung et al., 2017). Following PTSD, higher activity in the anterior cingulate cortex and right prefrontal cortex was detected during attention-switching tests conducted in the presence of distraction (Dibbets et al., 2020).

The exposure to stressful circumstances frequently among firefighters may contribute to their elevated risk of suicide. A sad heart is not unusual among firefighters when they respond to situations in which they witness the actual or imminent death—or themselves (Smith et al., 2017). PTSD is defined by the Diagnostic and Statistical Manual of Mental Disorders, Fifth Edition (DSM-5; American Psychiatric Association) as a condition that may fit Criterion A of the diagnostic criteria when it comes to work-related trauma exposure (APA, 2017). To protect themselves and others, firefighters are at an increased risk of developing PTSD (Smith et al., 2017). The presence of symptoms associated with re-experiencing (intrusions), adverse changes in cognition and mood (NACM), avoidance, and changes in arousal and reaction time (AR) for at least one month following the exposure to the traumatic event in question is required for a DSM-5 PTSD diagnosis to be made (APA, 2017). In firefighters, there appears to be a significant prevalence of PTSD, according to estimates ranging from 6.5 to 30 percent (Berninger et al., 2020). These findings are significant because PTSD has been linked to many people's thinking about taking their own lives, including firefighters (Smith et al., 2017).

Suicide risk is strongly associated with (PTSD) in the general population, and rates of PTSD are higher among suicide attempters than suicide ideators (Bryan et al., 2017). A study conducted by Boffa et al. (2017) found that among 893 firefighter participants in the United States, PTSD symptoms related to greater levels of SI and a history of suicide attempts (Sumińska et al., 2020). It is unclear why people in the fire service have PTSD symptoms and suicidal thoughts, but further research could help the fire service fight suicide more.

The high prevalence of posttraumatic stress disorder (PTSD) symptoms and suicidal ideation, as well as the linkage between these symptoms and suicidal ideation among firefighters, raises questions about possible treatment targets that may minimize their psychological effect on the firefighters (Williams-Bell et al., 2018). To achieve this goal, identifying a maintenance factor for posttraumatic stress disorder (PTSD) and suicidal thoughts is a crucial first step. A maintenance factor is a component of these disorders associated with their long-term persistence. One promising therapeutic target is anxiety sensitivity when treating posttraumatic stress disorder (PTSD) and suicide ideation (Greenlee et al., 2018). Anxiety sensitivity is characterized as an excessive apprehension about the possible repercussions of anxious arousal (Greenlee et al., 2018). When anxiety symptoms are considered a hierarchical construct, they can be divided into three lower-order dimensions: a generalized dread of anxious arousal, fear of physical and social repercussions of anxious arousal, and a fear of social consequences of anxious arousal (Wu et al., 2019). A fear of AS mental worries is a reflection of one's belief that attention problems indicate the onset of "becoming insane" and perception of somatic feelings (such as a hurting stomach or constriction in the throat) as signs of disease or death is exacerbated when anxiety sensitivity and physical anxieties are raised (Ye et al., 2022). Firefighters experience many anxiety symptoms because of their occupation so further research needs to be conducted on how best to address these symptoms.

Research has been conducted on the relationship between anxiety and PTSD. In a study conducted by Boffa et al. (2018), they discovered a positive relationship between anxiety sensitivity and PTSD symptoms in samples of active-duty police officers, motor-vehicle accident survivors, undergraduates exposed to campus shootings, and victims of interpersonal violence. According to the literature on suicide attempts, global AS is associated with current suicide attempts and a history of suicide attempts in the past (Allan et al., 2018). In other research, however, it appears that AS cognitive concerns maybe the most strongly connected with SI and prior suicide attempts (Capron et al., 2017). It is particularly relevant as a risk reduction mechanism in communities with a high frequency of (PTSD) symptoms and suicidal thoughts because it has shown lasting correlations with these symptoms (i.e., protective service workers) (Capron et al., 2017). Research on AS cognitive concerns needs to be conducted on firefighters.

Research has been conducted on the relationship between anxiety and PTSD but studies have also been conducted to explore the relationship between anxiety sensitivity and suicide risk. To investigate whether there is a link between anxiety sensitivity and suicide risk in a sample of 254 female firefighters, Stanley et al. (2017) conducted a follow-up study. They looked at the possibility of a link between AS and suicide risk in a sample of 254 female firefighters. Anxiety sensitivity was discovered by Stanley et al. (2017) to serve as a mediator of the relationship between posttraumatic stress disorder (PTSD) symptoms and global suicide risk, even after controlling for the presence of depressive symptoms. In a study that followed previous findings, cognitive problems were the most strongly associated with posttraumatic stress disorder symptoms, including the DSM-5 PTSD symptom clusters and suicide risk (Stanley et al., 2017). This was confirmed in a sample of male veterans participating in a study following previous findings (Raines et al., 2017). This study is significant since it identified a modifiable susceptibility factor contributing to the higher risk of suicide among protective service workers, such as firefighters, who suffer from posttraumatic stress disorder symptoms. However, further examination is required, notably, because the research conducted on firefighters included only female participants (Stanley et al., 2017), limiting its generalizability to the fire service, which is predominantly male (more than 90 percent of firefighters) (Lindström & Försth, 2018).

Firefighters appear to have a higher incidence of posttraumatic stress disorder (PTSD) and suicide than the general population when compared to other occupations, according to research. Research increases the likelihood of developing several ailments, particularly in the general population and veterans (Lindström & Försth, 2018). The presence of cognitive problems is significant in this case. The symptoms of posttraumatic stress disorder (PTSD) and the risk of suicide among firefighters are being investigated in the same way as before, emphasizing the influence of AS. Firefighters may benefit from portable AS-specific therapy that helps them improve their mental health and minimize their risk of suicide to reduce the likelihood of experiencing PTSD symptoms and suicidal ideation (Barr et al., 2020). Only a few studies have specifically assessed cognitive function modifications in firefighters in replicated frequent firefighting environments to determine the Impact of live-fire activities on firefighters" cognitive function. Several studies have demonstrated that firefighting simulations negatively influence cognitive performance (Abrard et al., 2019). It was discovered that simulating firefighting actions had an impact on cognitive impairment and an increase in cognitive function errors in the participants. So, firefighters must be physically and physiologically competent to carry out their responsibilities and minimize the harm caused by fire control techniques. Firefighters must have a specific set of cognitive talents to communicate successfully with command and their fellow firefighters during a fire (Aisbett et al., 2019). Also necessary is the ability to recall different regions of the fire to be able to flee in the event of an emergency. Those involved in search and rescue activities and those who work in other high-stress and life-or-death situations must have the ability to process information cognitively quickly.

Cognitive Ability

Previous research used visual assessments of cognitive skills (e.g., sustained attention, working memory, and information processing) after firefighting operations to determine their effectiveness (Boffa et al., 2018). Firefighters are expected to perform a diverse range of physically demanding tasks. We can illustrate this by looking at the example of firefighters involved in firefighting and rescue operations (Cvirn et al., 2019). They must maintain regular contact with commanders and other fire service employees to report the situation and receive necessary aid to save lives. Rescue activities in the ensuing pandemonium, such as searching for victims and locating individuals who have become trapped inside the burning structure, are essential. For example, hearing and communicating with victims in smoky and dark environments is critical to protect and rescue their lives and property as soon and precisely as possible (Hemmatjo et al., 2017). A high level of auditory cognitive function proficiency is required for firefighters to do these demanding tasks. Firefighters must engage in regular physical activity, and the weather significantly impacts their ability to perform their duties. Heat-related disorders, such as heat stroke, can arise due to prolonged exposure to high temperatures in the workplace, particularly in the summer. Workers who suffer from occupational heat sickness are more likely to be involved in an accident (Cvirn et al., 2019). This provides evidence of the urgency to address occupational heat sickness in firefighters.

Dehydration is an important element in firefighting and in the cognitive ability of firefighters. Some studies have demonstrated that dehydration decreases a person's ability to endure adverse situations and severely impacts cognitive and cardiovascular function (Angerer et al., 2018). Water deficit rates are regulated by environmental parameters like temperature and humidity, among other things (Canetti et al., 2022). It is possible to quantify the amount of fluid lost through sweating by observing changes in body weight after a sporting event (Canetti et al., 2022). Angerer et al. (2018) conducted 30-minute structural firefighting tests and discovered that hydration was satisfactorily maintained with no fluid consumption during the test period (Angerer et al., 2018). Their 30-minute structure firefighting trials discovered that hydration could be maintained adequately without needing fluid absorption. In the absence of adequate fluid intake, it is possible to lose between 1 and 2 percent of one's total body weight during a sporting event (Angerer et al., 2018). In this study, even though the weight loss was within this range, it was discovered that weight loss was only moderately associated with post-task motivation and weariness. Additionally, the hydration state did not affect or predict tolerance time or cognition in high-stress environments (Canetti et al., 2022). Per these findings, tympanic temperature fluctuations are more crucial in developing fatigue than changes in hydration status. Earlier research revealed a relationship between the rate of heat storage and the time required to exhaustion, as well as the fact that an individual's ability to withstand heat stress decreased as the rate of heat storage rose (Huang et al., 2019). Previous research has demonstrated that the rate of heat storage and the time required to reach fatigue are directly related. This is an important factor to consider in firefighting as heat storage from protective equipment can affect fatigue and directly correlate with cognitive function.

Experiences of Exhaustion, Motivation, and Weariness

Firefighters" sentiments of weariness 20 minutes after a shift were found to be strongly connected with their experiences of exhaustion immediately following the shift (Lindholm et al., 2018). When taken immediately after and 20 minutes after task completion, changes in tympanic temperature were found to predict weariness by 45 and 57 percent, respectively (Lindholm et al., 2018). Commonly performed tasks of firefighters such as victim search and rescue, stair and ladder climbing, and carrying heavy equipment have a high energy cost (Canetti et al., 2022). These tasks also contribute to cardiovascular and thermal strain (Canetti et al., 2022). According to previous studies, firefighters" core temperatures increased during passive recovery after 20 minutes of heat chamber search and rescue simulation (Canetti et al., 2022). Active recovery measures were inefficient in lowering the core temperature of firefighters to a safe level, allowing them to return to the fire scene (Canetti et al., 2022). Walker et al. (2017) enabled firefighters to remove their protective equipment and drink .6 liters of room temperature water, which is noteworthy because it directly conflicts with the present findings. Despite using these techniques, one's physical and cognitive capacities may be permanently compromised. Following fire suppression, researchers have investigated the visual and auditory abnormalities that firefighters experience (Walker et al., 2017). According to the results of cognitive tests, visual and auditory perception accuracy was diminished dramatically (Walker et al. (2017). The study by Walker et al. (2017) also demonstrated that an increase in thermal strain in firefighters was present when they were asked to re-enter fire scenes particularly when only passive cooling protocols were used. This has significant implications for firefighters when they are out in the field and during simulated firefighting activities. Walker et al. (2017) suggested that relying on individual perceptions of well-being may be insufficient to ensure the safety of firefighters when they re-enter fire scenes.

The effects of motivation and weariness on cognitive function have been proven in other studies (Nam et al., 2018). Stress-related factors or affective reactions to on-going stress such as burnout can diminish the safety of firefighters. According to Smith et al. (2018) burnout diminishes an individual's desire to participate in work activities and is negatively associated with job performance. The study by Smith et al. (2018) confirmed that burnout negatively impacts safety performance in firefighting. When a firefighter is enraged, they are more likely to react slowly, become less aware of their surroundings, and make poor decisions (Walker et al., 2017). Canetti et al. (2022) concluded that 15 minutes of exposure to a 7323.8 F (.984 ft. above ground) and 53.1 percent relative humidity increased the participant's" tympanic temperature and tiredness. Firefighters are routinely exposed to temperatures ranging from 20 to 70 degrees Celsius. They are frequently exposed for up to 20 minutes at a time. The study by Park (2019) concluded that variations in tympanic membrane temperature following a task related to decreased motivation, weariness, and test scores. According to the findings of an occupational field study, workers in the automotive industry who were exposed to temperatures between 86 and 95 degrees Fahrenheit had a decrease in speed and accuracy when doing cognitive tests (Robinson et al., 2017). Those exposed to the chemical also had higher levels of adrenaline, noradrenaline, and cortisol in their blood than those who had not been exposed (Robinson et al., 2017). As a result of their exhaustion and decreased cognitive function, firefighters returning to a potentially dangerous thermal environment (158–572 degrees Fahrenheit) is a matter of concern since it may impair their decision-making and safety (Canetti et al., 2022). Additional research needs to be conducted to determine the most effective ways to lower the body temperature after consecutive exposure to heat to increase cognitive function.

Protective Gear and Cognitive Deficits

Previous research has shown that firefighter protection gear has specific qualities (such as heavy, thick, and oversized) that help reduce evaporation and increase metabolism (Stout et al., 2020). Interruptions in body temperature regulation might result in heat accumulation and cognitive deficits in firefighters" cognitive performance. It has been demonstrated that firefighter" protective helmets have deleterious impacts on cognitive function, such as reduced sustained attention and reduced response times (Walker et al., 2017). Because of the increased danger of harm associated with firefighting operations, the body needs to adapt to the higher stress of firefighting operations (Walker et al., 2017) (Walker et al., 2017). As a result, it is possible that information processing and decision-making will be impaired. The body's release of stress hormones in response to various stressors makes it possible to experience various side effects (Walker et al., 2017). Stress causes the creation of steroids, which can cross the blood-brain barrier and influence the brain once they have reached the area where they are needed (Walker et al., 2017). Learning and memory processes may be altered if they bind to receptors in certain parts of the brain where those receptors are activated (Walker et al., 2017).

RESEARCH METHODOLOGY

Search Criteria

For this content analysis literature review, only the most relevant literature was used to analyze studies on firefighting operations, cooling strategies, and cognitive functions. Several databases were searched to find relevant literature such as CINAHL, PsychINFO, PubMed, MDPI, Science Direct, National Library of Medicine, Springer, SAGE, Emerald Insight, and BMC Medical Education. To search these databases keywords such as firefighters, cognitive stress, neurocognitive performance, work stress, cooling strategies for firefighters, cognitive deficiencies, and transient symptom depression were used. Only articles that were published after 2017 were included in the literature review. The abstracts of each article were scanned to determine whether they were relevant to the study topic and were actual studies conducted and not systematic or meta-analysis literature reviews.

Total Number of Works Cited = 30

Total Number of Cited Works Published between 2018 – 2022 = 30

1. Abrard, S., Bertrand, M., De Valence, T., & Schaupp, T. (2019).
2. Angerer, P., Kadlez-Gebhardt, S., Delius, M., Raluca, P., & Nowak, D. (2018).
3. Armstrong, D., Shakespeare-finch, J., & Shochet, I. (2019).
4. Barr, D., Gregson, W., & Reilly, T. (2020).
5. Bartlett, B., Jardin, C., Martin, C., Tran, J., Buser, S., Anestis, M., & Vujanovic, A. (2018).
6. Berninger, A., Webber, M. P., Cohen, H. W., Gustave, J., Lee, R., Niles, J. K., Chiu, S., Zeig-Owens, R., Soo, J., Kelly, K., & Prezant, D. J. (2020).
7. Boffa, J. W., King, S. L., Turecki, G., & Schmidt, N. B. (2018).
8. Canetti, E. F., Gayton, S., Schram, B., Pope, R., & Orr, R. M. (2022).
9. Carr, A. (2019).
10. Chiang, E. S., Riordan, K. M., Ponder, J., Johnson, C., & Cox, K. S. (2020).
11. Cvirn, M., Dorrian, J., Smith, B., Vincent, G., Jay, S., & Roach, G. et al. (2019).
12. Denkova, E., Zanesco, A., Rogers, S., & Jha, A. (2020).
13. Greenlee, T. A., Horn, G., Smith, D. L., Fahey, G., Goldstein, E., & Petruzzello, S. J. (2019).
14. Hemmatjo, R., Hajaghazadeh, M., Allahyari, T., Zare, S., & Kazemi, R. (2020).
15. Heydari, P., Babamiri, M., Tapak, L., Golmohammadi, R., & Kalatpour, O. (2022).
16. Hudson, A. N., Van Dongen, H., & Honn, K. A. (2020).

17. Huang, Q., Zhang, Q., An, Y., & Xu, W. (2019).

18. Klimley, K. E., Van Hasselt, V. B., & Stripling, A. M. (2018).

19. Kujawski, S., Słomko, J., Tafil-Klawe, M., Zawadka-Kunikowska, M., Szrajda, J., Newton, J. L., Zalewski, P., & Klawe, J. J. (2018).

20. Lindholm, H., Punakallio, A., Lusa, S., Sainio, M., Ponocny, E., & Winker, R. (2018).

21. Lindström, J., & Försth, M. (2018).

22. Nowak, K., & Łukomska, B. (2021).

23. Park, J. (2019).

24. Scott, D., Ratiliff, B., & English, C. (2022).

25. Song, Y., Ha, J., & Jue, J. (2020).

26. Stanley, I. H., Smith, L. J., Boffa, J. W., Tran, J. K., Schmidt, N. B., Joiner, T. E., & Vujanovic, A. A. (2018).

27. Stout, J., Beidel, D., Brush, D., & Bowers, C. (2020).

28. Sumińska, S., Nowak, K., Łukomska, B., & Cygan, H. (2020).

29. Wu, T., Yuan, K., Yen, D., & Xu, T. (2019).

30. Zare, S., Hemmatjo, R., Allahyari, T., Hajaghazadeh, M., Hajivandi, A., Aghabeigi, M., & Kazemi, R. (2018).

CONCLUSION AND RECOMMENDATIONS

Effective firefighting requires certain physical and physiological traits. Transient symptom depression (TSD) may hinder performance, especially when cognitive function tests are tedious and lengthy (Smith et al., 2017). Sleep deprivation impairs focus, according to mounting data (Aisbett et al., 2019). Neuroimaging research indicated that sleep-deprived people's attention test patterns varied from "normal" sleep (Jung et al., 2017). Heated work settings reduce physical and mental performance, increasing job-related accidents (Kujawski et al., 2018). Understanding the consequences of heated work settings and actively finding solutions to reduce the physical and mental strain it causes, will benefit firefighters and fire departments.

Firefighters conduct physically strenuous activities and prolonged exposure to high temperatures may cause heat-related diseases, including heat stroke. Previous research has also concluded that dehydration impairs cognitive and cardiovascular function and reduces a person's resilience (Angerer et al., 2018). Without enough fluids, a person might lose 1-2 percent of their body weight during a sport and firefighting (Angerer et al., 2018). From the studies that were reviewed in this section, it can be concluded that additional research needs to be conducted on the cognitive consequences of heat exposure, what effective treatments there are to reduce declines in function, and what practices can be employed for firefighters after they are exposed to extreme heat.

Recommendations for Future Study

Cognitive Therapy: A therapist will help one analyze and modify one's perceptions of the traumatic incident and its aftermath (Johnson et al., 2020). He or she must learn to recognize which thoughts about a traumatic event contribute to stress and worsening symptoms (Johnson et al., 2020). They will learn the tools to swap out these misconceptions with ones more grounded in reality and less likely to bring one distress. While remembering or discussing the past, one will pay attention to things other than their thoughts, such as eye movements, hand tapping, and sounds. The therapist may, for instance, move his hand and instruct one to gaze after it.

Medications: To alleviate depressive symptoms, doctors may prescribe selective serotonin reuptake inhibitors (SSRIs). All these things may help one feel better and less stressed. They give off a feeling of being helpful, and studies have shown they may be useful in improving the lives of specific individuals (Zare et al., 2018). Citalopram (Celexa), fluoxetine (Prozac), paroxetine (Paxil), and sertraline are all examples of selective serotonin reuptake inhibitors (Zoloft) (Zare et al., 2018). It is wise to talk to a primary care doctor about which medications might be the most helpful.

Exposure Therapy: Here, the subject aims toward a state of mind in which one's recollections cause less stress. Having several talks with a therapist about the traumatic experience may increase one's capacity to exercise control over their thoughts and emotions regarding the event. In the beginning, this may not be easy. In time, though, one will be able to cope with the situation better. Desensitization describes this method (Zhang et al., 2018).

Family Therapy: There is a chance that loved ones, including a person's children and spouse, do not entirely understand one's emotional swings and the pressures a person is facing. Because of a person's disease, they may feel responsible, afraid, or even angry (Carr, 2019). Talking to a therapist may help a person and their loved ones maintain healthy relationships, communicate more effectively, and cope with stressful emotions. Members of their families and friends may learn more about PTSD and available treatments.

Competing Interests

The author of this article declares there are no competing interest.

Funding

This research received no specific grant from any funding agency in the public, commercial, or not-for-profit sectors. Funding for this research was covered by DeAnjelo J.L. Bradley.

REFERENCES

Abrard, S., Bertrand, M., De Valence, T., & Schaupp, T. (2019). Physiological, cognitive, and neuromuscular effects of heat exposure on firefighters after a live training scenario. *International Journal of Occupational Safety and Ergonomics*, 27(1), 185–193. doi:10.1080/10803548.2018.1550899 PMID:30507358

Aisbett, B., Wolkow, A., Sprajcer, M., & Ferguson, S. (2012). "Awake, smoky, and hot": Providing an evidence-base for managing the risks associated with occupational stressors encountered by wildland firefighters. *Applied Ergonomics*, 43(5), 916–925. doi:10.1016/j.apergo.2011.12.013 PMID:22264875

Allan, N. P., Short, N. A., Albanese, B. J., Keough, M. E., & Schmidt, N. B. (2015). An anxiety sensitivity intervention's direct and mediating effects on posttraumatic stress disorder symptoms in trauma-exposed individuals. *Cognitive Behaviour Therapy*, 44(6), 512–524. doi:10.1080/16506073.2015.1075227 PMID:26427912

Angerer, P., Kadlez-Gebhardt, S., Delius, M., Raluca, P., & Nowak, D. (2018). Comparison of Cardiocirculatory and thermal strain of male firefighters during fire suppression to exercise stress test and aerobic exercise testing. *The American Journal of Cardiology*, *102*(11), 1551–1556. doi:10.1016/j.amjcard.2008.07.052 PMID:19026313

Arbona, C., & Schwartz, J. P. (2017). Posttraumatic stress disorder symptom clusters, depression, alcohol abuse, and general stress among Hispanic male firefighters. *Hispanic Journal of Behavioral Sciences*, *38*(4), 507–522. doi:10.1177/0739986316661328

Armstrong, D., Shakespeare-finch, J., & Shochet, I. (2019). Predicting posttraumatic growth and posttraumatic stress in firefighters. *Australian Journal of Psychology*, *66*(1), 38–46. doi:10.1111/ajpy.12032

Barr, D., Gregson, W., & Reilly, T. (2020). The thermal ergonomics of firefighting reviewed. *Applied Ergonomics*, *41*(1), 161–172. doi:10.1016/j.apergo.2009.07.001 PMID:19664755

Barros, B., Oliveira, M., & Morais, S. (2021). Firefighters' occupational exposure: Contribution from biomarkers of effect to assess health risks. *Environment International*, *156*, 106704. doi:10.1016/j.envint.2021.106704 PMID:34161906

Bartlett, B., Jardin, C., Martin, C., Tran, J., Buser, S., Anestis, M., & Vujanovic, A. (2018). Posttraumatic Stress and Suicidality Among Firefighters: The Moderating Role of Distress Tolerance. *Cognitive Therapy and Research*, *42*(4), 483–496. doi:10.100710608-018-9892-y

Baumann, M., Gohm, C., & Bonner, B. (2017). Phased Training for High-Reliability Occupations. *Human Factors*, *53*(5), 548–557. doi:10.1177/0018720811418224 PMID:22046726

Berninger, A., Webber, M. P., Cohen, H. W., Gustave, J., Lee, R., Niles, J. K., Chiu, S., Zeig-Owens, R., Soo, J., Kelly, K., & Prezant, D. J. (2020). Trends of elevated PTSD risk in firefighters exposed to the World Trade Center disaster: 2001–2005. *Public Health Reports*, *125*(4), 556–566. doi:10.1177/003335491012500411 PMID:20597456

Boffa, J. W., King, S. L., Turecki, G., & Schmidt, N. B. (2018). Investigating the role of hopelessness in the relationship between PTSD symptom change and suicidality. *Journal of Affective Disorders*, *225*, 298–301. doi:10.1016/j.jad.2017.08.004 PMID:28843079

Bryan, C. J., Grove, J. L., & Kimbrel, N. A. (2017). Theory-driven models of self-directed violence among individuals with PTSD. *Current Opinion in Psychology*, *14*, 12–17. doi:10.1016/j.copsyc.2016.09.007 PMID:28813309

Canetti, E. F., Gayton, S., Schram, B., Pope, R., & Orr, R. M. (2022). Psychological, physical, and heat stress indicators prior to and after a 15-Minute structural firefighting task. *Biology (Basel)*, *11*(1), 104. doi:10.3390/biology11010104 PMID:35053102

Capron, D. W., Lamis, D. A., & Schmidt, N. B. (2017). Test of the depression distress amplification model in young adults with elevated risk of current suicidality. *Psychiatry Research*, *219*(3), 531–535. doi:10.1016/j.psychres.2014.07.005 PMID:25063018

Carr, A. (2019). Couple therapy, family therapy and systemic interventions for adult-focused problems: The current evidence base. *Journal of Family Therapy*, *41*(4), 492–536. doi:10.1111/1467-6427.12225

Chiang, E. S., Riordan, K. M., Ponder, J., Johnson, C., & Cox, K. S. (2020). Distinguishing firefighters with subthreshold PTSD from firefighters with probable PTSD or low symptoms. *Journal of Loss and Trauma, 26*(1), 65–77. doi:10.1080/15325024.2020.1728494

Choi, H. (2018). Effects of empowerment and family function on the depression of firefighters. *Fire Science and Engineering, 32*(2), 116-121. doi:10.7731/KIFSE.2018.32.1.116

Colquitt, J., LePine, J., Zapata, C., & Wild, R. (2018). Trust in Typical and High-Reliability Contexts: Building and Reacting to Trust among Firefighters. *Academy of Management Journal, 54*(5), 999–1015. doi:10.5465/amj.2006.0241

Cvirn, M., Dorrian, J., Smith, B., Vincent, G., Jay, S., Roach, G., Sargent, C., Larsen, B., Aisbett, B., & Ferguson, S. A. (2019). The effects of hydration on cognitive performance during a simulated wild-fire suppression shift in temperate and hot conditions. *Applied Ergonomics, 77*, 9–15. doi:10.1016/j.apergo.2018.12.018 PMID:30832782

Denkova, E., Zanesco, A., Rogers, S., & Jha, A. (2020). Is resilience trainable? An initial study comparing mindfulness and relaxation training in firefighters. *Psychiatry Research, 285*, 112794. doi:10.1016/j.psychres.2020.112794 PMID:32078885

Dibbets, P., Evers, E. A., Hurks, P. P., Bakker, K., & Jolles, J. (2020). Differential brain activation patterns in adult attention-deficit hyperactivity disorder (ADHD) associated with task switching. *Neuropsychology, 24*(4), 413–423. doi:10.1037/a0018997 PMID:20604616

Greenlee, T., Horn, G., Smith, D., Fahey, G., Goldstein, E., & Petruzzello, S. (2018). The influence of short-term firefighting activity on information processing performance. *Ergonomics, 57*(5), 764–773. doi:10.1080/00140139.2014.897375 PMID:24670047

Greenlee, T. A., Horn, G., Smith, D. L., Fahey, G., Goldstein, E., & Petruzzello, S. J. (2019). The influence of short-term firefighting activity on information processing performance. *Ergonomics, 57*(5), 764–773. doi:10.1080/00140139.2014.897375 PMID:24670047

Hemmatjo, R., Hajaghazadeh, M., Allahyari, T., Zare, S., & Kazemi, R. (2020). The effects of live-fire drills on visual and auditory cognitive performance among firefighters. *Annals of Global Health, 86*(1), 144. Advance online publication. doi:10.5334/aogh.2626 PMID:33262933

Hemmatjo, R., Motamedzade, M., Aliabadi, M., Kalatpour, O., & Farhadian, M. (2017). The effect of artificial smoke compound on physiological responses, cognitive functions and work performance during firefighting activities in a smoke-diving room: An intervention study. *International Journal of Occupational Safety and Ergonomics, 24*(3), 358–365. doi:10.1080/10803548.2017.1299995 PMID:28278005

Heydari, P., Babamiri, M., Tapak, L., Golmohammadi, R., & Kalatpour, O. (2022). Weighing and prioritization of individual factors affecting the performance of industries firefighters. *Fire Safety Journal, 127*, 103512. doi:10.1016/j.firesaf.2021.103512

Horn, G. P., Stewart, J. W., Kesler, R. M., DeBlois, J. P., Kerber, S., Fent, K. W., Scott, W. S., Fernhall, B., & Smith, D. L. (2019). Firefighter and fire instructor's physiological responses and safety in various training fire environments. *Safety Science, 116*, 287–294. doi:10.1016/j.ssci.2019.03.017

Huang, Q., Zhang, Q., An, Y., & Xu, W. (2019). The relationship between dispositional mindfulness and PTSD/PTG among firefighters: The mediating role of emotion regulation. *Personality and Individual Differences, 151,* 109492. doi:10.1016/j.paid.2019.07.002

Hudson, A. N., Van Dongen, H., & Honn, K. A. (2020). Sleep deprivation, vigilant attention, and brain function: A review. *Neuropsychopharmacology, 45*(1), 21–30. doi:10.103841386-019-0432-6 PMID:31176308

Igboanugo, S., Bigelow, P. L., & Mielke, J. G. (2021). Health outcomes of psychosocial stress within firefighters: A systematic review of the research landscape. *Journal of Occupational Health, 63*(1), e12219. doi:10.1002/1348-9585.12219 PMID:33780075

Jeon, S. G., Han, J., Jo, Y., & Han, K. (2019, November). Being more focused and engaged in firefighting training: Applying user-centered design to VR system development. In *25th ACM Symposium on Virtual Reality Software and Technology* (pp. 1-11). 10.1145/3359996.3364268

Johnson, C. C., Vega, L., Kohalmi, A. L., Roth, J. C., Howell, B. R., & Van Hasselt, V. B. (2020). Enhancing mental health treatment for the firefighter population: Understanding fire culture, treatment barriers, practice implications, and research directions. *Professional Psychology, Research and Practice, 51*(3), 304–311. doi:10.1037/pro0000266

Jung, Y., Lee, J., & Shin, W. (2017). Sustained attention performance during sleep deprivation and following nap: Associated with trait-like vulnerability. *Sleep Medicine, 40,* e151. doi:10.1016/j.sleep.2017.11.442

Kim, S., & Yook, S. (2018). The Influence of Posttraumatic Stress on Suicidal Ideation in Firefighters: Cognitive Emotion Regulation as a Moderator. *Fire Science and Engineering, 32*(2), 92–101. doi:10.7731/KIFSE.2018.32.2.092

Kim, Y., Kim, W., Bae, M., Choi, J., Kim, M., Oh, S., Park, K. S., Park, S., Lee, S.-K., Koh, S.-B., & Kim, C. (2022). The effect of polycyclic aromatic hydrocarbons on changes in the brain structure of firefighters: An analysis using data from the Firefighters Research on Enhancement of Safety & Health study. *The Science of the Total Environment, 816,* 151655. doi:10.1016/j.scitotenv.2021.151655 PMID:34785224

Klimley, K. E., Van Hasselt, V. B., & Stripling, A. M. (2018). Posttraumatic stress disorder in police, firefighters, and emergency dispatchers. *Aggression and Violent Behavior, 43,* 33–44. doi:10.1016/j.avb.2018.08.005

Kujawski, S., Słomko, J., Tafil-Klawe, M., Zawadka-Kunikowska, M., Szrajda, J., Newton, J. L., Zalewski, P., & Klawe, J. J. (2018). The Impact of total sleep deprivation upon cognitive functioning in firefighters. *Neuropsychiatric Disease and Treatment, 14,* 1171–1181. doi:10.2147/NDT.S156501 PMID:29773948

Langner, R., & Eickhoff, S. B. (2017). Sustaining attention to simple tasks: A meta-analytic review of the neural mechanisms of vigilant attention. *Psychological Bulletin, 139*(4), 870–900. doi:10.1037/a0030694 PMID:23163491

Lindholm, H., Punakallio, A., Lusa, S., Sainio, M., Ponocny, E., & Winker, R. (2018). Association of cardio-ankle vascular index with physical fitness and cognitive symptoms in aging Finnish firefighters. *International Archives of Occupational and Environmental Health*, *85*(4), 397–403. doi:10.100700420-011-0681-0 PMID:21789686

Lindström, J., & Försth, M. (2018). Fire test of profile plank for transformer pit fire protection. *Fire Technology*, *52*(2), 309–319. doi:10.100710694-014-0409-2

Martin, C. E., Tran, J. K., & Buser, S. J. (2017). Correlates of suicidality in firefighter/EMS personnel. *Journal of Affective Disorders*, *208*, 177–183. doi:10.1016/j.jad.2016.08.078 PMID:27788381

Nam, C., Kim, H., & Kwon, S. (2018). Effects of a Stress Management Program Providing Cognitive Behavior Therapy on Problem-focused Coping, Job Stress, and Depression in Firefighters. *Journal of Korean Academy of Psychiatric and Mental Health Nursing*, *22*(1), 12. doi:10.12934/jkpmhn.2013.22.1.12

Nowak, K., & Łukomska, B. (2021). The Impact of shift work on the well-being and subjective levels of alertness and sleepiness in firefighters and rescue service workers. *International Journal of Occupational Safety and Ergonomics*, *27*(4), 1056–1063. doi:10.1080/10803548.2021.1933320 PMID:34082652

Park, J. (2019). The adverse Impact of personal protective equipment on firefighters' cognitive functioning. *The Research Journal of The Costume Culture*, *27*(1), 1–10. doi:10.29049/rjcc.2019.27.1.001

Raines, A. M., Capron, D. W., Stentz, L. A., Walton, J. L., Allan, N. P., McManus, E. S., Uddo, M., True, G., & Franklin, C. L. (2017). Posttraumatic stress disorder and suicidal ideation, plans, and impulses: The mediating role of anxiety sensitivity cognitive concerns among veterans. *Journal of Affective Disorders*, *222*, 57–62. doi:10.1016/j.jad.2017.06.035 PMID:28672180

Robinson, S., Leach, J., Owen-Lynch, P., & Sünram-Lea, S. (2017). Stress Reactivity and Cognitive Performance in a Simulated Firefighting Emergency. *Aviation, Space, and Environmental Medicine*, *84*(6), 592–599. doi:10.3357/ASEM.3391.2013 PMID:23745287

Scott, D., Ratiliff, B., & English, C. (2022). Sounding the alarm: Firefighter behavioral health and suicide prevention. *International Journal of Integrated Care*, *22*(S2), 16. Advance online publication. doi:10.5334/ijic.ICIC21290

Semmens, E., Domitrovich, J., Conway, K., & Noonan, C. (2016). A cross-sectional survey of occupational history as a wildland firefighter and health. *American Journal of Industrial Medicine*, *59*(4), 330–335. doi:10.1002/ajim.22566 PMID:26792645

Sliter, M., Kale, A., & Yuan, Z. (2018). Is humor the best medicine? The buffering effect of coping humor on traumatic stressors in firefighters. *Journal of Organizational Behavior*, *35*(2), 257–272. doi:10.1002/job.1868

Smith, D., Manning, T., & Petruzzello, S. (2017). Effect of strenuous live-fire drills on cardiovascular and psychological responses of recruit firefighters. *Ergonomics*, *44*(3), 244–254. doi:10.1080/00140130121115 PMID:11219758

Smith, T. D., Hughes, K., DeJoy, D. M., & Dyal, M. A. (2018). Assessment of relationships between work stress, work-family conflict, burnout and firefighter safety behavior outcomes. *Safety Science, 103,* 287–292. doi:10.1016/j.ssci.2017.12.005

Song, Y., Ha, J., & Jue, J. (2020). Examining the Relative Influences of the Risk Factors and Protective Factors That Affect Firefighter Resilience. *SAGE Open, 10*(4), 215824402098261. doi:10.1177/2158244020982610

Stanley, I., Hom, M., Spencer-Thomas, S., & Joiner, T. (2017). Examining anxiety sensitivity as a mediator of the association between PTSD symptoms and suicide risk among women firefighters. *Journal of Anxiety Disorders, 50,* 94–102. doi:10.1016/j.janxdis.2017.06.003 PMID:28645017

Stanley, I. H., Boffa, J. W., Hom, M. A., Kimbrel, N. A., & Joiner, T. E. (2017). Differences in psychiatric symptoms and barriers to mental health care between volunteer and career firefighters. *Psychiatry Research, 247,* 236–242. doi:10.1016/j.psychres.2016.11.037 PMID:27930964

Stanley, I. H., Smith, L. J., Boffa, J. W., Tran, J. K., Schmidt, N. B., Joiner, T. E., & Vujanovic, A. A. (2018). Anxiety sensitivity and suicide risk among firefighters: A test of the depression-distress amplification model. *Comprehensive Psychiatry, 84,* 39–46. doi:10.1016/j.comppsych.2018.03.014 PMID:29684659

Stout, J., Beidel, D., Brush, D., & Bowers, C. (2020). Sleep disturbance and cognitive functioning among firefighters. *Journal of Health Psychology, 26*(12), 2248–2259. doi:10.1177/1359105320909861 PMID:32126834

Sumińska, S., Nowak, K., Łukomska, B., & Cygan, H. (2020). Cognitive functions of shift workers: Paramedics and firefighters – an electroencephalography study. *International Journal of Occupational Safety and Ergonomics, 27*(3), 686–697. doi:10.1080/10803548.2020.1773117 PMID:32436781

Walker, A., Argus, C., Driller, M., & Rattray, B. (2017). Repeat work bouts increase thermal strain for Australian firefighters working in the heat. *International Journal of Occupational and Environmental Health, 21*(4), 285–293. doi:10.1179/2049396715Y.0000000006 PMID:25849044

Williams-Bell F. McLellan T. Murphy B. (2018). The effects of exercise-induced heat stress on cognitive function in firefighters. doi:10.7287/peerj.preprints.2524v1

Wu, T., Yuan, K., Yen, D., & Xu, T. (2019). Building up resources in the relationship between work-family conflict and burnout among firefighters: Moderators of guanxi and emotion regulation strategies. *European Journal of Work and Organizational Psychology, 28*(3), 430–441. doi:10.1080/1359432X.2019.1596081

Ye, Y., Shi, Y., Xia, P., Kang, J., Tyagi, O., Mehta, R., & Du, J. (2022). Cognitive characteristics in firefighter wayfinding Tasks: An Eye-Tracking analysis. *Advanced Engineering Informatics, 53,* 101668. doi:10.1016/j.aei.2022.101668

Zare, S., Hemmatjo, R., Allahyari, T., Hajaghazadeh, M., Hajivandi, A., Aghabeigi, M., & Kazemi, R. (2018). Comparison of the effect of typical firefighting activities, live-fire drills and rescue operations at height on firefighters' physiological responses and cognitive function. *Ergonomics, 61*(10), 1334–1344. doi:10.1080/00140139.2018.1484524 PMID:29862929

Zhang, Y., Balilionis, G., Casaru, C., Geary, C., Schumacker, R., Neggers, Y., Curtner-Smith, M. D., Richardson, M. T., Bishop, P. A., & Green, J. M. (2014). Effects of caffeine and menthol on cognition and mood during simulated firefighting in the heat. *Applied Ergonomics*, *45*(3), 510–514. doi:10.1016/j.apergo.2013.07.005 PMID:23891504

Chapter 9
Applying the Triple Bottom Line for Corporate Sustainability Toward Zero Environmental, Social, and Economic Footprints in Corporate Practice

Emad Rahim
https://orcid.org/0000-0002-9391-747X
Bellevue University, USA

ABSTRACT

The mystification of the term sustainability with society's desiderata, desegregate sustainability into three types: social, economic, and environmental. The triple bottom line needs to be integrated into every stratum of the business for corporate responsibility. The optimal performance ensures sustainability and brings together strategies that relate to the environment and society. This chapter serves as a road map to bring about a zero triple bottom line, thus ensuring a sustainable business ecosystem. A sustainability strategy aligns business sustainability goals with environmental and social stewardship goals. Corporations need to create a synergistic relationship with key stakeholders and the global communities regarding the biosphere. A call of duty requires that corporations/firms need go beyond product stewardship into beneficial relationships relating to the communities and the Earth. Ample opportunities and significant challenges abound for organizations globally.

INTRODUCTION

The term sustainability has become increasingly important in the corporate world today. Sustainability is defined as "meeting the needs of the present without compromising the ability of future generations to meet their own needs" (WBCSD, 2020). As companies become more aware of the environmental and social impacts of their operations, they are now making sustainability a priority in order to remain

DOI: 10.4018/979-8-3693-1630-6.ch009

competitive and ensure their long-term survival. This paper will discuss why sustainability is important to companies and what it looks like in terms of operational activities.

Sustainability is important to companies for a number of reasons. One of the most important is that it is a requirement for doing business in a competitive and global economy. Investors, customers, and consumers are now demanding that companies demonstrate their commitment to sustainability by taking steps to reduce their environmental footprint and increase their social responsibility. Companies that do not incorporate sustainability into their operations are at risk of losing their competitive edge (Lüdeke-Freund, et al., 2019). Another reason why sustainability is important to companies is that it can help them to save money. Companies can reduce their overhead costs by incorporating sustainability initiatives into their operations. For example, they can invest in energy-efficient technologies and practices, such as LED lighting, renewable energy sources, and the use of recycled materials. These investments can help to reduce energy and water consumption, resulting in long-term savings for the company (Kemfert, 2014). In addition, sustainability is important to companies because it can help to improve their brand image and reputation. Consumers are now more likely to purchase from companies that are committed to sustainability. Companies can build trust and loyalty with their customers by demonstrating their commitment to sustainability through their operations and initiatives (Henderson, 2015). Finally, sustainability is important to companies because it can help to improve their ability to attract and retain talent. Employees want to work for companies that are committed to sustainability, and companies that are able to demonstrate this commitment are more likely to be able to attract and retain the best talent (Gardner, 2017).

Sustainability in terms of operational activities refers to the implementation of practices that are designed to reduce the environmental and social impacts of a company's operations. Companies can do this by incorporating sustainability initiatives into their operations. One way to do this is by investing in energy-efficient technologies and practices. This can include the use of LED lighting, renewable energy sources, and the reuse of materials. These investments can help to reduce energy and water consumption, resulting in long-term savings for the company (Kemfert, 2014). Another way to incorporate sustainability into operations is through the use of sustainable materials. Companies can invest in recycled and renewable materials, such as recycled paper and plant-based plastics, in order to reduce their environmental impact. Companies can also look for ways to reduce their waste and use natural resources more efficiently (Kubala, 2018). In addition, companies can also incorporate sustainability into their operations by investing in green transportation initiatives. This can include investing in electric vehicles, carpooling, or using public transportation. This can help to reduce emissions and improve air quality (Kemfert, 2014). Finally, companies can also incorporate sustainability into their operations by looking for ways to reduce their carbon footprint. This can include investing in carbon offset programs, such as investing in renewable energy sources or replanting forests. This can help to reduce the environmental impact of the company's operations (Kubala, 2018).

Goodland and Daly (1996) posited that sustainability must not become a landfill dump for everyone's environmental and social list. Because of varying definitions of sustainability, the three types of sustainability (social, economic, and environmental) are best understood when they are treated disaggregated and separately (Rutting., Vervoort & Mees, 2022). There has been a global consensus that sustainable development should encompass at least economic growth, social progress, and stewardship of the environment (Tanzil & Beloff, 2006). Sustainability is often considered in terms of three pillars, economic, social, and environmental (ESE) considerations (Morrisson-Saunders & Therivel, 2006). Although the number of dimensions is changeable, the main idea is to translate each sustainable issue into a traceable reference based on ESE concerns. These three dimensions of sustainable development have long been separately managed, and each dimension has been measured under a discrete-dimensional approach (Shin, 2006). According to Halme, et al. (2006), the three dimensions of sustainability must be addressed simultaneously.

The Significance of This Paper and the Topic

There are a variety of sustainability numbers that can be used to measure a company's performance. These include environmental metrics such as carbon footprint, energy efficiency, and water use; social metrics such as employee engagement and diversity; and governance metrics such as board diversity and executive compensation. Additionally, there are a variety of industry-specific sustainability numbers that can be used to measure performance in specific areas, such as water use in the agricultural industry or energy efficiency in the manufacturing industry. Sustainability numbers can be used in a variety of ways to help companies measure and improve their performance in terms of sustainability. Companies can use sustainability numbers to set goals, identify areas for improvement, track progress over time, and compare their performance to that of other companies in their industry. Additionally, sustainability numbers can be used to demonstrate to stakeholders, such as investors and consumers, that the company is taking steps to address environmental, social, and governance issues.

Contexts From the Literature

Achieving economic growth and development without depleting or compromising the world's natural resources for future generations became a concern of the United Nations after the leaders read the *Our Common Future* report from the World Commission on Environmental Development, also known as the Brundtland Commission, in 1987 (Gladwin, et al., 1996). Sustainable development, as termed by the Brundtland Commission, represents the "development that meets the needs of the present without compromising the ability of future generations to meet their own needs (World Commission on Environment and Development, 1987).

As major industries began to recognize the threats associated with *Our Common Future* they began to review the impact of this phenomenon on the organization's business operation. According to Harvard Business School Publishing (2005) "strategy creation typically begins with extensive research and should be approached as a process." The process has awakened many organizations to think about the social and environmental impacts of their business practices; although progress has been made, the strategies do not properly connect the performance goals to the sustainability strategy (Rutting., Vervoort & Mees, 2022). Thus, a successful sustainability strategy should clearly communicate the contribution from each business unit and the benefits; that is, what's in it for me. The plan should communicate these three things:

- The corporate social responsibility
- Sustainability training and development
- The energy efficiency benefits for stakeholders

STRATEGIC MANAGEMENT

The strategic management tools, methods and models that organizations implore in the driving wheels of its core activities help in the determination of the sustainability solution of the organization. These strategic elements—if well developed, with considerable understanding of environmental, political, economic, and social factors—gives an organization the desired competitive advantage necessary to dominate its market and the industry as a whole. To have a sustainable competitive advantage in an organization, the stakeholders, as well as the individuals in the organization, must learn first before the organizational learning can occur. Garvin (2000) defined a learning organization (LO) as "an organization skilled at creating, acquiring, interpreting, transferring and retaining knowledge, and at purposefully modifying its behavior to reflect new knowledge and insights." An organization that wants to gear toward zero corporate sustainability also must be very mindful of the social and economic impact in the local communities (Bolton, 2022). The profitability is vital to the stakeholders. Corporate sustainability has diverse stakeholders that include the employees, top management, directors, customers, and the local communities they serve (Carrera, 2022). Amongst all of the different stakeholders, sustainability underpins the social, economic, and environmental concerns.

CORPORATE SUSTAINABILITY AND LEADERSHIP

Organizations gearing toward sustainability should embark on social strategies and environmental stewardship, efficient operation, and strategic applications of its resources (energy, people, and materials). These measures will ultimately make them productive while minimizing environmental pollution and waste. Corporations have always been measured traditionally in terms of financial metrics; however, social and environmental impact assessment has become widespread (Carrera, 2022). Haugh and Talwar (2010) posited that "societal demands for greater accountability and transparency have brought about innovations in measuring and communicating the broader impact of corporations on different stakeholder groups." Operational efficiency and respect for the environment are part of the strategy inherent in organizational culture and a business approach toward zero environmental, social, and economic footprints in business practice. For example, according to the United States Environmental Protection Agency (EPA), "it is mandated by regulation that every airline in the industry must contribute 2% of its revenue towards environmental project in response to the U.S. Greenhouse Gas Emissions (GHGs)." By taking these actions, the airline industry is starting to use social and environmental accounting tools (GRI, 2000), and environmental impact measures (ISO, 14001) are part of a gradual movement toward designing standardized methods to calculate social and environmental impact (Lehman, 1999); all of these measures help to reduce the air emissions associated with its flight within the environment.

Managing human resources, training, and development are key components to rolling out a successful sustainability strategy. Hays (2011) suggested attaining a greater degree of sustainability in modern society will require involvements and action from individuals, and as a result, good leadership is needed. Hays (2011) further suggested that "transformational learning is needed among those who interact with leaders, as this challenges people to change their belief systems and behavioral patterns; to be more effective, this can be coupled with contextual learning, which 'makes the learning relevant to the experience'". Thus, implementing a successful sustainability strategy requires employee awareness of the corporate sustainability initiatives and growth opportunities for employees to gain experience through development and training relating to the sustainability strategy (Duca & Gherghina, 2019). Some corporations will face challenges as they aim to implement the sustainability initiatives into the culture of the organization. According to Haugh and Talwar (2010) "these challenges demand new knowledge, and learning lies at the heart of such organizational transformations. Changing employee attitudes to appreciate that sustainability is a key driver of the organization, not an optional add-on, will require investment," and the employees must learn and accept the relationships between sustainability and the organization. Thus, gaining practical experience at work in the content area of sustainability can be valuable learning opportunities for managers and employees.

Thus, as corporations seek to use technology to advance their sustainability strategies, employees can enhance their skills through the alliances that are formed with stakeholders in an effort to develop products or services or use advancements in technology to increase sustainability value. Nidumolu, et al. (2009) contended that "executives are waking up to the fact that a sizable number of consumers prefer eco-friendly offerings, and that their business can score over rivals by being the first to redesign existing products or develop new ones." Staying current with market trends and technology provides an opportunity for companies to design and implement sustainable products and services by listening and understanding the consumer needs and reviewing the organization's product life cycle. This type of opportunity exposes employees to higher levels of management and key decision makers outside of the organization. Thus, "the creation of structures and opportunities for technical action, and social learning have the potential to transform individual learning about sustainability into organizational learning" (Haugh & Talwar, 2010).

CORPORATE SOCIAL RESPONSIBILITY

The attention received by many corporations regarding being environmentally friendly in their business operations came by surprise from the public (Duca & Gherghina, 2019). Consumers and nongovernmental stakeholders expressed a growing need to conduct business with organizations that were environmentally conscious in their business practices. Consumers expected corporations to align their business priorities with the new forces at play in the world, be socially responsible for pollutants generated from the organization's business operations, and be sensitive to labor relations issues. Although many companies have made great efforts to improve the social and environmental initiatives in their business practices, internal and external opposition can impede the process. Porter and Kramer (2006) argued that companies do not have a clear understanding of the interconnection between the corporate social responsibilities with the corporate strategic plan. As a result, the framework and planning involved in the corporate strategic plan are not used to position the corporate social responsibility strategy; this disconnect prohibits organizations from identifying the opportunities and competitive market advantage that socially responsible goals in an organization can achieve.

Several researchers have contended that there are positive influences associated with a company's value as a result of corporate social responsibility engagement. In an empirical study Jo and Harjoto (2011) revealed that "activities that address internal social enhancement within the firm, such as employees diversity, [the] firm['s] relationship with its employees, and product quality, enhance the value of [the] firm more than other CSR subcategories for broader external social enhancement." Thus, an effective corporate social responsibility plan will uphold the corporate governance, conduct the business of the organization as desired by the shareholders, and promote sound business practices in an effort to ensure corporate sustainability (Carrera, 2022). Collaboration with all shareholders can also create a firm's value. Hill et al. (2007) suggested that there is a hierarchical order to corporate social responsibility and that ranking involves economic, legal, moral, and philanthropic actions of firms, and these actions have an impact on all stakeholders. In an effort to enhance a firm's value, Esteves and Barclay (2011) contended that corporations should establish a conceptual agreement with key community partners that allow the company to monitor their partnership performance to achieve program objectives that are key sustainability initiatives for the organization. Esteves and Barclay (2011) also contended that the responsibility does not rest entirely on a firm and that the organization's management should take an interest in all the stakeholder group members to ensure that the high performance in sustainability is be achieved by all parties. Full disclosure is a key component to building trusting relationships. Michelon (2011) contended that there is a relation between sustainability disclosure by a firm and reputational risk. Companies that collaborate with their stakeholder on the company's sustainability initiatives are more transparent and have a better relationship with their stakeholder than organizations that do not engage or disclose the information (Correia, 2019). Thus, the impact of corporate social responsibility on a firm's value is a great concern for shareholders.

ALIGNING GOALS TO SUPPORT A SUSTAINABILITY STRATEGY

According to Harvey (2006) alignment is a term that "describes the continuous process of mobilizing enterprise resources to execute company objectives." Ideally, every level of management can articulate the organization's strategic plans and the contribution of each employee is responsible to meet that target goal. However, Kruse and Lundbergh (2010) contended that "sustainability is often still not included as part of performance management across the entire company." Kruse and Lundbergh (2010) pointed out that since incentives are in place to encourage senior management to achieve key strategic performance initiatives the "sustainability targets should be tied to executive remuneration."

Thus, a definition of corporate sustainability should be defined. Fairfield et al. (2010) stated that "corporate sustainability" may be considered as a "company's ability to achieve its business goals and increase long-term shareholder value by integrating economic, environmental, and social opportunities into its business strategies." There are many environmental, social, and economic factors that challenge the corporation's business practices as the world becomes increasingly concerned about the future of the world's natural resources and the people who live in it (Prakash, 2020). Aligning business priorities with the new forces at play in the world becomes the social responsibility of an organization and vital to its long-term success. The extent to which an organization implements sustainability practices will be dependent on the issues that are perceived as critical factors that contribute to the overall success of the organization. Sustainability strategies can vary in practice from one organization to another. According to Fairfield et al. (2010):

Many practices relate to improving eco-efficiency and reducing environmental 'footprint' through energy conservation and the like. Other practices aim to create more sustainable and effective workplaces by focusing on worker health and safety, employee engagement, and civic volunteerism, while slowly infusing sustainability criteria into talent and performance management systems. Other practices focus on sustainability-related product innovation, market development, and branding, while still others emphasize stakeholder engagement.

In a similar manner, Alesi (2008) provided an integrated business model as to how organizations can create a culture of resiliency so that the business plan establishes accountability and authority for every employee. Alesi (2008) contended that every employee should play an intricate part in the change process and should have access to the overall corporate plan. Therefore, success is achieved by having a course of action to review the business goals and deliverables regularly, and the model must be integrated into the day-to-day operations.

COST REDUCTION THROUGH ENERGY EFFICIENCY

The status quo and business-as-usual philosophy will not position an organization to stay competitive to meet the future demands of the customers. Continuous change must become a part of the organizational culture for the organization to survive in the marketplace. Thus, reducing greenhouse gases has become one of the main concerns in the United States. Environmental innovations can involve new or modified processes, business practices, or products and services that result in a reduction of environmental depletion of resources in the business. For example, the electric utility sector is the largest emitter of greenhouse gases (GHG) in the United States. Fossil fuel has been the primary source to generate electricity in the industry and the business structure supports this type of infrastructure. However, new technology can help the industry reduce its carbon footprint and become eco-friendly.

The electric utility industry in the 21st century has begun to realign its corporate goals to integrate a sustainability strategy that involves improving energy efficiency, conserving energy, and reducing its carbon footprint in its business practices. The energy efficiency programs and technology not only help consumers to save on their electric bill but also lower emissions, thus reducing the need to build power plants in the future. The industry is using various technologies to integrate an eco-efficiency and environmental emission goal in its business practices.

Electric utility companies have started to introduce smart meter technology into the business operation in an effort to reduce greenhouse gas levels associated with removing vehicles off the road that were being used to drive around and read energy meters. In addition, according to Spaur (2008) "the smart meters advanced data collection and demand-response capabilities, enable utilities to work with their customers to reduce their energy when energy prices are high…. the load reduction during peak time-based pricing empowers customers and reduces new generation needs." The smart grid and meter technology will be a critical component of survival from firms that are in the industry. Spaurs (2008) also contended that the new technology will be a costly investment to utilities; however, the technology will help to reduce energy use—for example, in California, residents tap into their smart homes while they are away to control appliances and lights using smart meters and smart phones.

Aras and Crowther (2008) argued that "sustainability is actually based on efficiency measures of sustainability [that] would consider the rate at which resources are consumed by the organization in relation to the rate at which resources can be regenerated." As corporations seek to create stakeholder value, measuring the sustainability performance provides feedback to the management on the efficiency and effectiveness of the strategy.

LEARNING ORGANIZATION

Senge (1990) defined a learning organization (LO) "as a place where leaderships create an environment for flourishing, where people continually expand their capacity to generate desired results, where new and valuable patterns of thinking are nurtured, where collective aspiration is set free, where people are continually learning how to learn, and where people are bonded firmly in the same boat with clear future destiny." The many strategies put in place by organizations will indeed be used to sustain zero environmental, social, and economic footprints in business practice against competitors. These strategies must align with the vision, mission, values, and culture of the corporation (O'Rourke, 2004). According to Porter (2008), "understanding the competitive forces, and their underlying causes, reveals the roots of an industry's current profitability while providing a framework for anticipating and influencing competition (and profitability) over time."

Clarkson (1995) notes that "a corporation's survival and continuing success depends on the ability of its management to create sufficient wealth, value, or satisfaction for all primary stakeholder groups." Additionally, Clarkson (1995) argues that "the economic and social purpose of the corporation is to create and distribute increased wealth and value to all its primary stakeholder groups, without favoring one group at the expense of others." Similarly, Jones and Wicks (1999) argue that "the interests of all (legitimate) stakeholders have intrinsic value, and no set of interests is assumed to dominate the others." Corporate sustainability that gears towards zero environmental, social, economic footprints in business practice can be implemented by designing company structures and policies that embody the principles of economic, social, and environmental sustainability (Bansal, 2002). Furthermore, Haugh and Talwar (2010) posited that integrating sustainability principles into an organization requires decisions concerning with whom, where, and how this responsibility will be managed. The society's hope is that corporations can and should pursue sustainable solutions to social and environmental problems by engaging in more influential strategies (Lepineux, 2009) in the way business are conducted.

STRATEGIC PLANNING AND IMPLEMENTATION

Corporations looking for sustainability solutions engage their business both in economic performance and social responsibility strategies that have a direct relationship despite organizational and environmental differences (Carrera, 2022). Southwest Airlines (SWA) found the relationship of social responsibility and economic performance enviable, positive (Sturtevant & Ginter, 1977), and a performing strategy that has sustained both internal and external stakeholders, surrounding communities inclusive while also responding to environmental differences. Stakeholders have enjoyed significant dividends based on the corporate strategic planning and strategic implementation that tie down to the vision, mission, value, and culture of the organization. Furthermore, Meznar et al. (1991) stated that "Freeman's classification is parsimonious, appears to be collectively exhaustive (the 'Narrow' and 'Utilitarian' categories alone are capable of embracing all combinations of stakeholders), and seems to be timeless."

Freeman (1984) "has gone a step further by developing a better understanding of the scope of a firm's 'social-legitimacy concerns' using the stakeholder approach." SWA combined stakeholder and utilitarian strategy (maximize benefits to society) to create an excellent sustainable organization culture that stands out in the entire aviation world. Parra (2008) considered "social responsibilities as the possibility to find new economic opportunity and economic benefit.''

Corporations should maintain their strategies that have sustained them in economic performance and in their environmental stewardship. Their core values, goals, mission, vision, and culture has been sustained regardless. In assessing the enterprise level strategy of a corporation, Freeman (1984), defines enterprise strategy as "what a firm stands for." Corporations stand for so many things, such as the environmental steward across their systems, and they want to provide their employees with a stable working environment with equal opportunity for learning and personal growth. In addition, a corporation's vision is to have a sustainable future that balances the business model between its employees, the community, the environment, and primarily its financial viability.

Mezner et al. (1991) explain "how the firm attempts to add value to its stakeholders in order to legitimize its existence and ensure its future." Brue (2006) defines Six Sigma as "a problem-solving methodology that reduces costs and improves customer satisfaction by greatly reducing waste in all the processes involved in the creation and delivery of products and/or services." Corporations should apply lean Six Sigma strategy in their business dealings that gear toward zero environmental, social, economic footprints in business practice. According to Grubbs-West (2005), "people give as good as they get." This is like the golden rule in the Bible that says, "do to others what you would [have] them do to you" (KJB, 2008). Similarly, Deep and Sussman (1995) stated that "in today's world, employees' commitment or loyalty to their customers, their employer, and their work translates into millions of dollars of revenue." Corporations known for their environmental stewardship stand out as pioneers in so many programs that affect their social responsibility to their stakeholders, customers, communities, suppliers, and all other partners associated with physical environment such as EPA.

ENVIRONMENTAL SUSTAINABILITY

According to Senge (1990), "effective organizational learning is very likely to lead to improved strategic management responsiveness, efficiency, and effectiveness." Similarly, Porter (2008) stated that "technological development must accompany a company's efforts at growth during periods of great change." Corporate publications, social media tools that brings awareness of sustainability (Meckel, 2010), employee training courses, and workshops are effective methods (Armstrong & Sadler-Smith, 2008), and company visits enable employees to interact with and learn from other organizations that have successfully implemented sustainability initiatives (Haugh & Talwar, 2005). Proponents of environmental sustainability have now taken this thesis one step further with the argument that environmentally conscious and ecologically friendly strategies could, in fact, lead to competitive advantages and superior financial performance (Engardio, 2007; Hart, 2005). While earlier views were dominated by notions that environmental objectives were a constraint to the economic goals of a business or that the economic objectives of a business were a direct threat to environmental conservation, the recent approach treats both economics and ecology as two sides of the same coin. Hart (2005) argued that when properly focused, the profit motive of business can accelerate the transformation toward global sustainability, with nonprofits, governments, and multilateral agencies all playing crucial roles as collaborators. Savitz and Weber (2006) suggest that a sustainable corporation is one that creates profit. Recently, Lash and Wellington (2007) suggested that firms will be at a competitive disadvantage if they do not pay attention to sustainability issues.

According to Porter and Kramer (2006), the starting point for environmental sustainability is surprisingly simple: If everyone recognizes that ecosystems and natural resources are limited, economic decisions can be so oriented that the end products of economic actions are environmentally sustainable as well.

Figure 1. CSM framework for telecommunications services
Source: Porter and Kramer (2006)

Halme et al. (2006) suggested that the fast-changing, dynamic global business environment requires firms to be more flexible to quickly adapt and respond to market changes. Among the forces that drive changes, requirements for corporate responsibility and sustainability are getting more urgent (Beerannavar, 2020). During such a difficult time as this economic downturn, companies are faced with hard choices to survive. Research has acknowledged that addressing sustainability issues is critical to the long-term existence and thriving of companies (Porter and Kramer, 2006).

The Triple Bottom Line (TBL) is an approach to corporate sustainability that puts equal emphasis on the financial, social, and environmental aspects of a company's operations. The TBL framework has been adopted by many organizations with the goal of improving their sustainability performance, while also providing long-term economic value. This paper will discuss the concept of the TBL and how it can be applied in corporate sustainability plans. The Concept of Triple Bottom Line The Triple Bottom Line (TBL) was first proposed by John Elkington in 1994 and is defined as "the three dimensions of performance—economic, environmental and social—that determine a company's long-term success" (Elkington, 1994). This concept is based on the idea that economic, environmental, and social performance are all important aspects of an organization's operations and should be given equal consideration in decision-making. By taking into account all three elements of performance, an organization can ensure that its operations are sustainable and aligned with its mission, values, and goals.

The TBL framework is often represented as a triangle, with economic performance at the bottom, environmental performance in the middle, and social performance at the top. The idea is that an organization should strive to achieve balance between the three aspects of performance, and that strong performance in one area should not come at the expense of performance in another (Elkington, 1994).

The TBL framework has been widely adopted by organizations as a way to improve their sustainability performance. Applying the TBL in corporate sustainability plans involves assessing the organization's current performance in each of the three areas and then setting goals for improvement in each area (Elkington, 1994). The first step in applying the TBL is to assess the organization's current performance in each of the three areas. This assessment should include an evaluation of the organization's economic performance, such as its financial health, profitability, and ability to meet customer needs. It should also evaluate the organization's environmental performance, such as its energy consumption, emissions, and waste management practices. Finally, it should evaluate the organization's social performance, such as its commitment to employee satisfaction and involvement in community initiatives. Once the assessment has been completed, the organization should set goals for improvement in each of the three areas. These goals should be specific, measurable, and achievable. For example, an organization might set a goal to reduce its energy consumption by 10%, to increase its profits by 5%, or to increase its involvement in community initiatives. The organization should then create a plan to achieve these goals. The plan should include strategies for improving performance in each of the three areas, as well as timelines and milestones for progress. The plan should be designed to ensure that the goals are met in a sustainable manner, with consideration given to the long-term economic, environmental, and social impacts of the organization's operations (Elkington, 1994).

Organizational culture is an important factor in the long-term success of any organization attempting to engage in sustainability activities. Culture is the shared beliefs, values, and practices that characterize an organization and form its identity (Bergström & Källström, 2019). When organizations seek to make changes to their culture, it is the responsibility of leaders to provide the guidance, support, and guidance needed in order to successfully implement and maintain those changes (Bergström & Källström, 2019). One of the most important leadership practices when it comes to organizational cultural change is communication (Bergström & Källström, 2019).

Effective communication is key to helping ensure that all members of the organization understand and accept the changes. Leaders should be clear and concise about the goals and expectations of the change, and make sure that everyone is on the same page (Bergström & Källström, 2019).To facilitate this process, leaders should actively listen to feedback from employees and use those insights to inform their communication and decision-making. Leaders should also provide ongoing support and guidance throughout the process, offering resources, coaching, and mentorship to help employees adjust to the new culture (Bergström & Källström, 2019).

Leaders should also practice transparency when it comes to cultural change. Leaders should be open about their plans, and share information about the change with all stakeholders. This will help to build trust with employees, and also demonstrate that the change is supported by upper-level management. Leaders should also be open to feedback, and be willing to consider alternative approaches and solutions (Bergström & Källström, 2019). This will help to ensure that the change is successful, and that employees are on board with the process. Leaders should also demonstrate commitment to the change, and be willing to take responsibility for any mistakes that may occur during the transition. This includes being willing to make the necessary adjustments to ensure that the change is implemented successfully. This demonstrates to employees that the leader is invested in the process and is committed to making the change successful. It also shows employees that the leader is willing to take responsibility for any mistakes that may occur. Leaders should also practice accountability when it comes to organizational cultural change (Bergström & Källström, 2019).

Leaders must be willing to hold themselves and their team members accountable for implementing the change successfully. This includes setting clear goals and expectations, and providing feedback and support when needed (Bergström & Källström, 2019). It also means holding team members accountable for any mistakes that may occur, and taking corrective action when necessary. This ensures that everyone involved is taking the change seriously, and is committed to making it successful (Bergström & Källström, 2019). Finally, leaders should practice continuous improvement when it comes to organizational culture. They should actively seek out feedback and adjust their approach as needed. This includes understanding the needs of their team members, and making adjustments to the change process as needed. This helps to ensure that the change is successful, and that the organization is continuously improving (Bergström & Källström, 2019).

CONCLUSION

Corporate sustainability plans are an increasingly popular way for companies to measure and manage their environmental, social, and economic impacts. Sustainable practices are beneficial to both a company's bottom line and the environment, and are becoming increasingly important in the corporate world. It is critical that organizations establish plans, engage in actions, and measure results.

Step 1: Set Goals

The first step in measuring a corporate sustainability plan is to set goals. These goals should be measurable and achievable. They should also be tailored to the specific company and its desired outcomes. For example, a company may set a goal to reduce carbon emissions by a certain percentage over a set period of time. Additionally, goals should be relevant to the company's core business and operations. (Kemp, 2018). Setting clear and achievable goals is essential in order to measure the success of a sustainability plan.

Step 2: Establish a Baseline

The next step is to establish a baseline in order to measure progress against the set goals. Establishing a baseline involves collecting data on the current environmental, social, and economic impacts of the company. This information can be used to identify areas of improvement, as well as to measure progress over time. Additionally, it is important to track any changes in the baseline over time in order to accurately assess the success of the sustainability plan. (Hammami, et al., 2017).

Step 3: Develop a Monitoring Plan

After setting goals and establishing a baseline, the next step is to develop a monitoring plan. This plan should outline the data that needs to be collected and the frequency with which it should be collected. Additionally, the plan should specify how the data will be analyzed and what metrics will be used to measure progress. Finally, the plan should include a timeline for achieving the set goals. (Grenz, 2017).

Step 4: Implement the Plan

Once the monitoring plan has been established, it is time to implement the plan. This involves collecting the necessary data, analyzing it, and comparing it to the baseline data. Additionally, it is important to track changes over time in order to accurately measure progress. (Hammami, et al., 2017).

Step 5: Evaluate Results

The final step is to evaluate the results. This involves comparing the data collected to the baseline data and measuring progress against the set goals. If the goals have been met, then the sustainability plan is deemed successful. Additionally, it is important to identify any areas of improvement in order to make the sustainability plan more effective. (Grenz, 2017). Conclusion In conclusion, measuring a corporate sustainability plan requires several steps. These include setting goals, establishing a baseline, developing a monitoring plan, implementing the plan, and evaluating the results. Following these steps will ensure that the sustainability plan is successful in achieving its desired outcomes.

Sustainability is important for companies since it increases their potential for long-term success. Companies that are able to reduce their environmental impact and use resources more efficiently can create a more sustainable future. This will make them more attractive to investors and customers, as they will be seen as a company that is investing in the future. Additionally, companies that engage in sustainability effort can benefit from cost savings, as they are able to reduce their energy, water, and other resource costs. In the long run, these savings can add up to significant amounts, allowing companies to make larger investments in sustainable technologies, such as renewable energy, or increase profits for shareholders (Halme & Väänänen, 2018). Sustainability can also be beneficial for companies from a public relations standpoint. Companies that are seen as attempting to reduce their environmental impact and create a more sustainable future can have a positive impact on their reputation. This can lead to increased customer loyalty, increased sales, and increased investments, as investors are more likely to invest in a company with a good reputation (Gond, Lahiri, Reddy & Suman, 2018). How Companies can Implement Sustainability There are a number of different ways that companies can implement sustainability initiatives. One way is to reduce their carbon emissions through energy efficiency measures, such as installing efficient lighting, heating, and air conditioning systems (Hoffmann, 2018).

Companies can also invest in renewable energy sources, such as wind and solar power, to reduce their reliance on fossil fuels and reduce their carbon footprint. Additionally, companies can reduce their water use by installing water-saving devices, such as low-flow toilets and showers, and using water-efficient irrigation systems for landscaping (Holm, 2018). Companies can also invest in sustainable practices such as recycling and composting. By recycling and composting, companies can reduce their waste output and save money on waste disposal costs (Saravanan, 2018). Additionally, companies can reduce their use of toxic chemicals and pollutants by using natural and organic products for cleaning and manufacturing processes (Liu, 2018). Benefits of Sustainability Initiatives There are a number of potential benefits that companies can gain from engaging in sustainability initiatives. One of the most important benefits is cost savings, as companies can save money on energy, water, and other resource costs by investing in efficient technologies and recycling and composting programs (Halme & Väänänen, 2018). Additionally, companies can benefit from increased customer loyalty and increased sales, as customers are more likely to buy products and services from a company that is making an effort to reduce its environmental impact (Gond, Lahiri, Reddy & Suman, 2018). Finally, companies can benefit from increased investments, as investors are more likely to invest in companies that are investing in sustainability initiatives (Halme & Väänänen, 2018). Additionally, companies can benefit from improved public relations and corporate reputation, as they will be seen as a company that is attempting to create a more sustainable future (Gond, Lahiri, Reddy & Suman, 2018)

Sustainability and the success of the societal economy will drastically be affected if organizations do not take environmental responsibility of business seriously. More research is needed to examine this correlation in the present context of business strategic goals and environmental responsibility. It is apparent that the social and environmental issues need to be redefined, knowing that these issues are not going away anytime soon. The survival of business organizations depends largely on their leadership. Leadership that starts from the top with all-inclusive strategy is critical for sustainability. According to Werbach (2011), "organizations today have a choice: They can either innovate differently and win or innovate narrowly and lose." Sustainability of the future moves beyond the relentless pursuits of short-term gain and toward long-term sustainability (Werbach, 2011). True sustainability comes from everyone in the organizations and not just the innovative leadership. Essentially, this creates horizontal and vertical information flow, thereby building a social relationship that allows new collaborations to occur (Werbach, 2011).

According to Yip and Makipere (2008) "all organizations should push towards achieving a higher level of corporate sustainability against all three sustainability components: economic, environment and social." Mirchandani and Ikerd (2008) stated that organizations should move beyond pollution prevention and product stewardship into a sustainable vision strategy and clean technology. Organizational change is rarely smooth (Haugh & Talwar, 2005). To attain corporate sustainability that gears toward zero triple bottom lines, sustainability ought to be all-inclusive. Therefore, further research should examine how corporate sustainability cuts across business functions from production, manufacturing, supply chains and distribution, marketing and selling, to finance and management control (Haugh & Talwar, 2005).

REFERENCES

Alesi, P. (2008). Building enterprise-wide resilience by integrating business continuity capability into day-to-day business culture and technology. *Journal of Business Continuity & Emergency Planning*, 2(3), 214–220. PMID:21339108

Aras, G., & Crowther, D. (2008). Evaluating sustainability: A need for standards. *Issues In Social & Environmental Accounting*, 2(1), 19–35. doi:10.22164/isea.v2i1.23

Armstrong, S. J., & Sadler-Smith, E. (2008). Learning on demand at your own pace, in rapid bite-sized chunks: The future shape of management development? *Academy of Management Learning & Education*, 7(4), 571–586. doi:10.5465/amle.2008.35882197

Bansal, P. (2002). The corporate challenges of sustainable development. *The Academy of Management Perspectives, 21*(1), 122–131. doi:10.5465/ame.2002.7173572

Bauer, R., Eichholtz, P., Kok, N., & Quigley, J. M. (2011). How green is your property portfolio? The global real estate sustainability benchmark. *Rotman International Journal of Pension Management, 4*(1), 34–43.

Baumgartner, R. J., & Ebner, D. (2010). Corporate sustainability strategies: Sustainability profiles and maturity levels. *Sustainable Development (Bradford), 18*(2), 76–89. doi:10.1002d.447

Beerannavar, C. (2020). The Role of Corporations in Achieving Ecological Sustainability: Evaluating the Environmental Performance of Corporations. In *Interdisciplinary Approaches to Public Policy and Sustainability*. (pp. 228-247). IGI Global Publisher. https://www.igi-global.com/book/interdisciplinary-approaches-public-policy-sustainability/227626

Bergström, A., & Källström, E. (2019). Leadership behavior and communication in organizational change. *Leadership and Organization Development Journal, 40*(4), 545–559. doi:10.1108/LODJ-06-2018-0203

Bolton, M. (2022). A system leverage points approach to governance for sustainable development. *Sustainability Science, 17*(6), 2427–2457. doi:10.100711625-022-01188-x

Carrera, L. (2022). Corporate social responsibility. A strategy for social and territorial sustainability. *Int J Corporate Soc Responsibility, 7*(7), 7. Advance online publication. doi:10.118640991-022-00074-0

Cheung, A. W. (2011). Do stock investors value corporate sustainability? Evidence from an event study. *Journal of Business Ethics, 99*(2), 145–165. doi:10.100710551-010-0646-3

Clarkson, M. B. (1995). A stakeholder framework for analyzing and evaluating corporate social performance. *Academy of Management Review, 20*(1), 92–117. doi:10.2307/258888

Correia, M. (2019). Sustainability: An Overview of the Triple Bottom Line and Sustainability Implementation. *International Journal of Strategic Engineering, 2*(1), 29–38. doi:10.4018/IJoSE.2019010103

Deep, S., & Sussman, L. (1995). *Smart moves for people in charge: 130 checklists to help you be a better leader*. Perseus Books Group.

Duca, I., & Gherghina, R. (2019). CSR Initiatives: An Opportunity for the Business Environment. In *Corporate Social Responsibility: Concepts, Methodologies, Tools, and Applications* (pp. 127-142). IGI Global Publisher. https://www.igi-global.com/book/corporate-social-responsibility/197763

Ekins, P. (2010). Eco-innovation for environmental sustainability: Concepts, progress, and policies. *International Economics and Economic Policy, 7*(2/3), 267–290. doi:10.100710368-010-0162-z

Elkington, J. (1994). Towards the sustainable corporation: Win–win–win business strategies for sustainable development. *California Management Review, 36*(2), 90–100. doi:10.2307/41165746

Esteves, A., & Barclay, M. (2011). New approaches to evaluating the performance of corporate-community partnerships: A case study from the minerals sector. *Journal of Business Ethics, 103*(2), 189–202. doi:10.100710551-011-0860-7

Fairfield, K. D., Harmon, J., & Benson, S. (2010). Influences on the organizational implementation of sustainability: An integrative model. *Academy of Management Annual Meeting Proceedings*, 1-6. 10.5465/ambpp.2010.54497867

Freeman, E. (1984). *Strategic management: A stakeholder approach*. Pitman.

Gardner, T. (2017). *The value of sustainability to an organization*. Retrieved from https://hbr.org/2017/09/the-value-of-sustainability-to-an-organization

Garvin, D. A. (2000). *Learning in action: A guide to putting the learning organization to work*. Harvard Business School Press.

Global Reporting Initiative. (2000). *Sustainability reporting guidelines (Amsterdam)*. U.S. Government Printing Office.

Gond, J. P., Lahiri, S., Reddy, P. R., & Suman, D. (2018). Sustainable strategies for competitive advantage: Role of corporate social responsibility (CSR). *International Journal of Business and Management*, *13*(3), 66–74.

Goodland, R., & Daly, H. (1996). Environmental sustainability: Universal and non-negotiable. *Ecological Applications, 6*(4), 1002-1017. Retrieved from http://links.jstor.org/sici=1051-0761%28199611%

Grenz, S. (2017). *Sustainability measurement: A toolkit for assessing corporate sustainability performance*. Routledge.

Grubbs-West, L. (2005). *Lessons in loyalty*. Cornerstone Leadership Institute.

Halme, M., Anttonen, M., Hrauda, G., & Kortman, J. (2006). Sustainability evaluation of European household services. *Journal of Cleaner Production, 14*(17), 1529–1540. doi:10.1016/j.jclepro.2006.01.021

Halme, M., & Väänänen, K. (2018). Benefits of sustainability: An empirical assessment of the impact of sustainability on firm performance. *Business Strategy and the Environment, 27*(3), 658–670.

Hammami, A., Hammami, S., Naffrechoux, E., & Lecompte, J. F. (2017). Measuring corporate sustainability performance: State of the art and directions for future research. *Sustainability, 9*(11), 2091.

Hart, S. L. (2005). *Capitalism at the crossroads: The unlimited business opportunities in solving the world's most difficult problems*. Wharton School Publishing.

Harvey, J. (2006). Understanding goal alignment models. *Chief Learning Officer, 5*(5), 24–63.

Haugh, H. M., & Talwar, A. (2010). How do corporations embed sustainability across the organization? *Academy of Management Learning & Education, 9*(3), 384–396. doi:10.5465/amle.9.3.zqr384

Hay, R. (2010). The relevance of ecocentrism, personal development, and transformational leadership to sustainability and identity. *Sustainable Development (Bradford), 18*(3), 163–171. doi:10.1002d.456

Henderson, C. (2015). *How sustainability improves brand loyalty*. Retrieved from https://www.forbes.com/sites/christopherhenderson/2015/07/15/how-sustainability-improves-brand-loyalty/#1f2f7c3d3d14

Hill, R. P., Ainscough, T., Shank, T., & Manullang, D. (2007). Corporate social responsibility and socially responsible investing: A global perspective. *Journal of Business Ethics, 70*(2), 165–174. doi:10.100710551-006-9103-8

Hoffmann, V. (2018). How to reduce your company's carbon emissions. *Harvard Business Review.*

Holm, M. (2018). 5 strategies to reduce water use in your business. *Harvard Business Review.*

Jaros, S. (2010). Commitment to organizational change: A critical review. *Journal of Change Management, 10*(1), 79–108. doi:10.1080/14697010903549457

Jo, H., & Harjoto, M. (2011). Corporate governance and firm value: The impact of corporate social responsibility. *Journal of Business Ethics, 103*(3), 351–383. doi:10.100710551-011-0869-y

Kemfert, C. (2014). Energy efficiency and renewable energy – key to sustainability. *DIW Economic Bulletin*, (4), 24-29.

Kemp, R. (2018). How to Measure Corporate Sustainability. *Harvard Business Review.* Retrieved from https://hbr.org/2018/06/how-to-measure-corporate-sustainability

Ketola, T. (2009, December 11). Five leaps to corporate sustainability through a corporate responsibility portfolio matrix. *Corporate Social Responsibility and Environmental Management, 17*(6), 320–336. doi:10.1002/csr.219

King, M. C. (2008, April). What sustainability should mean. *Challenge, 51*(2), 27–39. doi:10.2753/0577-5132510204

Kondrasuk, J., Bailey, D., & Sheeks, M. (2005). Leadership in the 21st century: Understanding global terrorism. *Employee Responsibilities and Rights Journal, 17*(4), 263–279. doi:10.100710672-005-9054-8

Kruse, C., & Lundbergh, S. (2010). The governance of corporate sustainability. *Rotman International Journal of Pension Management, 3*(2), 46–51.

Kubala, J. (2018). *5 ways to make your company more sustainable.* Retrieved from https://www.businessnewsdaily.com/7813-sustainable-business-practices.html

Kuhn, T. R. (2010). The advancement of technology. *Electric Perspectives, 35*(3), 6.

Laine, M. (2010). Towards sustaining the status quo: Business talk of sustainability in Finnish corporate disclosures 1987-2005. *European Accounting Review, 19*(2), 247–274. doi:10.1080/09638180903136258

Lash, J., & Wellington, F. (2007). Competitive advantage on a warming climate. *Harvard Business Review, 85*(3), 94–103. PMID:17348173

Linnenluecke, M. K., Russell, S. V., & Griffiths, A. (2007). Subcultures and sustainability practices: The impact on understanding corporate sustainability. *Business Strategy and the Environment, 18*(7), 432–452. doi:10.1002/bse.609

Liu, G. (2018). 5 ways to reduce toxic chemicals in your business. *Harvard Business Review.*

Lüdeke-Freund, F. (2019). Business and sustainability: Understanding the scope and nature of the field. *Journal of Cleaner Production, 208*, 463–479.

Makipere, K., & Yip, G. S. (2008). Sustainable leadership. *Business Strategy Review*, *19*(1), 64–67. doi:10.1111/j.1467-8616.2008.00521.x

Méndez, P. F., Clement, F., Palau-Salvador, G., Diaz-Delgado, R., & Villamayor-Tomas, S. (2022). Understanding the governance of sustainability pathways: Hydraulic megaprojects, social–ecological traps, and power in networks of action situations. *Sustainability Science*. Advance online publication. doi:10.100711625-022-01258-0

Meznar, M. B., Carroll, A. B., & Chrisman, J. J. (1991). Social responsibility and strategic management: Towards an enterprise strategy classification. *Business and Professional Ethics Journal, 10*(1), 47-67. Retrieved from http://www.pdcnet.org

Michelon, G. (2011). Sustainability disclosure and reputation: A comparative study. *Corporate Reputation Review*, *14*(2), 79–96. doi:10.1057/crr.2011.10

Mirchandani, D., & Ikerd, J. (2008). Building and maintaining sustainable organizations. *Organizational Management Journal*, *5*(1), 40–51. doi:10.1057/omj.2008.6

Morrisson-Saunders, A., & Therivel, R. (2006). Sustainability integration and assessment. *Journal of Environmental Assessment Policy and Management*, *8*(3), 281–298. doi:10.1142/S1464333206002529

Nidumolu, R., Prahalad, C. K., & Rangaswami, M. R. (2009). Why sustainability is now the key driver of innovation. *Harvard Business Review*, *87*(9), 56–64.

O'Rourke, D. (2004). *Opportunities and obstacles for corporate social responsibility reporting in developing countries*. World Bank Group.

Parra, C. M. (2008). Quality of life market. *Journal of Human Development*, *9*(2), 207–227. doi:10.1080/14649880802078751

Porter, M., & Kramer, R. M. (2006). Strategy and society: The link between competitive advantage and corporate social responsibility. *Harvard Business Review*, *82*(12), 78–92. PMID:17183795

Prakash, O. (2020). History, Policy Making, and Sustainability. In *Interdisciplinary Approaches to Public Policy and Sustainability* (pp. 1-17). IGI Global Publisher. https://www.igi-global.com/book/interdisciplinary-approaches-public-policy-sustainability/227626

Rutting, L., Vervoort, J., & Mees, H. (2022). Disruptive seeds: a scenario approach to explore power shifts in sustainability transformations. In *Sustainability Science*. Springer. https://link.springer.com/article/10.1007/s11625-022-01251-7#citeas

Saravanan, S. (2018). 6 tips to reduce waste output in your business. *Harvard Business Review*.

Senge, P. M. (1990). *The fifth discipline: The art and practice of the learning organization*. Doubleday Currency.

Shin, D. H. (2006). VOLP: A debate over information service or telephone application in US. *Telematics and Informatics*, *23*(2), 57–73. doi:10.1016/j.tele.2005.04.001

Spaur, M. (2008). Smart meter infrastructure is keystone of smart grid. *Natural Gas & Electricity*, *25*(3), 23–27.

Strategy: Create and implement the best strategy for your business. (2005). Harvard Business School Publishing Corporation.

Tanzil, D., & Beloff, B. R. (2006). Assessing impacts: Overview on sustainability indicators and metrics. *Environmental Quality Management, 15*(4), 41–56. doi:10.1002/tqem.20101

Watson, M. (2011). Doing well by doing good: Ray C. Anderson as evangelist for corporate sustainability. *Business Communication Quarterly, 74*(1), 63–67. doi:10.1177/1080569910395567

World Business Council for Sustainable Development. (2020). *What is sustainability?* Retrieved from https://www.wbcsd.org/Topics/Sustainability/What-is-Sustainability

Chapter 10
Analysis of User Authentication Experience in Electronic Banking

Chinyere Igwe
ICT University, Cameroon

Foluso Ayeni
ⓘD https://orcid.org/0000-0003-0989-7056
Metro State University, USA

Victor Mbarika
East Carolina University, USA

ABSTRACT

The evolution of technology has brought about a transformation in the delivery and utilization of financial services. Companies have leveraged technology to create value in the digital realm, presenting innovative opportunities that prioritize customer-centric approaches. Despite the numerous benefits of e-banking, the user experience during authentication has had an impact on its adoption in developing economies. Hence, this study investigated the authentication experience of users in the realm of e-banking using Nigeria as a case study. The research used five constructs of UTAUT2 to analyze this phenomenon.

INTRODUCTION

Electronic banking brought about innovative opportunities that focused more on customers. It is a payment system that allows customers to conduct financial transactions over the Internet (Carranza et al., 2021). It offers valued services that created competitive benefits such as checking account balances, paying bills, transfers, and text message notifications (Mostafa, 2020; Khan, 2017). E-banking enabled banking activities to be performed without being physically present in the bank (Malaquias et al., 2019). It is flexible and can be accessed 24/7 from any location (Worku et al., 2016). It is cost-saving and helps customers to compare products and services among banks (Asiyanbi, & Ishola, 2018). E-banking has

DOI: 10.4018/979-8-3693-1630-6.ch010

added value to several businesses (Baabdullah et al., 2019). Internet services provided opportunities for interaction with companies that allow consumers to participate in the development and improvement of products and services (Carranza et al., 2021). Mobile devices and desktops are the tools customers use in e-banking to pay for products and services (Zhang et al., 2018).

Studies showed that previous works considered issues that influenced the adoption of e-banking (Mostafa, 2020). The adoption rate of e-banking is still low despite its numerous benefits (Shankar et al., 2020). Many consumers are not using e-banking facilities as they are not at ease with the authentication methods used by banks. They lack confidence in its safety and privacy. Authentication is a method that is used to identify and grant users access to transactions. It is used to ensure that access is granted to the right person (Djellali B. et al., 2014). This process is important because of the prevalence of fraud and criminal activities experienced in e-banking (Asiyanbi, & Ishola, 2018). Authentication involves a two-step process: Identification and Verification.

Bank authentication guarantees the confidentiality of delicate banking information, helps to reduce fraud, and identity theft crimes, and increases customers' trust in the institution (Orji, 2019; Sepczuk, & Kotulski, 2018; Balfe et al., 2015). However, users' or customers' experience during the authentication process is that it does not allow for a long time before the expiration of the code generated (Gerea, & Herskovic, 2022; Reese et al., 2019). For example, in the One-Time-Password (OTP) authentication method the time allow for user authentication in this process is small, which delays the success of the code provided. Sometimes the code needs to be changed severally before authentication is allowed or becomes successful. This makes the whole process of code authentication tedious, boring, tiring, and cumbersome, as well as complex for users and customers alike (Fujimoto, & Omote, 2022). The generated one-time password (authentication code) is sent to the phone number or email of the requesting user for immediate use. Since the authentication code provided often needs to be changed at any transaction due to possible login failure, customers find it inconvenience and discomforting, therefore, want to discontinue the use of the technology (Okpa et al., 2022; Inder et al., 2022). Hence, most bank customers find the process of code authentication unacceptable and lose confidence in the entire process due to login failure, and prefer transacting across the counter. Login failure occurs in the event of the expiration of the 30-second count for the user to supply the authentication code (Chen et al., 2022; Wang et al., 2022; Reese et al. 2019). The authentication process is repeated to generate the authentication code needed to complete the login session (Ogbanufe, & Kim, 2018).

User experience is a reaction that developed from the use of a product, service, or structure (ISO 9241-210, International standard). It includes feelings about the use of a specific device, the experience of practical elements like its usefulness, simplicity of use, and the effectiveness of the system. User experience is important because it indicates how a person feels when interacting with a system and it produces some definite result. It is important in justifying the money spent on technologies as the world is becoming Internet-centric and e-enabled.

The advent of technological payment systems made banking activities easier for customers (Kelvin, 2012). The flexibility experienced in e-banking brought about the increase in payment, collection, and development of different applications that helps users to conduct financial activities 24/7 from any location. The effectiveness of e-banking products and services made user experience important. E-banking made buying and selling easy and to be conducted from any location through the Internet (Tijani & Ilugbemi, 2015). It brought about efficiency in service delivery and as well offered value-added services and made it easy for customers to compare products and services among banks and obtain information from banks' websites about their products, services, and policies (Vaciago et al, 2016). This is unlike the conventional banking system where people visit the bank physically, queue, and spent a lot of time carrying out banking transactions.

The development of digital banking in Nigeria dates back to 1986 during the Structural adjustment program (SAP) era. During this period, banks in Nigeria were deregulated and electronic banking customers' taste in service delivery changed posing serious challenges to the banks. The banks provided Automated Teller Machines (ATMs) to ease the constraints which caused more customer satisfaction and increased revenue for banks. In Nigeria today, bank customers can use their smart devices to conduct banking activities from any location (Okoye et al., 2019).

Nigeria is in West Africa and has different climates. Her outstanding feature is her people. She has a population of over 200 million people. The country is blessed with abundant natural resources. Notably among the resources are large deposits of oil and gas. Her Telecom Market is growing fasts across the country (Nigeria Telecommunication Market Report, 2020-2025). Nigeria has about 136,203,231 internet users in 2020 (Telecoms Data, Q1, 2020). According to Nigerian Communications Commission (NCC), internet users in Nigeria have hit 91 million (NCC, 2017). In 2020, 66 percent of the Nigerian population is linked to the internet. The ICT sector alone contributed 18.44%t to Nigeria's Gross Domestic Product (GDP) in 2022 (National Bureau of Statistics 2022).

Electronic banking platforms are exposed to various abuses and intrusions which made banks focus on securing e-banking applications. Hence a user is required to be identified through authentication before he/she is allowed to access his/her account. In 2003, the Central Bank of Nigeria (CBN) issued Electronic Banking procedures for electronic payment channels. The service providers were mandated to follow the guidelines when assessing or executing electronic transactions. Though the guidelines are centered on risk management and Internet channels, it is also relevant to all electronic banking activities. The guideline approved the two-factor authentication process as the minimum requirement to access services involving customers' information and movement of funds. It further stipulates that the authentication methods used by any bank must be appropriate to the risks involved. The risk assessments carried out showed that single-factor authentication is insufficient hence the need for multifactor authentication to lessen the risks (CBN, 2018).

Electronic banking is a web-based application accessed through the Internet. This makes bank customers a target for criminal-minded individuals. Most Banks in Nigeria use e-banking transaction processing for their operation. The biggest task in e-processing is the authentication of consumers, security, and the fast-developing cyber-crime. This characterizes a task, not only for the customers who use such services but also for the establishments offering the services (Dixit, 2016). It has numerous benefits like nurturing customer loyalty, help in expanding the output of businesses and lessening human errors etc. In spite of all the benefits, the adoption rate is still low (Shankar et al., 2020). Many consumers are not at ease with the authentication methods used by banks. They lack confidence in the safety and privacy the methods. The authentications methods use in Nigerian e-banking system are Passwords, PINs, Tokens and One-Time passwords. In the study case of Nigeria, most bank customers are uninterested due to the process of authentication with the OTP (One-Time-Password) code (Tarhini et al., 2015). The One-Time-Password most times, is not easily accessed due to network issues, poor knowledge of the user in accessing email to get the code sent. Each password generated is different and is used only once. The generated code expires within 30 seconds thereby forcing the customer to start the process all over again (Gerea, & Herskovic, 2022; Reese et al., 2019). Hence, most bank customers do not want to use online banking apps as they need to enter security codes many times due to constant login failure (Wang et al., 2020; Jibril et al., 2020). The complex safety measure implemented by banks exposes customers to the habit that might invalidate the safety procedures (French, 2012). User experience is dependent on consumers' expectations while interacting with a firm or organization (Sheng M.L. and Teo T. S. H., 2012).Hence value creation includes emotions, beliefs, preferences, and responses during and after using a service (Hsu C.-L, Chen M. –C.,2018). Therefore, security and privacy on e-banking platforms is a major problem to positive user experience as the security features affect the ease of use (Kim & Yi, 2015).

The study examined user authentication experience in e-banking in FCT Nigeria using five UTAUT2 variables of performance expectance, effort expectance, social influence, facilitating conditions and hedonic motivation as independent variables and one dependent variable (E-banking).

THEORETICAL REVIEW

The Unified theory of acceptance and use of technology (UTAUT2) theory was developed by Venkatesh et al., (2012). It was developed to understand factors that influence technology adoption from consumers' perspective. UTAUT2 theory has not been used to investigate user authentication experience in e-banking in Nigeria. Theory of Reasoned Action (TRA), Technology Acceptance Model (TAM), and Unified Theory of Acceptance and usage of Technology (UTAUT) are three research models established to describe the elements that influence the interest and usage of an information technology system. It is the second most popular theoretical model in understanding user behavior (Patil et al., 2017; Tarhini et al. 2016; Gupta and Arora 2019). It is used to predict consumer acceptance of Internet banking (Alalwan et al., 2018; Tarhini et al., 2016), to examine consumers' mobile payment acceptance (Patil et al., 2020). Scholars believed the new factors could upturn the borderlines. Venkatesh et al. (2003b) theorize that consumer decision-making on technology adoption varies across background. Hence, the need to investigate technology acceptance in a specific context. Venkatesh et al., (2012) recommended extending the model in different technological context hence the choice of the model. Based on this knowledge, the researcher adopted UTAUT2 theoretical model for the study and also, because of its high explanatory power.

In the study case of Nigeria, the bank customers that desire to use the technology of authentication became uninterested due to the difficulty of authentication with the OTP code (Tarhini et al., 2015). Most people in Nigeria currently are discouraged from using online banking apps because of the need to enter security codes many times due to constant login failure (Wang et al., 2020; Jibril et al., 2020). This problem has persisted because the e-banking service providers have not taken time to identify user's experience in authentication, low education of customers on the basics of internet security, absence of a legal framework, and lack of enabling infrastructure. The researcher is not a way of any government regulation on user authentication experience in e-banking in Nigeria.

The purpose of the study is to establish user authentication experience and e-banking adoption in FCT Nigeria and proffer a solution that is simple, fast and seamless to use. To accomplish this, the following research questions were asked:

i.   What is the impact of performance expectancy on e-banking adoption in FCT Nigeria?
ii.   What is the effect of effort expectancy on e-banking adoption in FCT Nigeria?
iii. What impact does social influence have on e-banking adoption in FCT Nigeria?
iv.   What is the impact of facilitating conditions on e-banking adoption in FCT Nigeria?
v.   What influence does hedonic motivation have on e-banking adoption in FCT Nigeria?

The research objectives are to:

i. Examine the influence of performance expectancy on e-banking adoption of selected bank customers in FCT.

ii) Assess the extent to which effort expectancy affects e-banking adoption of selected bank customers in FCT.

iii) Evaluate the impact of social influence on e-banking adoption of selected bank customers in FCT.

iv) Evaluate the impact of facilitating conditions on e-banking adoption of selected bank customers in FCT.

v). Assess the influence of hedonic motivation on e-banking adoption of selected bank customers in FCT.

The study contributed to the existing body of knowledge, will assist banks in implement authentication methods that enhanced positive user authentication experience. The study has provided banks with Policy formulation and goals settings decision-making that are advantageous to all and as well revealed users' challenge with the authentication methods. The outcome of the study is useful to researchers who wish to carry out further investigation on the phenomenon of study. Other developing countries have learned from Nigeria's experience. An improved authentication method help users' confidence in e-banking, increase patronage, customer retention, and increase banks' liquidity ratio thus making loans available to medium and small-scale businesses. And encourage the adoption of a cashless policy as all these will have a positive effect on the economy.

Study Implication to Customers

Technology usage brings about easiness and reliability" and "customer service" affects customer satisfaction positively and significantly. In fact provision of proper customer service shapes the consumer behavior patterns significantly. Our result also conforms to this fact as "customer service" dimension has relatively higher impact on customer satisfaction than "technology usage easiness and reliability". We also found that customer satisfaction has a positive and significant impact on customer loyalty (Shirshendu Ganguli Sanjit Kumar Roy, (2011). Sulin Ba and Wayne C. Johansson (2008) also identified that perceived ease of use influences customer satisfaction through service value.

Study Implication to Banks

ICT help banks improve the efficiency and effectiveness of services offered to customers and enhances business processes, managerial decision-making, and workgroup collaborations, which strengthens their competitive positions in rapidly changing and emerging economies. It is also important to note that ICT enables banks to meet regulatory requirement.

Banks are to select a based on customers' acceptance, confidence, risk level, deployment and maintenance cost, simplify user login experience, implement block chain-based multi-factor authentication, offer detailed communication on steps taken to secure personal data and protect user, identify and document customers experience with authentication to determine customers perspective on authentication process at each interaction and its effect on overall customers satisfaction.

Study Implication to the Government

ICT development is meant to contribute to increased and faster communications and exchanges between and across functional units, more efficient service delivery, and increase citizen participation in governance (i.e. e-voting, e-participation, e-tax filing and e-registration). Additionally, "governments have become aware that it is not enough to introduce ICT to their existing internal processes, but to use ICT to assist the re-engineering process in government organizations concurrently with some other e-government initiatives" (Obi, 2009, p. 173). Such initiatives include the development of novel administrative features that enables a more effective alignment of vertical and horizontal organizational structures in ways that improves transparency, accountability, and timely responsiveness to citizen needs.

Theoretical Implications

The use of UTAUT2 theory provided a comprehensive framework that explained user authentication experience in e-banking in FCT Nigeria. The structures of user authentication experience in e-banking are consistent with the existing theoretical debates and literature. Hence ICT infrastructure usage is a combination of availability, accessibility, user-ability

The study was limited to One-Time-Password (OTP) authentication process authentication process.

Literature Review

Systematic review was considered appropriate research method to achieve the aim of this research. A total of 135 articles were reviewed. These articles were screened for availability as full articles and downloaded. The reviewed was done using key words like e-banking acceptance, e-banking usage, e-banking challenges and prospects, authentication methods used in e-banking, user authentication experience etc. The works of literature reviewed on user authentication experience in e-banking are from databases like Elsevier, IEEE, Science Direct, Springer Link, Journals from the African Journal of Computing and ICT, American Journal of computer technology and Application, Google Scholar, Emerald, EBSCOHOST and chartered institute of Bankers of Nigeria. The study used only papers from peer-reviewed journals. Articles reviewed was based on the following: region, theories applied, constructs, methodology, data analysis tools used, future research and study context. Literature review was guided by the research objectives. The review guided the development of research questions, hypotheses, development/refinement of the conceptual framework and getting the operational definitions of the constructs.

Europa, MasterCard and Visa (EMV) have been commercially accessible for the past 14 years and are currently being widely implemented despite the limited amount of research that has been published on its security. In 1999, Van & Jelmol, assessed the suitability of EMV for Internet payments and noted the difficulty of not being able to tell if the Verify command was ever executed because it is not verified. This was a problem because it prevented them from knowing whether or not EMV was suitable for Internet payments. They recommended a payment system that would be based on the Internet and indicated that the ARQC should only be generated if the Verify command had been completed without error. However, their study did not take into account the fact that the result of PIN verification is contained in the IAD, nor did it take into account the possibility that a man-in-the-middle may alter the Verify message during a point-of-sale transaction.

Kafle, V. P., et al., (2016), proposed an ID-based conversation that uses Internet Protocol (IP) address to find hosts, route traffic, and identify hosts and services and Veeraraghavan, P. et al., (2016) suggested shrewd image-based authentication. Islam, S. H., et al., (2014) proposed remote user authentications with a key settlement scheme while Fujimoto, S., & Omote, K. (2022) Proposal smart contract-based security token management system. Reese, Ken, et al. (2019), studied "A usability study of five two-factor authentication methods" and Ogbanufe, O., & Kim, D. J. (2018) Compared fingerprint-based biometrics authentication versus traditional authentication methods for e-payment

The risk assessments carried out by Central bank of Nigeria in 2018, showed that single-factor authentication is insufficient hence the need for multifactor authentication to lessen the risks (CBN, 2018).

The literature reviewed shows that users' experience with authentication might harm e-banking. As customer experience in e-banking starts from access to services and it is the customer's feeling after use of product or service. User experience is continuous process valued by the user in each transaction and a decent experience will affect banks value and its services recommended to others. In implementing bank authentication, speed and convenience for the user should be considered. Users want their security to be guaranteed and data protected. Therefore, authentication methods should be designed in such a way that it is easy to access and secured. They must build trust in their choice of technology and ensure that it is simple, fast and seamless to use.

Several scholars have researched the issues that affect adoption, and technology usage but the researcher is not aware of any study on user authentication experience in FCT Nigeria. The identified gaps in literatures reviewed are (i) minimum time required for user's authentication which is 30 seconds (ii) several times of login attempts that may be required and (iii) login failure during the process of users' authentication and (iv) password provision.

Research Methodology

The research method was quantitative (Williams, (2011) approach and the ontology of the research is objectivism (Polit and Beck 2012:13) while the epistemology is positivisms (Wasik, 2016). The axiology of the research is of no bias (Li, 2016). The research approach used is deductive (Bryman & Bell, 2015) and conclusive research design was adopted. The target population is bank customers in FCT Nigeria. The sampling technique is purposeful (Palinkas, L.A et al., 2015) and the sapling size is 396 calculated using Cochran's (1977) formula. Data collection was primary source (Martins et al.., 2018) and structured questionnaire designed in Likert 5 point scale format was used for data collection (Rabin, 2009). Data was analyzed using SPSS23 and AMOS23 statistical software. The validity and reliability of the data was tested using the cronbach alpha (Drost, 2012). For ethical consideration-informed consent and voluntary participation, anonymity and confidentiality of participants and respect for intellectual property were observed.

Results

Data was collection was through questionnaire, and the responses were analyzed using SPSS23 and Amos23 statistics software. The survey questionnaire was shared through proportional sampling to selected banks customers. A total of four hundred [400] questionnaires was distributed and three hundred and eighty-eight [388] responses were received. A total of thirteen [13] questionnaires were not returned, and after cleaning and filtering, 388 responses were considered valid for analysis.

The sample comprised of 191 males, 190 females, with age ranging from 21 to 65 years. The majority of the participants (34.3%) were aged between 36 and above, while 21.1% were below 25 years, and 24.5% were above 30 years. The participants were from different educational backgrounds, with 70.9% having a higher education. The measurement criteria was based on ordinal and binary data. The parameters include: Gender = [Male & Female], Location = [Amac, Bwari, Kuje, Gwagwalada, Kwali & Abaji], Age range = [21-25, 26-30, 31-35, 36 and above, Occupation = [Employed, Unemployed and Self-employed] and Qualification= [FLC, SSCE, Degree, Master, and PhD]. There was no occurrence of missing data in the analysis of participants' background information as all the three hundred and eighty-eight [388] respondents answered the questions.

The six area councils in FCT Nigeria were sampled and this include Bwari, Kuje, Gwagwalada, Kwali and Abaji. The sample representation for each community was consistently distributed as follows: Amac 112[28.9%], Bwari 51[13.1%], and Kuje 59 [15.%], Gwagwalada 68[17.6%], Kwali 47 [12.1%] and Abaji 51(13.%]. This distribution was decided to ensure appropriate and unbiased representations of the sample. The six area councils share similar socio-cultural orientations and experience similar economic realities. The gender representation consists of one hundred and ninety-one [191] male and one hundred and ninety [190] females representing a sample of three hundred and eighty-eight [388] respondents. The inclusion of gender perspectives enhanced the validity and reliability of the study.

The employment status was measured using four levels of ordinal data: Employed, Self-employed, Unemployed and Retired. The academic level is summed up by the intellectual status of the respondents, which is based on school-level achievement involving learning and thinking. The academic level was measured using five levels of ordinal data: the first school level (FLC), Senior Secondary Certificate Examination, Degree, Masters, and PhD. This helps avoid the case of bias and invalid samples.

The missing data identified were treated using appropriate statistical techniques. The Little's MCAR test was ran to confirm that data missing in the datasheet were missing completely at random and not being influenced by any deliberate intention. The Chi-Square [X2] =660.990, Degree of Freedom = .586, and μ = Sig. =0.17> 0.05] suggesting insignificant statistical evidence to reject the null hypothesis. And conclude that missing data as observed in the dataset was completely at random.

Each specific independent construct was measured to ascertain the consistent or inconsistent measurement of variables using exploratory factor analysis (EFA). The Kaiser-Meyer-Olkin Measure of Sampling Adequacy of the study is .885 > 0.5 showing that the sample size is adequate. Bartlett's Test of Sphericity - Chi-square (X2) = 2908.239 with; Degree of Freedom (DF) = 153 and sig. = 0.00 < 0.01 indicating the existence of at least one [1] significant correlation amongst observed items. Principal Component Analysis was used for extraction and Verimax for rotation method with Kaiser Normalization converged in five iterations. Smaller coefficients of less than 0.4 with Eigenvalue greater than one [Eigen Value ≥ 1] was rejected. A total of seventeen [17] indicators were retained and eleven [11] was rejected. Factor loadings for retained indicators did not cross-load and have coefficient factor loading of at least 0.5. Indicators with factor loading < 0.5 and cross-loaded were rejected. There is no factor with a coefficient of < 0.5 and no cross-loading amongst loaded components. A total of thirty-32 [32] indicators was used to measure the independent latent constructs. Based on the dimension reduction analysis, a total of seventeen [17] indicators were retained and eleven [11] were rejected.

Five indicators were used to measure the latent construct e-banking. The Kaiser-Meyer-Olkin Measure of Sampling Adequacy was 0.669 greater than 0.5 [KMO = .696 > 0.5] indicating an appropriate sample size for the analysis. Bartlett's Test of Sphericity - Chi-square [X 2] = 236.448; Degree of Freedom [DF] = 6 and P-value = 0.00 < 0.01 indicating at least one [1] significant correlation amongst the items. There was no cross-loading or the coefficient of factor loadings being less than 0.5.

Construct validity was tested using Exploratory Factor Analysis [EFA] and Confirmatory Factor Analysis [CFA] to assess the degree operationalization of construct measured the theoretical constructs. The reliability was tested using Cronbach's alpha coefficient. Factors whose alpha scores were below .7 thresholds were dropped. Additional data cleaning was conducted for the independent latent construct using confirmatory factor analysis. CFA model did not meet the model fitness specifications and not all factor loadings for the respective indicators were appropriate. The minimum requirement for factor loadings is 0.5. Based on this limitation, CFA was inconclusive as the model did not fit the data. Some further downsizing was conducted by removing inappropriate data.

Outlier test was conducted using the box plot methods. The process repeated until no outlier was identified. Normality test was carried out using histograms, normality plots, ShapiroWilk Test, and the skewness, and kurtosis test. The assumption of multivariate normality based on skewness and the kurtosis was observed as both coefficients lie between -3 and 3 for all variables in the model. If the P-value of the Shapiro-Wilk test is > .05, the data is normally distributed and if P-value < .05 then the data significantly deviates from a normal distribution. All the latent constructs for this study were normally distributed. P-P plots were used by plotting the two cumulative distribution functions against each other. The P-P plot and Q-Q plot formed a straight line along with a normal distribution. As shown in Figure 1, the normality was tested using histogram which provided a visual assessment and pattern of outliers.

Figure 1. Testing for normality using histograms Peat and Barton

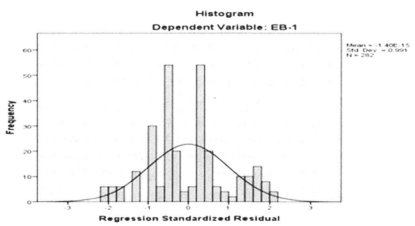

The multicollinearity was assessed using the tolerance value (TV) and the variance inflation factor (VIF). The result showed VIF < 10 and Tolerance > 0.1. There is no existence of multicollinearity for all the dependent latent constructs measuring e-banking. The Homogeneity of Variance was carried out to ensure the dependent variable demonstrates equal levels of variance across independent variables. The Levene test was used to assess equal variance distribution. The result showed a non-significant Levene statistic [P>.05]. The test of homoscedasticity was also based on a scatter plot of the residuals.

The result shows a random displacement of scores, no clustering or systematic pattern. The assumption of equal variance was met for all the dependent latent constructs measuring e-banking.

The structural model developed was examined using regression weights and path coefficients explained by standardized estimates (β coefficients) to determine the extent the independent variables affects User authentication experience in E-banking.

CB-SEM

CMIN = 149.284, DF = 6, P = .000, CMIN/DF =24.881, GFI =.890, IFI = .496, TLI = -.301, CFI = .480, RMSEA = .248

Table 1. Regression weights

Dependent Variable	Effects	Latent Construct	Estimate	S.E	C.R	P	Label
E-banking	<---	Performance expectancy	.092	.070	1.309	.191	PE1
E-banking	<---	Effort expectancy	.123	'065	1.874	.061	EE1
E-banking	<---	Social influence	0.30	.058	.530	.596	SI1
E-banking	<---	Facilitating conditions	.016	.048	.326	.774	FC4
E-banking	<---	Hedonic motivation	.154	.050	3.086	.002	HM1

Source: Field data

Table 2. Standardized regression weights

Endogenous Variable	Effects	Exogenous Variable	Estimate
E-banking	<---	Performance expectancy	.072
E-banking	<---	Effort expectancy	.104
E-banking	<---	Social influence	.027
E-banking	<---	Facilitating conditions	.017
E-banking	<---	Hedonic motivation	.154

Source: Field data

Table 3. Harmonized test of hypotheses

Hypotheses	P-Value at 95% (CI)	Decision / Conclusion
H1: There is no significant relationship between performance expectancy and e-banking adoption in FCT Nigeria.	[H0: μ= .191 > 0.05, β = - .072, CI =95%]. positive statistically	We fail to reject the null hypothesis and conclude that there is statistical evidence to suggest that Performance expectancy [PE] has a positive effect on e-banking adoption in FCT Nigeria
H2: There is no significant relationship between effort expectancy and e-banking adoption in FCT Nigeria.	[H0: μ= 0.61 > 0.05, β = -.104, CI =95%]. positive statistically	We fail to reject the null hypothesis and conclude that there is statistical evidence to suggest that Effort expectancy [EE] has a positive effect on e-banking adoption in FCT Nigeria
H3: There is no significant relationship between social influence and e-banking adoption in FCT Nigeria.	[H0: μ= .596 > 0.05, β = .027, CI =95%]. positive statistically	We fail to reject the null hypothesis and conclude that there is statistical evidence to suggest that Social influence [SI] has a positive effect on e-banking adoption in FCT Nigeria
H4: There is no significant relationship between Facilitating conditions and e-banking adoption in FCT Nigeria.	[H0: μ= .774 > 0.05, β = - .017, CI =95%]. positive statistically	We fail to reject the null hypothesis and conclude that there is statistical evidence to suggest that Facilitating conditions [FC] has a positive effect on e-banking in FCT Nigeria
H5: There is no significant relationship between hedonic motivation and e-banking adoption in FCT Nigeria.	H0: μ= 0.002 < 0.005, β = . 154, CI =95%]. CI =95%]. Negative statistically significant	Reject the null hypothesis and conclude that there is significant statistical evidence to suggest that Hedonic motivation [HM] has a positive significant effect on e-banking adoption in FCT Nigeria

The study used five variables of UTAUT2 to investigated user authentication experience in e-banking in FCT Nigeria. The variables are: Performance expectancy, Effort expectancy, Social influence, Facilitating conditions and Hedonic motivation as the independent variables that predict e-banking the dependent construct. The outcome of the study is argued through extensive literature, theoretical concepts, and empirical expositions. The discussions includes analysis of the distributional characteristics of background information, missing data analysis, dimension reduction, test of parametric assumptions, and test of hypotheses using Covariance-Based Structural Equation Model.

The findings include descriptive and hypothetic deductive statistics. The descriptive statistics are: location, gender, age, occupation and qualification. While hypothetic deductive statistics discussed results the relationships between independent and dependent variable. The study is focused on the Federal Capital Territory (FCT) Nigeria which comprises six area council: Abuja Municipal Area Council(AMAC), Kuje, Bwari, Abaji, Kwali and Gwagwalada. A comparable distribution was decided to ensure appropriate and unbiased representations of the sample. The sample representation for each community was consistently distributed: AMAC - 112[28.9%], Gwagwalada-68[17.6%], Kuje 59[15%], Abaji 51[13%] and Kwali 47[12.1%]. All the area councils share similar socio-cultural orientations and experience similar economic realities. The involvements of all the area councils in FCT representing diverse opinions on the issue of discussion, shows that the sample is well represented.

DISCUSSION

The gender representation consists of one hundred and ninety-one [191] males and one hundred and ninety [190] females. The inclusion of gender perspectives views enhanced validity and reliability of the study. Employment status was measured using four [4] levels of nominal data of employed, self-employed, unemployed, and retired. The specifications of being employed or not being employed can influence whether to bank or not. The opinion expressed in this study is the representative of participants' view. The academic level of participants were measured using levels of nominal data - first school level, SSCE, Degree, Master and PhD level. The participants were from different educational backgrounds, with 70.9% having a higher education. Therefore, it could be concluded that the opinion expressed in this study is representative of participants. Also, the age of participants were measured using non-categorical data: [21-25] [26-30], [31-35] and [36 and above]. The overall sample represented a population of young and older adults with experience on e-banking.

The five variables of UTAUT2 used in examining users authentication experience in FCT Nigeria are performance expectancy, effort expectancy, social influence, facilitating conditions and hedonic motivation.

Performance Expectancy (PE)

It was hypothesis; there is no significant relationship between performance expectancy and e-banking adoption in FCT Nigeria. The findings revealed statistical evidence that suggests Performance expectancy has positive effect on e-banking adoption by customers in FCT Nigeria. Studies carried out by scholars confirmed that the PE is a significant element of technology acceptance. This is be true in the case of smart watch acceptance (Hong et al., 2017; Wu et al., 2016; Hsiao, 2017;Choi and Kim, 2016; Chuah et al., 2016; Mani and Chouk, 2017). Consumers will accept a technology when perceived convenient in performing their task.

Effort Expectancy (EE)

Hence it was hypothesis; there is no significant relationship between effort expectancy and e-banking adoption in FCT Nigeria. Findings revealed that there is statistical evidence to suggest that effort expectancy has a positive effect on e-banking adoption in FCT Nigeria.

Studies carried out revealed that effort expectance play a role in technology acceptance (Chuah et al., 2016). This is seen in smart watch adoption in Malaysian and South Korean. It is believed that if technology is easy to use more people will be eager to use it.

Social Influence (SI)

It was hypothesis; there is no significant relationship between social influence and e-banking adoption in FCT Nigeria. Findings revealed that there is statistical evidence to suggest that effort expectancy has a positive effect on e-banking adoption in FCT Nigeria. SI is a determinant element in information systems research. It is found to have link with smart watch use (Wu et al., 2016; Hsiao, 2017).

Facilitating Condition (FC)

It was hypothesis that there is no significant relationship between facilitating conditions and e-banking adoption in FCT Nigeria. Findings revealed that there is statistical evidence to suggest that facilitating conditions has a positive effect on e-banking adoption in FCT Nigeria. It is believed that the accessibility of resources will enrich the preference of consumers. Facilitating conditions played a significant part on wearable device adoption (Spagnolli et al., 2014).

Hedonic Motivation (HM)

Hence it was hypothesis; there is no significant relationship between hedonic motivation and e-banking adoption in FCT Nigeria. Findings revealed that there is statistical evidence to suggest that hedonic motivation has a significant positive effect on e-banking adoption in FCT Nigeria. It was found to influence the smart watch adoption in South Korean users (Wu et al., 2016; Hong et al., 2017). It is believed that an individual will be interested in using a technology when they are absorbed. Therefore individuals, who find using a technology pleasurable, will to adopt it. It is hypothesized:

CONCLUSION

Performance Expectancy, Effort Expectancy, Social Influence and facilitating conditions has positive effects on e-banking adoption in FCT Nigeria while hedonic motivation has a positively significant effect on e-banking in FCT Nigeria. The analysis shows that majority of e-banking customers in FCT Nigeria find the services useful, but believe there is still room for improvement as they want the providers of e-banking services to implement more authentication methods that is fast, simple and seamless to use.

REFERENCES

Abdullah, M. (2019). Consumer use of mobile banking (M-Banking) in Saudi Arabia: Towards an integrated model. *International Journal of Information Management, 44*(February), 38–52. doi:10.1016/j.ijinfomgt.2018.09.002

Adisu, Z. (2018). *E-Banking Service Practices And Its Challenges On Trade Activities In Selected Commercial Banks (In Case Of Debre Berhan)* [Doctoral Dissertation].

Adrian, T. (2021). *BigTech in financial services.* Academic Press.

Afshan, & Sharif, A. (2016, May). Acceptance of mobile banking framework in Pakistan. *Telematics and Informatics, 33*(2), 370–387. doi:10.1016/j.tele.2015.09.005

Akinola Kayode, E. (2017). Internet Banking In Nigeria: Authentication Methods, Weaknesses and Security Strength. *American Journal of Engineering Research, 6*(9), 226-231.

Alalwan. (2017). Social Media in Marketing: A Review and Analysis of the Existing Literature. *Telematics and Informatics, 34*(7). doi:10.1016/j.tele.2017.05.008

Alvi, M. H. (2016). *A Manual for Selecting Sampling Techniques in Research*. https://mpra.ub.uni-muenchen.de/70218/

Apuke, O. D. (2016). Social and Traditional Mainstream Media of Communication: Synergy and Variance Perspective. *Journal of New Media and Mass Communication, 53*, 83–86. www.iiste.org

Asiyanbi, H., & Ishola, A. (2018). E-banking services impact and customer satisfaction in selected bank branches in Ibadan metropolis, Oyo state, Nigeria. *Accounting, 4*(4), 153–160. doi:10.5267/j.ac.2018.3.001

Basilaia, G., & Kvavadze, D. (2020). Transition to Online Education in Schools during a SARS-CoV-2 Coronavirus (COVID-19) Pandemic in Georgia. *Pedagogical Research, 5*(4), em0060. Advance online publication. doi:10.29333/pr/7937

Carranza, R., Díaz, E., Sánchez-Camacho, C., & Martín-Consuegra, D. (2021). e-Banking adoption: An opportunity for customer value co-creation. *Frontiers in Psychology, 11*, 621248. doi:10.3389/fpsyg.2020.621248 PMID:33519647

CBN. (2019). *Regulation on electronic payments and collection for public and private sectors in Nigeria*. CBN.

Chen & Lin. (2019). Understanding the effect of social media marketing activities: The mediation of social identification, perceived value, and satisfaction. *Journal Technological Forecasting and Social Change, 140*, 22-32.

Chen, F., Xiao, Z., Xiang, T., Fan, J., & Truong, H. L. (2022). A full lifecycle authentication scheme for large-scale smart IoT applications. *IEEE Transactions on Dependable and Secure Computing*, 1. doi:10.1109/TDSC.2022.3178115

Choi, J. R., & Kim, S. (2016). Is the smart watch an IT product or a fashion product? A study on factors affecting the intention to use smart watches. *Computers in Human Behavior, 63*, 777–786. doi:10.1016/j.chb.2016.06.007

Chuah, Rauschnabel, P. A., Krey, N., Nguyen, B., Ramayah, T., & Lade, S. (2016). Wearable technologies: The role of usefulness and visibility in smart watch adoption. *Computers in Human Behavior, 65*, 276–284. doi:10.1016/j.chb.2016.07.047

Dagnachew, A. (2021). *Electronic Banking Service Practice and Challenges On Trade Activities (In Case Of Debre Berhan)* [Doctoral dissertation].

Fermor, P. (2022). *Customer experience: key pillars for continuous improvement*. https://International-bankers.com/Technology/customerexperience-key-pillar-for-continuous-improvement

Fujimoto, S., & Omote, K. (2022, August). Proposal of a smart contract-based security token management system. In *2022 IEEE International Conference on Blockchain (Blockchain)* (pp. 419-426). IEEE. 10.1109/Blockchain55522.2022.00065

Gerea, C., & Herskovic, V. (2022). Transitioning from multichannel to Omnichannel customer experience in service-based companies: Challenges and coping strategies. *Journal of Theoretical and Applied Electronic Commerce Research, 17*(2), 394–413. doi:10.3390/jtaer17020021

Gope, P., & Hwang, T. (2016). A Realistic Lightweight Anonymous Authentication Protocol for Securing Real-Time Application Data Access in Wireless Sensor Networks. *IEEE Transactions on Industrial Electronics, 63*(11).

Gupta, K., & Arora, N. (2019). Investigating consumer intention to accept mobile payment systems through unified theory of acceptance model: An Indian perspective November 2019. *South Asian Journal of Business Studies*. doi:10.1108/SAJBS-03-2019-0037

Haac. (2017, March). The IceCube Neutrino Observatory: Instrumentation and online systems. *Journal of Instrumentation : An IOP and SISSA Journal, 12*.

Inder, S., Sood, K., & Grima, S. (2022). Antecedents of behavioral intention to adopt Internet banking using structural equation modeling. *Journal of Risk and Financial Management, 15*(4), 157. doi:10.3390/jrfm15040157

ISO 9241 is a multi-part standard from the International Organization for Standardization (ISO) covering ergonomics of human-computer interaction.

Jolly, V. (2016). The Influence of Internet Banking on the Efficiency and Cost Savings for Banks' Customers. *International Journal of Social Sciences and Management, 3*(3), 163–170. doi:10.3126/ijssm.v3i3.15257

Kafle Ved, P. (2016). Internet of things standardization in ITU and prospective networking technologies. *IEEE Communications Magazine, 54*(9), 43–49. doi:10.1109/MCOM.2016.7565271

Kayode, Ehiwe, & Olawale. (2016). *Secured Models for Online Bank Vulnerabilities in Nigeria*. https://www.semanticscholar.org/paper/Secured-Models-for-Online-Bank-Vulnerabilities-in-Kayode- Ehiwe/c7c9d6c3487003bd7bc791a72985978d53ef6d10.SemanticScholar

Khan, H. F. (2017). E-banking: Benefits and issues. *American Research Journal of Business and Management, 3*(1), 1–7.

Kim, K., & Shin, D.-H. (2015). An acceptance model for smart watches: Implications for the adoption of future wearable technology. *Internet Research, 25*(4), 527–541. Advance online publication. doi:10.1108/IntR-05-2014-0126

Kumar, S., Xiao, J. J., Pattnaik, D., Lim, W. M., & Rasul, T. (2022). Past, present and future of bank marketing: A bibliometric analysis of International Journal of Bank Marketing (1983–2020). *International Journal of Bank Marketing, 40*(2), 341–383. doi:10.1108/IJBM-07-2021-0351

Malinka, K., Hujňák, O., Hanáček, P., & Hellebrandt, L. (2022). E-Banking Security Study—10 Years Later. *IEEE Access : Practical Innovations, Open Solutions, 10*, 16681–16699. doi:10.1109/ACCESS.2022.3149475

Mani & & Chou. (2017). Drivers of consumers' resistance to smart products. *Journal of Marketing Management, 33*(1-2).

Mostafa, S.G. (2020). Transformational Leadership, Information Technology, Knowledge management, firm performance: How are they linked? *The Journal of Value-Based Leadership, 13*(2).

National Bureau of Statistics. (2020). *Telecoms Data: Active Voice and Internet per State, Porting and Tariff Information*. Author.

Ogbanufe, O., & Kim, D. J. (2018). Comparing fingerprint-based biometrics authentication versus traditional authentication methods for e-payment. *Decision Support Systems*, *106*, 1–14. doi:10.1016/j.dss.2017.11.003

Okoye. (2019). Customer service delivery in the Nigerian banking sector through engineering and technology-based channels. *International Journal of Civil Engineering and Technology*, *10*(1), 2156–2169.

Okpa, J. T., Ajah, B. O., Nzeakor, O. F., Eshiotse, E., & Abang, T. A. (2022). Business e-mail compromise scam, cyber victimization, and economic sustainability of corporate organizations in Nigeria. *Security Journal*, 1–23.

Olowookere. (2021). *Nigerian Banks' e-banking Income Drops 27.3% Despite high Transactions*. Academic Press.

Orji, U. J. (2019). Protecting Consumers from Cybercrime in the Banking and Financial Sector: An Analysis of the Legal Response in Nigeria. *Tilburg Law Review, 24*(1).

Partala, T., & Saari, T. (2015). Understanding the most influential user experiences in successful and unsuccessful technology adoptions. *Computers in Human Behavior*, *53*, 381–395. doi:10.1016/j.chb.2015.07.012

Patil, P. P., Dwivedi, Y. K., & Rana, N. P. (2017). Digital Payments Adoption: An Analysis of Literature. In *Conference on e-Business, e-Services and e-Society* (pp. 61-70). Springer.

Reese, K., & ... 2019). A usability study of five two-factor authentication methods. *Proceedings of the Fifteenth Symposium on Usable Privacy and Security*.

Rodrigo, Malaquiasa, & Hwangb. (2019). Mobile banking use: A comparative study with Brazilian and U.S. participants. *International Journal of Information Management*. www.elsevier.com/locate/ijinfomgt

Rovetta, A., & Bhagavathula, A.S. (2020). COVID-19-Related Web Search Behaviors and infodemic Attitudes in Italy: Infodemiological Study. *JMIR Public Health Surveill, 6*(2) doi: :32338613PM-CID:7202310 doi:10.2196/19374PMID

Sepczuk, M., & Kotulski, Z. (2018). A new risk-based authentication management model oriented on user's experience. *Computers & Security*, *73*, 17–33. doi:10.1016/j.cose.2017.10.002

Sepehri, A. (2019). An application of DEMATEL for transaction authentication in online banking. *International Journal of Data and Network Science, 3*(2), 71-76. doi:10.5267/j.ijdns.2019.1.002

Shankar, A., & Jebarajakirthy, C. (2019). The influence of e-banking service quality on customer loyalty: A moderated mediation approach. *International Journal of Bank Marketing*, *37*(1), 1119–1142. Advance online publication. doi:10.1108/IJBM-03-2018-0063

Singh, I. & Srivastava, R.K. (2020). Understanding the intention to use mobile banking by existing online banking customers: an empirical study. *Journal of Financial Services Marketing, 3*, 86-96.

Soderberg, G., Bechara, M. M., Bossu, W., Che, M. N. X., Davidovic, S., Kiff, M. J., ... Yoshinaga, A. (2022). *Behind the scenes of central bank digital currency: Emerging trends, insights, and policy lessons*. Academic Press.

Sutton, J., & Austin, Z. (2015, May-June). Qualitative Research: Data Collection, Analysis, and Management. *The Canadian Journal of Hospital Pharmacy*, *68*(3), 226–231. doi:10.4212/cjhp.v68i3.1456 PMID:26157184

Tarhini, El-Masri, Ali, & Serrano. (2016). Extending the UTAUT model to understand the customers' acceptance and use of internet banking in Lebanon: A structural equation modeling approach. *Information Technology & People*.

Tijani, J. A., & Ilugbemi, A. O. (2015). Electronic Payment Channels in the Nigeria Banking Sector and Its Impacts on National Development. *Asian Economic and Financial Review*, *5*(3), 521–531. doi:10.18488/journal.aefr/2015.5.3/102.3.521.531

Veeraraghavan. (2016, September 10). A hybrid computational strategy to address WGS variant analysis in >5000 samples. *BMC Bioinformatics*, *17*(1), 361. doi:10.118612859-016-1211-6 PMID:27612449

Venkatesh. (2003). User Acceptance of Information Technology: Toward a Unified View. *MIS Quarterly, 27*(3), 425-478.

Venkatesh. (2012). Consumer Acceptance and Use of Information Technology: Extending the Unified Theory of Acceptance and Use of Technology. *MIS Quarterly, 36*(1), 157-178.

Wang, V., Nnaji, H., & Jung, J. (2020). Internet banking in Nigeria: Cyber security breaches, practices and capability. *International Journal of Law, Crime and Justice*, *62*, 100415. doi:10.1016/j.ijlcj.2020.100415

Wang, W., Huang, H., Yin, Z., Gadekallu, T. R., Alazab, M., & Su, C. (2022). Smart contract token-based privacy-preserving access control system for industrial Internet of Things. *Digital Communications and Networks*.

Worku, G., Tilahun, A., & Tafa, M. A. (2016). The impact of electronic banking on customers' satisfaction in Ethiopian banking industry (The Case of Customers of Dashen and Wogagen Banks in Gondar City). *Journal of Business & Financial Affairs*, *5*(2), 1–18.

Wu. (2019). *Behavior Regularized Offline Reinforcement Learning*. doi:https://doi.org/10.48550/arXiv.1911.11361

Chapter 11

An Analysis of How Cognitive Cities Better Address Sustainability and Equity Concerns in Society as Compared to Smart Cities

Kevin Richardson

https://orcid.org/0009-0002-3212-8669

Edward Waters University, USA

ABSTRACT

More than half the population today lives in urban areas. The UN predicts with 80% confidence that the global population will get to between 9.6 billion and 12.3 billion people within the 21st century. Population increase leads to more people in the city. More people in the city translates to new challenges that need addressing. When addressing the new challenges, cities evolve by improving the efficiency of services. Eventually, cities change in both structure and composition. In helping show how the cities have changed, the authors utilized the industrial revolution theory which occurred in stages from the first industrial revolution to Industry 5.0. Just like the industrial revolution, cities evolve in stages with the latter stage using the success of the former stage as building blocks. Smart cities which are characterized by progressive city plans and state-of-the-art infrastructure act as a building block for cognitive cities which are characterized by the ability to have connectivity, and common data architecture for people to share and drive innovation.

DOI: 10.4018/979-8-3693-1630-6.ch011

INTRODUCTION

The 21st century is an era of daunting challenges including but not limited to population growth, climate change, urban densification, poverty, and inequality (Lomborg, 2020). According to the United Nations, for instance, the population will continue growing throughout the 21st century (Webb & Buratini, 2018). The UN predicts with 80% confidence that the global population will get to between 9.6 billion and 12.3 billion people within the 21st century (Webb & Buratini, 2018). The United Nations posit that population increase can exacerbate the challenge of ensuring sustainable and inclusive development in the future (Wilmoth et al., 2022). The beauty of society is that it never lacks challenges and therefore, people are always busy trying solve these problems (Norton, 2022). Norton (2022) notes that the ugly part of the society is that solutions to problems are not applied equitably. A section of the society benefits at the expense of others. An example of a solution created to solve society challenges is government (Gourevitch & Rousseau, 2018). Governments exist through a social contract where people delegate their sovereign rights to the government (Besley, 2020). The government is expected to conduct its business in accordance to the social contract and observing the rights of each individual (Besley, 2020). The government acting as a solution to societal challenges creates institutions that are meant to serve the people. In these institutions, bias decision making lead to unequal service delivery in society (Battaglio et al., 2019). Racism is also heavily embedded in these institutions, a testament of the unsustainability of institutionalism (Johnson, 2020).

The concept of smart cities was engineered to help solve some of the societal challenges facing the world today (Orlowski & Romanowska, 2019). Smart cities according to IBM is a city that utilizes interconnected information and communication that is made available in optimizing the limited resources at its disposal (Okai et al., 2018). Smart cities are characterized by infrastructural development that revolves around technology (Kasznar et al., 2021). An important concept of smart cities is the implementation of industry 5.0 (Sharma et al., 2020). Industry 5.0 involves the addition of a human touch to technological collaboration (Xu et al., 2021). Smart cities have, for instance, through electric vehicles helped promote sustainability in society (). As part of solutions to the societal challenges, the concept of cognitive cities has been created. Cognitive cities according to Professor Tadhg O'Donovan, Deputy Vice-Principal, Academic Leadership and the Head of the School of Engineering and Physical Sciences at Heriot-Watt University Dubai is the next phase of smart cities (Dcunha, 2022). According to Dcunha (2022), cognitive cities can be viewed as smart cities on steroids. While smart cities incorporate the use of data, the main concern is on how the data is used and not on how much data is utilized (LEAPandInnovate, 2022). Smart cities utilize 5% of available data while cognitive utilize over 95% of available data (LEAPandInnovate, 2022). Cognitive cities help solve the societal challenges through creating an environment that is highly efficient and technologically connected (TED Institute, 2014). Such an environment is able to predict demand and offer innovative and sustainable solutions (Haldorai et al., 2019). For instance, the electric vehicle as envisioned by smart cities solved some aspects in society and created new challenges. Communities dominated by people of color have, for instance, been turned to charging deserts (Zhou et al., 2022). The lack of charging stations means that people from these communities cannot enjoy the benefits associated with electric vehicles (Kuiper et al., 2022). This inequality is part of the problems that the society seeks to solve. Through cognitive cities, investors are able to predict the demand in a given area and provide the needed support-infrastructure creating a win-win situation for investors and the community (Oleksyk et al., 2020).

Problem Statement

The challenges of lack of sustainability and equity in society today are to a large extent caused by bias decision making (Knittel et al., 2022). The finite pool of worry hypothesis, a behavioral bias, for instance, during hard times such as war or economic crisis forces people to stop thinking about climate change and focus on how to survive past these crises (Botzen et al., 2021). Implicit bias has continued to perpetuate racism in the country as evidenced in the Amy Cooper case (Davies, 2020). On seeing Christian Cooper, Amy Cooper threatened to call police saying, "I'm going to tell them there's an African American man threatening my life" (Vera & Ly, 2020). Black people have been reported to the police for mundane reasons with some ending up dead (Shrikan & Sambaraju, 2021). The solution to the lack of sustainability and equity in society therefore must effectively address the biases that have been created and established over time. The general problem is identifying the best placed model to effectively help address consequences of the bias decisions humans make. The specific problem involves the understanding of how cognitive cities are better placed in addressing the biases that cause lack of sustainability and equity in society compared to smart cities. Overall, the primary focus will be to investigate the myriad of opportunities that cognitive cities offer that smart cities lack and also investigate any positives that smart cities have over cognitive cities in addressing sustainability and equity in society.

Purpose Statement

The purpose of this qualitative study is to explore the effectiveness of cognitive cities versus smart cities in addressing modern challenges in society which are largely caused by the bias decisions people make. This study aims at establishing the better model between smart cities and cognitive cities. This study targets people of color specifically the black community seeing that most of the bias decisions in society end up hurting this community more. The independent variables in this study are cognitive cities and smart cities. The dependent variables include sustainability and equity while the independent variables are smart cities and cognitive cities.

Theoretical Framework

The shift from smart cities to cognitive cities is in itself a revolution that can only be compared to the industrial revolution. The industrial revolution theory describes a scenario characterized by a changed from an agrarian and handicraft society to a society dominated by industries and machine manufacturing (Xu et al., 2018). Industrial revolution did not occur overnight. The changes occurred gradual with one change paving way to another (Chowdhury & Murzi, 2020). The shift from common cities to smart cities and now to cognitive cities takes similar shape to industrial revolution. Different aspects of cities have been changing leading to the emergence of new cities that are more effective. The shift to smart cities entailed heavily investing and relying on technology to build state-of-the-art infrastructure (Amini et al., 2019). Smart cities also saw the growth of confident and progressive city plans (Pozdniakova, 2018). The success of smart cities heavily relies on the relationship between public and private entities (Clement et al., 2022). The private entities depend on the public entities to share data which is then used to improve the society (Broccardo et al., 2019). The shift to cognitive cities signifies a paradigm shift in the usage of data. While smart cities heavily rely on public entities to supply data, cognitive cities rely on the whole city to provide data and use data (Zhu et al., 2022). Data flows from citizens to city management, citizen to citizen, and citizen to system (Schmid, 2018; Mitchell & Krulicky, 2021). With such an elaborative mechanism of data sharing, cognitive cities promote the art of learning continuously thus changing the society. The large sharing of data in cognitive cities help eliminate bias decision making as people and institutions act from a point of knowledge.

The second theory to help in determining the better model between smart cities and cognitive cities in addressing sustainability and equity issues in society is cognitive bias theory. In 1970s, Amos Tversky and Daniel Kahneman coined the term cognitive bias as they described the systemic and flawed judgement and decision making (Park, 2020). Korteling and Toet (2022) define cognitive bias as, "Cognitive biases are systematic cognitive dispositions or inclinations in human thinking and reasoning that often do not comply with the tenets of logic, probability reasoning, and plausibility." How people act, therefore, is informed by these biases. This theory will help in linking different social injustices to systemic and flawed decisions made by both individuals and by institutions.

LITERATURE REVIEW

Cognitive and Smart City Concepts

According to Machin and Solanas (2018), the cognitive concept in cognitive city refers to the creation of efficiency in a complex environment based on past and present data that helps in making predictions about the city. Cognitive city differentiates itself from other forms of urban settlement in the sense that it involves continuous learning and adapting "its behavior based on past experiences and is able to sense, understand and respond to changes in its environment" (Machin & Solanas, 2018). In addition, the cognitive concept allows the monitoring of reactions besides drawing additional lessons from the same. The fact that a cognitive city allows continuous interaction between humans and technology sets it apart and in elevation compared to a smart city. Considering the current constant changes in the environment, a cognitive city approach is appropriate for timely adaptability to changes due to its power of predictability thus enabling it to tackle issues on sustainability and equity (TED Institute, 2014). The cognitive concept applies in diverse sectors of an urban setting including electricity and water systems, the monitoring of seismic activities, environmental monitoring, transportation, surveillance, healthcare, and law enforcement among several others.

One of the ways in which a cognitive city ensures sustainability and equity is visible in the transportation sector. Through an intelligence-embedded transport system, a cognitive city is able to solve transportation problems such as traffic congestion and road accidents that are common in urban areas (Dimitrakopoulos & Demestichas, 2010). A cognitive city's transport system relies on data from different players thus making it extremely connected to the happenings of the city (Mostashari et al., 2011). The efficient use of data helps enables this model to establish sustainable traffic control (Zhao et al., 2022). Traffic congestion in urban areas is a source of lack of sustainability and equity as it is associated with economic loss amongst other problems. The Intelligent Transport System (ITS) of a cognitive city is associated with a reduction in the number of accidents besides ensuring that transportation is efficient through electronic sensors, conveyance of data and intelligent control (Malygin et al., 2018). The ITS utilizes technology such as Big Data, the Internet of Things (IoT), and cloud computing. These technologies facilitate prompt detection of flaws in the transport system and, as a result, a timely response (Miz & Hahanov, 2014). Since ITS relies on big data, it is not biased, thus promoting sustainability and equity. Moreover, the intelligent transport system of a cognitive city offers data continuously which is then used cognitively to improve the system over time.

Urban settings requires strategic management of resources to ensure that any form of bias that exists is withdrawn and to embrace sustainability and equity. A smart city may lack in terms of attaining strategic management but with the application of cognitive technologies, sustainability, efficiency and equity are attained. Cognitive technologies are applied in big data to elevate the concept of a smart city to a cognitive city. Research reveals that to solve the various problems that are associated with urban management of smart cities the application of cognitive technologies is instrumental (Giela, 2022). Cognitive technologies in strategic urban management facilitate the consideration of the human mind and how it operates. Strategic management is, thus automated and improved leading to the betterment of life in urban settings and creating sustainability and equity. Just like major business decisions utilize cognitive technologies such as deep learning to decipher decisions, strategic management in the same context works similarly (Giela, 2022). Algorithms in big data helps in minimizing human flaws that could be associated with strategic management of a cognitive city (Ahuja & Khosla, 2019). The algorithms also assist in establishing solutions to existing human problems at a local level, thus, contributing to human intelligence involved in strategic management. Therefore, cognitive technologies which advance a smart city into a cognitive city only complement human intelligence but do not replace it (Tayeb et al., 2018). If human intelligence fails to liaise with artificial intelligence in a cognitive city setting then the whole concept of cognition fails (Herath & Mittal, 2022).

In a basic smart city that is void of the cognitive aspect data is still generated from the technological processes and patterns that exist. However, only 5% of the data is utilized thus about 95% of data is not utilized leading to a failure of extracting meaningful information contained in the big data sets (TED Institute, 2014). The data that is drawn is dynamic in nature which calls for highly adaptable mechanisms for operability. Unlabeled data is especially more vulnerable to waste which calls for closer monitoring. Smart cities lack in terms of the interaction of technology with humanity, the failure to use data for improvement of previous state, failure to embrace continual learning and in consequence, adaptability to changes that occur (Mohammadi & Al-Fuqaha, 2018).

Bias Decision Making

As of July 2018, the U.S. population according to data from the U.S. Census Bureau comprised of 61% white (non-Hispanic or Latino), 18% Hispanic, 13% black, and 5.7$ Asian (Walker & Nauman, 2017). In an equitable industry, these percentages would be reflected in the workforce. The financial service industry in the United States, for instance, does not mirror the ethnical and racial structure of the nation (Davies, 2020). In the asset management industry, the executive committee level comprises of 88.6% White, 5.4% Asian, 3.0% Black, 2.4% Hispanic, and 0.6% being people with two or more races (Walker & Nauman, 2017). According to Walker and Nauman (2017), the managing directors position in the same industry comprises of 86.4% White, 6.9 Asian, 3.7 Hispanic, 1.5% Black, 0.7% people belonging to two or more races, 0.7% people from other races, and 0.1% representing American Indians or Alaska Natives. According to Davies (2020), a study done on 14 consulting firms which together represented $1.4 trillion in asset under management, Blacks and Latinos were under represented as they comprised 5.7% and 5% respectively. Davies (2020) mentions that under representation is not the only cause of inequality. In the financial industry, there is a problem in gauging the competence of racially diverse groups (Lyons-Padilla et al., 2019). The industry is also highly characterized by bias regarding the performance level of minorities. Lack of information has made players in the industry believe that hiring diverse firms would compromise investment returns (Lyons-Padilla et al., 2019).

According to Davies (2020), under representation and other forms of inequality is not unique to the financial industry. It has spread to other industries and affects public institutions as well. This lack of equity and sustainability is caused by bias decision making. The bias decisions end up becoming policy and practice a factor that reinforces and perpetuate bias (Davies, 2020). The cyclic nature of bias decisions cause lack of equity and sustainability in society. For instance, the cyclic nature of bias decisions create and allow institutional racism to thrive (Derous & Ryan, 2019). Because bias decisions dictate policy and practice in an institution, it is common for people to bias even without knowing.

BEHAVIORAL BIASES

Simplification

It is common for people to make decisions after making considerations of the probability of a disaster occurring or after gauging the potential consequences (Li & Wei, 2019). This happens at the expense of making rational assessment of the risks involved and their distribution (Botzen et al., 2021). When dealing with situations such as climate change, risks such as natural disasters have a low probability of occurring. This leads to people assuming that the risks are zero. The consequence of the bias decisions people make on climate change continues to affect the society.

Availability

According to Clarke et al. (2020), one of the main reasons why President Donald Trump lost his re-election is because of how he handled the pandemic. The pandemic started in China and took close to two months before reaching the U.S (Baker, 2020). Clarke et al. (2020) notes that had President Trump acted quickly before the pandemic reached the country, many lives would have been saved. President trump only acted after the covid-19 had reached the country. This is what Botzen et al., (2021) refers to availability bias. Not everyone feels or understands discrimination. As a result, not everyone will understand the extent to which racism affects people. It is only after people experience how discrimination in any form that one starts to understand how minority groups and women are affected.

Finite pool of worry

According to Sisco et al. (2020) people have a limited pool of emotional resources. This is to mean that people tend to emotionally connect to one issue at a time. When one an individual focuses so much on one issue, concern about other issues plummets (Sisco et al., 2020). After the death of George Floyd, the issue on police brutality became the highlight for many media stations as well as the social media (Mocatta & Hawley, 2020). As the pandemic continued ravaging people's lives, concern on the police brutality gradually issue declined. Climate change concerns seem to rise when there are ravaging floods or other natural calamities. When other major events come up such as economic recession, people forget about climate change concerns (Botzen et al., 2021).

Myopia

According to Kasdan (2018), people have "the tendency to focus on the short-term rather than the long-term implications of our actions." Botzen et al. (2018) terms this as myopia bias. Myopia bias influence people to act on urgent near-term risks. When looking at pollution, people only consider what they see and forget about what they see will lead to in the future. Air pollution may not seem serious as people continue living without disturbance, However, in the future, the same people risk contracting respiratory diseases.

Herding

In the Amy Cooper case, many people came out to castigate her actions (Ransom, 2020). Many people could not believe that such things happen. Had the Amy Cooper case not been highlighted on national, international, and social media, very few people would come out acknowledging the existence of racism. The tendency of individual choices being influenced by the behavior of others is referred to as the herding bias (Ding & Li, 2019). Herding bias explains why during covid-19, people agreed to observe the measures put in place to curb the spread of the virus (Botzen et al., 2018). People tend to follow what the masses believe in. Dealing with lack of sustainable development and equity in society can be achieved by triggering social norms which can stimulate action from the masses.

DISCUSSION

Today, more than half the population lives in urban areas (Kite, 2020). Kite projects that by 2050, 70% of total human population will be living in urban areas. Ten thousand years ago, living in urban areas was not common (Ritchie & Roser, 2018). It is not until humans learned how to grow food that semi-permanent houses were built (Kite, 2020). As people increasingly progressed technologically, urbanization started taking shape. The first cities had infrastructural challenges. The Roman Empire managed to solve some of these problems including the developments of roads (De Benedictis et al., 2022). Cities however, started taking the modern shape during the industrial revolution.

The industrial revolution occurred in intervals. The first industrial revolution was responsible for transforming the society from agricultural based to industrial based (Chowdhury & Murzi, 2020). This entailed the mechanization of processes. The second industrial revolution started the replacement of coal and introduced new forms of energy including electricity, gas, and oil (Mohajan, 2019). The third industrial revolution saw the introduction of nuclear energy in 1969 (Chowdhury & Murzi, 2020). The forth industrial revolution saw emphasis created on the use of renewable energy. The biggest development of the fourth revolution, however, was the acceleration of digital technology (Xu et al., 2018). Just like the industrial revolution, cities have evolved in stages. With each revolution, the society saw some of its challenges settled while others such as pollution exacerbated. Cities continue to evolve changing in structure and composition (Des Roches et al., 2021). As cities evolve, some challenges are solved while new ones are created. For instance, job opportunities are created but employment lacks similar to racial and ethical balance (Mohl, 2021). First organized settlement was a village and it started with semi-permanent structures when people discovered they could grow crops instead of hunting and gathering (Kite, 2020). Food surplus allowed the development of cities. Cities created opportunities and new challenges including overcrowding and lack of infrastructure. The Roman Empire solved some of these problems including creating a road network (De Benedictis et al., 2022). It is the industrial revolution, however, that accelerated the development of cities to what is common today.

Cities evolve as the needs of the society change. For instance, the vertical growth reduced congestion in cities and ensured cities do not extend horizontally to unmanageable sizes (Zambon et al., 2019). Nevertheless, cities continuously need to change so as to handle the demands of the society. The smart city model is characterized by heavy infrastructural growth. Infrastructure is seen as critical part in growing the economy as well as enhancing social and cultural urban development (Kasznar et al., 2021). Smart cities according to Amini et al. (2019) seek to create competitive environment through provision of needed support infrastructure. Smart cities, therefore, focuses on growth through utilizing new resources and creating new structures. Unlike smart cities, cognitive focuses on utilizing exhaustively whatever is available. This is made possible through the collection and utilization of data. Smart cities also do collect data from residents. However, smart cities are okay collecting 5% of available data and using it to improve safety and efficiency of public service (LEAPandInnovate, 2022). Cognitive cities, on the other hand, are more concerned with utilizing the available data exhaustively to improve the wellbeing and prosperity of the people. Cognitive cities utilize 95% of available data to solve societal problems wholesomely (LEAPandInnovate, 2022). In cognitive cities, data flows from citizen to the system and from the system to citizens. Data also flows from citizens to the city management and from the city management to citizens (Schmid, 2018). To enhance the flow of data, cognitive city also promotes the flow of data from citizen to citizen (Ranchordás, 2020). A major difference between cognitive city and smart city is that in smart cities, data is collected and utilized and it ends at that while in cognitive cities the whole city generates and consumes data helping the city to continuously learn and evolve as it continues to learn.

Many wrongs and injustice in society can be attributed to bias decisions. According to TED Institute (2014), cognitive cities help eliminate bias in society. This happens through sharing of information. Cognitive cities subject every decision to analysis of available data so as to come up with solutions that fits the society (Mohammadi & Al-Fuqaha, 2018). For example, smart cities promote vertical gardening as a way to reduce pollution and increase food production. Cognitive cities build on this and collect data from building owners, vertical farmers, consumers and other stakeholders (Schmid, 2018). The collected data helps know what types of crops can be planted in buildings, what crops are in demand in the market, what crops need to be grown, and the crops that do not grow well on building. With this information, cognitive cities promote sustainable development. Smart cities are known for their sharp focus on infrastructural technology (Amini et al., 2018). Smart cities boost of progressive city plans and state-of-the-art infrastructure. These development is a huge step. Nonetheless, it is not sustainable considering that cities continue to witness high population growth. The lack of considering the long-term changes is a form of myopia bias (Botzen et al., 2021). Decisions influenced by the myopia bias forces the cities to look for new solutions. Cognitive cities take into consideration the rate at which the city will grow before embarking on infrastructural development. Cognitive cities also involves the sharing of information between different stake holders thus it is easy for instance, to know when a particular road is busy and when the road is not busy (TED Institute, 2014). With such information, it becomes easy to direct traffic to the less busy roads thus reducing traffic jams without necessarily having to construct new roads. Cognitive cities promise to end inequality in society. This is based on the high level of data sharing and data analysis. In industries where minorities are underrepresented, cognitive cities through data analysis promises to change this as the management relying on cognitive technology will be advised to enhance ethnic and racial diversity at their organizations.

GAPS IN LITERATURE

Cognitive city builds on the success of smart cities (Finger & Portmann, 2016). Without smart cities, collecting information would still be a daunting task. For cognitive city to solve problems in society, it heavily relies on the available data from different disciplines and sectors. It is for this reason that research suggests that cognitive technology promises to end lack of sustainable development and lack of in society (Sangwan & Bhatia, 2020; Xu et al., 2021). There are so many ills in society including but not limited to climate change, mass incarcerations, racism, gun violence, corruption, illegal immigration, poverty, and unemployment. For these vices to occur, some decisions are made leading to the emergence or continuation of these challenges. Research has not addressed the decisions whether political, social, or economic that perpetuate these vices. More research needs to be done so that for each challenge, the bias decisions involved is known and ways to address them is identified.

CONCLUSION

The society is changing at a very fast rate thanks to technology. About 10,000 years ago, there never existed a city in the world. After the domestication of crops and animals, there was food surplus and villages started to erupt. Soon cities were made and they continued to evolve to up to what is common in contemporary society. As cities evolve, more people shift to these urban centers searching for better opportunities to improve their lives. Meanwhile, demand for services increase in cities due to the rapid population growth. Technology in smart cities has been at the forefront in helping the society deal with these challenges. Through infrastructural revamp and the incorporation of people through industry 5.0, urban centers have been redefined and solutions for challenges therein found. Cognitive cities build on the success of smart cities. Through data analysis and collaboration among citizens, private sector, and public institutions, cognitive technology is able to address the root course of a problem (Schmid, 2018). As a result, it is able to correct the biases that perpetuate different challenges in society including lack of sustainability and equity. Smart cities attempt to address lack of sustainability and equity in society but lack of utilization of available data often leads to the emergence of new challenges. Cognitive cities has the whole city generating and consuming data thus helping the city to continuously learn and evolve as it continues to learn.

REFERENCES

Ahuja, K., & Khosla, A. (Eds.). (2019). *Driving the Development, Management, and Sustainability of Cognitive Cities*. IGI Global. doi:10.4018/978-1-5225-8085-0

Amini, M. H., Arasteh, H., & Siano, P. (2019). Sustainable smart cities through the lens of complex interdependent infrastructures: panorama and state-of-the-art. In *Sustainable interdependent networks II* (pp. 45–68). Springer. doi:10.1007/978-3-319-98923-5_3

Baker, M. (2020, May 15). When did the Coronavirus arrive in the U.s.? Here's a review of the evidence. *The New York Times.* https://www.nytimes.com/2020/05/15/us/coronavirus-first-case-snohomish-antibodies.html

Battaglio, R. P. Jr, Belardinelli, P., Bellé, N., & Cantarelli, P. (2019). Behavioral public administration ad fontes: A synthesis of research on bounded rationality, cognitive biases, and nudging in public organizations. *Public Administration Review*, *79*(3), 304–320. doi:10.1111/puar.12994

Besley, T. (2020). State capacity, reciprocity, and the social contract. *Econometrica*, *88*(4), 1307–1335. doi:10.3982/ECTA16863

Botzen, W., Duijndam, S., & van Beukering, P. (2021). Lessons for climate policy from behavioral biases towards COVID-19 and climate change risks. *World Development*, *137*, 105214. doi:10.1016/j.worlddev.2020.105214 PMID:32994663

Broccardo, L., Culasso, F., & Mauro, S. G. (2019). Smart city governance: Exploring the institutional work of multiple actors towards collaboration. *International Journal of Public Sector Management*, *32*(4), 367–387. doi:10.1108/IJPSM-05-2018-0126

Chowdhury, T. M., & Murzi, H. (2020, June). The evolution of teamwork in the engineering workplace from the First Industrial Revolution to Industry 4.0: A literature review. *2020 ASEE Virtual Annual Conference Content Access.* 10.18260/1-2--35318

Clarke, H., Stewart, M. C., & Ho, K. (2021). Did Covid-19 Kill Trump Politically? The Pandemic and Voting in the 2020 Presidential Election. *Social Science Quarterly*, *102*(5), 2194–2209. doi:10.1111squ.12992 PMID:34226770

Clement, J., Manjon, M., & Crutzen, N. (2022). Factors for collaboration amongst smart city stakeholders: A local government perspective. *Government Information Quarterly*, *39*(4), 101746. doi:10.1016/j.giq.2022.101746

Davies, E. S. (2020, July 2). *Bias has consequences: Disrupting the cycle of everyday racism.* Beeck Center. https://beeckcenter.georgetown.edu/bias-has-consequences-disrupting-the-cycle-of-everyday-racism/

Dcunha, S. D. (2022, August 18). *What will a cognitive city look like? Are we ready for it? - Fast Company Middle East.* Fast Company Middle East. https://fastcompanyme.com/technology/what-will-a-cognitive-city-look-like-are-we-ready-for-it/

De Benedictis, L., Licio, V., & Pinna, A. (2022). *From the historical Roman road network to modern infrastructure in Italy.* arXiv preprint arXiv:2208.06675.

Derous, E., & Ryan, A. M. (2019). When your resume is (not) turning you down: Modelling ethnic bias in resume screening. *Human Resource Management Journal*, *29*(2), 113–130. doi:10.1111/1748-8583.12217

Des Roches, S., Brans, K. I., Lambert, M. R., Rivkin, L. R., Savage, A. M., Schell, C. J., Correa, C., De Meester, L., Diamond, S. E., Grimm, N. B., Harris, N. C., Govaert, L., Hendry, A. P., Johnson, M. T. J., Munshi-South, J., Palkovacs, E. P., Szulkin, M., Urban, M. C., Verrelli, B. C., & Alberti, M. (2021). Socio-eco-evolutionary dynamics in cities. *Evolutionary Applications, 14*(1), 248–267. doi:10.1111/eva.13065 PMID:33519968

Ding, A. W., & Li, S. (2019). Herding in the consumption and purchase of digital goods and moderators of the herding bias. *Journal of the Academy of Marketing Science, 47*(3), 460–478. doi:10.100711747-018-0619-0

Finger, M., & Portmann, E. (2016). What are cognitive cities? In *Towards Cognitive Cities* (pp. 1–11). Springer. doi:10.1007/978-3-319-33798-2_1

Giela, M. (2022). Cognitive Technologies in Smart City Services as the Future in Strategic Management of Cities. *Management Systems in Production Engineering, 30*(3), 276–281. doi:10.2478/mspe-2022-0035

Gourevitch, V., & Rousseau, J. J. (2018). *Rousseau: the Social Contract and other later political writings*. Cambridge University Press. doi:10.1017/9781316584606

Haldorai, A., Ramu, A., & Chow, C. O. (2019). Big data innovation for sustainable cognitive computing. *Mobile Networks and Applications, 24*(1), 221–223. doi:10.100711036-018-1198-5

Johnson, T. J. (2020). Intersection of bias, structural racism, and social determinants with health care inequities. *Pediatrics, 146*(2), e2020003657. doi:10.1542/peds.2020-003657 PMID:32690807

Kasdan, D. O. (2018). The ostrich paradox: why we underprepare for disasters. *Disaster Prevention and Management: An International Journal*.

Kasznar, A. P. P., Hammad, A. W., Najjar, M., Linhares Qualharini, E., Figueiredo, K., Soares, C. A. P., & Haddad, A. N. (2021). Multiple dimensions of smart cities' infrastructure: A review. *Buildings, 11*(2), 73. doi:10.3390/buildings11020073

Kite, V. (2020, February 28). *Urbanization and the evolution of cities across 10,000 years*. Academic Press.

Knittel, B., Coile, A., Zou, A., Saxena, S., Brenzel, L., Orobaton, N., Bartel, D., Williams, C. A., Kambarami, R., Tiwari, D. P., Husain, I., Sikipa, G., Achan, J., Ajiwohwodoma, J. O., Banerjee, B., & Kasungami, D. (2022). Critical barriers to sustainable capacity strengthening in global health: A systems perspective on development assistance. *Gates Open Research, 6*(116), 116. doi:10.12688/gatesopenres.13632.1 PMID:36415884

Kuiper, J. A., Wu, X., Zhou, Y., & Rood, M. A. (2022). Modeling Electric Vehicle Charging Station Siting Suitability with a Focus on Equity (No. ANL-22/33). Argonne National Lab.

Li, P., & Wei, C. (2019). An emergency decision-making method based on DS evidence theory for probabilistic linguistic term sets. *International Journal of Disaster Risk Reduction, 37*, 101178. doi:10.1016/j.ijdrr.2019.101178

Lomborg, B. (2020). Welfare in the 21st century: Increasing development, reducing inequality, the impact of climate change, and the cost of climate policies. *Technological Forecasting and Social Change, 156,* 119981. doi:10.1016/j.techfore.2020.119981

Lyons-Padilla, S., Markus, H. R., Monk, A., Radhakrishna, S., Shah, R., Dodson, N. A. D. IV, & Eberhardt, J. L. (2019). Race influences professional investors' financial judgments. *Proceedings of the National Academy of Sciences of the United States of America, 116*(35), 17225–17230. doi:10.1073/pnas.1822052116 PMID:31405967

Machin, J., & Solanas, A. (2018, July). A review on the meaning of cognitive cities. In *2018 9th International Conference on Information, Intelligence, Systems and Applications (IISA)* (pp. 1-5). IEEE. 10.1109/IISA.2018.8633654

Malygin, I., Komashinskiy, V., & Korolev, O. (2018). Cognitive technologies for providing road traffic safety in intelligent transport systems. *Transportation Research Procedia, 36,* 487–492. doi:10.1016/j.trpro.2018.12.134

Mitchell, T., & Krulicky, T. (2021). Big data-driven urban geopolitics, interconnected sensor networks, and spatial cognition algorithms in smart city software systems. *Geopolitics, History, and International Relations, 13*(2), 9–22. doi:10.22381/GHIR13220211

Miz, V., & Hahanov, V. (2014, September). Smart traffic light in terms of the cognitive road traffic management system (CTMS) based on the Internet of Things. In *Proceedings of IEEE east-west design & test symposium (EWDTS 2014)* (pp. 1-5). IEEE. 10.1109/EWDTS.2014.7027102

Mocatta, G., & Hawley, E. (2020). covid19? The coronavirus crisis as tipping point: Communicating the environment in a time of pandemic. *Media International Australia, Incorporating Culture & Policy, 177*(1), 119–124. doi:10.1177/1329878X20950030

Mohajan, H. (2019). *The second industrial revolution has brought modern social and economic developments.* Academic Press.

Mohammadi, M., & Al-Fuqaha, A. (2018). Enabling cognitive smart cities using big data and machine learning: Approaches and challenges. *IEEE Communications Magazine, 56*(2), 94–101. doi:10.1109/MCOM.2018.1700298

Norton, R. D. (2022). *Structural Inequality: Origins and Quests for Solutions in Old Worlds and New.* Springer Nature. doi:10.1007/978-3-031-08633-5

Okai, E., Feng, X., & Sant, P. (2018, June). Smart cities survey. In *2018 IEEE 20th international conference on high performance computing and communications; IEEE 16th international conference on smart city; IEEE 4th international conference on data science and systems (HPCC/SmartCity/DSS)* (pp. 1726-1730). IEEE. 10.1109/HPCC/SmartCity/DSS.2018.00282

Orlowski, A., & Romanowska, P. (2019). Smart cities concept: Smart mobility indicator. *Cybernetics and Systems, 50*(2), 118–131. doi:10.1080/01969722.2019.1565120

Park, J. J. (2020). Do We Really Know What We See? The Role of Cognitive Bias in How We View Race in Higher Education. *Change, 52*(2), 46–49. doi:10.1080/00091383.2020.1732776

Pozdniakova, A. M. (2018). Smart city strategies "London-Stockholm-Vienna-Kyiv": In search of common ground and best practices. *Acta Innovations*.

Ranchordás, S. (2020). Nudging citizens through technology in smart cities. *International Review of Law Computers & Technology, 34*(3), 254–276. doi:10.1080/13600869.2019.1590928

Ransom, J. (2020, July 6). Amy Cooper faces charges after calling police on black bird-watcher. *The New York Times*. https://www.nytimes.com/2020/07/06/nyregion/amy-cooper-false-report-charge.html

Ritchie, H., & Roser, M. (2018). Urbanization. *Our World in Data*.

Sangwan, S. R., & Bhatia, M. P. S. (2020). Sustainable development in industry 4.0. In *A Roadmap to Industry 4.0: Smart Production, Sharp Business and Sustainable Development* (pp. 39–56). Springer. doi:10.1007/978-3-030-14544-6_3

Schmid, A. (2018, January 23). *From Smart to Savvy: The transition to Cognitive Cities (Part 3 of 3)*. Qognify: Safeguarding Your World. https://www.qognify.com/from-smart-to-savvy-the-transition-to-cognitive-cities-part-3-of-3/

Sharma, I., Garg, I., & Kiran, D. (2020). Industry 5.0 and smart cities: A futuristic approach. *European Journal of Molecular and Clinical Medicine, 7*(08), 2515–8260.

Shrikant, N., & Sambaraju, R. (2021). 'A police officer shot a black man': Racial categorization, racism, and mundane culpability in news reports of police shootings of black people in the United States of America. *British Journal of Social Psychology, 60*(4), 1196–1217. doi:10.1111/bjso.12490 PMID:34350606

SiscoM. R.ConstantinoS. M.GaoY.TavoniM.CoopermanA. D.BosettiV.WeberE. U. (2020). A finite pool of worry or a finite pool of attention? evidence and qualifications. *Preprint]. , 3*. doi:10.21203/rs.3.rs-98481/v1

TED Institute [tedinstitute]. (2014, December 22). *Dario Gil: Cognitive systems and the future of expertise*. Youtube. https://www.youtube.com/watch?v=0heqP8d6vtQ

Walker, D., & Nauman, B. (2017). *Ethnic and Racial Diversity at Asset Management Firms*. https://www.mminst.org/sites/default/files/file_attach/MMI-FF%20Diversity_in_Asset_Mgmt_Full-Report-FINAL.pdf

Webb, R., & Buratini, J. (2018). Global challenges for the 21st century: The role and strategy of the agri-food sector. *Animal Reproduction, 13*(3), 133–142. doi:10.21451/1984-3143-AR882

Wilmoth, M. J., Menozzi, M. C., & Bassarsky, M. L. (2022). *Why population growth matters for sustainable development*. Academic Press.

Xu, M., David, J. M., & Kim, S. H. (2018). The fourth industrial revolution: Opportunities and challenges. *International Journal of Financial Research, 9*(2), 90-95.

Xu, X., Lu, Y., Vogel-Heuser, B., & Wang, L. (2021). Industry 4.0 and Industry 5.0—Inception, conception and perception. *Journal of Manufacturing Systems, 61*, 530–535. doi:10.1016/j.jmsy.2021.10.006

Xu, X., Lu, Y., Vogel-Heuser, B., & Wang, L. (2021). Industry 4.0 and Industry 5.0—Inception, conception and perception. *Journal of Manufacturing Systems, 61*, 530–535. doi:10.1016/j.jmsy.2021.10.006

Zambon, I., Colantoni, A., & Salvati, L. (2019). Horizontal vs vertical growth: Understanding latent patterns of urban expansion in large metropolitan regions. *The Science of the Total Environment*, *654*, 778–785. doi:10.1016/j.scitotenv.2018.11.182 PMID:30448668

Zhou, Y., Gohlke, D., Sansone, M., Kuiper, J., & Smith, M. P. (2022). Using Mapping Tools to Prioritize Electric Vehicle Charger Benefits to Underserved Communities (No. ANL/ESD-22/10). Argonne National Lab.

Zhu, W., Yan, R., & Song, Y. (2022). Analysing the impact of smart city service quality on citizen engagement in a public emergency. *Cities (London, England)*, *120*, 103439. doi:10.1016/j.cities.2021.103439 PMID:34539020

Chapter 12
Counseling Supervisors' Clinical Healthcare Leadership Development:
A Phenomenological Study

John Grady
New York University, USA

William Quisenberry
Purdue University Global, USA

Robert H. Kitzinger Jr.
 https://orcid.org/0000-0002-4314-5002
Kean University, USA

ABSTRACT

Leadership development and clinical counseling supervision have an established position in the literature. Counseling leadership development has been researched by Chang et al. and Peters et al. while clinical counseling supervision has been explored by Bernard and Goodyear and Elswick et al. This study defined leadership as a biodirectional social influence process that features a supervisor questing for willing involvement of supervisees to realize organizational objectives while also demonstrating managerial leadership in the organization's structure. Research has focused on the convergence of these disciplines. However, a 20-year metastudy of publication characteristics in Counselor Education and Supervision found no direct category featuring on organizational leadership or business topics. This qualitative phenomenological study explored the clinical healthcare leadership development experiences of eight clinical counseling supervisors.

DOI: 10.4018/979-8-3693-1630-6.ch012

Clinical counseling supervision is an important component to the counseling field. Counseling supervision is centered on bolstering the clinical capabilities and understanding of counselors (Curtis & Sherlock, 2006). A need has long existed for sufficient counseling supervision (Elswick et al., 2018; Morrison et al., 2022; Watkins, 1990). Organizations naturally turn to clinical supervisors to lead clinical mental health and addictions programs. Counseling program directors are often tasked with both clinical and clinical healthcare leadership responsibilities (Evans et al., 2016). Despite the importance of administrative supervision as part of a clinical healthcare leadership position, clinical supervisors are generally not formally prepared (e.g., adequate coursework or workshops regarding leadership topics) for clinical healthcare leadership roles.

As a result of this lack of formal preparedness, clinical supervisors also struggle to navigate increasingly demanding competitive and macro environmental settings that continue to diversify, and require sound inclusive leadership strategies. This study explored how clinical counseling supervisors developed their organizational leadership skills in their healthcare settings and provides some considerations regarding how healthcare professionals in clinical environments can improve their leadership skills and be better prepared to properly serve multicultural stakeholders.

Clinical Counseling Supervision

Clinical counseling supervision may be described in multiple manners. Counseling supervision is a vital and complicated subject that has been well explored in counseling research (Curtis & Sherlock, 2006; Kocyigit, 2022). Bernard and Goodyear's (1992) venerable definition of the term, supervision, views it as an intervention conducted by a more established professional in a field to a less established professional in the same field. Bernard and Goodyear's (1992) definition of "supervision" has served as a foundation upon which these and other researchers have built.

Counseling supervision is a primary educational approach employed to assess counselor development and responsibility (Anderson et al., 2022; Baltrinic & Wachter Morris, 2020; Gazzola et al., 2013). Counseling supervision consists of supervisory actions that assist or inform the counseling interventions performed by supervisees (ACES, 2011). Counseling supervision is the medium to prepare, educate, and assess treatment quality provided by supervisees (Evans et al., 2016). Supervision is a long term evaluative and hierarchical relationship between a senior professional and a junior colleague, one that monitors and evaluates the professional services of the junior professional (Bernard & Goodyear, 2018). The employment of both counseling supervision and counseling is influenced by multicultural considerations and competencies.

Multicultural Clinical Counseling

Cultural diversity and inclusivity should not be ignored in any context, including leadership, clinical supervision, and counseling. Culture has an impact on organizational activities as it is a significant factor in worker management (Rodriguez-Rivero et al., 2022). The counseling literature has emphasized diversity issues and concerns in supervisory settings (Broadwater et al., 2022; Kemer et al., 2022; La Guardia, 2020). From a clinical psychotherapy angle, multicultural competency in counseling has garnered support in regard to how counselors, who are different from clients, consider those differences and ensure that clients are receiving the support and care that they need. Support for multicultural competence in counseling has resulted in a meaningful number of scholarly explorations regarding multicultural dynamics in counseling settings.

Clinical psychology literature embraces the importance and need of multicultural training and development, and competency models such as Multicultural Competence (MCC) have been developed and encouraged as a result (Henry & Li, 2022; Gundel et al., 2020; Sue et al., 1992). Counselors who are competent in multiculturalism can be far more effective and efficient at both individual and group supervision (Watkins et al., 2022). Adequate multicultural training and development can help counselors improve as individuals, professionals, and healthcare practitioners, while adequately serving clients, and even contribute to positive social and systemic change (Pope-Davis et al., 2002; Sue & Sue, 2008; Hayes et al., 2016; Imel et al., 2011). The benefits of multicularly-informed counseling can inform advocates beyond the counseling office.

Ultimately, embracing concepts and methods that align with MCC and inclusive clinical counseling practices is a social justice issue, and hence, a lack of multicultural consideration in this regard results is a form of social injustice (Grzanka & Cole, 2021; Huminuik et al., 2022; Cohen et al., 2022). However, despite the benefits and empirical evidence that supports multicultural training, development, and competency for clinical counselors, there can still be struggles leveraging the research in a practical fashion and sustainably maintaining sound inclusive methods.

There is ample support for clinical counselors and therapists being equipped to adequately serve diverse populations in an inclusive manner both clinically as counselors, and also as counseling supervisors. Since the 1970's, counseling graduate programs and literature have increasingly addressed the need for enhancing multicultural competencies, understanding, and awareness (Sue et al., 1992). The American Counseling Association (2014) Code of Ethics calls for counselors and counseling supervisors to address multicultural and diversity-related dynamics in their professional roles. Counseling-related professions have prominently emphasized multicultural counseling competence (Mollen et al., 2021). Counselors have traditionally assumed responsibility for constructing culturally informed clinical services moreso than the organizations for whom they toil (Center for Substance Abuse Treatment, 2014). However, healthcare organizations must ensure that they are properly equipped with the leadership skills, knowledge regarding multiculturalism and inclusivity, and also held accountability to apply this knowledge in a practical fashion. Ultimately, this means that healthcare organizations must provide formal leadership development training for counseling supervisors to ensure that these practices and methods are embraced by therapists.

Dual Supervisory Roles

Clinical healthcare leadership responsibilities may also be tasked to clinical supervisors. Most organizations' assign administrative and counseling supervision responsibilities to the same professional (ACES, 2011; Center for Substance Abuse Treatment, 2009; Evans et al., 2016). Administrative and counseling supervision responsibilities can overlap in counseling agencies (ACES, 2011; Berna; Center for Substance Abuse Treatment, 2009; Friedmann et al., 2010; Henderson, 1994). Clinical supervisors often possess administrative duties that include team development, time management, enforcing organizational policies, documentation, hiring and disciplining of employees, performance assessment, adherence to state and legal expectations, managing monetary problems, and facilitating communications (Center for Substance Abuse Treatment, 2009). Assuming clinical healthcare leadership demands after years of clinical counseling work can be challenging to the novice clinical supervisor.

Clinical Healthcare Leadership Training

Clinical counseling leaders assume service roles and statuses (McKibben et al., 2017; Meany-Walen et al., 2013; Storlie et al., 2015; Storlie & Wood, 2014) and are frequently expected to assume leadership roles in academic environments and beyond (McGinn, 2022; Fassinger & Shullman, 2017; Lockard et al., 2014).Successful leadership appears vital to any organization, school, or business (Puyo, 2022; Storlie & Herlihy, 2022; Phillips et al., 2017), yet clinical supervisors generally do not receive organization leadership training.

In fact, the past 15 years have witnessed multiple calls for improved clinical supervision training. Most clinical supervisors have not received supervision training (Glosoff et al., 2011; Kocyigit, 2022). The literature has uncovered the need for a dependable, nationwide curriculum for supervision training of counselors (American Counseling Association [ACA], 2014; Council for Accreditation of Counseling & Related Educational Programs [CACREP], 2016; Henderson et al., 2016). The counseling field clearly requires novel approaches to training clinical and administrative supervisors (Evans et al., 2016). A more prominent scholarly focus on the topic may uncover the extent of the problem and insights into the benefits of addressing it.

Leadership and Leadership Training

An exploration of leadership can commence with a review of its meaning. It is important to define counseling leadership (Woo et al., 2016). Leadership is a broad term that has been described in myriad ways (Gabel, 2013). There are many ways to define leadership, both in general and as it applies to clinical counseling settings. This study defined leadership as a biodirectional social influence process that features a supervisor questing for supervisees to realize organizational objectives while also demonstrating managerial leadership in the organization's structure (Center for Substance Abuse Treatment, 2007). The literature has additional ways to define leadership.

Barreto (2012) conceptualizes leadership as the interaction of physical, spiritual, mental, and emotional energy that strives to evolve and flourish. Yukl (2013) defines adaptive leadership as "an emergent process that occurs when people with different knowledge, beliefs, and preferences interact in an attempt to solve problems and resolve conflicts" (p. 296). Leaders are a holistic integration of managing, educating, and motivating (Barreto, 2012). Healthcare leaders ethically and successfully influence others for their patients' well-being (Harget et al., 2017). Healthcare leaders can impact subordinate emotional labours through their management and training approaches (Oleksa-Marewska & Tokar, 2022). Such leadership views can be applied to myriad healthcare settings, including clinical counseling settings.

Psychologists are trained to participate in leadership roles associated with clinical services (American Psychological Association, 2013). Consistent with their field's value system, successful social worker leaders focus on the environments, processes, and interventions associated with client needs (Sullivan, 2016). Licensed social workers' training guidelines call for leadership that bolsters service quality and champions social and economic justice (McGinn, 2022; Lockard et al., 2014). Substance abuse counseling leadership is a primary focus in improving client care (Broome et al., 2009). Some effective leadership traits may even mirror those of effective college counselors (DeDiego, 2022; Jacob et al., 2017). Leadership in counseling settings may manifest in multiple ways, regardless of a professional's particular field, and mirror leadership expressed in more traditional (e.g., business) settings.

RESEARCH DESIGN AND METHOD

This phenomenological research study's purpose explored how clinical counseling supervisors develop clinical healthcare leadership skills. Phenomenology is a philosophical branch founded upon the study of personal experience and human consciousness (Arbnor & Bjerke, 2009). There appears to be a literature gap regarding the proposed study's topic. Contemporary literature on training and guiding the application of counseling supervision and education is limited yet burgeoning (Böhm et al., 2022; APA, 2015; Holt et al., 2015). An investigation of how counseling supervisors develop clinical healthcare leadership skills may identify insufficiencies in this process.

More specifically, a key focus of the proposed study is to explore how clinical supervisors construct clinical healthcare leadership abilities despite the dearth of formal training in this expertise (or in addition to it). Findings helped to bolster current best practices for the clinical healthcare leadership development of clinical supervisors, identify shortcomings in the developmental process and practices, while highlighting multicultural considerations that can improve the literature's attention to these topics.

Phenomenological Research

A foremost research task is the identification of specific research approaches to effectively study the targeted phenomenon. Psychological researchers can utilize qualitative approaches to inquiry (Imogen et al., 2022). Phenomenology is one such example. Phenomenology was established in the early 1900s and has been utilized as a research approach in multiple social science fields (Spencer et al., 2014). The origin of phenomenology can be traced back to Edmund Husserl (Houston, 2022; Puta, 2022). Heidegger introduced existential phenomenology, a holistic view of existence that consists of reciprocal interdependence between oneself, others, and things that penetrates one's awareness when needed (Klenke, 2008). Heidegger's hermeneutics principles create space to illuminate what science has covered up (Bentz & Shapiro, 1998). Subsequent phenomenological researchers have built upon this foundation by identifying literature gaps and addressing them.

Problem Statement

The proposed study was prompted by the dearth of professional development regarding clinical counseling supervisors' clinical healthcare leadership training. Although it is an important topic, leadership has not been prominently featured in the counseling literature (Fassinger et al., 2017; Gabel, 2013). More leadership research is needed throughout the behavioral health fields, including counselor education (McKibben et al., 2017), social work (Elswick et al., 2018), counseling psychology (Fassinger et al., 2017; Fassinger & Shullman, 2017), school counseling (Dolan, 2022; Kneale et al., 2018), and substance abuse (Friedmann et al., 2010; Kimberly & McLellan, 2006). Clinical healthcare leadership may be a reasonably novel research focus (Curtis & Sherlock, 2006; McKibben et al., 2017). While leadership is of vital importance in counseling psychology's development, present status, and future, there is a dearth of research on the topic (Fassinger et al., 2017; Fassinger & Shullman, 2017). The limited amount of research is an unfortunate reality that has been acknowledged throughout the past two decades.

Most counseling education programs do not address business leadership procedures such as executing performance, addressing colleague work performance, and being responsible for workgroup cohesiveness and productivity (Curtis & Sherlock, 2006). Curriculum infusion can educate clinical students in targeted subjects, prepare them for non-academic work, and prepare them for future leadership roles (Dewitt et al., 2017; Elswick et al., 2018). Leadership training and development should be prioritized in academic settings (McGinn, 2022; Lockard et al., 2014). Leadership training programs are valuable (Evans et al., 2016). Enhancing leadership skill development can occur if the topic is more thoroughly explored in graduate school programs (Elswick et al., 2018). There is a literature gap regarding how clinical supervisors develop clinical healthcare leadership skills. Additionally, formal leadership development programs for clinical supervisors appear to be insufficient.

Conceptual Framework

This phenomenological study design's conceptual framework consisted of adaptive leadership theory and systems leadership theory. These theories frame the research study's novel investigation of how clinical supervisors develop clinical healthcare leadership skills. The adaptive leadership framework may be a formidable approach to developing and assessing novel interventions to complicated issues by discovering and utilizing the adaptive abilities of healthcare providers, clients, and clients' families (Bailey et al., 2012). Yukl's (2013) systems model of leadership development consists of separate but overlapping categories that inform how leaders evolve. Yukle's model provides a framework to understand leadership development processes that clinical supervisors may experience.

Clinical supervisors who assume clinical healthcare leadership roles generally adapt to having business-related responsibilities. Comprehending managerial effectiveness is vital to producing successful counseling programs (Curtis & Sherlock, 2006). Leader-subordinate communication frequency and quality are important for healthcare organizations' operations (Maritsa et al., 2022). Clinical supervisors are called upon to adapt to their administrative leadership roles. Adaptive leadership behaviors require a modification in principles, beliefs, and actions (Lennon et al., 2022; Heifetz, 1994). As with their clinical counseling and supervision responsibilities, clinical supervisors must consider followers in their clinical healthcare leadership actions.

Considering followers' responses to leadership decisions is congruent with adaptive leadership theory. Adaptive leadership theory's foundation concerns how leadership behaviors impact followers' behaviors (Northouse, 2015). Clinical supervisors' expertise in diagnosing mental health and addictions ailments may uniquely qualify them to best understand and employ adaptive leadership theory's approach to diagnosing organizational afflictions. A systematic, evidence-based diagnostic process, one that is similar to the medical field's diagnostic processes, is required by organizational leaders to best identify challenges and to create needed actions to rectify them (McFillen et al., 2013). Adherents to systems leadership theories may also see congruent dynamics regarding clinical supervisors' adaption to clinical healthcare leadership roles.

Systems leadership theory permits for the acknowledgement that the whole organization should be served even though all decisions and actions may not appeal to each member, and align more with inclusive leadership, instead of traditional, non-adaptive and exclusive leadership approaches. An operational organization needs to function according to the interests of the whole population and a variety of stakeholder groups, which is not always the most beneficial to one or more systemic components at any one time (Chaudhry, 2022; Pfiffner, 2022; Vik et al., 2022). Clinical supervisors in clinical healthcare leadership positions possess both clinical and administrative supervisory responsibilities, which sometimes conflict. A systems approach to leadership development may help inform clinical supervisors how to appeal to the needs of independent organizational segments. Clinical supervisors' counseling experiences and formal education may enable them to quickly adhere to systems leadership theory principles.

Systems leadership theory is also similar to many counselors' fundamental trainings. Educated in family counseling (which oftentimes emphasizes systems thinking), clinical supervisors are familiar with systems theory and may apply such knowledge to non-counseling situations (e.g., personal leadership development, training others in leadership situations). Family systems theory explains human family dynamics and offers a foundation for family counseling, but its insights are also applicable to non-family groups, human society, and even non-human species (Calatrava et al., 2022; Kerr, 2003). Such diversity of application suggests that systems theory insights can be applied to leadership development, and help better equip counseling supervisors with capabilities befitting to Diversity, Equity, and Inclusion (DEI).

Systems leadership theory and related concepts is an integral focus in public health literature (Bigland et al., 2020). A systems approach to clinical healthcare leadership development can include distinct but overlapping leadership competency methods where each interrelate in complicated but learning-enhancing ways (Yukl, 2013). For example, Fernandez et al.'s (2021) study indicated that leadership training based on leadership competencies benefitted the systems associated with its population of mid-to-senior Maternal and Child Health Leader population. Combined, adaptive leadership and systems leadership theories informed the study (see Figure 1 below) to holistically consider contrasting forces in a clinical supervisor's clinical healthcare leadership development.

Figure 1. Conceptual framework

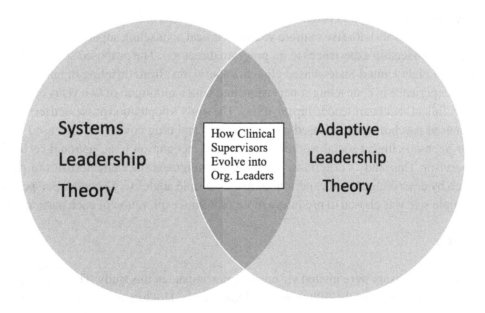

Research Questions and their Rationales

The overall research question guiding this study was: How do clinical supervisors develop clinical healthcare leadership skills? Leadership is defined as a process consisting of multiple individuals who communicate both directly and indirectly in diverse manners (McKibben et al., 2017). The study was further established by two sub questions and informed by The Adaptive Leadership Questionnaire (Northouse, 2015), adaptive leadership principles, and Yukl's (2013) systems model of leadership development:

1. How do clinical supervisors develop leadership skills for clinical healthcare leadership (e.g., program director, executive director) roles?
2. How do clinical supervisors learn to address unforeseen business challenges (e.g., low census) while leading clinical programs?

Population and Sample

The proposed study's participant population consisted of eight counseling supervisors with clinical healthcare leadership experiences. Phenomenological studies have been conducted on leaders and their lived leadership-related experiences (Atli Osbas & Kovanci, 2022; Hite & Milbourne, 2022; Thomas & Grafsky, 2021). Congruent with the phenomenological emphasis on lived experiences, the counseling leaders were asked how they developed their clinical healthcare leadership skills. Phenomenological researchers investigate everyday happenings where individuals live through phenomena in real circumstances (Giorgi, 1985). The following provides more detail about the study's population.

Research Participants

Participation criteria was created to better ensure that interviewees consisted of established counseling supervisors (i.e., supervisors with five or more years of clinical counseling supervision experience) with clinical healthcare leadership experiences (e.g., program directors). The proposed study's sample population consisted of eight United States-based clinical supervisors, from differing organizations, with at least 5 years of experience in counseling supervision, and with a minimum of two years of experience in administrative/clinical healthcare leadership positions. The study's population possessed terminal licenses (e.g., state-licensed psychologists, licensed clinical alcohol and drug counselors, licensed professional counselors, or licensed clinical social workers) and formal recognition (e.g., national certification) as a clinical supervisor. This study's criteria were designed to augment the characteristics of phenomenological research by describing shared experiences from multiple angles (e.g., gender perspectives). The population sample size was chosen to produce a more profound exploration of each participant's views.

Demographics

Over 500 clinical supervisors were invited via email to participate in this study. The researcher screened 13 professionals of whom 8 met the following required criteria: Holding a terminal clinical counseling license, at least five years of counseling supervision experience, and a minimum of 2 years of administrative/clinical healthcare leadership. The following questions screened respondents:

- Are you a terminally licensed counseling professional?
- Are you a certified clinical supervisor?
- Do you have at least five years of counseling supervision experience?
- Do you have at least two years of clinical healthcare leadership experience?

All eight qualified professionals agreed to participate in the study and signed informed consent forms. The study's participant population reported to have accumulated vast years of counseling, supervision, and leadership experience; to have worked in multiple levels of care (i.e., partial hospitalization programs, intensive outpatient programs, and outpatient programs); and to have earned a range of licenses and certifications. Licenses include Licensed Psychologist (PsyD), Licensed Professional Counselor (LPC), Licensed Clinical Alcohol and Drug Counselor (LCADC), and Licensed Rehabilitation Counselor (LRC). Supervision certifications include Approved Clinical Supervisor (ACS) and Certified Clinical Supervisor (CCS). Counseling certifications include Student Assistance Coordinator (SAC), Certified Tobacco Treatment Specialist (CTTS), Certified Clinical Hypnotherapist (CCH), and National Certified Counselor (NCC). Additional credentials included a medical professional (vaguely described to help protect confidentiality), School Counselor, and Psychological Associate (PA). The table below summarizes each participant's professional credentials and provides average years of experience as a counselor, supervisor, and leader.

Table 1. Counseling, supervision, and leadership experiences and credentials

Participant	Years as Counselor	Years as Clinical Supervisor	Years as Organizational Leader	Clinical Licenses and Supervision Certifications	Other Credentials
P1	16	6	8	PsyD, LPC, ACS	NCC, (medical professional)
P2	(40)	(35)	(35)	LPC, LRC, ACS	CTTS, PsyA, CCH
P3	30	12	13	LPC, LCADC, ACS, CCS	NCC, CCH
P4	38	36	36	LPC, LCADC, ACS	NCC
P5	13	5	3	LPC, ACS	NCC, School Counselor
P6	31	23	25	LPC, ACS	NCC
P7	15	9	5	LPC, LCADC, ACS, (CCS)	NCC
P8	8	5	3	LPC, LCADC, ACS	NCC, SAC, School Counselor

Note. To protect confidentiality, participant 1's specific medical background was not specified due to the uniqueness of her credentials.
Note. Participant 2 did not provide specific statistics. Numbers were estimated based on participant's graduation date for Master's degree (for years as counselor) and testimony regarding when she commenced counseling supervision and clinical healthcare leadership roles.
Note. Participant 7 reported to be in the process of earning her CCS.

As illustrated in Table 1, all participants possessed at least a Master's degree with one participant holding a doctorate degree. All participants earned their LPC (100%) while 5 of 8 (63%) participants earned two licenses. 7 of 8 (88%) participants reported to be nationally certified counselors (i.e., NCC). All participants earned their ACS (100%) while 2 of 8 (25%) also earned, or were in the process of earning, their CCS. As depicted in the following table, the participant population averaged 24 years in the counseling industry, 16 years as a clinical supervisor, and 16 years as an organizational leader.

PROCEDURES

This study's procedures were guided by a phenomenological focus. Phenomenology's objective is to comprehend phenomena in its own element and to offer an account of human experience according to the person (Bentz & Shapiro, 1998; Houston, 2022). Counseling researchers use phenomenological methods to underscore broad partners and general variations across individual understandings of an identifiable subjective experience (Hanna et al., 2017). The targeted phenomenon of this study is explored through the lens of how the participant experienced it. A phenomenon describes how entities appear in human consciousness (Willis et al., 2016). Exploring phenomena through the phenomenological lens is well-justified. Knowledge regarding how human beings think and feel is most directly derived from phenomenology (Bentz & Shapiro, 1998). While this view is debatable depending upon one's philosophical persuasion, phenomenology unquestionably attempts to capture the unique experiences of the participant.

Data Collection

Permission to conduct research with the targeted population was secured from The Chicago School of Professional Psychology's Institutional Review Board (IRB). Consent forms from respondents were obtained to speak with clinical leaders at each site location. This research study used a modified descriptive phenomenological strategy to data collection. Descriptive pre-transcendental Husserlian phenomenology researchers secure descriptions regarding a phenomenon as experienced by an individual to establish a holistic psychological understanding of it, re-visits the data to establish is units of meaning, transforms each unit of meaning into expressions that communicate the psychological meaning of the participant's self-reports, and summarizes the phenomena (Giorgi & Giorgi, 2008). The descriptive pre-transcendental Husserlian phenomenological process was employed to capture data and create meaningful themes.

The researchers also considered important core phenomenological research ideals. True to Husserl's (1900/1970) central phenomenological theme of describing phenomena strictly through the lens of those who are living the phenomena, one may contend that descriptive phenomenology typically does not invite other theories into its framework lest its bracketing for pre-perceptions be impacted. According to Heidegger (1971), anything that comes between the researcher and the studied phenomenon must be cast aside. In fact, Hursserl's phenomenological method for research was designed to include the researcher's own experiences rather than consulting with others to explore their experiences with the phenomenon (Hanna et al., 2017). These standards do not permit for external influences guiding the researcher's interpretation of the studied phenomenon.

However, although Husserl constructed the primary structure of phenomenological study, many followers have modified it to some degree (Giorgi et al., 2017). For example, many phenomenologists contend that pure bracketing is neither pragmatic nor possible (Klenke, 2008). All complicated phenomena cannot be completely explained by a particular theoretical framework, or that framework will be challenged to increase its borders to include the phenomena (Gabel, 2013). These perspectives are aligned with this study's use of bracketing and a conceptual framework to understand the data. This descriptive phenomenological study used Adaptive and System Leadership Theories to inform interview queries so that the studied phenomenon could be more wholly described.

Data Collection Approach

This study's unit of analysis was clinical supervisors. Data was secured through semi-structured, open-ended question interviews of eight current or former clinical supervisors who have also assumed clinical healthcare leadership roles (e.g., directors of clinical counseling programs). Phenomenological studies generally gather data through extended interviews regarding the study's subject and question (Moustakas, 1994). Interviews were conducted and video recorded via the HIPAA-approved online medium Zoom. com, and transcribed with MAXQDA technology. The semi-structured interview approach was selected to provide flexibility for exploration while being grounded with quality questions that are not provided in unstructured interviews. The semi-structured format is designed to generate important data about the studied phenomenon.

This study utilized trustworthiness to help ensure validity and reliability. The influential work of Lincoln and Guba (1985) replaced validity and reliability with the analogous term, trustworthiness, that consisted of four components: credibility, dependability, transferability, and confirmability (Morse, 2015). The authors utilized reflexivity to identify how they influenced data acquisition and interpretation, bracketed researcher bias throughout the study, utilized composed epochs, triangulated information, and constructed a expansive description of data. Combined, these efforts helped to establish the level of objectivity required to establish sound findings.

Interviews were conducted via Zoom videos until saturation was reached and sufficient data was accumulated. Each semi-structured interview was scheduled for 30-60 minutes, but three lasted beyond this time frame due to detailed responses. The first author transcribed or reviewed each spoken word, utilized exact quotes to generate themes to realize validity and transparency of the participants' lived experiences. Information from the interviews was then inserted into MAXQDA for analysis.

Data Analysis

The first author employed content analysis of the participant testimonies. In leadership research, content analysis underscores the importance of language with words, sentences, and paragraphs serving as analytic formulations (Klenke, 2008). Dramaturgical coding was used to capture themes throughout the interviews. According to Saldana (2021), dramaturgical coding harmonizes the researcher to the participant's qualities, viewpoints, and drives. Dramaturgical categories were chosen because they provided a holistic format to investigate reported experiences. Dramaturgical categories were used to create meaning units. These categories were: Objectives (OBJ); conflicts (CON); tactics (TAC); attitudes (ATT); emotions (EMO); and subtexts (SUB). Each category boasted definitions that helped to harness themes conveyed across participant testimonies. Table 3 below summarizes these definitions. Transcribed interviews were reviewed and tagged with these broad categories and the specific subcategories created by this writer. Findings will be presented in the "Results" section below.

Table 2. Dramaturgical coding categories

Codes	Definitions
Objectives (OBJ)	Organization-related motives expressed via action verbs (e.g., learning)
Conflicts (CON)	Obstacles encountered by participants that prevented him or her from achieving leadership-related objectives
Tactics (TAC)	Leadership efforts to resolve conflicts or overcome obstacles to leadership-development objectives
Attitudes (ATT)	Participant perspectives towards leadership-development environments, individuals (e.g., mentors), or conflicts
Emotions (EMO)	Participant feelings regarding leadership-development dynamics
Subtexts (SUB)	Gerunds (e.g., "ing" words) to highlight action words related to leadership-development thoughts or impressions.

Themes uncovered in dramaturgical coding were constructed and represented the lived-meanings as described by the participants. Triangulation of the initial screen, structured questions, public advertisements of private practices (i.e., Psychology Today's "Find a Therapist), LinkedIn profiles, and open-ended queries were used to generate data. Clustering was used to link similar data. Epoch, mindful reflection, and reflective journal writing best ensured objectivity throughout the interview, data collection, and data analysis. Code construction was guided by the definitions described in Table 3 and according to my assessment of the participant descriptive reports. One coding cycle was sufficient as themes become clear and pervasive throughout the participant population. Themes articulated in all or most interviews were identified in the next section (i.e., "Results").

RESULTS

623 codes were recorded across eight semi-structured interviews. These codes were categorized in sections as per dramaturgical coding guidelines (see Table Three). Objectives (OBJ) included reports of clinical healthcare leadership-related motivations. Conflicts (CON) consisted of obstacles to leadership development-related objectives. Tactics (TAC) encompassed efforts to resolve conflicts or overcome obstacles to leadership-development objectives. Attitudes (ATT) included participant attitudes towards leadership-development environments, individuals (e.g. mentors), or conflicts. Emotions (EMO) captured participant feelings regarding leadership-development dynamics. Subtexts (SUB) consisted of gerunds (e.g., "ing" words) to highlight action words related to leadership-development thoughts or impressions. The table below summarizes the number of codes in each category:

Table 3. Category and code frequency

Dramaturgical Category	Number of Codes (Percentage of Total Codes)
Objectives (OBJ)	85 (14%)
Conflicts (CON)	48 (8%)
Tactics (TAC)	274 (44%)
Attitudes (ATT)	65 (10%)
Emotions (EMO)	34 (2%)
Subtexts (SUB)	117 (19%)

These themes were identified by 1) the number of participants that reported the theme and 2) the number of times the code was recorded. A minimum of seven participants reported the code, as I considered this indicative of the code's pervasiveness across the participant population's reported lived experiences. A minimum of seven participants was also utilized to rule out themes with artificially high numbers of codes (i.e., codes that were repeated very frequently by a few participants). A frequency of 41 was considered the threshold as all codes below this number were reported by six or less participants.

Table 4. Themes

Theme (and Category)	Number of Participants Reporting Theme (and Percentage)	Number of Times Theme Was Communicated
Learning Leadership Through Experience (Tactics)	8 (100%)	109 (17%)
Sub Theme: Learning to Improve Agency's Business Procedures (Objectives)	7 (88%)	64 (10%)
Learning Leadership Approaches via Mentors, Superiors, Peers (Tactics)	8 (100%)	76 (12%)
Learning Leadership Through Bad Leadership (Tactics)	7 (88%)	41 (7%)
Lack of Formal Leadership Training (Conflicts)	8 (100%)	50 (8%)
Being a Natural Leader (Subtext)	8 (100%)	73 (12%)
Balancing Business Leadership and Clinical Supervisor Roles (Subtext)	8 (100%)	53 (8%)

Theme One: Learning Leadership Through Experience

All eight (100%) participants discussed this theme, which consisted of 109 (17% of total number) codes. Theme One consisted of descriptions of leadership development through the participants' own experiences. Theme One consists of descriptions of encountering novel leadership demands, addressing them to the best of his or her ability, and learning through the consequences of his or her leadership decisions and actions. Examples of these leadership demands include evaluating subordinates, providing resources to subordinates, and learning time management tactics so that the participant can address fundamental leadership needs (e.g., assigning clients to counselors, ensuring that counseling groups are conducted by counselors, reviewing charts to ensure that clinical notes are authored correctly to ensure insurance payment, etc.).

Sub Theme: Learning to Improve Agency's Business Procedures

Seven of eight (88%) of the participant population discussed this theme, which consisted of 64 (10% of total number) codes. The sub theme included efforts to develop the counseling program or agency's financial strength, bolster census, or money-related issues (e.g., developing effective billing practices). These novel leadership actions describe unanticipated business management aspects of clinical healthcare leadership. Seven of eight (88%) of the participant population discussed how learning to improve business procedures was an aspect of their leadership development. These expectations were described as being placed upon them by organizational superiors.

Theme Two: Learning Leadership Approaches via Mentors, Supervisors, Peers

All eight (100%) of participants discussed this theme, which consisted of 76 (12% of total number) codes. Theme Two describes participants' leadership development via encountering unforeseen business challenges and learning from mentors, supervisors, or peers. These experiences include participants describing having been educated by leaders of equal or higher organizational status.

Theme Three: Learning Leadership Through Bad Leadership

Seven of eight (88%) participants discussed this theme, which consisted of 41 (% of total number) codes. Theme Three consisted of participant descriptions of learning through experiencing "bad leadership" (as defined by the participant). These experiences consisted of the participant describing being led by what they considered to be poor leadership. The emphasis was not on unsuccessful leadership decisions, but more permanent traits of poor leadership. How this was specifically defined varied across the participant population. These experiences reportedly informed the participant of what not to do – or be – as a leader.

Theme Four: Lack of Formal Leadership Training

Eight of eight (100%) participants discussed this theme, which consisted of 50 (8% of total number) codes. Theme 4 consisted of participant reports of having no time for formal training, no finances for formal leadership training, and almost no opportunities for formal leadership training (e.g., university classes, workshops) conducted by counseling professionals. Theme Four manifested as participants recounted how they learned to address unforeseen business challenges and to develop leadership skills. Several described engaging in leadership training provided by non-counseling programs or agencies and personal research efforts.

Theme Five: Being a Natural Leader

Eight of eight (100%) participants discussed this theme, which consisted of 73 (12%) codes. The study's next prominent theme included discussions on innate leadership traits and leading through intuition (when confronted with unforeseen business challenges). That is, participants reported that, based on their lived experiences, leadership development was heavily dependent on personality traits and instinct. While leadership experts have long concluded that the natural born leader concept is myth (Steinhoff, 2015), some researchers suggest that natural leaders possess innate leadership qualities that can be enhanced through experience, research, and training (ul Amin & Kamal, 2016). Such qualities include foundational skills (e.g. building rapport), leadership direction qualities (e.g. guiding and developing others), and leadership influence skills (e.g. establishing commitment from followers) (Blank, 2001). Natural leader characteristics also included, as defined by the study population, the ability to adapt to situations' leadership needs, cultivate relationships with others (i.e., subordinates, peers, superiors), and maintain temperament in stressful circumstances. While other themes focused on learning through experiences and interactions with others, the theme of "being a leader" emphasized innate capabilities.

Theme Six: Balancing Business Leadership and Clinical Supervisor Roles

Eight of eight (100%) participants discussed this theme. 53 (8%) of the total number of themes were represented in this category. This study's final prominent theme describes the participants' experience of balancing clinical healthcare leadership and counseling supervision roles as part of their leadership development. Novel clinical healthcare leadership tasks were largely interpreted to be administrative in nature (e.g., scheduling subordinates, creating budgets), which differs from counseling supervision responsibilities. The latter was viewed as centered exclusively on the supervisee's clinical services (e.g., helping the supervisee to improve treatment approaches) to clients.

Minor Themes in Dramaturgical Coding Categories

The above major themes distinguished themselves from many other more minor codes/themes via 1) pervasiveness reported throughout the participant population and 2) the volume number of reports in the participants' testimonies. However, many minor codes/themes were added to the data. They are also indirectly represented in the "Findings" section as the researchers holistically considered the themes, to which all codes belong, through the lens of the dramaturgical coding categories. Table 6 summarizes each dramaturgical coding category, its themes, and the number of codes per category.

Table 5. Code system and all major and minor themes

Code System Category	Themes (and Subthemes)	Total Number of Themes and Subthemes per Category	Total Number of Codes Per Category (Percentage of Total Codes)
Objectives	Improve Agency Business Procedures (subtheme of Learning Leadership Through Experience); Improve Services to Subordinates	Two	85 (14%)
Conflicts	Youth; Lack of External Support; Lack of Formal Leadership (Learning Leadership Formally via Non-Counseling Sources)	Three	48 (8%)
Tactics	Learning Leadership Approaches Via Mentors, Supervisors, Peers; Learning from Bad Leadership; Self-Teaching Leadership; Learn Leadership Through Experience (Learning to Improve Agency's Business Procedures)	Four	274 (44%)
Attitudes	Role Model; Genuine; Positivity; Determined; Responsible; Entrepreneurial; Humble	Seven	65 (10%)
Emotions	Positive; Fear; Negative; Grateful; Compassionate; Concerned; Proud; Confused	Eight	34 (2%)
Subtexts	Balancing Business and counseling supervision Roles; Learning Leadership/Business Approaches Via Other Professions; Being a Natural Leader; Leading Leadership Formally	Four	117 (19%)

The study produced six major themes and one sub-theme that were communicated 1) by all or most (i.e., seven of eight) participants and 2) expressed at least 41 times. The latter standard was identified because all other minor themes were communicated by six or less participants. These minor themes and two sub themes combine to number 21 in total, or 75% of the total number of codes. However, these 21 minor themes represented only 200 of 623 (32%) total codes. While there is a significant difference between the number of codes applied to the major and minor themes (see Table Seven), the provided minor themes were important as evidenced by their being reported as part of the participants' experiences. These themes may have emerged to a larger degree in a study boasting a larger sample population, suggesting a place in this summary's findings is indicated. They are represented in the conclusions' exploration of the dramaturgical coding-inspired interpretation of findings.

Table 6. Theme frequency summary

6 Major Themes and Subtheme: Total Number of Codes (and % of Total Codes)	Average Number of Codes per Major Theme (and Subtheme)	19 Minor Themes and 2 Subthemes: Total Number of Codes (and % of Total Codes)	Average Number of Codes per Minor Theme (and Subthemes)
423 of 623 (68%)	60.4	200 of 623 (32%)	9.5

DISCUSSION AND CONCLUSIONS

Analysis of the participant population's semi-structured interviews produced five major themes from 623 codes. The themes include learning leadership through experience (with a sub theme of learning to improve agency's business procedures); learning leadership approaches via mentors, superior, peers; learning leadership through bad leadership; lack of formal leadership training; and being a natural leader. These findings were considered within the context of the study's contextual framework (i.e., adaptive leadership theory and systems leadership theory).

The dramaturgical coding categories were chosen because it offers a holistic list of categories that represent every single code (100%) uncovered in the study. In contrast, the themes represented 413 of 623 codes (66%). Dramaturgical coding was paired with systems leadership theory because of the latter's emphasis on each organizational component contributing to the whole's structure. All are interdependent and related. Systems adherents value every influence as being a cause and an effect, believing that everything is influenced in both directions (Senge, 2006). Since the bracketing process prevented my beliefs from influencing the investigated phenomenon, the study's developed themes were unexpected. Discussion of the findings are presented in the following sections.

RECOMMENDATIONS

Scholarly exploration of a subject should represent one of myriad efforts to generate understanding. Science may be viewed as a cultural institution committed to the quest to acquire the greatest amount of sound knowledge pertaining to world phenomena (Giorgi, 1997). The current study contributed to the literature gap regarding how clinical counseling supervisors develop their clinical healthcare leadership skills. However, the dearth of data on this topic indicates that additional qualitative research is needed. Qualitative research of leadership may produce meaningful outcomes such as uncovering issues that have been omitted in the literature (Bryman et al., 1988). Additional qualitative studies may validate the themes and insights produced in this study and/or create new themes that can augment this study's findings.

Future studies may build upon this study's findings by using a phenomenological design to generate additional data. More and novel data may replicate this study's themes, thus suggesting that they may be experienced by many clinical supervisors who transition to leadership roles. It is advised that qualitative research designs be used due to the study's unique focus. Such designs can be useful for under-studied topics. Future investigators may utilize the framework employed in this study to narrow its focus to clinical supervisors from specific fields (e.g., counseling, social work, psychology). They may also broaden the topic to explore the experiences of supervisors in other health care professions (e.g., nursing). All scholarly explorations of how helpers develop their clinical healthcare leadership skills can help uncover those forces that bolster and obstruct leadership and management development. Future studies may also explore clinical leaders' perceived needs for clinical healthcare leadership development based on their experiences.

Additional scholarly endeavors may also seek out pragmatic solutions to multiple challenges described in this study. Such challenges include the near-absolute reliance on on-the-job experience for leadership development and the lack of leadership preparedness described by the participants. Such a focus can include investigating the potential consequences (if any) of no formal leadership experiences on the quality of clinical services. Another possible focus is exploring clinical supervisors' emotions (e.g., degrees of feeling safe and supported in the work environment) during their on-the-job leadership development experiences. Such a study might identify how emotions both fuel and obstruct leadership development and the solving of novel business challenges.

It is also recommended that counseling scholars and practitioners consider how to solve the study-identified issue of few leadership training opportunities. While the participants' established the themes of learning via experience and the lack of participating in formal leadership training, they did not theorize as to how to break this cycle. How to improve healthcare leadership training may be a literature gap that can also impact the leadership development of future clinical supervisors (e.g., proactive efforts by counseling supervision certification organizations to include leadership training in their curriculum). Counseling leaders in the field may wish to empower their careers by advocating for more leadership development opportunities. By extension, counselor trainers/entrepreneurs may find a new niche by providing leadership trainings (e.g., marketing, creating budgets) dedicated to healthcare professionals in general and counseling professionals in particular. Below is a summary of these recommendations and the insights they may address.

Table 7. Recommendations summary

Study-Derived Theme or Insight	Possible Impact on Leadership Development	Recommendation (and Benefits)
Dearth of Scholarly Attention to Leadership Development of Clinical Supervisors	Unidentified Issues with Leadership Development of Clinical Supervisors	Additional Phenomenological Studies to Validate this Study's Findings, Uncover Additional Insights to Leadership Development Obstacles and Catalysts
Near-Exclusive Reliance on On-The-Job Related Experiences for Leadership Development	Compromised Preparedness for clinical healthcare leadership Positions	Additional Studies to Explore the Consequences of this Theme, Both in Terms of Experienced Stressor Severity and Leadership Development.
Dearth of Formal Leadership Training Opportunities	Obstacle to Ideal Leadership Development of Clinical Supervisors	Counselor Trainers/Entrepreneurs Develop Leadership Development Training Programs

LIMITATIONS

Limitations plague all scholarly explorations of topics. Three limitations were prominent in this study: 1) the possibility for subjectivity and bias influencing data collection and interpretation, 2) the limited number of participants making conclusions difficult to generalize to larger populations, and 3) the recruitment strategy resulted in a population who were all trained in clinical supervision from a singular source. The following paragraphs summarize these limitations.

The first author's counseling practices have included many years of mindfulness exercises and reflection sessions. These efforts likely empowered him to be more aware of the following possible limitations than many researchers. Even so, there are multiple potential limitations to this phenomenological study. These limitations may be a concern with most similarly structured studies. While a bracketing and reflective journal was employed throughout the data collection and analysis procedures, it is possible that subjectivity infiltrated the study. For example, researcher bias may have impacted the data collection and its interpretation. Because the researcher is a primary instrument for qualitative research, scholarly intuition may have somewhat guided the determination of themes. It is possible that another researcher may have interpreted different themes from the same reported experiences.

The study's limitations include the number of participants. The limited number of participants (i.e., 8) disallows its findings to generalize to the larger population of clinical supervisors who assume clinical healthcare leadership roles. The first author's familiarity with the topic and understanding of the counseling supervision and clinical healthcare leadership processes may have unknowingly influenced data collection (e.g., unconsciously leading my unplanned queries). The first author's presence during data collection may have impacted the participant responses, thus altering the authenticity of the presented data.

The study's limitations may include its participant recruitment strategy. While hundreds of clinical supervisors were invited, the source was singular in nature (i.e., a clinical supervisor training organization). The participant recruitment strategy resulted in a population exclusively trained in counseling supervision in their post-graduation years. Clinical supervisors trained via counseling supervision graduate school courses were not included. The study also included an entire population of clinical supervisors from a singular field, counseling (one participant also had a doctorate in psychology). Clinical supervisors with social work or clinical psychology licenses were not included. A more diversified participant population may have provided additional insights into how clinical leaders can develop clinical healthcare leadership skills. Finally, every participant hailed from a singular state (i.e., New Jersey). It is possible that clinical supervisors from different regions may have reported additional themes.

SIGNIFICANCE AND IMPLICATIONS OF THE STUDY

The study's findings provide insights into how clinical counseling supervisors develop clinical healthcare leadership skills and adapt to novel leadership roles. Participant descriptions of how they learned to lead organizations highlighted themes that may be pervasive across mental health and addictions counseling fields. Further, the reported experiences may be similar to professionals in other healthcare professions (e.g., nursing, physical therapists, medical doctors, etc.). More specifically, all participants communicated that the counseling field lacked formal education or training regarding clinical healthcare leadership and business management strategies. Additional studies may validate this finding and perhaps inspire efforts to address it.

The lack of formal training not only can contribute to mishaps and decreased performance in regard to management decision-making and supervisory requirements, but also limit counseling supervisors' abilities to accurately leverage more inclusive leadership techniques. An organization's leadership team has more leverage to initiate and sustain culturally-informed clinical programs than its clinical counselors (Center for Substance Abuse Treatment, 2014). In today's oftentimes globalized and complex work environment where various disciplines intersect, asking for counseling supervisors to practice complex utilitarianism without formal training and development could be problematic, and vastly decrease multicultural development and stakeholder consideration within healthcare settings, even if the exclusive implications are not necessarily intentional.

Participants described their leadership development and adaptation to novel business challenges largely relied on learning strategies via experiences and through relationships. Leadership development influenced predominantly on experience and through relationships implies that clinical supervisors are expected to develop their clinical healthcare leadership skills "on-the-job" and without any formal guidance. Since there has been virtually no impetus to alter reliance on learning via experience and mentorship, one may conclude that the current system is effective. However, just as counseling supervision has evolved from similar reliance to increasingly develop into its own discipline, participant responses in this study regarding formal leadership opportunities imply that the counseling field should include leadership development training.

The study's findings offer additional implications. Perhaps most prominently, the outcomes highlight the prudence for additional studies to explore how to optimally prepare clinical supervisors for their leadership roles. Leadership preparation may include investigating what successful clinical supervisors with clinical healthcare leadership experience consider to be the most effective leadership development dynamics. By better understanding this population's leadership development experiences and their resulting conclusions on how best to train novel leaders, graduate school courses may emphasize leadership development in an established course (e.g. counseling supervision) and in counseling supervision workshops for certified clinical supervisors. More effective leadership may result in more efficiently and ethically run counseling programs that produce higher quality clinical care for clients, the ultimate intention for all counseling professionals.

Practitioners planning to assume counseling supervision roles may consider these findings in reflections about leadership development. Knowing the key themes of lack of formal education in business practices and learning through experiences, aspiring clinical supervisors can seek out business education courses prior to assuming leadership roles. They may also be more alert to the need to have resources (e.g. mentors) established before taking on clinical healthcare leadership responsibilities. Agency owners may also consider these findings and support business and leadership development of their clinical supervisors.

CONCLUSION

Clinical healthcare leadership is a critical contributor to successful mental health services, yet there is a lack of formal leadership learning and development for counseling supervisors in clinical environments. Not providing formal leadership learning and development for counseling supervisors who come from healthcare backgrounds and possess hard, clinical skills alone, but lack leadership skills can lead to many stakeholder groups ultimately being underserved. The authors intentionally used the language "leadership skills" in this conclusion, despite some participants and previous researchers seeing leading as engraved, characteristics (born theory), because leading oftentimes comes down to behaviors, what we do, not personality or character traits alone, and we can learn new skills to improve our ability to execute and behave in a healthy, successful manner (made theory).

Accounting for Multicultural Competency (MCC) while providing clinical healthcare leadership learning and development is also critical, because leaders and therapists on the frontlines both require the capabilities to engage a diverse set of clients that could be very different from themselves. Not emphasizing and accounting for MCC can produce implications where counseling injustice emerges for underserved, minority people groups and unhealthy ripple effects in communities of need. These are issues that have often been overlooked in regard to formal leadership learning and development efforts for clinical healthcare leaders, as counseling supervisors have been expected to develop leadership knowledge and skills on their own or to just "go with the flow," while healthcare organizations emphasized clinical psychotherapy development instead.

This qualitative phenomenological study sought to take a significant step in the right direction when it comes to addressing this gap in literature and practice by first answering these research questions: "How do clinical supervisors develop leadership skills for clinical healthcare leadership (e.g., program director, executive director) roles?" and "How do clinical supervisors learn to address unforeseen business challenges (e.g., low census) while leading clinical programs?". The former question produced insights that featured learning through directly encountering leadership experiences and learning through interactions with others. Both themes implied the need for the leader, him or herself, to initiate developmental and educational dynamics (e.g., seeking mentorship from others). The second question produced the similar themes of simply experiencing novel leadership experiences, reflecting upon the outcomes, and using lessons to inform future leadership decisions.

While clinical healthcare leaders showed adaptive leadership and intuitive initiative to address leadership challenges, the study still identified the sheer lack of formal leadership development in clinical healthcare environments and shed light on the practices being leveraged by counseling supervisors, which may not necessarily rise to the level of being competent or responsible, especially in such a challenging environment (clinical healthcare). The lack of formal leadership support for clinical healthcare leaders points to a major risk factor, and something that healthcare organizations must be aware of to ensure that they're mitigating these gaps and risks, while providing adequate support and services for all people groups. When there is a lack of leadership competency on behalf of counseling supervisors, ultimately, the care, services, direction, and practices of the therapists reporting to these leaders can diminish, leading to underperformance and execution. Underperformance and execution in this context does not necessarily just mean that the "bottom line" will suffer, but more importantly, that patients seeking care and support could be underserved and not achieve adequate treatment and health, which contributes to human suffering.

In conclusion, the study uncovered six major themes describing how clinical supervisors develop clinical healthcare leadership skills and adapt to the novel demands of leadership positions. These clinical supervisors learned through encountering new leadership challenges, intuitively managing leadership demands, and discussing these experiences informally with others. Understanding these shared experiences can lead to additional studies to validate these themes and hopefully lead to reform efforts. More specifically, to dedicate time and resources to better prepare clinical supervisors for the leadership demands that they will encounter as organizational leaders, so they can be better prepared to serve stakeholders.

REFERENCES

American Counseling Association. (2014). *2014 ACA code of ethics*. Author.

American Psychological Association. (2013). Guidelines for psychological practice in health care delivery systems. *The American Psychologist*, *68*(1), 1–6. doi:10.1037/a0029890 PMID:23025748

Anderson, L. S., Page, J., & Zahl, M. (2022). The status of clinical supervision in therapeutic recreation in 2020. *Therapeutic Recreation Journal*, *56*(1), 55–82. doi:10.18666/TRJ-2022-V56-I1-11189

Arbnor, I., & Bjerke, B. (2009). *Methodology for creating business knowledge* (3rd ed.). SAGE Publications. doi:10.4135/9780857024473

Atli Ozbas, A., & Kovanci, M. S. (2022). The experience of moral distress by chief nurse officers during the covid-19 pandemic: A descriptive phenomenological study. *Journal of Nursing Management*, *30*(7), 2383–2393. doi:10.1111/jonm.13780 PMID:36044440

Bailey, D. Jr, Docherty, S. L., Adams, J. A., Carthron, D. L., Corazzini, K., Day, J. R., Neglia, E., Thygeson, M., & Anderson, R. A. (2012). Studying the clinical encounter with the adaptive leadership framework. *Journal of Healthcare Leadership*, *4*, 83–91. doi:10.2147/JHL.S32686 PMID:24409083

Baltrinic, E. R., & Wachter Morris, C. (2020). Signature pedagogies: A framework for pedagogical foundations in counselor education. *Teaching and Supervision in Counseling*, *2*(2).

Barreto, A. (2012). Counseling for the training of leaders and leadership development: A commentary. *The Professional Counselor*, *2*(3), 226–234. doi:10.15241/abb.2.3.226

Bentz, V., & Shapiro, J. (1998). *Mindful inquiry in social research*. Sage Publications. doi:10.4135/9781452243412

Bernard, J. M., & Goodyear, R. K. (1992). *Fundamentals of clinical supervision*. Allyn & Bacon.

Bernard, J. M., & Goodyear, R. K. (2018). *Fundamentals of clinical supervision* (6th ed.). Pearson Education, Inc.

Bigland, C., Evans, D., Bolden, R., & Rae, M. (2020). Systems leadership in practice: Thematic insights from three public health case studies. *BMC Public Health*, *20*(1), 1–14. doi:10.118612889-020-09641-1 PMID:33203397

Blank, W. (2001). *The 108 skills of natural born leaders*. AMACOM.

Böhm, B., Palma, M., Ousley, J., & Keane, G. (2022). Competency-based mental health supervision: Evidence-based tool needs for the humanitarian context. *Global Mental Health (Cambridge, England)*, 1–2.

Broadwater, A. R., Brown, C. L., & Moore, M. (2022). An integrative pedagogical approach to teaching counseling supervision. *The Journal of Counselor Preparation and Supervisor*, *15*(2), 53–79.

Broome, K. M., Knight, D. K., Edwards, J. R., & Flynn, P. M. (2009). Leadership, burnout, and job satisfaction in outpatient drug-free treatment programs. *Journal of Substance Abuse Treatment*, *37*(2), 160–170. doi:10.1016/j.jsat.2008.12.002 PMID:19339143

Bryman, A., Bresnen, M., Beardsworth, A., & Keil, T. (1988). Qualitative research and the study of leadership. *Human Relations*, *41*(1), 13–30. doi:10.1177/001872678804100102

Bush, T. (2014). Instructional and transformational leadership: Alternative and complementary models? *Educational Management Administration & Leadership*, *45*(2), 193–195. doi:10.1177/1741143216686723

CACREP 2016 standards. (n.d.). https://www.cacrep.org/for-programs/2016-cacrep-standards/

Calatrava, M., Martins, M. V., Schweer-Collins, M., Duch-Ceballos, C., & Rodríguez-González, M. (2022). Differentiation of self: A scoping review of Bowen Family Systems Theory's core construct. *Clinical Psychology Review*, *91*, 102101. doi:10.1016/j.cpr.2021.102101 PMID:34823190

Center for Substance Abuse Treatment. (2007). *Competencies for substance abuse treatment clinical supervisors: Technical assistance publication (TAP) series 21-A*. Substance Abuse and Mental Health Services Administration.

Center for Substance Abuse Treatment. (2009). *Clinical supervision and professional development of the substance abuse counselor*. Substance Abuse and Mental Health Services Administration.

Center for Substance Abuse Treatment. (2014). *TIP 59: Improving Cultural Competence*. Substance Abuse and Mental Health Services Administration.

Chaudhry, I. S. (2022). Viable system model: A tool for managing sustainable development holistically. *Management & Sustainability: An Arab Review*, *1*(1), 50–65. doi:10.1108/MSAR-01-2022-0008

Cohen, J. A., Kassan, A., Wada, K., Arthur, N., & Goopy, S. (2022). Enhancing multicultural and social justice competencies in Canadian counselling psychology training. *Canadian Psychology*, *63*(3), 298–312. doi:10.1037/cap0000287

Curtis, R., & Sherlock, J. J. (2006). Wearing two hats: Counselors working as managerial leaders in agencies and schools. *Journal of Counseling and Development*, *84*(1), 120–126. doi:10.1002/j.1556-6678.2006.tb00386.x

DeDiego, A. C., Chan, C. D., & Basma, D. (2022). Emerging leaders: Leadership development experiences of counselor education doctoral students. *Counselor Education and Supervision*, *61*(3), 262–275. doi:10.1002/ceas.12241

Dolan, A. (2022). *Beliefs Matter: School Counselor Self-Assessment of Perceived Advocacy, Collaboration, and Leadership Mindset* [Doctoral dissertation].

Elswick, S. E., Cuellar, M. J., & Mason, S. E. (2018). Leadership and school social work in the usa: A qualitative assessment. *School Mental Health, 29*, 1-14.

Evans, A. M., Wright, S., Murphy, P., & Maki, J. (2016). *Incorporating leadership models into counseling supervision: Recommendations to strengthen services*. Retrieved June 9, 2020, from https://www.counseling.org/docs/default-source/vistas /article_5124f227f16116603abcacff0000bee5e7.pdf?sfvrsn=4&sfvrsn=4

Fassinger, R. E., Buki, L. P., & Shullman, S. L. (2017). Leadership in counseling psychology: Introduction to the special issue. *The Counseling Psychologist*, *45*(6), 742–751. doi:10.1177/0011000017729755

Fassinger, R. E., & Shullman, S. L. (2017). Leadership and counseling psychology: What should we know? Where could we go? *The Counseling Psychologist*, *45*(7), 927–964. doi:10.1177/0011000017744253

Fernandez, C. S. P., Noble, C. C., & Garman, L. (2021). A qualitative analysis of maternal and child health public health leadership institute (mch phli) leaders: Assessing the application of leadership skills at the "others" and "wider community" levesl of the mch leadership competencies 4.0. *Maternal and Child Health Journal*, *25*(9), 1437–1446. doi:10.100710995-021-03134-2 PMID:33950326

Fricdmann, P. D., Jiang, L., & Alexander, J. A. (2010). Top manager effects on buprenorphine adoption in outpatient substance abuse treatment programs. *The Journal of Behavioral Health Services & Research*, *37*(3), 322–337. doi:10.100711414-009-9169-z PMID:19296223

Gabel, S. (2013). Transformational leadership and healthcare. *Medical Science Educator*, *23*(1), 55–60. doi:10.1007/BF03341803

Gazzola, N., De Stefano, J., Theriault, A., & Audet, C. (2013). Learning to be supervisors: A qualitative investigation of difficulties experienced by supervisors-in-training. *The Clinical Supervisor, 32*(1), 15–39. doi:10.1080/07325223.2013.778678

Gibson, D. M., Dollarhide, C. T., & McCallum, L. J. (2010). Nontenured assistant professors as American counseling association division presidents: The new look of leadership in counseling. *Journal of Counseling and Development, 88*(3), 285–292. doi:10.1002/j.1556-6678.2010.tb00024.x

Giorgi, A. (1985). Introduction. In A. Giorgi (Ed.), *Phenomenology and psychological research* (pp. 1–7). Duquesne University Press.

Giorgi, A. (1997). The theory, practice, and evaluation of the phenomenological method as a qualitative research procedure. *Journal of Phenomenological Psychology, 28*(2), 235–260. doi:10.1163/156916297X00103

Giorgi, A., & Giorgi, B. (2008). Phenomenological psychology. In C. Willig & W. Stainton-Rogers (Eds.), *The sage handbook of qualitative research in psychology* (pp. 165–178). Sage Publications. doi:10.4135/9781848607927.n10

Giorgi, A., Giorgi, B., & Morley, J. (2017). The descriptive phenomenological psychological method. In C. Willig & W. Stainton-Rogers (Eds.), *The sage handbook of qualitative research in psychology* (2nd ed., pp. 176–192). Sage Publications. doi:10.4135/9781526405555.n11

Glosoff, H. L., Durham, J. C., & Whittaker, J. E. (2011). Supervision to prepare counselors as leaders and social justice advocates. In C. Y. Chang, C. A. Barrio Minton, A. Dixon, J. E. Myers, & T. J. Sweeney (Eds.), *Professional counseling excellence through leadership and advocacy* (pp. 185–205). Routledge.

Grzanka, P. R., & Cole, E. R. (2021). An argument for bad psychology: Disciplinary disruption, public engagement, and social transformation. *The American Psychologist, 76*(8), 1334–1345. doi:10.1037/amp0000853 PMID:35113597

Gundel, B. E., Bartholomew, T. T., & Scheel, M. J. (2020). Culture and care: An illustration of multicultural processes in a counseling dyad. *Practice Innovations (Washington, D.C.), 5*(1), 19–31. doi:10.1037/pri0000104

Hargett, C.W., Doty, J.P., Hauck, J.N., Webb, A.M.B., Cook, S.H., Tsipis, N.E., Neumann, J.A., , Andolsek, K. M., & Taylor, D. C. (2017). Developing a model for effective leadership in healthcare: A concept mapping approach. *Journal of Healthcare Leadership, 9*, 69–78. doi:10.2147/JHL.S141664 PMID:29355249

Hayes, J. A., McAleavey, A. A., Castonguay, L. G., & Locke, B. D. (2016). Psychotherapists' outcomes with White and racial/ethnic minority clients: First, the good news. *Journal of Counseling Psychology, 63*(3), 261–268. doi:10.1037/cou0000098 PMID:27078197

Heidegger, M. (1971). *The origin of the work of art*. Harper Books.

Heifetz, R. A. (1994). *Leadership without easy answers*. Belknap Press. doi:10.4159/9780674038479

Henderson, P. (1994). *Administrative skills in counseling supervision*. ERIC Digest. ERIC database. (ED372356)

Henderson, S. E., Henricksen, R. C., Jr., Liang, Y.-W. M., & Marks, D. F. (2016). *Counselor licensure supervision across the United States: A comparative look.* https://www.counseling.org/docs/defaultsource/vistas/article_09ccbf24f16116603abcacff0000bee5e7.pdf?sfvrsn=52a9442c_4

Henry, H. L., & Li, C.-S. (2022). Religious identity development and multicultural competence: A correlational study of counseling students. *Counseling and Values, 67*(1), 116–137.

Hite, R. L., & Milbourne, J. D. (2022). Divining the professional development experiences of K-12 stem master teacher leaders in the united states. *Professional Development in Education, 48*(3), 476–492. doi:10.1080/19415257.2021.1955733

Holt, H., Beutler, L. E., Kimpara, S., Macias, S., Haug, N. A., Shiloff, N., & Stein, M. (2015). Evidence-based supervision: Tracking outcome and teaching principles of change in clinical supervision to bring science to integrative practice. *Psychotherapy (Chicago, Ill.), 52*(2), 185–189. doi:10.1037/a0038732 PMID:25985042

Houston, C. (2022). Why social scientists still need phenomenology. *Thesis Eleven, 168*(1), 37–54. doi:10.1177/07255136211064326

HuminuikK.O'ConnorM.DockettK.KallivayalilD. J.McFarlandS. G.WyndhamJ.

Husserl, E. (1970). *Logical investigations* (J. Findlay, Trans.). Humanities Press. (Original publication 1900)

Imel, Z. E., Baldwin, S., Atkins, D. C., Owen, J., Baardseth, T., & Wampold, B. E. (2011). Racial/ethnic disparities in therapist effectiveness: A conceptualization and initial study of cultural competence. *Journal of Counseling Psychology, 58*(3), 290–298. doi:10.1037/a0023284 PMID:21534654

Imogen, F., Orr, C., & Thielking, M. (2022). Apply the framework method to qualitative psychological research: Methodological overview and worked example. *Qualitative Psychology.* Advance online publication. doi:10.1037/qup0000238

Jacob, C. J., Stoler, J., & Roth, G. (2017). A pilot study of transformational leadership and college counseling outcomes. *Journal of Creativity in Mental Health, 12*(2), 180–191. doi:10.1080/15401383.2016.1201033

Kemer, G., Li, C., Attia, M., Chan, C. D., Chung, M., Li, D., Colburn, A. N., Peters, H. C., Ramaswamy, A., & Sunal, Z. (2021). Multicultural supervision in counseling: A content analysis of peer-reviewed literature. *Counselor Education and Supervision, 61*(1), 2–14. doi:10.1002/ceas.12220

Kerr, M. (2003). Multigenerational family systems: Theory of bowen and its application. In G. G. Sholevar & L. D. Schwoeri (Eds.), *Textbook of family and couples therapy: Clinical applications* (pp. 103–126). American Psychiatric Publishing.

Kimberly, J. R., & McLellan, A. T. (2006). The business of addiction treatment: A research agenda. *Journal of Substance Abuse Treatment, 31*(3), 213–219. doi:10.1016/j.jsat.2006.06.018 PMID:16996384

Klenke, K. (2008). *Qualitative research in the study of leadership.* Emerald Group Publishing Limited.

Kneale, M. G. M., Young, A. A., & Dollarhide, C. T. (2018). Cultivating counseling leaders through district leadership cohorts. *Professional School Counseling*, *21*(1b), 1–9.

Kocyigit, M. (2022). Challenges and ethical issues in counseling supervision from faculty supervisors' perspectives. *Participatory Educational Research*, *9*(5), 305–329. doi:10.17275/per.22.116.9.5

La Guardia, A. C. (2020). Counselor education and supervision: 2019 Annual Review. *Counselor Education and Supervision*, *60*(1), 2–21. doi:10.1002/ceas.12192

Lennon, E., Hopkins, L., Einboden, R., McCloughen, A., Dawson, L., & Buus, N. (2022). Organizational Change in Complex Systems: Organizational and Leadership Factors in the Introduction of Open Dialogue to Mental Health Care Services. *Community Mental Health Journal*, ●●●, 1–10. PMID:35585467

Lincoln, Y. S. (1995). Emerging criteria for quality in qualitative and interpretive research. *Qualitative Inquiry*, *1*(3), 275–289. doi:10.1177/107780049500100301

Lockard, F. W. III, Laux, J. M., Ritchie, M., Piazza, N., & Haefner, J. (2014). Perceived leadership preparation in counselor education doctoral students who are members of the American counseling association in cacrep-accredited programs. *The Clinical Supervisor*, *33*(2), 228–242. doi:10.1080/073 25223.2014.992270

M. (2022). Moving human rights to the forefront of psychology: Summary of the final report of the APA task force on human rights. *American Psychologist, 77*(4), 589.

Mann, S. T., & Merced, M. (2018). Preparing for entry-level practice in supervision. *Professional Psychology, Research and Practice*, *49*(1), 98–106. doi:10.1037/pro0000171

Maritsa, E., Goula, A., Psychogios, A., & Pierrakos, G. (2022). Leadership development: Exploring relational leadership implications in healthcare organizations. *International Journal of Environmental Research and Public Health*, *19*(23), 1–14. doi:10.3390/ijerph192315971 PMID:36498040

McFillen, J. M., O'Neil, D. A., Balzer, W. K., & Varney, G. H. (2013). Organizational diagnosis: An evidence-based approach. *Journal of Change Management*, *13*(2), 223–246. doi:10.1080/14697017.2 012.679290

McGinn, J. M. (2022). Engaging and Leading Future Counseling Leaders. *MSJCC 10 Building Mindful Community 12 Peer Support in Times of COVID and Beyond 14 Navigating Trauma Utilizing*, *17*(2), 1–24.

McKibben, W. B., Umstead, L. K., & Borders, L. D. (2017). Identifying dynamics of counseling leadership: A content analysis study. *Journal of Counseling and Development*, *95*(2), 192–202. doi:10.1002/jcad.12131

Meany-Walen, K. K., Carnes-Holt, K., Barrio-Minton, C. A., Purswell, K., & Pronchenko-Jain, Y. (2013). An exploration of counselors' professional leadership development. *Journal of Counseling and Development*, *91*(2), 206–215. doi:10.1002/j.1556-6676.2013.00087.x

Mollen, D., & Ridley, C. R. (2021). Rethinking multicultural counseling competence: An introduction to the major contribution. *The Counseling Psychologist*, *49*(4), 490–503. doi:10.1177/0011000020986543

Morrison, P., Spofford, J., & Carswell, M. (2022). Supervision of cognitive behavioral therapy for substance use disorders. In E. A. Storch, J. S. Abramowitz, & D. McKay (Eds.), *Training and supervision in specialized cognitive behavior therapy: Methods, settings, and populations* (pp. 319–336). American Psychological Association. doi:10.1037/0000314-022

Morse, J. M. (2015). Critical Analysis of strategies for determining rigor in qualitative inquiry. *Qualitative Health Research*, *25*(9), 1212–1222. doi:10.1177/1049732315588501 PMID:26184336

Moustakas, C. (1994). *Phenomenological research methods*. Sage Publications. doi:10.4135/9781412995658

Northouse, P. G. (2015). *Leadership: Theory and practice* (7th ed.). Sage.

Oleksa-Marewska, K., & Tokar, J. (2022). Facing the post-pandemic challenges: The role of leadership effectiveness in shaping the affective well-being of healthcare providers working in a hybrid work mode. *International Journal of Environmental Research and Public Health*, *19*(21), 1–19. doi:10.3390/ijerph192114388 PMID:36361264

Pfiffner, M. (2022). *The Neurology of Business: Implementing the Viable System Model*. Springer Nature. doi:10.1007/978-3-031-14260-4

Phillips, J. C., Hargons, C., Chung, Y. B., Forrest, L., Oh, K. H., & Westefeld, J. (2017). Society of counseling psychology leadership academy: Cultivating leadership competence and community. *The Counseling Psychologist*, *45*(7), 965–991. doi:10.1177/0011000017736141

Pope-Davis, D. B., Toporek, R. L., Ortega-Villalobos, L., Ligiéro, D. P., Brittan-Powell, C. S., Liu, W. M., Bashshur, M. R., Codrington, J. N., & Liang, C. T. H. (2002). Client perspectives of multicultural counseling competence: A qualitative examination. *The Counseling Psychologist*, *30*(3), 355–393. doi:10.1177/0011000002303001

Puta, B. (2022). Does phenomenology (still) matter? Three phenomenological traditions and sociological theory. *International Journal of Politics Culture and Society*, *35*(3), 41–431.

Puyo, J. G. B. (2022). Ethical Leadership in Education: A Uniting View Through Ethics of Care, Justice, Critique, and Heartful Education. *Journal of Culture and Values in Education*, *5*(2), 140–151. doi:10.46303/jcve.2022.24

Rodriguez-Rivero, R., Ortiz-Marcos, I., & Patino-Arenas, V. E. (2022). Exploring the influence of culture in the present and future of multicultural organizations: Comparing the case of spain and latin america. *Sustainability (Basel)*, *14*(4), 1–15. doi:10.3390u14042327

Saldana, J. (2021). *The coding manual for qualitative researchers* (4th ed.). Sage.

Senge, P. M. (2006). *The fifth discipline: The art & practice of the learning organization*. Doubleday.

Steinhoff, R. L. (2015). Natural born leaders: Use of a self-assessment tool and benefits to coaching and development. *Journal of Practical Consulting*, *5*(2), 19–28.

Storlie, C. A., & Herlihy, B. E. (2022). *Counseling leaders & advocates: Strengthening the future of the profession*. American Counseling Association.

Storlie, C. A., Parker-Wright, M., & Woo, H. (2015). Multicultural leadership development: A phenomenological exploration of emerging leaders in counselor education. *Journal of Counselor Leadership & Advocacy*, *2*, 154–169. doi:10.1080/2326716X.2015.1054078

Storlie, C. A., & Wood, S. M. (2014). Developing social justice leaders through Chi Sigma Iota: A phenomenological exploration of chapter leader experiences, Part 1. *Journal of Counselor Leadership & Advocacy*, *1*(2), 160–180. doi:10.1080/2326716X.2014.935984

Sue, D. W., Arredondo, P., & McDavis, R. J. (1992). Multicultural counseling competencies and standards: A call to the profession. *Journal of Multicultural Counseling and Development*, *20*(2), 64–88. doi:10.1002/j.2161-1912.1992.tb00563.x

Sue, D. W., & Sue, D. (2008). *Counseling the culturally diverse: Theory and practice*. Wiley.

Sullivan, P. (2016). Leadership in social work: Where are we? *Journal of Social Work Education*, *52*(51), 551–561. doi:10.1080/10437797.2016.1174644

Thomas, E. M., & Grafsky, E. L. (2021). Appalachian church leaders: An interpretive phenomenological analysis study to understand how substance use impacts their communities. *Pastoral Psychology*, *70*(4), 379–397. doi:10.100711089-021-00956-3

ul Amin, S., & Kamal, Y. (2016). Impact of natural born leader qualities on the project team performance: The influences of demographics (gender and age). *International Journal of Management, Accounting, and Economics, 3*(5), 306-318.

Vik, M. B., Finnestrand, H., & Flood, R. L. (2022). Systemic Problem Structuring in a Complex Hospital Environment using Viable System Diagnosis–Keeping the Blood Flowing. *Systemic Practice and Action Research*, *35*(2), 203–226. doi:10.100711213-021-09569-6 PMID:33935483

Watkins, C. E. (1990). Development of the psychotherapy supervisor. *Psychotherapy (Chicago, Ill.)*, *27*(4), 553–560. doi:10.1037/0033-3204.27.4.553

Watkins, C. E., Hook, J. N., DeBlaere, C., Davis, D. E., Wilcox, M. M., & Owen, J. (2022). Extending multicultural orientation to the group supervision of psychotherapy: Practical applications. *Practice Innovations (Washington, D.C.)*, *7*(3), 255–267. doi:10.1037/pri0000185

Willis, D. G., Sullivan-Bolyai, S., Knafl, K., & Zichi-Cohen, M. (2016). Distinguishing features and similarities between descriptive phenomenological and qualitative description research. *Western Journal of Nursing Research*, *38*(9), 1–20. doi:10.1177/0193945916645499 PMID:27106878

Woo, H., Storlie, C. A., & Balrinic, E. R. (2016). Perceptions of professional identity development from counselor educators in leadership positions. *Counselor Education and Supervision*, *55*(4), 278–293. doi:10.1002/ceas.12054

Yukl, G. (2013). *Leadership in organizations* (8th ed.). Prentice Hall.

Chapter 13
Current Ethical Issues in Healthcare Settings

Jo Hall

https://orcid.org/0009-0004-8082-4305

Marymount University, USA

ABSTRACT

The healthcare industry is one of the industries that has undergone a substantial digital transformation. The paperwork initially used by hospitals has been changed to cloud services, smart devices, and the introduction of the internet of medical things (IoMT). Electronic health records have improved health-care quality, among other factors. The increased cyber security in the healthcare system and workers' limited knowledge of cyber security has been attributed to workers' negligence. The inability to secure healthcare information and data has intense implications for the healthcare organization. These threats may be limited through ethical decision-making models and organizational culture models. The leader-ship theory, decision-making model, strategy model theory, change managerial theory, and desired state of the organizational culture are some of the methodologies that can be used in securing cyber threats. The topic concerning the various methods of protecting healthcare information from cyberbullies is important because it protects all data categories from damage and theft.

INTRODUCTION

Background

It has been discovered that a group of employees at Nice One Hospital are accessing the hospital's medical records and patients' credit card information and are selling it on the dark web. The informa-tion has been reported in the Washington Post and on CNN in the wake of this discovery. According to preliminary investigations and media reports, approximately 65% of the patients' records have been leaked to the dark web, adversely exposing them to stigmatization, discrimination, and psychological, emotional, and financial harm. It is estimated that the affected patients have lost between \$20 and \$50 million. As a result of the internal unauthorized disclosure of patient information, there is a massive

DOI: 10.4018/979-8-3693-1630-6.ch013

public outcry against the hospital and its administration, citing improper mechanisms in collecting, storing, and retrieving patients' information and data. Besides, numerous campaigns have emerged pushing the Department of Health and Human Services, through their Office for Civil Rights (DHHSOCR), to suspend the hospital's operating license for failing to uphold the Health Insurance Portability and Accountability Act (HIPAA).

The hashtag #boycottniceonehospital has been trending on major social media platforms, including Facebook, Twitter, Instagram, and TikTok, as people share their experiences following the exposé. Prominent human rights activists sponsor the trends. Accordingly, the number of visits has drastically reduced from a daily average of six hundred patients to barely forty. Moreover, as the levels of suspicion and claims of negligence increase, there is massive discontentment among workers in the medical and support departments. The presence of investigators and media practitioners in the hospital facilities aggravates the uneasiness. The hospital management has also been invited to record statements on the extent of exposure affecting patients' data.

Scope and the Objectives

Based on the Nice One Hospital case, the primary objective of this paper is to explore strategies or ways to reduce data breaches in hospitals to protect patient health information. It explores how the leadership theory, decision-making model, strategy model theory, change organizational theory, and desired state of the corporate culture can be used to reduce cyber threats. The paper also explores the financial, social, and psychological implications of healthcare data breaches.

Specifically, the paper aims at addressing the following objectives:

i.   To determine the financial, social, and psychological implications of healthcare data breaches.
ii. To evaluate strategies that can be used to reduce healthcare data breaches based on various theories and models.

Problem Statement

The healthcare industry is undergoing a massive, disruptive digital transformation (Chernyshev et al., 2019). The introduction of the Internet of Medical Things (IoMT), information systems, smart devices, and cloud services have actualized the digitization of healthcare services, replacing paper-based medical recording systems with electronic health records (EHRs) (Seh et al., 2020). While these developments have improved the quality of care and levels of accessibility for patients, the digitized healthcare environment has become a primary target for internal and external attacks. Health information is an increasingly attractive target for cybercriminals given its inherent sensitivity, the risk to patients' lives, the high value of patients' records, and the potential for financial gains through patients' credit card details.

According to Seh et al. (2020), about 249.09 million have been directly affected by data breaches in the healthcare sector between 2005 and 2019. The study also revealed that healthcare is the worst industry affected by data breaches, as about 41.2 million healthcare data records were stolen in 2019 alone across the globe (Seh et al., 2020). The USA is one of the countries that are worst affected by healthcare data breaches. The number of attacks on U.S. hospitals each year doubled between 2016 and 2021, from 43 to 91, according to research published in the Journal of the American Medical Association (Wetsman et al., 2023). A patient survey that was conducted in the USA found that 75% of patients are worried about the privacy and confidentiality of their personal information (Raghupathi, Raghupathi & Saharia, 2023).

While workers are critical organizational assets, their negligence, whether deliberate or not, and their lack of information security knowledge are prominent cybersecurity threats (Ramluckan et al., 2020). Insider attackers at Nice One Hospital damaged the protected health information and disclosed the patients' sensitive healthcare data to dark web operationists. Internal healthcare data breaches are increasingly becoming a concern, especially based on the findings of the survey by the Ponemon Institute in 2022. The survey revealed that 42% of healthcare data breaches are caused internally by employees (Raghupathi, Raghupathi & Saharia, 2023). Employee error or negligence is the leading cause of healthcare data breaches, leading to increased hacking. The same survey by Ponemon Institute showed that 60% of organizations believe that their employees lack sufficient knowledge about cybersecurity risks (Raghupathi, Raghupathi & Saharia, 2023). Yeo and Banfield (2022) add that healthcare data breaches mainly result from unintentional human factors, which include ignorance, negligence, and carelessness.

With data breaches, clients, organizations, stakeholders, and businesses are deleteriously affected (Seh et al., 2020). Data breaches are linked to significant financial costs. For instance, in the USA, the cost of a breach per record is estimated to be US $242 while the global average cost is $150 (Lee & Choi, 2021). Data breaches are also associated with reduced quality of healthcare services offered by hospitals, including time wastage to solve the problem. The clients are the main losers in this data breach. There is also a higher possibility of the Nice One Hospital facing litigation, paying fines and penalties, and incurring additional costs on system upgrades. Scripps Health in San Diego reached a $3.5 million proposed settlement to resolve a class action lawsuit stemming from a May 2021 ransomware attack and subsequent breach that impacted 2.1 million individuals (McKeon, 2023).

Significance Statement

Healthcare data breaches remain to be a problem despite various legal, technical, and strategic interventions to address the issue. Many hospitals like Nice One Hospital are still facing significant cybersecurity threats, which substantially affect individual patients, hospitals, and the larger society. There is a need to conduct further studies to determine evidence-based strategies that can be used to secure healthcare data, particularly concerning patient health information (PHI). Thus, this paper is important because it contributes to understanding ways of reducing healthcare data breaches, especially based on various theories or models. It explains strategies that hospitals like Nice One Hospital can use to reduce data breaches while providing the evidence-based and theoretical background for policymaking around enhancing cybersecurity in the healthcare industry.

LITERATURE REVIEW

Current State of the Organization

The insider data breaches and the subsequent sale of patients' data on the dark web have positioned Nice One Hospital, its patients, stakeholders, and business associates in an increasingly dire situation. Since the media reports by Washington Post and on CNN, the hospital has experienced negative publicity that has eroded its trust and reputation as a leading healthcare organization in the region. Nice One Hospital is also experiencing an unprecedented backlash on social media following claims that one of our patients lost an estimated $2.5 million to dark web operatives. According to Smith (2022), data breaches are the primary enablers of fraud, where personal or organizational information is used to commit fraud. Various human rights activities, using #boycottniceonehospital, have championed the hospital's closure until an independent commission establishes its suitability to continue operating. This eventuality could compound the organization's current challenges. Moreover, the DHHSOCR has also been notified about the case, with three human rights organizations calling for the penalization of the hospital for noncompliance with HIPAA regulations.

Nice One Hospital is experiencing the worst operational downtime since its inception. Following the exposé, business operations have been extensively disrupted. Accordingly, the number of visits has largely plummeted, with the hospital registering a 93.33% decline in visitations. With this eventuality, the organization is staring at a massive loss in revenue collection. In addition to the loss in the number of patients, the hospital has lost key partners financing the expansion of the hospital's renal and cardiology units. The hospital had anticipated that expanding these units would help position the healthcare facility as the region's referral center for kidney and heart conditions. Nonetheless, the internally instigated data breaches eroded the sponsors' trust in the facility. Additionally, in the wake of the data breaches, the hospital administration has received approximately twenty-five resignations from employees at managerial levels and thirteen from nurses and general practitioner specialists.

Risks of not Fixing the Data Breaches

Failure to secure healthcare data and information has massive implications for organizations. Reputational damage could negatively affect the organization's corporate brand, affecting its long-term business positioning. According to Nobanee et al. (2021), reputation is a critical commodity to any organization and a lack of it can lead to low customer satisfaction, low employee morale, and poor relationship with stakeholders. With the information on the data breach shared on social media and in *CNN* and the *Washington Post*, the company's search engine results are "poisoned." Additionally, the reputational damage will push the organization's business prospects down, reducing the number of patients seeking medical care from the facility (Biresaw et al., 2021). With sustained loss-making, the organization will be forced to cease operations altogether. Besides, failure to fix the data breaches would expose the organization to unexpected expenditures as the hospital seeks to repair its damaged reputation. Besides, lawsuits-related costs would further push the expenses higher.

Failure to fix the data breaches would make the organization less attractive to workers. In this case, employees would resign from their positions, culminating in higher employee turnover, especially among employees in the executive. Other workers will leave the organization because of increased workplace conflicts and stresses arising from the blame game and accusations on who was responsible for selling patients' data to the dark web, which often leads to job insecurity (Ghani et al., 2022). Low employee morale could also culminate in employee disengagement, workplace anxiety, and job dissatisfaction, culminating in the loss of experienced and committed workers. Consequently, a study by Juma'h and Alnsour (2020) revealed that data breaches significantly impact organizational performance, as such events indicate weakness in the organization's internal control or management.

In addition, failure to fix data breaches can result in significant financial costs to individuals and hospitals. According to Seh et al. (2020), 83% of data security breaches in the healthcare sector are financially motivated, meaning that perpetrators aim at making money with such events. This explains why healthcare is the leading industry in terms of the financial cost of data breaches. For instance, based on a study by Bohn and Schiereck (2022), the average cost of a data breach per record in the healthcare sector is $380 compared to $71 and $223 in the public and finance sectors respectively. The analysis by the Health Sector Cybersecurity Coordination Center (HC3) on the cost of data breaches in the sector reveals that hospitals and individual patients incur significant burdens due to cybersecurity issues. Based on the analysis, the cost per record in the USA was $408 in 2018 and this keeps increasing (HC3, 2019). Thus, data breaches result in substantial financial costs.

Data breaches are also linked to psychological problems, particularly among victims. According to Budimir, Fontaine, and Roesch (2021), many victims of data breaches suffer from severe affective stress due to fear and uncertainty about the consequences of such events. Kilovaty (2021) adds that such victims are likely to experience psychological or mental problems like depression and anxiety, and sometimes post-traumatic stress disorder (PTSD). However, the psychological effects may not be immediate or they can be delayed. As a result, the psychological effects of data breaches are often ignored or not recognized (Solove & Citron, 2017). It is important to recognize the psychological effects of data breaches on victims because they affect their health and well-being. However, the psychological effects of data breaches in the healthcare industry are yet to be comprehensively researched by experts and scholars, as it has limited evidence-based information or data.

Ethical Decision-Making Theories and Model

The first thing Nice One Hospital must do is conduct a thorough forensic investigation to ascertain the existence of a cybersecurity breach and the sale of patients' data on the dark web. This process will help understand which systems were compromised and the extent of corrupted patient data (Kabir et al., 2018). In this case, the organization must delegate various critical aspects of the investigation to its lead information technologists and initiate containment measures to prevent further damage before the threat is wholly eradicated (Coburn et al., 2018).

The virtue approach and the duty-based approach can help actualize this process. According to the duty-based (deontological approach), people must act accordingly irrespective of the consequences that could be triggered (BBC, n.d.). In this case, the hospital administration must send all workers in the information technology department on mandatory leave tasked with managing patients' medical records and credit card information until the investigation is complete. If found liable, the employees must be terminated, and legal proceedings must be opened against them. Moreover, the virtue approach will allow whistle-blowers with information on the real perpetrators of data breaches to share critical information with investigators. In this case, by sharing the crucial details concerning the sale of patients' data to the dark web, the workers will exercise their morality, honesty, and virtuous deeds for the organization's good (Brown, 2020).

Organizational Culture Theories and Models

Nice One Hospital must develop initiatives to evaluate its workers' efforts in achieving organizational effectiveness. The ongoing data breach shows that the employees are diversely influenced by organizational and personal factors, prompting them to disclose and sell patients' medical records and credit card information to operatives on the dark web. Accordingly, the organization has to use the competing values framework and the canoe theory to push the hospital from the reputational and trust loss. According to

Osei et al. (2023), in the competing values framework (CVF), the various organizational and individual factors are grouped into four quadrants: clan, adhocracy, hierarchical, and market. To overcome the current challenges of data breaches, Nice One Hospital can implement a hierarchical framework to achieve an increased internal focus based on processes and policies through a concerted top-down approach (Beus et al., 2020; Tarbouriech et al., 2022). In this case, the Nice One Hospital will develop policies and processes for managing patients' data and information, provide elaborate supervision on data usage, and transparent mechanisms to deal with non-compliant workers.

In headachy culture, Nice One Hospital is like to have clear and defined decision-making authority, standard rules and procedures to be followed, and high levels of accountability that can help in reducing cases of data breaches (Maximini, 2018). Such a culture can enable the organization to develop formalized and structured workplace. However, according to Maximini (2018), a hierarchy culture is only effective where leaders can effectively organize and coordinate employees while maintaining smooth management of the organization. There are concerns that hierarchical culture is bullying and autocratic, preventing employees from voicing their concerns and actively participating in decision-making. Nonetheless, this culture is effective in times of crisis or emergency like the one Nice One Hospital is in (Fernandopulle, 2021). It helps in holding employees, including the management, accountable for the problems faced by the organization. But it is still important for the organization to embrace a flat hierarchy instead of the traditional one because the latter will make it responsive to change. A flat hierarchy promotes teamwork and sharing of knowledge due to close and beneficial interactions between staff and management (Fernandopulle, 2021).

The canoe theory could restructure the missing links in the organization (Zhonghai, 2023). The case analysis shows that the organization lacks teamwork arrangements, allowing the employees to seek individual accomplishments at the expense of the common organizational objective. Juliana et al. (2021) suggest that the canoe theory can enhance teamwork and unity in the workplace to address the fallout among workers and teams before and after the data breach incident. According to canoe theory, employees and management must work together to achieve the intended or common goal (Males, Hudson & Kerr, 2018). This theory will change the organizational culture to ensure that every employee plays a legitimate role in protecting patients' data from possible breaches. The perspectives by Madimenos et al. (2022) on the effectiveness of the canoe theory in allowing the "members to row together" could help eliminate workplace conflict and disagreements among the workers at Nice One Hospital. With the canoe theory, the team will avoid the blame game and work toward securing patients' data and fortifying the organization's cybersecurity systems (Banda, 2022).

Leadership Theories and Decision Models

Nice One Hospital must implement various policies, training, and senior leadership support changes to prevent data breaches in the future. With these changes, the healthcare facility can achieve massive transformation in growth and productivity. The leader-member exchange theory (LMX theory) and transformational leadership theory will help manage organizational activities to enhance the senior leadership support on the hospital's strategic plan (MasterClass, 2022). According to the LMX theory, the leaders and team members will have high-quality relationships, allowing the workers to perform their tasks according to their job description (Comstock et al., 2021). With a practical LMX theory, the leader will develop and communicate the organization's policies with the team members (Xu & Zhang, 2020). Moreover, the workers will be adequately trained to meet the current requirements. With a high-quality relationship, the leaders will understand the gaps in training and knowledge required to deal with data breaches.

High-quality LMX implies that favorable relationships between leaders and subordinates are beneficial in eliminating the inclination to "punish" the administration by selling confidential patients' data on the dark web (Arrasyid et al., 2019). According to Comstock et al. (2021), trust, obligation, and respect under the LMX theory are the principles under which a constructive and transformational working relationship between the leader and their subjects is founded. In this case, the workers must uphold the work ethics and organizational culture, effectively monitoring and preventing data breaches in the future. With the LMX theory, the organization will reduce its high turnover rates because it improves the employees' emotional intelligence, turnover intentions, and overall job satisfaction (AlHashmi et al., 2019). It is worth noting that workers leave an organization due to problems with their supervisors, inadequate compensation, work benefits, organizational issues, and lack of internal collaboration (AlHashmi et al., 2019). However, given the effective relationship and communication between the leader and the subjects, the management is adequately informed of the workers' needs and initiates mechanisms to address them. The high-quality exchanges between the leader and the team will ensure that the employees work to support the leader's vision, hence reducing the occurrence of data breaches in the future. Therefore, the LMX theory can play a significant role in preventing the occurrence of data breaches in the future since the employees are committed to pleasing their leader.

The organization can use transformational leadership theory to improve interactions among leaders and their subjects (Lancefield & Rangen, 2021). Through this leadership approach, Nice One Hospital can instigate change among individual workers and social systems, creating valuable and positive transformation in the followers. Merviö (2022) postulates that transformational leaders inspire their followers to be creative and innovative by interrogating assumptions, reframing difficulties, and approaching old circumstances in new ways. In this case, the management at Nice One Hospital can use transformational leadership to change their employees' perspectives, performance, and culture, effectively avoiding the occurrence of data breaches in the future (Pham, 2021). In this case, transformational leadership will allow the leaders to focus on what motivates and influences the employees to sell patients' medical data and credit card information to dark web operatives. As evidenced by Cleveland & Cleveland (2018), the leadership will initiate measures to progressively coach the workers on improving their performance and understanding the information technology strategy in the organization. Through this approach, the organization will succeed in "transforming" the workers to "value" organizational objectives, including protecting patients and organizational data from breaches.

Strategy Models Theories and the Desired State of the Organizational Culture

Developing resilient software to fortify patients' medical records and credit card information is another critical step for Nice One Hospital. McKinsey's strategic horizons can be extended to inspire organizational change concerning resilient technological development. According to Markopoulos et al. (2020), McKinsey's 3 Horizon Model is founded on the need to address continuous organizational growth and innovation by exploring the opportunities for future growth without disregarding the present performance. In this case, Nice One Hospital can use this model to examine robust data-loss-prevention (DLP) practices to prevent data breaches in the future while improving their current collection, storage, and retrieval of patient information in the hospital setting. Under this model, the organization's primary focus should be to maintain and defend its core business in the healthcare industry. According to Hinterhuber (2022), the

Hospital must install an enabling technology to support its digital transformation. In horizon two, which focuses on nurturing emerging businesses, the organization has to use technology as the building blocks to prevent possible data breaches. Here, the Hospital has to partner with technology companies to install breach meters and detectors to monitor employees' activities on the Hospital's information technology system. In this regard, analytics and artificial intelligence (AI) capabilities can help the organization achieve automated monitoring and identification of data breaches (Bogdanoski, 2022). This could include the development of in-house advanced analytics and AI capabilities to provide data-management solutions to detect and prevent unauthorized data sharing quickly. In horizon three, the organization can create new roles, especially in the information and technology and medical informatics department, to supervise the employees' conduct and activities in the hospital's system. This will include a team tasked with encrypting credit card information according to the organization's security policies (Kosseff, 2022).

Additionally, the IT team can conduct a reverse test to understand the system's ability to withstand hacking incidents in the future and create appropriate fortifications. Kosseff (2022) advises organizations to routinely conduct audits and penetration testing to ascertain the strength of the information system against hackers. Through this approach, the organization will develop a less-complex information system that is less vulnerable to external or internal hackers.

Cooperation among stakeholders is envisioned as an outcome of organizational changes. Nice One Hospital can use the stakeholder theory framework to change its corporate strategy to communicate with its stakeholders on the status of the recovery process following the data breach to demonstrate a resilient response against cybersecurity threats (Coburn et al., 2018). Deursen (2022) states that organizations cannot isolate their various stakeholders when implementing a change in their strategies since each stakeholder is essential for successfully operationalizing the business. The organization can induce the stakeholder theory framework to achieve a uniform approach concerning the incidence of data breaches and subsequent losses in the stakeholders' interests. Through stakeholder analysis, the organization will determine its respective stakes in the change strategy (Deursen, 2022). Since the issue of data breaches at the hospital is now a matter of public interest, the organization has to conduct extensive stakeholder analysis and formulate a stakeholder communication plan to determine their interests and levels of influence and keep them informed of the various stages of the organization's strategic changes. Officials from DHHSOCR and other investigating officials could influence the implementation of strategic changes in the organization. Accordingly, the hospital will determine the best approach to relate with them and the best communication channel to utilize when providing compliance reports.

Change Management Theories and Models

Altering organizational and individual cultures is imperative in avoiding data breaches in the future. Accordingly, Nice One Hospital can kickstart its change strategy using the nudge theory and the ADKAR change management model. The nudge theory is increasingly influential in changing the staff's behavior. According to Deursen (2022), a nudge refers to a slight change to the context in which decisions are made that alters their behavior. In cybersecurity, nudges are used to influence behavior change among end-users. Coburn et al. (2018) contend that, even without corresponding compensation or penalties, the nudge principle could help encourage good cyber hygiene in the workplace, avoiding instances of data breaches in the future. In this case, the organization can use markers to remind the staff of the appropriate use of information technologies in healthcare settings. Besides, holding regular conversations on the overall security apparatus in the organization could instigate a positive nudging tone among the workforce to achieve a mutually beneficial relationship between the workers and the organization. Xu et al. (2018) assert that the nudge will help improve the workers' motivation, efficiency, and effectiveness in their workplaces as they are not forced to change their working behaviors. Besides, the nudge can be easily scaled up within the organization, reducing the time to implement change (Tams, 2018).

The organization can implement the ADKAR change management model to assess the security culture among the workers and implement related changes (Vasileiou & Furnell, 2019). Through the ADKAR change management model, Nice One Hospital will take the employees through a five-phased process: awareness, desire, knowledge, ability, and reinforcement (Vasileiou & Furnell, 2019, p. 81). The drive for awareness will inform the workers about the necessity of achieving change, which is to avoid the occurrence of data breaches in the future. In this case, all workers in the hospital must receive proper communication about the vision of the proposed changes (Ramluckan et al., 2020). Workers' desire will also be exemplified by the willingness to be part of and support the initiated change processes in the organization. In this regard, the organization must eliminate any dissatisfaction or demotivation among the workers to ensure the successful implementation of the change process (Ramluckan et al., 2020).

About 70% of change programs fail mainly due to employee resistance (Furxhi, 2021; Darmawan & Azizah, 2020), and Nice One Hospital can reduce this risk of change failure by actively involving workers in the entire change process. According to Furxhi (2021), effective communication, reducing mistrust, and addressing the emotional needs of employees can reduce resistance to change significantly. Also, the organization should reduce cynicism to create a comfortable work environment while guaranteeing workers of job security (Darmawan & Azizah, 2020). The organization must address the risks of employee resistance to successfully implement the proposed change initiative. Additionally, Nice One Hospital should embrace modern technology in its change management. Technology-mediated change management (TMCM) effectively engages and influences key stakeholders to ensure the successful execution of the change (Kanitz & Gonzalez, 2021). For instance, it can use TalentLMS and Docebo tools to empower employees while getting them up to speed to ensure the timely execution of the change. Such tools can enable the organization to quickly understand and monitor stakeholders' behaviors, and faster feedback. Thus, incorporating technology ensures adaptability, personalization, and openness in the change process (Kanitz & Gonzalez, 2021).

The ADKAR change management model can inform the organization of regular training sessions on cybersecurity hygiene (Scherer, 2022). Knowledge, which is the know-how to achieve change, will be achieved through extensive training for all employees on the effective utilization of information technologies in the healthcare sector and mechanisms to enhance cybersecurity hygiene to avoid data breaches in the future. As Vasileiou and Furnell (2019) show, the organization will use the knowledge acquired from the investigation data and findings to create awareness of the need for change. Kosseff (2022) contends that regular training on processing sensitive information is vital in sustaining the required behavior among workers. Imperatively, the negative aspects of the data breach will form the bases of the knowledge shared, emphasizing what not to do when working on the hospital premises.

Lastly, the organization must maintain its capability to implement change. In this case, the hospital must support its ability to change by deploying various management resources to monitor its implementation and the impacts on business operations (Vasileiou & Furnell, 2019). Leaders of the organization must demonstrate the right change leadership behaviors, particularly by providing a compelling mission and vision, providing the required resources, and closely monitoring the execution of the change (Engida, Alemu & Mulugeta, 2022). Importantly, they should enhance employees' readiness for the proposed change. The same should be reinforced to guarantee sustained improvement in the organization's cybersecurity apparatus. Besides, given the extent of the data breach and the subsequent media reports, the hospital's management must be extensively prepared to reinform efforts to improve their cybersecurity by offering recognition, rewards, or compensation to end-users who maintain the highest levels of cybersecurity hygiene.

METHODOLOGY

After the data leakage at Nice One Hospital, this research aims to understand the financial, social, and psychological implications of unauthorized access to patients' information. A qualitative research methodology was adopted to collect primary data through interviews and an online survey involving questionnaires.

First, face-to-face interviews were done with the affected patients and hospital staff to understand the magnitude of exposure and the financial and psychological implications of the data leakage (Hasan et al., 2023). The interviews also involved health and human rights pursuits to gain more insight into the presence of the breach. This was done to understand the public complaints against the hospital. Specifically, semi-structured interviews were used to collect data from the participants. Semi-structured interviews were preferred in this case because it could effectively be used for exploratory data and helped in generating new concepts or ideas (DeJonckheere & Vaughn, 2019). Also, it is ideal for qualitative research while allowing the researcher to explore participants' beliefs, feelings, and thoughts, particularly on sensitive issues. Interviews involved open-ended questions and each lasted for about 30 minutes.

Then, an online survey was hosted to collect more data from a wider population. The survey consisted of queries on the loss of finances incurred by the sick, the magnitude of public trust in the health center, and the presence of substitute healthcare facilities in the area. Online survey participants were required to respond to questions contained in the questionnaires. 250 people participated in the online survey, and they provided useful responses that complemented data collected through interviews.

In addition, a critical literature review was used to gain perceptions of the statutory fallout of the breach of information and the orders established to safeguard private particulars. The literature scan yielded a profound grasp of the Health Insurance Portability and Liability Act (HIPAA) and the purpose of the DHHS OCR in such happenstances. The discoveries of the quest will be gauged and explained employing illustrative data and apposite solutions. The consequences will be harnessed to secure an enhanced understanding of the ramifications of the information rupture and to form tactics to decrease the hazards of parallel episodes in the time to come.

RECOMMENDATIONS

First, hospital management should act right now to strengthen its data security architecture in order to address the current issue. To protect patient data, the hospital should first invest in new security systems that follow HIPAA regulations and use technologies such as encryption and authentication. Also, the hospital should create a thorough data breach response strategy to help it cope with data-related issues in the future (Jimo et al., 2023). Also, to strengthen its data security, Nice One Hospital should adopt effective cryptographic techniques. Encryption is one of the effective ways to secure data, especially against unauthorized access and use (Hassan et al., 2022).

Secondly, the hospital should also hold regular staff training sessions to ensure everyone knows the value of data security and the repercussions of any unlawful access. Findings from the literature review revealed that many employees are not knowledgeable of data security techniques. The training should be aimed at equipping employees with the knowledge and skills to ensure effective data security hygiene in the organization (Haney & Lutters, 2020). Also, the training should be used to create data security awareness among employees.

Thirdly, by taking in public relations operations and explaining the procedure they are doing to secure the security of patient data, the hospital should also take measures to reclaim the public's trust. The hospital needs to restore public trust to achieve long-term and sustainable success (Karhapää, Savolainen & Malkamäki, 2022). To regain public trust, the hospital first needs to take responsibility for the consequences of data breaches, and this should be clearly communicated by the top leadership. Secondly, it needs to explain the action it has taken to rectify the mistake. It should assure the public that such events will not happen in the future.

Finally, the hospital should consider hiring outside specialists to conduct a thorough examination of the hospital's security policies and practices. Internal employees were involved in data breaches and external specialists are required in this case to ensure proper investigation and impartiality in the entire process (Files & Liu, 2022). Unlike internal specialists, external investigators are not connected to employees, enabling them to conduct a thorough and impartial investigation. Also, external specialists are likely to inject a lot of expertise and experience in the entire investigation process, leading to useful findings that can help in addressing the process while helping the organization to strongly move forward. The Hospital will be able to find any security system holes as a result and take action to close them.

CONCLUSION

Nice One Hospital's data breach confirms the increasing cybersecurity threats facing many hospitals globally, including in the USA. It reveals that the problem indeed exists and needs to be addressed. Importantly, healthcare data breaches result in adverse effects, particularly financial and psychological effects. Many hospitals are losing and incurring millions of dollars due to such breaches while victims are subjected to great psychological problems like stress, anxiety, and depression. The first major step to addressing data breaches is to get the root cause of the problem by conducting an effective and impartial investigation. Also, organizations should introduce relevant organizational culture to help in addressing cybersecurity threats. Hierarchical culture may be appropriate for many organizations because it ensures formalized procedures and structures in data management. Effective leadership is also essential in securing healthcare data. Human, organizational, and technical factors should be considered when hospitals are developing plans to boost healthcare data security.

REFERENCES

AlHashmi, M., Jabeen, F., & Papastathopoulos, A. (2019). Impact of leader–member exchange and perceived organizational support on turnover intention. *Policing*, *42*(4), 520–536. doi:10.1108/PI-JPSM-06-2018-0081

Arrasyid, M., Amaliyah, A., & Pandin, M. (2019). *Review on Leader-Member Exchange Theory: Antecedent and The Effect on Employee Performance.* Academic Press.

Banda, R. (2022). *The role of the state and non-state actors in ensuring security: The case of Luangwa district.* Academic Press.

BBC. (n.d.). *Ethics – Introduction to ethics: Duty-based ethics.* Retrieved from https://www.bbc.co.uk/ethics/introduction/duty_1.shtml

Beus, J. M., Solomon, S. J., Taylor, E. C., & Esken, C. A. (2020). Making sense of climate: A meta-analytic extension of the competing values framework. *Organizational Psychology Review, 10*(3-4), 136–168. doi:10.1177/2041386620914707

Biresaw, H., Mulugeta, H., Endalamaw, A., Yesuf, N. N., & Alemu, Y. (2021). Patient satisfaction towards health care services provided in Ethiopian health institutions: A systematic review and meta-analysis. *Health Services Insights, 14*(1), 1–11. doi:10.1177/11786329211040689 PMID:34511929

Bischoff, P. (2020, February 11). *Ransomware Attacks on US Healthcare Organizations Cost $20.8bn in 2020.* Comparitech. https://www.comparitech.com/blog/information-security/ransomware-attacks-hospitals-data/

Bogdanoski, M. (2022). *Building cyber resilience against hybrid threats.* IOS Press. doi:10.3233/NICSP61

Bohn, L., & Schiereck, D. (2022). Regulation of data breach publication: The case of US healthcare and the HITECH act. *Journal of Economics and Finance,* 1–14.

Brown, J. (2020, May 9). *What is the virtue approach?* The Knowledge Burrow. Retrieved from https://knowledgeburrow.com/what-is-the-virtue-approach/

Budimir, S., Fontaine, J. R., & Roesch, E. B. (2021). Emotional experiences of cybersecurity breach victims. *Cyberpsychology, Behavior, and Social Networking, 24*(9), 612–616. doi:10.1089/cyber.2020.0525 PMID:34185598

Chernyshev, M., Zeadally, S., & Baig, Z. (2018). Healthcare data breaches: Implications for digital forensic readiness. *Journal of Medical Systems, 43*(1), 7. Advance online publication. doi:10.100710916-018-1123-2 PMID:30488291

Cleveland, S., & Cleveland, M. (2018). Toward cybersecurity leadership framework. *Proceedings of the Thirteenth Midwest Association for Information Systems Conference.*

Comstock, M., Supovitz, J., & Kaul, M. (2021). Exchange quality in teacher leadership ties: Examining relational quality using social network and leader-member exchange theories. *Journal of Professional Capital and Community, 6*(4), 395–409. doi:10.1108/JPCC-01-2021-0002

Darmawan, A. H., & Azizah, S. (2020, January). Resistance to change: Causes and strategies as an organizational challenge. In *5th ASEAN Conference on Psychology, Counselling, and Humanities (ACPCH 2019)* (pp. 49-53). Atlantis Press.

DeJonckheere, M., & Vaughn, L. M. (2019). Semistructured interviewing in primary care research: A balance of relationship and rigour. *Family Medicine and Community Health, 7*(2), e000057. doi:10.1136/fmch-2018-000057 PMID:32148704

Deursen, N. V. (2022). *Visual Communication for Cybersecurity: Beyond Awareness to Advocacy.* River Publishers. doi:10.1201/9781003340027

Dhasarathan, C., Hasan, M. K., Islam, S., Abdullah, S., Mokhtar, U. A., Javed, A. R., & Goundar, S. (2023). COVID-19 health data analysis and personal data preserving: A homomorphic privacy enforcement approach. *Computer Communications, 199,* 87–97. doi:10.1016/j.comcom.2022.12.004 PMID:36531214

Engida, Z. M., Alemu, A. E., & Mulugeta, M. A. (2022). The effect of change leadership on employees' readiness to change: The mediating role of organizational culture. *Future Business Journal, 8*(1), 1–13. doi:10.118643093-022-00148-2

Fernandopulle, N. (2021). To what extent does hierarchical leadership affect healthcare outcomes? *Medical Journal of the Islamic Republic of Iran, 35*(1), 1–11. PMID:34956963

Files, R., & Liu, M. (2022). Unraveling financial fraud: The role of the board of directors and external advisors in conducting independent internal investigations. *Contemporary Accounting Research, 39*(3), 1905–1948. doi:10.1111/1911-3846.12784

Furxhi, G. (2021). Employee's Resistance and Organizational Change Factors. *European Journal of Business and Management Research, 6*(2), 30–32.

Ghani, B., Memon, K. R., Han, H., Ariza-Montes, A., & Arjona-Fuentes, J. M. (2022). Work stress, technological changes, and job insecurity in the retail organization context. *Frontiers in Psychology, 13*(1), 1–14. doi:10.3389/fpsyg.2022.918065 PMID:36483719

Haney, J., & Lutters, W. (2020). Security awareness training for the workforce: Moving beyond "check-the-box" compliance. *Computer, 53*(10), 1–11. doi:10.1109/MC.2020.3001959 PMID:34131349

Hassan, J., Shehzad, D., Habib, U., Aftab, M. U., Ahmad, M., Kuleev, R., & Mazzara, M. (2022). The rise of cloud computing: Data protection, privacy, and open research challenges—a systematic literature review (SLR). *Computational Intelligence and Neuroscience, 2022,* 2022. doi:10.1155/2022/8303504 PMID:35712069

Hinterhuber, A. (2022). Digital transformation, the Holy Grail, and the disruption of business models: An interview with Michael Nilles. *Business Horizons, 65*(3), 261–265. doi:10.1016/j.bushor.2021.02.042

Jimo, S., Abdullah, T., & Jamal, A. (2023, January). IoE Security Risk Analysis in a Modern Hospital Ecosystem. In *Cybersecurity in the Age of Smart Societies: Proceedings of the 14th International Conference on Global Security, Safety and Sustainability, London, September 2022* (pp. 451-467). Cham: Springer International Publishing. 10.1007/978-3-031-20160-8_26

Juliana, J., Stella, B., Austine, C. V., Budiono, E. D., & Klarissa, K. (2021). Antecedents on Customer Satisfaction Tuku Coffee Shop: A Perspective Expectation-Confirmation Theory and Kano's Model. *International Journal of Social, Policy, and Law, 2*(3), 1–11.

Juma'h, A. H., & Alnsour, Y. (2020). The effect of data breaches on company performance. *International Journal of Accounting & Information Management, 1*(1), 1–26. doi:10.1108/IJAIM-01-2019-0006

Kabir, U. Y., Ezekekwu, E., Bhuyan, S. S., Mahmood, A., & Dobalian, A. (2020). Trends and best practices in health care cybersecurity insurance policy. *Journal of Healthcare Risk Management, 40*(2), 10–14. doi:10.1002/jhrm.21414 PMID:32441812

Kanitz, R., & Gonzalez, K. (2021). Are we stuck in the predigital age? embracing technology-mediated change management in organizational change research. *The Journal of Applied Behavioral Science, 57*(4), 447–458. doi:10.1177/00218863211042896

Karhapää, S. J., Savolainen, T., & Malkamäki, K. (2022). Trust and performance: A contextual study of management change in private and public organisation. *Baltic Journal of Management, 17*(6), 35–51. doi:10.1108/BJM-06-2022-0212

Kilovaty, I. (2021). Psychological data breach harms. *North Carolina Journal of Law & Technology, 23*(1), 1–66.

Kosseff, J. (2022). *Cybersecurity law*. John Wiley & Sons.

Lancefield, D., & Rangen, C. (2021, May 5). 4 actions transformational leaders take. *Harvard Business Review*. Retrieved from https://hbr.org/2021/05/4-actions-transformational-leaders-take

Lee, J., & Choi, S. J. (2021). Hospital Productivity After Data Breaches: Difference-in-Differences Analysis. *Journal of Medical Internet Research, 23*(7), 1–8. doi:10.2196/26157 PMID:34255672

Lehto, M., & Neittaanmäki, P. (2018). *Cyber security: Power and technology*. Springer. doi:10.1007/978-3-319-75307-2

Madimenos, F. C., Gildner, T. E., Eick, G. N., Sugiyama, L. S., & Snodgrass, J. J. (2022). Bringing the lab bench to the field: Point-of-care testing for enhancing health research and stakeholder engagement in rural/remote, indigenous, and resource-limited contexts. *American Journal of Human Biology, 34*(11), e23808. doi:10.1002/ajhb.23808 PMID:36166487

Males, J. R., Hudson, J., & Kerr, J. H. (2018). Application of an innovative performance demand model with canoe slalom athletes and their coach. *Journal of Sport Psychology in Action, 9*(1), 63–71. doi:10.1080/21520704.2017.1326429

Management Daily. (n.d.). Retrieved from https://www.businessmanagementdaily.com

Markopoulos, E., Aggarwal, V., & Vanharanta, H. (2019). Democratization of intrapreneurship and corporate entrepreneurship within the McKinsey's three horizons innovation space. *Human Systems Engineering and Design, II*, 1007–1017. doi:10.1007/978-3-030-27928-8_150

MasterClass. (2022, May 19). *What is lmx theory? The leader-member exchange at work - 2023 - MasterClass*. Retrieved from https://www.masterclass.com/articles/lmx

Maximini, D. (2018). Organizational culture models. In *The Scrum Culture: Introducing agile methods in organizations* (pp. 187–204). Springer. doi:10.1007/978-3-319-73842-0_18

McKeon, J. (2023, January 3). Scripps Health Reaches $3.5M Settlement After Ransomware Attack. *HealthITSecurity*. https://healthitsecurity.com/news/scripps-health-reaches-3.5 m-settlement-after-ransomware-attack

Merviö, M. (2020). *Global issues and innovative solutions in healthcare, culture, and the environment.* IGI Global. doi:10.4018/978-1-7998-3576-9

Nobanee, H., Alhajjar, M., Abushairah, G., & Al Harbi, S. (2021). Reputational risk and sustainability: A bibliometric analysis of relevant literature. *Risks*, *9*(7), 1–13. doi:10.3390/risks9070134

Osei, M. B., Papadopoulos, T., Acquaye, A., & Stamati, T. (2023). Improving sustainable supply chain performance through organizational culture: A competing values framework approach. *Journal of Purchasing and Supply Management*, *29*(2), 100821. doi:10.1016/j.pursup.2023.100821

Pham, T. (2021). *The Role of External Mechanisms and Transformational Leadership in Information Security Policy Effectiveness: A Managerial Perspective of Financial Industry in Vietnam* [Doctoral dissertation]. Auckland University of Technology.

Raghupathi, W., Raghupathi, V., & Saharia, A. (2023). Analyzing Health Data Breaches: A Visual Analytics Approach. *AppliedMath*, *3*(1), 175–199. doi:10.3390/appliedmath3010011

Ramluckan, T., Van Niekerk, B., & Martins, I. (n.d.). A change management perspective to implementing a cybersecurity culture. *ECCWS 2020 20th European Conference on Cyber Warfare and Security*, 442-448.

Scherer, M. (2022, July 12). Understanding the adkar change management model. *Business (Atlanta, Ga.).*

Seh, A. H., Zarour, M., Alenezi, M., Sarkar, A. K., Agrawal, A., Kumar, R., & Ahmad Khan, R. (2020, May). Healthcare data breaches: insights and implications. In *Healthcare* (vol. 8, no. 2, p. 133). MDPI. https://www.ncbi.nlm.nih.gov/pmc/articles/PMC7349636/

Smith, D. (2022). *Fraud and corruption: Cases and materials.* Springer Nature. doi:10.1007/978-3-031-10063-5

Solove, D. J., & Citron, D. K. (2017). Risk and anxiety: A theory of data-breach harms. *Texas Law Review*, *96*(2), 1–38.

Tams, C. (2018, February 22). *Small Is Beautiful: Using gentle nudges to change organizations.* Forbes. Retrieved from https://www.forbes.com/sites/carstentams/

Tarbouriech, S., Navarro, B., Fraisse, P., Crosnier, A., Cherubini, A., & Sallé, D. (2022). An admittance-based hierarchical control framework for dual-arm robots. *Mechatronics*, *86*(1), 1–10.

The Health Sector Cybersecurity Coordination Center (HC3). (2019, April 12). *A Cost Analysis of Healthcare Sector Data Breaches*. https://www.hhs.gov/sites/default/files/cost-analysis-of-hea lthcare-sector-data-breaches.pdf

Vasileiou, I., & Furnell, S. (2019). *Cybersecurity education for awareness and compliance.* IGI Global. doi:10.4018/978-1-5225-7847-5

Wetsman, N., Dwyer, D., & Herndon, S. (2023, May 11). Cyberattacks on hospitals are growing threats to patient safety, experts say. *ABC News*. https://abcnews.go.com/Health/cyberattacks-hospitals-growing-threats-patient-safety-experts/story?id=99115898

Xu, J., Cooke, F. L., Gen, M., & Ahmed, S. E. (2018). *Proceedings of the twelfth international conference on management science and engineering management*. Springer.

Xu, Y., & Zhang, R. (2020). Key staff management in M & A based on Lmx Theory. In *International Conference on Social Science and Education Research* (pp. 608-617). Academic Press.

Yeo, L. H., & Banfield, J. (2022). Human factors in electronic health records cybersecurity breach: An exploratory analysis. *Perspectives in Health Information Management*, *19*(1). https://www.ncbi.nlm.nih.gov/pmc/articles/PMC9123525/ PMID:35692854

Zhonghai, Z. (2023). The ritual process of the canoe dragon boat in the Qingshui river basin. *Traditions and Cultural Heritage: Genesis, Reproduction, and Preservation*, 116-125.

Chapter 14
Corporate Financial Risk Case Study

Leeshawn Buhr
Marymount University, USA

ABSTRACT

This case study begins with a company purchase card audit that brought years of unethical purchasing practices to light. The author discusses how the purchases impacted organizational culture, leadership, and employee well-being. Risk management policies are examined to determine the best methods to reduce employee fallout impacting the organization. Change management, organizational culture, and leadership theories are analyzed to mitigate the negative impact unethical leadership has on the overall health of an organization.

OVERVIEW

Recently, an audit was performed by the financial board of an organization. The results of the audit shed light on several hundred thousand dollars' worth of personal purchases made on corporate purchase cards. Audits are tools that organizations around the globe use daily to determine the health of their organization (DeFond & Zhang, 2014). The most astounding part of the investigation was 85 percent of the organization's top leadership was involved in illegal/unethical purchases. Upon further investigation, the auditing team discovered the organization does not currently have any policies or training programs regarding financial risk management or organizational purchase cards.

Additional research on the unethical purchases proved that the issues were known and reported by the Chief Financial Officer (CFO) of the agency. The complaints fell on deaf ears and eventually led the CFO to leave the agency. After the investigation, every organizational head was replaced, and the new regime promptly wanted to implement a risk management program.

My responsibility as the director of risk management is to implement risk control measures and create a risk management program that guarantees unethical purchases do not occur again. To implement this program, we will look at several business models and strategies that guarantee the sustainability of an organizational risk management program.

DOI: 10.4018/979-8-3693-1630-6.ch014

IDENTIFYING THE ISSUE

The organization has a lengthy history of unethical organizational credit card purchases made by senior leadership within the organization. Everyone was aware of the illegal purchasing activities, but mitigation efforts were not taken to stop or reduce illegitimate purchases. Without a financial risk policy, the organization will continuously lose hundreds of thousands of dollars annually in fraudulent purchases.

LITERATURE REVIEW

The Importance of Auditing

"Auditing that Matters: Case Studies (Marks, 2020)" provides several terms that help us gain a more thorough understanding of the auditing process. The purpose of this analysis is to explore auditing terms that correlate with risk management. Audits are broken down into sections such as financial, property, IT, etc., and the ratings for each section are combined to provide management and CEOs data showing their strengths, weaknesses, and where they rank against their competitors.

Changes are Necessary for Organizational Improvements

Throughout our studies of risk management policies and reduction, we have learned individual and organizational flexibility to change is necessary. Clarity is essential in every aspect of life; it is even more important when implementing organizational changes. The organization, employees, managers, and customers must understand what is expected from every entity to ensure the transition goes well (Bevan, 2015). When the purpose goes unidentified, stakeholders become dissatisfied and may negatively impact the change management process.

Risk Management Essentials

The textbook, "Enterprise Risk Management Straight to the Point (Decker & Galer, 2013)" provides several key risk management terms and concepts to guide individuals, management, and organizations. Ultimately, the purpose of effective risk management is to mitigate risks identified by organizations and security. Risk management also uses strategy to mitigate risks identified by the organization. Strategic tactics are utilized by managers and organizations to outline the steps that must be taken to achieve corporate goals and strategies (Decker & Galer, 2013).

Managing Risks in the Workplace

This article thoroughly explained that no matter how hard you try to mitigate risks in an organization, unforeseen risks can still have disastrous effects. Mr. Hayward, the CEO of BP, spent a lot of time mitigating risk in his organization. His methods were non-traditional but seemingly thorough. One of the many risk reduction measures he implemented was not allowing employees to drink beverages without a lid (Kaplan & Mikes, 2012). Although Hayward spent extended periods implementing guidelines to reduce employee risk, one of the most devastating oil rig accidents in history occurred under his watch.

Organizations and management teams need to remember policies and regulations do not mitigate every risk; disastrous risks can still affect the organization regardless of their procedures.

Open communication and risk strategy are two solutions Kaplan and Mikes proposed in this article. Organizations often have difficulties discussing risk and become overconfident in their ability to keep risk under control (Kaplan & Mikes, 2012). The impacts of uncontrollable risks are devastating and can destroy the company.

WHAT ARE THE REPERCUSSIONS?

Now that we have identified the first two W's in the equation, we are now going to research the why. To understand the why, we must have a thorough understanding of potential organizational repercussions if the correct change strategies are not implemented in a timely fashion. Unethical purchases fall into several risk categories that can tarnish and crumble the organization if the issues are untouched. The risks associated with their actions are reputational, catastrophic, legal, and strategic (Decker & Galer, 2013).

A high turnover rate was a repercussion the organization felt immediately as most of the veteran leadership was laid off or quit. The CFO left the organization because her warnings of improper use fell on deaf ears and refused to tarnish her reputation. Significant turnovers in an organization lead to low employee morale and job dissatisfaction (Caldalora, 2018). Senior leaders were asked to leave the organization to reduce the reputational risk impacts of their unethical purchases contributing to the high turnover rate.

Legal ramifications of the purchases were not visible due to the organization's lack of financial risk training and policies. The CFO informed management their purchases were illegal for several years. Annual ethics training is a requirement for senior leaders in the organization; erroneous purchases are part of the training. It is hard to take legal action against members of an organization when a policy is not in place.

The agency's reputation deteriorated at the organizational, employee, customer, and competitor levels. It takes several years to build a good reputation and one bad situation to ruin it (Eccles et al., 2007). Every employee will have a negative light on them regardless of their participation in unethical activities.

ORGANIZATIONAL IMPACT

The impacts of unethical leadership are low-employee morale, high turnover rates, decreased performance, increased unethical behavior, and negative attitudes in the workplace. Poor leadership reduces employees' moral compass and causes them to reevaluate their workplace activities (Gan et al., 2019). The results are job dissatisfaction for employees as it causes them to question whether their personal choices were correct. Employee performance rates fall along with productivity and discipline (Hassan et al., 2022).

Many executives and leaders recently left the organization due to unethical charges; another round of turnovers would stall the organization's structural and cultural overhaul. Employees may react negatively to new policies by engaging in counterproductive vengeful behaviors because of the stress imposed on the organization (Lasakova & Remisova, 2015). Changes must occur to change the negative workplace culture and create a positive and productive workplace.

SOLUTIONS

Now that we have identified the impact unethical leadership has on organizational culture, employees, and management, it is time to enact solutions to ensure the sustainability of the organization. The first step is to create a purchase card policy. Leaders will receive training from an external instructor on programs other agencies utilize to reduce unethical purchases. After training, the leaders and I will create a strategy to implement a financial risk management program that includes a purchase card policy.

We will meet with employees at every level of the organization to gauge employees' feelings about management, the purchase program, risk management, and organizational health. Feedback will be considered, and innovative ideas will be added to our risk management/purchase card policy. Policy implementation will be gradual to ensure all employees are comfortable with the system before the program is released.

Management will hold biweekly meetings with employees to ensure all issues are identified before D-day. Incentives and bonuses will be offered to employees who stay with the company for a year after the organizational overhaul. Internal audits will occur quarterly to tell us the health of the program and if we have any shortfalls in the program.

LIGHT AT THE END OF THE TUNNEL

My ideal outcome for the organization is to create a purchase card policy and financial risk management program. The process will bring the broken organization back together and raise employee morale. Management will gain employees' trust back and organizational culture will become positive. Censing sessions and team-building exercises will help rebuild the culture. The changes will not happen immediately, but employees will believe in themselves, their leaders, and the organization. Everyone will use these situations as a learning experience and overcome them.

CHANGE MANAGEMENT STRATEGIES

. The strategy models I would use to implement the changes identified above are Lewin's change management model and the McKinsey 7-step model. Both models analyze current and past business processes and use the data to create a viable strategy for the future

Lewin's change model is a three-step process that involves unfreezing, moving, and refreezing (Sarayreh et al., 2013). Unfreezing analyzes the organization's current state and is the beginning of communication between you and your employees. This is the kickoff event for the impending change and lets everyone know where they stand. Step 2 is the moving or changing part of the process. Open communication is essential to the success of the process. The final step is refreezing which is key in ensuring changes are maintained.

The McKinsey 7-step model analyzes seven aspects of the organization during the change process. The steps analyze organizational strategy, structure, systems, skills, staff, style, and shared values (Ravanfar, 2015). This process is thorough and fits the changes we currently need in the organization. The high turnover rate coupled with employee dissatisfaction requires an extensive look at all aspects of the organization and McKinsey's model answers those requirements.

STRATEGY MODELS

The strategy models I will use to implement the financial risk management program and purchase card policies are the balanced score card and Theory of Constraint (TOC) models. These strategies focus on achieving goals by analyzing goals and objectives.

The Balanced Score Card uses financial, consumer, internal processes, and employee skillsets to form a strategy (Kaplan & Norton, 2010). This method is beneficial to our current situation as all the components of a balanced scorecard are part of our organization. Projects are incentivized in this method which creates a common goal for the organization to work towards.

TOC analyzes the constraints that can affect your project or task (Lea & Min, 2010). In this case, we are working on multiple issues which means multiple factors can inhibit the success of our project. The TOC identifies constraints before they become an issue and strategizes how you will overcome the obstacles that may stop you from completing the mission.

ORGANIZATIONAL CULTURE THEORIES

The deteriorating culture of the organization has been one of the biggest impacts of this case study. Employees at all levels of the organization have felt the culture nosedive with the unethical activity and high turnover rates. I will utilize the Canoe theory and cultural iceberg model to mitigate these issues.

The Canoe Theory says everyone is in one canoe, and you must work together to travel to the next destination (Hibbard et al., 2006). If people don't pull their weight, the canoe may capsize, or you will not go anywhere. Everyone in the organization must work together to ensure the new programs and processes create a healthy organizational culture.

Cultural Iceberg is a theory that people only show you ten percent of themselves in the workplace, and the other 90 percent remains below the surface. To gain a complete understanding of the people you are working with, you must immerse yourself in them. Before you make assumptions about people based on their behaviors, spend time with them and build a trusting relationship.

DECISION MAKING THEORIES

To achieve the organization's desired results, I would take a utilitarian and common good approach to decision-making. Our goal is to ensure the sustainability of the organization, its employees, and our customers. We cannot achieve our goals if we do not make good decisions regarding the health of the organization.

A utilitarian makes decisions with the best interests of the organization in mind. Happiness and the greater good are at the focal point of decisions and they increase positive emotions and culture (Tardi, 2022). Employees need happiness to heal from unethical leadership and the negative workplace culture.

The common good approach focuses on decisions that better employees. Examples are catered lunches, holistic activities, etc. (Hussain, 2018). I would make decisions for the organization based on what is most beneficial for the organization. This satisfies employees needs to feel included in the decision-making process.

LEADERSHIP THEORIES

The leadership theories I find effective in management are transformational and situational. Situational leaders change their leadership style to match the situation at hand (Cherry, 2023). One size does not fit all when it comes to leadership, and you must know when to make the switch to effectively lead certain employees.

Transformational leaders lead from the front. Their job title or stature does not get in the way of working right beside their employees (Cherry, 2023). Everyone around a transformational leader is motivated to get the job done and work towards their common goal simply because of their go getter attitude.

Employees in the organization have seen unethical leadership, poor decisions, and a litany of other offenses. I will be the leader this organization needs to sustain our customers, employees, and leaders. The new policies we plan to implement will be a direct reflection of the leadership and decision-making techniques we chose to incorporate into our organization.

REFERENCES

Bevan, R. (2015). *The Changemaking checklists: Planning, leading, and sustaining change*. Academic Press.

Caldarola, N. T. (2010). *The effects of organizational and occupational commitment on job embeddedness and the individual's intent to stay* (Order No. 3411018). http://proxymu.wrlc.org/login?url=https://www.proquest.com/dissertations-theses/effects-organizational-occupational-commitment-on/docview/504844967/se-2

Cherry, K. (2023a, June 25). *The situational theory of leadership*. Verywell Mind. https://www.verywellmind.com/what-is-the-situational-theory-of-leadership-2795321

Cherry, K. (2023b, May 21). *What is transformational leadership?* Verywell Mind. https://www.verywellmind.com/what-is-transformational-leadership-2795313

Decker, A., & Galer, D. (2013). *Enterprise risk management - Straight to the point: An implementation guide function by function*. Academic Press.

DeFond, M, Zhang, J, (2014) *A review of archival auditing research*. . doi:10.1016/j.jacceco.2014.09.002

Eccles, R., Newquist, S., & Schatz, R. (2007) *Reputation and its Risks* https://hbr.org/2007/02/reputation-and-its-risks

Gan, C., Guo, W., Chai, Y., & Wang, D. (2019). Unethical leader behavior and employee performance: A deontic justice perspec-tive. *Personnel Review*, *49*(1), 188–201. doi:10.1108/PR-08-2018-0290

Hassan, S., Puneet, P., Muchiri, M., & Ogbonnaya, C. (2022). Unethical Leadership: Review, Synthesis and Directions for Future Research. *Journal of Business Ethics*, *183*(2), 511–550. Advance online publication. doi:10.100710551-022-05081-6

Hibbard, D., Hibbard, M., & Stockman, J. W. (2006). *The canoe theory: A business success strategy for leaders and associates*. iUniverse.

Hussain, W. (2018). The Common Good. *The Stanford Encyclopedia of Philosophy*. https://plato.stanford.edu/archives/spr2018/entries/common-good

Kaplan, R., & Mikes, A. (2012, June 1). Managing risks: A new framework. *Harvard Business Review*. https://hbr.org/2012/06/managing-risks-a-new-framework

Kaplan, R. S., & Norton, D. P. (2005). *The balanced scorecard: Measures that drive performance*. Academic Press.

Lašáková, A., & Remišová, A. (2015). *Unethical Leadership: Current Theoretical Trends and Conceptualization*. . doi:10.1016/S2212-5671(15)01636-6

Lea, B.-R., & Min, H. (2003). Selection of management accounting systems in Just-In-Time and Theory of Constraints-based manufacturing. *International Journal of Production Research*, *41*(13), 2879–2910. doi:10.1080/0020754031000109134

Marks, N. (2020). *Auditing that matters: Case studies discussion guide*. Independently Published.

Pascual-Ezama, D., Dunfield, D., Gil-Gómez de Liaño, B., & Prelec, D. (2015). Peer Effects in Unethical Behavior: Standing or Reputation? *PLoS One*, *10*(4), e0122305. doi:10.1371/journal.pone.0122305 PMID:25853716

Tardi, C. (2022, June 26). *Utilitarianism: What it is, founders, and main principles*. https://www.investopedia.com/terms/u/utilitarianism.asp

Chapter 15
Diversity, Transformational Leadership, and Public Governance

Dana-Marie Ramjit

ⓘ https://orcid.org/0000-0003-1369-8121

Adler University, Canada

ABSTRACT

The modern public sector confronts myriad crises, which demand sound decision-making in turbulent systems. More and more contemporary problems reveal long-held systemic injustices, inequity, and the inadequacy of public policies to create genuine social change. Still, modern society considers pluralism and diversity as unimpressive and toxic. Public administration must prioritize the ethnic mosaic to contribute to practical and effective global policymaking. Transformational leadership proposes a cultural metamorphosis focusing on approach and values to achieve institutional effectiveness. This framework is relevant to contemporary public leadership as it concentrates on moral and ethical markers, dynamism in the global economy, culture as the backdrop of change, innovation through ingenuity and intellectual motivation, and optimal performance through public service inspiration. This chapter explores the potential of transformational leadership to promote diversity in the public room and build a just and impactful society.

INTRODUCTION

Policymakers are challenged by the demand to make some of the toughest policy decisions in the history of modern society. In recent decades the public policy sector has struggled with inaction, where policymakers fail to act to tackle public concerns (McConnell & t' Hart, 2019). Moreover, current crises have revealed inequity and deficiencies in public policies safeguarding marginalized populations, reflecting a climate of uncertainty among policymakers (Blyth, 2002; Boin & Hart, 2022; Bali et al., 2022; Capano et al., 2022). Extensive crises exacerbate social and economic disparities and the state's fiscal capacity (Béland, Jingwei He & Ramesh, 2022). One relevant example is the COVID-19 pandemic which led

DOI: 10.4018/979-8-3693-1630-6.ch015

to widespread loss of income, lack of access to healthcare, isolation, lost opportunities, and increased global poverty among vulnerable populations (Sumner et al., 2020).

The pandemic alone led to a glaring increase in inequalities. OECD (2021) found that women's employment and income were impacted significantly, especially mothers, ethnic minorities, and people with low education and income faced a greater risk of infection and mortality, while youth unemployment increased by over 26% in OECD countries. The drive for diversity, equity, and inclusion is fuelled by a history of exclusion of these voices critical to the decision-making processes that directly impact them.

Though some progress in diverse representation in Canada's policy leadership is perceptible, many institutions still face the underrepresentation of women, minorities, and Indigenous leaders (Griffith, 2020). In the United States, while federal institutions incorporate diversity, equity, and inclusion in their strategic plans, employees of color represent only 32% of the professional workforce and are underrepresented in the executive branch (Partnership for Public Service, 2020). The European public dismissed diversity as an asset to their region. Merely a third of the populations in Sweden (36%), the UK (33%), and Spain (31%) consider diversity as profitable (Pew Research, 2016). Moreover, France, Germany, and the Netherlands primarily regard pluralism as unimpactful. More than half of Greece (63%) and Italy (53%) view diversity as destructive (Pew Research, 2016). These prevalent mindsets signal persistent inequality and bias in the global space.

Our turbulent society is burdened by superwicked problems, such as pandemics, wars, political tensions, global economic downturns, and environmental and humanitarian disasters, to name a few. Managing a crisis is not simply about a response. It is a process of intelligent and resourceful leadership that involves managing risk and prevention, preparedness, detection and recognition, rescue, normalization, assessments and learning from past efforts (Hannah, Baekkeskov, Tubakovic, 2022). The future of policymaking rests on leaders' ability to create a more just society by confronting public ostracism and intentionally designing diverse policy solutions that can improve the quality of life for citizens (Lynch, 2020).

Public sector leadership has implications for social inequalities. Policy design can shape and reshape inequality imprints over time; thus, leaders should focus on tackling inequalities throughout the policy-making process (Béland, Jingwei He & Ramesh, 2022). This discussion aims to summarize and review the patterns of inequality while stressing the importance of effective leadership and policy design as it intersects with these patterns. The chapter stresses that the persistence of inequity emphasizes the need for a transformation in public sector leadership, focusing on designing diverse policies in response to current crises. I emphasize transformational leadership in prioritizing multiculturalism and ethnic inclusivity in the public sector. Transformational leadership concentrates on altering the processes and values of individuals and groups to achieve organizational outcomes (Hay, 2006; Bass & Riggio, 2006; Ytterstad & Olaisen, 2023). Process and values are crucial in advancing social justice, developing creative policies to produce positive results, and cultivating a relevant public culture responsive to change (Collins, Bruce & McKee, 2019). With its emphasis on a re-evaluation of approach, an examination of inherent prejudices, a focus on cultural competence, and a mission to elevate the standard of fairness and justice, transformational leadership is a realistic model of contemporary governance (Shields & Hesbol, 2020).

Finally, this chapter proposes that only public institutions with a sound vision, mission, and strategy can successfully adapt to organizational diversity. Change is unreachable without innovative leadership, the main avenue through which leaders and followers achieve organizational goals (Bass & Avolio, 1993; Opiyo, 2019; Gélinas-Proulx & Shields, 2022). Through a review of literature on transformational leadership discussing the core themes of diversity, practice, culture, organizational change, and public governance, the chapter demonstrates the potential of transformational leadership to promote diversity in the public sector, leading toward a more just and equitable society.

OVERVIEW OF THE PROBLEM

It is indisputable that concepts like diversity and cross-culturalism are relevant to an ever-changing and complex society. Diversity enables societies to adapt to future challenges and increase productivity (Bourke & Dillion, 2018). A diverse workforce leads to public integrity and citizen-centric emphasis, trust, democracy, and innovation, as different mindsets and competencies contribute to designing pragmatic solutions to policy challenges (Australian Public Service Commission, 2022; Nolan-Flecha, 2019). The civil service optimally performs when it mirrors a country's diversity and is sensitized to public needs. Yet, one significant public sector weakness is its lack of diversity. Despite international and domestic inclusion and anti-discrimination policies, people continue to face prejudice, exclusion, and harassment because of their ethnic origins, gender, age, and disabilities, which confound actions to enhance opportunities and living standards (FRA, 2018). The general problem is that policymakers fail to design adequate policies that address some of the most pressing concerns for modern society due to a lack of multiculturalism and diversity. More specifically, the public sector requires transformative leadership and must re-organize its process and values if it should be a pertinent mechanism of public governance in the future.

SIGNIFICANCE

The modern world features complex crises, further exacerbating inequity and justifying the need for more responsive policy. Gender disparities exemplify social inequality and particularly the burden of crises on women (Bambra et al., 2021; Bettinger-Lopez & Bro, 2020; Mittal & Singh, 2020; Nieves et al., 2020). Racial inequalities persist when ethnic minorities, compounded by economic challenges, lack political representation and leadership (Emrich et al., 2020; McLoughlin et al., 2020; Wright & Merritt, 2020). People with low education and income are vulnerable to health and economic crises (Heggebø et al., 2019). Crises impact youth and the elderly in distinct ways, such as increasing unemployment, competing job markets, income decline, and higher death rates (Béland & Marier, 2020; Ciminelli & Garcia-Mandicó, 2020). Crisis imposes additional hardships on the disabled, such as access to facilities, services, assistance, and community support (Chakraborty et al.; Jesus et al., 2021).

While the number of women employees is rising, the extent to which women hold senior organizational positions varies extensively, and very few countries achieve gender equality. In Poland, Greece, Iceland, and Latvia, women in senior positions remain the highest (50-54%), while the lowest is in Japan (3%), Korea (6%), and Turkey (8%) (Poulsen, 2023). COVID-19 has aggravated the existing work equity gaps. Women's jobs are 1.8 times more vulnerable than men's, and women comprise 39% of global employment but account for 54% of general job losses (Madgavkar, White, Krishnan, Mahajan & Azcue, 2023). Black and minority students are less likely to graduate with a degree than white students (National Center for Education Statistics, 2019). 44% of Black and 61% of Hispanics experienced job and wage loss throughout the pandemic (Strada, 2020).

The impact of a lack of diversity in the design of effective public policies remains underestimated. Furthermore, the role of transformative leadership for diversity in the contemporary public sector is understudied. While decades of research on transformational leadership reflect its benefits to society, such as motivation, innovation, team creativity, and moral development, few studies have explored the importance of process and value transformation in achieving diverse outcomes (Bass and Riggio, 2010; Tichy & Devanna, 1986; Bryman, Grint & Collison, 2011). This chapter examines the core elements of transformational leadership from a diversity perspective. These ideas will help to improve public sector governance and the design of diverse policies that solve real-world problems. The ideas presented in this chapter will contribute several critical insights regarding diversity in the public sector. First, it leads to understanding the importance of recognizing and removing bias to increase opportunities for all. Second, it reveals strategies to minimize antagonism between public sector leaders and the public. Third, it uncovers the role of values and culture in promoting new organizational structures and facilitating new ways of thinking and working.

LITERATURE REVIEW

Transformational Practice

Transformational leadership was coined by Burns (1978) as a style of governance that promotes effective change through individualized consideration, inspirational motivation, idealized influence, and intellectual stimulation. These features of transformational leadership focus on attending to others to provide support and accommodation, articulating a unified vision that inspires others to a sense of purpose and optimism, modeling morals to achieve respect and trust, and challenging assumptions, taking risks, and encouraging participation and creativity to derive multiple solutions to problems (Bass & Riggio, 2005). Transformational leadership generates collective action and empowers those involved in the process (Bass, 1999; Stajkovic & Sergent, 2019). Transformative leadership stimulates hope, energy, and optimism, allowing for a redefinition of mission and vision, renewed commitment, and restructuring systems for goal realization (Leithwood & Poplin, 1992). As a leadership model, it engenders diversity as it requires individuals to re-evaluate their perspectives of differences, prejudices, and faults. Additionally, leaders who maintain an environment of support and cultural change, stimulate justice and fairness and ultimately, greater buy-in from followers (Feyes, 2018).

Transformational leadership appears to be a relevant approach across the various sectors of society. In the education sector, facilitative power has proven more effective in advancing change throughout institutions (Leithwood & Poplin, 1992; Anderson, 2017; Jovanovica & Ciricb, 2016). In healthcare, transformational leadership has counteracted the negative consequences of job stressors, serving as a resource for employees, instilling a positive patient safety climate and acting as a role model for safety behaviours (Seljemo, Viksveen, & Ree, 2020; Leithwood & Poplin, 1992).

Transformational leadership is consistent with the changing nature of the global economy. Exceptional leadership is needed to manage cultural shifts, create new visions, gather support and buy-in from stakeholders, and guide organizations through a transformative phase to institutionalize these changes (Tichy & Ulrich, 2008). For instance, the United States economy in the early 1980s evoked the need to revise organizational culture to ensure that institutions remained competitive in the world market much like the contemporary global economy today.

While a transactional leader may adjust the organizational tripod of mission, structure, and human resources, a transformational leader promotes radical changes in the organization's political and cultural approaches (Tichy & Ulrich, 2008). The impact of globalization on leadership outcomes appears to be a relevant example. The blurring of boundaries, increasing connections and inter-relatedness has fused global, political, economic, and cultural realms with significant socio-economic implications (Boston & Peterson, 2017). Global business demands global transformational leadership which considers gross imbalances in health, education, and living conditions, as well as exponential profits of global industries. Transformational leaders are equipped with cross-cultural acumen needed to navigate globalization dynamics.

Transformational leadership deviates from transactional leadership, which is based on an exchange of services that the leader dictates to incentivize individuals when they endeavor to progress. In this context, transformational leadership is value-added as leaders continually support teams to develop and maintain a collaborative, professional organizational culture (Leithwood & Poplin, 1992).

Transformational leadership is key to diversity since it encourages a new vision, mobilizes commitment to that vision, and initiates changes by assessing and revamping organizational culture (Tichy & Ulrich, 2008). Innovative leadership depends on the capacity of leaders to delineate the organizational dynamics of change and effectively manage the structure, culture, and people that build an institution.

Diversity

Diversity has become a buzzword in modern society with the rise of various movements that promote social justice and equity. The ideals of diversity and equity are fundamental as increasing awareness of the role of diverse perspectives, processes, and solutions develops solid teams and realistic answers to the world's most challenging problems (Jones, Carter, Davis & Wang, 2023). Definitions of diversity vary across the canon, but it is generally agreed that diversity is the practice of including people of different races and cultures in a group or organization, a composition of multifarious facets or qualities.

Diversity practices have resulted in increased benefits for institutions across the public sector. In the workplace, diversity has contributed innovative solutions to problem-solving, for instance, improved healthcare outcomes among minority populations (Feyes, 2018). Diversity has enabled education administrators to confront complex emotional conversations, equipping students with the tools to address inequities and create openness and understanding (Kite & Clark, 2022). Diversity in law enforcement has developed critical thinking and problem-solving, cross-cultural competence, and a global approach to policing (Flavin, 2018). Diversity in the financial services sector has allowed firms to acknowledge the importance of responsiveness to changing client demographics while remaining competitive in the world market (CFA Institute, 2022). Ultimately, diversity leads to tolerance and a more profound sense of security in modern society (Ramsay, 2021).

Expanding diversity requires across-the-board institutional transformation (Griffin, 2020). Institutional renovation to achieve success in diversity outcomes involves structure (policies and praxis), engagement (workforce involvement in decision-making), and culture (workplace climate) (Anicha, Bilen-Green, Burnett, Froelich & Holbrook, 2017). Leaders play a vital role in transforming the workplace atmosphere, enabling all people to thrive, contribute, and reinforce organizational values and objectives creatively and freely. Podsakoff, Mackenzie, and Boomer (1996) outline the six core traits of transformational leaders that can generate meaningful organizational transformation: conveying a vision, adopting a relevant approach, encouraging team goals, creating high-performance expectations, offering personal guidance, and philosophic inspiration. These traits produce transformational behaviors such as flexibility, agility, motivation, individual attention, and intellectual impulse, which build a culture of diversity and impartiality across communities (Ashikali & Groeneveld, 2015; Brown, Brown & Nandedkar, 2019).

Transformational leadership prioritizes ethics. A blend of diversity and ethics promotes creativity, innovation, and efficiency in institutions (Hofstede, 2003). Ethical responsibility in the public sector encompasses stakeholders' concerns, relationship-building, respect, and care. Diversity and ethics in the workplace promote equity for all and advancement not based on race, gender, or creed but on merit (Dagogo, 2019). Innovative organizations use diversified teams to solve problems due to their ability to produce countless ideas, experiences, and perspectives (Kanter, 2006; Kreitner & Kinichi, 2004). Transformational leaders are role models who embody high ethical values and responsibility (Bass, 1985; Kalshoven, Den Hartog, and De Hoogh, 2011; Moon & Christensen, 2022). Moral attributes and ethical standards create confidence and promote integrity among followers. Leaders with an exceptional ability to rouse, influence, and gain followers' trust are well-positioned to promote diversity and cultural transformation in organizations (Northhouse, 2016).

Transformational leaders are charismatic, confident, and exceptional communicators who can quickly earn support and respect from followers (Bass & Riggio, 2006). Undoubtedly, transformational leaders are distinguished by their ability to present change and offer support and guidance, which is crucial in transition periods.

Cultural Transformation

Organizational culture originates from its leadership and impacts leadership potential as transformational leaders change their culture by understanding it and realigning their philosophy with new vision, assumptions, values, and norms (Bass & Avolio, 1993). Effective organizations require tactical, strategic thinking and culture generation, which builds future vision (Hilton, Madilo, Awaah, & Arkorful, 2023). Indubitably, culture is the vicinity within which the vision is formed, and consequently, the vision defines the landscapes of the organization's culture (Bass & Avolio, 1993; Xenikou & Simosi, 2006; Ghasabeh, 2021).

Cultural evolution is a necessity for organizations to thrive in contemporary society. Innovation capacity refers to the generation of novel ideas and attitudes in systems, processes, products, services, and policies, leading to competitive advantage and expedient solutions for modern organizations (Yang et al., 2018; Lathong et al., 2021; Jia et al., 2018; Hoang & Ngoc, 2019; Gui et al., 2022; Sijabat et al., 2022). For instance, transformational leadership has proven one of the most effective approaches for managing the healthcare sector as vigorous transformations in culture and structure lead to increased morale, job satisfaction, resilience, intrinsic motivation, optimal service delivery, and reduced burn-out (Robbins & Davidhizar, 2020; Curado & Santos, 2022; Chen, Ghardallou, Comite, Ahmad, Ryu, Ariza-Montes, Han, 2022).

The public sector suffers an 80% failure rate in meeting its objectives, with 75% of public organizations facing below-average health (Checinski, Dillon, Hieronimus & Klier, 2019). Since public organizations are impacted by a risk-averse culture, bureaucracy, and political mandates, transformations require strong leaders who prioritize change.

Four popular attributes of transformational leaders are idealized influence, inspirational motivation, intellectual stimulation, and individualized consideration (Bass & Avolio, 1993). Transformational leaders integrate creative insight, persistence, energy, intuition, and sensitivity to the needs of others to generate a creative culture for their organizations (Bass & Avolio, 1993; Reinhardt, Anita, Leon, Teresa, Summers & Ochart, 2022). In a highly innovative and gratifying organizational culture, transformational leaders build on assumptions such as people are trustworthy and purposeful and make unique contributions, as complex problems are tackled from the ground up where the most significant visibility lies (Bass, 1985; Funding, 2019; Goodman, 2019; Craig, 2019).

Transformational leaders accept responsibility for developing the maximum potential of their followers (Bass & Avolio, 1993). Leaders who build a growth culture among followers reveal a sense of vision and purpose, aligning others around the vision and empowering them to take greater responsibility for achieving it. Instead of simply maintaining the status quo, transformational leaders are defined by their ability to nurture, lead, and cultivate a culture of inventive change and maturation (Bass & Riggio, 2006); Mach, Ferreira & Abrantes, 2021). This requires building teams across multicultural settings. Transformational leadership excels in diverse teams since transformational behaviors facilitate team identification and task-relevant information elaboration, leading to higher performance (Lisak, 2021).

Organizational Change

A transformational leader is a growth enabler and supporter responsive to diverse needs, empowering people, and creating alignment among the objectives and goals of individuals, leaders, and stakeholders within an organization (Bass & Avolio, 1993; Sayyadi, 2021). A vital component of this process is change. Change represents a shift from a present state to a new one. Organizational change reflects internal shifts made by an organization in response to external transitions, such as globalization and its creation of increased markets and prospects for growth. Organizational transformation involves changing the corporate culture (Chau, Tran & Le, 2022; Tsaousis & Vakola, 2018; Karasvirta & Teerikangas, 2022). Corporate culture is an organization's average and accepted behavior, atmosphere, values, attitudes, dress, practices, and philosophy (Bass & Avolio, 1993; Assens-Serra, Boada-Cuerva, Serrano-Fernández, & Agulló-Tomás, 2021).

Organizational change is vital to competitive advantage and survival (Burnes, 2004; By, 2005; Fugate et al., 2012). Unrestricted and flexible organizations attract, select, and retain like-minded talent (Weick, 2000; Thundiyil et al., 2015; Beus et al., 2020). Change includes external adaptation through which organizations can modernize and adjust their departments, policies, and services in response to dynamism and societal turbulence (Nneji & Asikhia, 2021).

The COVID-19 pandemic jeopardized gender and racial diversity in the global workforce. The tension and anxieties of the pandemic forced women to leave their jobs or downshift and increased fatigue, burnout, and distress among women at higher rates than men (D'Agostino, Ellingrud, Gardner, Kraemer, & O'Rourke, 2020). Specific groups that encountered unique and amplified problems were senior professional women, Black women, and young mothers (D'Agostino, Ellingrud, Gardner, Kraemer, & O'Rourke, 2020).

Resistance to change translates into a lack of diversity in the current workforce. Visionary leadership requires dedicated leaders committed to building and retaining diverse teams and an all-encompassing environment. D'Agostino, Ellingrud, Gardner, Kraemer, and O'Rourke (2020) established a link between vibrant diversity initiatives and organizational performance and outcomes, such as enhanced decision-making, creativity, and innovation. Additionally, a positive correlation was found between gender diversity and rich organizational health. McKinsey (2022) revealed that organizations perceived as committed to diversity are approximately 75 percent more likely to sustain a collaborative leadership culture.

Transformational leaders can boast improved success in advancing diversity and recasting their organization's culture (Feyes, 2018). Transformational leaders maintain a goal of ethics and integrity, design precise goals, and exemplify the morals they expect from their followers (Northouse, 2016). This leadership approach augments diversity with its focus on the benefits of multi-faceted teams. Transformational leaders stimulate followers to confront their prejudices and biases and to re-envision traditional perspectives and long-held assumptions to create authentic change (Feyes, 2018).

Transformational leadership is an innovative model of governance and change management. Leaders encourage followers to be creative by shaping organizational culture, emphasizing problem-solving and empowerment, and creating cultural alignment (Moynihan, Pandey, and Wright, 2012; Rainey, 2009; Sarros, Cooper & Santora, 2008; Yukl, 2008). Employees feel comfortable working in new scenarios, utilizing outside-of-the-box thinking and risk-taking without fear of adverse outcomes (Aboramadan, Albashiti, Alharazin & Zaidoune, 2020). The transformational trait of intellectual stimulation engages followers in the autonomy of ideas, providing them with authorization, acceptance, and importance (Amabile et al., 1996; García-Morales, Jiménez-Barrionuevo, and Gutiérrez-Gutiérrez 2012).

Transformational leaders steer followers into a unique skillset required in the modern workforce, cultivating the attitudes and values that create a humane, fair, and just community for all people (Northouse, 2016). As constant as change is, transformational leaders, grasp the dynamism of contemporary society, polishing their lifelong education mindset critical to embracing diversity and cultural competence.

Transforming Public Governance

Public governance, good governance, and global governance are important themes as modern societies navigate wicked crises. Public organizations provide significant public services that build and protect the social fabric of communities (Tran et al., 2021; Võ & Löfgren, 2019). As society evolves, these organizations are pressed to make structural and governance changes to maintain innovation, diversity, and resilience (Tetteh et al., 2021; Van Der Wal & Demircioglu, 2020). Hence, public leaders must clinch to change philosophies to support staff and boost organizational performance (Dartey-Baah et al., 2021).

Transformational leadership in the public sector addresses democratic norms and the role of citizens in formulating and realizing shared goals (Denhardt & Campbell, 2006). Though leadership literature is vast and varied, there has been a growing emphasis on the exploration of transformational models to understand the role leaders play in achieving institutional change. Transformational leaders were found to influence creative role identity and innovative work behavior through recurrent role-modeling, active listening, and constructive criticism (Tan, van Dun & Wilderom, 2023). Chau, Tran & Le (2022) discovered that transformational skills create a results-oriented culture, which leads to higher organizational performance. Bhatti, Ahmad, Akram & Ahmad (2021) found a positive relationship exists between transformational behaviors and job satisfaction and employee empowerment in the public sector. Bakri & Elmasry (2018) found transformational leadership to significantly influence good governance among public sector leaders in the developing world.

Transformational leaders are visionaries and catalysts of change who market their ideas and successfully reshape and reinvent their organizations (Denhardt & Campbell, 2006). The concept of transformation depicts movement. In the public sector, leadership is the vehicle for accomplishing change in the most innovative, effective, and efficient ways possible. Public leaders must consider both the means and ends of change. Transformation in the public context involves fundamental and unavoidable questions surrounding citizenship, democratic values, and service in the public interest that demand attention and can only be addressed by adopting a transformational blueprint (Denhardt & Campbell, 2006).

Bass (1984) deems transformational leadership as higher-level leadership execution. Transformational leadership occurs when leaders broaden and elevate the interests of their employees; generate awareness and acceptance of the purposes and mission of the group; and stir their employees to look beyond their self-interest to the group's greater good (Bass, 1985). Transformational leaders achieve these results in several ways. First, they are charismatic and influential, thus inspiring their followership. Second, they attend to the emotional needs of their teams, which in turn intellectually stimulates their followers. Finally, transformational leaders are individually considerate; they pay close attention to diversity among their employees and act as mentors to those who need help to mature and expand (Bass, 1985).

As a value-based framework, transformational leadership outlines strategies to help leaders incorporate public service motivation values across management systems to enhance employee and organizational performance (Paarlberg & Lavigna, 2010; Park & Rainy, 2008). In a world of constant change, transformational leaders can leverage on intrinsic motivation to create openness to change (Gennaro, 2019). A favorable relationship exists between transformational leadership and various employee performance measures and satisfaction in private and public organizations. Dvir et al. (2002) found that Israeli military leaders trained in transformational leadership reported higher development among followers, specifically regarding military readiness indicators. Grant (2012) discovered that transformational leadership was associated with higher performance ratings of supervisors by employees, while Belle (2013) found that leadership training principles improved the performance of nurses.

Transformational leaders communicate a compelling vision that arouses powerful emotions. They serve as ethical and principled role models, raising followers' consciousness about idealized goals and encouraging followers to transcend their self-interest for more extensive, collective goals (Paarlberg & Lavigna, 2010). They identify critical management practices and related theoretical concepts that allow leaders to harness employees' values. Transformational leaders create shared organizational value through inspirational communication, onboarding practices, setting meaningful goals, and designing significant work. Finally, transformational leaders empower employees to act on their values and serve as positive exemplars (Paarlberg & Lavigna, 2010).

Wright and Pandey (2010) investigated the effect of organizational structure on the transformational leadership practices of municipal chief administrative officers and found that transformational leadership is one of the most prominent theories of organizational behavior. In contrast to leadership based on individual gain and the exchange of rewards for effort, transformational leaders motivate behavior by changing their followers' attitudes and assumptions (Wright & Pandey, 2010). To direct and inspire individual effort, these leaders transform their followers by raising their awareness of the importance of organizational outcomes, thus activating their higher-order needs, and inducing them to transcend their self-interest for the sake of the organization (Wright & Pandey, 2010). Successful leaders augment their use of beneficial transactional behaviors with more transformational ones (Wright & Pandey, 2010). The result is public service motivation, goal, and mission clarity, ultimately building pride among organizations.

Stãnescu and Rosca (2010) viewed effective public service leadership for contemporary society as being politically neutral and professionally trained in modern principles and values of public sector governance). New leadership requests have a growing focus on transformational leadership in the context of a diversified labor market and the global economic slump. Transformational leaders motivate others to do more than they originally intended and often more than they thought possible as they set more challenging expectations and typically achieve higher performances (Gennaro, 2019). These leaders also tend to have more committed and satisfied followers.

Transformational leaders empower followers to pay attention to their individual needs and personal development, enabling them to develop leadership potential. Followers are inspired to commit to an organization's shared vision and goals, are challenged to be innovative problem solvers, and develop leadership capacity through coaching, mentoring, and support (Stănescu & Rosca, 2010). Hence, followers are stimulated to achieve prime objectives.

Transformational leadership was found to have extensive benefits in the healthcare industry. Medley and Larochelle (1995) studied the relationship of head nurse leadership style to staff nurse job satisfaction by using the leadership paradigm of transformational and transactional leadership. Registered staff nurses were selected using simple random sampling and presented a questionnaire to measure the leadership style of nurse managers as perceived by staff nurses. A positive, moderate correlation was revealed between the job satisfaction of registered staff nurses and the transformational leadership of nurse managers. An inverse, weak relationship existed between registered staff nurses' job satisfaction and nurse managers' transactional leadership (Medley & Larochelle, 1995). Bhatti, Ahmad, Akram, & Ahmad (2021) discovered a positive relationship between the features of transformational leadership such as handling uncertainty, guidance and support, risk management, and teambuilding, and job satisfaction among public sector employees during COVID-19. Undoubtedly, transformational leaders are influential especially during unexpected and complex health crises.

Transformational leadership describes an environment in which leaders and followers lift one another to higher levels of motivation and morality (Medley & Larochelle, 1995, Campbell, 2018). Transformational leadership involves leaders listening to concerns, providing helpful advice for development, teaching, and coaching, focusing on developing followers' strengths, treating followers as individuals, giving personal attention to followers who seem neglected, and promoting self-development (Medley & Larochelle, 1995).

Transformational leadership has been given the most attention in leadership literature, particularly in public administration, because of its consistently positive outcomes (Backhaus & Vogel, 2022). Yet, research is lacking in terms of organizational structure and chain of command and power within hierarchical transformative models. Since transformative change in the state sector involves managing complex scenarios, a balanced approach incorporating performance and administrative longevity can support public leaders to solve real-world problems through transformational efforts (Blackburn, 2021).

CONCLUSION & RECOMMENDATIONS

State entities and public leaders are impeded by administrative control mechanisms such as centralization, formalization, and routinization (Wright & Pandey, 2010). For transformational behaviors to thrive in contemporary society, a culture of diversity must be enacted. Heterogeneity enriches institutional legitimacy and acceptance of diversification (Andrews et al., 2005; Groeneveld & Van de Walle, 2010; Pitts et al., 2010). However, diversity efforts in hiring policies, workplace practices and benefits alone are insufficient. Instead, public institutions must foster a climate of diversity that requires systemic organizational change to include diverse perspectives in crucial decision-making processes. The following recommendations prove useful in building diverse organizations through transformation.

First, public organizations must encourage leaders to adopt a glocal perspective of their team and society through cross-cultural leadership training to improve sensitivity to differences. Second, leaders should promote cultural diversity, belonging and cohesiveness in achieving organizational goals. Training in this area should focus on the role of cultural transformation in enhancing performance of culturally diverse teams. Third, along with transformational leadership, this paper advances Stemoh leadership, a relatively new perspective of leadership which focuses on humility and service. When leaders first serve others with humility, they become influential to varying groups in society. Two highlights of this model are adaptability and respect (Ramjit, 2021). Powerful leaders can connect with people of diverse values, beliefs, ages, and backgrounds, cultivating compatibility and accessibility (Ramjit, 2021). When leaders treat their teams with respect and courtesy, regardless of who they are, followers are inspired and motivated to follow their lead. Stemoh leadership advances the five core behaviors of integrity, insight, agility, flexibility, and resilience, all of which prove effective in managing complex and dynamic systems (Ramjit, 2021).

Diverse leadership is paramount in discussing effective public management strategies for modern society. Leadership impacts the organizational atmosphere, which in turn affects governance mechanisms. A diverse leader's most extraordinary power is creating a favorable work habitat. Transformational leaders provide direction, implement plans, recast mindsets, support, and motivate; ultimately, people are inspired and energized to perform optimally in a transformational climate.

REFERENCES

Aboramadan, M., Albashiti, B., Alharazin, H., & Zaidoune, S. (2020). Organizational culture, innovation and performance: A study from a non-western context. *Journal of Management Development, 39*(4), 437–451. doi:10.1108/JMD-06-2019-0253

Akpa, V., Asikhia, O., & Nneji, N. (2021). Organizational culture and organizational performance: A review of literature. *International Journal of Advances in Engineering and Management, 3*(1), 361–372. doi:10.35629/5252-0301361372

Anderson, M. (2017). Transformational leadership in education: A review of existing literature. *International Social Science Review, 93*(1), 1–13.

Anicha, C. L., Bilen-Green, C., Burnett, A., Froelich, K., & Holbrook, S. (2017). Institutional transformation: Toward a diversity-positive campus culture. *Journal of Women and Minorities in Science and Engineering, 23*(2), 147–167. doi:10.1615/JWomenMinorScienEng.2017017021

APSC. (2022, September 27). *Diversity and inclusion report 2022.* https://www.apsc.gov.au/working-aps/diversity-and-inclusion/diversity-and-inclusion-report-2022

Ashikali, T., & Groeneveld, S. (2015). Diversity management in public organizations and its effect on employees' affective commitment: The role of transformational leadership and the inclusiveness of the organizational culture. *Review of Public Personnel Administration, 35*(2), 146–168. doi:10.1177/0734371X13511088

Assens-Serra, J., Boada-Cuerva, M., Serrano-Fernández, M.-J., & Agulló-Tomás, E. (2021). Gaining a Better Understanding of the Types of Organizational Culture to Manage Suffering at Work. *Frontiers in Psychology*, *12*, 782488. Advance online publication. doi:10.3389/fpsyg.2021.782488 PMID:34880819

Balestra, C., & Fleischer, L. (2018). Diversity statistics in the OECD: How do OECD countries collect data on ethnic, racial and indigenous identity? *OCED iLibrary*. doi:10.1787/18152031

Bambra, C., Lynch, J., & Smith, K. E. (2021). The unequal pandemic: COVID-19 and health inequalities. Policy Press. doi:10.1007/978-3-031-21824-8_8

Bass, B. M. (1985). Leadership: Good, better, best. *Organizational Dynamics*, *13*(3), 26–40. doi:10.1016/0090-2616(85)90028-2

Bass, B. M. (1999). Two decades of research and development in transformational leadership. *European Journal of Work and Organizational Psychology*, *8*(1), 9–32. doi:10.1080/135943299398410

Bass, B. M., & Avolio, B. J. (1993). Transformational leadership and organizational culture. *Public Administration Quarterly*, 112–121.

Bass, B. M., & Riggio, R. E. (2006). *Transformational leadership*. Academic Press.

Bass, B. M., & Riggio, R. E. (2010). The transformational model of leadership. *Leading organizations: Perspectives for a new era, 2*(1), 76-86.

Béland, D., He, A. J., & Ramesh, M. (2022). *COVID-19, crisis responses, and public policies: from the persistence of inequalities to the importance of policy design.* doi:10.1093/polsoc/puac021

Bettinger-Lopez, C., & Bro, A. (2020). A double pandemic: Domestic violence in the age of COVID-19. *Council on Foreign Relations*, *13*, 1–7.

Bhatti. (2021). Role of employee Empowerment. *Journal of Contemporary Issues in Business and Government*, *27*(4), 112. doi:10.47750/cibg.2021.27.04.012

Bourke, J., & Dillon, B. (2018). Eight truths about diversity and inclusion at work| Deloitte Insights. *Deloitte*, (January), 22.

Bradley, R. (2020). Reviewing Transformational Leadership and Change Management in United States of America. *Stratford Journals, 4*(6), 56-65. https://stratfordjournals.org/journals/index.php/journal-of-human-resource/article/view/689

Brown, M., Brown, R. S., & Nandedkar, A. (2019). Transformational leadership theory and exploring the perceptions of diversity management in higher education. *Journal of Higher Education Theory and Practice*, *19*(7).

Bryman, A., Collinson, D., Grint, K., Jackson, B., & Uhl-Bien, M. (2011). *The SAGE Handbook of Leadership*. SAGE.

Capgemini. (n.d.). *The key to designing inclusive tech.* https://www.capgemini.com/insights/research-library/the-key-to-designing-inclusive-tech/

Chau, T. H. P., Tran, Y. T., & Le, T. D. (2022). How does transformational leadership influence on the performance of public service organizations in a developing country? The interventional roles of NPM cultural orientations. *Cogent Business & Management*, *9*(1), 2140746. Advance online publication. doi:10.1080/23311975.2022.2140746

Checinski, M., Dillon, R., Hieronimus, S., & Klier, J. (2019, March 5). *Putting people at the heart of public-sector transformations*. McKinsey & Company. https://www.mckinsey.com/industries/public-and-social-sector/our-insights/putting-people-at-the-heart-of-public-sector-transformations

Chen, J., Ghardallou, W., Comite, U., Ahmad, N., Ryu, H. B., Ariza-Montes, A., & Han, H. (2022). Managing Hospital Employees' Burnout through Transformational Leadership: The Role of Resilience, Role Clarity, and Intrinsic Motivation. *International Journal of Environmental Research and Public Health*, *19*(17), 10941. doi:10.3390/ijerph191710941 PMID:36078657

Ciminelli, G., & Garcia-Mandicó, S. (2020). COVID-19 in Italy: An analysis of death registry data. *Journal of Public Health (Oxford, England)*, *42*(4), 723–730. doi:10.1093/pubmed/fdaa165 PMID:32935849

Collins, D. P., Bruce, J., & McKee, K. (2019). Teaching Transformative Leadership for Social Justice: Using Literature Circles to Enhance Learning and Create Deeper Meaning. *Journal of Leadership Education*, *18*(3), 158–166. doi:10.12806/V18/I3/A1

Curado, C., & Santos, R. (2022). Transformational leadership and work performance in health care: The mediating role of job satisfaction. *Leadership in Health Services*, *35*(2), 160–173. doi:10.1108/LHS-06-2021-0051 PMID:34767323

Emrich, C. T., Tate, E., Larson, S. E., & Zhou, Y. (2020). Measuring social equity in flood recovery funding. *Environmental Hazards*, *19*(3), 228–250. doi:10.1080/17477891.2019.1675578

Errida, A., & Lotfi, B. (2021). The determinants of organizational change management success: Literature review and case study. *International Journal of Engineering Business Management*, *13*, 1–15. doi:10.1177/18479790211016273

Gélinas-Proulx, A., & Shields, C. M. (2022). *Leading for equity and social justice: Systemic transformation in Canadian education*. University of Toronto Press.

Ghasabeh, M. S. (2021). Transformational Leadership: Implementing a Cultural Approach in Organizations. *The Journal of Values Based Leadership*, *14*(1), 101–118. doi:10.22543/0733.141.1340

GOV.UK. (2022, May 10). *Civil Service Diversity and Inclusion Dashboard*. https://www.gov.uk/government/publications/civil-service-diversity-inclusion-dashboard/civil-service-diversity-and-inclusion-dashboard

Griffin, K. A. (2019). Institutional barriers, strategies, and benefits to increasing the representation of women and men of color in the professoriate: looking beyond the pipeline. In *Higher Education: Handbook of Theory and Research* (Vol. 35, pp. 1-73). https://diversity.ucdavis.edu/sites/g/files/dgvnsk731/files/inline-files/InstitutionalBarriersStrategies2020.pdf

Griffith, A. (2020, October 21). *What new disaggregated data tells us about federal public service diversity*. Policy Options. https://policyoptions.irpp.org/magazines/october-2020/what-new-disaggregated-data-tells-us-about-federal-public-service-diversity/

Hannah, A., Baekkeskov, E., & Tubakovic, T. (2022). Ideas and crisis in policy and administration: Existing links and research frontiers. *Public Administration, 100*(3), 571–584. doi:10.1111/padm.12862

Heggebø, K., Tøge, A. G., Dahl, E., & Berg, J. E. (2019). Socioeconomic inequalities in health during the Great Recession: A scoping review of the research literature. *Scandinavian Journal of Public Health, 47*(6), 635–654. doi:10.1177/1403494818801637 PMID:30301437

Hilton, S. K., Madilo, W., Awaah, F., & Arkorful, H. (2023). Dimensions of transformational leadership and organizational performance: The mediating effect of job satisfaction. *Management Research Review, 46*(1), 1–19. doi:10.1108/MRR-02-2021-0152

InStride. (2021, February 19). *Diversity in the workplace statistics you need to know in 2023*. https://www.instride.com/insights/workplace-diversity-and-inclusion-statistics/

Kaase, M., & Newton, K. (1995). *Theories of Crisis and Catastrophe, Change and Transformation*. Academic. doi:10.1093/0198294727.003.0002

Kalnicky, E. (2022, December 8). *Race, gender and public service leadership: Major findings from 360 assessment data*. Partner for Public Service. https://ourpublicservice.org/publications/race-gender-and-public-service-leadership-major-findings-from-our-360-data/

Kearney, E., & Gebert, D. (2009). Managing diversity and enhancing team outcomes: The promise of transformational leadership. *The Journal of Applied Psychology, 94*(1), 77–89. doi:10.1037/a0013077 PMID:19186897

Mach, M., Ferreira, A. I., & Abrantes, A. C. (2022). Transformational leadership and team performance in sports teams: A conditional indirect model. *Applied Psychology, 71*(2), 662–694. doi:10.1111/apps.12342

Madgavkar, A., Krishnan, M., White, O., Mahajan, D., & Azcue, X. (2020, July 15). *COVID-19 and gender equality: Countering the regressive effects*. McKinsey. https://www.mckinsey.com/featured-insights/future-of-work/covid-19-and-gender-equality-countering-the-regressive-effects

McConnell, A., & t Hart, P. (2019). Inaction and public policy: Understanding why policymakers 'do nothing'. *Policy Sciences, 52*(4), 645–661. doi:10.100711077-019-09362-2

Mittal, S., & Singh, T. (2020). Gender-based violence during COVID-19 pandemic: A mini-review. *Frontiers in Global Women's Health, 1*, 4. doi:10.3389/fgwh.2020.00004 PMID:34816149

NCES. (2019, February). *Educational Attainment*. https://nces.ed.gov/programs/raceindicators/indicator_RFA.asp

Nolan-Flecha, N. (2019). Next generation diversity and inclusion policies in the public service: Ensuring public services reflect the societies they serve. Academic Press. doi:10.1007/978-3-031-21824-8_8

OECD. (2021). Diversity and inclusion in the public service. In Government at a Glance 2021. doi:10.1787/1c258f55-en

Opiyo, R. A. (2019). Inclusive practice and transformative leadership are entwined: Lessons for professional development of school leaders in Kenya. *Global Journal of Transformative Education*, *1*(1), 52–67. doi:10.14434/gjte.v1i1.25981

Paarlberg, L. E., & Lavigna, B. (2010). Transformational leadership and public service motivation: Driving individual and organizational performance. *Public Administration Review*, *70*(5), 710–718. doi:10.1111/j.1540-6210.2010.02199.x

Piper, M. (2022, June 3). *Why the public sector needs a more diverse tech workforce*. Capgemini. https://www.capgemini.com/insights/expert-perspectives/why-the-public-sector-needs-a-more-diverse-tech-workforce/

Poulsen, S. (n.d.). *Innovation and diversity in the public sector*. THNK. https://www.thnk.org/blog/innovation-and-diversity-in-the-public-sector/

Ramjit, D. (2021). Stemoh Leadership: A Multicultural Christian Approach to Contemporary Leadership. *International Journal of Responsible Leadership and Ethical Decision-Making*, *3*(2), 17–37. doi:10.4018/IJRLEDM.2021070102

Reinhardt, A. C., Leon, T. G., & Summers, L. O. (2022). The Transformational Leader in Nursing Practice–an approach to retain nursing staff. *Administrative Issues Journal*, *12*(1), 2. doi:10.5929/2022.12.1.1

Seljemo, C., Viksveen, P., & Ree, E. (2020). The role of transformational leadership, job demands and job resources for patient safety culture in Norwegian nursing homes: A cross-sectional study. *BMC Health Services Research*, *20*(1), 1–8. doi:10.118612913-020-05671-y PMID:32847598

Shields, C. M. (2010). Transformative leadership: Working for equity in diverse contexts. *Educational Administration Quarterly*, *46*(4), 558–589. doi:10.1177/0013161X10375609

Shields, C. M., & Hesbol, K. A. (2020). Transformative leadership approaches to inclusion, equity, and social justice. *Journal of School Leadership*, *30*(1), 3–22. doi:10.1177/1052684619873343

Sijabat, R. (2022). The association of economic growth, foreign aid, foreign direct investment and gross capital formation in Indonesia: Evidence from the Toda–Yamamoto approach. *Economies*, *10*(4), 93. doi:10.3390/economies10040093

Smith, C. (2021, December 9). *Has the Public Sector Done Enough to Create a Diverse Workforce?* Governing. https://www.governing.com/work/has-the-public-sector-done-enough-to-create-a-diverse-workforce

Strada. (2020, June 10). *Public Viewpoint: COVID-19 Work and Education Survey*. http://stradaeducation.org/wp-content/uploads/2020/06/Public-Viewpoint-Report-Week-9.pdf

Sumner, A., Hoy, C., & Ortiz-Juarez, E. (2020). *Estimates of the impact of COVID-19 on global poverty* (No. 2020/43). WIDER Working Paper.

Tamunomiebi, M. D., & Ehior, I. E. (2019). Diversity and ethical issues in the organizations. *International Journal of Academic Research in Business & Social Sciences*, *9*(2), 839–864. doi:10.6007/IJARBSS/v9-i2/5620

Tan, A. B. C., van Dun, D. H., & Wilderom, C. (2023). Lean innovation training and transformational leadership for employee creative role identity and innovative work behavior in a public service organization. *International Journal of Lean Six Sigma*. Advance online publication. doi:10.1108/IJLSS-06-2022-0126

Teetzen, F., Bürkner, P.-C., Gregersen, S., & Vincent-Höper, S. (2022). The mediating effects of work characteristics on the relationship between transformational leadership and employee well-being: A meta-analytic investigation. *International Journal of Environmental Research and Public Health, 19*(5), 3133. doi:10.3390/ijerph19053133 PMID:35270825

Thibault, T., Gulseren, D. B., & Kelloway, E. K. (2019). The benefits of transformational leadership and transformational leadership training on health and safety outcomes. In *Increasing occupational health and safety in workplaces* (pp. 334–348). Edward Elgar Publishing. doi:10.4337/9781788118095.00027

Tichy, N. M., & Devanna, M. A. (1986). The transformational leader. *Training and Development Journal*.

United Nations CEPA. (2019, October). *CEPA Strategy Guidance Note: Promotion of public sector workforce diversity*. https://unpan.un.org/sites/unpan.un.org/files/Draft%20strategy%20note%20%20 -%20public%20sector%20workforce%20diversity.pdf

Wenzelburger, G., & Wolf, F. (2015). *Policy theories in the crisis?* Academic Press. doi:10.1108/02683940610684409

Wright, J. E. II, & Merritt, C. C. (2020). Social equity and COVID-19: The case of African Americans. *Public Administration Review, 80*(5), 820–826. doi:10.1111/puar.13251 PMID:32836453

Xenikou, A., & Simosi, M. (2006). Organizational culture and transformational leadership as predictors of business unit performance. *Journal of Managerial Psychology, 21*(6), 566–579. doi:10.1108/02683940610684409

Ytterstad, S., & Olaisen, J. (2023). The Relationship Between Sternberg's Learning Style and Transformational Leadership. In Learning Transformational Leadership: A Pedagogical and Practical Perspective (pp. 141-151). Springer. doi:10.1007/978-3-031-21824-8_8

Chapter 16

Executive Coaching as an Effective Leadership Development Tool in Law Enforcement and Police Departments

Amalisha Aridi
https://orcid.org/0000-0002-7869-5530
Capitol Technology University, USA

Darrell Norman Burrell
https://orcid.org/0000-0002-4675-9544
Marymount University, USA

Kevin Richardson
https://orcid.org/0009-0002-3212-8669
Capitol Technology University, USA

ABSTRACT

Executive leadership coaching can have significant benefits for police officers and law enforcement agencies in addressing critical issues such as race relations, misconduct, and professionalism. Leadership coaches can help police officers develop a deeper understanding of their own biases and improve their cultural competence. This increased self-awareness enables leaders to foster a more inclusive and respectful work environment, promoting better relationships between officers and diverse communities. Additionally, coaching can help officers enhance their decision-making skills, encouraging them to implement fair and just policies that prioritize accountability and transparency. Ultimately, executive leadership coaching empowers police officers and their superiors to create a more equitable and trustworthy law enforcement system, benefiting both the officers and the communities they serve. This chapter uses theories and research from the literature to argue for the viability of the deployment of executive coaching as a tool to develop better police leaders at every level.

DOI: 10.4018/979-8-3693-1630-6.ch016

INTRODUCTION

Police leadership misconduct is an issue that has been reported in the news recently, with a variety of examples of poor leadership and abuse of power (Vasilenko, 2015). The role of police leadership is to serve as a model for other officers, demonstrate good ethical practices, and ensure that the police force is held to the highest standards of integrity (Vasilenko, 2015). Police leadership misconduct is "any behavior by a police supervisor or leader that is not in accordance with accepted ethical standards or departmental policy and procedures" (Vasilenko, 2015, p. 4). This includes any violations of the law, unethical behavior, or misuse of authority. Examples of police leadership misconduct include improper use of force, abuse of authority, corruption, and discrimination (Vasilenko, 2015).

The improper use of force is one of the most common forms of police misconduct (Vasilenko, 2015). This includes any physical or psychological force used against a person deemed excessive or unnecessary (Vasilenko, 2015). This can include physical force, such as striking a person with a baton or using pepper spray(Vasilenko, 2015). It can also include psychological force, such as threats of violence or verbal abuse (Vasilenko, 2015). The improper use of force can significantly impact police-community relationships and lead to a lack of trust in the police force (Vasilenko, 2015).

Abuse of authority is another form of police misconduct (Vasilenko, 2015; Stinson & Ross, 2017). This includes any actions taken by police officers that are not in line with their duties or the law (Vasilenko, 2015). This can include verbal or physical intimidation, threats or coercion, or the misuse of police resources (Vasilenko, 2015; Stinson & Ross, 2017). This type of misconduct can harm police-community relationships, leading to a lack of trust and respect for the police force (Vasilenko, 2015; Stinson & Ross, 2017). Corruption is another form of police misconduct. This includes any illegal or unethical behavior by police officers intended to gain financial or personal gain. This can include bribery, extortion, and the misuse of police resources. Corruption can significantly impact police-community relationships, leading to a lack of trust and respect for the police force (Vasilenko, 2015).

Discrimination is another form of police misconduct. This includes any action taken by police officers based on race, gender, religion, sexual orientation, or any other protected class (Vasilenko, 2015). Discrimination can significantly impact police-community relationships, leading to a lack of trust and respect for the police force (Vasilenko, 2015).

Police leadership misconduct can have a significant impact on police-community relationships. This impact can be both direct and indirect. Directly, police misconduct can lead to a lack of trust and respect for the police force (Vasilenko, 2015). For example, if a police officer uses excessive force, it can erode the trust between the police and the community. Similarly, if a police officer is found to have engaged in corruption, it can lead to a lack of trust in the police force (Vasilenko, 2015).

On an indirect level, police misconduct can lead to a sense of mistrust and alienation in the community (Vasilenko, 2015). This can manifest in various ways, such as decreased cooperation with police investigations or a reluctance to report crimes. This can lead to a breakdown in the relationship between the police and the community, harming public safety (Vasilenko, 2015).

PROBLEM STATEMENT

The statistics on police misconduct and arrests of law enforcement officers in the last five years are troubling and revealing. According to the National Police Misconduct Reporting Project (NPMRP), there were over 8,700 reported cases of police misconduct in the United States in the last five years (2016-2020) (National Police Misconduct Reporting Project, 2020). Of these, over 5,700 cases resulted in an arrest of the offending officer. This represents an increase of over 11% in reported cases of police misconduct since 2016 (National Police Misconduct Reporting Project, 2020).

The types of misconduct reported also varied significantly. The most common type of misconduct reported was excessive force (3,570 cases), followed by sexual misconduct (1,988 cases), false arrest (1,291 cases), and false imprisonment (1,068 cases). Other types of misconduct reported included racial slurs, improper search and seizure, and civil rights violations (National Police Misconduct Reporting Project, 2020).

The issue of police misconduct and arrests of law enforcement officers has significantly impacted the public's trust in law enforcement. According to a recent Pew Research Center survey, only half of Americans (50%) say they trust the police to do the right thing "all or most of the time" (Pew Research Center, 2020). This is a decrease of 10 percentage points since 2015 when 60% of Americans said they trusted the police to do the right thing "all or most of the time" (Pew Research Center, 2020).

This lack of trust in law enforcement has been particularly pronounced among minority groups. Only 30% of African Americans trust the police to do the right thing "all or most of the time" (Pew Research Center, 2020). This is a decrease of 17 percentage points since 2015 when 47% of African Americans said they trusted the police to do the right thing "all or most of the time" (Pew Research Center, 2020).

Leadership has long been recognized as one of the most critical factors determining the professionalism and conduct of police departments. Effective leadership can lead to greater efficiency and effectiveness, improved morale and productivity, and reduced citizen complaints (Laut, 2019). However, effective leaders are only sometimes born, and leadership development is essential to ensure that police departments are staffed with adequate and competent leaders at every level. Executive leadership coaching has been identified as an essential tool for developing leadership skills in law enforcement professionals (Laut, 2019). This conceptual paper explores the viability and practicality of employing executive leadership coaching as a leadership development tool in law enforcement.

Method

The method employed was a review of the literature. A literature review serves several essential functions, including providing the reader with a comprehensive understanding of the relevant literature and its implications for the topic at hand, giving a sense of the current state of knowledge on the topic, and helping to identify gaps in existing knowledge (Fink, 2014). A literature review can also provide solutions in a conceptual academic paper by synthesizing the various research findings and providing a framework for applying the solutions to real-world problems (Fink, 2014).

The information and data utilized in the literature review mainly originated from academic, business, criminal justice, and psychology resource. The research is exclusive to executive coaching professional management previous literature and expertise and does not include any other types of coaching such as sports, spiritual, political, or /and religious coaches. The literature review includes a) the previous studies and theories about executive coaching; b) the review presents a historical review of the development of the executive coaching practice and the significant stages that affected its popularity and evolvement; c) it provides a theoretical point of view and definition to generate a coaching-competency framework to validate the verify the characteristics and skills of effective coaches; d) exploration the connection of coaches competencies and qualifications to qualifications to the psychological and non-psychological theory basis.

Leadership Failures in Law Enforcement

In recent years, the United States has seen increased police misconduct. The prevalence of police misconduct has led to the arrest of various police chiefs and other high-ranking law enforcement officers nationwide.

The arrest of Payne Springs, Texas, Chief of Police Shawn Denning in April 2014 resulted from a criminal investigation into allegations of misuse of public funds. Denning was accused of using city funds to purchase items for himself and his family and paying himself for work he did not perform. He was also accused of using city funds to pay for travel expenses and to purchase items for his personal collection. Denning was subsequently charged with two counts of felony theft and two counts of official oppression. He was later found guilty of all charges and sentenced to four years in prison and a $10,000 fine (Texas Tribune, 2014).

The arrest of Payne Springs Chief of Police Shawn Denning raises several questions about police leadership and accountability. First, it raises the question of whether or not there is sufficient oversight of police chiefs and other high-ranking law enforcement officers. The lack of oversight, in this case, allowed Denning to misuse public funds for his own personal gain, and the situation could have been avoided with better oversight from the city. Second, the case raises questions about the effectiveness of internal controls and accountability systems in police departments. If the department had a system in place to detect and prevent such misuse of funds, it could have prevented the criminal activity from occurring in the first place. Finally, the case raises questions about the level of transparency and accountability that is expected of police chiefs. Denning's actions violated the public trust, and his arrest serves as a reminder that police chiefs must always act with integrity and transparency.

The arrest of Greensburg, Pennsylvania Police Chief William B. Fuller in November 2016 resulted from a criminal investigation into allegations of corruption and misuse of public funds. Fuller was accused of using city funds to purchase items for himself and his family and using city funds to pay for travel expenses. He was also accused of using city funds to pay for personal services, such as attorney fees and consulting services. Fuller was subsequently charged with two counts of felony theft, two counts of official oppression, and one count of conspiracy. He was later found guilty of all charges and sentenced to four years in prison and a $10,000 fine (PennLive, 2016).

The arrest of Greensburg Police Chief William B. Fuller raises similar questions to those raised by the arrest of Payne Springs Chief of Police Shawn Denning. First, it raises the question of whether or not there is sufficient oversight of police chiefs and other high-ranking law enforcement officers. The lack of oversight, in this case, allowed Fuller to misuse public funds for his own personal gain, and the situation could have been avoided with better oversight from the city. Second, the case raises questions about the effectiveness of internal controls and accountability systems in police departments. If the department had a system in place to detect and prevent such misuse of funds, it could have prevented the criminal activity from occurring in the first place. Finally, the case raises questions about the level of transparency and accountability that is expected of police chiefs. Fuller's actions violated the public trust, and his arrest serves as a reminder that police chiefs must always act with integrity and transparency.

The arrest of Homerville, Georgia, Police Chief Dearin "Mack" Drury in October 2016 resulted from a criminal investigation into allegations of misuse of public funds and abuse of power. Drury was accused of using city funds to purchase items for himself and his family and using city funds to pay for travel expenses. He was also accused of using his position to threaten and intimidate city officials. Drury was subsequently charged with two counts of felony theft, two counts of official oppression, and one count of conspiracy. He was later found guilty of all charges and sentenced to four years in prison and a $10,000 fine (The Atlanta Journal-Constitution, 2016).

The arrest of Homerville Police Chief Dearin "Mack" Drury raises similar questions to those raised by the arrest of Payne Springs Chief of Police Shawn Denning and Greensburg Police Chief William B. Fuller. First, it raises the question of whether or not there is sufficient oversight of police chiefs and other high-ranking law enforcement officers. The lack of oversight, in this case, allowed Drury to misuse public funds and abuse his position of power, and the situation could have been avoided with better oversight from the city. Second, the case raises questions about the effectiveness of internal controls and accountability systems in police departments. If the department had a system in place to detect and prevent such misuse of funds and abuse of power, it could have prevented the criminal activity from occurring in the first place. Finally, the case raises questions about the level of transparency and accountability that is expected of police chiefs. Drury's actions violated the public trust, and his arrest serves as a reminder that police chiefs must always act with integrity and transparency.

The arrest of Biscayne Park, Florida Police Chief Raimundo Atesiano in June 2018 resulted from a criminal investigation into allegations of false arrests and civil rights violations. Atesiano was accused of ordering officers to falsify police reports to falsely arrest innocent individuals for improving the department's crime rate. He was subsequently charged with one count of conspiracy to deprive individuals of their civil rights and one count of deprivation of rights under color of law. Atesiano was later found guilty of both charges and sentenced to three years in prison and a $25,000 fine (The Miami Herald, 2018).

The arrest of Biscayne Park Police Chief Raimundo Atesiano raises many questions about police leadership and accountability. First, it raises the question of whether or not there is sufficient oversight of police chiefs and other high-ranking law enforcement officers. The lack of oversight, in this case, allowed Atesiano to order officers to make false arrests, and the situation could have been avoided with better oversight from the city. Second, the case raises questions about the effectiveness of internal controls and accountability systems in police departments. If the department had a system in place to detect and prevent such misuse of power, it could have prevented the criminal activity from occurring in the first place. Finally, the case raises questions about the level of transparency and accountability that is expected of police chiefs. Atesiano's actions violated the public trust, and his arrest serves as a reminder that police chiefs must always act with integrity and transparency.

Developing better and more effective leadership skills in law enforcement at every level is critical. The literature review presents an analytical summary of the documented academic data to investigate the effectiveness of executive coaching as a developmental method to increase productivity and develop leadership competency. The problem phenomenon is based and analyzed on the leadership development theory and self-determination theory.

EXECUTIVE COACHING HISTORY AND DEFINITION

Recently, executive coaching developed and become the trendiest practice for improving organizational effectiveness and efficiency (Newsom & Dent, 2011). Further, coaching became the most reputable management method to construct leadership development (Kampa- Kokesh & Anderson, 2005; Newsom & Dente, 2011).

According to Kampa-Kokesh et al., the executive coaching practice appeared in the late 1940s; the practice started to operate as an affiliation of the consulting profession and psychologist's science. Thus, researching the literature to explore the history of the coaching intervention leads to the discovery of six essential topics, including a) definitions and interpretations; (b) objectives and goals; (c) methodologies; (d) relevance to psychology; (e) therapy and coaching skills; (f) recipients and advantages of users (Kampa- Kokesh & Anderson, 2005).

Definition and Conceptual Understanding

Executive leadership coaching is a form of professional development involving a coach to assist leaders in developing their leadership capabilities (Laut, 2019). The coach is a mentor, helping leaders build their skills and abilities and providing support and guidance. The coach can provide valuable insights and guidance that can help the leader to develop their own unique style of leadership (Laut, 2019). The coach can also help the leader to identify areas of improvement and to develop strategies for addressing those areas.

As its broadest status, coaching is primarily defined as the "process of equipping people with tools, knowledge, and opportunities they need to develop them and become more effective" (Peterson & Hicks, 1995, p: 41). The coaching technically was classified as a technique or a tool that management can utilize to increase performance as a factor to achieve projects' success and law enforcement effectiveness (Saowalux & Peng, 2007). Further, in 1990 executive coaching emerged urgently as an intervention to change the management conduct of managers (Peterson & Hicks, 1995).

The leadership literature (Feldman, 2001) specified the three major essential factors of the executive coaching profession, including (a) one-on-one training and mentoring; (b) it requires the implementation of 360- feedback on managers; (c) coaching target to enhance executives, leaders, and police managers competencies and effectiveness. Similarly, the consulting psychology literature referred to the same factors as Feldman's identification to construct the definition and understanding of executive coaching (2001). Furthermore, Definitions and understanding of executive coaching vary in accordance with perspectives, philosophy, approach, and professional and contextual objectives and reasons for coaching (Newsom & Dent, 2011; Northouse, 2013).

Vugt, Hogan, and Kaiser (2008) discussed the abroad and different approaches researchers utilized to define leadership. Researchers expressed continuously that leadership has a long developing history. Vugt et al. argued that leadership might emerge as a therapy and solution to group and people and communication and collaboration challenges and difficulties (2008).

Senge, in his book The Fifth Discipline: The Art of & Practice of Learning Organization, quoted a statement for Confucius that had said more than twenty-five years ago,

"To become a leader, you must first become a human being" Confucius created a developmental theory dealing with the seven "meditative spaces" (2006). Senge (2006) delivered and explained Confucius's vision about the collateral connection between leadership and wisdom, assuring that wisdom is one of the oldest competencies of leadership. Unfortunately, the leadership perspective has almost lost the compass of leading effectively in law enforcement. The concept and logic of leadership have lost and needed more technical and contextual clarity under the difficult parturition of innovation and technology (Senge, 2006).

However, the evaluation of leadership coaching is significantly different from other approaches to leadership development. Leadership coaching is widely defined as the perception of the developmental relationship between a coach and a client, which requires enhancing the client's leadership competencies to be an effective manager (Ely, Boyce, Nelson, Zaccaro, Broome, and Whyman, 2010).

Coaching can help police leaders develop leadership competencies and skills. One of the most widely discussed models focused on leadership competency is the "Four C's Model ."This model suggests that influential leaders must have the ability to be creative, critical, communicative, and collaborative (Kouzes & Posner, 2017). This model emphasizes the importance of leaders having the ability to think creatively and to develop innovative solutions to problems (Kouzes & Posner, 2017). Additionally, this model suggests that leaders must be able to analyze situations critically and communicate their ideas effectively (Kouzes & Posner, 2017). Finally, this model suggests that leaders must be able to foster collaboration among their followers and create an environment of cooperation and trust (Kouzes & Posner, 2017). Executive coaching can play a significant role in helping leaders in law enforcement become more effective.

Another widely discussed model is the "Leadership Competency Model."This model suggests that effective leaders must have the ability to develop and implement strategic plans, manage resources effectively, lead teams effectively, and create an environment of trust and respect (Kouzes & Posner, 2017). This model emphasizes the importance of leaders managing change effectively, delegating tasks effectively, and creating an environment of collaboration and cooperation (Kouzes & Posner, 2017). Additionally, this model suggests that leaders must inspire and motivate their followers, effectively manage conflict, and foster a culture of innovation and creativity (Kouzes & Posner, 2017). Coaching interventions can play a significant role in developing leadership skills in police chiefs.

THE INTERRELATION BETWEEN COACHING AND PERFORMANCE AND POLICE MANAGEMENT

Executive leadership coaching offers a range of benefits for law enforcement professionals. First, executive leadership coaching can help build the leader's confidence, which can be beneficial in various ways. Confidence can help the leader to take risks, think strategically, and to make better decisions (Laut, 2019). It can also help reduce the stress and anxiety often associated with leadership positions. Second, executive leadership coaching can help leaders develop their communication skills, which can be particularly beneficial in law enforcement. Effective communication is essential for successful leadership, as it can help build trust and improve relationships with other officers and community members (Laut, 2019). Third, executive leadership coaching can help leaders develop their problem-solving and decision-making skills, which can be beneficial in a fast-paced and unpredictable law enforcement environment (Laut, 2019). Finally, executive leadership coaching can help leaders build their resilience and manage their emotions, which can be essential for managing stress and difficult situations (Laut, 2019).

In the literature examining coaching as an emerging intervention to accomplish police management success, many researchers tried to verify the aspects of coaching as an integrated leadership development phenomenon. Therefore, the aspects that are presented in the literature to study coaching as a police management practice include: (a) credentials or skills for choosing a coach; (b) personal and professional attributes of an effective executive coach; (d) pros and cons for an internal and external executive coach; (e), the perception of the engagement of executive coaching; (f), specifications of coaching techniques and tools; (f) signs of executive coaching success; (g), learning, conduct, and culture change resulted from executive coaching (Kampa- Kokesh & Anderson, 2005; Newsom & Dente, 2011).

METHODOLOGIES TO THE COACHING PROCESS IN POLICE MANAGEMENT

Although the standards of the coaching process are fairly the same among all, the approaches that coaches implement changes through executives, police managers, and organizational leadership culture mainly depend on the professional and technical background of coaches and their intellectual and academic philosophies. Hence, five main approaches for executive coaching were presented by Pettier (2001) and updated by Newsom and Dente (2011); the five approaches are: psychodynamic, behaviorist, person-centered, cognitive therapeutic, and system-oriented.

Psychodynamic Approach

In this approach, psychologists help executives obtain a psychological scientific background and competencies to increase their ability to understand how their people think, feel, and react in the workplace (Pettier, 2001; Lebihan, 2011). Additionally, with this approach, psychologists help executives and leaders to improve their vision of themselves and others and how to manage their employees effectively in accordance with this vision (Lebihan, 2011). In their research, Gary et al. argued that psychologists are the most qualified to be coaches (2011).

However, the qualifications of the coaching profession as a developmental tool are not regulated with a disciplinary competency frame (Feldman & Lankau, 2010). Therefore, some researchers stated that psychologists are most qualified for coaching. Thus, the characteristics and skills of psychologists are the qualifications required for an executive coaching role, such as professionalism, communication and listening skills, and understanding the psychology of human-inner are the characteristics that the coach should attain (Freeman & Perry, 2010; Feldman & Lankau, 2010). Feldman and Lankau (2010) achieved a study that tested 87 executive coaching participants and presented their findings that the necessary qualifications of executive coaching are identical to the psychologists' attributes and expertise in order to create the reorganizational development and change towards success and sustainability (Feldman & Lankau, 2010).

Behaviorist Approach

In this approach, the focus is on changing the behavior through observation rather than through the inner status of the coach (McCarthy, Milner, 2011). The practitioners suggested two leadership approaches to represent the behavioral approach, including transformational and transactional (Khan et al., 2012). According to Khan ct al. (2012), transformational and transactional are the best leadership style that executive coaches must implement to achieve the behavioral coaching approach. A survey was implemented by Khan Et.al (2012) to prove this vision; a number of 280 questionnaires were established to confirm this hypothesis.

Cognitive Therapy Approach

Cognitive psychology is based on the idea that our thoughts and beliefs influence our feelings and actions. The theory of cognitive psychology applies to executive coaching in several ways. First, executive coaches can use cognitive psychology to help clients identify and shift unhelpful thought patterns and beliefs that may hold them back (Pettier, 2001; Strang, 2011). By helping clients uncover and challenge negative thoughts and beliefs, executive coaches can help clients develop more balanced and effective ways of thinking (Pettier, 2001; Strang, 2011). Additionally, cognitive psychology can help clients set meaningful goals and create strategies for achieving them (Pettier, 2001; Strang, 2011). Finally, executive coaches can use cognitive psychology to help clients develop self-awareness and enhance their decision-making skills (Pettier, 2001; Strang, 2011). Strang confirmed that the cognitive psychology approach is an effective managerial development technique to achieve police management success. However, the validity of this approach requires executing a supportive mentoring strategy and a unique organizational culture (2011).

System-Oriented Approach

In this approach, the coach must understand the work atmosphere and the factors that might affect the supervisor's and employee's behavior (Peltier, 2001; Strang, 2011). In this approach, the coach needs to know the whole organizational system with its complexities, challenges, stakeholders, culture, and market requirements in order to be able to create an effective mentoring strategy that is system-oriented (Peltier, 2001; Strang, 2011).

EXECUTIVE COACHING COMPETENCIES' IMPACT ON STRATEGIC POLICE MANAGEMENT EFFECTIVENESS

The popularity of coaching is emerging worldwide in business and academia (Lebihan, 2011). The Chartered Institute of Personnel and Development (CIPD) (2010) survey regarding the prevalence of coaching as a practice to increase organizational effectiveness reflected that % 90 of participants claimed that coaching is a recommended tool for individual and organizational development (Candis & Magnolia, 2010). Researchers and scholars constantly debate the strategic credentials and attributes that coaching must possess to help achieve police management effectiveness and organizational sustainability. Therefore, the International Federation raised a deep concern regarding the unregulated system of competencies and skills for the executive coaching profession (McCarthy & Miller, 2011). Nevertheless, in strategic management, Laufer (2012) established nine managerial practices to support the guidance of the operational and strategic organizational development and to help systemize the executive coaching professional basis. Laufer's nine leadership practices are embraced by executive coaches in the strategic coaching process to improve organizational effectiveness and performance (Cunningham & McNally, 2003; Hannafey & Vitulano, 2013). Researchers consider the nine Laufer (2012) leadership practices as critical strategic practices for the executive coaching process (Hannafey & Vitulano, 2013). The nine leadership practices are: 1) Embrace the living order; 2) challenge the status quo; 3) Fit the police activities to the proper context; 4) Recruiting the right people is a priority; Create a productive culture;

5) Concentrate on practical communication skills, 6) Planning and monitoring are daily strategies; 8) Focus on results; and 9) lead by example in order to manage successfully.

Additionally, many researchers suggested a systematic coaching approach to create a systematical change in organizations (Feldman & Lankau, 2010; Journal of Management, 2005). Executives and top management could manage the systematic coaching change; however, they must execute a framework that includes systematic managerial practices to achieve the targeted change (Feldman & Landau). Laufer's managerial practices are tools and techniques that coaches might utilize to lead organizational systematic and organizational change (Laufer, 2012; Spector, 2011). Thus, the systematic change process is a strategic brand that systemizes logical integration through a coaching framework.

Nevertheless, the systematic coaching process requires the executive coaches to possess keen managerial skills in order to be able to implement the necessary coaching framework that Laufer suggested as a strategic leadership plan to create systematic change (2012). Further, the requirements for leaders and executive coaches to implement systematic change in organizations are multi-facet due to challenges and complexities (McCarthy & Miller, 2011). In addition, Luntz (2011) presented nine principles of the influential management profession "leading to manage," including people-centeredness; (b) paradigm-breaking; (c) passion; (d) perfection; (e) prioritization; (f) persistence; (g) persuasion; (h) partnership; and (g) principled-action (Luntz, 2011). Luntz's principles are factors for strategic police management to lead organizations to function effectively (Luntz, 2011; Ely, 2010). Executive coaches can implement the nine principles of Lutz to clarify the daily operational activities and mission vision. Additionally, in the coaching process of police management development, the executives are required to construct a particular coaching model that correlates with the internal organizational vision, mission, goals, and cultures; and that interact with the external opportunities, weakness, and challenges of the market (Mayfield & Mayfield, 2012; Feldman, 2010). Luntz's leadership principles might help identify a systematic culture of organizational learning (Walker-Frazer, 2011). For organizations, the value of coaching and mentoring exists in the quality culture that carries the organizational values, norms, and principles (Freeman &Perry, 2010). In other words, the Lutz leadership principles and Laufer practices are a strategic and practical coaching framework for organizational culture to enhance organizational learning of police management (Paul & Berry, 2013; Laufer, 2012; Lutz, 2011; Freeman & Perry, 2010).

Coaching as an Organizational Behavior and System Thinking

The seminal research documented effective outcomes of the success on the nature of the relationship between the behavioral system approach and executive coaching (Visser, 2010). The studies stated productive organizational and operational outcomes on performance and sustainability (Visser, 2010). According to skinner, the behavioral system approach includes an organization's culture and the system approach under the guidance of the coaching practice (2007). Skinner implemented a comprehensive theoretical framework that includes explaining and illustrating the development of the system approach under executive coaching (2007).

Effective organizational behavior is a strategic and operational activity that requires a behavioral transition in the police perception of its vision, goals, objectives, and culture to accomplish the targeted connectivity with organizational productivity and performance (Visser, 2010). In viewing the related basis of the coaching process and behavioral system, researchers state that executive coaching is a systemic behavioral practice. The behavioral system supported coaches with three systematic developmental lessons (Wasylyshyn, 2003). The first lesson reflects the importance of the daily interaction between the coach and the employees to change their thinking status and mental states (Wasylyshyn, 2003). Further, mentoring the daily operational interaction helps polish the human system thinking (Visser, 2010). The psychodynamic and cognitive approaches concentrate on the importance of coaching personal needs, desires, and attitudes to steer the success and productivity of policing (Wasylyshyn, 2003). Second, this lesson concentrates on the philosophy that the coach must give attention and mentor to the present time and setting behavior rather than building assumptions and judgments of the past behavior (Thomas et al., 2007). However, the psychodynamic and many other humanitarian approaches suggest the importance of analyzing the past causes and motives of the inner psychic to solve the present conflicts. Thus, the behavioral system approach coaches must consider it is the "now- and –here "theory in dealing with the present complexities and challenges (Thomas et al., 2007).

The third lesson states that the coach is allowed to be manipulative in order to achieve the success of the behavioral system approach (Thomas et al., 2007). Further, the behavioral system suggests manipulation as a coaching technique to improve and develop many organizational gaps (Thomas et al., 2007). However, psychodynamic and cognitive approaches object to using manipulation as a strategic tool to solve an operational problem and develop organizational and individual strategic gaps (Visser, 2010). The cognitive and psychodynamic approaches also considered the manipulative tool unethical and against professional and ethical values (Visser, 2010).

COACHING AND ORGANIZATIONAL RESISTANCE CHANGE

Organizational change is an organization's strategy to target a future movement toward a desired goal to increase its productivity, effectiveness, and operational and market development away from its present condition (Lunenburg, 2010). Further, organizations are urged to change due to global and national economic, technological, and market competitiveness pressure and challenges (Lunenburg, 2010). In this process, the role of executive coaching is strategically intense and diverse (Creemers, 2010). Police chiefs are responsible for leading their departments and are often required to manage complex and challenging situations. As a result, police chiefs must have the necessary leadership skills to be successful in their roles (Wenson, 2010). Executive leadership coaching can be a valuable tool for developing these skills. Executive leadership coaching can help the police chief to develop their communication skills, as well as their problem-solving and decision-making skills (Laut, 2019). It can also help the police chief develop their ability to lead by example and build relationships with other officers and community members (Laut, 2019). Finally, executive leadership coaching can help the police chief to develop emotional intelligence, which can be beneficial in managing difficult situations (Laut, 2019).

Leadership development in law enforcement is vital for a variety of reasons. First, it effectively provides law enforcement personnel with the necessary skills and abilities to lead their teams (Ranney, 2020). Practical leadership skills are essential for law enforcement personnel to communicate effectively, motivate, and manage their teams to achieve successful outcomes (Ranney, 2020). Through leadership development, law enforcement personnel can learn the necessary skills to develop and implement effective strategies, prioritize tasks, and provide guidance and direction to their teams (Ranney, 2020).

Leadership development in law enforcement is critical to ensure that law enforcement personnel have the necessary knowledge and understanding of the law and legal processes (Bryant, 2020). Law enforcement personnel must know the laws and regulations that govern their actions and be able to interpret and apply them correctly. Leadership development provides law enforcement personnel with the necessary knowledge and understanding of the law and legal processes to ensure their actions comply with it (Bryant, 2020).

Finally, leadership development in law enforcement is essential to ensure that law enforcement personnel can effectively manage their teams (Lanier, 2020). Law enforcement personnel must effectively manage their teams to ensure they can complete their tasks and meet their goals (Ranney, 2020). Leadership development gives law enforcement personnel the necessary skills and abilities to effectively manage their teams, allocate resources, and motivate them to achieve successful outcomes (Ranney, 2020).

In conclusion, executive leadership coaching can be a valuable tool for developing leadership skills in law enforcement professionals. Executive leadership coaching can build leaders' confidence and help them develop communication, problem-solving, and decision-making skills. It can also help the police chief to develop emotional intelligence and to lead by example. Executive leadership coaching can be essential for developing the leadership skills necessary for law enforcement success.

REFERENCES

Anderson, A. (2011). *Engaging resistance: How ordinary people successfully champion Change*. Stanford University Press.

Bryant, N. (2020). The importance of leadership development in law enforcement. *Law Enforcement Executive Forum*, *20*(2), 32–34.

Candis, B. (2010, February). Assessing Leadership Readiness Using Developmental Personality Style: A tool for leadership coaching. *International Journal of Evidence Based Coaching and Mentoring*, *8*(1).

Chartered Institute of Personnel and Development. (2010). *Learning and Development 2010. Survey report*. CIPD. Retrieved from: https://www.cipd.co.uk/binaries/5215_learning_talent_development%20survey_report.pd

Creemers, B. (2010). *Improving the quality of education: Dynamic Approaches to school Improvement*. Routledge.

Cunningham, L., & McNally, K. (2003). *Improving Organizational and Individual Performance through Coaching. A case Study*. Mosby, Inc. doi:10.1067/nrsi.2003.90

Ely, K., Boyce, L. A., Nelson, J. K., Zaccaro, S. J., Hernez-Broome, G., & Whyman, W. (2010). Evaluating leadership coaching: A review and integrated framework. *The Leadership Quarterly*, *21*(4), 585–599. doi:10.1016/j.leaqua.2010.06.003

Feldman, D. C. (2001). Career coaching: What H.R. professionals and managers need to know. *Human Resources Planning*, *24*, 26–35.

Feldman, D. C., & Lankau, M. J. (2010). Executive Coaching: A review and Agenda for Future Research. *Journal of Management*. Advance online publication. doi:10.1177/0149206305279599

Fink, A. (2014). *Conducting research literature reviews: From the Internet to paper* (4th ed.). Sage Publications.

Freeman, A. M., & Perry, J.A. (2010). Executive coaching under pressure: A case study. *Consulting Psychology Journal: Practice and Research, 6,* 189-202.

Hannafey, T., & Vitulano, L. A. (2013). Ethics and Executive Coaching: An Agency Theory Approach. *Journal of Business Ethics, 115*(3), 599–603. doi:10.100710551-012-1442-z

Kampa-Kokesh, S., & Anderson, M. Z. (2005). Executive Coaching: A comprehensive Review of the Literature. *Consulting Psychology Journal: Practice and Research, 53*(4), 205-228.

Khan, V., Hafeez, M. H., Rizfi, S. M., Hasanain, A., & Maria, A. (2012). the relationship of leadership styles, employee's commitment, and organization Performance. *European Journal of Economics, Finance, and Administration.*

Kouzes, J. M., & Posner, B. Z. (2017). *The leadership challenge: How to make extraordinary things happen in organizations.* Jossey-Bass.

Lanier, M. (2020). Leadership development in law enforcement. *International Journal of Law Enforcement, 21*(4), 36–40.

Laufer, A. (2012). *Mastering the leadership role in project management: Practices that deliver remarkable results.* FT Press.

Laut, J. (2019). The value of executive leadership coaching in law enforcement. *Police Chief Magazine, 86*(12), 16–19.

Lebihan, R. (2011). Business schools tap coaching trend. *Australian Financial Review.*

Lunenburg, F. C., & Ometein, A. O. (2010). *Educational administration: Concepts and practices.* Wadsworth/Cengage Learning.

Luntz, F. (2011). Win: The key principles to take your business from ordinary to extraordinary. Hachette UK.

Mayfield, J., & Mayfield, M. (2012). the leadership relation between leader Motivating language and employee self-efficacy. A partial least squares model analysis. *Journal of Business Communication.* Advance online publication. doi:10.1177/0021943612456036

McCarthy, G., & Milner, J. (2012). Managerial coaching: challenges, opportunities and Training. Journal of Management Development, 32(7), 768-779. doi:10.1108/JMD-11-2011-0113

National Police Misconduct Reporting Project. (2020). *Police misconduct statistics.* Retrieved from https://www.policecrimes.com/misconduct.html

Newsom & Dent. (2011). A Work Behavior Analysis of Executive Coaches. *International Journal of Evidence Based Coaching and Mentoring, 9*(2), 1.

Northouse, P. G. (2013). *Leadership Theory and Practice* (6th ed.). Western Michigan University.

Paul, G. W., & Berry, D. M. (2013). *The Importance of Executive Leadership in Creating a Post-Merged Organizational Culture Conducive to Effective Performance Management.* S.A. Journal of Human Resources Management.

Peltier, B. (2001). *The psychology of executive coaching: Theory and Application*. Sheridan Books.

PennLive. (2016, November 25). *Former Greensburg police chief pleads guilty to felony charges*. Retrieved from https://www.pennlive.com/news/2016/11/former_greensburg_police_chie.html

Peterson, D. B., & Hicks, M. D. (1995). *The leader as coach: Strategies for coaching and Developing others*. Personnel Decisions.

Pew Research Center. (2020). *Trust in police is down among all Americans, but especially among black people*. Retrieved from https://www.pewresearch.org/fact- tank/2020/08/17/trust-in-police-is-down-among-all-americans-but-especially-among- black-people/

Ranney, M. (2020). Leadership in law enforcement organizations. *International Journal of Police Science & Management*, 22(3), 21–25.

Saowalux, P. & Peng, C. (2007). *Impact of Leadership Style on Performance: A Study of Six Sigma Professionals in Thailand*. International DSI/Asia and Pacific DSI.

Senge, P. M. (2006). The Fifth Discipline: The Art and Practice of the Learning Organization. Academic Press.

Spector, B. (2011). *Implementing organizational change: Theory into practice-international edition*. Prentice Hall.

Stinson, P., & Ross, R. (2017). Inadequate training and supervision of police officers as a cause of police misconduct. *Journal of Criminal Law and Criminology, 107*, 885–922. doi:10.2139/ssrn.2596304

Strang, K. D. (2011). Leadership substitute and personality impact on time and quality in virtual new product development project. *Project Management Journal, 42*(1), 73–90. doi:10.1002/pmj.20208

The Atlanta Journal-Constitution. (2016, October 16). *Georgia police chief jailed for stealing from city*. Retrieved from https://www.ajc.com/news/state--regional-govt-- politics/georgia-police-chief-jailed-for-stealing-from-city/b5cX9ZJ5K5CYhGw8dzJP2H/

The Miami Herald. (2018, June 25). *Biscayne Park police chief pleads guilty in federal false arrest case*. Retrieved from https://www.miamiherald.com/news/local/community/miami-dade/biscayne- park/article213682024.html

Thomas, F. N., Waits, R. A., & Hartsfield, G. L. (2007). The influence of Gregory Bateson: Legacy or vestige? *Kybernetes, 36*(7/8), 871–883. doi:10.1108/03684920710777397

Tribune, T. (2014, April 6). *Payne Springs police chief pleads guilty to theft charges*. Retrieved from https://www.texastribune.org/2014/04/06/payne-springs-police-chief- pleads-guilty-theft/

Vasilenko, S. A. (2015). Police Leadership Misconduct: An Examination of the Problem and Potential Solutions. *Law Enforcement Executive Forum, 15*(1), 3–13.

Visser, M. (2010). System dynamics and group facilitation: Contributions from communication Theory. *System Dynamics Review, 23*(4), 453–463. doi:10.1002dr.391

Vugt, M. V., Hogan, R., & Kaiser, R. B. (2008). Leadership, Followership, and Evolution. American Psychologist Association, 63(3), 182-196. doi:10.1037/0003-066X.63.3.182

Walker-Fraser, A. (2011, August). An H.R. perspective on executive coaching for organizational Learning. *International Journal of Evidence Based Coaching and Mentoring*, *9*(2).

Wasylyshyn, K. M. (2003). Coaching and executive character: Core problems and basic approaches. *Consulting Psychology Journal*, *55*(2), 94–106. doi:10.1037/1061-4087.55.2.94

Wenson, E. (2010, November). After-coaching leadership skills and their impact on direct reports: Recommendations for organizations. *Human Resource Development International*, *13*(5), 607–616. doi:10.1080/13678868.2010.520485

Chapter 17
An Exploration of Smart Cities' and Electric Vehicles' Future Impact on People of Color

Kevin Richardson

iD https://orcid.org/0009-0002-3212-8669

Edward Waters University, USA

ABSTRACT

Researchers theorize that smart cities are a new concept aligned with the idea of sustainability. In understanding the significance of smart cities in enhanced sustainability, scholars purport that they are towns typified by residents' ability to securely gather, manage, and disseminate information that relates to their daily endeavors ubiquitously and sustainably. The bigger picture about smart cities is that they are linked to the Industry 5.0 theme, which is associated with personalization or adding a human touch to technological collaboration. The concept of Industry 5.0 begs the question of whether African Americans and other People of Color are indeed humans. If they are humans, for sustainability, smart cities need to treat them as humans by providing the needed infrastructure such as charging stations to allow for development in Black and People of Color-dominated neighborhoods. As a result, the concept of personalization in smart cities can be understood from the perspective of incorporating electric vehicles.

INTRODUCTION

Over the past decade, the world's focus on sustainability has sparked the debate concerning Industry 4.0 and 5.0 (Rosemann et al., 2020). The progression from Industry 4.0 to 5.0 is perceivably a move from smart production to smart consumption. Rosemann et al. (2020) expounds on this by showing that Industry 4.0 refers to the overarching design paradigm linked to comprehensive digitization of manufacturing process. On the other hand, Industry 5.0 is perceived as the next industrial evolution characterized by the objective to leverage humans' creativity in collaboration with intelligent, efficient, and accurate machines (Maddikunta et al., 2022). Thus, Industry 5.0 is perceivably a solution to the shortcomings of Industry 4.0 as it entails obtaining user-preferred and resource-efficient manufacturing. Though the Industry 5.0

DOI: 10.4018/979-8-3693-1630-6.ch017

concept is relatively new, Sharma et al. (2020) affirm that its assimilation involves adding a theme of personalization or human touch that will allow co-working and collaboration between humans and robots, and this aligns with the concept of smart cities. According to Jo et al. (2021), smart cities provide humans with a sustainable lifestyle typified by greener and safer environment. Additionally, Canizes et al. (2019) note that electric vehicles are an essential part of smart cities since the overall concept of sustainable energy systems helps lessen harmful emissions and improve resource usage. Therefore, this paper will critically examine the concept of Industry 5.0 in the context of how it impacts smart cities and electric cars, particularly the kind of changes to expect and how they contribute to sustainability.

Smart cities refer to towns typified by residents' ability to securely gather, manage, and disseminate information that relates to their daily endeavors ubiquitously and sustainably. According to (Ćukušić, 2021), the services provided to residents in smart cities are usually facilitated by information and communication technology. Thus, smart cities are characterized by different sectors, such as mobility, smart building, air and water quality, climate changes, and energy systems (Jo et al., 2021). Studies about smart cities show that the incorporation of electric vehicles is vital. The significance of this incorporation is that electric vehicles align with the goal of sustainable energy. In Canizes et al.'s (2019) opinion, electric vehicles are an essential part of smart cities since the overall concept of sustainable energy systems helps lessen harmful emissions and improve resource usage. Therefore, integrating electric vehicles in smart cities will benefit residents, resulting in efficient energy use and reduced pollution.

As of the current situation, the adoption of electric vehicles in smart cities was increasing rapidly and was roughly 5% in 2020 (Anthony Jnr., 2021). On this note, cities in the United States transforming into smart cities project that they will have minimized greenhouse gas emissions by roughly 80-90% in 2050 (Deloitte, 2022). Anthony Jnr.'s (2021) explanation affirms that such occurrences are likely to be achieved if electric vehicles are integrated as important exponents of smart cities. Sizeable investments are being made across the United States, including the introduction of supporting infrastructures that will reduce vehicular emissions and unlock additional opportunities for smart cities. Komninos et al. (2022) theorize that the opportunities linked to smart cities include solutions for energy use, mobility, wider urban systems, public services, and increased citizen engagement and behavior changes. Accelerated adoption of electric vehicles is perceivably beneficial to smart cities since it requires enhanced coordination across networks, consumers, and products (Anthony Jnr., 2021). For example, the smart cities' digitalization of the power grid is likely to amplify the value of services to consumers and other important stakeholders in the energy market. Razmjoo et al., (2022) expound on this concept by showing that using electric vehicles in smart cities is crucial as it challenges sustainability and both promotes and stimulates upgrading the society. Electric vehicles in smart cities are likely to revolutionize operations, especially because they will promote the development of the smart grid.

Further study by Hardman et al. (2021). expound on the idea that people of color experience significantly higher pollution rates than their white counterparts. Since this population deals with more pollution exposure, research suggests that adopting electric vehicles in these communities will likely reduce this environmental problem. The only barrier to this assimilation is that most black communities are characterized as charging deserts. The term charging desert refers to the fact that black neighborhoods lack the necessary areas to charge electric vehicles, which obstructs the likelihood of people of color adopting electric vehicles. Various factors contribute to this disparity, and institutional racism is arguably the major contributor to black communities' underinvestment, decades of redlining, and financial discrimination. Zhao et al.'s (2021) approach to the existing disparities helps expound on the concept further by showing that electric vehicles are seen as a fight for racial equality in middle-class communities across the United States. Therefore, with the right mainstream technology and policies, black communities can adopt electric vehicles in that it will help reduce emission levels, particularly if their communities are lucky enough to be part of smart cities in the nation.

Problem Statement

Smart cities are designed to use advanced technology and data analysis to optimize their infrastructure and services, making them more sustainable and efficient (Bibri, 2019). This includes the reduction of emissions, a key factor in achieving sustainable development. One way in which smart cities achieve this is through the use of electric vehicles (EVs) (Ruggieri et al., 2021). According to Ruggieri et al. (2021), by promoting the use of EVs, smart cities can significantly reduce carbon emissions from transportation. EVs produce far fewer emissions than traditional gas-powered vehicles, and they can also be charged using renewable energy sources such as solar or wind power. Additionally, smart cities can use data to optimize traffic flow, reducing congestion and emissions from idling vehicles (Zhao & Malikopoulos, 2020). By prioritizing sustainable transportation and utilizing advanced technology, smart cities through adoption of the industry 5.0 concept can make a significant contribution to the fight against climate change. The combination can also aid in the achievement of sustainable development goals (Kasinathan et al., 2022). Global pollution has been deteriorating, considering that greenhouse gas emissions in 2018 were roughly 11% higher than in 2010, and industry and transport sectors have been the major contributors to the increase (Lamb et al., 2021). Statistically, the United States, transforming into smart cities, will have minimized greenhouse gas emissions by roughly 80-90% in 2050 (Deloitte, 2022). Therefore, based on the identified possibility, the general problem will be understanding the overall correlation between smart cities and environmental sustainability. The specific problem will encapsulate an understanding of how incorporating electric vehicles will increase sustainable mobility and reduce vehicular pollution in black neighborhoods. Overall, the primary focus will be to identify opportunities linked to smart cities, such as solutions for energy use, mobility, wider urban systems, public services, and increased citizen engagement and behavior changes in communities of color. Accelerated adoption of electric vehicles is perceivably beneficial to smart cities since it requires enhanced coordination across networks, consumers, and products.

Purpose Statement

The purpose of this qualitative research is to explore the spread of smart cities in communities of color by looking at the rate of adoption of electric vehicles within these communities and how this relates to the environment.. The targeted population are the people of color. They are a suitable target population because they are disproportionately affected by unsustainable development such as environmental pollution. Identifying the problem among black neighborhoods will guide the exploration to identify why smart cities and electric vehicles are essential to reducing environmental racism/injustice within the country (Neville et al., 2021; Kojola & Pellow, 2021). Considering that the amount of information on how smart cities and electric vehicles will impact people of color is limited, the data/survey method will review secondary sources to understand smart cities and how electric vehicles can help achieve sustainable energy consumption and mobility as part of these towns. The specific materials included in this research are peer-reviewed types, particularly materials related to smart cities, electric vehicles, disparate effects of environmental pollution on blacks, and how smart cities and electric vehicles will impact blacks in the future. Besides, in searching for the relevant materials, the survey was searched through known scholarly sites, such as ScienceDirect, ProQuest, and Google Scholar. The independent variables for this analysis are smart cities and electric vehicles and their contribution to enhanced sustainability. On the other hand, the dependent variables are sustainable mobility and the impacts on African Americans.

Significance of the Study

The concept of smart cities and electric vehicles is undeniably vital regarding reduced environmental degradation. According to (Anthony Jnr., 2020), the shift to smart cities and the incorporation of electric vehicles represents technological and societal changes, which are at par with the industrial revolution that entails the digitalization of everything. From this perspective, smart cities and electric vehicles will have long-lasting effects on the economy and environment. In particular, the impacts of smart cities and electric vehicles ought to be understood in terms of how they will affect societies inhabited by people of color. Canizes et al.'s (2019) note that countless studies have highlighted the disproportionate effects of pollution and climate change among low-income earners and non-white communities. For example, African Americans are 75% more likely to be affected by pollution than whites (Villarosa, 2020). Their vulnerability is ascribed to living near commercial facilities that produce odor, noise, and emissions, directly affecting this population. Based on this conception, smart cities and electric vehicles could be utilized to benefit the black communities. (Yigitcanlar & Cugurullo, 2020) elaborate on this by theorizing that electric vehicles are now becoming attainable to average consumers following the government's incentives. Nonetheless, access to charging stations, especially in black neighborhoods, is still challenging, so the government should focus on installing charging stations in these locations.

Theoretical Framework

Theoretically, smart cities and electric vehicles have the potential to reduce environmental pollution and improve sustainability. Specifically, the theory of planned behavior suggests that high environmental pollution in black neighborhoods is ascribed to vehicular contamination. Thus, when relating the concept of smart cities and electric vehicles to enhanced sustainability in black communities, the theory of planned behavior supposes that people's purchasing behavior most likely influences the adoption of electric vehicles (Zhang et al., 2018; Tu & Yang, 2019). According to the theory, consumers' purchasing power will be influenced by multitudinous factors, such as service quality, customer value, and customer participation. Primarily, the theory of planned behavior maintains that black people's willingness to adopt electric vehicles will be influenced by their attitude towards subjective norms and perceived behavioral control. As a result, the attitude characterizes whether smart cities and electric vehicles will positively affect them.

The second theory is the liberation theory, which will help reflect on factors associated with environmental racism. The theory will critically explore the concept of disproportionate effects of environmental pollution among African Americans (Neville et al., 2021; Kojola & Pellow, 2021). The specifics of this theoretical framework are that it will focus on actions necessary to confront unintentional means of environmental racism and how they are perpetuated. The theory will also assist in revealing racist socialization, which entails advocating for liberation that takes place at collective levels of social action. Scholars approach this theory by noting that the practice of liberatory consciousness ought to be approached at individual and collective levels (Daystar, 2021).

LITERATURE REVIEW

The term smart cities describe the use of technology-based solutions to improve people's quality of life, which is made possible by improved sustainable development. Ruggieri et al. (2021) explication of smart cities supports this assertion by showing that smart cities are towns where economic, social, and environmental developmental factors are balanced. Besides, smart cities are linked via devolved processes, which allow them enhanced efficiency in managing key resources, assets, and urban flow for real-time procedures. According to Anthony Jnr's (2020), smart cities are also identifiable based on their overall design around information and communication technology (ICT) infrastructures. As a result, ICT helps support urban and social interconnectivity through citizens' interaction with the government. In the United States, and other parts of the world, smart cities are developing rapidly, which involves embracing the smart philosophy. Currently, technology expenditure on smart cities stands at roughly $158 billion. The high expenditure rate is tied to the idea that smart cities are environmentally friendly and will help reduce energy consumption and pollution.

For the past few years, researchers have been critically exploring the concept of smart cities and how adopting electric vehicles may improve the strategy even further. Sanguesa et al. (2021) argues that the adoption of electric vehicles in smart cities is important as it will help decrease urban carbon dioxide schemes. Several studies have tried to explore the integration of electric vehicles in smart cities and how it could help people of color and their disproportionate exposure to pollution. Kumar et al. (2022), in their article "Impact of Electric Vehicles on Energy Efficiency with Energy Boosters in Coordination for Sustainable Energy in Smart Cities," have explored this by focusing on how electric vehicles can be incorporated into smart cities using the enterprise architecture approach (Anthony Jnr, 2020). Apparently, this strategy is vital as it is more likely to facilitate the digital transformation of electric vehicles towards sustainable mobility. Barreto et al. (2022) agree with this strategy by showing that the primary objective in smart cities and the assimilation of electric vehicles is to achieve sustainability and mobility solutions from diverse systems and stakeholders. Several other studies have critically explored this by showing that optimal sustainable mobility in smart cities can be achieved by focusing on battery management to promote extensive integration of microgrids connected to electric vehicles.

A scholarly review of studies concerning integrating electric vehicles in smart cities and grids suppose that the main objective is achieving sustainable energy. Particularly, electric vehicles are considered service models in smart cities, which are considered the main actors towards sustainability and also the barriers to that impend effectiveness of smart cities. To understand this, Kar et al. (2019) focus on the backgrounds of smart cities and the roles of sustainable mobility. This point of analysis notes that nearly half the population inhabits urban cities worldwide. This trend suggests that by 2050, the number of people living in urban cities may have grown to approximately 6.3 residents (Ray & Shaw, 2019). A high number of people in urban towns translates to increased environmental challenges. Bearing this in mind, researchers believe that the worries associated with increased urban habitation are the reason for smart cities and electric vehicles gaining prominence. Specifically, smart cities are associated with improving environmental, financial, and social benefits based on the support of digitalization and technological innovations.

Vaidya and Mouftah's (2020) explanation about smart cities note that the implementation of digital innovations in the United States is paramount in providing citizens with smart services. The adoption of smart cities across the United States is significant as it will make life easier for the citizens. Improved lifestyle is because smart cities are digital transformations that involve the deployment of new business models and disruptive technologies. In that context, a substantial increase in urban population should be addressed by postulating how the transport sector can be revitalized so as to reduce vehicular pollution. The need to focus on sustainable mobility is based on the conception that an increase in urban population will also amplify the number of vehicles used in the cities. Without the right approach, which in this case refers to the adoption of electric vehicles, smart cities may still have to deal with increased vehicular pollution.

On the contrary, pollution can be mitigated by focusing on urban mobility from improved infrastructures. The importance of mobility infrastructures is that they help resolve economic, social, and environmental constraints to allow competitive and sustainable urban mobility systems. According to Acheampong et al. (2021), adopting electric vehicles is the possible alternative to achieve sustainable mobility in smart cities. Considering that the concept of smart cities and electric vehicles has not been thoroughly explored, researchers may ask the question of what roles electric vehicles play in smart cities. Yigitcanlar and Cugurullo (2020) posit that the primary role of electric vehicles in smart cities is to help cumber environmental concerns, such as being able to reduce the oil supply. Suppose smart cities are to achieve the sustainable goal. In that case, reducing the oil supply is necessary, and this can be attained by moving towards electrification of the entire transportation sector. Technological developments are already making this possible since they have led to the advanced adoption of electric vehicles across the United States.

From a general overview, the term electric vehicle refers to automobiles that use an electric motor for propulsion. In contemporary society, electric vehicles are categorized as necessary technological advancements as they will help the prevalent problem of environmental pollution. Gong et al. (2019) expound on how electric vehicles will help address this by showing that these automobiles involve storing electric energy as reserve energy. Thus, their use translates to reduced dependency on fuel-powered vehicles. However, the greatest challenge when using electric vehicles is that energy storage facilities are supposed to provide the needed flexibility. However, the unavailability of charging stations becomes a great hurdle toward effective smart grid operations. Regardless of this challenge, Anthony Jnr (2021) purport that electric vehicles remain unmatched technological advancements in smart cities as they will help with power factor regulation, renewable energy tracking, load balancing, and voltage support. Consequently, electric vehicles may play vital roles in society since they might be the missing connection between the transportation and energy sectors.

Further research about smart cities and electric vehicles affirms that EVs have great potential for reducing CO2 emissions and consumption of fossil fuels. The ability of electric vehicles to reduce environmental pollution is attributed to the fact that electric car owners can now directly charge their automobiles using renewable energy sources or solar photovoltaic panels, which have been installed in residential areas (Kubik, 2022). The electricity generated from renewable energy sources has been commercialized with the energy grid. Such flexibility is important as it supports the increased use of electric vehicles. From a scholarly perspective, the positive impacts of electric vehicles on reduced environmental pollution are because their connection to the grid contributes to increased generation as loads on demand increase. Nonetheless, incorporating electric vehicles in smart cities may not be that smooth since, for these towns to achieve sustainability, electric vehicles may not result in the expected impact because of overdependence on energy grids.

Nemoto et al., (2021) posit that the general concept of smart cities and electric vehicles and their roles in reducing environmental degradation should also be approached from how this will affect people of color. Bamwesigye and Hlavackova (2019) supports this by noting that current studies report disproportionate effects of environmental pollution among African Americans. Environmental racism has been quite prevalent in the United States, and it greatly affects the blacks more than the white population. According to Nardone et al. (2020), research findings explore the adverse effects of environmental racism on sustainability, which reveal that blacks are more likely to be subjected to environmental pollution than white counterparts because environmental injustice supports this. In the United States, environmental injustice refers to how African Americans are more likely to live in areas near roads and industrial factories. As a result, their closeness to these pollution sites means increased exposure to environmental pollution and disasters. For example, high exposure to environmental contamination results in blacks suffering from environmental-related health complications, such as cancer and asthma (Graves & Goodman, 2021).

Racial disparities are usually manifested in almost all facets of black lives. For instance, people of color are disproportionately likely to inhale contaminated air because of their neighborhoods' proximity to highways and factories. Further studies show that vehicular pollution is most notorious among black neighborhoods. The Motairek et al., (2022) explanation argues that the history of redlining subjected the black population to inhabitable areas because of high environmental contamination rates. A brief skimming into American history confirms this by showing that black communities are usually on the front line of this environmental degradation regardless of whether it is a surging tide in New Orleans or Flint. Therefore, the disparate exposure to environmental pollution links to the long line of injustices, which demands attention, especially when addressing the concept of smart cities and electric vehicles.

According to Kaufman and Hajat (2021), attention to African Americans' disproportionate environmental pollution exposure should focus on vehicular transportation. In his opinion, transportation is to blame for the extensive pollution and greenhouse emissions in black neighborhoods. Specifically, most blacks depend on cars, trucks, and buses, all of which spew harmful fumes into the environment. Fishback et al. (2022) explicated the reason behind this occurrence by noting that in the 1930s, the United States government redlined blacks into areas that resulted in ethnic enclaves typified by financial desperation. Not long after, in the 1950s, the government authorized the construction of freeways through these neighborhoods (Ware, 2021). The construction of freeways through these areas was detrimental as it replaced parks and homes with vehicular exhaust. Ware (2021) interprets this occurrence to show that the government's actions left black communities denuded of community spaces, green areas, and infrastructures to combat the ongoing environmental and climate crisis. This level of neglect has worsened the situation in black neighborhoods, more so because segregation laws have continued to put African Americans in a disadvantaged position compared to the white population.

The deliberate and sustained discrimination against blacks demands an opposite direction that will eventually entail the construction of networks of electric vehicle infrastructures. The big question about this approach is whether the progression towards smart cities and the integration of electric vehicles will help address the issue of environmental racism in black neighborhoods. According to Hardman et al (2021), efforts by Congress have approached the issue of electric vehicles as a tool to reduce environmental contamination in black neighborhoods by focusing on increased financial investment in sustainable mobility. As a result, approximately $7.5 billion have been set aside to build nationwide networks of approximately 500,000 electric vehicle charging outlets. Scholars argue that the move by President Biden is the first of such an investment in American history. Ostensibly, the move is commendable, but the question that lingers among most researchers is if the move will also benefit people of color.

Naik (2021) supposes that the move towards smart cities and electric vehicles will be beneficial if the black population is not left out. Sustainable development should be done equitably, which means African

Americans participate in electric vehicle charging initiatives. Collaboration from relevant stakeholders is crucial as it will help create sustainable mobility at levels that count, which include improvement of blacks' and browns' lives. As leaders continue to piece together a map regarding electric vehicle charging stations, the initiatives should start by focusing on areas that need the most help. A survey by Hsu and Fingerman (2021) suppose that if this approach does not prioritize equity during creating these reparative infrastructures, it will result in massive failure. Addressing past injustices among African Americans is the only way that the idea of smart cities and electric vehicles will materialize.

Electric vehicles, such as Prius, are being adopted by middle-class individuals as it is characterized as a new kind of electric vehicle. According to a report by Yigitcanlar et al. (2019), the adoption of electric vehicles may be rising but at a lower rate than expected since most consumers lack appropriate education. The situation is most prevalent in black communities since they believe buying electric cars is beyond their means. Several factors contribute to this, the most notable being that black communities are charging deserts and fuel-powered vehicles are perceivably cheaper than electric ones (Hardman et al., 2021). These individuals fail to realize that buying electric vehicles may be cheap, but their maintenance is costly. This misinformation is why the number of whites owning hybrid cars stands at 70%, while the number of blacks owning these cars is roughly 20%. People of color are more concerned about environmental pollution, but their concerns are not reflected in adopting electric vehicles. According to Adnan et al. (2016) and Nazari-Heris et al., (2022), such occurrences can be mitigated through improved consumer education and optimization of electric charging outlets in black communities.

Theory Relevant to Study

Theoretically, smart cities and electric vehicles have the potential to reduce environmental pollution and improve sustainability. Specifically, the theory of planned behavior suggests that high environmental pollution in black neighborhoods is ascribed to vehicular contamination. Thus, when relating the concept of smart cities and electric vehicles to enhanced sustainability in black communities, the theory of planned behavior supposes that people's purchasing behavior most likely influences the adoption of electric vehicles (Zhang et al., 2018; Tu & Yang, 2019). According to the theory, consumers' purchasing power will be influenced by multitudinous factors, such as service quality, customer value, and customer participation. Primarily, the theory of planned behavior maintains that black people's willingness to adopt electric vehicles will be influenced by their attitude towards subjective norms and perceived behavioral control. As a result, the attitude characterizes whether smart cities and electric vehicles will positively affect them.

The second theory is the liberation theory, which will help reflect on factors associated with environmental racism. The theory will critically explore the concept of disproportionate effects of environmental pollution among African Americans (Neville et al., 2021; Kojola & Pellow, 2021). The specifics of this theoretical framework are that it will focus on actions necessary to confront unintentional means of environmental racism and how they are perpetuated. The theory will also assist in revealing racist socialization, which entails advocating for liberation that takes place at collective levels of social action. Scholars approach this theory by noting that the practice of liberatory consciousness ought to be approached at individual and collective levels (Daystar, 2021).

Gap in Literature

From the abovementioned analysis, it is apparent that the concept of smart cities and the incorporation of electric vehicles is new. However, because of this area's significance in sustainable mobility, a lot of research has been conducted, with most scholars focusing on what smart cities entail and how the incorporation of electric vehicles may help with the overall goal of reducing the environmental pollution. According to Shaheen and Bouzaghrane (2019), literature has developed several studies which have critically explored smart cities. In their analysis, they note that smart cities use technology-based solutions to improve people's quality of life, which is made possible by improved sustainable development. On the same note, including electric vehicles will help achieve the stipulated goal of improved sustainability as they will reduce vehicular pollution. From this point of analysis, literature also identifies the disproportionate impacts of environmental pollution. Besides this identification, researchers have not critically explored how constructing a nationwide network of electric vehicle charge points will reduce the disparate effects of environmental pollution among blacks (Yang et al., 2022). Further research in the future should critically explore how the government will address the issue of black communities being charging deserts and how addressing this will impact African Americans in the future.

CONCLUSION AND RECOMMENDATIONS FROM EMERGING LITERATURE

Conclusion

In conclusion, exploring the concept of smart cities and connection to the integration of electric vehicles shows that it will greatly impact the lives of people of color in the future. The bigger picture of this analysis is that electric vehicles and smart cities are both environmentally beneficial. Researchers critically explore this supposition to show that integrating electric vehicles in smart cities will result in substantial changes, which include providing efficient transportation services and a shift in economies following the change from petroleum as the energy source to electricity. Besides, the changes may be significant since the concept of electric vehicles and smart cities will decrease environmental degradation. However, electric vehicles' effectiveness and incorporation in smart cities is crowded with uncertainties. The specific challenges are how to deploy the business models necessary to transform electric vehicles into a great source of economic value. Prior studies suggest that the challenges are most likely to be prevalent when dealing with the availability of charging systems for electric vehicles in certain societies. Their opinion is based on the understanding that black communities are disproportionately affected by pollution from cars and industries.

Besides the identification that smart cities and electric vehicles are likely to reduce CO2 reduction schemes, researchers have not critically explored how the construction of a nationwide network of electric vehicle charge points will reduce the disproportionate effects of environmental pollution among blacks. Future research should critically explore how smart cities and the incorporation of electric vehicles will address the issue of black communities being charging deserts and how addressing this will impact African Americans in the future. In particular, research should explore the possible optimization of electric vehicle charging outlets. This approach should consider how smart cities incorporating electric vehicles can utilize on-board and off-board charging, especially charging stations installed in parking lots of commercial buildings, residential spaces, and along roadsides.

Policy Recommendations

According to research, the past one decade is notable for accelerated digital transformation and transitions within industries. The shift is commonly referred to as the shift from Industry 4.0 to Industry 5.0 (Rosemann et al., 2020). The transition is categorized an evolutionary step that will change cities' development plans. For example, Industry 4.0 focused on smart production through revolutionized manufacturing. On the contrary, Industry 5.0 is about smart consumption, which emphasizes the collaboration between humans and machines to have a human-centric, inclusive, and frictionless operations (Greene et al., 2019). However, as Congresswoman Yvette D. Clarke (2022) puts it, building smart cities needs to address several aspects of equity, which will ensure inclusivity and connection of everybody including people of color. As of the current situation, it is undeniably clear that smart cities are revolutionizing as they drive efficient, spur economic development and mobility, as well as improve sustainability. The only problem is that even though smart cities may be beneficial, more attention towards black communities is necessary, more so because most of their basic needs have been left behind. According to Amsler (2008), the initiative can be achieved through initiatives that improve African-American engagement, particularly through inclusivity policies (Foley et al., 2022). These policies include:

1. African-Americans, as technological citizens, should be afforded rights, which include knowledge of technologies and how they affect them, as it improves their participating in decision-making process
2. The major challenge about smart cities among people of color is that it unveils the tension between democracy and technocracy, which is why blacks should have a better comprehension of social constructs, specifically issues pertaining to the connection between them and state.
3. Policies should shift towards a citizen-centric focus that facilitates several attempts by African-Americans to engage in diverse public processes.
4. Emphasize on digital inclusion as it brings out the concept of non-user problem, which can be resolved by ensuring that people of color feel the need to participate without necessarily feeling like they are losing control over how they want their lives.
5. Further consideration should focus on changing government policies and recent financial investment in smart cities and electric vehicles so as to understand how this concept will turn out in the next few years.

REFERENCES

Acheampong, R. A., Cugurullo, F., Gueriau, M., & Dusparic, I. (2021). Can autonomous vehicles enable sustainable mobility in future cities? Insights and policy challenges from user preferences over different urban transport options. *Cities (London, England), 112*, 103134. doi:10.1016/j.cities.2021.103134

Adnan, N., Nordin, S., Rahman, I., Vasant, P., & Noor, A. (2016). A comprehensive review on theoretical framework-based electric vehicle consumer adoption research. *International Journal of Energy Research, 41*(3), 317–335. doi:10.1002/er.3640

Amsler, T. (2008). Engaging African-Americans in the civic and political life of their communities. *Western City Magazine.* https://www.westerncity.com/article/engaging-african-americans-civic-and-political-life-their-communities

Anthony, B. Jnr. (2020a). Managing digital transformation of smart cities through enterprise architecture – a review and research agenda. *Enterprise Information Systems, 15*(3), 299–331. doi:10.1080/17 517575.2020.1812006

Anthony, B. Jnr. (2020b). Smart city data architecture for energy prosumption in municipalities: Concepts, requirements, and future directions. *International Journal of Green Energy, 17*(13), 827–845. do i:10.1080/15435075.2020.1791878

Anthony, B. Jnr. (2021). Integrating Electric Vehicles to Achieve Sustainable Energy as a Service Business Model in Smart Cities. *Frontiers In Sustainable Cities, 3,* 1–12. doi:10.3389/frsc.2021.685716

Bamwesigye, D., & Hlavackova, P. (2019). Analysis of Sustainable Transport for Smart Cities. *Sustainability (Basel), 11*(7), 2140. doi:10.3390u11072140

Barreto, R., Faria, P., & Vale, Z. (2022). Electric Mobility: An Overview of the Main Aspects Related to the Smart Grid. *Electronics (Basel), 11*(9), 1–19. doi:10.3390/electronics11091311

Bibri, S. E. (2019). On the sustainability of smart and smarter cities in the era of big data: An interdisciplinary and transdisciplinary literature review. *Journal of Big Data, 6*(1), 1–64. doi:10.118640537-019-0182-7

Canizes, B., Soares, J., Costa, A., Pinto, T., Lezama, F., Novais, P., & Vale, Z. (2019). Electric Vehicles' User Charging Behaviour Simulator for a Smart City. *Energies, 12*(8), 1470. doi:10.3390/en12081470

Clarke, Y. D. (2022). *Building Smart Cities of the Future With Inclusivity and Connectivity for All.* State of Black America. https://soba.iamempowered.com/building-smart-cities-future-inclusivity-and-connectivity-all

Ćukušić, M. (2021). Contributing to the current research agenda in digital transformation in the context of smart cities. *International Journal of Information Management, 58,* 102330. doi:10.1016/j.ijinfomgt.2021.102330

Daystar, M. (2021). Developing a Liberatory Consciousness. *Women and Leadership Development in College: A Facilitation Resource.*

Deloitte. (2022). *Smart and sustainable buildings and infrastructure.* https://www2.deloitte.com/global/en/pages/public-sector/articles/urban-future-with-a-purpose/smart-and-sustainable-buildings-and-infrastructure.html

Fishback, P., Rose, J., Snowden, K., & Storrs, T. (2022). New Evidence on Redlining by Federal Housing Programs in the 1930s. SSRN *Electronic Journal,* 103462. doi:10.21033/wp-2022-01

Foley, R. W., Nadjari, S., Eshirow, J., Adekunle, R., & Codjoe, P. (2022). Towards digital segregation? Problematizing the haves and have nots in the smart city. *Frontiers in Sustainable Cities, 4,* 706670. Advance online publication. doi:10.3389/frsc.2022.706670

Gong, B., Wang, J., & Cheng, J. (2019). Market Demand for Electric Vehicles under Technology Improvements and Tax Relief. *Emerging Markets Finance & Trade*, 56(8), 1715–1729. doi:10.1080/154 0496X.2019.1656606

Graves, J. L., & Goodman, A. H. (2021). Chapter Four. Why Do Races Differ In Disease Incidence? In Racism, Not Race (pp. 82-101). Columbia University Press.

Greene, S., MacDonald, G., Arena, O., Srini, T., Ruth, G., Ezike, R., & Stern, A. (2019). *Technology and equity in cities: Emerging challenges and opportunities*. Academic Press.

Hardman, S., Fleming, K., Khare, E., & Ramadan, M. M. (2021). A perspective on equity in the transition to electric vehicle. *MIT Science Policy Review*, 2, 46–54. doi:10.38105pr.e10rdoaoup

Hsu, C., & Fingerman, K. (2021). Public electric vehicle charger access disparities across race and income in California. *Transport Policy*, 100, 59–67. doi:10.1016/j.tranpol.2020.10.003

Jo, S., Han, H., Leem, Y., & Lee, S. (2021). Sustainable smart cities and industrial ecosystem: Structural and relational changes of the smart city industries in Korea. *Sustainability (Basel)*, 13(17), 9917. doi:10.3390u13179917

Kar, A., Ilavarasan, V., Gupta, M., Janssen, M., & Kothari, R. (2019). Moving beyond Smart Cities: Digital Nations for Social Innovation & Sustainability. *Information Systems Frontiers*, 21(3), 495–501. doi:10.100710796-019-09930-0

Kasinathan, P., Pugazhendhi, R., Elavarasan, R. M., Ramachandaramurthy, V. K., Ramanathan, V., Subramanian, S., Kumar, S., Nandhagopal, K., Raghavan, R. R. V., Rangasamy, S., Devendiran, R., & Alsharif, M. H. (2022). Realization of Sustainable Development Goals with Disruptive Technologies by Integrating Industry 5.0, Society 5.0, Smart Cities and Villages. *Sustainability (Basel)*, 14(22), 15258. doi:10.3390u142215258

Kaufman, J. D., & Hajat, A. (2021). Confronting environmental racism. *Environmental Health Perspectives*, 129(5), 051001. doi:10.1289/EHP9511 PMID:34014764

Kojola, E., & Pellow, D. N. (2021). New directions in environmental justice studies: Examining the state and violence. *Environmental Politics*, 30(1-2), 100–118. doi:10.1080/09644016.2020.1836898

Komninos, N., Kakderi, C., Mora, L., Panori, A., & Sefertzi, E. (2022). Towards high impact smart cities: A universal architecture based on connected intelligence spaces. *Journal of the Knowledge Economy*, 13(2), 1169–1197. doi:10.100713132-021-00767-0

Kubik, A. (2022). Impact of the Use of Electric Scooters from Shared Mobility Systems on the Users. *Smart Cities*, 5(3), 1079–1091. doi:10.3390martcities5030054

Kumar, P., Nikolovski, S., Ali, I., Thomas, M., & Ahuja, H. (2022). Impact of Electric Vehicles on Energy Efficiency with Energy Boosters in Coordination for Sustainable Energy in Smart Cities. *Processes (Basel, Switzerland)*, 10(8), 1593. doi:10.3390/pr10081593

Lamb, W. F., Wiedmann, T., Pongratz, J., Andrew, R., Crippa, M., Olivier, J. G., Wiedenhofer, D., Mattioli, G., Khourdajie, A. A., House, J., Pachauri, S., Figueroa, M., Saheb, Y., Slade, R., Hubacek, K., Sun, L., Ribeiro, S. K., Khennas, S., de la Rue du Can, S., ... Minx, J. (2021). A review of trends and drivers of greenhouse gas emissions by sector from 1990 to 2018. *Environmental Research Letters*, *16*(7), 1–32. doi:10.1088/1748-9326/abee4e

Maddikunta, P. K., Pham, Q. B. P., Deepa, N., Dev, K., Gadekallu, T. R., Ruby, R., & Liyanage, M. (2022). Industry 5.0: A survey on enabling technologies and potential applications. *Journal of Industrial Information Integration*, *26*, 100257. doi:10.1016/j.jii.2021.100257

Motairek, I., Chen, Z., Makhlouf, M. H., Rajagopalan, S., & Al-Kindi, S. (2022). Historical neighbourhood redlining and contemporary environmental racism. *Local Environment*, 1–11. doi:10.1080/13549 839.2022.2155942 PMID:37588138

Naik, M. (2021). Recent advancements and key challenges with energy storage technologies for electric vehicles. *International Journal Of Electric And Hybrid Vehicles*, *13*(3/4), 256–269. doi:10.1504/ IJEHV.2021.123480

Nardone, A., Rudolph, K., Morello-Frosch, R., & Casey, J. (2020). Redlines and greenspace: The relationship between historical redlining and 2010 greenspace across the United States. *ISEE Conference Abstracts*, *2020*(1). 10.1289/isee.2020.virtual.P-0061

Nazari-Heris, M., Loni, A., Asadi, S., & Mohammadi-ivatloo, B. (2022). Toward social equity access and mobile charging stations for electric vehicles: A case study in Los Angeles. *Applied Energy*, *311*, 118704. doi:10.1016/j.apenergy.2022.118704

Nemoto, E., Issaoui, R., Korbee, D., Jaroudi, I., & Fournier, G. (2021). How to measure the impacts of shared automated electric vehicles on urban mobility. *Transportation Research Part D, Transport and Environment*, *93*, 102766. doi:10.1016/j.trd.2021.102766

Neville, H. A., Ruedas-Gracia, N., Lee, B. A., Ogunfemi, N., Maghsoodi, A. H., Mosley, D. V., LaFromboise, T. D., & Fine, M. (2021). The public psychology for liberation training model: A call to transform the discipline. *The American Psychologist*, *76*(8), 1248–1265. doi:10.1037/amp0000887 PMID:35113591

Ray, B., & Shaw, R. (2019). Defining urban water insecurity: concepts and relevance. *Urban Drought: Emerging Water Challenges in Asia*, 1-15. doi:10.1007/978-981-10-8947-3_1

Razmjoo, A., Gandomi, A. H., Pazhoohesh, M., Mirjalili, S., & Rezaei, M. (2022). The key role of clean energy and technology in smart cities development. *Energy Strategy Reviews*, *44*, 100943. doi:10.1016/j. esr.2022.100943

Rosemann, M., Becker, J., & Chasin, F. (2020). City 5.0. *Business & Information Systems Engineering*, *63*(1), 71–77. doi:10.100712599-020-00674-9

Ruggieri, R., Ruggeri, M., Vinci, G., & Poponi, S. (2021). Electric Mobility in a Smart City: European Overview. *Energies*, *14*(2), 315–331. doi:10.3390/en14020315

Sanguesa, J., Torres-Sanz, V., Garrido, P., Martinez, F., & Marquez-Barja, J. (2021). A Review on Electric Vehicles: Technologies and Challenges. *Smart Cities*, *4*(1), 372–404. doi:10.3390martcities4010022

Shaheen, S., & Bouzaghrane, M. (2019). Mobility and Energy Impacts of Shared Automated Vehicles: A Review of Recent Literature. Current Sustainable/Renewable. *Energy Reports, 6*(4), 193–200. doi:10.100740518-019-00135-2

Sharma, I., Garg, I., & Kiran, D. (2020). Industry 5.0 and smart cities: A futuristic approach. *European Journal of Molecular and Clinical Medicine, 7*(08), 2515–8260. https://ejmcm.com/pdf_4786_fecb-7ce33d6d11d7edb41c14e699c263.html

Tu, J. C., & Yang, C. (2019). Key factors influencing consumers' purchase of electric vehicles. *Sustainability (Basel), 11*(14), 3863. doi:10.3390u11143863

Vaidya, B., & Mouftah, H. (2020). Smart electric vehicle charging management for smart cities. *IET Smart Cities, 2*(1), 4–13. doi:10.1049/iet-smc.2019.0076

Villarosa, L. (2020). Pollution is killing Black Americans. This community fought back. *The New York Times Magazine*, 28.

Ware, L. (2021). Plessy's Legacy: The Government's Role in the Development and Perpetuation of Segregated Neighborhoods. *The Russell Sage Foundation Journal of the Social Sciences : RSF, 7*(1), 92–109. doi:10.7758/rsf.2021.7.1.06

Yang, X., Zhuge, C., Shao, C., Huang, Y., Hayse Chiwing, G., Tang, J., & Sun, M. (2022). Characterizing mobility patterns of private electric vehicle users with trajectory data. *Applied Energy, 321*, 119417. doi:10.1016/j.apenergy.2022.119417

Yigitcanlar, T., & Cugurullo, F. (2020). The Sustainability of Artificial Intelligence: An Urbanistic Viewpoint from the Lens of Smart and Sustainable Cities. *Sustainability (Basel), 12*(20), 8548. doi:10.3390u12208548

Yigitcanlar, T., Kamruzzaman, M., Foth, M., Sabatini-Marques, J., da Costa, E., & Ioppolo, G. (2019). Can cities become smart without being sustainable? A systematic review of the literature. *Sustainable Cities and Society, 45*, 348–365. doi:10.1016/j.scs.2018.11.033

Zhang, K., Guo, H., Yao, G., Li, C., Zhang, Y., & Wang, W. (2018). Modeling Acceptance of Electric Vehicle Sharing Based on Theory of Planned Behavior. *Sustainability (Basel), 10*(12), 1–14. doi:10.3390u10124686

Zhao, J., Xi, X., Na, Q., Wang, S., Kadry, S. N., & Kumar, P. M. (2021). The technological innovation of hybrid and plug-in electric vehicles for environment carbon pollution control. *Environmental Impact Assessment Review, 86*, 106506. doi:10.1016/j.eiar.2020.106506

Zhao, L., & Malikopoulos, A. A. (2020). Enhanced mobility with connectivity and automation: A review of shared autonomous vehicle systems. *IEEE Intelligent Transportation Systems Magazine, 14*(1), 87–102. doi:10.1109/MITS.2019.2953526

Chapter 18
Anthropology in Socio-Intercultural Organizations

José G. Vargas-Hernandez

Postgraduate and Research Division, Tecnológico Suoerior de Jalisco Mario Molina Pasquel y Henríquez, Unidad Académica Zapopan, Mexico

Omar C. Vargas-González

🆔 https://orcid.org/0000-0002-6089-956X

Tecnológico Nacional de México, Ciudad Guzmán, Mexico

ABSTRACT

This chapter begins the analysis from the assumption that the study of anthropological disciplines applied to organizations is leading to influence the organizational socio-intercultural manifestations and expressions of the anthropology in organizations. The method employed is the analytic-descriptive inducing to the reflection on the main issues related to the theoretical and empirical literature review on the topic. The study concludes that organizational socio-interculture has been influenced by both the ethnographic and quantitative methodology used by the organizational anthropology.

INTRODUCTION

The organizations are micro-societies or social spaces where the actions of agents and actors represent the reality. Formation processes of organizations as living entities are considered in the professional field in which partners, workers, owners, and customers are interrelated to provide the foundations that enables the analysis of the integral organizational systems processes. Organizations are consciously structured to create a system and formed by elements concentrated on diverse needs, according to the organizational objectives and goals, the fulfillment of tasks and activities.

Recent organizational anthropology analyzes categories and methods of social groups which contribute to analyze organizations and entrepreneurs that contribute to enrich the anthropological perspective of organizations. Anthropology has studied and describes the phenomenon of leadership in primitive societies, the activities of leaders, qualities, traits and personality attributes required to carry out socio-political activities. Personal interaction with society and tolerance enhances the anthropological value

DOI: 10.4018/979-8-3693-1630-6.ch018

which leads to mutual interactions with non-unified socio-interculture environment leading to organizational socio-interculture.

Therefore, the environment and organizational climate are interrelated variables in organizational anthropology. Organizational socio-interculture regulates the relationships between people and socio-ecological systems in organizations becoming the basis of organizational anthropology analysis.

In other matters, to define anthropology as a science is a complex solution linked to demarcation problem fundamental in philosophy of science requiring evidence. Organizational anthropology is capable of postulating scientific theories by an induction problem to develop theories (Morales, 2020). Organizational theory can formulate laws and theories with predictive models. Organizational anthropology predicts phenomena to forecast the initial conditions of events and anticipate future occurrence (Barrett & Stanford, 2006). The concept of regularity in organizational anthropology is part of a discipline as the material substratum of the scientific law (Diener et al., 1980).

However, few academics claim the not scientific nature of anthropology superseded by the notion that science as a modo of enquire is obsolete. The epistemological myths stating that anthropology is not a science, are related to the knot use of quantitative methods and techniques, does not apply formal methods, use experimental designs, postulate theories, predict the phenomena, formulate laws, and interact with other sciences.

Organizational anthropology develops scientific theories supported by functionalism and structuralism such as for example the information goods theory use to analyze the psychological adaptations from socio-intercultural learning (Henrich & Gil-White, 2001); the costly signal theory (Sosis, 2003) used to examine the religious beliefs that decrease the costs of intragroup cooperation in ritual practices (Salali et al., 2015) explaining the emergence and evolution small human groups to form large groups. The socio-intercultural group selection theory analyzes cooperation between non-related individuals emerging into complex human societies (Richerson et al., 2016).

The etymological concept of anthropology is made up of the Greek words ἄνθρωπος which means a person, and logos of concept, a doctrine, a word, and reason, which was first used by Aristotle. Evolutionary anthropology studies the evolution of the human being complemented by other specialties in anthropological sciences, such as economic anthropology, political anthropology, gender anthropology, psychological anthropology genetic anthropology, cognitive anthropology, religious anthropology, music anthropology, urban anthropology, design anthropology, neuropathology, and criminal anthropology, etc.

On the other hand, social anthropology studies the social relationships and structures. Some other anthropology specialties are the cognitive anthropology (Kronenfeld et al., 2011), biological anthropology (Larsen, 2010) and evolutionary anthropology (Henrich, 2016). Besides, anthropology studies various phenomena including espionage as observing in coexistence a human group (Price, 2000).

The disciplines of anthropology, ethology, psychology, and sociology under a qualitative, historical, and analytical approach intercepts the administrative and management science, organizational socio-interculture, ethnology as in knowledge work, the organizations as society of organized communities and psychology related to psyche and personality in the behavior of knowledge work. The organizational anthropology of the contemporary model (ARC) analyzes traditional methods of knowledge production. The cultural brain theory sustains that the human brain has increased in size to store and process through adaptive knowledge via cultural learning (Muthukrishna et al., 2018). The cumulative hypothesis of cultural brain theory predicts the size of human brain (Muthukrishna et al., 2018).

There is a long standing debate on the nature of anthropology as being humanities or science (Inga, 2021). The dispute on the various anthropological approaches to conceptual and theoretical analysis of anthropology applied to organizations are associated to the notion of anthropology as science (Horowitz et al., 2019). Anthropology as a discipline encompasses socio-intercultural anthropology, physical anthropology, archeology, and linguistics. It seems that there is a controversial debate that anthropology resigned from being a science and questioning the scientific nature, which has reached by the media with newspaper articles, essays, interviews, etc. (Boellstorf, 2010; Wade, 2010; Landau, 2010) and the existent gap between cultural and biological anthropology (Kuper & Marks, 2011).

While, the debate on socio-intercultural variables within the organization has been taken up by the notion of administration. Organizational anthropology explains the basic regulations of socio-interculture development, functions, interactions, symbolic systems, etc. Organizational anthropology formulates theories. Organizational anthropological theories predictive power such as the information goods theory predicts skilled individuals gaining prestige (Henrich & Gil-White, 2001).

This study analyzes the anthropological socio-interculturality and organizational socio-interculture beginning with a description of the anthropology methods used in the study of organizations, to concentrate on the analysis of the socio-intercultural anthropology and its interrelations and implication with socio-interculture of organizations. Finally, some conclusions are presented.

ANTHROPOLOGY METHODS IN ORGANIZATIONS

Organizational anthropological research has a relationship with the direct and mediate results through comparative analysis between the experiences of registering the planning and interventions of imaginaries in participatory actions. Ethnography is the methodology of organizational anthropology which incorporates in research new epistemological and ontological approaches. Ethnography studies the human condition with limitations to address the anthropological field, questions the meaning concept understood as the means why which human beings inhabiting a social space agree on representation and actions (Augé & Colleyn, 2006). Ethnography has a holistic value of being analytical anthropology by breaking down in parts the phenomenon leading to synthetic and pre-huma biological aimed to study the various specialties aimed to make up the human being.

The paradigm of qualitative research is based on ethnography using techniques such as observation, informal conversations and semi structured interviews applied to the organization. Ethnography studies the events as representations that bring invisible principles of social ordering (Mauksch, 2017). Interviews is the fundamental ethnographic method. From the ethnographic methodology in organizational anthropology through participant observation and emic perspective analyzes the socio-intercultural differences of organizational contexts at global, national, regional, and local leading to the description of organizational socio-interculture and entrepreneurship based on the analysis of capabilities, resources, and knowledge. The process of knowledge transmission in the anthropological perspective using the ethnography methodology requires full time dedication.

In addition, organizational anthropology can apply formal methods such as componential analysis (Goodenough 1971) from linguistics and used for the analysis of kinship systems, a ground for the conformation of algebra of kinship (Barnes, 1980). The focus group is a technique of the qualitative perspective aimed to the study of complex social dynamics in organizations to approach the systematic processes of organizational transformation.

The ethnographic method relates to socio-intercultural categories in the analysis of organizations, companies, and entrepreneurial elites. Entrepreneurship studies on the analysis of elites based on anthropology tools and ethnologic methods are characterized by practices and references (Inga, 2021). The specialties if ethnology (Hamill, 1990) as well as ethnomathematics (Rosa et al., 2017) emerge from the relationships between anthropology, logic, and mathematics. The analytical anthropological perspective of organizations analyzes the elite as a collective identity of actors (Hernández, 2013). Entrepreneurial anthropology contributes to analyze the dynamics historical-institutional context, organizations, companies, and businessmen aimed to transform the economic sector and social processes (Santos & Gortari, 2021).

The ethnographic method used in organizational anthropologies contributes to the socio-intercultural analysis, interpretation and explanation of organizations, companies and entrepreneurship considering the stakeholders in their context (Peña, 2008). Field work in classical anthropology resolve the obstacles in making decisions to gathering information when conducting interviews aimed to describe the socio-intercultural issues, myths and clan formation within and around organizations.

On the other hand, challenges and contributions of organizational anthropology for business and entrepreneurship studies at a global level extending a reflection in organizational socio-interculture. Organizational business anthropology is a study object that remains relevant for a long time to the extent that organizational business elites are linked to regional conjunctural factors.

Organizational anthropology carries out experimental designs in science to test hypotheses and formulate scientific theories, such as pure and quasi-experiments, pre- and pseudo-experiments (Cash et al., 2016). Exprimental design are currently present in experimental anthropology research, natural and field cut, from the comparative method to racial categorization (Byrne et al., 1995; Harris et al., 1993).

There are anthropological experiments on cultural evolution (Boyd & Richerson, 2005), ritual behavior, neuroanthropology (Lende & Downey, 2012), on economic rationality (Chibnik, 2005; Henrich et al., 2005), collective effervescence (Xygalatas, 2014), cognitive systems (Kronenfeld, 2018), cognitive evolution (Gamble et al., 2014), social learning (Van Leeuwen et al., 2018), among others. Organizational anthropology can conduct experiments like the basic and natural sciences. Instruction in experimental methods in anthropology are carried out in laboratories as Bartlett (1937) recommends.

However, the increasing use of statistical techniques in the ethnographic analysis leading to question a humanist turn toward interpretive approaches in anthropology due to the lack of quantification (Chibnik, 1999; 1985). Since the origin of anthropology, it has been using quantitative techniques although anthropology is considered as the one of the least quantifying social sciences, the statistical concepts are employed (Driver, 1953).

Organizational anthropology uses quantitative tools for data management such as descriptive statistics, correlational and bivariate models, hypothesis testing, comparative models supported by software for statistical methods and quantitative techniques (Williams & Quave, 2019). Statistics constitutes an integral part of anthropological research as an approach to test hypothesis on the subject (Madrigal, 2012). Research manuals in anthropology shows the use of quantitative resources in the design of questionnaires, the construction of scales and multivariate analysis (Bernard, 2011). Quantitative techniques used in anthropology proceed to the concern with behavioral descriptions (Johnson, 1978).

Also, various organizational anthropology studies incorporate research techniques based on statistical techniques, data analysis and big data (Beuving, 2020; Krieg et al., 2017) which opposes the belief that organizational anthropology cannot be quantified. Quantitative methods have failed to be useful in organizational anthropology in the study of the relationship with organizational and corporate socio-interculture confirmed by Meyer, Allen, and Smith (1993) as very poor conclusions.

New methodologies are being provided by Marxism and critical analysis of power relations such as the institutional ethnography (Smith, 1986) showing anthropology and ethnography against the conscious agent of economic exploitation (Clifford, 1988). Logical, mathematical, and computational methods linked to complexity theories considered formal methods, models, and approaches in anthropology, such as dynamic systems, complex adaptive systems, non-equilibrium and chaos theory are correlated in social sciences (Reynoso, 2006) are useful in anthropology since self-regulated systems (Nadel, 1953, 1957), schizogenesis (Bateson, 1975) ecosystem (Rappaport, 1984, 1999), artificial societies (Lansing, 2002, 2003).

Socio-Intercultural Anthropology

There are divergent positions regarding the nature of anthropology is considered as natural science of human species as in natural sciences, as the study of socio-interculture arguing the difficulties to apply theoretical methods of natural sciences to social phenomena to different orders between the biological and socio-intercultural man (Silva Santisteban, 2018). In classical anthropology, culture is a way of life. Anthropology is a science of cultural identities and expressed cultural diversity (Geertz, 1996). Anthropological tools contribute for the study of organizational socio-interculture.

The origins of anthropology as the scientific discipline are immerse in the colonial mentality of naturalist and travelers appropriated with the positive method searching for scientific explanations beyond the dogmatism of religious principles contributed to anthropology consolidating the evolutionary principles of philosophy (Valentí, 2009). Evolutionary anthropology studies the evolution of human being. Anthropology emerged in the middle of the 19th century serving the colonial interest of empires and companies. The Manchester and French school of decolonization as anthropological sources are developed by Max Glukman and Georges Balandier (Gravano, 2005 and 2008a, b).

To understand similarities among peoples, anthropology is a science that analyzes how strange are other people to us in scientific categories. Anthropological tools contribute for the study of generic and specific organizational socio-interculture. Contributions of anthropological studies of organizations in the theoretical framework and methods incorporate variables related to knowledge economy and society, the new socio-intercultural relationships built from information and communication technologies, and other technologies such as artificial intelligence, which contribute to organizational change processes. Global markets and trade liberalization has deepened the economy and the organizations with the support of the industrial psychology and sociology involved in capitalist organizations as abiotic without people engagements.

Whereas, technology is at the center of business, public and non-profit organizational phenomena that articulates the meaning of members on certain aspects that surrounds technology and the workspaces (Cloutier & Ravasi, 2020). Technology is defined as the knowledge, processes, tools, and systems used in the creation and provision of goods and services which can be used as an input in another organizational system. The social meaning construction conceptualize technology as an organizational anthropological category built on sociotechnical and pragmatic permanent transformation to transcend the application of science and artifacts. Traditional technology has a relevant role in production process.

Technology is one of the organizational dimensions of human factors as part of public, private and non-profit space adopting new technologies, improving, and adapting the existing ones. The nature of technology posits categories of analysis to facilitate anthropological and ethnographic research in mechanical technologies, physical and human technologies (Roberts & Grabowski, 1996).

Technology is a control mechanism in organizational processes including instruments and other elements. A research opportunity for organizational theory should focus more on the use of traditional technologies as a means of adaptation to be analyzed from adaptation to the work environment and variables such as collaboration, institutionalism, entrepreneurship.

Meanwhile, organization theory and studies locate the anthropology and their relationships organizational socio-interculture leading to resort to other disciplines aimed to provide tools for the analysis of the organizational phenomenon. The socio-intercultural analysis is a system of interaction of symbols aimed to construct referential frameworks for international, national, regional, and local actions.

Ethnography approaches organizations as a socio-intercultural formation. Ethnographic studies contribute to affect corporations in the workplace with interactions and documentation that have an impact on the outside socio-interculture of organizations. Organizational anthropology documents differences in the realm of values, beliefs, social relationships, and practices (Urban & Koh, 2013). More countable organizational practices that become more dehumanized (Dufour, 1995), under the universality of the principles of anthropology framework deriving in more humane organizations leading to the enhancement instead of disruption of the dimensions of the human being.

Ethnography and translation in anthropological practice in interpretivism does not objectify the total processes criticized for losing the native in contradictory relations (Crapanzano, 1986). These processes are related to the perspectives of Practical Anthropology (Gravano, 1992), the anthropological imagination (Gravano, 1995) and culture concept of Anthropology (Gravano, 2008b).

Anthropological imagination is an anthropological approach aims to study the own socio-interculture of the analyst leading to question the guarantee of objectivity of the reality studied based on the premise of introducing into reality to record the own vision which may lead to conceptual building of an alienation relationship. An anthropological perspective is based on socio-intercultural and environmental education processes that promote understanding between socio-economic differences that characterize the discrimination against individuals converging in collective purposes and leading to organizational knowledge and learning (Cely-López, & Gómez-Niño, 2016).

Applied anthropology has interest on the expectations of population living in urban society in cities leading to socio-cultural and socio-ecological, practical, and symbolic continuities and ruptures which require to make processes towards achieving effectiveness on fair and equal societies through collaboration. Applied anthropology to organizations contributes and provide arguments to organizational studies and resolve milestones of the discipline developed from the studies of simple societies to analyze the ideological, social, socio-intercultural, and technological environment of closed corporations and communities.

By the way, mexican anthropology maintains a permanent level of identification on socio-cultural insertion in the national context through the history. The Mexican anthropology directed towards reflection of new contexts transverse by socio-intercultural relation leading to many people living transitions of migration from the rural to the large urban cities. This reflection led the discipline to action and to transcend the structuralist model to analyze the cultural change that occurs loss or fusion of cultural tradition with the irruption of modern issues aimed at repositioning people in society.

The anthropology of modern worlds (Augé, 1995) opens the present and modernity. In the other side, it can be ahistorical culturalism together with structural materialism. The crisis of representation and postmodernism reformulated the anthropological practices, a repudiation of great theory, leading to the redefinition of the notion of theory retreating towards ethnography and the repudiation of great theory (Ellen, 2010).

Anthropology for management articulates the vision and the practice in activities at the service of a plaintiff leading to create dilemmas in traditional teaching and research activities, concealing to the illusion to work for oneself, for the students or for neutral entities such as academy and science. Cross-cultural research analysis is based on anthropology and the leading role of quantification (Murdock, 1967; Ember & Ember, 2009). The organizational research on business and gender drew on critical management perspectives. The study of organizational and management has analyzed in critical approaches of the past, current state and future concerning organizational work and gender (Pullen et al. 2019).

ORGANIZATIONAL ANTHROPOLOGY AND SOCIO-INTERCULTURAL SYSTEMS

The term culture is polysemic that studies the complexity of organizational phenomena resorting to diverse disciplines. Culture is a collective phenomenon originated by the interactions of groups, creating shared products and learned based on common experiences of social units. The emergence of the cultural dimension of organizational studies is the synthesis of the theoretical currents of anthropology and organization considering the basic but complex dimensions of the human being. Socio-intercultural dimensions contribute from a meta theory as the macro reference concepts aimed to the diagnosis that enable to order human social behaviors from a holistic organizational perspective leading to overcome specialization problems and able to analyze the labor phenomena in the specific social environment.

Organizational anthropology is a specialty (Caulkins & Jordan, 2013). Other anthropological specialties are the psychological anthropology (Casey & Edgerton, 2007), cognitive anthropology (Kronenfeld et al., 2011), linguistic anthropology, criminological anthropology (Schneider & Schneider, 2008), forensic anthropology (Boyd & Boyd, 2018) anthropology of science (Nader, 2013), genetic anthropology (Gokcumen et al., 2011); psychiatric anthropology (Good, 1992), molecular anthropology (Stoneking, 2017), and neuro-anthropology (Lende & Downey, 2012), etc.

Organizational aanthropology theory and methods are recognized as added value in organizational studies (Harrison-Conwill, 2014). The theoretical systems contribute to science based on principles that have broken with linear causality demonstrated by Malinowski (1944) and Mauss (1925) instead the rudimentary and underdeveloped and elementary peoples and groups leading to create dynamic and complex economic and socio-intercultural systems. Organizational anthropology is a scientific knowledge that analyses individual patterns of interaction with the socioecological and natural environment of various socio-intercultural systems. Organizational anthropology constructs information to change the organizational social functions that benefit society and drawing attention toward the harmful effects (Urban & Koh, 2013).

Anthropological journeys make explicit connections between anthropology and the study of organizations (Kunda, 1986; Weeks, 2004). The analysis of anthropology of organizations in complex societies is based on categories such as socio-interculture, cultural relativism, emic perspective, comparative methods, networks, etc. Categories of organizational anthropology analysis, tools and methods contribute to study entrepreneurship, organizations and companies enhancing the discipline.

Entrepreneurship is a subject of organizational anthropology studies focusing on the relationships from the perspectives of elite and socioeconomic history since the 1980s (Cerutti, 2003; Lomnitz & Pérez-Lizaur, 1993) placing categories of organizational culture, cultural relativism, emic perspective, networks, etc. The network analysis describes the historical relationships with organizational anthropology and its contributions in the implementation of mixed-methods approach to the analysis of global organizing.

Socio-intercultural systems of values and norms are part of concrete social systems. Organizational anthropology is interested in values and intangible assets of socio-interculture and institutional communication. The multiple dimensional value model is dominated in business organizations (Morden, 1999). Institutions are evaluated by organizational anthropology including dialogical socio-intercultural, organizational, and environmental dynamics which has effects on organizational values, work environment, relationships, and communications with stakeholders. Anthropological approach of organizations serves as the watching eye on the interactions between the evaluators and evaluated (Hernández, 2012; Rivera, 2012). Organizational business is conceptualized from the perspective of new institutional theory as an institutional field formed by actors and organizations, including firms, customers, suppliers, consultants, activist, etc. (Baba, 2012).

Culture and organizations are theoretical elements of anthropology that has the purpose to analyze, compare and capture the social reality, to expand the human discourse and the natural human behavior (Geertz, 1992). The analysis of socio-intercultural and organizational anthropology, administration, and social accounting disciplines from the socio-intercultural anthropology perspective, contribute to understand reality, solve related problems and to value the relationships and theoretical elements of organizational elements (Cely-López, & Gómez-Niño, 2016). Organizational anthropology includes contributions of culture and socio-interculturality.

In other matters, from a historical perspective, the experiment of the Hawthorne Western Electric Co., between 1927 and 1932 used methodology from anthropology and administration before the theoretical and conceptual framework development of organizational socio-interculture movement in administration. The Hawthorne experiment is the founding myth in the analysis of the industrial society, carried out between 1927 and 1932, is regarded as a relevant anthropological analysis characterized by a linguistic and functionalist orientation to related issues such as monotony and job satisfaction in productivity (Chapple, 1953). The investigation related to human relations in administration introduced by Mayo led to a theory considered oppose to scientific management paradigm sustained by Taylor that dominated the organizational scene during the last century.

Anthropological studies on organizations, companies and entrepreneurs using the comparative method to analyze and explain similarities for local environments of companies inserted in global value chains and processes and references affecting organizational structures, socio-intercultural references, and technological innovations. The conscious organizational structure creates expectations among its members related to the organizational behavior. Socio-intercultural anthropology focuses on the characterizations of societies. Cultural and socio-intercultural anthropology and socio-educational relations developed in organizational contexts contribute to administrative and social accounting sciences. From a theoretical perspective, socio-intercultural anthropology in organizational administration and social accounting functions contribute to organizational knowledge and learning.

The conceptual framework of socio-interculture involves the reformulation of ideas governing organizational paradigms from being universalist, linear and homogenizing, etc., to become more substantially improved in the organization and society. A conceptual framework of socio-interculture integrates administration in organizational studies and the adoption of sociology, psychology, and anthropology to enhance human relationships in the organizational system and not to conduct a positive analysis of variables searching to raise quality and productivity. The ethics of the organizational administration can be analyzed as knowledge and as practice.

In institutional analysis, the anthropological approach to hyper deduction and hyper induction is linked to diverse areas and means of socio-intercultural action (Rosaldo, 1991) associated to the concept dialectical negativity (Lourau, 1979). The objective of the Administration is to put organizations to work, with the aim of managing social action.

The purpose of anthropology and socio-interculture aiming to broaden the human discourse, providing practical guidance and moral progress, and building a theoretical framework. Scholars in organizational anthropology coincide in assigning socio-intercultural qualities in which there is approval. Socio-intercultural anthropology studies the socio-intercultural manifestations such as beliefs, myths, customs, ceremonies, clothing, music, dialects, etc. On social anthropology academic programs, the theoretical framework sources are based on Durkheim and the Marxism focusing more on essentialist phenomenological socio-intercultural –historical approach on issues such as popular socio-interculture and folklore approached by essentialist functionalism.

Social anthropology has some objects of study already stigmatized such as the analysis of aboriginal and traditional populations freezing the historical development with contradictions leading to search for another perspective to analyze traditional popular socio-intercultures. However, the issues related to traditional popular socio-intercultures are considered reactionary and conservative. Social anthropology has moved the object of study towards urban issues and construction of otherness based on ethnographic methodology.

Anthropology studies the otherness and others by implication in the past and non-modernity. The Anthropology of the present studies the world of the past and alien to the society (Althabe, 1999). Organizational facilitation from organizational anthropology methodology supported using ethnographic method based on the category of socio-interculture as the project to record reality articulated with and epistemological construction of otherness.

The anthropological perspective of socio-interculture is the basic principle to achieve collective objectives instrument used for the satisfaction of needs. Socio-intercultural ecology applies tools from anthropology and biology to create knowledge of social organizations and analyze the interrelations among the forces conforming them. The socio-intercultural ecology of people framed by anthropology is linked with incentives with creativity in customs, literature, and arts as systems of social control of power. The anthropological organizational development model includes the socio-interculture of people and the climate of the organizational environment.

An organizational analysis including socio-interculture and productivity aimed to make more productive must be supported by organizational anthropology (Ortega, 2012). Organizational anthropology is underlined by socio-intercultural symbolic horizons in diverse contexts aimed to operate, reproduce, and historicize human and social life. A theoretical organizational anthropology sources approach should specify the relevant aspects and define the meanings guiding the research, such as socio-interculture and organizational socio-interculture.

In relation to the anthropology of markets including organizational anthropology is a socio-intercultural approach to the market agents. The functions of ethnomarketing are developed from a socio-intercultural framework approach including organizational anthropological to be applied by the different market agents including. The theoretical and practical guidelines are drawn for the anthropology of markets for the application of the functions of ethnomarketing (Baquero, 2006).

Organizational anthropology has concentrated on managing socio-cultural problems in complex societies beyond the pre-industrial and non-industrial communities (Trujillo, 2010). Dialectical articulation moving from research to facilitation processes of organizational anthropology in terms of methodological contributions aimed to transform or improve human interrelationships at work in organizations, according to the perspectives of organizational actors exchanging institutional power between the socio-intercultural otherness in management circularity. Organizational anthropology has the objective to compare the behavior of workers in anthropological terms, as for example in the relationship between work and organizational violence (Urrea & Celis 2016).

Organizational anthropology contributes to develop human resources supported by the ethnographic methodology to generate decisions on the value of socio-cultural relationships in specific organizational contexts, and to resolve organizational problems to become more productive. The contributions of organizational anthropology, socio-interculture and socio-interculturality are to identify the dynamics of socio-intercultural, socio-intercultural, and socio-educational relationships in specific organizational contexts. The elements of organizational anthropology are treated to explain and analyze organizational socio-interculture and climate.

The characterization of concerns in which organizational anthropology was born in Mexican and Spanish organizations to become influential entities in their own socio-intercultural transformation processes (Trujillo, 2010). The organizational anthropology in México appreciated the relationship between socio-interculture and population groups on concerns of migration and modernization with new forms of organization with capitalist changes in socio-intercultural and material work which cannot be separated from symbolic production.

Specifically, applied anthropology in the organizational studies in Mexican public entities based on techniques of interviews and participant observation (Llanque, 2002) around the socio -intercultural variables of the industry, established comparative considerations in regional perspectives on work culture (Durand, 1986). The interventions practices in organizational anthropology include the management and action anthropology, participatory action research, social marketing, etc. (Barfield, 2000), which are evident in the transition from anthropological studies to urban studies associated with the population growth affecting traditional forms of living and concentration in poverty, which has repercussions on anthropological concerns (Gipolla, 2003).

ORGANIZATIONAL SOCIO-INTERCULTURE

The organization creates symbolic artifacts expressed in beliefs, values, ideologies, traditions, rites rituals, ceremonies, stories, myths, and imaginary leading to create and develop meaning and identity in organizational socio-interculture. Organizations, companies, enterprises, and corporations are the narratives of its identity and vision of community expressing who are, what do, where they go in addition to its products and services (Sánchez, 1997). The organizational paradigm of Toyotism is based on the community as the social constructions with adaptable and flexible response to external changes and internal problems.

Organizational anthropology is an attractive academic and research perspective considering the socio-intercultural symbolic manifestations influencing scientific assumptions leading to anthropological disciplines in the study of organizational culture. Organizational socio-interculture is an evolving phenomenon that transforms between and within groups.

Organizational socio-interculture is analyzed from an anthropological perspective of the organizations according to the semiotic concept sustained by a system of networks of meanings which can be interpreted and negotiated by organizational actors (Wright, 2005; Gonnet, 2012). The interactions and transactions within the network consolidate organizational objectives (González & Basaldúa, 2007). Organizational socio-interculture has two different perspectives: the managerialist and the socio-anthropological vision which is supported by the symbolic interaccionism (Wright, 2005; Gonnet, 2012). Management introduced the concept and theoretical approach for organizational socio-intercultural concerns with Ochi, Schein, Smircich, Hatch, Peters & Waterman, Hofstede, Abravanel, Allaire, Firsirotu, Deal & Kennedy, Aktouf, among others.

The organizational socio-interculture and facilitation concepts are defined by a system of representations and practices sustained by values, beliefs, symbols, and rites, in collective processes and institutional action pursuing specific objectives in specific contexts, synthesized as the way of doing things (Gravano, 1992, 1997a, 2000a) approached from organizational anthropology.

Applied organizational anthropology provides the concept of organizational socio-interculture with the implications between the articulations between the representations and practices of facilitation and research. Mentality changes of socio-interculture lead to effective participatory and facilitation processes of organizational and management socio-interculture facilitating the emergence of ruptures aimed to fulfill the objectives of the process.

Socio-interculture of organizations is extended by research during the decade of the eighties with an incursion from other disciplines different of anthropology from the field of organizational anthropology introducing anthropological terminology related to organizational culture. Organizational socio-interculture is supported by anthropology, psychology sociology, ethnology, linguistics, among other social sciences.

Anthropology has entry into corporate or organizational socio-interculture confirming the existence and management of symbolic resources in identity, images, visions, and scenarios integrated to organizational processes adding values. The organizational anthropology perspective is related to countercultural characterization of administration and management.

From the organizational anthropology perspective, the concept and practices of socio-intercultural management and administration are based on cultural differences on labor interrelationships and their acceptance. Socio-interculturality is the relationship between different groups that accept differences of their cultures (Gauthey et al., 1988, García de la Torre, 2007). Organizational socio-interculture implies sociocultural organizations arises from human beings pursuing a purpose to establish values and norms that guide collective behavior leading to weave social imagineries (Cáceres-Rubio & Villacrés-Chaparro, 2010). Organizational socio-intercultural and socio-intercultural anthropology studies have an impact on management from the working environment perspective.

The expansion of the dimensions of organizational culture standing out the anthropological and cultural contributes to organizational studies and theory approaches and their relationships. Theoretical perspectives on culture and organizational socio-interculture are related to influence the individual behavior in organizations. The design of a diagnostic tool to identify and characterize the organizational behavior, leads to develop conceptual and methodological options related to climate and organizational socio-interculture. Time appeals the logic of management since this has influences on the organizational behavior.

Therefore, organizational climate and organizational socio-interculture are present in functions and actions of the members in any organization, driven by the resources and having an active role in formulating and implementing strategies, systems, structures which can be learned and developed.

CONCLUSION

The analysis on the anthropological socio-interculturality and organizational socio-interculture, departing from the assumption that the study of anthropological disciplines applied to organizations is leading to influence the organizational socio-intercultural manifestations and expressions of the anthropology in organizations, concludes that organizational socio-interculture has been influenced by both the ethnographic and quantitative methodology used by the organizational anthropology.

Organizations produce goods and services and disseminate socio-intercultural values which are received by society. Anthropological studies contribute to analyze the socio-intercultural specificities of organizations. Social and organizational anthropological research unifies individuals with society and nature in a variety of existence forms in harmony together developing organizational culture. Organizational anthropology contributes to companies and organizations in the socio-intercultural analysis to explain the social values and processes, the notion of elite and the role of entrepreneurship.

Analysis of human behavior in organizational environment and management sciences should be approached from an interdisciplinary and transdisciplinary research approaches based on the US of organizational anthropology with the joint unification of knowledge in organizational socio-intercultural analysis. The reflective hermeneutics and the holistic analysis of the best organizational practices require the organizational anthropology and socio-intercultural knowledge to be broaden and deepen through interdisciplinary processes to support an active design, formulation, and implementation of continuous organizational improvement.

Anthropological analyzes of socio-intercultural organizations add to other social science disciplines in building and transforming external and internal social relations. The organizational anthropology contributions have been developed from other disciplines, such as administration, psychology, sociology, etc. to be applied on the analysis of human relations and technological processes in organizations. Anthropological theory in organizations contribute with categories of analysis, topics, methods, and tools, for the study of organizational and entrepreneurship phenomena.

Methods in organizational anthropological and organizational socio-intercultural analysis involved in the development and transference of knowledge and technology between organizations, companies, and entrepreneurship. Anthropology of organizations and organizational socio-interculture as a science can use formal, logical, mathematical, and computational methods.

The analysis of organizational anthropology and organizational socio-intercultural challenges the methodology of framing the regional context perspective for the analysis of companies leading to transformation processes within world systems as an approach to opportunities and threats in global context. Economic global interconnection, knowledge transfer and socio-interdisciplinary work are methodological challenges of the organizational anthropology and organizational socio-intercultural that extends to other societal analysis with the difficulties to isolate groups for analysis. Anthropological organizational socio-intercultural studies raise the incidence of global interconnection, the construction of a world system and the analysis of social problems of local communities.

REFERENCES

Althabe, G. (1999). Hacia una Antropología del presente. In G. Althabe (Ed.), *Antropología del presente* (pp. 11–21). Edicial.

Augé, M. (1995). *Antropología de los mundos contemporáneos*. Gedisa.

Augé, M., & Colleyn, J.-P. (2006). *Qué es la antropología*. Paidós.

Baba, M. (2012). Anthropology and business: influence and interests. Journal of Business Anthropology, 1(1), 20-71.

Baquero, A. F. (2006). Comentario sobre el Primer Congreso Latinoamericano de Antropología. Memorias. *Revista Digital de Historia y Arqueología desde el Caribe*, (4).

Barfield, T. (Ed.). (2000). *Diccionario de Antropología*. Siglo XXI Editores.

Barnes, J. (1980). Kinship studies: Some impressions of the current state of play. *Man*, *15*(2), 293–303. doi:10.2307/2801672

Barrett, J., & Stanford, P. (2006). Prediction. In S. Sarkar & J. Pfeifer (Eds.), The philosophy of science: An encyclopedia (pp. 585–599). Academic Press.

Bartlett, F. (1937). Psychological methods and anthropological problems. *Africa*, *10*(4), 401–420. doi:10.2307/1155145

Bateson, G. (1975). *Steps to an ecology of mind*. Ballantine Books.

Bernard, H. (2011). *Research methods in anthropology: Qualitative and quantitative approaches*. AltaMira Press.

Beuving, J. (2020). Ethnography's future in the big data era. *Information Communication and Society*, *23*(11), 1625–1639. doi:10.1080/1369118X.2019.1602664

Boellstorf, T. (2010). The definition of science. *The New York Times*. https://www.nytimes.com/2010/12/14/opinion/l14anthro.html

Boyd, C., & Boyd, D. (2018). *Forensic anthropology*. Wiley. doi:10.1002/9781119226529

Boyd, R., & Richerson, P. (2005). *The origin and evolution of cultures*. Oxford University Press.

Byrne, B., Harris, M., Consorte, J., & Lang, J. (1995). What's in a name? The consequences of violating Brazilian emic color-race categories in estimates of social well-being. *Journal of Anthropological Research*, *51*(4), 389–397. doi:10.1086/jar.51.4.3630144

Cáceres-Rubio, F., & Villacrés-Chaparro, M. (2010). *Cultura organizacional y las fusiones empresariales*. Facultad de Psicología, Universidad de La Sabana. Disponible en: http://intellectum.unisabana.edu.co/bitstream/handle/10818/4045/131294. pdf?sequence=1

Casey, C., & Edgerton, R. (Eds.). (2007). *A companion to psychological anthropology*. Blackwell Publishing.

Cash, P., Stanković, T., & Štorga, M. (2016). *Experimental design research*. Springer. doi:10.1007/978-3-319-33781-4

Caulkins, D., & Jordan, A. T. (Eds.). (2013). *A Companion to Organizational Anthropology*. Wiley-Blackwell.

Cely-López, C. L., & Gómez-Niño, O. (2016). An anthropological perspective of organizations from sociocultural characterization, management, and social accounting. The case of a tertiary education institution. *Cuadernos de Contabilidad*, *17*(43), 184.

Cerutti, M. (2003) Los estudios empresariales en América Latina ¿el debate interminable? *Boletín de Historia Económica*, *1*, 3-9. Disponible en: https://www.audhe.org.uy/Boletin_Audhe/Boletin_2/Boletin_02_Cerutti.pdf

Chapple, E. D. (1953). Applied anthropology in industry. In A. L. Kroeber (Ed.), *Anthropology Today*. Chicago University Press.

Chibnik, M. (1985). The use of statistics in sociocultural anthropology. *Annual Review of Anthropology*, *14*(1), 135–157. doi:10.1146/annurev.an.14.100185.001031

Chibnik, M. (1999). Quantification and statistics in six anthropology journals. *Field Methods*, *11*(2), 146–157. doi:10.1177/1525822X9901100205

Chibnik, M. (2005). Experimental economics in anthropology: A critical assessment. *American Ethnologist*, *32*(2), 198–209. doi:10.1525/ae.2005.32.2.198

Clifford, J. (1988). *The Predicament of Culture*. Harvard U Press.

Cloutier, C., & Ravasi, D. (2020). Identity trajectories: Explaining long-term patterns of continuity and change in organizational identities. *Academy of Management Journal*, *63*(4), 1196–1235. doi:10.5465/amj.2017.1051

Crapanzano, V. (1986). Hermes' dilemma: the masking of subversion in etnographic description. In J. Clifford (Ed.), *Marcus, E. Writing culture: the poetics and politics of ethnography* (pp. 51–76). University of California Press. doi:10.1525/9780520946286-005

Diener, P., Nonini, D., & Robkin, E. (1980). Ecology and evolution in cultural anthropology. *Man*, *15*(1), 1–31. doi:10.2307/2802000

Driver, H. (1953). Statistics in anthropology. *American Anthropologist*, *55*(1), 42–59. doi:10.1525/aa.1953.55.1.02a00040

Dufour, P. (1995). Techno-Globalism and the Challenges to Science and Technology Policy. *Daedalus*, *124*(3), 219–235.

Durand, J. (1986). *Los obreros del Río Grande*. Colegio de Michoacán.

Ellen, R. (2010). Theories in anthropology and 'anthropological theory'. *Journal of the Royal Anthropological Institute*, *16*(2), 387–404. doi:10.1111/j.1467-9655.2010.01631.x

Ember, C., & Ember, M. (2009). *Crosscultural research methods*. AltaMira Press.

Gamble, C., Gowlett, J., & Dunbar, R. (2014). *Thinking big: How the evolution of social life shaped the human mind*. Thames & Hudson.

García de la Torre, C. (2007). Estudios sobre identidad y cultura en las organizaciones en América Latina. *Cuadernos de Administración*, *38*, 21-51. Disponible en: http://bibliotecadigital.univalle.edu.co/ bitstream/10893/2151/1/ESTUDIOS%20 SOBRE%20LA%20IDENTIDAD%20Y%20 LA%20 CULTURA.pdf

Gauthey, F., Ratiu, I., Rodgers, I., & Xardel, D. (1988). *Leaders sans frontières: Le défi des différences*. McGraw-Hill.

Geertz, C. (1992). *La interpretación de las culturas*. Gedisa.

Geertz, C. (1996). Anti-antirrelativismo. In C. Geertz (Ed.), *Los usos de la diversidad* (pp. 93–127). Paidós.

Gessaghi, V. (2011) La experiencia etnográfica y la clase alta. ¿Nuevos desafíos para la antropología? *Boletín de Antropología y Educación, 2,* 17-26. Disponible en: https://es.scribd.com/document/423538599/Laexperiencia-etnografica-y-la-clase-alta-nuevos-desafios-para-la-antropolog

Gipolla, C. (2003). *Historia económica de la Europa preindustrial*. Crítica.

Gokcumen, Ö., Gultekin, T., Alakoc, Y., Tug, A., Gulec, E., & Schurr, T. (2011). Biological ancestries, kinship connections, and projected identities in four central Anatolian settlements: Insights from culturally contextualized genetic anthropology. *American Anthropologist, 113*(1), 116–131. doi:10.1111/j.1548-1433.2010.01310.x PMID:21560269

Gonnet, J. P. (2012). Cultura, organizaciones y antropología. Una revisión crítica. Avá (Posadas), *Revista de Antropología, 21,* 1-20. Disponible en: http:// www.scielo.org.ar/pdf/ava/n21/n21a07. pdf, https://www.redalyc.org/articulo.oa?id=169030268008

González, C., & Basaldúa, M. (2007) La formación de redes sociales en el estudio de actores y familias. Perspectiva de estudio en historia y antropología. *Redes. Revista Hispana para el Análisis de Redes Sociales, 12,* 1-27. Disponible en: https://revistes.uab.cat/redes/article/view/v12-n1-gonzalez-basaldua

Good, B. (1992). Culture and psychopathology: Directions for psychiatric anthropology. In T. Schwartz, G. White, & C. Lutz (Eds.), *New directions in psychological anthropology* (pp. 181–205). Cambridge University Press.

Goodenough, W. (1971). *Culture, Language, and Society*. Addison Wesley.

Gravano, A. (1992). Antropología Práctica, muestra y posibilidades de la Antropología Organizacional. Publicar en Antropología y Ciencias Sociales, 1, 95-126.

Gravano, A. (1995). La imaginación antropológica; interpelaciones a la otredad construida y al método antropológico. Publicar en Antropología y Ciencias Sociales, 4, 71-91.

Gravano, A. (1997). La cultura organizacional como herramienta de mejoramiento. In *El marco del trabajo humano, distintas corrientes en el análisis institucional y organizacional* (pp. 71–76). Area de Estudios e Investigación en Ciencia, Cultura y Sociedad, Cultura de la Ciudad de Buenos Aires.

Gravano, A. (2000). *Plan urbano ambiental: el proceso participativo del plan*. GCBA.

Gravano, A. (2005). *El barrio en la teoría social*. Espacio Editorial.

Gravano, A. (Ed.). (2005). *Imaginarios de la ciudad media: emblemas, fragmentaciones y otredades urbanas, estudios de Antropología Urbana*. FACSO y SCYT de la UNICEN: Consejo Editor de la UNICEN.

Gravano, A. (2008a). *¿Vecinos o ciudadanos? el fenómeno NIMBY (Not In My Back Yard) o SPAN (Sí, Pero No Aquí) del imaginario urbano en un proceso de participación social y su tratamiento desde la facilitación organizacional antropológica.* Trabajo presentado en II Congreso de la Asociación Latinoamericana de Antropología (ALA), Universidad de Costa Rica, Simposio "Imaginarios urbanos y participación social".

Gravano, A. (2008b). La cultura como concepto central de la Antropología. In Apertura a la Antropología, alteridad, cultura, naturaleza humana (3rd ed.). Proyecto Editorial.

Hamill, J. (1990). *Ethno-logic: The anthropology of human reasoning.* University of Illinois.

Harris, M., Consorte, J., Lang, J., & Byrne, B. (1993). Who are the whites? Imposed census categories and the racial demography of Brazil. *Social Forces, 72*(2), 451–462. doi:10.2307/2579856

Harrison-Conwill, G. (2014). Informal ethnography in the corporate workplace: Applying foundational research methods in professional life. *Practical Anthropology, 36*(2), 17–21. doi:10.17730/praa.36.2.4g331p0142864nl6

Henrich, J. (2016). *The secret of our success: How culture is driving human evolution, domesticating our species, and making us smarter.* Princeton University Press. doi:10.1515/9781400873296

Henrich, J., Boyd, R., Bowles, S., Camerer, C., Fehr, E., Gintis, H., McElreath, R., Alvard, M., Barr, A., Ensminger, J., Henrich, N., Hill, K., Gil-White, F., Gurven, M., Marlowe, F., Patton, J., & Tracer, D. (2005). "Economic man" in cross-cultural perspective: Behavioral experiments in 15 small-scale societies. *Behavioral and Brain Sciences, 28*(6), 795–855. doi:10.1017/S0140525X05000142 PMID:16372952

Henrich, J., & Gil-White, F. (2001). The evolution of prestige: Freely conferred deference as a mechanism for enhancing the benefits of cultural transmission. *Evolution and Human Behavior, 22*(3), 165–196. doi:10.1016/S1090-5138(00)00071-4 PMID:11384884

Hernández, B. (2012). La selección de personal, algunas consideraciones frente a sus prácticas. *Semestre Económico, 15*(31), 173–186. doi:10.22395eec.v15n31a7

Hernández, V. (2013). Genealogía de una elite rural: elucidación antropológica de una práctica de poder. *Mundo Agrario, 13*(26). Disponible en: https://www.redalyc.org/pdf/845/84527468004.pdf

Horowitz, M., Yaworsky, W., & Kickham, K. (2019). Anthropology's science wars: Insights from a new survey. *Current Anthropology, 60*(5), 674–698. doi:10.1086/705409

Inga, S. M. (2021). The Seven epistemological myths of anthropology *Rev. Epistemol. Psychol. Science. Soc. (Arequipa), 4*, 89-103.

Johnson, A. (1978). *Quantification in cultural anthropology.* Stanford University Press.

Krieg, L., Berning, M., & Hardon, A. (2017). Anthropology with algorithms? An exploration of online drug knowledge using digital methods. *Medicine Anthropology Theory, 4*(3), 21–52.

Kronenfeld, D. (2018). *Culture as a system.* Routledge.

Kronenfeld, D., Bennardo, G., De Munck, V., & Fischer, M. (Eds.). (2011). *A companion to cognitive anthropology.* Wiley-Blackwell. doi:10.1002/9781444394931

Kunda, G. (1986). *Engineering culture: Control and commitment in a high-tech corporation.* Temple University Press.

Kuper, A., & Marks, J. (2011). Anthropologists unite! *Nature, 470*(7333), 166–168. doi:10.1038/470166a PMID:21307914

Landau, E. (2010). *Putting 'science' back in anthropology.* CNN. http://news.blogs.cnn.com/2010/12/03/putting-science-back-inanthropology

Lansing, S. (2002). 'Artificial societies' and the social sciences. *Artificial Life, 8*(3), 279–292. doi:10.1162/106454602320991864 PMID:12537687

Lansing, S. (2003). Complex adaptive systems. *Annual Review of Anthropology, 32*(1), 183–204. doi:10.1146/annurev.anthro.32.061002.093440

Larsen, C. (Ed.). (2010). *A companion to biological anthropology.* Wiley-Blackwell. doi:10.1002/9781444320039

Lende, D., & Downey, G. (Eds.). (2012). *The encultured brain: An introduction to neuroanthropology.* Massachusetts Institute of Technology. doi:10.7551/mitpress/9219.001.0001

Llanque Ferrufino, R. J. (2002). Redes sociales y cultura organizacional en entidades públicas. *Revista de Antropología Experimental, 2.* http://www.ujaen. es/huesped/rae/rae-02.pdf

Lomnitz, L., & Pérez-Lizaur, M. (1993). *Una familia de la élite mexicana, parentesco, clase y cultura 1820-1890.* Alianza Editorial.

Lourau, R. (1979). *El análisis institucional.* Amorrortu.

Madrigal, L. (2012). *Statistics for anthropology.* Cambridge University Press. doi:10.1017/CBO9781139022699

Malinowski, B. (1944). *A scientific theory of culture and other essays.* University of North Carolina Press.

Mauksch, S. (2017). Managing the dance of enchantment: An *ethnography* of social entrepreneurship events. *Organization, 24*(2), 133–153. doi:10.1177/1350508416644511

Mauss, M. (1925). *The gift: Forms and functions of exchange in archaic societies.* Norton Library.

Menéndez, E. (2006). Participación social en salud: las representaciones y las prácticas. In E. Menéndez (Ed.), *Spinelli, H.: Participación social ¿para qué?* (pp. 81–115). Lugar Editorial.

Meyer, J. P., Allen, N. J., & Smith, C. A. (1993). Commitment to organizations and occupation: Extensions and test of a three-component conceptualization. *The Journal of Applied Psychology, 78*(4), 538–551. doi:10.1037/0021-9010.78.4.538

Morales, S. (2020). El problema de la inducción y la formulación de teorías científicas en antropología. *Revista Peruana de Antropología, 5*(7), 128–142.

Morden, T. (1999). Models of National Culture – Management Review. *Cross Cultural Management, 6*(1), 19–44. doi:10.1108/13527609910796915

Murdock, G. (1967). *Ethnographic Atlas*. University of Pittsburgh Press.

Muthukrishna, M., Doebeli, M., Chudek, M., & Henrich, J. (2018). The cultural brain hypothesis: How culture drives brain expansion, sociality, and life history. *PLoS Computational Biology, 14*(11), e1006504. doi:10.1371/journal.pcbi.1006504 PMID:30408028

Nadel, S. (1953). Social control and self-regulation. *Social Forces, 31*(3), 265–273. doi:10.2307/2574226

Nadel, S. (1957). *The theory of social structure. The Free Press of Glencoe* (L. Nader, Ed.).

Nader, L. (Ed.). (2013). *Naked science: Anthropological inquiry into boundaries, power, and knowledge*. Routledge.

Ortega, R. (2012). *Antropología Organizacional* (L. O. Vargas, Entrevistador). Academic Press.

Peña, W. (2008) La etnografía, una metodología apropiada al diagnóstico de la responsabilidad social empresarial. *Univ. Empresa, 7*(15), 177-183. https://www.redalyc.org/pdf/1872/187214457008.pdf

Price, D. (2000, Nov. 20). Anthropologists as Spies. *The Nation*, 24.

Pullen, A., Lewis, P., & Ozkazanc-Pan, B. (2019). A critical moment: 25 years of gender, work and organization. *Gender, Work and Organization, 26*(1), 1–8. doi:10.1111/gwao.12335

Rappaport, R. (1984). *Pigs for ancestors: Ritual in the ecology of a New Guinea people*. Yale University Press.

Rappaport, R. (1999). *Ritual and religion in the making of humanity*. Cambridge University Press. doi:10.1017/CBO9780511814686

Reynoso, C. (2006). *Complejidad y caos: Una exploración antropológica*. Editorial Sb.

Richerson, P., Baldini, R., Bell, A., Demps, K., Frost, K., Hillis, V., Mathew, S., Newton, E., Naar, N., Newson, L., Ross, C., Smaldino, P., Waring, T., & Zefferman, M. (2016). Cultural group selection plays an essential role in explaining human cooperation: A sketch of the evidence. *Behavioral and Brain Sciences, 39*, e3. doi:10.1017/S0140525X1400106X PMID:25347943

Rivera, L. (2012). Hiring as cultural matching: The case of elite professional service firms. *American Sociological Review, 77*(6), 999–1022. doi:10.1177/0003122412463213

Roberts, K., & Grabowski, M. (1996). Organizations, Technology and Structuring. In S. Clegg, C. Hardy & W. Nord (Eds.), Handbook of Organization Studies (pp. 409-423). Sage.

Rosa, M., Shirley, L., Gavarrete, M., & Alangui, W. (Eds.). (2017). *Ethnomathematics and its diverse approaches for mathematics*. Springer. doi:10.1007/978-3-319-59220-6

Rosaldo, R. (1991). *Cultura y verdad, nueva propuesta de análisis social*. Grijalbo.

Salali, G., Whitehouse, H., & Hochberg, M. (2015). A life-cycle model of human social groups produces a U-shaped distribution in group size. *PLoS One, 10*(9), e0138496. doi:10.1371/journal.pone.0138496 PMID:26381745

SánchezE. (1997). http://uam. academia.edu

Santos, M. J., & de Gortari, R. (2021). Familia y empresas un análisis desde la antropología social. *Telos: Revista de Estudios Interdisciplinarios en Ciencias Sociales, 23*(3), 728–746. doi:10.36390/telos233.14

Schneider, J., & Schneider, P. (2008). The anthropology of crime and criminalization. *Annual Review of Anthropology, 37*(1), 351–373. doi:10.1146/annurev.anthro.36.081406.094316

Silva Santisteban, F. (2018). *Antropología.* Biblioteca de la Universidad de Lima.

Smith, D. (1986). Institutional ethnography: A feminist method. *Resources for Feminist Research, 15*(1), 6–13.

Sosis, R. (2003). Why aren't we all hutterites? Costly signaling theory and religious behavior. *Human Nature (Hawthorne, N.Y.), 14*(2), 91–127. doi:10.100712110-003-1000-6 PMID:26190055

Stoneking, M. (2017). *An introduction to molecular anthropology.* Wiley.

Trujillo, J. T. E. (2010). Anthropology in Mexico and Spain: Industry, work and organizations. *Journal of Anthropology and Sociology: Turns, 12,* 197–226.

Urban, G., & Koh, K. (2013). *Ethnographic research on modern business corporation. In Annual Review Anthropology* (Vol. 42). Estados Unidos.

Urrea, F., & Celis, J. (2016). Los estudios laborales en Colombia entre 1993 y 2014. In Los estudios laborales en América Latina. Orígenes, desarrollo y perspectivas. Universidad Autónoma Metropolitana – Iztapalapa y Anthropos Editorial.

Valentí, S. (2009). *Ideólogos, teorizantes y videntes.* Edward Burnett Tylor. https://www.filosofia.org/aut/svc/index.htm

Van Leeuwen, E., Cohen, E., Collier-Baker, E., Rapold, C., Schäfer, M., Schütte, S., & Haun, D. (2018). The development of human social learning across seven societies. *Nature Communications, 9*(1), 2076. doi:10.103841467-018-04468-2 PMID:29802252

Wade, N. (2010). Anthropology a science? Statement deepens a rift. *The New York Times.* https://www.nytimes.com/2010/12/10/science/10anthropology.html

Weeks, J. (2004). *Unpopular culture: The ritual of complaint in a British bank.* University of Chicago Press.

Williams, L., & Quave, K. (2019). *Quantitative anthropology.* Elsevier.

Wright, S. (Ed.). (2005). *Anthropology of organizations.* Routledge.

Xygalatas, D. (2014). The biosocial basis of collective effervescence: An experimental anthropological study of a fire-walking ritual. *Fieldwork in Religion, 9*(1), 53–67. doi:10.1558/fiel.v9i1.53

Chapter 19
Exploring the Cost–Benefit Factors, Technological Advancements, and Cybersecurity Impacts:
Analyzing ROI

Sharon L. Burton
ⓘ https://orcid.org/0000-0003-1653-9783
Capitol Technology University, USA

Yoshino W. White
Florida State University, USA

ABSTRACT

Online education is continuously evolving to enhance learning and reduce costs. In today's fast-paced world, technology is a driving force in education and business, making it crucial to understand the cost-saving benefits and efficiencies of e-learning. This requires careful planning and investment, similar to online business enterprises. Historical data can inform future strategies, but new information and process improvements are necessary to remain competitive. Aligning training with business objectives and evaluating business results are critical for success. Investing in online training benefits both learners and training professionals. Organizational learning capabilities can be tied to business values, and practitioners can learn about the key components needed to calculate ROI in a technology-driven 21st century. This chapter explores the importance of aligning ROI with training, business objectives, evaluating business results, and investing in online training.

DOI: 10.4018/979-8-3693-1630-6.ch019

INTRODUCTION

The 21st century has brought about unprecedented changes in technology, learning, and budget concerns, which have had a significant impact on the delivery of online education programs. The purpose of this chapter is to provide academicians, business professionals, and learners with ROI understood strategies and techniques that can be readily interpreted with ease of use regarding online education programs. This chapter begins with developing learning effectiveness plans that encompass Covey's second principle of personal leadership, *Begin with the End in Mind* (Covey, 1990). According to Covey, it is feasible to determine whether or not a goal can be physically created by first visualizing and producing it in the mind. It is essential to ensure that all education and training program objectives are clear, recognized, and understood before beginning education and training projects (Burrell, 2019). Additionally, it is critical to validate these objectives against business goals to be achieved (Katsinas, 2019).

The implementation of online education programs with reduced cost continues to drive learning effectiveness. Business leaders, institutions of higher learning, and learners are concerned with cost savings, cost-benefits, and cost efficiencies of e-learning and how to achieve these benefits without overspending their thin, overstretched, and uncertain budgets. Academics are struggling to understand how to deliver this information in a way that is not riddled with academic jargon and theories, and institutions of higher learning need to deliver this significant information in a format that can be immediately applied (Ferrell & Davis, 2019). Learners are seeking new knowledge, skills, abilities, and competencies in a rapidly transforming and technical climate. The present information and digital age is intertwined in networked substructures within working environments, and online learning is pushing the rules regarding the return-on-investment (ROI) as it requires more planned programs and investments (Katsinas, 2019). Therefore, it is essential to continuously review new information for process improvements and to justify training, attain new information through continuous and lifelong learning, and align training with business objectives (Moore, 2020).

The objectives of this chapter are to review the importance of aligning training with business objectives, tracking and evaluating business results, and defining terminology for education and training professionals. It is critical to understand that definitions signify and propel practice in a field, and a clear definition is required to understand a topic (Lee & Choi, 2020). Online education has multiple definitions and names, including online learning, e-learning, virtual education and learning, and web-based training, plus distance learning; it is important to agree on terminology usage before moving forward on any project.

FRAMEWORKS AND RESEARCH

This study proposes a framework for the design and implementation of online learning environments that integrates several key elements, including social constructivism, instructional design principles, and educational technologies. As given by Gergen (2020), and Healy & Short (2021), using a combination of old and new frameworks in a study can provide a comprehensive understanding of a research topic. It allows researchers to build upon established theories while also incorporating emerging perspectives and technologies. This mixed framework approach can enhance the reliability and validity of research findings and contribute to the advancement of knowledge in the field (Gergen, 2020; Healy & Short, 2021).

One recent study that aligns with the proposed framework is by Li et al., (2019), who developed an online learning platform that incorporates social constructivism, instructional design principles, and educational technologies. The study found that the platform significantly improved students' learning outcomes and satisfaction. Yes, learning environments that integrate social constructivism, instructional design principles, and educational technologies draw from the constructionist theory. The constructionist theory posits that people learn by constructing knowledge through active participation and interaction with the environment and others.

Recent research by Hu and Colleagues (2022) explored the design and implementation of a learning environment. This research incorporated social constructivism, instructional design principles, and educational technologies. The study found that the learning environment supported students in constructing knowledge through active participation and collaboration, which in turn enhanced their engagement and learning outcomes.

This researcher's framework also incorporates the principles of instructional design, which emphasize the importance of aligning learning objectives with instructional strategies, and of providing learners with feedback and support as they engage in the learning process (Morrison et al., 2013). The utilizing of multiple frameworks, such as the Morrison et al., (2013) research, helps to overcome limitations and biases of individual theories, leading to a more nuanced and holistic analysis (Rosenberg et al., 2022). In addition, the framework integrates educational technologies, such as learning management systems, online collaboration tools, and multimedia resources, which can enhance the effectiveness and efficiency of the learning environment (Dede, 2019).

In order to evaluate the success of the framework, this researcher will gather information from the literature on how well learners are satisfied, engaged, and performing. The study's findings will be put to use in future research on the best practices for online learning environments to improve the framework. All information will be gathered and examined in line with accepted research methods, including criteria for literature reviews and content analyses.

Limitations and Delimitations

The focus of this document is to explore the concept of ROI as it pertains to online learning and the technology associated with online learning. Specifically, it will examine how ROI can be used to measure cost-savings, cost-benefits, and cost efficiencies in these areas, and how it can help business leaders, institutions of higher learning, and learners achieve their objectives. While the document will not delve into the specifics of calculating ROI or maximizing it, it will serve as a valuable tool for understanding the key parameters needed to perform the calculation. Please note that the actual calculation of ROI and how to use the ROI formula will be covered in a separate text.

METHODOLOGY

In this study, a combination of content analysis of theoretical literature and a literature review approach was employed. As noted by Jones and Smith (2021), a literature review is a crucial tool in providing an extensive overview of previous research conducted in a specific field. By acknowledging the works of previous scholars, a literature review helps to assure the reader that the current study has been thoroughly researched. The literature review approach was chosen as the methodology to identify the need for further research in the area of study. Through this approach, the researcher established the relationship between various works in the context of their contribution to the research topic and other related research (Robinson & Cooper, 2020). Moreover, the literature review provided this researcher with an essential tool to navigate the increasing complexity of information (Bodolica & Spraggon, 2018). This study utilized a literature review approach to examine the existing literature on the research topic and identify gaps that required further exploration. The literature review helped to establish the context and background of the study, as well as the current state of knowledge in the field. This approach enabled the researcher to draw meaningful conclusions and recommendations for further research.

APPLICABLE THEORIES

This research is guided by three relevant theories: blended learning, adaptive learning, and Augmented Reality (AR) and Virtual Reality (VR). Blended learning suggests integrating online and face-to-face learning to create a more effective and flexible educational experience (Hamari & Sjöklint, 2021; Kizilcec & Halawa, 2020). This approach combines the advantages of both traditional and digital learning, promoting learner-centered learning and increasing engagement and motivation. The second theory is adaptive learning. According to Sharma and Srinivasan (2021), adaptive learning is a theory that suggests personalized educational experiences through the use of technology and data analysis. This technology-driven theory proposes that learners should have customized learning paths, feedback, and resources that adapt to their strengths, weaknesses, and learning preferences. The last and third theories are augmented reality (AR) and virtual reality (VR). Augmented reality (AR) and virtual reality (VR) suggest a new era of human-computer interaction that can enhance and transform the way we perceive and interact with the world around us. AR involves overlaying digital information on the real world, while VR immerses users in a completely virtual environment. According to a study by Zhang et al. (2019), AR and VR technologies have the potential to revolutionize education and training by providing interactive and immersive learning experiences.

Blended learning is a teaching approach that combines traditional classroom learning with online or digital learning. According to Kizilcec and Halawa (2020), blended learning can improve student performance, reduce dropout rates, and enhance the overall quality of education. This approach allows students to access content online at their own pace while also participating in face-to-face activities and discussions in the classroom. Blended learning is a popular method for teaching in a technological environment because it offers flexibility and can cater to different learning styles. It also allows for a more personalized learning experience, as students can work at their own pace and receive individualized support and feedback from teachers.

Adaptive learning is an approach that uses technology to personalize and adapt learning experiences to the needs and abilities of individual learners. According to Sharma and Srinivasan (2021), adaptive learning improved students' performance and engagement and concluded that it has the potential to enhance students' learning experiences. This research team examined the effectiveness of adaptive learning in enhancing students' learning outcomes in computer programming. This methodology leverages artificial intelligence and machine learning algorithms to create personalized learning paths and adjust the difficulty of content based on a learner's strengths and weaknesses.

Augmented reality (AR) and virtual reality (VR) are immersive technologies that can be used to create engaging and interactive learning experiences. AR allows learners to experience digital content overlaid on the real world, while VR provides a completely simulated environment. Both AR and VR can be used to create simulations, scenarios, and interactive games that help learners understand complex concepts and skills. AR and VR can also be used for remote learning and collaboration, providing a way for learners to connect and learn from anywhere.

UNDERSTANDING THE RETURN ON INVESTMENT (ROI)

ROI is used for higher education and organizational educational programs. The use of ROI in education and training initiatives was popularized in the 1950s by the work of Donald Kirkpatrick, who introduced the four levels of evaluation for training programs, with ROI being the fourth level (Kirkpatrick, 1959; Sung et al., 2019). Since then, ROI has been used to determine training initiatives' financial value and impact on an organization's bottom line. According to a survey by Training Industry, Inc. (2017), 94% of organizations surveyed indicated that they measure the impact of their training programs, with ROI being one of the most commonly used metrics. According to a report by the Association for Talent Development (ATD), the practice of ROI in training projects has developed as especially important as organizations grapple with the problems posed by the COVID-19 epidemic. (ATD, 2021).

ROI is an accounting formula used to determine the real or perceived future value of an expenditure or investment (Nguyen, 2020). The ROI calculates the profit before taxes and after depreciation from all investments made and is usually expressed as a percentage of the original total cost invested. In the education and training arenas, ROI is a metric that provides an immediate understanding of the economic payoff of an education initiative or training program (Bates & Khasawneh, 2019). To accurately calculate ROI, leaders and administrators must first ensure that faculty members are competent in andragogy, subject matter areas, and educational technologies (Miller, 2021). Inter-business unit congeniality, such as IT, human resources, and instructional design, is also necessary for success (Chen & Chen, 2020). Additionally, individual motivation is a crucial factor in the success of education and training programs (Bates & Khasawneh, 2019). To calculate ROI, the collective return can be calculated by comparing the profit inputs of all new products within the determined payback period against investment in product development. Review the ROI formula in Figure 1.

Figure 1. Return on Investment
Source: Adapted from Bates and Khasawneh (2019)

$$\textbf{ROI} = \textbf{Gain from Investment - Cost of Investment / Cost of Investment}$$

A study by Pappas et al. (2020), provides a comprehensive review of literature on the impact of IT investments on financial and non-financial performance measures. Also, this study highlights the importance of considering both financial and non-financial impacts when assessing the return on investment of IT projects. The calculation of ROI can provide valuable information to institutions and organizations in determining the success and effectiveness of education and training programs. ROI is an important metric that can provide insight into the economic payoff of education and training initiatives. To accurately calculate ROI, leaders and administrators must ensure that educators and trainers are competent and that inter-business unit congeniality is present.

In the context of education and training initiatives, ROI can provide insights into the economic payoff of these programs. By calculating the ROI of an education or training program, organizations can assess the value of their investment and determine whether it is worth continuing or expanding (Phillips & Phillips, 2019). The program's costs must be compared to the benefits it generates to calculate the ROI of an education or training program. Further, according to Phillips and Phillips (2019), the program's costs include the direct costs of delivering the program, such as instructor salaries and materials, as well as the indirect costs, such as the time spent by participants and the opportunity cost of not using that time for other activities. The program's benefits include increased productivity, improved job performance, and higher earnings potential (Phillips & Phillips, 2019). By comparing the costs and benefits of an education or training program, organizations can calculate the ROI of the program. If the ROI is positive, the program generates more benefits than costs and is therefore considered a good investment. If the ROI is negative, the program generates more costs than benefits and should be reconsidered.

In the study by Mishra and Sahoo (2020), the authors examined the impact of training and development programs on employee performance in Indian manufacturing firms. They found that such programs positively affected both individual and organizational performance. Furthermore, they recommended that organizations calculate these programs' return on investment (ROI) to evaluate their effectiveness.

For the Cheng and Li (2019) meta-analysis, the authors reviewed empirical studies on training effectiveness. They identified various factors that could influence the ROI of training programs, such as the type of training, training design, and evaluation methods. They also provided guidelines for measuring the ROI of training programs, which could help organizations to make informed decisions about their training investments.

There are several challenges to calculating the ROI of education and training initiatives, such as identifying and measuring the program's benefits and assigning a monetary value to those benefits. However, despite these challenges, ROI analysis can provide valuable insights into the economic payoff of education and training initiatives. Additionally, a comprehensive evaluation of the training program's objectives and outcomes should be conducted to measure the initiative's effectiveness on employee performance and organizational goals (Wang & Guo, 2019).

LITERATURE REVIEW

Aligning Technology and Training With Business Goals to Maximize Returns

In order to develop and implement effective training programs, human capital and learning strategists, as well as practitioners, must have a clear understanding of their organization's overall strategy, including technological changes and how they relate to specific business units and functions (Schuurman et al., 2021a). However, organizations may face challenges in developing training programs when there is a lack of clarity around corporate and business unit goals, which can make it difficult to align training initiatives with organizational objectives (Kowalski & Kelley, 2021; Schuurman et al., 2021c). To overcome these challenges, it is important for leadership to develop clear business objectives that are directly linked to their training strategy, taking into account technological changes and advancements.

For example, a shift to remote work due to technological changes may require training on virtual collaboration tools and communication software (Bashrum, 2019a; 2019b).

Martin and Caruso (2019) argue that higher education leaders must deeply understand their institution's strategic priorities and business units to lead effective change initiatives. Understanding the institution's strategic priorities and business units to lead effective change initiatives includes comprehending how technological changes impact various functions within the institution, such as teaching and learning, research, and administrative services. By understanding these dynamics, leaders can design and implement training programs that align with the institution's strategic goals and support the development of necessary skills and competencies.

To create successful training programs, it is essential first to decide who needs to be trained, why the individuals need to be trained, and what proportion of personnel and information should be offered for training. Industry regulators set compliance-driven training standards, while information-driven training is driven by organizational leadership and the needs of employees (Temples et al., 2019a). Organizations must adapt to technological advances and their influence on organizational objectives to flourish in today's fast-paced and ever-changing business environment (Chang et al., 2021). By doing so, organizations can develop training programs that drive employee performance and contribute to overall organizational success.

To succeed in today's fast-paced and ever-changing business environment, organizations must be able to adapt to technological changes and their impact on organizational objectives (Chang et al., 2021). Developing effective training programs that align with business goals, academic and organizational, is essential (Temples, 2019b). By identifying the training needs of employees, setting clear business objectives, and providing top-down support, organizations can ensure that their training initiatives drive employee performance and contribute to overall organizational success (Temples et al., 2019c).

Technological changes have become a critical factor in organizational success, significantly impacting operations. For instance, the adoption of artificial intelligence (AI) and machine learning (ML) technologies has transformed various industries, from education to healthcare and finance. Consequently, organizations must equip their employees with the necessary skills to use these technologies effectively. Gartner (2022) found that by 2025, 75% of organizations will have invested in employee retraining and upskilling to address the skills gaps arising from the increasing adoption of AI, ML, and other new technologies. Higher education institutions can be crucial in providing the necessary training and education to upskill and reskill the workforce. They are uniquely positioned to offer a wide range of programs and courses that align with the changing demands of the job market (O'Brien, 2021). As the demand for workers with AI and ML skills increases, universities and colleges can develop new curricula and programs that prepare students for these emerging careers and help organizations fill the skills gaps (Brown & Lam, 2019).

According to a study by the International Data Corporation, worldwide spending on AI is expected to reach $79.2 billion in 2022, a significant increase from the $24 billion spent in 2018. Similarly, the global market for machine learning is projected to grow from $1.41 billion in 2017 to $8.81 billion by 2022. Assessing the technology skills of the current workforce is an essential step for organizations to identify areas that need improvement and implement effective training programs. Based on this assessment of technology skills of the current workforce, organizations can design training programs that are tailored to their employees' needs and aligned with the organization's overall objectives. This process can also benefit higher education institutions by providing insight into the technological competencies that students should possess upon graduation to meet the demands of the modern workforce (Bryant &

Gray, 2019). Also, higher education institutions have a duty to work together with industry companions to recognize technology abilities that are in need in the workplace and then assimilate them into the curriculum. By aligning their educational offerings with industry needs, higher education institutions can better prepare their students for the job market and support the workforce development goals of organizations (Bryant & Gray, 2019). The Bryant and Gray research team offered that the ROI of training programs for technology skills is directly connected to this information, as organizations that invest in such programs can expect to see improved productivity, increased efficiency, and greater innovation, leading to increased profits and competitive advantage. Additionally, higher education institutions that align their educational offerings with industry needs can attract more students, increase enrollment, and strengthen their reputation, leading to increased funding and support (Bryant & Gray, 2019).

One way to assess the technology skills of the current workforce is through surveys and self-assessment tools. Another way is to conduct skills tests or evaluations. Another way to assess the technology skills, according to a study by the Society for Human Resource Management (SHRM), is to identify gaps in technology skills and determine the training needs of employees (SHRM, 2021a). Another study by the World Economic Forum recommends using skills assessments and mapping to identify skills gaps and prioritize training efforts (WEF, 2020). In higher education, identifying gaps in technology skills and determining training needs of students is crucial to prepare them for the workforce. Institutions can use skills assessments and mapping to determine the current level of technology skills of students and prioritize efforts to fill the gaps (WEF, 2020). This will ensure that students graduate with the necessary technology skills to be successful in their chosen fields (SHRM, 2021b).

Organizations and educational institutions must set clear business objectives that are aligned with the training programs they offer. This setting of clear business objectives ensures that the training programs contribute to achieving the organization's goals, and employees can apply the skills learned in their day-to-day work. Additionally, organizations must provide top-down support for their training initiatives, with senior management leading by example and encouraging employees to participate in training programs. In brief, organizations must adapt to technological changes to remain competitive in today's business environment. By designing technology-driven training programs that align with business objectives and providing top-down support, organizations can drive employee performance and contribute to overall organizational success.

Artificial Intelligence and Training ROI: Enhancing Business Results Through Measurable Training Outcomes

Artificial intelligence (AI) has transformed the way businesses operate, including how they approach training and measuring its effectiveness. AI-powered tools can help businesses to analyze training data, personalize training content, and track the impact of training on business results. In a report by Gartner, Inc., by the year 2025, half of all workplace learning will utilize AI to create, distribute and monitor personalized educational materials. (Gartner, 2019). In this chapter, we will discuss how AI connects with training and business results to measure training results for ROI, the positives, and negatives of this approach. Let us review three key points.

Initially, AI can assist in analyzing training data in academics and organizations. AI algorithms can analyze vast amounts of data from employee training programs to identify patterns and trends, making it easier to understand which training programs are most effective. A study by Towards Data Science found that the implementation of AI in learning and development programs by organizations has resulted in a 30-50% increase in employee engagement and a 22% boost in productivity (Towards Data Science, 2021). Academic institutions could benefit from implementing AI in their learning and development programs to improve engagement and productivity among students and faculty. One example is a study published in the Journal of Educational Computing Research in 2020, which found that incorporating AI-based personalized learning into a college-level programming course improved student engagement and performance (Mavridis & Giannakos, 2020). These analyses can help organizations to personalize training content and delivery methods to suit each individual employee's learning style.

Then, AI can help to personalize training content. Personalized training programs, tailored to each employee's unique learning style, have been shown to increase engagement and learning outcomes. AI can help to deliver customized learning experiences by analyzing employee data, including job roles, performance, and learning history. In a white paper by Docebo (2020), a learning management system provider, it was reported that utilizing AI-driven personalization can enhance engagement rates by up to 30%, which can ultimately result in improved training outcomes and higher rates of completion. Personalized training can also help employees to develop specific skills that are directly relevant to their job role, leading to better job performance and business results (Burton, 2019).

Third, AI can track the impact of training on business results. By analyzing employee performance data, businesses can evaluate the impact of training on business results (Kim et al., 2021). This approach can help organizations to determine the ROI of their training programs and identify areas for improvement. Additionally, AI-based tracking can provide insights into individual employee performance, identifying areas where additional training may be needed to improve overall business outcomes (Alam et al., 2021).

However, there are also potential negatives associated with using AI to measure training effectiveness. Firstly, there is the risk that the technology may not be accurate, leading to incorrect data analysis and misleading results (McKinsey, 2021). Secondly, the use of AI in training can raise ethical concerns, including concerns around employee privacy and the use of personal data (European Commission, 2021). Finally, there is a risk that AI-powered training programs may not be suitable for all employees, particularly those who prefer more traditional training methods. A study by Li and Liang (2022) found that some employees may resist the use of AI-powered training programs, preferring more traditional training methods. The study suggests that employers should consider employees' preferences and provide a range of training options. In addition, a study by the International Labor Organization (ILO) highlights the need for transparency and accountability in the use of AI in the workplace to ensure that employees are not subjected to discriminatory or biased decision-making processes (ILO, 2021).

To come to the point, AI has the potential to transform the way businesses approach training and measuring its effectiveness. AI can assist in analyzing training data, personalizing training content, and tracking the impact of training on business results. While there are potential negatives associated with using AI to measure training effectiveness, the positives, including improved training outcomes and ROI, outweigh the negatives. Companies must consider the benefits and risks when integrating AI into their training programs, taking a cautious approach to ensure the technology is used ethically and accurately.

Augmented Reality (AR) and Training ROI: Enhancing Business Results Through Measurable Training Outcomes

According to a report by Markets and Markets (2019), the global market size for AR in training is expected to reach USD 4.48 billion by 2023, with a CAGR of 36.2% from 2018 to 2023. AR, a powerful tool in training and development is being used in various fields such as education, manufacturing, and military (Markets & Markets, 2019), thereby offering a unique and engaging way for employees to learn new skills and improve their performance. AR has also been used for training and development in the healthcare industry (Market and Market, 2019). For example, AR can be used to simulate surgeries and allow medical professionals to practice procedures before performing them on actual patients. A study by Vázquez et al. (2021a) found that using AR in surgical training resulted in better performance and lower error rates among medical students. ROI is connected to this information as the growth in the AR training market indicates an increasing demand for AR-based training solutions, which can yield a positive ROI for companies investing in such technology (Vázquez et al., 2021b). The higher engagement and effectiveness of AR-based training can lead to improved employee performance and productivity, leading to a positive impact on the organization's bottom line.

Another advantage of AR-based training methods is its ability to enhance learning retention and engagement, and knowledge transfer compared to traditional training methods (Chen, Liang & Chen, 2021). This information highlights the potential benefits of using AR-based training methods in a business context, such as improving employee learning and knowledge transfer, which can ultimately lead to improved job performance and productivity.

According to a study by Liao et al. (2019), students who used AR in their anatomy classes had higher retention rates and better performance on exams than those who used traditional learning methods. AR can also make learning more interactive and engaging by allowing users to explore and manipulate virtual objects in real-time.

One of the key benefits of using AR for training is the increased engagement it provides. Studies have shown that the use of AR technology in training (business or education) can lead to higher levels of motivation and engagement among learners, as they are more likely to be immersed in the learning experience (Choi, 2019). This increased engagement can translate into improved learning outcomes, as learners are more likely to retain information and apply it to real-world situations. Also, AR training offers real-time feedback to learners. AR technology can track learners' actions and provide feedback on their performance, allowing them to identify areas for improvement and adjust their approach accordingly (Burton, 2020). This feedback can help learners to develop their skills more effectively and efficiently than traditional training methods, which may not offer such detailed feedback (Choi, 2019).

In terms of measuring training results for ROI, AR technology can provide valuable data on learners' performance and progress. For example, AR-enabled training modules can track learners' interactions with virtual objects, allowing educators and trainers to identify areas where learners are struggling and adjust their training accordingly (Zarei, 2019). This data can be used to measure the effectiveness of the training program and to make informed decisions about how to allocate resources for future training initiatives. Concisely, augmented reality technology has the potential to revolutionize the way we approach training and development, offering a range of benefits over traditional methods. AR can provide engaging, immersive learning experiences, real-time feedback, and valuable data on learners' performance.

Augmented Reality (AR) and Training ROI: The Drawbacks for Education and Business

Potential drawbacks exist to using AR for training. One primary concern is the cost of implementing AR technology, which can be high compared to traditional training methods (Alalwan et al., 2021a; Markets and Markets, 2021). This cost may be a barrier for some organizations, notably smaller businesses with limited budgets, high costs, and concerns around user experience. Additionally, some learners may find

AR technology too distracting or overwhelming, which could negatively impact their learning outcomes (Zarei, 2019). The potential high cost of implementing AR technology for training could affect the return on investment (ROI) of the training program, particularly for smaller businesses. Learners' negative perception of AR technology could also impact the ROI. (Alalwan et al., 2021a; Markets and Markets, 2021; Zarei, 2019).

Another potential drawback of using AR for training is the need for specialized technical skills to create and maintain AR applications. Companies may need to invest in training or hiring personnel with expertise in AR development, which can add to the overall cost of implementing the technology (Alalwan et al., 2021b). Additionally, the development process for AR training materials can be time-consuming, requiring extensive planning and design to ensure the technology is used effectively and efficiently (Zarei, 2019).

A different concern is the compatibility of AR technology with existing IT infrastructure. Companies may need to upgrade their hardware and software systems to support AR applications, which can significantly invest time and money (Markets and Markets, 2021). Moreover, not all learners may have access to the necessary hardware and software required to participate in AR training programs, which can create disparities in learning opportunities and outcomes.

Finally, there are privacy and security concerns surrounding AR technology. AR devices and applications can capture and store sensitive data, such as personal information and images of individuals, raising concerns about data privacy and security (Alalwan et al., 2021b). Companies must take steps to ensure that AR applications are secure and that user data is protected. Overall, organizations must consider AR technology's benefits and drawbacks before deciding whether to incorporate it into their training programs.

FUTURE RESEARCH DIRECTIONS

The duration of future research recommendations may vary depending on the specific field of study, research objectives, and the scope of the research project. However, in general, future research recommendations should cover a timeframe that allows for significant progress to be made towards the research objectives, while also being realistic in terms of the available resources and the current state of knowledge in the field. Based on current trends and challenges in the education and training industry, here are some future research recommendations for education and training practitioners, leaders, and administrators to prioritize the safeguarding of learning effectiveness and the application of Return on Investment (ROI) measures over the next six years:

- Investigate the impact of emerging technologies on learning effectiveness and ROI. With the increasing adoption of emerging technologies such as artificial intelligence, virtual and augmented reality, and gamification in education and training, there is a need to investigate their impact on learning effectiveness and ROI. This research should focus on understanding how these technologies can be used to enhance learning outcomes and provide a positive ROI for educational institutions and organizations.
- Analyze the effectiveness of personalized learning approaches: Personalized learning has become increasingly popular in recent years, with a focus on tailoring instruction to meet the needs of individual learners. However, there is a need to investigate the effectiveness of these approaches and

their impact on ROI. This research should aim to identify the most effective personalized learning strategies and how they can be scaled and implemented in different educational settings.

- Examine the role of learning analytics in improving learning effectiveness and ROI: Learning analytics can provide valuable insights into student performance and learning outcomes. However, there is a need to investigate how these analytics can be used to improve learning effectiveness and ROI. This research should focus on identifying the most effective learning analytics tools and how they can be integrated into educational institutions and organizations.

- Investigate the impact of soft skills training on learning effectiveness and ROI. Soft skills such as communication, collaboration, and critical thinking are becoming increasingly important in the workforce. There is a need to investigate the impact of soft skills training on learning effectiveness and ROI. This research should focus on identifying the most effective soft skills training strategies and how they can be integrated into educational programs and training initiatives.

- Analyze the effectiveness of online learning programs and their impact on ROI: Online learning programs have become increasingly popular in recent years, with many educational institutions and organizations offering online courses and training programs. However, there is a need to investigate the effectiveness of these programs and their impact on ROI. This research should aim to identify the most effective online learning strategies and how they can be used to provide a positive ROI for educational institutions and organizations.

Overall, these research recommendations can help education and training practitioners, leaders, and administrators to prioritize the safeguarding of learning effectiveness and the application of ROI measures over the next six years. By investigating the impact of emerging technologies, personalized learning, learning analytics, soft skills training, and online learning programs, educational institutions and organizations can make informed decisions that lead to better learning outcomes and a positive return on investment.

CONCLUSIONS AND RECOMMENDATIONS

The years 2019 to 2023 have seen an increasing need for education and training practitioners, leaders, and administrators to prioritize the safeguarding of learning effectiveness, including the application of Return on Investment (ROI) measures (Buchanan & Trinkle, 2019; Phillips & Phillips, 2019). Additionally, inter-business unit collaboration is essential to sustain congeniality and achieve organizational goals (Sitzmann et al., 2019; Friesen & Lowe, 2020; Geiger & Schaffhauser, 2020; Kim & Hwang, 2022; Li et al., 2022). Five recommendations apply.

- To achieve this, both business and education leaders must remain competent in technology and adult learning (Fernández-March et al., 2021; Reimers & Schleicher, 2019). Inter-business unit congeniality, particularly between IT, human resources, and instructional design departments, must also be sustained (Bates, 2020; Heo & Lee, 2020).

- To ensure that learning is effective, education and training practitioners should adopt blended learning approaches that combine online and offline learning (Hew & Cheung, 2021).

- They must also create a culture of continuous learning that encourages learners to engage in lifelong learning (Kostons et al., 2021).

- Also, education and training practitioners should utilize data analytics and learning analytics to measure the effectiveness of their programs (Khalil et al., 2021; Yoon & Kim, 2019).
- According to a study by the ATD, organizations can use a combination of traditional ROI metrics and more qualitative metrics to measure the impact of training on business outcomes (Measuring the ROI, 2019). The ATD study found that while cost savings and revenue growth are important ROI metrics, organizations should also consider other factors such as employee satisfaction and engagement to fully measure the effectiveness of training.

REFERENCES

Alalwan, A. A., Baabdullah, A. M., Rana, N. P., Tamilmani, K., & Dwivedi, Y. K. (2021b). The impact of augmented reality on training: An exploratory study. *Computers in Human Behavior*, *120*, 106767.

Alalwan, A. A., Rana, N. P., Dwivedi, Y. K., & Algharabat, R. (2021). Barriers to the adoption of Augmented Reality in training: An empirical investigation in the oil and gas industry. *Journal of Business Research*, *129*, 386–395. doi:10.1016/j.jbusres.2021.01.004

Alam, S. S., Ali, S., Khurshid, K., Hussain, M., & Chang, V. (2021). AI-based Performance Analysis for Efficient Employee Training and Development. *IEEE Access : Practical Innovations, Open Solutions*, *9*, 116330–116345.

Association for Talent Development (ATD). (2019). *Measuring the ROI of Learning and Development*. https://www.td.org/research-reports/measuring-the-roi-of-learning-and-development

Association for Talent Development (ATD). (2021). *Measuring the success of virtual training: ROI and beyond*. https://www.td.org/research-reports/measuring-the-success-of-virtual-training-roi-and-beyond

Bashrum, A. (2019). *The importance of training and development in the workplace*. https://www.business.com/articles/importance-of-training-and-development-in-the-workplace/

Bashrum, A. (2019). Aligning Training and Development Strategy with Corporate Strategy: A Study of Small Businesses in Saudi Arabia. *Journal of Applied Research in Higher Education*, *11*(4), 595–607.

Bates, R., & Khasawneh, S. (2019). Return on Investment (ROI) in Education and Training. In M. Khosrow-Pour (Ed.), *Encyclopedia of Information Science and Technology* (4th ed., pp. 4326–4335). IGI Global.

Bodolica, V., & Spraggon, M. (2018). The importance of literature reviews in academic field research. *Journal of Applied Research in Higher Education*, *10*(2), 183–194.

Brown, M., & Lam, A. (2019). Preparing students for the rise of AI and the gig economy. *EDUCAUSE Review*, *54*(3), 12–25.

Bryant, F. B., & Gray, E. K. (2019). *Handbook of positive psychology*. Oxford University Press.

Burrell, D. N. (2019). How hiring baby boomers can assist with the global cybersecurity employee shortage. *International Journal of Hyperconnectivity and the Internet of Things, 3*(2), 1–10. doi:10.4018/IJHIoT.2019070101

Burton, S. L. (2019). Grasping the cyber-world: Artificial intelligence and human capital meet to inform leadership. *International Journal of Economics, Commerce and Management, 7*(12), 707–759.

Burton, S. L. (2020). Augmented reality: Enhancing student engagement and learning. *Journal of Educational Technology Development and Exchange, 13*(1), 1–14.

Chang, D. Y., Park, J. H., & Chai, S. (2021). The effect of technological innovation on organizational performance: The role of absorptive capacity and dynamic capability. *Sustainability, 13*(1), 30. doi:10.3390u13010030

Chen, C.-H., Liang, J.-C., & Chen, W.-F. (2021). The effectiveness of augmented reality on knowledge acquisition and transfer in medical education: A systematic review and meta-analysis. *BMC Medical Education, 21*(1), 171. doi:10.118612909-021-02632-1 PMID:33740973

Chen, C. M., & Chen, C. Y. (2020). Designing an online professional learning program for instructional designers: A case study of interdepartmental collaboration. *The International Review of Research in Open and Distributed Learning, 21*(2), 88–107.

Cheng, L., & Li, Y. (2019). How to measure training effectiveness: A meta-analysis of empirical studies. *Human Resource Management Review, 29*(2), 203–218.

Covey, S. R. (1990). *The 7 Habits of Highly Effective People.* Simon & Schuster.

Dede, C. (2019). The role of emerging technologies in distance education. In R. Reiser & J. Dempsey (Eds.), *Trends and issues in instructional design and technology* (pp. 63–73). Pearson.

Deterding, S., Dixon, D., Khaled, R., & Nacke, L. (2019). From game design elements to gamefulness: defining "gamification". *Proceedings of the 15th International Academic Mindtrek Conference: Envisioning Future Media Environments,* 9-17.

Docebo. (2020). *Personalized learning with artificial intelligence: A new approach to employee training.* https://www.docebo.com/resource/personalized-learning-with-artificial-intelligence/

European Commission. (2021). *Proposal for a Regulation laying down harmonized rules on artificial intelligence (Artificial Intelligence Act) and amending certain Union legislative acts.* https://digital-strategy.ec.europa.eu/en/library/proposal-regulation-laying-down-harmonised-rules-artificial-intelligence-artificial-intelligence

Ferrell, G., & Davis, M. (2019). Higher education institutions and online programs: Understanding the importance of course delivery and student success. *Online Journal of Distance Learning Administration, 22*(2).

Fetaji, B., & Fetaji, M. (2009). The evaluation of e-learning and the cost-benefit analysis of distance learning education. *Journal of Applied Computer Science & Mathematics, 13*(7), 69–73.

Friesen, J. P., & Lowe, K. B. (2020). Team mental model convergence, interdependence, and collaboration: A multi-level investigation. *Journal of Business and Psychology, 35*(5), 611–629.

Gartner. (2019). *The future of employee training and development relies on AI.* https://www.gartner.com/en/documents/3942674/the-future-of-employee-training-and-development-relies

Gartner. (2022). *Gartner top strategic predictions for 2022 and beyond.* https://www.gartner.com/en/documents/4009644/gartner-top-strategic-predictions-for-2022-and-beyond

Geiger, B., & Schaffhauser-Linzatti, M. M. (2020). The influence of team diversity and conflict on team creativity and innovation: A meta-analytic review. *Journal of Business and Psychology, 35*(2), 123–139.

Hamari, J., & Sjöklint, M. (2021). The sharing economy gamified: An analysis of gamification features in peer-to-peer rental services. *Journal of Business Research, 122,* 624–634.

Hassan, R. (2019). Understanding the influence of technology on society. *Journal of Technology and Society, 1*(1), 1–10.

Hu, W., Wang, Y., Ren, Y., & Cui, G. (2022). Designing and implementing a constructionist learning environment: Integrating social constructivism, instructional design principles, and educational technologies. *Journal of Educational Technology Development and Exchange, 15*(1), 1–16. doi:10.18785/jetde.1501.01

International Labor Organization. (2021). *Global survey on AI and the future of work.* https://www.ilo.org/global/topics/future-of-work/publications/global-survey-on-ai/lang--en/index.htm

Jones, P. W., & Smith, T. S. (2021). A guide to writing a literature review. *Journal of Transportation Safety & Security, 13*(1), 28–43.

Jordan, K. (2021). Initial trends in enrolment and dropout of massive open online courses. *Distance Education, 42*(1), 14–28.

Katsinas, S. G. (2019). Understanding the costs and benefits of distance education. In *The Handbook of Distance Education* (pp. 147–166). Routledge.

Kim, H., Kim, M., & Lee, H. (2021). The effects of artificial intelligence on employee performance and organizational performance. *Journal of Business Research, 123,* 583–590. doi:10.1016/j.jbusres.2020.09.014

Kim, S., & Hwang, H. (2022). How transformational leadership facilitates knowledge sharing and innovation: The mediating role of inter-unit collaboration. *Journal of Business Research, 145,* 63–74.

Kirkpatrick, D. L. (1959). Techniques for evaluating training programs. *The Journal of the American Society of Training Directors, 13*(11), 3–9.

Kizilcec, R. F., & Halawa, S. A. (2020). Attrition and achievement gaps in online learning. *Proceedings of the sixth ACM conference on Learning @ Scale,* 215-218.

Kowalski, K., & Kelley, K. (2021). Developing Effective Training Programs. *Harvard Business Review.* https://hbr.org/2021/03/developing-effective-training-programs

Kowalski, R., & Kelley, R. (2021). The Challenge of Training Needs Assessment. *Journal of Management Development, 40*(2), 224–238.

Kowalski, S., & Kelley, M. (2013). Strategic planning for distance education in higher education. *Online Journal of Distance Learning Administration, 16*(4).

Lee, J., & Choi, S. (2020). A systematic review of online learning definitions, concepts, and theories. *Educational Research Review, 30*, 100326. doi:10.1016/j.edurev.2020.100326

Li, C., Yan, X., & Wang, J. (2022). Business unit boundary spanning and knowledge sharing in multinational corporations. *Journal of Knowledge Management, 26*(1), 139–159.

Li, J., & Liang, H. (2022). Employees' attitudes toward AI-powered training: The role of perceived usefulness, ease of use, and resistance to change. *International Journal of Human Resource Management,* •••, 1–24. doi:10.1080/09585192.2022.2021389

Li, Y., Li, H., & Liang, J. (2019). Design and implementation of an online learning platform based on social constructivism. *International Journal of Emerging Technologies in Learning, 14*(16), 4–18. doi:10.3991/ijet.v14i16.11106

Liao, Y., Chen, C., Chen, H., & Chen, G. (2019). The effects of augmented reality on learning outcomes and motivation in a flipped classroom environment. *Journal of Educational Technology & Society, 22*(3), 214–226.

Lievrouw, L. A. (2019). Technology and social change: The role of communication networks. *Journal of Communication, 69*(2), 266–276.

Markets and Markets. (2019). Augmented Reality in Training and Education Market by Component (Hardware and Software), Device Type (AR Headsets, AR Glasses, and AR Cards), and Geography (North America, Europe, APAC, and RoW). *Global Forecast to 2023.* https://www.marketsandmarkets.com/Market-Reports/augmented-reality-training-education-market-222455352.html

Markets and Markets. (2021). *Augmented Reality (AR) market by offering, device type, application, and geography - global forecast to 2025.* https://www.marketsandmarkets.com/Market-Reports/augmented-reality-virtual-reality-market-1185.html

Martin, M. M., & Caruso, C. (2019). *Leading academic change: Essential roles for senior leaders.* Stylus Publishing, LLC.

Mavridis, P., & Giannakos, M. (2020). Using AI-based personalized learning to enhance student engagement and performance. *Journal of Educational Computing Research, 58*(6), 1366–1388. doi:10.1177/0735633120905959

McKinsey & Company. (2019). *How artificial intelligence will impact the future of workforce learning.* https://www.mckinsey.com/business-functions/mckinsey-digital/our-insights/how-artificial-intelligence-will-impact-the-future-of-workforce-learning

McKinsey & Company. (2021). *The impact of AI in the learning organization.* https://www.mckinsey.com/business-functions/mckinsey-digital/our-insights/the-impact-of-ai-in-the-learning-organization

Miller, M. T. (2021). Competency-Based Education and Training: A Review of the Literature. *Journal of Vocational Education Research*, *46*(1), 1–16.

Mishra, S., & Sahoo, C. K. (2020). Impact of training and development on employee performance: Evidence from Indian manufacturing firms. *Journal of Advances in Management Research*, *17*(3), 365–382.

Morrison, G. R., Ross, S. M., & Kemp, J. E. (2013). *Designing effective instruction* (7th ed.). Wiley.

Nguyen, T. (2020). Return on investment (ROI). In K. L. Kreitner & C. Kinicki (Eds.), *Organizational behavior* (13th ed., pp. 654–656). McGraw-Hill Education.

O'Brien, K. (2021). Why higher education must help bridge the AI skills gap. *eCampus News*. https://www.ecampusnews.com/2021/01/26/why-higher-education-must-help-bridge-the-ai-skills-gap/

Pappas, P., Vlachopoulou, M., & Chrissikopoulos, V. (2020). Measuring the impact of IT investments on financial and non-financial performance: A literature review. *Information & Management*, *57*(2), 103168. doi:10.1016/j.im.2019.103168

Phillips, J. J., & Phillips, P. P. (2019). *Measuring the success of employee training: ROI and the value of learning*. Routledge.

Schuurman, D., Croon, M. A., & Hooft, E. A. J. (2021a). The role of strategic alignment in HRD and its contribution to organizational performance. *Human Resource Development Review*, *20*(3), 254–280. doi:10.1177/1534484321990326

Schuurman, D., Mulder, M., Veldkamp, B. P., Van Vianen, A. E., & De Lange, A. H. (2021). Learning climate, employee well-being, and performance: The mediating role of employees' self-regulation of learning. *Journal of Occupational and Organizational Psychology*, *94*(1), 219–239.

Schuurman, D., Van Rijswijk, J., & Plak, P. (2021). The impact of technological changes on the training and development of human capital. *Journal of Organizational Change Management*, *34*(2), 330–345.

Sharma, P., & Srinivasan, S. (2021). Adaptive Learning: Improving Student Performance and Engagement. *Journal of Educational Technology & Society*, *24*(1), 86–98.

Sitzmann, T., Ely, K., & Brown, K. G. (2019). A multilevel review of diversity, conflict, and synergy in teams: Challenges and opportunities for future research. *Annual Review of Organizational Psychology and Organizational Behavior*, *6*, 457–482.

Society for Human Resource Management. (2021a). *Assessing the Skills Gap and Workforce Readiness*. https://www.shrm.org/hr-today/trends-and-forecasting/research-and-surveys/Documents/Assessing-the-Skills-Gap-and-Workforce-Readiness.pdf

Society for Human Resource Management. (2021b). *Technology Skills Gap and Future of Work*. https://www.shrm.org/hr-today/trends-and-forecasting/research-and-surveys/pages/technology-skills-gap-future-of-work.aspx

Sung, S. Y., Cho, Y. J., & Kim, H. (2019). Exploring the Role of Return on Investment (ROI) in Human Resource Development. *Sustainability*, *11*(12), 3324. doi:10.3390u11123324

Temples, A., Simons, D., & Atkinson, M. (2019b). Training and development in the workplace. In R. Burke & C. Cooper (Eds.), *The Oxford Handbook of Training and Development* (pp. 377–394). Oxford University Press.

Temples, A., Simons, D., & Atkinson, M. (2019c). Strategic employee training and development in a changing world. *International Journal of Training and Development*, *23*(1), 1–10.

Temples, C., Simons, R., & Atkinson, L. (2019a). Using a needs assessment model to drive information-driven training for small business owners. *Journal of Workplace Learning*, *31*(5), 315–326. doi:10.1108/JWL-01-2019-0011

Towards Data Science. (2021). *How AI is Transforming Employee Training and Development*. https://towardsdatascience.com/how-ai-is-transforming-employee-training-and-development-4f36c7e55d4e

Training Industry, Inc. (2017). *Measuring the business impact of learning: Key findings from training industry's survey*. https://trainingindustry.com/research/measuring-the-business-impact-of-learning-key-findings-from-training-industrys-survey/

Vázquez, F., Pena, A., Sánchez-González, P., García-Solano, M., & Burgos, D. (2021). Augmented reality in surgical training: A systematic review and meta-analysis. *Surgical Innovation*, *28*(1), 77–88.

Vázquez, J., Arrebola, R., Mirón, F. J., Rojas-Sola, J. I., & Jiménez, M. F. (2021). Augmented reality as a tool for surgical training: A systematic review. *Surgical Endoscopy*, 1–11.

Wang, S., & Guo, X. (2019). Analysis of training program evaluation model based on ROI. In *3rd International Conference on Education and Multimedia Technology (ICEMT)* (pp. 266-270). IEEE.

World Economic Forum. (2020). *The Future of Jobs Report 2020*. https://www.weforum.org/reports/the-future-of-jobs-report-2020

Zarei, J. (2019). Augmented reality in education and training: A literature review. *Journal of Education and Practice*, *10*(22), 136–147.

Zhang, T., Raza, S. A., Ahmad, S., & Afzal, H. (2019). Augmented Reality and Virtual Reality in Education: Concepts, Applications and Trends. *Journal of Educational Technology & Society*, *22*(2), 255–267.

KEY TERMS AND DEFINITIONS

Artificial Intelligence: Artificial intelligence is a rapidly evolving field that involves the development of intelligent machines that can perform tasks that typically require human intelligence. AI is being used in a variety of applications, including natural language processing, computer vision, robotics, and data analysis, and has the potential to revolutionize many industries. However, there are also concerns about the impact of AI on jobs, privacy, and ethics, and it is important for researchers and policymakers to address these issues as AI continues to advance.

Augmented Reality: Augmented reality is a technology that superimposes digital information onto the physical world, enhancing the user's perception of reality. It can be used in various industries, such as gaming, education, and healthcare, to create immersive and interactive experiences.

Cost of Investment: Cost of investment refers to the total expenses incurred in acquiring and holding an asset or investment. It includes the purchase price, transaction fees, taxes, and other related expenses.

Education and Training: Education and training are essential for personal and professional growth, as they provide knowledge, skills, and experience needed to succeed in various fields. They also promote critical thinking, problem-solving, and creativity, which are important for innovation and progress. Moreover, education and training can enhance social mobility, reduce poverty, and foster economic development by preparing individuals for high-demand jobs and creating a skilled workforce. Additionally, lifelong learning is crucial in today's rapidly changing world, where new technologies and industries emerge constantly, requiring individuals to continuously update their knowledge and skills to stay relevant. Overall, education and training are key factors in improving individuals' lives and contributing to the progress and prosperity of societies.

Online Learning: Online learning refers to a mode of education where students use digital technology to access educational materials and interact with instructors and peers remotely. Online learning can take many forms, including video conferencing, webinars, online courses, and virtual classrooms. It offers a flexible and convenient way for people to acquire new knowledge and skills without the constraints of time and location. However, it also requires self-discipline and motivation on the part of the learner, as well as reliable internet access and digital literacy.

Return-on-Investment: Return-on-investment (ROI) is a financial metric used to evaluate the profitability of an investment relative to its cost over a specified period. It is calculated by dividing the net profit of an investment by the cost of the investment, and is often expressed as a percentage. ROI is a key factor in business decision-making and is used to assess the potential benefits and risks of different investment options.

Technological Advancement: Technological advancement is a continuous process of innovation, improvement, and integration of new tools, techniques, and systems to enhance efficiency, productivity, and convenience in various fields. It has revolutionized the way we live, work, and communicate, and has opened up new frontiers for exploration and discovery. However, it also poses significant challenges such as ethical dilemmas, job displacement, and information overload, which require thoughtful consideration and proactive solutions. Overall, technological advancement has the potential to bring tremendous benefits and positive changes to society, but it requires responsible and sustainable development to ensure a bright and equitable future for all.

Chapter 20
Exploring Sexual Harassment and Organizational Development in the Restaurant Industry

Amalisha Sabie Aridi
https://orcid.org/0000-0002-7869-5530
Capitol Technology University, USA

ABSTRACT

The Apex Restaurant Group recently went public with several allegations of sexual misconduct against the founder and other executives. The result of the allegations includes a class action complaint lodged by 25 women working within the organization. The whole senior leadership, which was all men, has been replaced by a management team of all women. An organizational development management consultant has been brought in to investigate and recommend viable solutions. This chapter explores the utility of intervention action research to find real-world solutions through the deployment of a consultant.

INTRODUCTION

Sexual harassment is a pervasive issue in the restaurant industry and is often overlooked due to its informal and unique work environment. This paper examines the prevalence and impact of sexual harassment in the restaurant industry, the effectiveness of current strategies to address sexual harassment, and the importance of implementing preventative measures to eliminate sexual harassment in the workplace. The restaurant industry is an important sector of the economy and employs diverse workers, including those from low-income backgrounds, immigrants, and women (Bureau of Labor Statistics, 2020). Unfortunately, the restaurant industry has a long history of sexual harassment, which can significantly impact restaurant workers' physical, mental, and economic well-being (Gorman, 2018). Although sexual harassment in the restaurant industry is well-documented, it is often overlooked due to its informal and unique workplace environment (Gorman, 2018).

DOI: 10.4018/979-8-3693-1630-6.ch020

The impact of sexual harassment in the restaurant industry is significant and can have far-reaching consequences for workers. Research has found that sexual harassment can lead to adverse mental health outcomes, including depression, anxiety, and post-traumatic stress disorder (Feeley, 2019). Additionally, sexual harassment can lead to decreased job satisfaction, increased job turnover, and decreased productivity (Feeley, 2019). Furthermore, sexual harassment in the restaurant industry can have economic repercussions, as victims may lose wages and benefits due to decreased productivity or job turnover (Feeley, 2019).

Recent developments in the #MeToo movement have shown how far-reaching the effects can be. The #MeToo movement has resulted in the resignations of multiple corporate executives, severe damage to workplace morale, and the erosion of positive workplace cultures (Noguchi, 2018). Organizational culture is "a system of shared meaning held by members that distinguish the organization from other organizations" (Robbins & Judge, 2017, p. 266). A positive workplace culture consists of a workplace that focuses on building upon the strengths of the individual employees and fosters growth and synergy (Robbins & Judge, 2017, p. 279). Sexual harassment in the workplace, especially when unaddressed, attacks the foundation of a positive organizational culture.

Sexual harassment allegations against the founding owner have primarily shaken the Apex Restaurant Group. Twenty-five female employees have accused the restaurant owner of belittling, fondling, and propositioning them in a tormenting workplace environment, and as a result, a management consulting intervention is taking place to attempt to change the organizational culture. The pre-intervention organizational culture was so centered around the acceptance of sexual harassment that if any employees made complaints about unwanted behavior, they were ignored, berated, or subject to retaliation (Anderson, 2017). Since the allegations became public, Apex has been replaced as Chief Executive Officer (CEO) by the former Chief Operations Officer (COO). New management immediately realized they needed consulting help to transform the corporate culture and cultivate an environment built on trust, respect, and communication. Trust and respect are essential elements of a healthy organizational culture (Robbins & Judge, 2017, p. 281). Effective organizations "are characterized by mutual trust, honesty, and openness" (Robbins & Judge, 2017, p. 281). White acknowledges that she needs to investigate claims, counsel staff, improve morale, and weed out employees resistant to cultural changes (Noguchi, 2018). However, improving corporate culture is not the only change that needs to be made. The Apex Restaurant Group needs to implement an organization-wide program that addresses and prevents sexual harassment. Before such a program can be developed, sexual harassment issues, laws, and regulations need to be examined.

Problem Statement

Prevalence and Impact of Sexual Harassment in the Restaurant Industry Sexual harassment is a pervasive issue in the restaurant industry, with most restaurant workers citing that they have experienced some form of sexual harassment (Gorman, 2018). Research has found that sexual harassment is particularly prevalent among female restaurant workers, with nearly 80% of female restaurant workers reporting that they have been subjected to sexual harassment in the workplace (Gorman, 2018). Furthermore, research has shown that sexual harassment in the restaurant industry is not limited to female workers, as male restaurant workers have also reported experiencing sexual harassment in their workplace (Gorman, 2018). This paper explores sexual harassment in the Apex Restaurant Group through intervention activities from a management consulting group.

Method

The method in this paper is intervention action research. The Apex Restaurant Group recently went public with several allegations of sexual misconduct against the founder and other executives. The result of the allegations includes a class action complaint lodged by 25 women working within the organization. The whole senior leadership, which was all men, has been replaced by a management team of all women. An organizational development management consultant has been brought to investigate and recommend viable solutions.

Intervention action research (IAR) is a methodical investigation strategy that analyzes real-world problems, establishes evidence, applies theories, collects data, presents verifiable results, and develops viable solutions (Ackermann & Eden, 2015). Consultants in management and organizational development use this practice (Ackermann & Eden, 2015). The capacity to combine practical and theoretical frameworks to analyze complex organizations in real-time shows this research method's value, importance, and worth (Ackermann & Eden, 2015). IAR helps organizations find and fix issues to increase performance (Ackermann & Eden, 2015). IAR involves the researcher working with the organization's stakeholders to identify areas for improvement and propose solutions (Ackermann & Eden, 2015). Data collection, analysis, problem identification, intervention planning, and implementation are all part of IAR (Ackermann & Eden, 2015). Organizations benefit from IAR (Coghlan & Brannick, 2014). First, IAR is a practical technique that helps organizations swiftly identify issues and create solutions (Ackermann & Eden, 2015). It is cheap and does not demand long-term commitments (Ackermann & Eden, 2015). Second, IAR engages stakeholders in problem identification and plan creation (Ackermann & Eden, 2015). This improves problem comprehension and solutions. Third, IAR is adaptable to many organizational contexts and scenarios (Ackermann & Eden, 2015). IAR can also assist organizations in creating new strategies and transformation (Ackermann & Eden, 2015).

SYSTEMS THEORY

The systems theory is a theoretical framework used to understand, analyze, and explain the behavior of complex systems (Heller, 2009). This approach focuses on the relationships between the parts and the whole of the system and how these relationships interact to create a behavior system more significant than the sum of its parts (Heller, 2009). By understanding the behaviors and dynamics of a system, a consultant can develop strategies to engage and support the system to create a more effective outcome.

Organizational systems theory is an ideal tool for organizational development consultants to use when addressing sexual harassment in the workplace. This approach focuses on understanding the dynamics of the organization and how the behaviors of the individuals and the system interact to create a more extensive system of behavior (Rosenfeld, 2011). By understanding the relationship between individual behaviors and the organizational culture, a consultant can create strategies to engage the organization in a productive discussion about sexual harassment and create a safe space to address the issue.

Engaging an Organization with Significant Sexual Harassment Problems When engaging an organization with significant sexual harassment issues, a consultant must consider the dynamics of the system and how they interact to create a more extensive system of behavior. The consultant should assess the organizational culture and the behaviors of the individuals within the organization and create an atmosphere of trust and safety. The consultant should also consider the power dynamics that may be present and create an environment of respect and understanding.

The consultant should also seek to understand the root causes of sexual harassment and develop strategies to address the issue. These strategies should focus on creating an organizational culture of respect and understanding and addressing the behaviors and dynamics contributing to the harassment. The consultant should also create channels for communication so that individuals can speak out about their experiences and have a platform to express their feelings and concerns.

SEXUAL HARASSMENT

Defining Sexual Harassment

Workplace sexual harassment is a complex problem involving multiple personal, corporate, cultural, and legal factors. Much thought and debate have gone into the simple act of defining sexual harassment. The textbook definition describes sexual harassment as "any unwanted activity of a sexual nature that affects an individual's employment or creates a hostile work environment" (Robbins & Judge, 2017, p. 215). Sexual harassment was initially defined in 1975 by Lin Farley as any repeated and unwanted sexual contact, remarks, or suggestions that are offensive and cause workplace discomfort (Hemel & Lund, 2018, p. 1594). The Equal Employment Opportunity Commission (EEOC) and federal courts have contended that sexual harassment includes any harassment based on sexual orientation (Hemel & Lund, 2018, p. 1596). It is generally accepted today that offensive behavior should not be repeated to be considered harassment (Hemel & Lund, 2018. P. 1596). Sexual harassment has been divided into two types: quid pro quo sexual harassment and hostile work environment (Crucet, Graells, Cabral, & Lane, 2010, p. 16). Quid pro quo sexual harassment involves harassment cases in which sexual activity is requested in exchange for employment incentives and opportunities (Hemel & Lund, 2018, p. 1596). According to Apodaca and Kleiner (2001):

A legal definition of [a hostile working environment] is {a} speech and/or conduct, {b}of a sexually discriminatory nature, {c} which was neither welcomed nor encouraged, {d} committed by or permitted by a supervisor, {e} which would be so offensive to a reasonable person as to {f} create an abusive working environment and/or {g} impair his/her job performance. (p. 5)

Per Lee and Greenlaw (1995), hostile work environment sexual harassment does not only include sexually charged behavior. The environment can be adversely impacted by inappropriate behavior targeting a specific gender without reference to sexual behavior (p. 359). To demonstrate the presence of a hostile work environment, it must be shown that the behavior involved was particularly severe or prevalent (Lee & Greenlaw, 1995, p. 360). Due to the spectrum of human behavior possibilities, developing specific guidelines for identifying a hostile work environment is practically impossible (Lee & Greenlaw, 1995, p. 360). The EEOC has a policy of addressing hostile work environment issues case-by-case (Lee & Greenlaw, 1995, p. 360). The EEOC has also stated the importance of looking into every facet of each situation (Lee & Greenlaw, 1995, p. 360).

Similarly, the Supreme Court has held that a hostile work environment can only be established after examining all instances of sexual harassment within an organization (Lee & Greenlaw, 1995, p. 360).

The EEOC guidelines state that questionable conduct will be evaluated using the reasonable person standard of what is considered socially acceptable (Lee & Greenlaw, 1995, p. 360). One issue with this standard is that each organization has a different measurement threshold for what is acceptable within its culture (Lee & Greenlaw, 1995, p. 360). Furthermore, what is reasonable to men differs from what women consider reasonable (Lee & Greenlaw, 1995, p. 360).

Sexual Harassment Issues

Sexual harassment in the workplace is not a new problem, but it does not appear to be going away. A study conducted in 1976 stated that 90 percent of women indicated they had been the victim of some form of sexual harassment at some point in their work experience (Martell & Sullivan, 1994, p. 5). As more women enter the workplace and ascend the corporate ladder, the potential for sexual harassment grows (Martell & Sullivan, 1994, p. 5). "Society expects employers to protect their workers on the job, including their physical, emotional, and economic well-being" (Martell & Sullivan, 1994, p. 5). Sexual harassment continues to be a problem, partly because no comprehensive test is available to establish that harassment has occurred quickly (Martel & Sullivan, 1994, p. 5). As the circumstances of sexual harassment involve many variables, it is essential to note that victims and perpetrators do not have to be of the opposite sex, harassers may not be in a position of power, and there may be victims other than the one harassed (Apodaca & Kleiner, 2001, p. 4).

Costs and Consequences

Whether realized or not, all workplace sexual harassment has costs and consequences for the victims, the perpetrators, the organizations, and society. It is estimated that for each employee that experiences sexual harassment, the organization loses approximately $22,500 in productivity (Hart, Crossley, & Correll, 2018, p. 1). Furthermore, sexual harassment leads to high turnover rates, low morale, and poor individual performance or attendance (Martell & Sullivan, 1994, p. 5). Sexual harassment has been identified as a cause of various adverse employee outcomes, including increased work-related stress, decreased engagement, and diminished job satisfaction (Madera, Guchait, and Dawson, 2018, p. 1211). Job satisfaction, a positive view of one's job and the organization in which one works, is a crucial element of a positive work environment and helps to increase job involvement, identification, and dedication (Robbins & Judge, 2017, p. 37). Similarly, employee engagement refers to an individual's enthusiasm for their work (Robbins & Judge, 2017, p. 38). On an individual level, victims can suffer significant harm to their careers, economic stability, and mental health (Lee & Greenlaw, 1995, p. 357).

THE WORKPLACE PSYCHOLOGICAL CONTRACT

The psychological contract, defined by Rousseau (1995) as "the unwritten expectations and understandings that shape the mutual obligations between an employer and employee" (p. 5), is an essential concept in the study of workplace dynamics. It is based on the idea that employers and employees have an unwritten agreement in which they each have certain expectations of the other. This agreement is based on trust, respect, and communication, and it affects the way that employees interact with each other and with their employer (Rousseau, 1995)

Sexual harassment in the workplace has a significant impact on the psychological contract between employer and employee (Smith, 1998). When an employee is sexually harassed, they feel a sense of betrayal, as they have been subjected to unwanted and inappropriate behavior from someone they believed they could trust (Smith, 1998). This feeling of betrayal can lead to reduced job satisfaction, commitment, and productivity (Smith, 1998). Furthermore, it can decrease communication and trust between employer and employee (Smith, 1998).

The effects of sexual harassment on the psychological contract can be seen in the work of Smith (1998), who found that employees who experienced sexual harassment felt an increased sense of alienation from their employer. They felt that their employer was not protecting them from the harassment and thus did not trust them or respect them. This feeling of alienation can harm the psychological contract, leading to decreased job satisfaction, commitment, and productivity (Smith, 1998).

The implications of sexual harassment on the psychological contract are significant for both employers and employees. For employers, it can lead to decreased job satisfaction and productivity and increased turnover, absenteeism, and legal costs (Smith, 1998). For employees, it can lead to decreased job satisfaction, commitment, and alienation from their employer(Smith, 1998).

LAWS AND REGULATIONS

Title VII

The foundation of laws and regulations about sexual harassment stems from discrimination laws. According to Hemel and Lund 2018:

The primary legal mechanism for regulating and remedying sexual harassment in the workplace is Title VII of the Civil Rights Act of 1964. The statute provides that "it shall be an unlawful employment practice for an employer . . . to discriminate against any individual concerning his compensation, terms, conditions, or privileges of employment, because of such individual's race, color, religion, sex, or national origin. (p. 1597)

The legal framework for sexual harassment in the workplace is essential in the fight against sexual harassment. In the United States, Title VII of the Civil Rights Act of 1964 and the Americans with Disabilities Act are two primary federal laws prohibiting workplace sexual harassment (Equal Employment Opportunity Commission, 2021). State and local laws may also provide additional protections for employees, so employers must be aware of these laws and ensure they are compliant.

EEOC

Title VII of the Civil Rights Act of 1964 is responsible for creating the EEOC and tasking it with the promulgation and enforcement of regulations related to civil rights law (Hemel & Lund, 2018, p. 1597). The EEOC has developed specific processes for complaints of sexual harassment (Hemel & Lund, 2018, p. 1597). As outlined by Hemel and Lund (2018):

If the EEOC finds in favor of the employee, it first seeks to settle the charge with the employer, and if that fails, the commission can sue the employer in federal court. If the commission decides not to file a lawsuit, it will issue a "right-to-sue" letter indicating that the employee has 90 days from receipt of the letter to bring a lawsuit to federal court. Alternatively, if the EEOC makes a "no probable cause" determination or dismisses the charge due to procedural irregularities, it will also send the employee a "dismissal and notice of rights" that informs the employee of his or her right to sue within 90 days. (pp. 1597 – 1598)

In 1980, the EEOC developed guidelines that officially classified sexual harassment as a form of sex discrimination (Hemel & Lund, 2018, p. 1599). These guidelines acknowledged the existence and classification of both quid pro quo sexual harassment and hostile work environment and deemed them unlawful employment practices under Title VII (Hemel & Lund, 2018, p. 1599).

Corporate Law

Corporate executives in charge of a company's operations act as corporate fiduciaries and are tasked with controlling the company's operations on behalf of the company's owners, the shareholders (Hemel & Lund, 2018, p. 1628). Corporate law exists to protect shareholders by holding corporate officers to their fiduciary duties of loyalty and care (Hemel & Lund, 2018, p. 1628). The duty of care requires corporate executives to engage in informed decision-making and steward the organization's resources (Hemel & Lund, 2018, p. 1628). Similarly, loyalty requires fiduciaries to act in good faith in the interest of shareholders and the organization (Hemel & Lund, 2018, p. 1629). If these fiduciary responsibilities are dishonored, shareholders may join and sue the organization (Hemel & Lund, 2018, p. 1628).

HUMAN RELATIONS THEORY

Human relations theory is a framework that seeks to explain how people interact with one another in the workplace (Saari & Judge, 2004). The theory emphasizes the importance of relationships between individuals in the workplace and how these relationships can influence motivation, job satisfaction, and performance. Additionally, human relations theory focuses on how individuals interact to foster healthy and productive relationships.

One way in which human relations theory can explain sexual harassment is through the concept of power and status. According to human relations theory, those with higher power and status have more influence over those with lower levels of power and status (Saari & Judge, 2004). This power dynamic can lead to situations where those with higher power and status attempt to take advantage of those with lower power and status, such as through sexual harassment. Additionally, studies have demonstrated that those in positions of power often have a greater willingness to engage in unethical behavior or take advantage of their subordinates (Berdahl & Moon, 2019).

Sexual harassment can significantly impact employees and organizations (Glomb & Richman, 2019). For employees, sexual harassment can lead to decreased job satisfaction and motivation and physical and psychological harm (Berdahl & Moon, 2019). For organizations, sexual harassment can lead to decreased productivity and increased employee turnover (Glomb & Richman, 2019).

Human relations theory can also be used to reduce or eliminate sexual harassment in the workplace. This can be done through policies that discourage using power and status to take advantage of others (Berdahl & Moon, 2019). Additionally, organizations can create a culture of respect and inclusivity that encourages employees to speak up when they feel their rights are violated (Glomb & Richman, 2019). Furthermore, organizations can implement training programs that teach employees about the effects of sexual harassment and how to prevent it (Berdahl & Moon, 2019).

O.D. Practices, and Approaches

Organizational Development (O.D.) is a multi-disciplinary approach to improving an organization's performance, effectiveness, and competitive advantage through planned interventions in the organization's processes and culture (Sawyer, 2017). O.D. interventions can be used to address a variety of workplace issues, including those related to sexual harassment. Research has identified several O.D. practices and approaches that can be used to address workplace culture issues such as sexual harassment.

One of the most effective O.D. approaches is organizational development consulting (ODC). ODC involves using an external consultant to help an organization identify and address issues related to workplace culture, such as sexual harassment. ODC can help an organization understand the underlying causes of sexual harassment and create a more respectful and inclusive workplace culture (Hosmer & Morin, 2018).

In addition, O.D. interventions can be used to create a more transparent and accountable workplace. Organizations can use O.D. interventions to develop and implement policies and procedures that clearly define expectations for workplace behavior and provide clear consequences for violations (Lewis, 2018). This can help an organization create a safe workplace culture for all employees and reduce the risk of sexual harassment.

Organizational Development interventions can also create a more diverse and inclusive workplace. Organizations can use O.D. interventions to create a workplace culture that respects all individuals and cultures and provides equal opportunities for all employees (Bennett et al., 2019). This can help to reduce the risk of sexual harassment by creating an environment where all individuals are respected and valued.

Finally, O.D. interventions can create an effective communication and feedback system. Organizations can use O.D. interventions to develop and implement effective communication systems and feedback processes that allow employees to openly discuss workplace issues, including those related to sexual harassment (Jameson et al., 2016). This can help an organization create a workplace culture that is safe, respectful, and supportive for all employees.

Sexual harassment creates a hostile workplace culture that must be addressed proactively to create a safe and respectful workplace for all employees. Organizational Development (O.D.) interventions can be used to effectively address this problem and create a workplace culture where sexual harassment and a hostile work environment are not tolerated.

Organizational culture is a crucial factor in the success of any organization. The workplace environment, the attitudes, beliefs, and behaviors of employees, and the norms and values that guide the organization's actions all contribute to the culture of an organization (Mishra & Mishra, 2011). When a toxic workplace culture exists, it can be damaging to organizational performance, morale, and productivity.

The first step an organizational development consultant would take when evaluating the organizational culture and recommending solutions is to identify the underlying causes of the toxic workplace culture (Mishra & Mishra, 2011). Several factors could contribute to the toxic culture, such as poor leadership, ineffective communication, a lack of trust, and clear organizational goals (Mishra & Mishra, 2011). Once the consultant has identified the underlying causes of the toxic culture, the consultant can then recommend strategies to address the root causes.

The second step an organizational development consultant would take when evaluating the organizational culture and recommending solutions is to engage employees in the process. Employee engagement is vital to successful organizational change (Mishra & Mishra, 2011). Employees must be involved in diagnosing the problem, developing solutions, and implementing changes to ensure they are invested in the process and the outcome (Mishra & Mishra, 2011). This can be done through surveys, focus groups, interviews, and other methods that allow employees to provide feedback and be part of the process (Mishra & Mishra, 2011).

The third step an organizational development consultant would take when evaluating the organizational culture and recommending solutions is to recommend specific strategies to improve the organizational culture. These strategies may include improving the organization's communication systems, developing and implementing a clear mission and vision, increasing employee trust and collaboration, and improving the organization's leadership (Mishra & Mishra, 2011). Additionally, the consultant may recommend strategies to improve employee engagement, such as providing employees with opportunities for professional development and career advancement, recognizing and rewarding employees for their contributions, and providing employees with tools and resources to help them succeed in their roles (Mishra & Mishra, 2011).

EMPLOYER ISSUES

Employer Responsibilities

As has been demonstrated above, sexual harassment can have vast implications that include negative publicity, production losses, and legal liability (Broadwater, 2006, p. 36). The 1980 EEOC guidelines show that employers are responsible for the actions of their agents and management employees (Lee & Greenlaw, 1995, p. 362). Furthermore, employers may be responsible for sexual harassment between nonemployees and non-management personnel (Lee & Greenlaw, 1995, p. 362). Employers can be legally liable for sexual harassment perpetrated by a supervisor if it involves employment activities such as quid pro-quo-related termination (Broadwater, 2006, p. 36). If not, the employer may avoid liability by demonstrating a reasonable amount of due care (Broadwater, 2006, p. 36).

Employer Actions

The best way to combat workplace sexual harassment is to attempt to prevent occurrences and have a system in place to address issues if they do occur. The best programs include a written policy, employee screening, orientation, a secure work environment, swift investigation, enforcement, and encouragement (Kleiner, 2012, p. 13).

Policy. Organizations must develop and publish a written sexual harassment policy (Kleiner, 2012, p. 13). The policy should clearly outline what is considered sexual harassment and express that it will not be tolerated (Kleiner, 2012, p. 13). It should include detailed procedures for confidential reporting and investigated claims (Kleiner, 2012, p. 13).

Employee screening. The Human Resources department should be well-trained in the hiring process and be able to check potential employees' backgrounds. Before hiring an employee, they should be screened to ensure there is no record of sexual harassment in the past (Kleiner, 2012, p. 13).

Orientation. New hire orientation is a chance to outline all regulations, procedures, processes, and expectations for incoming employees. New employees should be guided through the employee handbook, and the sexual harassment policy should be stressed (Kleiner, 2012, p. 13).

Secure Environment. Establishing a secure work environment (Kleiner, 2012, p. 13). Employees should feel completely secure and free to file a complaint of sexual harassment with the full support of the organization and no chance of retribution or retaliation (Kleiner, 2012, p. 13).

Investigations. It should be clear to all employees that every sexual harassment claim will be investigated thoroughly and swiftly (Kleiner, 2012, p. 13). "Once a conclusion has been reached, take corrective action" (Kleiner, 2012, p. 13). The punishment should be severe enough to signal that such behavior will not be tolerated (Kleiner, 2012, p. 13).

Enforcement. To enforce the sexual harassment policy, organizations can have regular meetings with employees to review the policy (Kleiner, 2012, p. 13). Employees should be required to sign a document stating that they have read and fully understand the policy (Kleiner, 2012, p. 13). "Everyone needs to be aware that sexual harassment is disrespectful, hurtful, and illegal" (Kleiner, 2012, p. 13).

Encouragement. Employees should be encouraged to report any occurrences of sexual harassment in the workplace (Kleiner, 2012, p. 13). If instances are not reported, management will not know there is a problem (Kleiner, 2012, p. 13).

SUGGESTIONS AND CONCLUSIONS

Unfortunately, the problem the Apex Restaurant Group is facing is not uncommon. Many companies face workplace cultures that foster improper behavior. The Apex Restaurant Group problems highlight that behavior and organizational culture are informed from the top down. As a result, the organizational development management consultant recommends the following practical solutions.

Prevention Strategies

A key to addressing sexual harassment in the workplace is prevention. Employers should adopt comprehensive prevention strategies to create a safe and respectful work environment. These strategies should include, but not be limited to, the following:

- Develop and enforce policies, procedures, and codes of conduct that prohibit sexual harassment and discrimination in the workplace.
- Provide clear procedures for reporting and responding to complaints of sexual harassment.
- Educate employees on acceptable workplace behavior and the consequences of sexual harassment.
- Monitor the workplace to ensure employees adhere to policies and procedures.
- Provide resources for victims of sexual harassment and other forms of discrimination.

Training and Education

Training and education are essential in preventing and addressing sexual harassment in the workplace. Employers should provide regular training to all employees on the definition of sexual harassment, appropriate workplace conduct, and their rights and responsibilities under the law. This training should be comprehensive, interactive, and tailored to the organization's needs. Additionally, employers should create opportunities for open, honest discussion and dialogue between employees and supervisors to ensure that all employees are comfortable voicing concerns and reporting any incidents of sexual harassment.

Consequences

Employers must have clear and consistent consequences for those who violate workplace policies and procedures regarding sexual harassment. Employers should ensure that all employees know the potential consequences of engaging in sexual harassment or other forms of discrimination and that any disciplinary action taken is consistent and fair.

REFERENCES

Ackermann, F., & Eden, C. (2015). Intervention action research: A method for studying and transforming practice. *Journal of Management Development*, *34*(1), 4–17.

Anderson, B. (2017, October 21). *John Besh restaurants fostered a culture of sexual harassment, 25 women say*. Retrieved from https://www.nola.com/business/2017/10/john_besh_restaurants_fostered.html

Apodaca, E., & Kleiner, B. H. (2001). Sexual harassment in the business environment. *The International Journal of Sociology and Social Policy*, *21*(8-10), 3–13. doi:10.1108/01443330110789763

Bennett, R. M., van der Vorst, Y., van den Bergh, J., & van den Berg, P. (2019). The effect of diversity management on sexual harassment: A meta-analysis. *Human Resource Management Review*, *29*(2), 233–249.

Berdahl, J., & Moon, S. (2019). The power of power: A meta-analysis of the effects of power on sexual harassment. *Psychological Bulletin*, *145*(2), 251–286.

Broadwater, H. J. (2006). Preventing workplace sexual harassment. *Rural Telecommunications, 25*(5), 34-36, 38. Retrieved from https://search.proquest.com/docview/202695333?accountid=10378

Bureau of Labor Statistics. (2020). *Restaurants and Food Services*. Retrieved from https://www.bls.gov/ooh/food-preparation-and-serving/restaurants-and-other-food-services.htm

Crucet, C., Graells, J., Cabral, S., & Lane, S. (2010). Sexual harassment in the workplace. *Academy of Legal, Ethical and Regulatory Issues, 14*(1), 16-20. Retrieved from https://search.proquest.com/docview/521205959?accountid=10378

Equal Employment Opportunity Commission. (2021). *Title VII of the Civil Rights Act of 1964*. Retrieved from https://www.eeoc.gov/laws/statutes/titlevii.cfm

Feeley, T. H. (2019). Defining Sexual Harassment in the Restaurant Industry. *Journal of Culinary Science & Technology, 17*(1), 1–20.

Glomb, T., & Richman, W. (2019). The effect of sexual harassment on employee outcomes: A meta-analysis. *The Journal of Applied Psychology, 104*(6), 858–879.

Gorman, E. (2018). Sexual Harassment in the Restaurant Industry. *Harvard Business Review*. Retrieved from https://hbr.org/2018/11/sexual-harassment-in-the-restaurant-industry

Hart, C., Crossley, A. D., & Correll, S. (2018). Study: When leaders take sexual harassment seriously, so do employees. *Harvard Business Review Digital Articles,* 1–5. Retrieved from https://hbr.org/2018/12/study-when-leaders-take-sexual-harassment-seriously-so-do-employees

Heller, M. (2009). *Systems theory: An introduction.* Sage.

Hemel, D., & Lund, D. S. (2018). Sexual harassment and corporate law. *Columbia Law Review, 118*(6), 1583–1680. https://search.ebscohost.com/login.aspx?direct=true&AuthType=shib&db=buh&AN=132610149&site=ehost-live&custid=s8501869

Hosmer, D. T., & Morin, J. (2018). *Organizational development consulting: A guide to internal and external consulting.* Sage.

Jameson, J. J., Thornton, G. C., & Byars-Winston, A. (2016). The role of organizational development in improving communication and feedback. *Human Resource Development Quarterly, 27*(4), 377–396.

Kleiner, K. (2012). What you need to know about sexual harassment: Understanding sexual harassment is crucial to assure a productive workplace and avoid lawsuits. *Nonprofit World, 30,* 12–13. Retrieved from https://search.proquest.com/docview/1115474277?accountid=10378

Lane, S. (2019). *1 in 4 U.S. women report workplace sexual harassment, study finds.* Retrieved from https://www.cnn.com/2019/01/17/health/workplace-sexual-harassment-study-bn/index.html

Lee, R. D., & Greenlaw, P. S. (1995). The legal evolution of sexual harassment. *Public Administration Review, 55*(4), 34–36, 33578. doi:10.2307/977127

Lewis, R. (2018). The role of organizational development in developing and implementing policies and procedures. *Human Resource Development International, 21*(2), 191–203.

Madera, J. M., Guchait, P., & Dawson, M. (2018). Managers' reactions to customer vs. coworker sexual harassment. *International Journal of Contemporary Hospitality Management, 30*(2), 1211–1227. doi:10.1108/IJCHM-02-2017-0081

Martell, K., & Sullivan, G. (1994). Strategies for managers to recognize and remedy sexual harassment. *Industrial Management (Des Plaines), 36*(3), 5. https://search.proquest.com/docview/211593867?accountid=10378

McCabe, M. P., & Hardman, L. (2005). Attitudes and perceptions of workers to sexual harassment. *The Journal of Social Psychology, 145*(6), 719–740. doi:10.3200/SOCP.145.6.719-740 PMID:16334516

Mishra, P., & Mishra, R. (2011). *Strategic organizational development: Practices and processes.* Sage Publications.

Noguchi, Y. (2018, November 20). *Work after #MeToo: A restaurant company tries to change its culture.* Retrieved from https://www.npr.org/sections/thesalt/2018/11/20/668211164/work-after-metoo-a-restaurant-company-tries-to-change-its-culture

Robbins, S. P., & Judge, T. A. (2017). *Essentials of Organizational Behavior: Student value edition. Place of publication not identified.* Prentice Hall.

Rosenfeld, P. (2011). Organizational systems theory: A framework for organizational development. *Consulting Psychology Journal, 63*(4), 289–301. doi:10.1037/a0023512

Rousseau, D. M. (1995). *Psychological contracts in organizations: Understanding written and unwritten agreements.* Sage. doi:10.4135/9781452231594

Saari, L., & Judge, T. (2004). Employee attitudes and job satisfaction. *Human Resource Management, 43*(4), 395–407. doi:10.1002/hrm.20032

Sawyer, J. E. (2017). *Organizational development: A process of learning and changing.* Jossey-Bass.

Smith, P. C. (1998). Sexual harassment and the psychological contract: Implications for organizational behavior. *Academy of Management Journal, 41*(4), 403–416.

Chapter 21
Identifying Reputable and Non-Reputable Journal Articles Using Machine Learning

Jennifer Ferreras-Perez

iD https://orcid.org/0009-0003-0972-1824

Marymount University, USA

Philip Shen

iD https://orcid.org/0000-0002-6308-2248

Marymount University, USA

Jesus Alberto Galvan

Universidad Autonoma de Nuevo Leon, Mexico

ABSTRACT

The presence of non-reputable journals and low-quality research publications has imposed the development of a machine learning-based system to facilitate the swift and accurate identification of reputable sources. Using Python libraries, such as Pandas and Scikit-learn, this research analyzed data from the Kaggle database collection to create a supervised learning model. The logistic regression classification algorithm was implemented as the basis of this model, while performance metrics were calculated using accuracy, precision, recall, and F1-scores. The results of this study demonstrate an accuracy of 0.9600 for the training data, an accuracy of 0.9433 for the testing data, and a k-5 score accuracy of 0.94. These findings indicate the effectiveness and reliability of the proposed system in recognizing reputable and non-reputable journals. By streamlining the literature review process, this machine learning-based approach can significantly improve students' ability to identify high-quality sources for their academic endeavors.

DOI: 10.4018/979-8-3693-1630-6.ch021

I. INTRODUCTION

Selecting reputable journal articles for dissertation writing can be time-consuming and challenging for student researchers. With the proliferation of journals available in various domains, it can be difficult to identify and sort through peer-reviewed and reputable journals that publish high-quality research papers (Jinha, 2010; Kovanis et al., 2016; Lu et al., 2022). Furthermore, non-reputable journals may publish low-quality or even fake research papers, which can diminish the researcher's credibility and disqualify the current research adding an extra layer of complexity for researchers (Alsheikh-Ali et al., 2011; Butler, 2013). Therefore, there is a need to develop a machine learning-based system that can assist student researchers in identifying reputable and non-reputable journals quickly and accurately.

Several studies have proposed different approaches for detecting non-reputable journals. For example, Beall's list of predatory journals was a popular resource for identifying non-reputable journals until it was discontinued in 2017 (Beall, 2017). Despite such resources' availability, manually sorting through journals remains a significant challenge for researchers. Machine learning algorithms offer a potential solution to this problem by automating sorting through journals and classifying them as reputable or non-reputable (Ben Jabeur et al., 2023; Hao & Ho, 2019).

This research proposes a machine learning-based system for assisting student researchers in identifying reputable and non-reputable journals for dissertation writing. By applying a supervised learning approach to a dataset of journal articles, the proposed system will classify articles as reputable or non-reputable. The system will use several classification algorithms, including logistic regression, to evaluate their performance based on accuracy, precision, recall, and F1-score metrics (Kamei et al., 2021; Rojalin et al., 2022).

II. PROBLEM STATEMENT

In today's rapidly evolving academic landscape, student researchers encounter increasing difficulties in navigating the abundance of publications and identifying high-quality sources for their research projects. In academia, there is a well-known expression, published or perish. This can entice scholars to publish in publications claiming to have peer review but only go through the motions or even no peer review. Many of these publishers are in the business because they can make a lot of money from the fees paid by the author to be included. Thirty-five leading scholars and publishers published a definition of predatory publishing in an article in Nature (Grudniewicz et al., 2019). Many predatory journals make it crucial to develop an innovative, machine learning-driven approach that enables swift and accurate determination of credible sources. This study aims to design an advanced system that harnesses the power of cutting-edge Python libraries, such as Pandas and Scikit-learn, and a unique classification algorithm to streamline the literature review process, ultimately ensuring that academic researchers can reliably differentiate between reputable and non-reputable journals to enhance the quality of their work.

III. SIGNIFICANCE

Developing a machine learning-driven system to identify reputable sources accurately holds immense potential to transform the academic research landscape. By streamlining the literature review process, this novel approach will significantly improve the efficiency of student researchers and other academics, allowing them to focus their time and energy on conducting high-quality research. Furthermore, the proposed system will bolster the integrity and credibility of academic research by reducing the reliance on low-quality or non-reputable sources. By enhancing the overall quality of research outputs, this innovative approach will contribute to advancing knowledge across various domains, facilitating the discovery of new insights and fostering progress in diverse fields of study. Ultimately, the significance of this study lies in its potential to empower academic researchers by providing them with a reliable, time-efficient method for identifying reputable sources and ensuring that their work is grounded in high-quality, trustworthy information.

IV. LITERATURE REVIEW

The literature review process is inherently extensive due to the research, note-taking, and classification procedures it demands. Moreover, determining the quality and reputability of the journals used within this process can significantly impact the validity and credibility of the research. Likewise, the proliferation of journals across various domains poses a challenge in identifying those that publish high-quality research papers (Jinha, 2010; Pyrczak & Tcherni-Buzzeo, 2018). Besides the inherent stress associated with the literature review process, recent years have witnessed increasing concerns surrounding predatory journals. These journals publish articles without proper peer review and are frequently deemed non-reputable, posing a significant challenge for students seeking reputable, high-quality sources for their literature reviews [6]. Scholars have identified various characteristics of predatory journals, including low-quality articles, unsolicited emails soliciting article submissions, and a lack of transparency in the review process [6], [12], [13]. This literature review aims to present an overview of the existing literature on distinguishing between reputable and non-reputable journal articles and explore the application of machine learning algorithms to address this issue.

A. Identifying Reputable and Non-Reputable Journals

Identifying reputable journals is crucial to ensuring researchers access high-quality research papers. Several approaches have been proposed in the literature for identifying reputable and non-reputable journals. One such approach is to consider the journal's impact factor, which measures the average number of citations received by articles published in the journal over a certain period (Ding et al., 2015; Guba & Tsivinskaya, 2023). Journals with high impact factors are considered reputable as they publish high-quality research papers cited frequently by other researchers (Abramo et al., 2017; Jennings, 2006) However, impact factors are domain specific, and some domains may not have high-impact journals. Therefore, researchers may need to consider other metrics, such as h-index or Eigenfactor score, for differentiation purposes (Guba & Tsivinskaya, 2023).

An alternative approach to identifying reputable journals involves utilizing journal blacklists and whitelists. Journal blacklists comprise journals deemed predatory or fraudulent, whereas whitelists consist of journals considered reputable and known for publishing high-quality research papers. Beall's List of Predatory Journals exemplifies journal blacklists, while the Directory of Open Access Journals (DOAJ) represents a journal whitelist (Beall, 2017; Ding et al., 2015; Goldfarb-Tarrant et al., 2020).

Although these lists can be helpful, they may not always be up-to-date or encompass all journals within a specific domain.

A final approach considers factors such as author reputations, review status, and the number of citations. While these individual data points are insufficient to categorize a journal as reputable or non-reputable, their combination contributes to a comprehensive score that can differentiate between reputable and non-reputable journals (Goldfarb-Tarrant et al., 2020).

B. Machine Learning Algorithms for Identifying Reputable and Non-Reputable Journals

Machine learning algorithms have emerged as a viable solution for rapidly and accurately identifying reputable and non-reputable journals (Ben Jabeur et al., 2023). These algorithms leverage various features, including impact factor, publisher, domain, citation counts, date, and review status, to classify journals accordingly (Brnabic & Hess, 2021; S. Zhao et al., 2018; Z. Zhao et al., 2019). By training the classification algorithm on a labeled dataset, where journals are designated as reputable or non-reputable, the algorithm can discern patterns in the data and generate predictions for new data (Géron, 2019; Rojalin et al., 2022; Xu et al., 2007). Numerous machine-learning algorithms have been proposed in the literature for purposes akin to this research, with logistic regression, decision trees, random forests, and support vector machines (SVM) commonly employed for such tasks. Some studies have also utilized deep learning algorithms like convolutional neural net-works (CNNs) for classification tasks, which could be applied to discerning the reputability of journals.

C. Evaluation Metrics for Machine Learning Algorithms

1. Pandas

Pandas is an open-source Python library for data manipulation and analysis. It provides data structures for efficiently storing and manipulating large and complex datasets and functions for data cleaning, filtering, and transformation (Géron, 2019; *Pandas User Guide*, 2023). Pandas' data manipulation functions are used in fields that deal with large and complex datasets. The library's main data structures are the Series and DataFrame, which allow users to work with one-dimensional and two-dimensional data, respectively. Additionally, Pandas offers robust time series functionality and integrates well with other data analysis libraries in Python, such as NumPy and Matplotlib.

2. Scikit-learn

Scikit-learn is a Python library that is open-source and specifically designed for machine learning and data science applications. It offers an array of algorithms for various tasks, including classification, regression, clustering, dimensionality reduction, model selection, and preprocessing, in addition to tools for assessing and fine-tuning model performance (Géron, 2019). Scikit-learn relies on other Python libraries, such as NumPy, SciPy, and Matplotlib, and is recognized for its accessible API, comprehensive documentation, and robust community backing (Géron, 2019; Hao & Ho, 2019).

3. Data Transformation With Scikit-learn

Data transformation plays a pivotal role in all aspects of data analysis. Commonly employed transformations, such as whitening transformation, differencing, and log-odds ratios, cater to a range of input variables. Scikit-learn offers many user-friendly functions for executing data transformations and pre-processing tasks. The primary data structure utilized in most Scikit-learn functions is the NumPy array.

The independent variables, often referred to as features in machine learning, are represented by an $N_o \times N_f$ array, where N_o corresponds to the number of observations and N_f to the number of features. On the other hand, dependent variables, also known as targets or labels, are represented by an $N_o \times N_l$ array, with N_l indicating the number of labels (Pang et al., 2020). A single label with multiple values is typically encountered in most supervised learning applications, rendering N_l as one. By convention, the uppercase X symbolizes the feature array, while the lowercase y represents the label array (Hao & Ho, 2019).

4. Supervised Learning

Supervised learning is a branch of machine learning algorithms that create associations between input features and corresponding target variables, given both features and labels are known. It comprises two categories: regression for continuous labels and classification for discrete labels. This review emphasizes classification, with the transition to regression being relatively straightforward by substituting classification functions with regression functions (Géron, 2019; Hao & Ho, 2019). Four widely-used classifiers—Support Vector Machines (SVM), Maximum Entropy (Multinomial Logistic Regression), Artificial Neural Networks, and Random Forests—are briefly introduced. For further details on these methods, readers are directed to relevant literature or books on supervised learning.

The Scikit-learn framework employs a three-step process for utilizing a classifier. Initially, establish the model by defining its hyperparameters. Subsequently, train the model using the provided data to ascertain the necessary parameters (Géron, 2019). Conclusively, apply the trained model to the test data to obtain the predicted classifications. The outline of these steps can be represented in pseudocode, where classifier() is an instance of one of the supervised learning methods (Hao & Ho, 2019).

Figure 1. Scikit-learn pseudocode as depicted by Hao and Ho, and Geron
Source: Géron (2019) and Hao and Ho (2019)

```
model = classifier(hyper-parameters = something)
model.fit(X_train, y_train)
y_test = model.predict(X_test)
```

To assess the performance of the machine learning algorithm, various metrics such as accuracy, precision, recall, and F1-score can be employed (Hao & Ho, 2019; Moslehi & Haeri, 2021). Accuracy evaluates the proportion of correctly classified journals, while precision quantifies the percentage of true positives (i.e., reputable journals) among all journals classified as positive. Recall calculates the percentage of true positives among all actual positive instances, and the F1-score represents the harmonic mean of precision and recall (Rojalin et al., 2022). Moreover, feature importance techniques, including permutation importance and SHapley Additive exPlanations (SHAP), can be utilized to identify key features with predictive power and understand the model's decision-making process. K-fold cross-validation can also serve to evaluate the model's performance by partitioning the dataset into training and testing sets, training the model on the former, and assessing its performance on the latter (Géron, 2019; Hao & Ho, 2019; Rojalin et al., 2022). Implementing these evaluation metrics and techniques can offer valuable insights into the strengths and weaknesses of the machine learning algorithm, ultimately helping to pinpoint areas for enhancement.

V. RESEARCH METHODOLOGY

This study aims to develop a machine learning-based system that can assist student researchers in identifying reputable and non-reputable journals quickly and accurately. Using the Python programming language's multiple libraries focusing on Pandas and Scikit-learn, the study analyzed data from the Kaggle database collection (Nasir, 2020). For this demonstration, the Impact-Factor-Rating database was used, which contains a series of parameters describing journals and publications, such as the number of citations, citation percentage, CiteScore, SNIP (Source Normalized Impact per Paper), SJR (SCImago Journal Rank), among others.

During the data ingestion process, several Python libraries, including Pandas and Scikit-learn (sklearn), were imported to enable data cleaning, filtering, normalization, and analysis. Subsequently, using the Pandas library, relevant data from the Impact-Factor-Ratings.csv file was extracted and transferred to a DataFrame for further manipulation. The information in the database underwent the initial normalization process to establish the criteria for classifying a journal as reputable or not.

The data cleaning and normalization process comprised several key steps, including identifying valuable text columns for analysis and transforming them into a representative value for each. Furthermore, the correlation between each column and others was validated to identify any possible redundant values. Any missing information within the DataFrame, as de-noted by NaN values, was addressed by either removing or completing it, depending on the necessity of the columns for the analysis (Izonin et al., 2022). Additionally, numerical columns were normalized, and weights were assigned to each column to facilitate subsequent analysis. Finally, based on the weight of each column and its corresponding value, the reputability of a given journal was determined.

Upon conducting an analysis of the information loaded into the DataFrame, it was observed that two text columns, namely "subject" and "Publisher," hold potential as representative numerical variables for the subsequent analysis. "Subject" identifies the field to which the journal belongs, while "Publisher" pertains to the author. In light of this, both columns will be transformed into representative numerical values to facilitate their integration into subsequent data analysis and algorithms. dimensionally. If you must use mixed units, clearly state the units for each quantity you use in an equation.

Figure 2. Table formatted, naturalized form data from impact-factor-rating dataset parsed using Ju-pyterLabs Windows desktop application
Source: Bektas (2023)

mber	Source title	citescore	subjects	subject_number	number_citations	number_documents	percent_cited	SNIP	SJR	Publisher	publisher_assigned_number	subjects_rep	Publisher_rep
1	Ca-A Cancer Journal for Clinicians	435.4	Oncology	213.0	47455	109	94	113.744	88.192	Wiley Blackwell		115	232	106
2	MMWR Recommendations and Reports	152.5	Health (social science)	207.0	2288	15	87	37.543	41.022	Centers for Disease Control and Prevention (CDC)	38	225	39
3	Nature Reviews Materials	123.7	Materials Chemistry	210.0	23868	193	96	15.261	36.691	Springer Nature	100	228	91
4	Chemical Reviews	100.5	General Chemistry	204.0	97295	968	96	12.832	20.847	American Chemical Society	7	222	9
5	Reviews of Modern Physics	75.8	General Physics and Astronomy	206.0	11906	157	92	14.948	21.938	American Physical Society	15	224	18
...	...	...	...	...	...	...	...	...	...	...	...	...	...
996	Environment and Behavior	8.8	\nHematology	117.0	1467	167	95	2.206	1.538	SAGE	95	118	86
997	Agronomy for Sustainable Development	8.8	\nInfectious Diseases	137.0	2202	251	82	2.288	1.779	Springer Nature	100	126	91
	Biology and		\nHardware							Springer			

Upon converting the text-based attributes into numerical representations, a comprehensive correlation analysis was conducted on key columns, which are instrumental in differentiating between reputable and non-reputable academic journals. For this purpose, the following attributes were utilized: ['citescore', 'subject_number', 'number_citations', 'number_documents', 'percent_cited', 'SNIP', 'SJR', 'publisher_assigned_number', 'subjects_rep', 'Publisher_rep'].

A correlation coefficient of 90% (0.9) or higher was set as the decisive criterion to establish the threshold for retaining or eliminating columns in the analysis. Upon examination, as demonstrated in Figure 2, it was observed that just the SNIP column displayed a robust correlation with the 'citescore' column. Consequently, the SNIP column was omitted from subsequent stages of the investigation.

Figure 3. Visual correlational representation of naturalized data from impact-factor-rating dataset by means of a heatmap
Source: Géron (2019), Hao and Ho (2019), and Xu et al. (2007)

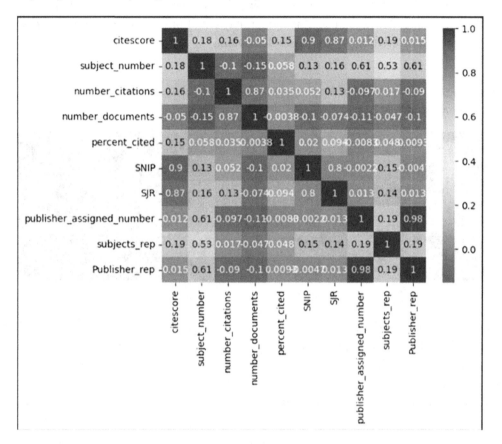

In order to advance with subsequent data manipulation and calculations, it was essential to address any missing or empty values present in the dataset. An in-depth analysis was undertaken to identify such values, and depending on their column location and validity, these entries were either discarded or completed with the mean value (Kang, 2013). This analysis identified Not a Number (NaN) values in the SNIP column; however, these were disregarded as this column is deemed irrelevant due to its strong correlation with the 'citescore' column. Similarly, NaN values in the 'subject_number' column were also dismissed as this column will not be utilized in further analysis. Lastly, NaN values identified within the SJR column were replaced with the mean value of the corresponding publisher's other elements in the same column, ensuring data consistency and integrity.

In assessing the reputation of a publication, it is crucial to allocate appropriate weights to each column, which will in turn dictate the relative influence of each parameter on the determination of a journal's reputability. As illustrated in Figure 4, emphasis was placed on the 'citescore', 'SNIP,' and 'SJR' columns by assigning them higher weights, as these values are derived from comprehensive statistical data. Conversely, the remaining columns receive lower weights in the analysis since they primarily encompass basic statistical metrics. This balanced weight distribution ensures a thorough and nuanced evaluation of the journal's overall reputation.

The data utilized in this model offers a tentative perspective of our objective. Nevertheless, the model is not confined to these data. In other words, if available, additional factors, such as peer review score, journal ranking, and author reputation, can be incorporated into the initial database before data processing takes place. An upgraded version of this model may entail publisher categorization based on their reputation for publishing credible or non-credible content.

Figure 4. The Python programming language was employed to assign weight values to each category within the normalized dataset

```python
weights = {'citescore_normalized': 0.3,
           'SNIP_normalized': 0.2,
           'SJR_normalized': 0.2,
           'number_documents_normalized': 0.1,
           'number_citations_normalized':0.1,
           'percent_cited_normalized': 0.1}

data['overall_score'] = (data[list(weights.keys())] * list(weights.values())).sum(axis=1)
data
```

The aforementioned classification equations were employed to implement the Logistic Regression classification algorithm, as it aligns optimally with the research objectives. Figure 5 illustrates the code used to train the algorithm effectively and partitiond the dataset, allocating 70% for the purpose of training the algorithm and reserving the remaining 30% to evaluate its performance. This approach facilitates a rigorous assessment of the algorithm's predictive capabilities and ensures a robust analysis. Furthermore, prior to incorporating our data into the model, it is imperative to refine the format of the values to guarantee seamless compatibility with the algorithm. To accomplish this, the 'scaler' function will be utilized for transforming our features X, while the 'ravel' function will be employed to reshape our targets y.

Figure 5. The classification code employed to partition the dataset into two distinct segments, with 70% dedicated to training data and the remaining 30% allocated for evaluation purposes

```python
features = ['citescore','number_citations','number_documents', 'percent_cited', 'SJR','subjects_rep','Publisher_rep']
target=['reputation_binary']

X = data[features].values
y = data[target].values
split_test_size = 0.30

X_train, X_test, y_train, y_test = train_test_split(X,y,test_size=split_test_size, random_state=42)
```

A comprehensive series of predictive assessments were conducted on both the training and testing datasets, encompassing an evaluation of performance metrics. The outcomes revealed an accuracy of 0.9600 for the training data, an accuracy of 0.9433 for the testing data, and a k-5 score accuracy of 0.94.

These results were further corroborated by the metrics delineated in Figure 6, thus substantiating the model's effectiveness and reliability.

Figure 6. The confusion matrix and classification report generated using normalized testing data derived from the impact-factor-rating dataset, demonstrating high levels of accuracy and precision

```
Confusion Matrix
[[100    7]
 [ 10 183]]

Classification_report
              precision    recall  f1-score   support

           0       0.91      0.93      0.92       107
           1       0.96      0.95      0.96       193

    accuracy                           0.94       300
   macro avg       0.94      0.94      0.94       300
weighted avg       0.94      0.94      0.94       300
```

VI. RESULTS

The primary objective of this study was to develop a machine learning-based system capable of aiding student researchers in accurately and efficiently identifying reputable and non-reputable journals. Utilizing various Python programming language libraries, with a particular emphasis on Pandas and Scikit-learn, the research analyzed data from the Kaggle database collection (Nasir, 2020). The Impact-Factor-Rating dataset, encompassing a range of parameters describing journals and publications, served as the foundation for this investigation.

During the initial data ingestion phase, Python libraries such as Pandas and Scikit-learn (sklearn) facilitated the necessary data cleaning, filtering, normalization, and analysis. Employing the Pandas library, relevant data was extracted from the Impact-Factor-Ratings.csv file and stored within a DataFrame for further processing. Subsequently, the information was normalized to establish classification criteria for journal reputability. This process involved several critical steps, including identifying and transforming valuable text columns into representative numerical values, validating inter-column correlations to detect redundancy, and addressing any missing data within the DataFrame, denoted by NaN values (Izonin et al., 2022). In addition, numerical columns were normalized, and weights were assigned to each column to aid in subsequent analysis. The reputability of a given journal was then determined based on the weight and corresponding value of each column.

After thoroughly examining the DataFrame, the "subject" and "Publisher" text columns were identified as potential numerical variables for further analysis. Consequently, these columns were transformed into representative numerical values to facilitate integration into subsequent data analysis and algorithms.

A comprehensive correlation analysis was then conducted, utilizing a decisive criterion of a 90% (0.9) correlation coefficient to eliminate redundant columns, excluding the SNIP column from the further investigation (Moslehi & Haeri, 2021). Data integrity was preserved throughout the analysis by addressing missing or empty values in the dataset through a rigorous identification process, which involved discarding or completing entries based on their column location and validity (Kang, 2013). Appropriate weights were allocated to each column, emphasizing the 'citescore', 'SNIP', and 'SJR' columns, as they were derived from comprehensive statistical data.

The Logistic Regression classification algorithm was implemented using the classification equation, as it optimally aligned with the research objectives. The dataset was partitioned into 70% for algorithm training and 30% for performance evaluation, ensuring a robust analysis. Prior to incorporating data into the model, the 'scaler' function was employed for transforming features X, while the 'ravel' function was used to reshape targets y.

The results reported indicate the performance of the machine learning model on both the training and testing datasets. The model's accuracy measures its ability to correctly classify reputable and non-reputable journals. The higher the accuracy, the better the model's performance. The model achieved an accuracy of 0.9600 (96%) for the training data, suggesting that it accurately classified 96% of the training samples. Additionally, the model achieved an accuracy of 0.9433 (94.33%) for the testing data, indicating that it accurately classified 94.33% of the testing samples. The high accuracy rates for training and testing data demonstrate that the model can effectively identify reputable and non-reputable journals with minimal errors. Furthermore, the k-5 score accuracy of 0.94 (94%) refers to the model's performance using a k-fold cross-validation method, where the dataset is split into five equal parts (k=5). In k-fold cross-validation, the model is trained and tested k times, with each part as the testing dataset once and the remaining parts as the training dataset. The reported k-5 score accuracy of 0.94 indicates that the model's performance remains consistently high across different dataset partitions, further validating the model's reliability and effectiveness in classifying reputable and non-reputable journals.

VII. LIMITATIONS OF THIS STUDY

This study acknowledges potential limitations primarily pertaining to the robustness of the data utilized in the machine learning algorithm. In the article "Citations, Citation Indicators, and Research Quality: An Overview of Basic Concepts and Theories," the authors discuss the approaches and constraints associated with citation indices. It is important to note that these databases are not uniform; a non-English journal with exceptional editorial standards and rigorous peer review processes may not be indexed. Additionally, a newly published paper might lack citations, while an older, less relevant paper might have numerous citations. Various methods and normalization schemes have been developed to address these and other factors.

The impact factor of a journal is derived from citation counts, and its significance was analyzed by Saha et al. (2003) in their research. They discovered a strong, albeit imperfect, correlation between a panel of subject matter experts and the impact factor for multiple medical journals. The correlation was stronger for researchers ($r^2 = 0.83$) as compared to practitioners ($r^2 = 0.62$). Serenko and Kohan (2011) conducted a comparative analysis of expert survey-based and citation impact-based journal ranking methodologies. Their findings revealed that researchers typically ranked journals with a focus on their current research interests more favorably, which aligns with the observations made in the Saha paper. Moreover, expert surveys demonstrated a tendency to favor journals with a higher publication frequency.

In summary, the predictive assessments on both training and testing datasets, the model demonstrated an accuracy of 0.9600 for the training data, an accuracy of 0.9433 for the testing data, and a k-5 score accuracy of 0.94. These results corroborate the model's effectiveness and reliability, aligning with previous studies that have successfully employed machine learning algorithms to identify and classify reputable and non-reputable sources (Ben Jabeur et al., 2023).

VIII. RECOMMENDATIONS AND CONCLUSION

This research successfully developed a machine learning-based system to assist student researchers in identifying reputable and non-reputable journals for dissertation writing. By employing a supervised learning approach with logistic regression on a dataset of journal articles, the model demonstrated strong performance in classifying articles as reputable or non-reputable. The model's accuracy reached 0.9600 for the training data and 0.9433 for the testing data, indicating its effectiveness and reliability. Improvements and enhancement in the algorithm's capabilities can be accomplished by incorporating additional parameters. A variety of approaches are characteristic of predatory journals (Grudniewicz, 2019). For example, non-reputable journals websites may contain false or misleading information. These journals do not follow best editorial and publication practices. There is frequently a lack of transparency when it comes to editorial procedures, fees and how the peer review process is conducted. These journals often are very aggressive in soliciting papers or reviewers. All of the aforementioned items should be considered as red flags. The author's reputation may be of help in evaluating the quality of an article and therefore the journal the article is published in. If it were possible to assess the quality of peer reviews that would greatly help to evaluate the quality of a journal but unfortunately there is no way to measure this. The successful addition of any of the above factors would enhance the accuracy of the study's algorithm. This study's findings provide valuable insights into utilizing machine learning algorithms to streamline the process of sorting through journals and enhancing the quality of research by reducing the risk of relying on non-reputable sources. Future research could explore other machine learning algorithms, such as deep learning techniques like convolutional neural networks (CNNs), to refine the classification process and improve the model's accuracy.

REFERENCES

Abramo, G., D'Angelo, C. A., & Soldatenkova, A. (2017). An investigation on the skewness patterns and fractal nature of research productivity distributions at field and discipline level. *Journal of Informetrics*, *11*(1), 324–335. doi:10.1016/j.joi.2017.02.001

Alsheikh-Ali, A. A., Qureshi, W., Al-Mallah, M. H., & Ioannidis, J. P. A. (2011). Public availability of published research data in high-impact journals. *PLoS One*, *6*(9), e24357. doi:10.1371/journal.pone.0024357 PMID:21915316

Beall, J. (2017). What I learned from predatory publishers. *Biochemia Medica*, *27*(2), 273–278. doi:10.11613/BM.2017.029 PMID:28694718

Bektas, M. (2023). *JupyerLab Desktop* (3.6.3) [Eng; Windows]. Jupyter. https://github.com/jupyterlab/jupyterlab-desktop

Ben Jabeur, S., Ballouk, H., Ben Arfi, W., & Sahut, J.-M. (2023). Artificial intelligence applications in fake review detection: Bibliometric analysis and future avenues for research. *Journal of Business Research, 158*, 113631. doi:10.1016/j.jbusres.2022.113631

Brnabic, A., & Hess, L. M. (2021). Systematic literature review of machine learning methods used in the analysis of real-world data for patient-provider decision making. *BMC Medical Informatics and Decision Making, 21*(1), 54. doi:10.118612911-021-01403-2 PMID:33588830

Butler, D. (2013). Investigating journals: The dark side of publishing. *Nature, 495*(7442), 433–435. doi:10.1038/495433a PMID:23538810

Ding, Y., Zhang, G., Chambers, T., Song, M., Wang, X., & Zhai, C. (2015). Content-based citation analysis: The next generation of citation analysis: Content-Based Citation Analysis: The Next Generation of Citation Analysis. *Journal of the Association for Information Science and Technology, 65*(9), 1820–1833. doi:10.1002/asi.23256

Géron, A. (2019). *Hands-on machine learning with Scikit-Learn, Keras, and TensorFlow: Concepts, tools, and techniques to build intelligent systems* (2nd ed.). O'Reilly Media, Inc.

Goldfarb-Tarrant, S., Robertson, A., Lazic, J., Tsouloufi, T., Donnison, L., & Smyth, K. (2020). Scaling Systematic Literature Reviews with Machine Learning Pipelines. *Proceedings of the First Workshop on Scholarly Document Processing*, 184–195. 10.18653/v1/2020.sdp-1.21

Grudniewicz, A., Moher, D., Cobey, K. D., Bryson, G. L., Cukier, S., Allen, K., Ardern, C., Balcom, L., Barros, T., Berger, M., Ciro, J. B., Cugusi, L., Donaldson, M. R., Egger, M., Graham, I. D., Hodgkinson, M., Khan, K. M., Mabizela, M., Manca, A., ... Lalu, M. M. (2019). Predatory journals: No definition, no defence. *Nature, 576*(7786), 210–212. doi:10.1038/d41586-019-03759-y PMID:31827288

Guba, K., & Tsivinskaya, A. (2023). Expert judgments versus publication-based metrics: Do the two methods produce identical results in measuring academic reputation? *The Journal of Documentation, 79*(1), 127–143. doi:10.1108/JD-02-2022-0039

Hao, J., & Ho, T. K. (2019). Machine learning made easy: A review of *scikit-learn* package in python programming language. *Journal of Educational and Behavioral Statistics, 44*(3), 348–361. doi:10.3102/1076998619832248

Izonin, I., Tkachenko, R., Shakhovska, N., Ilchyshyn, B., & Singh, K. K. (2022). A two-step data normalization approach for improving classification accuracy in the medical diagnosis domain. *Mathematics, 10*(11), 1942. doi:10.3390/math10111942

Jennings, C. (2006). Quality and value: The true purpose of peer review. *Nature*. Advance online publication. doi:10.1038/nature05032

Jinha, A. E. (2010). Article 50 million: An estimate of the number of scholarly articles in existence. *Learned Publishing, 23*(3), 258–263. doi:10.1087/20100308

Kamei, F., Wiese, I., Lima, C., Polato, I., Nepomuceno, V., Ferreira, W., Ribeiro, M., Pena, C., Cartaxo, B., Pinto, G., & Soares, S. (2021). Grey Literature in Software Engineering: A critical review. *Information and Software Technology*, *138*, 106609. doi:10.1016/j.infsof.2021.106609

Kang, H. (2013). The prevention and handling of the missing data. *Korean Journal of Anesthesiology*, *64*(5), 402. doi:10.4097/kjae.2013.64.5.402 PMID:23741561

Kovanis, M., Porcher, R., Ravaud, P., & Trinquart, L. (2016). The global burden of journal peer review in the biomedical literature: Strong imbalance in the collective enterprise. *PLoS One*, *11*(11), e0166387. doi:10.1371/journal.pone.0166387 PMID:27832157

Lu, E. P., Fischer, B. G., Plesac, M. A., & Olson, A. P. J. (2022). Research Methods: How to Perform an Effective Peer Review. *Hospital Pediatrics*, *12*(11), e409–e413. doi:10.1542/hpeds.2022-006764 PMID:36214067

Moslehi, F., & Haeri, A. (2021). A novel feature selection approach based on clustering algorithm. *Journal of Statistical Computation and Simulation*, *91*(3), 581–604. doi:10.1080/00949655.2020.1822358

Nasir, U. (2020). *Impact factor of top 1000 journals* (Version 2) [Csv]. Kaggle. https://www.kaggle.com/datasets/umairnasir14/impact-factor-of-top-1000-journals

Pandas User Guide. (2023). Pydata.Org. https://pandas.pydata.org/docs/user_guide/index.html

Pang, B., Nijkamp, E., & Wu, Y. N. (2020). Deep Learning With TensorFlow: A Review. *Journal of Educational and Behavioral Statistics*, *45*(2), 227–248. doi:10.3102/1076998619872761

Pyrczak, F., & Tcherni-Buzzeo, M. (2018). *Evaluating Research in Academic Journals: A Practical Guide to Realistic Evaluation* (7th ed.). Routledge. doi:10.4324/9781351260961

Rojalin, T., Antonio, D., Kulkarni, A., & Carney, R. P. (2022). Machine Learning-Assisted Sampling of Surfance-Enhanced Raman Scattering (SERS) Substrates Improve Data Collection Efficiency. *Applied Spectroscopy*, *76*(4), 485–495. doi:10.1177/00037028211034543 PMID:34342493

Saha, S., Saint, S., & Christakis, D. A. (2003). Impact factor: A valid measure of journal quality? *Journal of the Medical Library Association: JMLA*, *91*(1), 42–46. PMID:12572533

Serenko, A., & Dohan, M. (2011). Comparing the expert survey and citation impact journal ranking methods: Example from the field of Artificial Intelligence. *Journal of Informetrics*, *5*(4), 629–648. doi:10.1016/j.joi.2011.06.002

Xu, K., Tang, C., Liu, Y., Li, C., Wu, J., Zhu, J., & Dai, L. (2007). Improving selection methods for evolutionary algorithms by clustering. *Third International Conference on Natural Computation (ICNC 2007)*, *3*, 742–746. 10.1109/ICNC.2007.440

Zhao, S., Zhang, D., Duan, Z., Chen, J., Zhang, Y., & Tang, J. (2018). A novel classification method for paper-reviewer recommendation. *Scientometrics*, *115*(3), 1293–1313. doi:10.100711192-018-2726-6

Zhao, Z., Anand, R., & Wang, M. (2019). Maximum Relevance and Minimum Redundancy Feature Selection Methods for a Marketing Machine Learning Platform. *2019 IEEE International Conference on Data Science and Advanced Analytics (DSAA)*, 442–452. 10.1109/DSAA.2019.00059

Chapter 22
Analysis of ESG in Building New Business Models

Kevin Richardson

ⓘ https://orcid.org/0009-0002-3212-8669

Edward Waters University, USA

ABSTRACT

According to researchers, environmental, social, and governance (ESG) has been discussed extensively, specifically as a socially responsible investment. Regardless of this exploration, researchers have failed to critically examine the concept of ESG integration and how it impacts the transformation of business models from conventional to more sustainable ones. The chapter utilized a meta-analysis to critically examine previous research findings. The data collection method involved analyzing qualitative and quantitative research that allowed deriving generalized conclusions about ESG and building sustainable business models based on the existing literature. ESG integration benefits the pertinent firms. The advantages are apparent with the study showing that ESG integration results in positive returns on equity and assets. Organizations with strong ESG performance are ranked as best-performing firms and have a lower cost of debt. This benefit means that firms should focus on ESG integration and building new business models resulting in improved financial performance.

1. INTRODUCTION

In the recent past, environmental, social, and governance (ESG) has gained significant traction. According to Aldowaish et al. (2022), ESG is associated with growing interest by investors at domestic and international levels. Based on past research, scholars reveal that investors applauded companies with good ESG. Their appreciation was based on the conception that poorly disclosed ESG was an indicator of idiosyncratic risks. For example, the lack of ESG in a company is believably because of poorly-made investments, especially in high-risk areas. The high-risk areas, in this context, refer to sectors that may discriminate against workers or pollute the environment. Amel-Zadeh and Serafeim (2017) supports this idea by hypothesizing that integrating ESG into investment decisions is vital as it helps pertinent individuals make sound decisions that are guided by a company's overall performance rather than just

DOI: 10.4018/979-8-3693-1630-6.ch022

its financial performance. Friede et al.'s (2015) exploration of ESG implies that the approach embraced by investors is influenced by the fact that it refers to organizational obligations focused on improving social welfare. Improved social welfare translates to sustainable and equitable long-term wealth for the stakeholders.

The bigger picture about ESG and its integration into a firm's operation is that better governance, sustainable development, and environmental care characterize ESG-compliant organizations. In an attempt to understand the significance of ESG in businesses, Amel-Zadeh and Serafeim (2017) noted that related issues are gaining increased concern among the investor community. The approach by most investors is based on the understanding that organizations have increased their expectations about different stakeholders. They expect stakeholders to act right and embrace a proactive approach that helps manage ESG threats and opportunities and how they apply to existing business strategies. Precisely, the global investment community is currently more interested in ESG issues. Investors' interest in ESG is like the demand for corporate leaders to improve sustainable practices that benefit an organization's bottom line and impact the wider community. According to Brooks and Oikonomou (2018), investors' demands align with the current approach to ESG and its connection to corporate performance, particularly because the two are intrinsically intertwined. Thus, firms with commendable ESG performance have a high likelihood of talent retention, record better financial performance, and have long-term value creation.

As investments dedicated to ESG and sustainability continue to grow, organizations are incorporating ESG as part of their new business models. Câmara and Morais's (2022) survey of trends shows that the number of firms adopting ESG compliance is on the rise. An increase in the adoption is linked to the impacts of ESG on new business models. Specifically, the move by organizations towards improved sustainability is one of the factors behind the increased adoption of ESG in business models as it improves their corporate social responsibility. An entry by Aagaard (2018) presents ESG from the perspective of how it relates to business models. Spoz (2021) also examines this concept to show that ESG impacts business model outcomes, which explains the rush for its integration. The results from both surveys suggest that research about the integration of ESG in business models may not be that substantial. Still, it is undeniably clear that ESG incorporation in business models helps improve sustainability. A survey by Jørgensen and Pedersen (2018) highlight that in creating new sustainable business models, the implementation of ESG is necessary as it helps ensure that the embraced approaches are compatible with the primary goal of sustainability. As a result, firms that have integrated ESG into their business models are laudable since they are likely to adopt sustainability-related actions.

1.1 Problem Statement

The integration of environmental, social, and governance (ESG) factors into business models has become a crucial issue in recent times (Huang, 2021). Scholars have provided a conceptual understanding of the connection between ESG and business models; however, there is a lack of detailed case studies on the integration process and how firms can fully incorporate ESG to transform their business models into more sustainable ones. This gap in the literature has led to businesses' reluctance to adopt ESG and its holistic integration into existing business models (Aldowaishet al., 2022). This hinders their progress towards sustainability.

The general problem is that organizations are not fully integrating ESG factors into their core business models thus resulting in unsustainable business practices (Zeidan, 2022). These unsustainable practices are not aligned with society's changing demands and environmental concerns. Very few organizations consider ESG an integral part of the organization with many viewing it as a separate issue. This mindset creates a gap between the company's sustainability goals and its actual practices. The result is that businesses lack accountability and transparency. This mindset also results in missed opportunities to create value and achieve long-term success by aligning with stakeholders' values and expectations. The specific problem is that there exists a lack of understanding of the specific steps and processes required to fully integrate ESG into business models. While scholars have provided some theoretical frameworks, there is a need for more practical guidance on how to implement and monitor ESG integration effectively.

1.2 Purpose of the Study

The purpose of this study is significant in filling the existing literature gap regarding how firms can fully incorporate ESG to transform their business models into more sustainable ones. The study's contribution is the critical examination of how ESG incorporation is essential in transforming conventional business models into sustainable ones, with a focus on how ESG transforms business models to increase their advancement toward sustainability (Kaiser, 2020; Hu & Kee, 2022). From the study, readers will develop a deeper understanding of the roles and influence of ESG factors in building sustainable business models. This will help in revealing a positive connection between a firm's innovation and sustainable business models. The paper also highlights the benefits of ESG integration, such as positive returns on equity and assets, and a key indicator of a firm's profitability (Kaiser, 2020). The study's contribution provides a basis for organizations to embrace ESG integration into their existing business models to become more sustainable, contributing to the advancement of sustainable development goals.

1.3 Significance of the Study

The significance of this study is multifaceted. First, the study provides a comprehensive review of the literature on the integration of environmental, social, and governance (ESG) factors in conventional business models. This review highlights the importance of ESG integration in creating new business models that can translate to increased competitive advantage and enhanced corporate social responsibility (Ziolo, 2021). Additionally, the study underscores the role of sustainable business models in contributing to the firm's and society's sustainable development. Secondly, this study addresses a significant gap in the literature by providing detailed insights into how firms can integrate ESG factors into their existing business models to transform them into more sustainable ones. Thirdly, the study highlights the financial benefits of ESG integration and sustainable business models. The study underscores that firms with strong ESG performance are ranked as best-performing firms and have a lower cost of debt (Kotsantonis & Serafeim, 2019). Fourthly, this study provides valuable insights for policymakers and regulators. The study underscores the importance of ESG integration in creating more sustainable business models that can help address societal and environmental challenges.

1.4 Theoretical Framework

To understand the contribution of ESG in forming new business models, researchers purport that the stakeholder theory will help to critically examine the overall occurrence. According to Dmytriyev et al. (2021), the suitability of the stakeholder theory in this context is apparent in that it applies to three concepts that include normative interpretation of functions of a corporation, such as identification of philosophical and moral guidelines, empirical description and explanation of specific corporate behaviors and characteristics, and instrumental, which is used to identify the possible connections or their inexistence between stakeholder management and accomplishment of conventional corporate goals. This approach to stakeholder theory supposes that it is an effective way to theorize organizational operations, especially in meeting the demands of changing society and environment. This interpretation means that stakeholder theory helps justify the connection between an organization and the ideas of multiple stakeholders, such as their consumers, investors, and workers.

The second theory that applies in this research is the stewardship theory. The theory is specifically based on sociology, psychology, and leadership models. According to Contrafatto (2014), this theory is imperative in this research as it expounds on the possible alignment of principle agents with a psychological contact or connection. With that in place, the theory helps understand the agent's behavior, particularly in a community-focused manner that directs trustworthy moral behaviors of a firm and its shareholders. Based on this approach, the stewardship theory may be linked to how organizations are compelled to observe corporate social responsibility. This assertion is evident in that the theory describes the roles of an organization and its commitment to meet the tasks and responsibilities they are entrusted with.

2. LITERATURE REVIEW

The researcher's interest in sustainable business models has been growing. Specifically, sustainable business models are becoming important both from businesses' response to green consumerism and sustainable development goals (Kluza et al., 2021). According to Kluza et al. (2021), this occurrence may be attributed to searching for the connection between social, environmental, and financial performance. Existing literature gives a mixed picture concerning the overall connection. In particular, researchers are divided between whether the connection between social and environmental performance is positive, neutral, or negative. Regardless of the stand, what stands out is that the likelihood of a positive connection is higher than the other two. Cappucci (2018) confirmed this by examining the financial benefits of a company's corporate social and environmental responsibility. The positive connection is apparent in that sustainability and a company's financial performance are why firms have been venturing into new business models that align with the sustainability goal (Shabbir & Wisdom, 2020). Companies that have embraced this approach are also pressured to incorporate environmental, social, and governance (ESG) factors, especially in their decision-making process.

Aldowaish et al. (2022) note that since the introduction of the ESG concept by the United Nations in 2004, it has been integrated based on the conception that it helps them with achieving sustainability. Further exploration of ESG incorporation reveals that most firms are under pressure from investors, regulators, and stakeholders to disclose their ESG performance (Daugaard & Ding, 2022). The need to disclose ESG performance is meant to unearth how it has impacted a company's progression toward sustainability. The pressure has led to drawbacks, such as firms manipulating their ESG performance. The manipulation process has also given birth to value washing, greenwashing, and blue washing, and they are aimed at satisfying stakeholders and attracting investors. Value washing refers to the efforts by an organization that entails misinterpretation of their value outcomes. Greenwashing describes the manipulation of a company's sustainability reporting (Yu et al., 2020). Lastly, bluewashing denotes unethical behaviors by companies using the UN's Compact to gain legitimacy. Despite such drawbacks, Huang (2021) argues that ESG integration is paramount as it is linked to socially responsible investment and sustainable development. The correlation between ESG and these sustainability factors is apparent in that enhanced social responsibility is part of effective business operations.

ESG integration into socially responsible investment (SRI) is influenced by the organization's focus on environmental sustainability. According to Mohamad (2020), researchers' concerns over businesses' environmental impact have raised global awareness about sustainability. As a result, businesses have shifted from traditional investments to more modern strategies directed toward profit maximization as long as a firm supports sustainability. Kaiser (2020) expounds on this concept to show that the integration of ESG and sustainability in businesses' financial markets are what researchers call SRI. By definition, SRI describes ESG integration based on systematic and explicit considerations of social, environmental, and governance factors and how they impact the investment decision-making process. Kaiser breaks down the definition further to show that ESG integration and SRI can be understood based on three factors, which are environmental, social, and government. The environmental part of it encapsulates a company's performance as an agent of the natural environment. Secondly, the social factor approach examines how an organization manages its connection with its stakeholders, such as suppliers, customers, employees, and communities, in its operations. Lastly, governance factors help understand sustainability by focusing on a company's leadership and internal controls.

Empirical research about ESG and its impacts on the financial markets supposes that they represent a company's financial value and performance. A study by Hill (2020) critically examined the existing empirical findings to show that ESG is associated with positively impacting a company's corporate financial performance. Further, positive connections were found to exist between an organization's ESG disclosure and its profitability. The connection between ESG and profitability is usually construed to show the positive link between these factors and financial performance. Most researchers that evaluate the connection between ESG and financial outcomes have divided opinions, with some suggesting a positive relationship and others a negative correlation. Regardless of the divided opinions, Melas et al. (2017) note that being socially responsible is an organization's most essential strategy as it increases attraction to stakeholders. A more detailed explanation hypothesizes that investors play important roles in supporting ethical practices and ESG (Melas et al., 2017). The roles investors play is reflected in literature, particularly in the context of investor-based integration of ESG in a firm's decision-making procedures and investment that manages risks.

ESG integration into new business models can also be understood from a sustainable development perspective. Muñoz-Torres et al. (2018) explication shows that the integration of ESG and sustainability in a company's operations is scholarly, known as sustainable development (SD). In this context, sustainable development refers to the corporate activities used by an organization to balance current sustainability efforts with environmental, economic, and social factors necessary in addressing organizational systems (Rafiq et al., 2020). Several empirical studies have examined the effects of ESG on a company's operations. The findings of these studies reveal that they result in positive impacts that apply to a company's corporate governance and ESG reporting. The positive impacts linked to governance practices and reporting strategies help firms to become more proactive, particularly when addressing sustainability, improved relationships with external resources, and stakeholder engagement (Aureli et al., 2020). The bigger picture about the existing connection is that ESG is notably an indicator of a company's sustainability.

An understanding of the impacts of ESG on a firm's operation shows that their integration is vital in forming new business models. According to Muñoz-Torres et al. (2018), the integration of ESG into business models is most apparent in how value is created, distributed, and captured in a firm. Simply put,

ESG represents how organizations do their business and facilitate a critical understanding of how they are created. From a scientific approach, Widyawati (2019) theorizes that ESG can be examined across parameters that include performance and control, innovation, design, as well as change and evolution. Consequently, the extent of sustainable development puts an organization under pressure, which entails turning their business models into more sustainable ones. In Zaccone and Pedrini's (2020) opinion, the conventional business model is typified by the ability to achieve sustainability goals that encapsulate social, economic, and environmental. Based on this approach, Bocken et al. (2014) identified eight archetypes that can be used to create business models appropriate for sustainability. The significance of building sustainable business models is entrenched in the idea that they help capitalize on material and energy efficiency. In doing so, pertinent organizations deliver functionality and not ownership, create value from waste, encourage sufficiency, substitute with natural and renewables, embrace a stewardship role, and develop scale-up resolutions (Ćwiklicki & O'Riordan, 2018). In that case, managers are responsible for changing the business model to a sustainable one. Besides, leadership plays a crucial role in an organization that pushes it towards meeting sustainability ambitions.

An organization's growth opportunity characterizes the connection between ESG and the transformation of business models toward sustainability. Therefore, an organization that incorporates ESG into its operation and transforms its business model to a more sustainable one benefits from being successful. According to Khuen and Heng (2022), ESG is a key to a firm's success as it helps them address global issues sustainably. Scholarly examination of this occurrence affirms that the organizations that have not adopted ESG to transform their business models to more sustainable ones are because of the existing knowledge gap. Samans and Nelson's (2022) elaboration of this concept confirms that organizations are in a better position when the knowledge gap is addressed as they record stronger ESG performance characterized by fewer debts.

According to Kluza et al. (2021), an overall comprehension of ESG and its contribution to building new business models can be understood based on how long the term "business model" has existed. Various authors define the term business model differently, but none of the descriptions have been scientifically approved and accepted in the business community. Regardless of failed consensus, Bouma and Walters (2018) note that a business model is generally adopted as a strategy that describes how companies do their business. In other words, business models refer to ways in which an enterprise uses resources to operate and generate profits. The bigger picture about business models is that they are all united by having value creation as part of their operations (Freudenreich et al., 2020). Since organizations have been linked with causing negative impacts on society and the environment, they are obliged to integrate sustainability into their operations to ensure societies are more sustainable. As a result, traditional business models have been transformed to be more sustainable. Their transformation is ascribed to helping firms achieve stipulated corporate sustainability goals (Bouma & Walters, 2018). Thus, sustainable business models are reputable for incorporating a triple-bottom approach that helps take into account stakeholders' interests, including society and the environment.

3. MATERIALS AND METHODS

The article utilized a meta-analysis to assess and critically examine previous research findings. More precisely, the data collection method involved analyzing qualitative and quantitative research that allowed deriving generalized conclusions about ESG and building sustainable business models based on the existing literature. In that case, secondary research materials were used to study ESG factors, sustainable business models, and how they influenced organizational performance. In relation to the research question, the study's scope was to examine ESG integration in firms and how it helped build new business models. To examine the two based on existing literature, some keywords were used during searching for information in various scientific databases, such as Google Scholar, JSTOR, EBSCOhost, and Google Books. They included ESG integration, conventional business models, sustainable business models, corporate social responsibility, as well as environmental, social, and governance. The search for secondary materials also involved inclusion and exclusion criteria. The materials excluded from this survey were information from non-scientific sources, such as online periodicals. On the other hand, the inclusion criteria involved all materials accessed from scientific sites, such as Google Scholar, especially the peer-reviewed type.

4. RESULTS

The integration of ESG in conventional business models helps create new business models that translate to the increased competitive advantage of an organization. Enhanced competitive advantage is because sustainable business models result in higher customer value, contributing to the firm's and society's sustainable development. Schramade (2016) when they pointed out that a sustainable business model is a key component for sustainable value creation that helps organizations meet the demands of changing business environments echoed similar conclusions. A wide range of stakeholders has debated sustainable business models, and their approach agrees that it allows organizations to utilize limited resources and emphasize corporate social responsibility. A study by Tundys (2022) focused on small-and-medium enterprises (SMEs). It showed that sustainability is essential as it helps create value by achieving innovations in conventional business models. From this survey, Taticchi and Demartini (2020) also suggests that the main challenge in designing sustainable business models is for organizations to approach it from the point of whether they are focused on capturing economic value for themselves by focusing on how their operations benefit the environment and society. The deduced concept from this study is that sustainable business models are vital in running successful businesses. Still, organizations must consider how the integration of ESG contributes to their corporate sustainability.

The significance of ESG in building new business models extends beyond enhanced corporate social responsibility (Muñoz-Torres et al., 2019). Many studies critically explore this to show that the benefits of integrating the environment and sustainability in business processes may help determine and predict the financial performance of an organization. The main message about sustainability is that it influences a firm's creditworthiness, which is reflected in its financial performance. For example, investors and creditors are currently very sensitive about corporate social responsibility, particularly in the absence of collateral. The concerns by investors are based on the notion that sustainability affects the performance of an organization, especially its finances. Evidence supporting this assertion confirms that organizations with strong ESG performance are ranked as best-performing firms and have a lower cost of debt. Kumar and Firoz (2022) verified this assertion by noting that the financial performance of an organization is currently influenced by its environmental and sustainability impacts. From this perspective, it is evident that ESG integration is essential in creating new, more sustainable business models, and they help influence an organization's financial performance.

A critical examination of sustainable business models reveals that they are an extension of traditional business models. The only differentiation between traditional and new business models is the integration of ESG (Drei et al., 2019). ESG incorporation is imperative as it denotes an organization's need to create, deliver, and capture values by ensuring that social, economic, and cultural factors are addressed sustainably. An exploration of the literature by Kluza et al. (2021) affirms that new business models, which are sustainable, are modifications of conventional business models. The modification means that certain goals and characteristics are added and integrated as part of meeting sustainability. A deeper examination of sustainable business models also reveals that they combine value proposition, creation, and delivery into a single approach based on value and efficient use of resources (Cosenz et al., 2020). The outcomes of this strategy are that the products and services produced using this business model contribute to a more sustainable society. Hence, regardless of the model approach used to examine sustainable business models, scholars agree that they are critical components used by organizations to meet the constant demands of changing society and the environment.

5. DISCUSSION AND CONCLUSIONS

Based on existing literature, it is apparent that scholars have only provided a conceptual understanding of the connection between ESG and business models. As a result, the existing literature gap is that research lacks a detailed case of the integration process and an explanation of how firms can fully incorporate ESG to transform their business models into more sustainable ones. The gap in the literature has been the reason for businesses' reluctance to adopt ESG and its holistic integration into existing business models. Based on this understanding, this article has addressed these shortcomings by critically examining how ESG incorporation is essential in transforming conventional business models into sustainable ones. The article specifically focuses on how ESG transforms business models to increase their advancement toward sustainability. As a result, the article has made a significant contribution regarding integrating ESG into core business models and how the process will benefit organizations through improved financial performance following enhanced sustainability.

The article's examination of secondary research materials affirms that ESG integration benefits the pertinent firms. The advantages are apparent: ESG integration results in positive returns on equity and assets. In particular, ESG is a key indicator of a firm's profitability. Therefore, organizations are advised to embrace ESG integration into their existing business models as it will help them become more sustainable. Researchers have also studied the roles and influence of ESG factors in building sustainable business models, revealing a positive connection between a firm's innovation and sustainable business models. Besides, organizations with strong ESG performance are ranked as best-performing firms and have a lower cost of debt. This benefit means that firms should focus on ESG integration and building new business models resulting in improved financial performance, particularly because their environmental and sustainability impacts currently influence organizational success.

REFERENCES

Aagaard, A. (2018). *Sustainable business models: Innovation, implementation and success.* Springer. https://link.springer.com/book/10.1007/978-3-319-93275-0

Aldowaish, A., Kokuryo, J., Almazyad, O., & Goi, H. C. (2022). Environmental, social, and governance integration into the business model: Literature review and research agenda. *Sustainability (Basel)*, *14*(5), 2959. doi:10.3390u14052959

Amel-Zadeh, A., & Serafeim, G. (2017). Why and how investors use ESG information: Evidence from a global survey. SSRN *Electronic Journal*. doi:10.2139/ssrn.2925310

Aureli, S., Del Baldo, M., Lombardi, R., & Nappo, F. (2020). Nonfinancial reporting regulation and challenges in sustainability disclosure and corporate governance practices. *Business Strategy and the Environment*, *29*(6), 2392–2403. doi:10.1002/bse.2509

Bocken, N., Short, S., Rana, P., & Evans, S. (2014). A literature and practice review to develop sustainable business model archetypes. *Journal of Cleaner Production*, *65*, 42–56. doi:10.1016/j.jclepro.2013.11.039

Bouma, J. J., & Walters, T. (2018). *Corporate sustainability: The next steps towards a sustainable world*. Routledge. doi:10.4324/9781315639185

Brooks, C., & Oikonomou, I. (2018). The effects of environmental, social and governance disclosures and performance on firm value: A review of the literature in accounting and finance. *The British Accounting Review*, *50*(1), 1–15. doi:10.1016/j.bar.2017.11.005

Câmara, P., & Morais, F. (2022). *The palgrave handbook of ESG and corporate governance*. Springer Nature. https://link.springer.com/book/10.1007/978-3-030-99468-6?noAccess=true

Cappucci, M. (2018). The ESG integration paradox. *The Bank of America Journal of Applied Corporate Finance*, *30*(2), 22–28. doi:10.1111/jacf.12296

Contrafatto, M. (2014). Stewardship theory: Approaches and perspectives. *Advances in Public Interest Accounting*, 177-196. doi:10.1108/S1041-706020140000017007

Cosenz, F., Rodrigues, V. P., & Rosati, F. (2020). Dynamic business modeling for sustainability: Exploring a system dynamics perspective to develop sustainable business models. *Business Strategy and the Environment*, *29*(2), 651–664. doi:10.1002/bse.2395

. Ćwiklicki, M., & O'Riordan, L. (2018). Creating value via sustainable business models and reverse innovation. *CSR, Sustainability, Ethics & Governance*, 151-167. doi:10.1007/978-3-319-73503-0_8

Daugaard, D., & Ding, A. (2022). Global drivers for ESG performance: The body of knowledge. *Sustainability (Basel)*, *14*(4), 2322. doi:10.3390u14042322

Dmytriyev, S. D., Freeman, R. E., & Hörisch, J. (2021). The relationship between stakeholder theory and corporate social responsibility: Differences, similarities, and implications for social issues in management. *Journal of Management Studies*, *58*(6), 1441–1470. doi:10.1111/joms.12684

DreiA.Le GuenedalT.LepetitF.MortierV.RoncalliT.SekineT. (2019). ESG investing in recent years: New insights from old challenges. *Available at* SSRN 3683469. doi:10.2139/ssrn.3683469

Freudenreich, B., Lüdeke-Freund, F., & Schaltegger, S. (2020). A stakeholder theory perspective on business models: Value creation for sustainability. *Journal of Business Ethics*, *166*(1), 3–18. doi:10.100710551-019-04112-z

Friede, G., Busch, T., & Bassen, A. (2015). ESG and financial performance: Aggregated evidence from more than 2000 empirical studies. *Journal of Sustainable Finance & Investment*, *5*(4), 210–233. doi:10.1080/20430795.2015.1118917

Hill, J. (2020). Defining and measuring ESG performance. *Environmental, Social, and Governance (ESG) Investing*, 167-183. doi:10.1016/B978-0-12-818692-3.00009-8

Hu, M. K., & Kee, D. M. H. (2022). Global institutions and ESG integration to accelerate SME development and sustainability. In *Handbook of Research on Global Institutional Roles for Inclusive Development* (pp. 139–156). IGI Global. doi:10.4018/978-1-6684-2448-3.ch008

Huang, D. Z. (2021). Environmental, social and governance (ESG) activity and firm performance: A review and consolidation. *Accounting and Finance*, *61*(1), 335–360. doi:10.1111/acfi.12569

Huang, D. Z. (2021). Environmental, social and governance factors and assessing firm value: Valuation, signalling and stakeholder perspectives. *Accounting and Finance*, *62*(S1), 1983–2010. doi:10.1111/acfi.12849

Jørgensen, S., & Pedersen, L. J. (2018). *Restart sustainable business model innovation*. Springer., doi:10.1007/978-3-319-91971-3

Kaiser, L. (2020). ESG integration: Value, growth and momentum. *Journal of Asset Management*, *21*(1), 32–51. doi:10.105741260-019-00148-y

Khuen, W. W., & Heng, T. B. (2022). Revisiting external stakeholders' role in environmental, social and governance (ESG) disclosure: A systematic literature review and research agenda. *ACBPP Official Conference Proceedings*. 10.22492/issn.2189-1001.2022.3

Kluza, K., Ziolo, M., & Spoz, A. (2021). Innovation and environmental, social, and governance factors influencing sustainable business models - meta-analysis. *Journal of Cleaner Production*, *303*, 127015. doi:10.1016/j.jclepro.2021.127015

Kotsantonis, S., & Serafeim, G. (2019). Four things no one will tell you about ESG data. *The Bank of America Journal of Applied Corporate Finance*, *31*(2), 50–58. doi:10.1111/jacf.12346

Kumar, P., & Firoz, M. (2022). Does accounting-based financial performance value environmental, social and governance (ESG) disclosures? A detailed note on a corporate sustainability perspective. *Australasian Business. Accounting and Finance Journal*, *16*(1), 41–72. doi:10.14453/aabfj.v16i1.4

Melas, D., Nagy, Z., & Kulkarni, P. (2017). Factor investing and ESG integration. *Factor Investing*, 389-413. doi:10.1016/B978-1-78548-201-4.50015-5

Mohamad, N. E. (2020). Environmental, social and governance (Esg) disclosure and financial performance. *European Proceedings of Social and Behavioural Sciences*. doi:10.15405/epsbs.2020.12.05.57

Muñoz-Torres, M. J., Fernández-Izquierdo, M. Á., Rivera-Lirio, J. M., & Escrig-Olmedo, E. (2018). Can environmental, social, and governance rating agencies favor business models that promote a more sustainable development? *Corporate Social Responsibility and Environmental Management*, *26*(2), 439–452. doi:10.1002/csr.1695

Rafiq, M., Zhang, X., Yuan, J., Naz, S., & Maqbool, S. (2020). Impact of a balanced scorecard as a strategic management system tool to improve sustainable development: Measuring the mediation of organizational performance through PLS-smart. *Sustainability (Basel)*, *12*(4), 1365. doi:10.3390u12041365

Samans, R., & Nelson, J. (2022). *Sustainable enterprise value creation: Implementing stakeholder capitalism through full ESG integration.* Palgrave Macmillan. doi:10.1007/978-3-030-93560-3

Schramade, W. (2016). Integrating ESG into valuation models and investment decisions: The value driver adjustment approach. SSRN *Electronic Journal*. doi:10.2139/ssrn.2749626

Shabbir, M. S., & Wisdom, O. (2020). The relationship between corporate social responsibility, environmental investments and financial performance: Evidence from manufacturing companies. *Environmental Science and Pollution Research International*, *27*(32), 39946–39957. doi:10.100711356-020-10217-0 PMID:32797400

Spoz, A. (2021). Sustainable business models of companies. *Advances in Business Information Systems and Analytics*, 44–60. doi:10.4018/978-1-7998-6788-3.ch003

Taticchi, P., & Demartini, M. (2020). *Corporate sustainability in practice: A guide for strategy development and implementation.* Springer. https://link.springer.com/book/10.1007/978-3-030-56344-8

Tundys, B. (2022). Business models for sustainable value creation in companies and financial markets. *Fostering Sustainable Business Models through Financial Markets*, 125-152. doi:10.1007/978-3-031-07398-4_6

Widyawati, L. (2019). A systematic literature review of socially responsible investment and environmental social governance metrics. *Business Strategy and the Environment*, *29*(2), 619–637. doi:10.1002/bse.2393

Yu, E. P., Luu, B. V., & Chen, C. H. (2020). Greenwashing in environmental, social and governance disclosures. *Research in International Business and Finance*, *52*, 101192. doi:10.1016/j.ribaf.2020.101192

Zaccone, M. C., & Pedrini, M. (2020). ESG factor integration into private equity. *Sustainability (Basel)*, *12*(14), 5725. doi:10.3390u12145725

Zeidan, R. (2022). Why don't asset managers accelerate ESG investing? A sentiment analysis based on 13,000 messages from finance professionals. *Business Strategy and the Environment*, *31*(7), 3028–3039. doi:10.1002/bse.3062

Ziolo, M. (2021). *Adapting and mitigating environmental, social, and governance risk in business.* IGI Global. doi:10.4018/978-1-7998-6788-3

Ziolo, M. (2021). Business Models of Banks Toward Sustainability and ESG Risk. In *Sustainability in Bank and Corporate Business Models: The Link between ESG Risk Assessment and Corporate Sustainability* (pp. 185–209). Springer International Publishing. doi:10.1007/978-3-030-72098-8_7

Chapter 23
Changing Health Policy Practices and Evaluation of Specialist Physicians Towards City Hospitals

Busra Saylan
 https://orcid.org/0000-0002-1296-1824
Hacettepe University, Turkey

Songul Cinaroglu
 https://orcid.org/0000-0001-5699-8402
Hacettepe University, Turkey

ABSTRACT

Strategic changes and policy implementation have a significant impact on health and health-related issues. The motivation of this study is to evaluate the opinions of specialist physicians towards city hospitals, which is a new and controversial policy action, and to analyze the findings obtained from these opinions by using various classification and machine learning methods. In order to evaluate their views on city hospitals, specialist physicians were divided into three groups using hierarchical clustering method in terms of health service quality and efficiency, coordination of care components, interdisciplinary care teams, and integration of health services dimensions. The differences between these groups were found to be statistically significant in terms of four dimensions ($p < 0.0001$). Naïve Bayes (AUC=0.896, F1=0.757), one of the machine learning techniques used to predict clusters obtained from four dimensions obtained from the evaluations of specialist physicians, was found to be the best predictor of four-dimensional classroom evaluations.

DOI: 10.4018/979-8-3693-1630-6.ch023

INTRODUCTION

With the changing and developing world conditions, the needs and expectations of people have begun to differentiate. To keep up with this development and change, the states have started to take steps to realize some transformations to ensure sustainable development in the cities and to improve the health, comfort, and quality of life standards of the people living in the cities (Dhyani et al., 2018). The sustainability in question is not only about the health of the environment of cities but also about the health of people living in cities (Mason, 2022). In this context, Turkey has taken an important step that will directly affect the country's health. It has put into operation the large and complex structures called the integrated health campuses (city hospitals), which were taken from England and built with the public-private partnership (PPP) model (Savas et al., 2020). Unlike public hospitals and training and research hospitals operating in Turkey, city hospitals are structured as large regional medical centers. The purpose of establishing these large health complexes is to meet the health needs of the people of the region with the latest technology, medical facilities, and qualified health personnel by having various health units (Atasever, 2018).

A New Strategic Change Application for Healthcare Systems: City Hospitals

City hospitals are defined as the integration of multi-part structures of health institutions in terms of management processes, which are built with the PPP model and strategic cooperation with health sector organizations and stakeholders (Ministry of Development, 2018; Kiviliene & Blazeviciene, 2019). These city hospitals, which serve in various regions in Turkey, have brought a new perspective to the country's health system and have begun to be implemented as a new reform (Kayral, 2019). This is the new and visible health policy action in Turkey, which has become one of the most controversial issues in the Turkish health system in recent years. The main purpose of putting city hospitals into operation is to combine small-capacity health facilities under larger campuses, to build more modern and functional health facilities, to provide high standards of service to increase the quality and effectiveness of health services, and to share the risks by reflecting the cost of health services to private sector entrepreneurs (World Bank, 2016; Uysal, 2020; Ministry of Health, 2022). In addition, the increase in the number of applications made to hospitals and the demand for health services over the years, as well as the increase in the need for the number of qualified health personnel to meet the demands, are also cited among the reasons for the implementation of this project (Ministry of Health, 2021). For this reason, in 2017, the first implementation of the city hospitals project, which undertakes the construction of large hospital complexes with the PPP model and will be operated in cooperation with the public sector for 25 years, have been implemented (Ministry of Health, 2021; Yılmaz & Aktas, 2021). In city hospitals, interdisciplinary working environments and multidisciplinary teamwork are prevalent. To provide high-quality patient care, these hospitals provide interdisciplinary, transdisciplinary, and effective collaborative practices (Ika et al., 2019; Okoh et al., 2020). Health policymakers need to understand the attitudes and intentions of health professionals regarding health system regulations so that they can design policies that improve the efficiency, effectiveness, and quality of health care (Rowe et al., 2018; Schot et al., 2020). For this reason, determining the opinions of certain occupational groups, such as specialist physicians, has critical importance for health policymakers to better respond to the needs in the health sector and to determine better policy practices.

Impact of City Hospitals Application on Healthcare

Due to the widespread use of city hospitals in the health services sector, the concept of health tourism, one of the areas where the health sector contributes directly to the economy, has recently started to take place in the agenda of Turkey frequently. Tourism also plays an important role in the socioeconomic development of societies and is considered a transformative force with a significant impact on the world (Siakwah, 2018). Health tourism, on the other hand, is defined as people traveling to another place to seek and receive health, medical, and/or wellness services for different reasons (Wong & Hazley, 2020).

Health tourism is seen as the strong driving force of the economy and society in cities and the economic pillars of developed countries (Lee & Li, 2019). Turkey is a country where health tourism has developed and made significant progress in recent years, both in terms of urbanization and in terms of risky moves in the health sector (Aksu & Bayar, 2019). This situation was evaluated as an opportunity for the further development of health tourism in city hospitals, and in this context, it was emphasized that the need for units and personnel for health tourism in city hospitals should be defined to ensure that Turkey is among the leading countries in health tourism in the 2019-2023 Strategic Plan. At the same time, it is aimed to create appropriate infrastructure and processes in city hospitals for an effective health tourism service (Ministry of Health, 2022).

Problem Statement

City hospitals have become one of the most current issues in the Turkish health system in recent years. While these projects raise many questions that need to be answered, they attract all the attention. Participation in such large-scale projects inevitably affects economic, social, and political relations and is a new reform. The problem addressed by this study is the ignorance of the long-term effects of a new policy change, such as city hospitals, on health care delivery. The problem is the lack of taking the opinions of health workers for city hospitals and evaluating the conditions of the use of designs in the world and in Turkey (Yesiltas, 2020). Therefore, in this study, the attitudes of a specific group, such as specialist physicians, who play an active role in the provision of health services, towards city hospitals were evaluated, considering the lack of multidimensional evaluations of health professionals for city hospitals. For this reason, for the first time, the attitudes of specialist physicians, who play an important role in service delivery, towards these complex structures were evaluated. Within the scope of the study, it is thought that these evaluations of specialist physicians will contribute to the accumulation of knowledge as an interdisciplinary approach to predict the long-term effects of city hospitals on the provision of health services and to increase sustainability.

Applicable Theories and Research From the Literature

New Public Management (NPM) policies in health care have been implemented in many OECD countries since the 1980s to address the complexity of health institutions as well as concerns about aging populations, increasing health expenditures, and technological and medical advances (Alonso et al., 2015; Ciani et al., 2018). NPM theory expresses a non-bureaucratic management style that minimizes centralization as much as possible, implements authorized projects, provides sensitivity training as well as corporate development, and prioritizes responsibility (Frederickson, 2015).

The spread of NPM on a global scale and the transition from traditional public service understandings to new public service understandings led to the emergence of a model like PPP in the service delivery process (Ozer, 2016). PPP practices, which are accepted as an extension of the NPM change agenda, have started to pave the way for meeting the financing needs of alternative sources in order to maintain quality, and undelayed health services. In this way, health services will be expanded, their efficiency will be increased, regional development will be provided and cost-effective medical care will be provided (Lamba et al., 2014; Ciani et al., 2018). Efforts to increase the effectiveness of new public investments to improve the performance of health services are critical for the sustainability of health systems (Chabrol et al., 2019).

Significance of the Study Statement

This study aims to evaluate the opinions of specialist physicians about city hospitals, which is a strategy and policy implementation that has just started to be implemented with the PPP model in Turkey and is of great importance in terms of health services. Within the scope of this study, which is based on the lack of evaluations of a specific group for city hospitals, the attitudes of specialist physicians towards city hospitals are discussed. Evaluation of the attitudes of specialist physicians towards city hospitals was handled in a multifaceted way with dimensions such as health service quality and efficiency, coordination of care components, interdisciplinary care teams, and integration of health services in city hospitals, and comparisons were made using different analysis techniques. The original contribution of this study is as follows; (i) understanding the attitudes of specialist physicians towards city hospitals, which has emerged as a new policy method, (ii) multidimensional consideration of the opinions of specialist physicians in terms of health service quality and efficiency, coordination of care components, interdisciplinary care teams, and integration of health services in city hospitals and (iii) classification performances of modern machine learning (ML) techniques such as Neural Network (NN), Random Forests (RF), Naïve Bayes (NB), and k-Nearest Neighbors (k-NN) are compared to predict the groupings of specialist physicians in terms of four dimensions of the ATIHC scale.

METHODS AND MATERIALS

Data Collection

In the scope of the study, the attitudes of specialist physicians working in a city hospital operating in Turkey towards city hospitals were evaluated. This study is a quantitative study that represents an analytical cross-sectional field study. The data set used in this research was obtained by applying a face-to-face survey method to specialist physicians. The "Initial Attitudes Toward Integrated Health Care Scale (ATIHC)" questionnaire developed by Zvonkovic (2015) was used to create the data set. Descriptive information about age, gender, marital status, time of work in the profession, and branches of work were obtained from the specialist physicians within the scope of the study. Then, these specialist physicians were asked to evaluate city hospitals in terms of health care quality and efficiency, coordination of care components, interdisciplinary care teams, and integration of health services dimensions. As a result of the study, 185 specialist physicians working in the city hospital participated in the study. Orange ML data mining program, and SPSS 25 program was used to evaluate the opinions of specialist physicians about city hospitals.

Grouping of Specialist Physicians in Terms of Four Dimensions: Hierarchical Clustering

In this study, the hierarchical clustering method was used to group the dimension classes of city hospitals and health service quality and efficiency, coordination of care components, interdisciplinary care teams, and integration of health services. In addition, the ANOVA test was used to determine whether the differences in the evaluations of the specialist physician groups towards city hospitals in terms of four dimensions were statistically significant.

Hierarchical Clustering (HC) consists of recursively dividing a dataset into successively smaller clusters (Cohen-Addad et al., 2019). The HC is a weighted graph representing a rooted tree that consists of building a binary joining tree starting from data items stored in leaves and continuing by combining the 'nearest' subsets by twos until reaching the root (Nielsen, 2016). By combining the most similar patterns in the cluster to create a larger cluster, HC produces high-quality clusters, but is rather time-consuming, which is a problem (Bouguettaya et al., 2015). HC, which is used to analyze, preprocess and classify large datasets, is very important for developing efficient and robust algorithms in various research fields such as big data analysis, machine learning, and bioinformatics (Cohen-Addad et al., 2019). Dendrogram, which is derived from the Greek 'dendron' meaning tree and 'gramma' meaning to draw, is used to display hierarchical clusters (Nielsen, 2016; Shetty & Singh, 2021). Different proximity measures are used to combine clusters in HC. The Ward method, also used in this study, is a frequently used hierarchical method (Jolliffe & Philipp, 2010). The Ward connection (Ward Jr, 1963), which is defined as the smallest increase in the sum of squares within the cluster due to the merging of the two clusters, shows the distance between the two clusters A and B with the ward's a and b centers and frequencies nA and nB as follows (Govender & Sivakumar, 2020) (See Equation 1):

$$d\left(A,B\right)=\frac{d\left(a,b\right)^{2}}{n_{A}^{-1}+n_{B}^{-1}} \tag{1}$$

Machine Learning Predictors of Four-Dimensional Classes Towards City Hospitals

In this study, ML predictors such as NN, RF, NB, and k-NN were used to discover the best predictors for the health care quality and efficiency, coordination of care components, interdisciplinary care teams, and integration of health services dimension classes for city hospitals. By comparing the estimation performances of the ML techniques, the best estimators of the four-dimension classes were determined.

NN is a set of algorithms that mimic the way the human brain works while trying to recognize fundamental relationships in a set of data. NNs, which have their roots in artificial intelligence, is a type of supervised learning (Mahesh, 2020; Qi et al., 2019). Referring to neuron systems, organic or artificial in nature, NNs produce the best possible result without the need to redesign the output criteria, as they can adapt to changing inputs (Mahesh, 2020). As one of the nonlinear statistical modeling tools, NN has strong evaluation capabilities to represent complex relationships between input and output properties (Goldberg, 2017). In the input layer, the number of neurons represents the variables used to predict the output. In the output layer, neurons represent the predicted variables (Amita et al., 2015). The following formula is used to calculate the output of a neuron with n inputs (Equation 2) (Beale et al., 2015). Y represents output, x_i represents input, w_i represents weight, b represents bias, and f represents a transfer function (Amita et al., 2015).

$$Y = f\left(\sum\nolimits_{i=1}^{n} w_i x_i + b\right) \tag{2}$$

RF, a supervised learning algorithm and is considered one of the most popular methods or frameworks used in data science, is used in regression and classification problems (Aung & Min, 2017; Karthika et al., 2019). The RF algorithm consists of multiple decision trees, which are different from each other (Karthika et al., 2019). In this algorithm, decision trees are created for a data set, and then the best solution is selected by guessing each and eventually voting (Zakariazadeh, 2022). The accuracy and reliability of prediction results increase with more decision trees (Lin et al., 2017). RF is recognized as one of the best-performing algorithms among classification algorithms. It is used to accurately classify large amounts of data and analyze complex data structures (Aung & Min, 2017). Applied for feature subset selection and incomplete data assignment, RF works very efficiently and can perform well for future data insertion. Following certain guidelines for tree growing, self-testing, tree combination, and finishing, the RF is robust to overfitting. It is also said to be more stable than other ML algorithms in very high-dimensional parameter spaces and the presence of outliers (Sarica et al., 2017). Formally, the tree is grown by using the formula Equation 3. In this model, the regions Rj and the coefficients βj are estimated from the data. Rj is typically discrete, and βj represents the mean of the Y values in Rj.

$$Y = \sum\nolimits_{j=1}^{r} \beta_j \mathrm{I}\left(x \in R_j\right) + \varepsilon \tag{3}$$

The main purpose of NB, a supervised classification method based on the assumption of class conditional independence, is to find the best match between a set of new data and a set of classifications within a given problem domain (Pham et al., 2017; Shirzadi et al., 2017; Yang, 2018). For this match to be probabilistic, it is necessary to convert the joint probabilities into the products of the previous probabilities and the conditional probabilities (Yang, 2018). NB is a classification algorithm based on Bayes' theorem and applying a 'naïve' conditional independence assumption between each pair of variables used. Using a set of arguments in this method, the posterior probability is generated for each possible class (Valdiviezo-Diaz et al., 2019). Since NB can calculate posterior probabilities for each variable used, multi-class density-based classification is frequently used in solving problems; and in this method, the value of a particular property is independent of the value of any other property given to the class variable (Niazi et al., 2019). NB has three most obvious advantages over other classifiers. The first is that NB is a very strong (naive) assumption of independence from any condition or event. Second, in this model, the structure is predefined and is easy and simple to construct. Lastly, the model is efficient and applicable to large datasets, especially when there is no strong correlation between features (Feng et al., 2018; Salmi & Rustam, 2019). The basis of the NB theorem used is the Bayesian formula as follows (Salmi & Rustam, 2019). (See Equation 4)

$$P(C \mid X) = \frac{P(X \mid C).P(C)}{P(X)} \tag{4}$$

P(C | X) is the posterior probability,
P(X | C) is probability,
P(C) is the pre-class probability,
P(X) is the predictive preliminary probability.

The k-NN algorithm is a supervised ML technique used in solving classification and regression problems (Mahesh, 2020). k-NN, which does not make assumptions about the basic data distribution, can perform very well in predictive and pattern recognition analysis. For a new data point, k-NN first ranks the data points closest to it in terms of distance from the destination data point (Gareth et al., 2013). This distance, which can be measured in various ways, is the Euclidean distance, as suggested and widely used by researchers (Islam et al., 2017). The k-NN algorithm, which is one of the simplest among other ML techniques, is a non-parametric method that is easy to implement and understand, and effective in managing both regression and classification problems (Islam et al., 2017; Mahesh, 2020). Despite its simplicity and easy implementation, the k-NN algorithm is known to perform well in a wide variety of problems (Triguero et al., 2019). k-NN is formulated as follows (Equation 5). The number of dimensions or features is n, x_i is the feature i in the data test, and y_i is the feature i in the data train (Daeli & Adiwijaya, 2020).

$$dist(x, y) = \sqrt{\sum_{i=1}^{n}(x_i - y_i)^2} \tag{5}$$

Investigating the relationship between the sensitivity and specificity of the binary classifier, the ROC curve is a performance measure used for classification problems at various threshold settings (Flach, 2016; Narkhede, 2018). ROC represents a probability curve and the Area Under the ROC Curve (AUC) represents the measure or degree of separability. The higher the AUC value, the better the model performs in predicting the classes, while providing information about how well the model distinguishes the classes (Narkhede, 2018). One of the most popular and widely used performance evaluation metrics in the ML community, ROC is highly consistent, especially when dealing with unstable datasets (Halimu et al., 2019).

RESULTS

Descriptive Statistics

The descriptive research findings regarding the personal characteristics and professional knowledge of the specialist physicians within the scope of the research are shown in Table 1. According to these findings, it was determined that 39.5% of the specialist physicians were between the ages of 30-37, 30.8% were between the ages of 38-45, 20.5% were between the ages of 46-53, and 9.2% were between the ages of

54 and over. While 62.2% of the specialist physicians working in the city hospital within the scope of the study were male, 37.8% were female, it was determined that 86.5% were married and 13.5% were single. Considering the findings regarding the working hours, it is seen that 28.7% of the specialist physicians have worked in the profession for 21 years and above, 23.2% have worked for 11-15 years, 23.2% have worked for 6-10 years, 17.3% have worked for 16-20 years and 7.6% of them have worked 1-5 years. While 84.3% of the specialist physicians gave a positive opinion on the eligibility of city hospitals for the health sector, 15.7% expressed a negative opinion. When the fields of specialization of the 185 specialist physicians included in the study are analyzed according to internal and surgical branches, it is seen that 53.5% of the physicians have specialization in internal branches and 46.5% in surgical branches.

Table 1. Descriptive statistics of specialist physicians

	n	%
Age		
30-37	73	39.5
38-45	57	30.8
46-53	38	20.5
54+	17	9.2
Sex		
Male	115	62.2
Female	70	37.8
Marital Status		
Single	25	13.5
Married	160	86.5
Time of Work in the Profession		
1-5 years	14	7.6
6-10 years	43	23.2
11-15 years	43	23.2
16-20 years	32	17.3
21+ years	53	28.6
Eligibility of Integrated Health Campuses		
Yes	156	84.3
No	29	15.7
Internal/Surgical Branches		
Internal	99	53.5
Surgery	86	46.5
Total	**185**	**100**

Grouping of Specialist Physicians in Terms of Four Dimensions: Hierarchical Clustering

Expert physician evaluations regarding the dimensions of health care quality and efficiency, coordination of care components, interdisciplinary care teams, and integration of health services were classified using the hierarchical clustering method. Ward's method, one of the proximity measures used to combine the clusters, was used. Accordingly, the optimal number of clusters was determined as three, and the number of specialist physicians was balanced within each group. The dendrogram corresponding to the clustering of the relationship between the clusters obtained as a result of hierarchical clustering and the four dimensions is shown in Figure 1. Then, the ANOVA test was used to determine whether the three clusters we obtained were different from each other in terms of four dimensions. The results of the ANOVA test in Table 2 showed that the differences between the evaluations of the three specialist physician groups in terms of health care quality and efficiency (F=134.363; p<0.01), coordination of care components (F=193.758; p<0.01), interdisciplinary care teams (F=138.381; p<0.01) and integration of health services (F=132.463; p<0.01) dimensions were statistically significant.

Figure 1. Hierarchical clustering

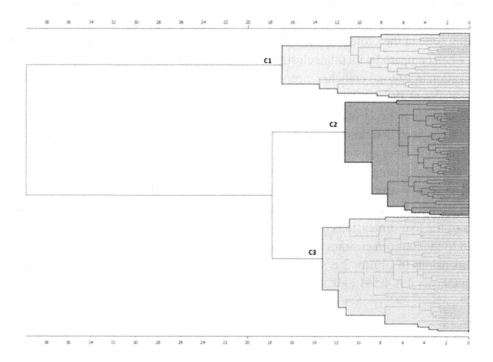

Table 2. ANOVA test

		Sum of Squares	df	Mean Square	F	Sig.
Health Care Quality and Efficiency	Between Groups	87.632	2	43.816	134.363	**p<0.0001**
	Within Groups	59.350	182	.326		
	Total	146.982	184			
Coordination of Care Components	Between Groups	114.717	2	57.359	193.758	**p<0.0001**
	Within Groups	53.878	182	.296		
	Total	168.595	184			
Interdisciplinary Care Teams	Between Groups	50.868	2	25.434	138.381	**p<0.0001**
	Within Groups	33.451	182	.184		
	Total	84.319	184			
Integration of Health Services	Between Groups	39.423	2	19.712	132.463	**p<0.0001**
	Within Groups	27.083	182	.149		
	Total	66.507	184			

Table 3 shows the descriptive statistics of the specialist physician groups in terms of four dimensions. Accordingly, the frequencies and percentages of the three specialist physician groups regarding age, gender, working time in the profession, and the surgical/internal branch specializations are presented. Accordingly, when compared with other clusters, it was seen that 64% of specialist physicians in Cluster 1 had specialization in internal branches, according to internal and surgical branches. Again, it has been observed that 39.2% of the specialist physicians in Cluster 2, within these three cluster groups, have worked in the profession for 21 or more years. When the ages of the specialist physicians in Cluster 3 are examined, it has been determined that the majority of the physicians in this group are in the 30-37 age range compared to other clusters. In the continuation of the table, the averages of the answers given by three specialist physician groups to the questions related to the four dimensions are given by using a 6-point Likert scale (1 = strongly disagree; 2 = disagree; 3 = somewhat disagree; 4 = somewhat agree; 5 = agree; 6 = strongly agree). Accordingly, when the general average of the answers given to the questions in terms of the four dimensions of the specialist physician groups is examined, the average of the answers given to the four dimensions in Cluster 1 is 3.335 ($\pm$0.098), the average of the answers given to the four dimensions in Cluster 2 is 4.981 ($\pm$0.385) and the average of the answers given to the four dimensions in Cluster 3 is 4.551 ($\pm$0.303).

Table 3. Basic statistics of specialist physicians' attitudes towards city hospitals exists in three clusters

	Cluster 1		Cluster 2		Cluster 3	
	n	%	n	%	n	%
Age						
30-37	15	38.5	25	33.8	33	45.8
38-45	15	38.5	21	28.4	21	29.2
46-53	3	7.7	20	27	15	20.8
54+	6	15.4	8	10.8	3	4.2
Sex						
Male	23	59	49	66.2	43	59.7
Female	16	41	25	33.8	29	40.3
Time of Working in the Profession						
1-5 years	2	5.1	5	6.8	7	9.7
6-10 years	12	30.8	14	18.9	17	23.6
11-15 years	8	20.5	14	18.9	21	29.2
16-20 years	9	23.1	12	16.2	11	15.3
21+ years	8	20.5	29	39.2	16	22.2
Internal/Surgical Branches						
Internal	25	64.1	36	48.6	38	52.8
Surgical	14	35.9	38	51.4	34	42.2
Four Dimensions						
	Mean	sd	Mean	sd	Mean	sd
Health Care Quality and Efficiency	3.343	0.70	5.191	0.524	4.647	0.538
Coordination of Care Components	3.271	0.754	5.370	0.466	4.872	0.479
Interdisciplinary Care Teams	3.472	0.685	4.868	0.356	4.543	0.299
Integration of Health Services	3.256	0.567	4.494	0.386	4.145	0.235
Total	3.335	0.098	4.981	0.385	4.551	0.303

In the next step, in Figure 2, there are figures in which the answers of three specialist physician groups using 6-point Likert scales are evaluated in terms of four dimensions of the ATIHC scale. Accordingly, while the y-axis indicates the probability of four dimensions, the x-axis indicates the Likert scale ranging from 1 to 6. According to Figure 2, the blue color represents cluster 1, the red color represents Cluster 2, and the green color represents Cluster 3. Considering the dimensions of quality and effectiveness in health services, it was seen that the majority of the physicians in Cluster 1 preferred the options of 'disagree' and 'somewhat disagree', and the experts in Cluster 2 preferred the options of 'agree' and 'strongly agree', and the majority of the experts in Cluster 3 preferred the options of 'somewhat agree' and 'agree'. When we look at the integration of the health services dimension, which is another dimension of the ATIHC scale, it is seen that almost all of the specialist physicians that exist in Cluster 1 choose the 'disagree' and 'somewhat disagree' options, the specialists that exist in Cluster 2 mostly choose the 'agree' option, and almost all of the specialists that exist in Cluster 3 choose the 'somewhat agree' and 'agree' option. In addition, it should be noted in Figure 2 that no one chooses the option '1 = strongly disagree' in any specialist physician group. Accordingly, it can be said that the evaluations of the specialist physicians forming Cluster 1 on the four dimensions are mostly 'strongly agree', the evaluations of the specialist physicians forming Cluster 2 are mostly 'disagree' and 'somewhat disagree' and finally the evaluations of the specialist physicians forming the Cluster 3 are mostly 'somewhat agree' and 'agree'.

Figure 2. Evaluation of the answers of three specialist physician groups in terms of four dimensions of the ATIHC scale

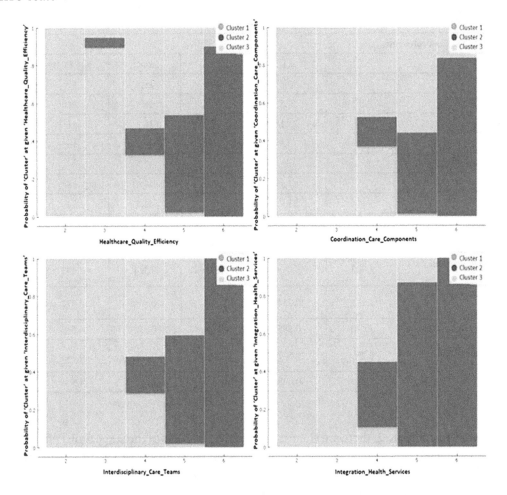

Machine Learning Predictors of Four-Dimensional Classes Towards City Hospitals

One of the objectives of this study is to find the best ML technique to estimate the clusters obtained from the dimensions of health care quality and efficiency, coordination of care components, interdisciplinary care teams, and integration of health services from the evaluations of specialist physicians for city hospitals. ML techniques such as NN, RF, NB, and k-NN were used to make these performance comparisons. The performance values of the compared ML techniques are seen in Table 4. In Table 4, the prediction performance results obtained from NN, RF, NB, and k-NN algorithms are compared. The performance of each model in the table was evaluated in terms of Area Under the ROC Curve (AUC), Classification Accuracy (CA), F1, Precision, and Recall values in the data set. AUC, CA, F1, precision, and recall values are frequently used to compare the prediction performance of learning algorithms in the presence of multiclass prediction variables (Deng et al., 2021). The fact that the scores obtained from these values are close to 1 means that the model performances perform well (Grandini et al., 2020). According to the findings obtained as a result of the study, it was seen that NB performed better than other predictors and the scores were closer to 1.

Table 4. Comparison of machine learning techniques prediction models performances

Model	AUC	CA	F1	Precision	Recall
Naïve Bayes	0.896	0.757	0.756	0.755	0.757
Random Forest (Number of trees=10)	0.853	0.735	0.735	0.736	0.735
Neural Network	0.850	0.735	0.737	0.738	0.735
k-Nearest Neighbor	0.845	0.714	0.716	0.720	0.714
Abbreviations: AUC: Area Under the ROC Curve; CA: Classification Accuracy					

According to the findings of this study, NB has the highest predictive performance (AUC=0.896; CA=0.757). RF (number of trees=10) and NN have performance values close to each other. RF performed as the second-best predictor (AUC=0.853; CA=0.735) and NN as the third-best predictor (AUC=0.850; CA=0.735). Among the ML techniques used, the technique with the lowest performance value was k-NN (AUC=0.845; CA=0.714). As a result of the results obtained, it has been confirmed that NB has higher classification performances for estimating the four-dimensional classes of multi-class specialist physicians' evaluations compared to other ML techniques.

Figure 3. ROC curve

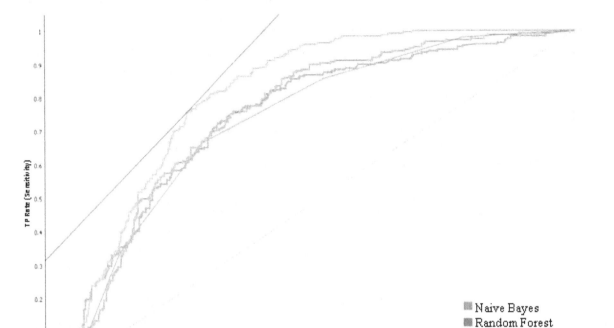

The ROC curve of the ML prediction models is shown in Figure 3. Accordingly, it is seen that NB performs better than other classifiers. Again, it is seen that RF and NN perform close to each other, but RF provides the best performance with a small advantage. Finally, it has been determined that k-NN has the lowest performance compared to the other three alternative classifiers. As a result, it can be said that NB best distinguishes the evaluations of specialist physicians for city hospitals in terms of four dimensions.

DISCUSSION

In recent years, there has been an increase in demand for modern and converted hospitals in Turkey as well as in the rest of the world, depending on the changing health conditions (Oguz, 2020). The expiration of the economic life of the old hospital buildings that are currently in operation, the obsolete architectural design of these buildings, the deterioration of their physical conditions, and inadequacies of infrastructure have prevented other health workers, especially physicians, from applying technological innovations and have caused efficiency losses in the provision of health services (Atasever et al., 2018). The findings obtained as a result of this study provide very important information for a better understanding of the evaluations of the specialist physicians, who are in the group directly affected by both strategy and policy changes and the transformation of health institutions in cities, towards city hospitals. When the findings of the study are examined, it is seen that the majority of the specialist physicians within the scope of the study are between the ages of 30-37 and they have been working in the health sector for more than 10 years. In this case, it is possible to say that the specialist physicians within the scope of the study have worked in the health sector for many years and have closely witnessed the changing health policy actions. Again, according to the findings of this study, it was determined that the majority of the opinions of specialist physicians about the suitability of city hospitals for the health sector were positive (84.3%). Despite these positive evaluations, city hospitals built with the PPP model, which includes the private sector in the health services that should be provided by the public, have been subjected to many criticisms since the first days. Before the establishment of city hospitals, the cities where these facilities will be established, population, geographical structure, transportation, and the habit of the people to receive health services were considered. With this planning application, the Ministry of Health aimed to improve physical access opportunities to health services so that every citizen's health service needs are met at the closest distance, and to balance the distribution of health resources across the country by expanding health services in each region (Health Services Planning Department, 2017). However, the transportation problem, due to the construction of these structures away from the city centers, the efficiency problems of high-capacity city hospitals, the challenges of internal transport due to large hospital buildings, and the unforeseen consequences of these facilities in the long term are among the most criticized issues of city hospitals (Savas et al., 2020; Turkish Medical Association, 2018). Although city hospitals have been under intense criticism, they have started to serve since 2017; there are currently 13 city hospitals operating in Turkey (General Directorate of Public Hospitals, 2022; Ministry of Health, 2021). Despite all these criticisms, city hospitals, which were built as world-class, ultra-luxurious, thousands of beds, state-of-the-art hospitals, serve as huge health complexes and gigantic centers where compact services will be provided for both national and foreign health tourism patients (Dogan & Aslan, 2019; Yılmaz & Aktas, 2021).

In our study, specialist physicians working in city hospitals were divided into three groups using the hierarchical clustering method according to the dimensions of quality, and efficiency of health services, coordination of care components, interdisciplinary care teams, and integration of health services. ANOVA was applied to test whether the groups formed with this clustering approach were statistically significant in terms of four dimensions. As a result of the test, it was seen that there were statistically significant differences between the evaluations of the specialist physician groups in terms of four dimensions. In the next stage of our study, we tried to find the best ML technique to estimate the clusters obtained from the four dimensions of the evaluations of the three specialist physician groups for city hospitals. In this context, the best-performing technique was tried to be determined by using ML techniques such as NN, RF, NB, and k-NN. Among these techniques, the technique with the highest prediction performance was NB (AUC=0.896; CA=0.757), followed by RF (AUC=0.853; CA=0.735), NN (AUC=0.850; CA=0.735) and k-NN (AUC=0.845; CA=0.714). This showed that NB distinguishes the evaluations of specialist physicians towards city hospitals in the best way in four dimensions.

Limitations

Considering the limitations of this study, only one city hospital operating in Turkey was included in the study. Another limitation is that only specialist physicians were included in the study. For this reason, it is one of the most important limitations of the research to evaluate the attitudes of health personnel towards city hospitals only from the eyes of specialist physicians. Since the research was conducted with a specific group of health professionals, it is not recommended to generalize the findings of the study to the behavior of all specialist physicians working in city hospitals throughout Turkey.

Strength of Study

The strongest aspect of this study is that it examines the evaluations of specialist physician groups for city hospitals in terms of four dimensions using modern ML prediction techniques. Another strength of this study, in which the opinions of specialist physicians for city hospitals were evaluated, is that NB showed the highest estimation performance as a result of the comparison of the performance indicators of the evaluations made in terms of the physician group and four dimensions using ML techniques. In this study, the opinions of specialist physicians for city hospitals, which started to be implemented as a new policy method in the health sector, were evaluated with versatile and different analysis techniques in terms of these strategic changes. It is expected that this study, which is carried out with this different perspective and analysis techniques, will make original contributions to the literature.

CONCLUSION AND RECOMMENDATIONS

In this study, the results of the evaluations for city hospitals, which started to be implemented with the PPP model in Turkey and became the focus of many discussions and criticisms, were discussed. According to the findings obtained because of the study, it was determined that the majority of specialist physicians had positive opinions about the suitability of city hospitals for the health sector. The findings obtained because of the research showed that specialist physicians working in city hospitals consist of three different groups in terms of health service quality and efficiency, coordination of care components, interdisciplinary care teams, and integration of health services. In the further analysis stage, it was determined that NB, among the ML techniques used to find the best predictors of the evaluations of specialist physician groups in terms of four dimensions, was the best-performing learning technique. The positive evaluations and criticisms of city hospitals by physicians who are experts in the integration of health services should be considered in the planning of city hospitals.

As city hospitals are an innovative policy action, they bring with them a lot of unknowns. The returns of this strategic change cannot be understood in the short term. For this reason, the positive evaluations and criticisms of physicians who are experts in the integration of health services should be considered in the planning of city hospitals. Within the framework of the evaluation of these views, it is recommended to include other professional communities in future studies and to create study designs that include questions about strategic and political changes in the health sector. It is also recommended to carry out international studies in which the evaluations obtained from the health facilities built with the PPP model in other countries as well as in Turkey are compared with the evaluations obtained from the city hospitals in Turkey. In studies where international comparisons are carried out, it is recommended to evaluate the opinions of service users, as well as health service providers, on a country basis, to better understand projects such as city hospitals and to provide health services effectively and efficiently.

Declaration of Interest

None of the authors has any conflict of interest to disclose.

Funding

No funding was received for this study.

ACKNOWLEDGMENT

This study was produced by Saylan B. (2022) from a part of the master's thesis named "Comparison of health professionals' attitudes towards integrated health campuses (city hospitals)" approved by Hacettepe University, Social Sciences Institute, Health Management Department, Ankara, Turkey.

REFERENCES

Aksu, A., & Bayar, K. (2019). Development of health tourism in Turkey: SWOT analysis of Antalya province. *Journal of Tourism Management Research*, *6*(2), 134–154. doi:10.18488/journal.31.2019.62.134.154

Alonso, J. M., Clifton, J., & Díaz-Fuentes, D. (2015). The impact of New Public Management on efficiency: An analysis of Madrid's hospitals. *Health Policy (Amsterdam)*, *119*(3), 333–340. doi:10.1016/j.healthpol.2014.12.001 PMID:25533550

Amita, J., Singh, J. S., & Kumar, G. P. (2015). Prediction of bus travel time using artificial neural network. *IJTTE. International Journal for Traffic and Transport Engineering*, *5*(4), 410–424. doi:10.7708/ijtte.2015.5(4).06

Atasever, M., Gözlü, M., Özaydın, M. M., Güler, H., Örnek, M., Barkan, O. B., Kavak, Y., & İlhan, N. (2018). *City Hospitals Research* [Şehir Hastaneleri Araştırması]. SAGLIK-SEN Strategic Research Center (SASAM).

Aung, Y. Y., & Min, M. M. (2017). An analysis of random forest algorithm based network intrusion detection system. In *2017 18th IEEE/ACIS International Conference on Software Engineering, Artificial Intelligence, Networking and Parallel/Distributed Computing (SNPD)* (pp. 127-132). IEEE.

Beale, M. H., Hagan, M. T., & Demuth, H. B. (2015). Neural network toolbox user's guide. The Math-Works Inc.

Bouguettaya, A., Yu, Q., Liu, X., Zhou, X., & Song, A. (2015). Efficient agglomerative hierarchical clustering. *Expert Systems with Applications*, *42*(5), 2785–2797. doi:10.1016/j.eswa.2014.09.054

Chabrol, F., Albert, L., & Ridde, V. (2019). 40 years after Alma-Ata, is building new hospitals in low-income and lower-middle-income countries beneficial? *BMJ Global Health*, *22*(3, Suppl 3), 1–5. doi:10.1136/bmjgh-2018-001293 PMID:31168419

Ciani, O., Torbica, A., Lecci, F., Morelli, M., Drummond, M., Tarricone, R., & Bene, L. D. (2018). Myth #5: Health Care Is Rightly Left to the Private Sector, for the Sake of Efficiency. In P. Adinolfi & E. Borgonovi (Eds.), *The Myths of Health Care* (pp. 123–154). Springer. doi:10.1007/978-3-319-53600-2_8

Cohen-Addad, V., Kanade, V., Mallmann-Trenn, F., & Mathieu, C. (2019). Hierarchical clustering: Objective functions and algorithms. *Journal of the Association for Computing Machinery, 66*(4), 1–42. doi:10.1145/3321386

Daeli, N. O. F., & Adiwijaya, A. (2020). Sentiment analysis on movie reviews using Information gain and K-nearest neighbor. *Journal of Data Science and Its Applications, 3*(1), 1–7.

Deng, F., Huang, J., Yuan, X., Cheng, C., & Zhang, L. (2021). Performance and efficiency of machine learning algorithms for analyzing rectangular biomedical data. *Laboratory Investigation, 101*(4), 430–441. doi:10.103841374-020-00525-x PMID:33574440

Dhyani, S., Lahoti, S., Khare, S., Pujari, P., & Verma, P. (2018). Ecosystem based Disaster Risk Reduction approaches (EbDRR) as a prerequisite for inclusive urban transformation of Nagpur City, India. *International Journal of Disaster Risk Reduction, 32*, 95–105. doi:10.1016/j.ijdrr.2018.01.018

Dogan, B. B., & Aslan, A. (2019). Current status of health tourism in Turkey and its impact on the economy of the country [Türkiye'de sağlık turizminin mevcut durumu ve ülke ekonomisine katkıları]. *Journal of Dicle University Economics and Administrative Sciences, 9*(18), 390–418.

Feng, X., Li, S., Yuan, C., Zeng, P., & Sun, Y. (2018). Prediction of slope stability using naive Bayes classifier. *KSCE Journal of Civil Engineering, 22*(3), 941–950. doi:10.100712205-018-1337-3

Flach, P. A. (2016). ROC analysis. In *Encyclopedia of machine learning and data mining* (pp. 1–8). Springer.

Frederickson, H. G. (2015). Toward a New Public Administration. In J. M. Shafritz & A. C. Hyde (Eds.), *Classics of Public Administration*. Eight Edition.

Gareth, J., Daniela, W., Trevor, H., & Robert, T. (2013). Springer texts in statistics. In G. Casella, S. Fienberg, & I. Olkin (Eds.), *An introduction to statistical learning* (1st ed., pp. 203–264).

General Directorate of Public Hospitals. (2022). *City hospitals* [Şehir hastaneleri]. Retrieved 07.09.2022 from https://khgmsehirhastaneleridb.saglik.gov.tr/TR-43796/sehir-hastanelerimiz.html

Goldberg, Y. (2017). Neural network methods for natural language processing. *Synthesis Lectures on Human Language Technologies, 10*(1), 1-309.

Govender, P., & Sivakumar, V. (2020). Application of k-means and hierarchical clustering techniques for analysis of air pollution: A review (1980–2019). *Atmospheric Pollution Research, 11*(1), 40–56. doi:10.1016/j.apr.2019.09.009

Grandini, M., Bagli, E., & Visani, G. (2020). *Metrics for multi-class classification: an overview.* arXiv preprint arXiv:2008.05756.

Halimu, C., Kasem, A., & Newaz, S. S. (2019). Empirical comparison of area under ROC curve (AUC) and Mathew correlation coefficient (MCC) for evaluating machine learning algorithms on imbalanced datasets for binary classification. *Proceedings of the 3rd international conference on machine learning and soft computing*, 1-6. 10.1145/3310986.3311023

Health Services Planning Department. (2017). *Health service area* [Sağlık hizmet bölgesi]. Retrieved 01.09.2022 from https://planlamadb.saglik.gov.tr/TR,5708/saglik-hizmet-bolgesi.html

Ika, C., Novieastari, E., & Nuraini, T. (2019). The role of a head nurses in preventing interdisciplinary conflicts. *Enfermeria Clinica, 29*, 123–127. doi:10.1016/j.enfcli.2019.04.019

Islam, M. M., Iqbal, H., Haque, M. R., & Hasan, M. K. (2017). *Prediction of breast cancer using support vector machine and K-Nearest neighbors. In 2017 IEEE Region 10 Humanitarian Technology Conference (R10-HTC).* IEEE.

Jolliffe, I. T., & Philipp, A. (2010). Some recent developments in cluster analysis. *Physics and Chemistry of the Earth Parts A/B/C, 35*(9-12), 309–315. doi:10.1016/j.pce.2009.07.014

Karthika, P., Murugeswari, R., & Manoranjithem, R. (2019). *Sentiment analysis of social media network using random forest algorithm. In 2019 IEEE international conference on intelligent techniques in control, optimization and signal processing (INCOS).* IEEE.

Kayral, İ. H. (2019). Can the theory of broken windows be used for patient safety in city hospitals management model? [Kırık pencereler teorisi, şehir hastaneleri yönetim modelinde hasta güvenliği için kullanılabilir mi?]. *Hacettepe Journal of Health Administration, 22*(3), 677–694.

Kiviliene, J., & Blazeviciene, A. (2019). Review of complex adaptive systems in nursing practice. *Journal of Complexity in Health Sciences, 2*(2), 46–50. doi:10.21595/chs.2019.21169

Lamba, M., Altan, Y., Aktel, M., & Kerman, U. (2014). Reconstruction in the Ministry of Health: An evaluation in terms of the new public management [Sağlık Bakanlığı'nda yeniden yapılanma: yeni kamu yönetimi açısından bir değerlendirme]. *Amme Idaresi Dergisi, 47*(1), 53–78.

Lee, C.-W., & Li, C. (2019). The process of constructing a health tourism destination index. *International Journal of Environmental Research and Public Health, 16*(22), 4579. doi:10.3390/ijerph16224579 PMID:31752340

Lin, W., Wu, Z., Lin, L., Wen, A., & Li, J. (2017). An ensemble random forest algorithm for insurance big data analysis. *IEEE Access : Practical Innovations, Open Solutions, 5*, 16568–16575. doi:10.1109/ACCESS.2017.2738069

Mahesh, B. (2020). Machine learning algorithms-a review. *International Journal of Science and Research, 9*, 381-386.

Mason, M. (2022). *What is sustainability and why is it important?* Retrieved 12.09.2022 from https://www.environmentalscience.org/sustainability

Ministry of Development. (2018). *Developments in public-private partnership practices in the world and in Turkey 2017.* Retrieved from 18.01.2023 from https://www.sbb.gov.tr/wp-content/uploads/2019/05/Kamu-Ozel_Isbirligi_Raporu-2018.pdf

Ministry of Health. (2021). *Health statistics yearbook 2019.* Retrieved 09.09.2022 from https://sbsgm.saglik.gov.tr/eklenti/40566/0/health-statistics-yearbook-2019pdf.pdf

Ministry of Health. (2022). *2019-2023 strategic plan updated version* [2019-2023 stratejik planı güncellenmiş versiyonu]. Retrieved 10.09.2022 from https://sgb.saglik.gov.tr/TR-61668/tc-saglik-bakanligi-2019-2023--stratejik-plani-guncellenmis-versiyonu.html

Narkhede, S. (2018). Understanding auc-roc curve. *Towards Data Science*, *26*(1), 220–227.

Niazi, K. A. K., Akhtar, W., Khan, H. A., Yang, Y., & Athar, S. (2019). Hotspot diagnosis for solar photovoltaic modules using a Naive Bayes classifier. *Solar Energy*, *190*, 34–43. doi:10.1016/j.solener.2019.07.063

Nielsen, F. (2016). *Introduction to HPC with MPI for Data Science*. Springer. doi:10.1007/978-3-319-21903-5

Oguz, A. B. (2020). Turkish health policies: Past, present, and future. *Social Work in Public Health*, *35*(6), 456–472. doi:10.1080/19371918.2020.1806167 PMID:32811368

Okoh, A. E., Akinrolie, O., Bell-Gam, H. I., Adandom, I., Ibekaku, M. C., & Kalu, M. E. (2020). Nigerian healthcare workers' perception of transdisciplinary approach to older adults' care: A qualitative case study. *International Journal of Care Coordination*, *23*(2-3), 92–106. doi:10.1177/2053434520954362

Ozer, M. A. (2016). A New Service Delivery Model in Health Sector: Public Private Partnership [Sağlık Sektöründe Yeni Bir Hizmet Sunum Modeli: Kamu Özel Ortaklığı]. *Journal of Social Security*, *6*(1), 9–38.

Pham, B. T., Tien Bui, D., Pourghasemi, H. R., Indra, P., & Dholakia, M. (2017). Landslide susceptibility assesssment in the Uttarakhand area (India) using GIS: A comparison study of prediction capability of naïve bayes, multilayer perceptron neural networks, and functional trees methods. *Theoretical and Applied Climatology*, *128*(1), 255–273. doi:10.100700704-015-1702-9

Qi, X., Chen, G., Li, Y., Cheng, X., & Li, C. (2019). Applying neural-network-based machine learning to additive manufacturing: Current applications, challenges, and future perspectives. *Engineering (Beijing)*, *5*(4), 721–729. doi:10.1016/j.eng.2019.04.012

Rowe, A. K., Rowe, S. Y., Peters, D. H., Holloway, K. A., Chalker, J., & Ross-Degnan, D. (2018). Effectiveness of strategies to improve health-care provider practices in low-income and middle-income countries: A systematic review. *The Lancet. Global Health*, *6*(11), e1163–e1175. doi:10.1016/S2214-109X(18)30398-X PMID:30309799

Salmi, N., & Rustam, Z. (2019). Naïve Bayes classifier models for predicting the colon cancer. *IOP Conference Series. Materials Science and Engineering*, *546*(5), 052068. doi:10.1088/1757-899X/546/5/052068

Sarica, A., Cerasa, A., & Quattrone, A. (2017). Random forest algorithm for the classification of neuroimaging data in Alzheimer's disease: A systematic review. *Frontiers in Aging Neuroscience*, *9*, 329. doi:10.3389/fnagi.2017.00329 PMID:29056906

Savas, T., Keles, R., & Goktas, B. (2020). Public private partnership model: Ankara city hospital example [Kamu özel işbirliği modeli Ankara şehir hastanesi örneği]. *Journal of Health Sciences, 9*(2), 22-31.

Schot, E., Tummers, L., & Noordegraaf, M. (2020). Working on working together. A systematic review on how healthcare professionals contribute to interprofessional collaboration. *Journal of Interprofessional Care*, *34*(3), 332–342. doi:10.1080/13561820.2019.1636007 PMID:31329469

Shetty, P., & Singh, S. (2021). Hierarchical clustering: A survey. *International Journal of Applied Research*, *7*(4), 178–181. doi:10.22271/allresearch.2021.v7.i4c.8484

Shirzadi, A., Bui, D. T., Pham, B. T., Solaimani, K., Chapi, K., Kavian, A., Shahabi, H., & Revhaug, I. (2017). Shallow landslide susceptibility assessment using a novel hybrid intelligence approach. *Environmental Earth Sciences*, *76*(2), 1–18. doi:10.100712665-016-6374-y

Siakwah, P. (2018). Tourism geographies and spatial distribution of tourist sites in Ghana. *African Journal of Hospitality, Tourism and Leisure*, *7*(1), 1–19.

Triguero, I., García-Gil, D., Maillo, J., Luengo, J., García, S., & Herrera, F. (2019). Transforming big data into smart data: An insight on the use of the k-nearest neighbors algorithm to obtain quality data. *Wiley Interdisciplinary Reviews. Data Mining and Knowledge Discovery*, *9*(2), e1289. doi:10.1002/widm.1289

Turkish Medical Association. (2018). *Hidden privatization in treatment services: city hospitals workshop report* [Tedavi hizmetlerinde gizli özelleştirme: şehir hastaneleri çalıştay raporu]. https://ato.org.tr/files/documents/0673367001518504406.pdf

Uysal, Y. (2020). The private sector incentive factors in public-private partnership model: Case of city hospitals. *MANAS Journal of Social Studies*, *9*(1), 386–401.

Valdiviezo-Diaz, P., Ortega, F., Cobos, E., & Lara-Cabrera, R. (2019). A collaborative filtering approach based on Naïve Bayes classifier. *IEEE Access : Practical Innovations, Open Solutions*, *7*, 108581–108592. doi:10.1109/ACCESS.2019.2933048

Ward, J. H. Jr. (1963). Hierarchical grouping to optimize an objective function. *Journal of the American Statistical Association*, *58*(301), 236–244. doi:10.1080/01621459.1963.10500845

Wong, B. K. M., & Hazley, S. A. S. A. (2020). The future of health tourism in the industrial revolution 4.0 era. *Journal of Tourism Futures*, *7*(2), 267–272. doi:10.1108/JTF-01-2020-0006

World Bank. (2016). *Public-private partnerships in health: World Bank group engagement in health PPPs*. World Bank Washington.

Yang, F.-J. (2018). An implementation of naive bayes classifier. In *2018 International conference on computational science and computational intelligence (CSCI)*. IEEE.

Yesiltas, A. (2020). Public private partnership in the health sector: An evaluation on city hospitals [Sağlık sektöründe kamu özel ortaklığı: Şehir hastaneleri üzerine bir değerlendirme]. *International Journal of Health Management and Strategies Research*, *6*(1), 15–28.

Yılmaz, V., & Aktas, P. (2021). The making of a global medical tourism destination: From state-supported privatisation to state entrepreneurialism in healthcare in Turkey. *Global Social Policy*, *21*(2), 301–318. doi:10.1177/1468018120981423

Zakariazadeh, A. (2022). Smart meter data classification using optimized random forest algorithm. *ISA Transactions*, *126*, 361–369. doi:10.1016/j.isatra.2021.07.051 PMID:34389178

Zvonkovic, J. N. (2015). *Development of the attitudes toward integrated health care scale* [Master's thesis]. Southern Illinois University.

Compilation of References

Types of Risk Management Strategies to Follow in 2021. (2021, February 18). AuditBoard. https://www.auditboard.com/blog/10-risk-management-strategies-2021/

Aagaard, A. (2018). *Sustainable business models: Innovation, implementation and success*. Springer. https://link.springer.com/book/10.1007/978-3-319-93275-0

Abdullah, M. (2019). Consumer use of mobile banking (M-Banking) in Saudi Arabia: Towards an integrated model. *International Journal of Information Management*, *44*(February), 38–52. doi:10.1016/j.ijinfomgt.2018.09.002

Aboramadan, M., Albashiti, B., Alharazin, H., & Zaidoune, S. (2020). Organizational culture, innovation and performance: A study from a non-western context. *Journal of Management Development*, *39*(4), 437–451. doi:10.1108/JMD-06-2019-0253

Abramo, G., D'Angelo, C. A., & Soldatenkova, A. (2017). An investigation on the skewness patterns and fractal nature of research productivity distributions at field and discipline level. *Journal of Informetrics*, *11*(1), 324–335. doi:10.1016/j.joi.2017.02.001

Abrard, S., Bertrand, M., De Valence, T., & Schaupp, T. (2019). Physiological, cognitive, and neuromuscular effects of heat exposure on firefighters after a live training scenario. *International Journal of Occupational Safety and Ergonomics*, *27*(1), 185–193. doi:10.1080/10803548.2018.1550899 PMID:30507358

Acheampong, R. A., Cugurullo, F., Gueriau, M., & Dusparic, I. (2021). Can autonomous vehicles enable sustainable mobility in future cities? Insights and policy challenges from user preferences over different urban transport options. *Cities (London, England)*, *112*, 103134. doi:10.1016/j.cities.2021.103134

Ackermann, F., & Eden, C. (2015). Intervention action research: A method for studying and transforming practice. *Journal of Management Development*, *34*(1), 4–17.

Adisu, Z. (2018). *E-Banking Service Practices And Its Challenges On Trade Activities In Selected Commercial Banks (In Case Of Debre Berhan)* [Doctoral Dissertation].

Adnan, N., Nordin, S., Rahman, I., Vasant, P., & Noor, A. (2016). A comprehensive review on theoretical framework-based electric vehicle consumer adoption research. *International Journal of Energy Research*, *41*(3), 317–335. doi:10.1002/er.3640

Adrian, T. (2021). *BigTech in financial services*. Academic Press.

Adu, P. (2019). *A step-by-step guide to qualitative data coding* (1st ed.). Routledge. doi:10.4324/9781351044516

Advantages and Disadvantages. (2020, April 26). *Advantages and disadvantages of qualitative research*. https://www.advantages-disadvantages.co/pros-and-cons-of-qualitative-research-benefits/

Afshan, & Sharif, A. (2016, May). Acceptance of mobile banking framework in Pakistan. *Telematics and Informatics*, *33*(2), 370–387. doi:10.1016/j.tele.2015.09.005

After reading, writing and arithmetic, the 4th "r" of literacy is cyber-risk. (2023, January 5). World Economic Forum. https://www.weforum.org/agenda/2020/12/cyber-risk-cyber-security-education

Agarwal, S., Makkar, S., & Tran, D.-T. (Eds.). (2020). *Privacy Vulnerabilities and Data Security Challenges in the IoT* (1st ed.). CRC Press. doi:10.1201/9780429322969

Agyeman, J., Schlosberg, D., Craven, L., & Matthews, C. (2016). Trends and directions in environmental justice: From inequity to everyday life, community, and just Sustainabilities. *Annual Review of Environment and Resources*, *41*(1), 321–340. doi:10.1146/annurev-environ-110615-090052

Ahmed, U. A., Aktar, M. A., & Alam, M. M. (2021). Racial discrimination and poverty reduction for sustainable development. Encyclopedia of the UN Sustainable Development Goals, 741-750. https://doi.org/ doi:10.1007/978-3-319-95714-2_10

Ahmed, S. (2014). Not in the Mood. *New Formations*, *82*(82), 13–28. doi:10.3898/NeWF.82.01.2014

Ahuja, K., & Khosla, A. (Eds.). (2019). *Driving the Development, Management, and Sustainability of Cognitive Cities*. IGI Global. doi:10.4018/978-1-5225-8085-0

Aisbett, B., Wolkow, A., Sprajcer, M., & Ferguson, S. (2012). "Awake, smoky, and hot": Providing an evidence-base for managing the risks associated with occupational stressors encountered by wildland firefighters. *Applied Ergonomics*, *43*(5), 916–925. doi:10.1016/j.apergo.2011.12.013 PMID:22264875

Akinola Kayode, E. (2017). Internet Banking In Nigeria: Authentication Methods, Weaknesses and Security Strength. *American Journal of Engineering Research, 6*(9), 226-231.

Akpa, V. O., Asikhia, O. U., & Nneji, N. E. (2021). Organizational Culture and Organizational Performance: A Review of Literature. *International Journal of Advances in Engineering and Management*, *3*(1), 361–372. doi:10.35629/5252-0301361372

Aksu, A., & Bayar, K. (2019). Development of health tourism in Turkey: SWOT analysis of Antalya province. *Journal of Tourism Management Research*, *6*(2), 134–154. doi:10.18488/journal.31.2019.62.134.154

Alahmari, A., & Duncan, B. (2020, June). Cybersecurity risk management in small and medium-sized enterprises: A systematic review of recent evidence. In 2020 international conference on cyber situational awareness, data analytics and assessment (CyberSA) (pp. 1-5). IEEE.

Alalwan. (2017). Social Media in Marketing: A Review and Analysis of the Existing Literature. *Telematics and Informatics, 34*(7). doi:10.1016/j.tele.2017.05.008

Alalwan, A. A., Baabdullah, A. M., Rana, N. P., Tamilmani, K., & Dwivedi, Y. K. (2021b). The impact of augmented reality on training: An exploratory study. *Computers in Human Behavior, 120*, 106767.

Alalwan, A. A., Rana, N. P., Dwivedi, Y. K., & Algharabat, R. (2021). Barriers to the adoption of Augmented Reality in training: An empirical investigation in the oil and gas industry. *Journal of Business Research*, *129*, 386–395. doi:10.1016/j.jbusres.2021.01.004

Alam, S. S., Ali, S., Khurshid, K., Hussain, M., & Chang, V. (2021). AI-based Performance Analysis for Efficient Employee Training and Development. *IEEE Access : Practical Innovations, Open Solutions*, *9*, 116330–116345.

Alassaf, M., & Alkhalifah, A. (2021). Exploring the Influence of Direct and Indirect Factors on Information Security Policy Compliance: A Systematic Literature Review. *IEEE Access : Practical Innovations, Open Solutions*, 9, 162687–162705. doi:10.1109/ACCESS.2021.3132574

Aldowaish, A., Kokuryo, J., Almazyad, O., & Goi, H. C. (2022). Environmental, social, and governance integration into the business model: Literature review and research agenda. *Sustainability (Basel)*, 14(5), 2959. doi:10.3390u14052959

Alesi, P. (2008). Building enterprise-wide resilience by integrating business continuity capability into day-to-day business culture and technology. *Journal of Business Continuity & Emergency Planning*, 2(3), 214–220. PMID:21339108

Algarni, A., Thayananthan, V., & Malaiya, Y. K. (2021). Quantitative Assessment of Cybersecurity Risks for Mitigating Data Breaches in Business Systems. *Applied Sciences (Basel, Switzerland)*, 11(8), 3678. doi:10.3390/app11083678

AlHashmi, M., Jabeen, F., & Papastathopoulos, A. (2019). Impact of leader–member exchange and perceived organizational support on turnover intention. *Policing*, 42(4), 520–536. doi:10.1108/PIJPSM-06-2018-0081

Ali, H. (2018). Coping strategies to lead and succeed as a minority woman. *Forbes*. https://www.forbes.com/sites/ellevate/2018/04/23/coping-strategies-to-lead-and-succeed-as-a-minority-woman/#583f548f3dbb

Ali, N. A., Kanesan, J., Anis Salwa, M. K., Irfan, A. B., Kamangar, S., Hussien, M., & Maughal Ahmed, A. B. (2023). Training Multilayer Neural Network Based on Optimal Control Theory for Limited Computational Resources. *Mathematics*, 11(3), 778. doi:10.3390/math11030778

Ali, R. F., Dominic, P. D. D., Ali, S. F., Rehman, M., & Sohail, A. (2021). Information Security Behavior and Information Security Policy Compliance: A Systematic Literature Review for Identifying the Transformation Process from Noncompliance to Compliance. *Applied Sciences (Basel, Switzerland)*, 11(8), 3383. doi:10.3390/app11083383

Allan, N. P., Short, N. A., Albanese, B. J., Keough, M. E., & Schmidt, N. B. (2015). An anxiety sensitivity intervention's direct and mediating effects on posttraumatic stress disorder symptoms in trauma-exposed individuals. *Cognitive Behaviour Therapy*, 44(6), 512–524. doi:10.1080/16506073.2015.1075227 PMID:26427912

Alonso, J. M., Clifton, J., & Díaz-Fuentes, D. (2015). The impact of New Public Management on efficiency: An analysis of Madrid's hospitals. *Health Policy (Amsterdam)*, 119(3), 333–340. doi:10.1016/j.healthpol.2014.12.001 PMID:25533550

Alsharif, M. G., Mishra, S., & Alshehri, M. (2022). Impact of Human Vulnerabilities on Cybersecurity. *Computer Systems Science and Engineering*, 40(3), 1153–1166. doi:10.32604/csse.2022.019938

Alsheikh-Ali, A. A., Qureshi, W., Al-Mallah, M. H., & Ioannidis, J. P. A. (2011). Public availability of published research data in high-impact journals. *PLoS One*, 6(9), e24357. doi:10.1371/journal.pone.0024357 PMID:21915316

Althabe, G. (1999). Hacia una Antropología del presente. In G. Althabe (Ed.), *Antropología del presente* (pp. 11–21). Edicial.

Althor, G., & Witt, B. (2020). A quantitative systematic review of distributive environmental justice literature: A rich history and the need for an enterprising future. *Journal of Environmental Studies and Sciences*, 10(1), 91–103. doi:10.100713412-019-00582-9

Alvi, M. H. (2016). *A Manual for Selecting Sampling Techniques in Research*. https://mpra.ub.uni-muenchen.de/70218/

Amel-Zadeh, A., & Serafeim, G. (2017). Why and how investors use ESG information: Evidence from a global survey. SSRN *Electronic Journal*. doi:10.2139/ssrn.2925310

American Counseling Association. (2014). *2014 ACA code of ethics*. Author.

American Psychological Association. (2011, August 18). *Study finds sex differences in mental illness* [Press release]. http://www.apa.org/news/press/releases/2011/08/mental-illness

American Psychological Association. (2013). Guidelines for psychological practice in health care delivery systems. *The American Psychologist*, *68*(1), 1–6. doi:10.1037/a0029890 PMID:23025748

American Psychological Association. (2022). Publication manual of the American psychological association. American Psychological Association.

American Psychology Association. (n.d.). *Inclusive Language Guidelines*. Retrieved April 13, 2023, from https://www.apa.org/about/apa/equity-diversity-inclusion/language-guidelines

American Society for Quality. (n.d.). *PDCA Cycle - What is the Plan-Do-Check-Act Cycle?* https://asq.org/quality-resources/pdca-cycle

Amini, M. H., Arasteh, H., & Siano, P. (2019). Sustainable smart cities through the lens of complex interdependent infrastructures: panorama and state-of-the-art. In *Sustainable interdependent networks II* (pp. 45–68). Springer. doi:10.1007/978-3-319-98923-5_3

Amita, J., Singh, J. S., & Kumar, G. P. (2015). Prediction of bus travel time using artificial neural network. *IJTTE. International Journal for Traffic and Transport Engineering*, *5*(4), 410–424. doi:10.7708/ijtte.2015.5(4).06

Amsler, T. (2008). Engaging African-Americans in the civic and political life of their communities. *Western City Magazine*. https://www.westerncity.com/article/engaging-african-americans-civic-and-political-life-their-communities

Anderson, B. (2017, October 21). *John Besh restaurants fostered a culture of sexual harassment, 25 women say*. Retrieved from https://www.nola.com/business/2017/10/john_besh_restaurants_fostered.html

Anderson, A. (2011). *Engaging resistance: How ordinary people successfully champion Change*. Stanford University Press.

Anderson, L. S., Page, J., & Zahl, M. (2022). The status of clinical supervision in therapeutic recreation in 2020. *Therapeutic Recreation Journal*, *56*(1), 55–82. doi:10.18666/TRJ-2022-V56-I1-11189

Anderson, M. (2017). Transformational leadership in education: A review of existing literature. *International Social Science Review*, *93*(1), 1–13.

Aneshensel, C. S. (1992). Social stress: Theory and research. *Annual Review of Sociology*, *18*(1), 15–38. doi:10.1146/annurev.so.18.080192.000311

Angerer, P., Kadlez-Gebhardt, S., Delius, M., Raluca, P., & Nowak, D. (2018). Comparison of Cardiocirculatory and thermal strain of male firefighters during fire suppression to exercise stress test and aerobic exercise testing. *The American Journal of Cardiology*, *102*(11), 1551–1556. doi:10.1016/j.amjcard.2008.07.052 PMID:19026313

Anicha, C. L., Bilen-Green, C., Burnett, A., Froelich, K., & Holbrook, S. (2017). Institutional transformation: Toward a diversity-positive campus culture. *Journal of Women and Minorities in Science and Engineering*, *23*(2), 147–167. doi:10.1615/JWomenMinorScienEng.2017017021

Anshari, M., Syafrudin, M., Fitriyani, N. L., & Razzaq, A. (2022). Ethical Responsibility and Sustainability (ERS) Development in a Metaverse Business Model. *Sustainability (Basel)*, *14*(23), 15805. doi:10.3390u142315805

Anthony, B. Jnr. (2020a). Managing digital transformation of smart cities through enterprise architecture – a review and research agenda. *Enterprise Information Systems*, *15*(3), 299–331. doi:10.1080/17517575.2020.1812006

Anthony, B. Jnr. (2020b). Smart city data architecture for energy prosumption in municipalities: Concepts, requirements, and future directions. *International Journal of Green Energy*, *17*(13), 827–845. doi:10.1080/15435075.2020.1791878

Anthony, B. Jnr. (2021). Integrating Electric Vehicles to Achieve Sustainable Energy as a Service Business Model in Smart Cities. *Frontiers In Sustainable Cities*, *3*, 1–12. doi:10.3389/frsc.2021.685716

Apodaca, E., & Kleiner, B. H. (2001). Sexual harassment in the business environment. *The International Journal of Sociology and Social Policy*, *21*(8-10), 3–13. doi:10.1108/01443330110789763

APSC. (2022, September 27). *Diversity and inclusion report 2022*. https://www.apsc.gov.au/working-aps/diversity-and-inclusion/diversity-and-inclusion-report-2022

Apuke, O. D. (2016). Social and Traditional Mainstream Media of Communication: Synergy and Variance Perspective. *Journal of New Media and Mass Communication*, *53*, 83–86. www.iiste.org

Aras, G., & Crowther, D. (2008). Evaluating sustainability: A need for standards. *Issues In Social & Environmental Accounting*, *2*(1), 19–35. doi:10.22164/isea.v2i1.23

Arbnor, I., & Bjerke, B. (2009). *Methodology for creating business knowledge* (3rd ed.). SAGE Publications. doi:10.4135/9780857024473

Arbona, C., & Schwartz, J. P. (2017). Posttraumatic stress disorder symptom clusters, depression, alcohol abuse, and general stress among Hispanic male firefighters. *Hispanic Journal of Behavioral Sciences*, *38*(4), 507–522. doi:10.1177/0739986316661328

Arianna, T., Kamps, J., Akartuna, E. A., Hetzel, F. J., Bennett, K., Davies, T., & Johnson, S. D. (2022). Cryptocurrencies and future financial crime. *Crime Science*, *11*(1), 1. Advance online publication. doi:10.118640163-021-00163-8 PMID:35013699

Armstrong, V. (2019, July 8). *Stigma regarding mental illness among people of color*. National Council for Behavioral Health. https://www.thenationalcouncil.org/BH365/2019/07/08/stigma-regarding-mental-illness-among-people-of-color/

Armstrong, D., Shakespeare-finch, J., & Shochet, I. (2019). Predicting posttraumatic growth and posttraumatic stress in firefighters. *Australian Journal of Psychology*, *66*(1), 38–46. doi:10.1111/ajpy.12032

Armstrong, S. J., & Sadler-Smith, E. (2008). Learning on demand at your own pace, in rapid bite-sized chunks: The future shape of management development? *Academy of Management Learning & Education*, *7*(4), 571–586. doi:10.5465/amle.2008.35882197

Arora, N. K., Fatima, T., Mishra, I., Verma, M., Mishra, J., & Mishra, V. (2018). Environmental sustainability: Challenges and viable solutions. *Environmental Sustainability*, *1*(4), 309–340. doi:10.100742398-018-00038-w

Arrasyid, M., Amaliyah, A., & Pandin, M. (2019). *Review on Leader-Member Exchange Theory: Antecedent and The Effect on Employee Performance*. Academic Press.

Arredondo-Soto, K. C., Blanco-Fernández, J., Miranda-Ackerman, M. A., Solis-Quinteros, M. M., Realyvásquez-Vargas, A., & García-Alcaraz, J. L. (2021). A Plan-Do-Check-Act Based Process Improvement Intervention for Quality Improvement. *IEEE Access : Practical Innovations, Open Solutions*, *9*, 132779–132790. doi:10.1109/ACCESS.2021.3112948

Asadzadeh, A., Mohammadzadeh, Z., Fathifar, Z., Jahangiri-Mirshekarlou, S., & Rezaei-Hachesu, P. (2022). A framework for information technology-based management against COVID-19 in Iran. *BMC Public Health*, *22*(1), 402. doi:10.118612889-022-12781-1 PMID:35219292

Ashcraft, K. L. (2017). 'Submission' to the rule of excellence: Ordinary affect and precarious resistance in the labor of organization and management studies. *Organization*, *24*(1), 36–58. doi:10.1177/1350508416668188

Ashikali, T., & Groeneveld, S. (2015). Diversity management in public organizations and its effect on employees' affective commitment: The role of transformational leadership and the inclusiveness of the organizational culture. *Review of Public Personnel Administration*, *35*(2), 146–168. doi:10.1177/0734371X13511088

Ash, M., & Boyce, J. K. (2018). Racial disparities in pollution exposure and employment at US industrial facilities. *Proceedings of the National Academy of Sciences of the United States of America*, *115*(42), 10636–10641. doi:10.1073/pnas.1721640115 PMID:30275295

Asiyanbi, H., & Ishola, A. (2018). E-banking services impact and customer satisfaction in selected bank branches in Ibadan metropolis, Oyo state, Nigeria. *Accounting*, *4*(4), 153–160. doi:10.5267/j.ac.2018.3.001

Assens-Serra, J., Boada-Cuerva, M., Serrano-Fernández, M.-J., & Agulló-Tomás, E. (2021). Gaining a Better Understanding of the Types of Organizational Culture to Manage Suffering at Work. *Frontiers in Psychology*, *12*, 782488. Advance online publication. doi:10.3389/fpsyg.2021.782488 PMID:34880819

Association for Talent Development (ATD). (2019). *Measuring the ROI of Learning and Development.* https://www.td.org/research-reports/measuring-the-roi-of-learning-and-development

Association for Talent Development (ATD). (2021). *Measuring the success of virtual training: ROI and beyond.* https://www.td.org/research-reports/measuring-the-success-of-virtual-training-roi-and-beyond

Atasever, M., Gözlü, M., Özaydın, M. M., Güler, H., Örnek, M., Barkan, O. B., Kavak, Y., & İlhan, N. (2018). *City Hospitals Research* [Şehir Hastaneleri Araştırması]. SAGLIK-SEN Strategic Research Center (SASAM).

Atli Ozbas, A., & Kovanci, M. S. (2022). The experience of moral distress by chief nurse officers during the covid-19 pandemic: A descriptive phenomenological study. *Journal of Nursing Management*, *30*(7), 2383–2393. doi:10.1111/jonm.13780 PMID:36044440

Augé, M. (1995). *Antropología de los mundos contemporáneos*. Gedisa.

Augé, M., & Colleyn, J.-P. (2006). *Qué es la antropología*. Paidós.

Aung, Y. Y., & Min, M. M. (2017). An analysis of random forest algorithm based network intrusion detection system. In *2017 18th IEEE/ACIS International Conference on Software Engineering, Artificial Intelligence, Networking and Parallel/Distributed Computing (SNPD)* (pp. 127-132). IEEE.

Aureli, S., Del Baldo, M., Lombardi, R., & Nappo, F. (2020). Nonfinancial reporting regulation and challenges in sustainability disclosure and corporate governance practices. *Business Strategy and the Environment*, *29*(6), 2392–2403. doi:10.1002/bse.2509

Baba, M. (2012). Anthropology and business: influence and interests. Journal of Business Anthropology, 1(1), 20-71.

Bailey, D. Jr, Docherty, S. L., Adams, J. A., Carthron, D. L., Corazzini, K., Day, J. R., Neglia, E., Thygeson, M., & Anderson, R. A. (2012). Studying the clinical encounter with the adaptive leadership framework. *Journal of Healthcare Leadership*, *4*, 83–91. doi:10.2147/JHL.S32686 PMID:24409083

Baker, M. (2020, May 15). When did the Coronavirus arrive in the U.s.? Here's a review of the evidence. *The New York Times.* https://www.nytimes.com/2020/05/15/us/coronavirus-first-case-snohomish-antibodies.html

Baker, J., & Cangemi, J. (2016). Why are there so few women CEOs and senior leaders in corporate America? *Organization Development Journal*, *34*(2), 31–43. https://tcsedsystem.idm.oclc.org/login?url=https://search-proquest-com.tcsedsystem.idm.oclc.org/docview/1791020833?accountid=34120

Balestra, C., & Fleischer, L. (2018). Diversity statistics in the OECD: How do OECD countries collect data on ethnic, racial and indigenous identity? *OCED iLibrary.* doi:10.1787/18152031

Baltrinic, E. R., & Wachter Morris, C. (2020). Signature pedagogies: A framework for pedagogical foundations in counselor education. *Teaching and Supervision in Counseling, 2*(2).

Bambra, C., Lynch, J., & Smith, K. E. (2021). The unequal pandemic: COVID-19 and health inequalities. Policy Press. doi:10.1007/978-3-031-21824-8_8

Bamwesigye, D., & Hlavackova, P. (2019). Analysis of Sustainable Transport for Smart Cities. *Sustainability (Basel), 11*(7), 2140. doi:10.3390u11072140

Banda, R. (2022). *The role of the state and non-state actors in ensuring security: The case of Luangwa district.* Academic Press.

Bansal, P. (2002). The corporate challenges of sustainable development. *The Academy of Management Perspectives, 21*(1), 122–131. doi:10.5465/ame.2002.7173572

Banzhaf, H. S., Ma, L., & Timmins, C. (2019). Environmental justice: Establishing causal relationships. *Annual Review of Resource Economics, 11*(1), 377–398. doi:10.1146/annurev-resource-100518-094131

Banzhaf, S., Ma, L., & Timmins, C. (2019). Environmental justice: The economics of race, place, and pollution. *The Journal of Economic Perspectives, 33*(1), 185–208. doi:10.1257/jep.33.1.185 PMID:30707005

Baquero, A. F. (2006). Comentario sobre el Primer Congreso Latinoamericano de Antropología. Memorias. *Revista Digital de Historia y Arqueología desde el Caribe*, (4).

Barfield, T. (Ed.). (2000). *Diccionario de Antropología.* Siglo XXI Editores.

Barnes, J. (1980). Kinship studies: Some impressions of the current state of play. *Man, 15*(2), 293–303. doi:10.2307/2801672

Barr, D., Gregson, W., & Reilly, T. (2020). The thermal ergonomics of firefighting reviewed. *Applied Ergonomics, 41*(1), 161–172. doi:10.1016/j.apergo.2009.07.001 PMID:19664755

Barreto, A. (2012). Counseling for the training of leaders and leadership development: A commentary. *The Professional Counselor, 2*(3), 226–234. doi:10.15241/abb.2.3.226

Barreto, R., Faria, P., & Vale, Z. (2022). Electric Mobility: An Overview of the Main Aspects Related to the Smart Grid. *Electronics (Basel), 11*(9), 1–19. doi:10.3390/electronics11091311

Barrett, J., & Stanford, P. (2006). Prediction. In S. Sarkar & J. Pfeifer (Eds.), The philosophy of science: An encyclopedia (pp. 585–599). Academic Press.

Barros, B., Oliveira, M., & Morais, S. (2021). Firefighters' occupational exposure: Contribution from biomarkers of effect to assess health risks. *Environment International, 156*, 106704. doi:10.1016/j.envint.2021.106704 PMID:34161906

Bartlett, B., Jardin, C., Martin, C., Tran, J., Buser, S., Anestis, M., & Vujanovic, A. (2018). Posttraumatic Stress and Suicidality Among Firefighters: The Moderating Role of Distress Tolerance. *Cognitive Therapy and Research, 42*(4), 483–496. doi:10.100710608-018-9892-y

Bartlett, F. (1937). Psychological methods and anthropological problems. *Africa, 10*(4), 401–420. doi:10.2307/1155145

Bashrum, A. (2019). *The importance of training and development in the workplace.* https://www.business.com/articles/importance-of-training-and-development-in-the-workplace/

Bashrum, A. (2019). Aligning Training and Development Strategy with Corporate Strategy: A Study of Small Businesses in Saudi Arabia. *Journal of Applied Research in Higher Education, 11*(4), 595–607.

Basilaia, G., & Kvavadze, D. (2020). Transition to Online Education in Schools during a SARS-CoV-2 Coronavirus (CO-VID-19) Pandemic in Georgia. *Pedagogical Research, 5*(4), em0060. Advance online publication. doi:10.29333/pr/7937

Bass, B. M., & Riggio, R. E. (2006). *Transformational leadership.* Academic Press.

Bass, B. M., & Riggio, R. E. (2010). The transformational model of leadership. *Leading organizations: Perspectives for a new era, 2*(1), 76-86.

Bass, B. M. (1985). Leadership: Good, better, best. *Organizational Dynamics, 13*(3), 26–40. doi:10.1016/0090-2616(85)90028-2

Bass, B. M. (1999). Two Decades of Research and Development in Transformational Leadership. *European Journal of Work and Organizational Psychology, 8*(1), 9–32. doi:10.1080/135943299398410

Bass, B. M., & Avolio, B. J. (1993). Transformational leadership and organizational culture. *Public Administration Quarterly*, 112–121.

Bateson, G. (1975). *Steps to an ecology of mind.* Ballantine Books.

Bates, R., & Khasawneh, S. (2019). Return on Investment (ROI) in Education and Training. In M. Khosrow-Pour (Ed.), *Encyclopedia of Information Science and Technology* (4th ed., pp. 4326–4335). IGI Global.

Battaglio, R. P. Jr, Belardinelli, P., Bellé, N., & Cantarelli, P. (2019). Behavioral public administration ad fontes: A synthesis of research on bounded rationality, cognitive biases, and nudging in public organizations. *Public Administration Review, 79*(3), 304–320. doi:10.1111/puar.12994

Bauer, R., Eichholtz, P., Kok, N., & Quigley, J. M. (2011). How green is your property portfolio? The global real estate sustainability benchmark. *Rotman International Journal of Pension Management, 4*(1), 34–43.

Baumann, M., Gohm, C., & Bonner, B. (2017). Phased Training for High-Reliability Occupations. *Human Factors, 53*(5), 548–557. doi:10.1177/0018720811418224 PMID:22046726

Baumgartner, R. J., & Ebner, D. (2010). Corporate sustainability strategies: Sustainability profiles and maturity levels. *Sustainable Development (Bradford), 18*(2), 76–89. doi:10.1002d.447

BBC. (n.d.). *Ethics – Introduction to ethics: Duty-based ethics.* Retrieved from https://www.bbc.co.uk/ethics/introduction/duty_1.shtml

Beale, M. H., Hagan, M. T., & Demuth, H. B. (2015). Neural network toolbox user's guide. The MathWorks Inc.

Beall, J. (2017). What I learned from predatory publishers. *Biochemia Medica, 27*(2), 273–278. doi:10.11613/BM.2017.029 PMID:28694718

Bearden, J. E. (2018). Diversity in the power elite: Ironies and unfulfilled promises. *Choice (Chicago, Ill.), 56*(1), 134.

Beerannavai, C. (2020). The Role of Corporations in Achieving Ecological Sustainability: Evaluating the Environmental Performance of Corporations. In *Interdisciplinary Approaches to Public Policy and Sustainability.* (pp. 228-247). IGI Global Publisher. https://www.igi-global.com/book/interdisciplinary-approaches-public-policy-sustainability/227626

Bektas, M. (2023). *JupyerLab Desktop* (3.6.3) [Eng; Windows]. Jupyter. https://github.com/jupyterlab/jupyterlab-desktop

Béland, D., He, A. J., & Ramesh, M. (2022). *COVID-19, crisis responses, and public policies: from the persistence of inequalities to the importance of policy design.* doi:10.1093/polsoc/puac021

Belasen, A., & Belasen, A. R. (2016). Value in the middle: Cultivating middle managers in healthcare organizations. *Journal of Management Development*, *35*(9), 1149–1162. doi:10.1108/JMD-12-2015-0173

Bell, J. M., & Hartmann, D. (2007). Diversity in Everyday Discourse: The Cultural Ambiguities and Consequences of "Happy Talk.". *American Sociological Review*, *72*(6), 895–914. doi:10.1177/000312240707200603

Bello, A., Jahan, S., Farid, F., & Ahamed, F. (2023). A Systemic Review of the Cybersecurity Challenges in Australian Water Infrastructure Management. *Water (Basel)*, *15*(1), 168. doi:10.3390/w15010168

Ben Jabeur, S., Ballouk, H., Ben Arfi, W., & Sahut, J.-M. (2023). Artificial intelligence applications in fake review detection: Bibliometric analysis and future avenues for research. *Journal of Business Research*, *158*, 113631. doi:10.1016/j.jbusres.2022.113631

Bennett, R. M., van der Vorst, Y., van den Bergh, J., & van den Berg, P. (2019). The effect of diversity management on sexual harassment: A meta-analysis. *Human Resource Management Review*, *29*(2), 233–249.

Bentz, V., & Shapiro, J. (1998). *Mindful inquiry in social research*. Sage Publications. doi:10.4135/9781452243412

Benz, T. A. (2017). Toxic cities: Neoliberalism and environmental racism in Flint and Detroit Michigan. *Critical Sociology*, *45*(1), 49–62. doi:10.1177/0896920517708339

Beqiri, G. (2018, March 8). Managing anxiety and stress in the workplace. *Virtual Speech*. https://virtualspeech.com/blog/managing-anxiety-stress-workplace

Berdahl, J., & Moon, S. (2019). The power of power: A meta-analysis of the effects of power on sexual harassment. *Psychological Bulletin*, *145*(2), 251–286.

Berdahl, J., & Moore, C. (2006). Workplace harassment: Double jeopardy for minority women. *The Journal of Applied Psychology*, *91*(2), 426–426. doi:10.1037/0021-9010.91.2.426 PMID:16551193

Berger, R. (2015). Now I see it, now I don't: Researcher's position and reflexivity in qualitative research. *Qualitative Research*, *15*(2), 219–234. doi:10.1177/1468794112468475

Bergström, A., & Källström, E. (2019). Leadership behavior and communication in organizational change. *Leadership and Organization Development Journal*, *40*(4), 545–559. doi:10.1108/LODJ-06-2018-0203

Berman, J. (2018, March 3). When a woman or person of color becomes CEO, white men have a strange reaction. *Marketwatch*. https://www.marketwatch.com/story/when-a-woman-or-person-of-color-becomes-ceo-white-men-have-a-strange-reaction-2018-02-23

Bernard, H. (2011). *Research methods in anthropology: Qualitative and quantitative approaches*. AltaMira Press.

Bernard, J. M., & Goodyear, R. K. (1992). *Fundamentals of clinical supervision*. Allyn & Bacon.

Berninger, A., Webber, M. P., Cohen, H. W., Gustave, J., Lee, R., Niles, J. K., Chiu, S., Zeig-Owens, R., Soo, J., Kelly, K., & Prezant, D. J. (2020). Trends of elevated PTSD risk in firefighters exposed to the World Trade Center disaster: 2001–2005. *Public Health Reports*, *125*(4), 556–566. doi:10.1177/003335491012500411 PMID:20597456

Beshears, J. (2015). Leaders as Decision Architects. *Harvard Business Review*, 2–11.

Besley, T. (2020). State capacity, reciprocity, and the social contract. *Econometrica*, *88*(4), 1307–1335. doi:10.3982/ECTA16863

Bettinger-Lopez, C., & Bro, A. (2020). A double pandemic: Domestic violence in the age of COVID-19. *Council on Foreign Relations*, *13*, 1–7.

Beus, J. M., Solomon, S. J., Taylor, E. C., & Esken, C. A. (2020). Making sense of climate: A meta-analytic extension of the competing values framework. *Organizational Psychology Review*, *10*(3-4), 136–168. doi:10.1177/2041386620914707

Beuving, J. (2020). Ethnography's future in the big data era. *Information Communication and Society*, *23*(11), 1625–1639. doi:10.1080/1369118X.2019.1602664

Bevan, R. (2013). *Changemaking: Tactics and resources for managing organizational change.* eBookIt.com.

Bevan, R. (2015). *The Changemaking checklists: Planning, leading, and sustaining change.* Academic Press.

Bevan, R. (n.d.). *The Changemaking Checklists: A Toolkit for Planning, Leading, and Sustaining Change.* Changestart Press.

Bhatti. (2021). Role of employee Empowerment. *Journal of Contemporary Issues in Business and Government*, *27*(4), 112. doi:10.47750/cibg.2021.27.04.012

Bibri, S. E. (2019). On the sustainability of smart and smarter cities in the era of big data: An interdisciplinary and transdisciplinary literature review. *Journal of Big Data*, *6*(1), 1–64. doi:10.118640537-019-0182-7

Bigland, C., Evans, D., Bolden, R., & Rae, M. (2020). Systems leadership in practice: Thematic insights from three public health case studies. *BMC Public Health*, *20*(1), 1–14. doi:10.118612889-020-09641-1 PMID:33203397

Biresaw, H., Mulugeta, H., Endalamaw, A., Yesuf, N. N., & Alemu, Y. (2021). Patient satisfaction towards health care services provided in Ethiopian health institutions: A systematic review and meta-analysis. *Health Services Insights*, *14*(1), 1–11. doi:10.1177/11786329211040689 PMID:34511929

Bischoff, P. (2020, February 11). *Ransomware Attacks on US Healthcare Organizations Cost $20.8bn in 2020.* Comparitech. https://www.comparitech.com/blog/information-security/ransomware-attacks-hospitals-data/

Blank, W. (2001). *The 108 skills of natural born leaders.* AMACOM.

Boal, K., & Schultz, P. (2007). Storytelling, time, and evolution: The role of strategic leadership in complex adaptive systems. *The Leadership Quarterly*, *18*(4), 411–428. doi:10.1016/j.leaqua.2007.04.008

Bocken, N., Short, S., Rana, P., & Evans, S. (2014). A literature and practice review to develop sustainable business model archetypes. *Journal of Cleaner Production*, *65*, 42–56. doi:10.1016/j.jclepro.2013.11.039

Bock, L. (2015). *Work Rules! Insights from Inside Google That Will Transform How You Live and Lead.* Twelve.

Bodolica, V., & Spraggon, M. (2018). The importance of literature reviews in academic field research. *Journal of Applied Research in Higher Education*, *10*(2), 183–194.

Boellstorf, T. (2010). The definition of science. *The New York Times.* https://www.nytimes.com/2010/12/14/opinion/114anthro.html

Boffa, J. W., King, S. L., Turecki, G., & Schmidt, N. B. (2018). Investigating the role of hopelessness in the relationship between PTSD symptom change and suicidality. *Journal of Affective Disorders*, *225*, 298–301. doi:10.1016/j.jad.2017.08.004 PMID:28843079

Bogdanoski, M. (2022). *Building cyber resilience against hybrid threats.* IOS Press. doi:10.3233/NICSP61

Böhm, B., Palma, M., Ousley, J., & Keane, G. (2022). Competency-based mental health supervision: Evidence-based tool needs for the humanitarian context. *Global Mental Health (Cambridge, England)*, 1–2.

Bohn, L., & Schiereck, D. (2022). Regulation of data breach publication: The case of US healthcare and the HITECH act. *Journal of Economics and Finance*, 1–14.

Bolden-Barnett, V. (2017, August 11). Study: Turnover costs employers $15,000 per worker. *HRDive*. https://www.hrdive.com/news/study-turnover-costs-employers-15000-per-worker/449142/

Bolton, M. (2022). A system leverage points approach to governance for sustainable development. *Sustainability Science*, *17*(6), 2427–2457. doi:10.100711625-022-01188-x

Bond, M., & Haynes, M. (2014). Workplace diversity: A social-ecological framework and policy implications. *Social Issues and Policy Review*, *8*(1), 167–201. doi:10.1111ipr.12005

Boone, C. G., Buckley, G. L., Grove, J. M., & Sister, C. (2009). Parks and people: An environmental justice inquiry in Baltimore, Maryland. *Annals of the Association of American Geographers*, *99*(4), 767–787. doi:10.1080/00045600903102949

Bostic, R. W., & Martin, R. W. (2003). Black home-owners as a gentrifying force? Neighbourhood dynamics in the context of minority home-ownership. *Urban Studies (Edinburgh, Scotland)*, *40*(12), 2427–2449. doi:10.1080/0042098032000136147

Botzen, W., Duijndam, S., & van Beukering, P. (2021). Lessons for climate policy from behavioral biases towards COVID-19 and climate change risks. *World Development*, *137*, 105214. doi:10.1016/j.worlddev.2020.105214 PMID:32994663

Bouguettaya, A., Yu, Q., Liu, X., Zhou, X., & Song, A. (2015). Efficient agglomerative hierarchical clustering. *Expert Systems with Applications*, *42*(5), 2785–2797. doi:10.1016/j.eswa.2014.09.054

Bouma, J. J., & Walters, T. (2018). *Corporate sustainability: The next steps towards a sustainable world*. Routledge. doi:10.4324/9781315639185

Bourke, J., & Dillon, B. (2018). Eight truths about diversity and inclusion at work| Deloitte Insights. *Deloitte*, (January), 22.

Boyd, C., & Boyd, D. (2018). *Forensic anthropology*. Wiley. doi:10.1002/9781119226529

Boyd, R., & Richerson, P. (2005). *The origin and evolution of cultures*. Oxford University Press.

Boyle, M., & Deveau, S. (2019, October 9). Bed Bath and Beyond taps target's top merchant as its new CEO. *Bloomberg*. https://www.bloomberg.com/news/articles/2019-10-09/bed-bath-beyond-names-target-s-tritton-as-its-new-ceo

Bradley, R. (2020). Reviewing Transformational Leadership and Change Management in United States of America. *Stratford Journals*, *4*(6), 56-65. https://stratfordjournals.org/journals/index.php/journal-of-human-resource/article/view/689

Brnabic, A., & Hess, L. M. (2021). Systematic literature review of machine learning methods used in the analysis of real-world data for patient-provider decision making. *BMC Medical Informatics and Decision Making*, *21*(1), 54. doi:10.118612911-021-01403-2 PMID:33588830

Broadwater, H. J. (2006). Preventing workplace sexual harassment. *Rural Telecommunications, 25*(5), 34-36, 38. Retrieved from https://search.proquest.com/docview/202695333?accountid=10378

Broadwater, A. R., Brown, C. L., & Moore, M. (2022). An integrative pedagogical approach to teaching counseling supervision. *The Journal of Counselor Preparation and Supervisor*, *15*(2), 53–79.

Broccardo, L., Culasso, F., & Mauro, S. G. (2019). Smart city governance: Exploring the institutional work of multiple actors towards collaboration. *International Journal of Public Sector Management*, *32*(4), 367–387. doi:10.1108/IJPSM-05-2018-0126

Bronk, C., & Jones, N. (2023). Cyber Cases: The PICCA Framework for Documenting Geopolitically Relevant Cyber Action. *Journal of Strategic Security*, *16*(1), 72–89. doi:10.5038/1944-0472.16.1.2068

Brooks, C., & Oikonomou, I. (2018). The effects of environmental, social and governance disclosures and performance on firm value: A review of the literature in accounting and finance. *The British Accounting Review*, *50*(1), 1–15. doi:10.1016/j.bar.2017.11.005

Broome, K. M., Knight, D. K., Edwards, J. R., & Flynn, P. M. (2009). Leadership, burnout, and job satisfaction in outpatient drug-free treatment programs. *Journal of Substance Abuse Treatment*, *37*(2), 160–170. doi:10.1016/j.jsat.2008.12.002 PMID:19339143

Brown, D. T. (2018). *Investigating Information Security Policy Characteristics: Do Quality, Enforcement and Compliance Reduce Organizational Fraud?* DigitalCommons@Kennesaw State University. https://digitalcommons.kennesaw.edu/dba_etd/40/

Brown, J. (2020, May 9). *What is the virtue approach?* The Knowledge Burrow. Retrieved from https://knowledgeburrow.com/what-is-the-virtue-approach/

Brown, M., Brown, R. S., & Nandedkar, A. (2019). Transformational leadership theory and exploring the perceptions of diversity management in higher education. *Journal of Higher Education Theory and Practice*, *19*(7).

Brown, M., & Lam, A. (2019). Preparing students for the rise of AI and the gig economy. *EDUCAUSE Review*, *54*(3), 12–25.

Brulle, R. J., & Pellow, D. N. (2006). Environmental justice: Human health and environmental inequalities. *Annual Review of Public Health*, *27*(1), 103–124. doi:10.1146/annurev.publhealth.27.021405.102124 PMID:16533111

Brunnermeier, M., Papakonstantinou, F., & Parker, J. (2016). Optimal time-inconsistent beliefs: Misplanning, procrastination, and commitment. *Management Science*, 1-65.

Bryan, C. J., Grove, J. L., & Kimbrel, N. A. (2017). Theory-driven models of self-directed violence among individuals with PTSD. *Current Opinion in Psychology*, *14*, 12–17. doi:10.1016/j.copsyc.2016.09.007 PMID:28813309

Bryant, F. B., & Gray, E. K. (2019). *Handbook of positive psychology*. Oxford University Press.

Bryant, N. (2020). The importance of leadership development in law enforcement. *Law Enforcement Executive Forum*, *20*(2), 32–34.

Bryman, A., Bresnen, M., Beardsworth, A., & Keil, T. (1988). Qualitative research and the study of leadership. *Human Relations*, *41*(1), 13–30. doi:10.1177/001872678804100102

Bryman, A., Collinson, D., Grint, K., Jackson, B., & Uhl-Bien, M. (2011). *The SAGE Handbook of Leadership*. SAGE.

Buchanan, N., & Settles, I. (2019). Managing (in)visibility and hypervisibility in the workplace. *Journal of Vocational Behavior*, *113*, 1–5. doi:10.1016/j.jvb.2018.11.001

Buchanan, T. W. (2007). Retrieval of emotional memories. *Psychological Bulletin*, *133*(5), 761–779. doi:10.1037/0033-2909.133.5.761 PMID:17723029

Budimir, S., Fontaine, J. R., & Roesch, E. B. (2021). Emotional experiences of cybersecurity breach victims. *Cyberpsychology, Behavior, and Social Networking*, *24*(9), 612–616. doi:10.1089/cyber.2020.0525 PMID:34185598

Buiten, M., & Hartmann, A. (2013). Public-Private Partnerships: Cognitive Biases in the Field. In *Engineering Project Organization Conference* (pp. 1-24). EPOS.

Bullard, R. D. (2002). Confronting environmental racism in the twenty-first century. *Global Dialogue*, *4*(1), 34. https://www.proquest.com/openview/639d07e04d3cbf5beab4a8cbcbf3c406/1?pq-origsite=gscholar&cbl=55193

Bureau of Labor Statistics, U.S. Department of Labor. (2019, February 26). Black women made up 53 percent of the Black labor force in 2018 on the Internet. *The Economics Daily.* https://www.bls.gov/opub/ted/2019/black-women-made-up-53-percent-of-the-black-labor-force-in-2018.htm

Bureau of Labor Statistics. (2020). *Restaurants and Food Services.* Retrieved from https://www.bls.gov/ooh/food-preparation-and-serving/restaurants-and-other-food-services.htm

Burrell, D. N., Aridi, A. S., & Nobles, C. (2018, March). The critical need for formal leadership development programs for cybersecurity and information technology professionals. In *International Conference on Cyber Warfare and Security* (pp. 82-91). Academic Conferences International Limited.

Burrell, D. N. (2019). How hiring baby boomers can assist with the global cybersecurity employee shortage. *International Journal of Hyperconnectivity and the Internet of Things, 3*(2), 1–10. doi:10.4018/IJHIoT.2019070101

Burton, S. L. (2022). *Cybersecurity Leadership from a Telemedicine/Telehealth Knowledge and Organizational Development Examination* [Doctoral dissertation]. Capitol Technology University.

Burton, S. L. (2019). Grasping the cyber-world: Artificial intelligence and human capital meet to inform leadership. *International Journal of Economics, Commerce and Management, 7*(12), 707–759.

Burton, S. L. (2020). Augmented reality: Enhancing student engagement and learning. *Journal of Educational Technology Development and Exchange, 13*(1), 1–14.

Bush, G. W. (2008). *National Security National Directive/Homeland Security Presidential Directive: Cybersecurity Policy* (NSPD-54/HSPD-23). The White House. https://irp.fas.org/offdocs/nspd/nspd-54.pdf

Bush, T. (2014). Instructional and transformational leadership: Alternative and complementary models? *Educational Management Administration & Leadership, 45*(2), 193–195. doi:10.1177/1741143216686723

Butler, D. (2013). Investigating journals: The dark side of publishing. *Nature, 495*(7442), 433–435. doi:10.1038/495433a PMID:23538810

Byrne, B., Harris, M., Consorte, J., & Lang, J. (1995). What's in a name? The consequences of violating Brazilian emic color-race categories in estimates of social well-being. *Journal of Anthropological Research, 51*(4), 389–397. doi:10.1086/jar.51.4.3630144

Byrnes, W. M. (2013). Climate justice, Hurricane Katrina, and African American environmentalism. *Journal of African American Studies, 18*(3), 305–314. doi:10.100712111-013-9270-5

Cáceres-Rubio, F., & Villacrés-Chaparro, M. (2010). *Cultura organizacional y las fusiones empresariales.* Facultad de Psicología, Universidad de La Sabana. Disponible en: http://intellectum.unisabana.edu.co/bitstream/handle/10818/4045/131294. pdf?sequence=1

CACREP 2016 standards. (n.d.). https://www.cacrep.org/for-programs/2016-cacrep-standards/

Cai, C., & Zhao, L. (2023). Information sharing and deferral option in cybersecurity investment. *PLoS One, 18*(2), e0281314. Advance online publication. doi:10.1371/journal.pone.0281314 PMID:36745656

Calatrava, M., Martins, M. V., Schweer-Collins, M., Duch-Ceballos, C., & Rodríguez-González, M. (2022). Differentiation of self: A scoping review of Bowen Family Systems Theory's core construct. *Clinical Psychology Review, 91*, 102101. doi:10.1016/j.cpr.2021.102101 PMID:34823190

Caldarola, N. T. (2010). *The effects of organizational and occupational commitment on job embeddedness and the individual's intent to stay* (Order No. 3411018). http://proxymu.wrlc.org/login?url=https://www.proquest.com/dissertations-theses/effects-organizational-occupational-commitment-on/docview/504844967/se-2

Câmara, P., & Morais, F. (2022). *The palgrave handbook of ESG and corporate governance.* Springer Nature. https://link.springer.com/book/10.1007/978-3-030-99468-6?noAccess=true

Cameron, E., & Green, M. (2019). *Making sense of change management: A complete guide to the models, tools and techniques of organizational change.* Kogan Page Publishers.

Campean, S. (2019). The Human Factor at the Center of a Cyber Security Culture. *International Journal of Information Security and Cybercrime.* doi:10.19107/IJISC.2019.01.07

Candis, B. (2010, February). Assessing Leadership Readiness Using Developmental Personality Style: A tool for leadership coaching. *International Journal of Evidence Based Coaching and Mentoring, 8*(1).

Canetti, E. F., Gayton, S., Schram, B., Pope, R., & Orr, R. M. (2022). Psychological, physical, and heat stress indicators prior to and after a 15-Minute structural firefighting task. *Biology (Basel), 11*(1), 104. doi:10.3390/biology11010104 PMID:35053102

Canizes, B., Soares, J., Costa, A., Pinto, T., Lezama, F., Novais, P., & Vale, Z. (2019). Electric Vehicles' User Charging Behaviour Simulator for a Smart City. *Energies, 12*(8), 1470. doi:10.3390/en12081470

Capgemini. (n.d.). *The key to designing inclusive tech.* https://www.capgemini.com/insights/research-library/the-key-to-designing-inclusive-tech/

Cappucci, M. (2018). The ESG integration paradox. *The Bank of America Journal of Applied Corporate Finance, 30*(2), 22–28. doi:10.1111/jacf.12296

Capron, D. W., Lamis, D. A., & Schmidt, N. B. (2017). Test of the depression distress amplification model in young adults with elevated risk of current suicidality. *Psychiatry Research, 219*(3), 531–535. doi:10.1016/j.psychres.2014.07.005 PMID:25063018

Carr, A. (2019). Couple therapy, family therapy and systemic interventions for adult-focused problems: The current evidence base. *Journal of Family Therapy, 41*(4), 492–536. doi:10.1111/1467-6427.12225

Carranza, R., Díaz, E., Sánchez-Camacho, C., & Martín-Consuegra, D. (2021). e-Banking adoption: An opportunity for customer value co-creation. *Frontiers in Psychology, 11*, 621248. doi:10.3389/fpsyg.2020.621248 PMID:33519647

Carrera, L. (2022). Corporate social responsibility. A strategy for social and territorial sustainability. *Int J Corporate Soc Responsibility, 7*(7), 7. Advance online publication. doi:10.118640991-022-00074-0

Casali, G. L. (2007). A Quest for Ethical Decision Making: Searching for the Holy Grail, and Finding the Sacred Trinity in Ethical Decision-Making by Managers. *Social Responsibility Journal, 3*(3), 50–59. doi:10.1108/17471110710835581

Casey, C., & Edgerton, R. (Eds.). (2007). *A companion to psychological anthropology.* Blackwell Publishing.

Cash, P., Stanković, T., & Štorga, M. (2016). *Experimental design research.* Springer. doi:10.1007/978-3-319-33781-4

Castro, A., De Giovannini, U., Sato, S. A., Hübener, H., & Rubio, A. (2023). Floquet engineering with quantum optimal control theory. *New Journal of Physics, 25*(4), 043023. doi:10.1088/1367-2630/accb05

Caughron, J., & Mumford, M. (2012). Embedded leadership: How do a leader's superiors impact middle-management performance. *The Leadership Quarterly, 23*(3), 342–353. doi:10.1016/j.leaqua.2011.08.008

Caulkins, D., & Jordan, A. T. (Eds.). (2013). *A Companion to Organizational Anthropology.* Wiley-Blackwell.

CBN. (2019). *Regulation on electronic payments and collection for public and private sectors in Nigeria.* CBN.

Cely-López, C. L., & Gómez-Niño, O. (2016). An anthropological perspective of organizations from sociocultural characterization, management, and social accounting. The case of a tertiary education institution. *Cuadernos de Contabilidad, 17*(43), 184.

Center for Substance Abuse Treatment. (2007). *Competencies for substance abuse treatment clinical supervisors: Technical assistance publication (TAP) series 21-A.* Substance Abuse and Mental Health Services Administration.

Center for Substance Abuse Treatment. (2009). *Clinical supervision and professional development of the substance abuse counselor.* Substance Abuse and Mental Health Services Administration.

Center for Substance Abuse Treatment. (2014). *TIP 59: Improving Cultural Competence.* Substance Abuse and Mental Health Services Administration.

Cerutti, M. (2003) Los estudios empresariales en América Latina ¿el debate interminable? *Boletín de Historia Económica, 1,* 3-9. Disponible en: https://www.audhe.org.uy/Boletin_Audhe/Boletin_2/Boletin_02_Cerutti.pdf

Chabrol, F., Albert, L., & Ridde, V. (2019). 40 years after Alma-Ata, is building new hospitals in low-income and lower-middle-income countries beneficial? *BMJ Global Health, 22*(3, Suppl 3), 1–5. doi:10.1136/bmjgh-2018-001293 PMID:31168419

Chang, D. Y., Park, J. H., & Chai, S. (2021). The effect of technological innovation on organizational performance: The role of absorptive capacity and dynamic capability. *Sustainability, 13*(1), 30. doi:10.3390u13010030

Chanland, D., & Murphy, W. (2018). Propelling diverse leaders to the top: A developmental network approach. *Human Resource Management, 57*(1), 111–126. doi:10.1002/hrm.21842

Chapple, E. D. (1953). Applied anthropology in industry. In A. L. Kroeber (Ed.), *Anthropology Today.* Chicago University Press.

Chartered Institute of Personnel and Development. (2010). *Learning and Development 2010. Survey report.* CIPD. Retrieved from: https://www.cipd.co.uk/binaries/5215_learning_talent_development%20survey_report.pd

Chaudhry, I. S. (2022). Viable system model: A tool for managing sustainable development holistically. *Management & Sustainability: An Arab Review, 1*(1), 50–65. doi:10.1108/MSAR-01-2022-0008

Chau, T. H. P., Tran, Y. T., & Le, T. D. (2022). How does transformational leadership influence on the performance of public service organizations in a developing country? The interventional roles of NPM cultural orientations. *Cogent Business & Management, 9*(1), 2140746. Advance online publication. doi:10.1080/23311975.2022.2140746

Checinski, M., Dillon, R., Hieronimus, S., & Klier, J. (2019, March 5). *Putting people at the heart of public-sector transformations.* McKinsey & Company. https://www.mckinsey.com/industries/public-and-social-sector/our-insights/putting-people-at-the-heart-of-public-sector-transformations

Check Point Research. (2023, March 16). *2023 Security Report: Cyberattacks reach an all-time high in response to geo-political conflict, and the rise of 'disruption and destruction' malware.* https://research.checkpoint.com/2023/2023-security-report-cyberattacks-reach-an-all-time-high-in-response-to-geo-political-conflict-and-the-rise-of-disruption-and-destruction-malware/

Chen & Lin. (2019). Understanding the effect of social media marketing activities: The mediation of social identification, perceived value, and satisfaction. *Journal Technological Forecasting and Social Change, 140,* 22-32.

Chen, C. M., & Chen, C. Y. (2020). Designing an online professional learning program for instructional designers: A case study of interdepartmental collaboration. *The International Review of Research in Open and Distributed Learning*, *21*(2), 88–107.

Chen, C.-H., Liang, J.-C., & Chen, W.-F. (2021). The effectiveness of augmented reality on knowledge acquisition and transfer in medical education: A systematic review and meta-analysis. *BMC Medical Education*, *21*(1), 171. doi:10.118612909-021-02632-1 PMID:33740973

Chen, F., Xiao, Z., Xiang, T., Fan, J., & Truong, H. L. (2022). A full lifecycle authentication scheme for large-scale smart IoT applications. *IEEE Transactions on Dependable and Secure Computing*, 1. doi:10.1109/TDSC.2022.3178115

Cheng, L., & Li, Y. (2019). How to measure training effectiveness: A meta-analysis of empirical studies. *Human Resource Management Review*, *29*(2), 203–218.

Chen, J., Ghardallou, W., Comite, U., Ahmad, N., Ryu, H. B., Ariza-Montes, A., & Han, H. (2022). Managing Hospital Employees' Burnout through Transformational Leadership: The Role of Resilience, Role Clarity, and Intrinsic Motivation. *International Journal of Environmental Research and Public Health*, *19*(17), 10941. doi:10.3390/ijerph191710941 PMID:36078657

Chen, S., Hao, M., Ding, F., Jiang, D., Dong, J., Zhang, S., Guo, Q., & Gao, C. (2023). Exploring the global geography of cybercrime and its driving forces. *Humanities & Social Sciences Communications*, *10*(1), 71. doi:10.105741599-023-01560-x PMID:36852135

Chernyshev, M., Zeadally, S., & Baig, Z. (2018). Healthcare data breaches: Implications for digital forensic readiness. *Journal of Medical Systems*, *43*(1), 7. Advance online publication. doi:10.100710916-018-1123-2 PMID:30488291

Cherry, K. (2023a, June 25). *The situational theory of leadership*. Verywell Mind. https://www.verywellmind.com/what-is-the-situational-theory-of-leadership-2795321

Cherry, K. (2023b, May 21). *What is transformational leadership?* Verywell Mind. https://www.verywellmind.com/what-is-transformational-leadership-2795313

Cheung, A. W. (2011). Do stock investors value corporate sustainability? Evidence from an event study. *Journal of Business Ethics*, *99*(2), 145–165. doi:10.100710551-010-0646-3

Chiang, E. S., Riordan, K. M., Ponder, J., Johnson, C., & Cox, K. S. (2020). Distinguishing firefighters with subthreshold PTSD from firefighters with probable PTSD or low symptoms. *Journal of Loss and Trauma*, *26*(1), 65–77. doi:10.1080/15325024.2020.1728494

Chibnik, M. (1985). The use of statistics in sociocultural anthropology. *Annual Review of Anthropology*, *14*(1), 135–157. doi:10.1146/annurev.an.14.100185.001031

Chibnik, M. (1999). Quantification and statistics in six anthropology journals. *Field Methods*, *11*(2), 146–157. doi:10.1177/1525822X9901100205

Chibnik, M. (2005). Experimental economics in anthropology: A critical assessment. *American Ethnologist*, *32*(2), 198–209. doi:10.1525/ac.2005.32.2.198

Chinn, J., Martin, I., & Redmond, N. (2021). Health Equity Among Black Women in the United States. *Journal of Women's Health*, *30*(2), 212–219. doi:10.1089/jwh.2020.8868 PMID:33237831

Choi, H. (2018). Effects of empowerment and family function on the depression of firefighters. *Fire Science and Engineering*, *32*(2), 116-121. doi:10.7731/KIFSE.2018.32.1.116

Choi, J. R., & Kim, S. (2016). Is the smart watch an IT product or a fashion product? A study on factors affecting the intention to use smart watches. *Computers in Human Behavior*, *63*, 777–786. doi:10.1016/j.chb.2016.06.007

Choi, M., Lee, J., & Hwang, K. (2018). Information systems security (ISS) of E-Government for sustainability: A dual path model of ISS influenced by institutional isomorphism. *Sustainability (Basel)*, *10*(5), 1555. doi:10.3390u10051555

Chowdhury, T. M., & Murzi, H. (2020, June). The evolution of teamwork in the engineering workplace from the First Industrial Revolution to Industry 4.0: A literature review. *2020 ASEE Virtual Annual Conference Content Access*. 10.18260/1-2--35318

Chuah, Rauschnabel, P. A., Krey, N., Nguyen, B., Ramayah, T., & Lade, S. (2016). Wearable technologies: The role of usefulness and visibility in smart watch adoption. *Computers in Human Behavior*, *65*, 276–284. doi:10.1016/j.chb.2016.07.047

Ciani, O., Torbica, A., Lecci, F., Morelli, M., Drummond, M., Tarricone, R., & Bene, L. D. (2018). Myth #5: Health Care Is Rightly Left to the Private Sector, for the Sake of Efficiency. In P. Adinolfi & E. Borgonovi (Eds.), *The Myths of Health Care* (pp. 123–154). Springer. doi:10.1007/978-3-319-53600-2_8

Ciminelli, G., & Garcia-Mandicó, S. (2020). COVID-19 in Italy: An analysis of death registry data. *Journal of Public Health (Oxford, England)*, *42*(4), 723–730. doi:10.1093/pubmed/fdaa165 PMID:32935849

Cisco Secure. (2023). *Cisco Cybersecurity Readiness Index: Resilience in a Hybrid World*. https://www.cisco.com/c/dam/m/en_us/products/security/cybersecurity-reports/cybersecurity-readiness-index/2023/cybersecurity-readiness-index-report.pdf

Clarke, Y. D. (2022). *Building Smart Cities of the Future With Inclusivity and Connectivity for All*. State of Black America. https://soba.iamempowered.com/building-smart-cities-future-inclusivity-and-connectivity-all

Clarke, H., Stewart, M. C., & Ho, K. (2021). Did Covid-19 Kill Trump Politically? The Pandemic and Voting in the 2020 Presidential Election. *Social Science Quarterly*, *102*(5), 2194–2209. doi:10.1111squ.12992 PMID:34226770

Clarkson, M. B. (1995). A stakeholder framework for analyzing and evaluating corporate social performance. *Academy of Management Review*, *20*(1), 92–117. doi:10.2307/258888

Clayton, S. (2003). Environmental identity: A conceptual and an operational definition. *Identity and the natural environment: The psychological significance of nature*, 45-65.

Clement, J., Manjon, M., & Crutzen, N. (2022). Factors for collaboration amongst smart city stakeholders: A local government perspective. *Government Information Quarterly*, *39*(4), 101746. doi:10.1016/j.giq.2022.101746

Cleveland, S., & Cleveland, M. (2018). Toward cybersecurity leadership framework. *Proceedings of the Thirteenth Midwest Association for Information Systems Conference*.

Clifford, J. (1988). *The Predicament of Culture*. Harvard U Press.

Clough, E. (2018). Environmental justice and fracking: A review. *Current Opinion in Environmental Science & Health*, *3*, 14–18. doi:10.1016/j.coesh.2018.02.005

Cloutier, C., & Ravasi, D. (2020). Identity trajectories: Explaining long-term patterns of continuity and change in organizational identities. *Academy of Management Journal*, *63*(4), 1196–1235. doi:10.5465/amj.2017.1051

Cohen-Addad, V., Kanade, V., Mallmann-Trenn, F., & Mathieu, C. (2019). Hierarchical clustering: Objective functions and algorithms. *Journal of the Association for Computing Machinery*, *66*(4), 1–42. doi:10.1145/3321386

Cohen, J. A., Kassan, A., Wada, K., Arthur, N., & Goopy, S. (2022). Enhancing multicultural and social justice competencies in Canadian counselling psychology training. *Canadian Psychology, 63*(3), 298–312. doi:10.1037/cap0000287

Collins, D. P., Bruce, J., & McKee, K. (2019). Teaching Transformative Leadership for Social Justice: Using Literature Circles to Enhance Learning and Create Deeper Meaning. *Journal of Leadership Education, 18*(3), 158–166. doi:10.12806/V18/I3/A1

Collins, P. H. (2015). Intersectionality's definitional dilemmas. *Annual Review of Sociology, 41*(1), 1–20. doi:10.1146/annurev-soc-073014-112142

Collins, T. W., & Grineski, S. E. (2019). Environmental injustice and religion: Outdoor air pollution disparities in metropolitan Salt Lake City, Utah. *Annals of the American Association of Geographers, 109*(5), 1597–1617. doi:10.1080/24694452.2018.1546568

Colquitt, J., LePine, J., Zapata, C., & Wild, R. (2018). Trust in Typical and High-Reliability Contexts: Building and Reacting to Trust among Firefighters. *Academy of Management Journal, 54*(5), 999–1015. doi:10.5465/amj.2006.0241

Combs, G. M., Milosevic, I., & Bilimoria, D. (2019). Introduction to the Special Topic Forum: Critical Discourse: Envisioning the Place and Future of Diversity and Inclusion in Organizations. *Journal of Leadership & Organizational Studies, 26*(3), 277–286. doi:10.1177/1548051819857739

Comstock, M., Supovitz, J., & Kaul, M. (2021). Exchange quality in teacher leadership ties: Examining relational quality using social network and leader-member exchange theories. *Journal of Professional Capital and Community, 6*(4), 395–409. doi:10.1108/JPCC-01-2021-0002

Conklin, J. (2005). Wicked Problems & Social Complexity. In J. Conklin (Ed.), *Dialogue Mapping: Building Shared Understanding of Wicked Problems*. Wiley.

Contrafatto, M. (2014). Stewardship theory: Approaches and perspectives. *Advances in Public Interest Accounting*, 177-196. doi:10.1108/S1041-706020140000017007

Cook, A., & Glass, C. (2014). Above the glass ceiling: When are women and racial/ethnic minorities promoted to CEO? *Strategic Management Journal, 35*(7), 1080–1089. doi:10.1002mj.2161

Cooper, M. (2000). Towards a model of safety culture. *Safety Science, 36*(2), 111–136. doi:10.1016/S0925-7535(00)00035-7

Correia, M. (2019). Sustainability: An Overview of the Triple Bottom Line and Sustainability Implementation. *International Journal of Strategic Engineering, 2*(1), 29–38. doi:10.4018/IJoSE.2019010103

Cosenz, F., Rodrigues, V. P., & Rosati, F. (2020). Dynamic business modeling for sustainability: Exploring a system dynamics perspective to develop sustainable business models. *Business Strategy and the Environment, 29*(2), 651–664. doi:10.1002/bse.2395

Cossette, P. (2015). Heuristics and cognitive biases in entrepreneurs: a review of the research. *Journal of the Canadian Council for Small Business & Entrepreneurship, 27*(5), 471-496. http://dx.DOI.org/10.1080/08276331.2015.1105732

Cost of a data breach 2022. (n.d.). IBM. Retrieved April 22, 2023, from https://www.ibm.com/reports/data-breach

Covey, S. R. (1990). *The 7 Habits of Highly Effective People*. Simon & Schuster.

Crapanzano, V. (1986). Hermes' dilemma: the masking of subversion in etnographic description. In J. Clifford (Ed.), *Marcus, E. Writing culture: the poetics and politics of ethnography* (pp. 51–76). University of California Press. doi:10.1525/9780520946286-005

Creemers, B. (2010). *Improving the quality of education: Dynamic Approaches to school Improvement*. Routledge.

Crenshaw, K. (2015, September 24). Why intersectionality can't wait. *The Washington Post.* https://www.washingtonpost.com/news/in-theory/wp/2015/09/24/why-intersectionality-cant-wait/

Creswell, J. (2007). *Qualitative inquiry and research design: Choosing among five approaches* (2nd ed.). Sage Publications.

Creswell, J. W. (2014). *Research design: Qualitative, quantitative, and mixed methods approaches* (4th ed.). Sage.

CrowdStrike. (2023, February 28). *2023 Global Threat Report | CrowdStrike.* crowdstrike.com. https://www.crowdstrike.com/global-threat-report/

Crucet, C., Graells, J., Cabral, S., & Lane, S. (2010). Sexual harassment in the workplace. *Academy of Legal, Ethical and Regulatory Issues, 14*(1), 16-20. Retrieved from https://search.proquest.com/docview/521205959?accountid=10378

Cuadra, D. (2022). Why professional development and upskilling is vital to women of color. *Employee Benefit News.* https://www.proquest.com/docview/2705282255/abstract/B207D99311A94633PQ/1

Ćukušić, M. (2021). Contributing to the current research agenda in digital transformation in the context of smart cities. *International Journal of Information Management, 58,* 102330. doi:10.1016/j.ijinfomgt.2021.10330

Cunningham, L., & McNally, K. (2003). *Improving Organizational and Individual Performance through Coaching. A case Study.* Mosby, Inc. doi:10.1067/nrsi.2003.90

Curado, C., & Santos, R. (2022). Transformational leadership and work performance in health care: The mediating role of job satisfaction. *Leadership in Health Services, 35*(2), 160–173. doi:10.1108/LHS-06-2021-0051 PMID:34767323

Curtis, R., & Sherlock, J. J. (2006). Wearing two hats: Counselors working as managerial leaders in agencies and schools. *Journal of Counseling and Development, 84*(1), 120–126. doi:10.1002/j.1556-6678.2006.tb00386.x

Cushing, L. J., Faust, J., August, L. M., Cendak, R., Wieland, W., & Alexeeff, G. (2015). Racial/Ethnic disparities in cumulative environmental health impacts in California: Evidence from a statewide environmental justice screening tool (Calenviroscreen 1.1). *ISEE Conference Abstracts, 2015*(1), 1790. 10.1289/isee.2015.2015-1790

Cvirn, M., Dorrian, J., Smith, B., Vincent, G., Jay, S., Roach, G., Sargent, C., Larsen, B., Aisbett, B., & Ferguson, S. A. (2019). The effects of hydration on cognitive performance during a simulated wildfire suppression shift in temperate and hot conditions. *Applied Ergonomics, 77,* 9–15. doi:10.1016/j.apergo.2018.12.018 PMID:30832782

Cybersecurity & Infrastructure Security Agency (CISA). (2022). *America's Cyber Defense Agency.* The Facts. https://www.cisa.gov/be-cyber-smart/facts https://connect.comptia.org/blog/cyber-security-stats-facts doi:10.1016/j.cogr.2021.05.001

Daeli, N. O. F., & Adiwijaya, A. (2020). Sentiment analysis on movie reviews using Information gain and K-nearest neighbor. *Journal of Data Science and Its Applications, 3*(1), 1–7.

Dagnachew, A. (2021). *Electronic Banking Service Practice and Challenges On Trade Activities (In Case Of Debre Berhan)* [Doctoral dissertation].

Darmawan, A. H., & Azizah, S. (2020, January). Resistance to change: Causes and strategies as an organizational challenge. In *5th ASEAN Conference on Psychology, Counselling, and Humanities (ACPCH 2019)* (pp. 49-53). Atlantis Press.

Daugaard, D., & Ding, A. (2022). Global drivers for ESG performance: The body of knowledge. *Sustainability (Basel), 14*(4), 2322. doi:10.3390u14042322

Davies, E. S. (2020, July 2). *Bias has consequences: Disrupting the cycle of everyday racism.* Beeck Center. https://beeckcenter.georgetown.edu/bias-has-consequences-disrupting-the-cycle-of-everyday-racism/

Davis, D. R., & Maldonado-Daniels, C. (2015). Shattering the glass ceiling: The leadership development of African American women in higher education. *Advancing Women in Leadership Journal, 35*, 48–64. doi:10.21423/awlj-v35.a125

Daystar, M. (2021). Developing a Liberatory Consciousness. *Women and Leadership Development in College: A Facilitation Resource.*

Dcunha, S. D. (2022, August 18). *What will a cognitive city look like? Are we ready for it? - Fast Company Middle East.* Fast Company Middle East. https://fastcompanyme.com/technology/what-will-a-cognitive-city-look-like-are-we-ready-for-it/

De Benedictis, L., Licio, V., & Pinna, A. (2022). *From the historical Roman road network to modern infrastructure in Italy.* arXiv preprint arXiv:2208.06675.

Deal, T. E., & Kennedy, A. (1983). Culture: A New Look Through Old Lenses. *The Journal of Applied Behavioral Science, 19*(4), 498–505. doi:10.1177/002188638301900411

Deal, T. E., & Kennedy, A. A. (1982). *Corporate Cultures: The Rites and Rituals of Corporate Life.* Addison Wesley.

Deal, T. E., & Kennedy, A. A. (2000). *The New Corporate Cultures: Revitalizing The Workplace After Downsizing, Mergers, And Reengineering.* Basic Books.

Decker, A., & Galer, D. (2013). *Enterprise risk management - Straight to the point: An implementation guide function by function.* Academic Press.

Decker, A., & Galer, D. (2013). *Enterprise Risk Management - Straight to the Point: An Implementation Guide Function by Function.* Createspace Independent Publishing Platform.

Dede, C. (2019). The role of emerging technologies in distance education. In R. Reiser & J. Dempsey (Eds.), *Trends and issues in instructional design and technology* (pp. 63–73). Pearson.

DeDiego, A. C., Chan, C. D., & Basma, D. (2022). Emerging leaders: Leadership development experiences of counselor education doctoral students. *Counselor Education and Supervision, 61*(3), 262–275. doi:10.1002/ceas.12241

Deep, S., & Sussman, L. (1995). *Smart moves for people in charge: 130 checklists to help you be a better leader.* Perseus Books Group.

DeFond, M, Zhang, J, (2014) *A review of archival auditing research.* . doi:10.1016/j.jacceco.2014.09.002

Deitch, E. A., Barsky, A., Butz, R. M., Chan, S., Brief, A. P., & Bradley, J. C. (2003). Subtle yet significant: The existence and impact of everyday racial discrimination in the workplace. *Human Relations, 56*(11), 1299–1324. doi:10.1177/00187267035611002

DeJonckheere, M., & Vaughn, L. M. (2019). Semistructured interviewing in primary care research: A balance of relationship and rigour. *Family Medicine and Community Health, 7*(2), e000057. doi:10.1136/fmch-2018-000057 PMID:32148704

Deloitte. (2022). *Smart and sustainable buildings and infrastructure.* https://www2.deloitte.com/global/en/pages/public-sector/articles/urban-future-with-a-purpose/smart-and-sustainable-buildings-and-infrastructure.html

Deng, F., Huang, J., Yuan, X., Cheng, C., & Zhang, L. (2021). Performance and efficiency of machine learning algorithms for analyzing rectangular biomedical data. *Laboratory Investigation, 101*(4), 430–441. doi:10.103841374-020-00525-x PMID:33574440

Denkova, E., Zanesco, A., Rogers, S., & Jha, A. (2020). Is resilience trainable? An initial study comparing mindfulness and relaxation training in firefighters. *Psychiatry Research, 285*, 112794. doi:10.1016/j.psychres.2020.112794 PMID:32078885

Depression in women: Understanding the gender gap. (2019, January 29). *Mayo Clinic.* https://www.mayoclinic.org/diseases-conditions/depression/in-depth/depression/art-20047725

Derous, E., & Ryan, A. M. (2019). When your resume is (not) turning you down: Modelling ethnic bias in resume screening. *Human Resource Management Journal, 29*(2), 113–130. doi:10.1111/1748-8583.12217

Des Roches, S., Brans, K. I., Lambert, M. R., Rivkin, L. R., Savage, A. M., Schell, C. J., Correa, C., De Meester, L., Diamond, S. E., Grimm, N. B., Harris, N. C., Govaert, L., Hendry, A. P., Johnson, M. T. J., Munshi-South, J., Palkovacs, E. P., Szulkin, M., Urban, M. C., Verrelli, B. C., & Alberti, M. (2021). Socio-eco-evolutionary dynamics in cities. *Evolutionary Applications, 14*(1), 248–267. doi:10.1111/eva.13065 PMID:33519968

Desmond, J., & Wilson, F. (2019). Democracy and worker representation in the management of change: Lessons from Kurt Lewin and the Harwood studies. *Human Relations, 72*(11), 1805–1830. doi:10.1177/0018726718812168

Deterding, S., Dixon, D., Khaled, R., & Nacke, L. (2019). From game design elements to gamefulness: defining "gamification". *Proceedings of the 15th International Academic Mindtrek Conference: Envisioning Future Media Environments,* 9-17.

Deursen, N. V. (2022). *Visual Communication for Cybersecurity: Beyond Awareness to Advocacy.* River Publishers. doi:10.1201/9781003340027

Dhasarathan, C., Hasan, M. K., Islam, S., Abdullah, S., Mokhtar, U. A., Javed, A. R., & Goundar, S. (2023). COVID-19 health data analysis and personal data preserving: A homomorphic privacy enforcement approach. *Computer Communications, 199,* 87–97. doi:10.1016/j.comcom.2022.12.004 PMID:36531214

Dhyani, S., Lahoti, S., Khare, S., Pujari, P., & Verma, P. (2018). Ecosystem based Disaster Risk Reduction approaches (EbDRR) as a prerequisite for inclusive urban transformation of Nagpur City, India. *International Journal of Disaster Risk Reduction, 32,* 95–105. doi:10.1016/j.ijdrr.2018.01.018

Dibbets, P., Evers, E. A., Hurks, P. P., Bakker, K., & Jolles, J. (2020). Differential brain activation patterns in adult attention-deficit hyperactivity disorder (ADHD) associated with task switching. *Neuropsychology, 24*(4), 413–423. doi:10.1037/a0018997 PMID:20604616

Dickens, D.D., & Chavez, E.L. (2017). Navigating the workplace: The costs and benefits of shifting identities at work among early career U.S. Black women. *Sex Roles, 78,* 760–774. doi:10.1007/s11199-017-0844-x

Dickens, D., Womack, V., & Dimes, T. (2019). Managing hypervisibility: An exploration of theory and research on identity shifting strategies in the workplace among Black women. *Journal of Vocational Behavior, 113,* 153–153. doi:10.1016/j.jvb.2018.10.008

Diener, P., Nonini, D., & Robkin, E. (1980). Ecology and evolution in cultural anthropology. *Man, 15*(1), 1–31. doi:10.2307/2802000

Ding, L., & Hwang, J. (2020). *Effects of gentrification on homeowners: Evidence from a natural experiment.* Working paper (Federal Reserve Bank of Philadelphia). doi:10.21799/frbp.wp

Ding, A. W., & Li, S. (2019). Herding in the consumption and purchase of digital goods and moderators of the herding bias. *Journal of the Academy of Marketing Science, 47*(3), 460–478. doi:10.100711747-018-0619-0

Ding, Y., Zhang, G., Chambers, T., Song, M., Wang, X., & Zhai, C. (2015). Content-based citation analysis: The next generation of citation analysis: Content-Based Citation Analysis: The Next Generation of Citation Analysis. *Journal of the Association for Information Science and Technology, 65*(9), 1820–1833. doi:10.1002/asi.23256

Dlugosch, O., Brandt, T., & Neumann, D. (2020). Combining analytics and simulation methods to assess the impact of shared, autonomous electric vehicles on sustainable urban mobility. *Information & Management,* 103285.

Dmytriyev, S. D., Freeman, R. E., & Hörisch, J. (2021). The relationship between stakeholder theory and corporate social responsibility: Differences, similarities, and implications for social issues in management. *Journal of Management Studies*, *58*(6), 1441–1470. doi:10.1111/joms.12684

Docebo. (2020). *Personalized learning with artificial intelligence: A new approach to employee training*. https://www.docebo.com/resource/personalized-learning-with-artificial-intelligence/

Dodgson, J. E. (2019). Reflexivity in qualitative research. *Journal of Human Lactation*, *35*(2), 220–222. doi:10.1177/0890334419830990 PMID:30849272

Dogan, B. B., & Aslan, A. (2019). Current status of health tourism in Turkey and its impact on the economy of the country [Türkiye'de sağlık turizminin mevcut durumu ve ülke ekonomisine katkıları]. *Journal of Dicle University Economics and Administrative Sciences*, *9*(18), 390–418.

Dolan, A. (2022). *Beliefs Matter: School Counselor Self-Assessment of Perceived Advocacy, Collaboration, and Leadership Mindset* [Doctoral dissertation].

Dovidio, J. F., Gaertner, S. E., Kawakami, K., & Hodson, G. (2002). Why can't we just get along? Interpersonal biases and interracial distrust. *Cultural Diversity & Ethnic Minority Psychology*, *8*(2), 88–102. doi:10.1037/1099-9809.8.2.88 PMID:11987594

Downey, L. (2006). Environmental racial inequality in Detroit. *Social Forces*, *85*(2), 771–796. doi:10.1353of.2007.0003 PMID:21874071

Dragicevic, P. a. (2014). *Visualization-Mediated Alleviation of the Planning Fallacy. In Decisive: Workshop on Dealing with Cognitive Biases in Visualizations*. IEEE. Retrieved from http://nbn-resolving.de/urn:nbn:de:bsz:352-0-329469

DreiA.Le GuenedalT.LepetitF.MortierV.RoncalliT.SekineT. (2019). ESG investing in recent years: New insights from old challenges. *Available at* SSRN 3683469. doi:10.2139/ssrn.3683469

Driver, H. (1953). Statistics in anthropology. *American Anthropologist*, *55*(1), 42–59. doi:10.1525/aa.1953.55.1.02a00040

Duca, I., & Gherghina, R. (2019). CSR Initiatives: An Opportunity for the Business Environment. In *Corporate Social Responsibility: Concepts, Methodologies, Tools, and Applications* (pp. 127-142). IGI Global Publisher. https://www.igi-global.com/book/corporate-social-responsibility/197763

Dufour, P. (1995). Techno-Globalism and the Challenges to Science and Technology Policy. *Daedalus*, *124*(3), 219–235.

Durand, J. (1986). *Los obreros del Río Grande*. Colegio de Michoacán.

Eagly, A., & Karau, S. (2002). Role congruity theory and prejudice towards female leaders. *Psychological Review*, *109*(3), 573–598. doi:10.1037/0033-295X.109.3.573 PMID:12088246

Eccles, R., Newquist, S., & Schatz, R. (2007) *Reputation and its Risks* https://hbr.org/2007/02/reputation-and-its-risks

Egede, L. E., & Walker, R. J. (2020). Structural racism, social risk factors, and Covid-19—A dangerous convergence for Black Americans. *The New England Journal of Medicine*, *383*(12), e77. doi:10.1056/NEJMp2023616 PMID:32706952

Eigenberg, H., & Min Park, S. (2016). Marginalization and invisibility of women of color: A content analysis of race and gender images in introductory criminal justice and criminology texts. *Race and Justice*, *6*(3), 257–279. doi:10.1177/2153368715600223

Ekins, P. (2010). Eco-innovation for environmental sustainability: Concepts, progress, and policies. *International Economics and Economic Policy*, *7*(2/3), 267–290. doi:10.100710368-010-0162-z

Elkington, J. (1994). Towards the sustainable corporation: Win–win–win business strategies for sustainable development. *California Management Review, 36*(2), 90–100. doi:10.2307/41165746

Ellen, R. (2010). Theories in anthropology and 'anthropological theory'. *Journal of the Royal Anthropological Institute, 16*(2), 387–404. doi:10.1111/j.1467-9655.2010.01631.x

Elswick, S. E., Cuellar, M. J., & Mason, S. E. (2018). Leadership and school social work in the usa: A qualitative assessment. *School Mental Health, 29*, 1-14.

Ely, K., Boyce, L. A., Nelson, J. K., Zaccaro, S. J., Hernez-Broome, G., & Whyman, W. (2010). Evaluating leadership coaching: A review and integrated framework. *The Leadership Quarterly, 21*(4), 585–599. doi:10.1016/j.leaqua.2010.06.003

Ember, C., & Ember, M. (2009). *Crosscultural research methods*. AltaMira Press.

Emrich, C. T., Tate, E., Larson, S. E., & Zhou, Y. (2020). Measuring social equity in flood recovery funding. *Environmental Hazards, 19*(3), 228–250. doi:10.1080/17477891.2019.1675578

Engida, Z. M., Alemu, A. E., & Mulugeta, M. A. (2022). The effect of change leadership on employees' readiness to change: The mediating role of organizational culture. *Future Business Journal, 8*(1), 1–13. doi:10.118643093-022-00148-2

Equal Employment Opportunity Commission. (2021). *Charge Statistics (Charges filed with EEOC) FY 1997 Through FY 2021*. US EEOC. https://www.eeoc.gov/data/charge-statistics-charges-filed-eeoc-fy-1997-through-fy-2021

Equal Employment Opportunity Commission. (2021). *Title VII of the Civil Rights Act of 1964*. Retrieved from https://www.eeoc.gov/laws/statutes/titlevii.cfm

Errida, A., & Lotfi, B. (2021). The determinants of organizational change management success: Literature review and case study. *International Journal of Engineering Business Management, 13*, 1–15. doi:10.1177/18479790211016273

ErtanA.CrosslandG.HeathC.DennyD.JensenR. (2018). Everyday Cyber Security in Organisations. arXiv:2004.11768.

Esteves, A., & Barclay, M. (2011). New approaches to evaluating the performance of corporate-community partnerships: A case study from the minerals sector. *Journal of Business Ethics, 103*(2), 189–202. doi:10.100710551-011-0860-7

European Commission. (2021). *Proposal for a Regulation laying down harmonized rules on artificial intelligence (Artificial Intelligence Act) and amending certain Union legislative acts*. https://digital-strategy.ec.europa.eu/en/library/proposal-regulation-laying-down-harmonised-rules-artificial-intelligence-artificial-intelligence

Evans, A. M., Wright, S., Murphy, P., & Maki, J. (2016). *Incorporating leadership models into counseling supervision: Recommendations to strengthen services*. Retrieved June 9, 2020, from https://www.counseling.org/docs/default-source/vistas/article_5124f227f16116603abcacff0000bee5e7.pdf?sfvrsn=4&sfvrsn=4

Fadun, S. (2021). *Cybersecurity Risk and Cybersecurity Risk Management (Cyber, Security, Risk, & Cyber Security)* [Video]. YouTube. https://www.youtube.com/watch?v=tZ7LfWinbu0

Fairfield, K. D., Harmon, J., & Benson, S. (2010). Influences on the organizational implementation of sustainability: An integrative model. *Academy of Management Annual Meeting Proceedings*, 1-6. 10.5465/ambpp.2010.54497867

Falch, M., Olesen, H., Skouby, K. E., Tadayoni, R., & Williams, I. (2022). Cybersecurity in SMEs in the Baltic Sea Region. *International Telecommunications Society 31th European Conference 2022*.

Fassinger, R. E., Buki, L. P., & Shullman, S. L. (2017). Leadership in counseling psychology: Introduction to the special issue. *The Counseling Psychologist, 45*(6), 742–751. doi:10.1177/0011000017729755

Fassinger, R. E., & Shullman, S. L. (2017). Leadership and counseling psychology: What should we know? Where could we go? *The Counseling Psychologist*, *45*(7), 927–964. doi:10.1177/0011000017744253

Fay, B. (1987). *Critical Social Science: Liberation and its Limits*. Cornell University Press.

Feagin, J. (2013). *Systemic racism: A theory of oppression*. Routledge. doi:10.4324/9781315880938

Feeley, T. H. (2019). Defining Sexual Harassment in the Restaurant Industry. *Journal of Culinary Science & Technology*, *17*(1), 1–20.

Feldman, D. C. (2001). Career coaching: What H.R. professionals and managers need to know. *Human Resources Planning*, *24*, 26–35.

Feldman, D. C., & Lankau, M. J. (2010). Executive Coaching: A review and Agenda for Future Research. *Journal of Management*. Advance online publication. doi:10.1177/0149206305279599

Feng, X., Li, S., Yuan, C., Zeng, P., & Sun, Y. (2018). Prediction of slope stability using naive Bayes classifier. *KSCE Journal of Civil Engineering*, *22*(3), 941–950. doi:10.100712205-018-1337-3

Fermor, P. (2022). *Customer experience: key pillars for continuous improvement*. https://Internationalbankers.com/Technology/customerexperience-key-pillar-for-continuous-improvement

Fernandes, L., & Alsaeed, N. (2014). African Americans and workplace discrimination. *European Journal of English Language and Literature Studies*, *2*(2), 56–76.

Fernandez, C. S. P., Noble, C. C., & Garman, L. (2021). A qualitative analysis of maternal and child health public health leadership institute (mch phli) leaders: Assessing the application of leadership skills at the "others" and "wider community" levesl of the mch leadership competencies 4.0. *Maternal and Child Health Journal*, *25*(9), 1437–1446. doi:10.100710995-021-03134-2 PMID:33950326

Fernandopulle, N. (2021). To what extent does hierarchical leadership affect healthcare outcomes? *Medical Journal of the Islamic Republic of Iran*, *35*(1), 1–11. PMID:34956963

Ferrell, G., & Davis, M. (2019). Higher education institutions and online programs: Understanding the importance of course delivery and student success. *Online Journal of Distance Learning Administration*, *22*(2).

Fetaji, B., & Fetaji, M. (2009). The evaluation of e-learning and the cost-benefit analysis of distance learning education. *Journal of Applied Computer Science & Mathematics*, *13*(7), 69–73.

Files, R., & Liu, M. (2022). Unraveling financial fraud: The role of the board of directors and external advisors in conducting independent internal investigations. *Contemporary Accounting Research*, *39*(3), 1905–1948. doi:10.1111/1911-3846.12784

Finger, M., & Portmann, E. (2016). What are cognitive cities? In *Towards Cognitive Cities* (pp. 1–11). Springer. doi:10.1007/978-3-319-33798-2_1

Fink, A. (2014). *Conducting research literature reviews: From the Internet to paper* (4th ed.). Sage Publications.

Fishback, P., Rose, J., Snowden, K., & Storrs, T. (2022). New Evidence on Redlining by Federal Housing Programs in the 1930s. SSRN *Electronic Journal*, 103462. doi:10.21033/wp-2022-01

Fisher, R., Porod, C., & Peterson, S. (2021). Motivating employees and organizations to adopt a cybersecurity-focused culture. *Journal of Organizational Psychology*, *21*(1), 114–131.

Fitzsimmons, T. W., & Callan, V. J. (2020). The diversity gap in leadership: What are we missing in current theorizing? *The Leadership Quarterly*, *31*(4), 101347. doi:10.1016/j.leaqua.2019.101347

Flach, P. A. (2016). ROC analysis. In *Encyclopedia of machine learning and data mining* (pp. 1–8). Springer.

Flynn, J. (2022, October 31). 30+ Alarming Employment Discrimination Statistics [2023]: Recent Employment Discrimination Cases. *Zippia*. https://www.zippia.com/advice/employment-discrimination-statistics/

Flyvbjerg, B., & Sunstein, C. (2015). The Principle of the Malevolent Hiding Hand; or the Planning Fallacy Writ Large. *SSRN*, 1–18. doi:10.2139srn.2654217

Foley, R. W., Nadjari, S., Eshirow, J., Adekunle, R., & Codjoe, P. (2022). Towards digital segregation? Problematizing the haves and have nots in the smart city. *Frontiers in Sustainable Cities*, *4*, 706670. Advance online publication. doi:10.3389/frsc.2022.706670

Ford, M., Cerasoli, C., Higgins, J., & Decesare, A. (2011). Relationships between psychological, physical, and behavioural health and work performance: A review and meta-analysis. *Work and Stress*, *25*(3), 185–204. doi:10.1080/0267 8373.2011.609035

Fraser, J. F., & Simkins, B. J. (2010). Enterprise Risk Management: An Introduction and Overview. In Enterprise Risk Management: Today's Leading Research and Best Practices for Tomorrow's Executives (1st ed.). Wiley. doi:10.1002/9781118267080.ch1

Frederickson, H. G. (2015). Toward a New Public Administration. In J. M. Shafritz & A. C. Hyde (Eds.), *Classics of Public Administration*. Eight Edition.

Freeman, A. M., & Perry, J.A. (2010). Executive coaching under pressure: A case study. *Consulting Psychology Journal: Practice and Research, 6,* 189-202.

Freeman, E. (1984). *Strategic management: A stakeholder approach*. Pitman.

Freudenreich, B., Lüdeke-Freund, F., & Schaltegger, S. (2020). A stakeholder theory perspective on business models: Value creation for sustainability. *Journal of Business Ethics*, *166*(1), 3–18. doi:10.100710551-019-04112-z

Friede, G., Busch, T., & Bassen, A. (2015). ESG and financial performance: Aggregated evidence from more than 2000 empirical studies. *Journal of Sustainable Finance & Investment*, *5*(4), 210–233. doi:10.1080/20430795.2015.1118917

Friedmann, P. D., Jiang, L., & Alexander, J. A. (2010). Top manager effects on buprenorphine adoption in outpatient substance abuse treatment programs. *The Journal of Behavioral Health Services & Research*, *37*(3), 322–337. doi:10.100711414-009-9169-z PMID:19296223

Friesen, J. P., & Lowe, K. B. (2020). Team mental model convergence, interdependence, and collaboration: A multi-level investigation. *Journal of Business and Psychology*, *35*(5), 611–629.

Frost, D. (2017). The benefits and challenges of health disparities and social stress frameworks for research on sexual and gender minority health. *The Journal of Social Issues*, *73*(3), 462–476. doi:10.1111/josi.12226

Fujimoto, S., & Omote, K. (2022, August). Proposal of a smart contract-based security token management system. In *2022 IEEE International Conference on Blockchain (Blockchain)* (pp. 419-426). IEEE. 10.1109/Blockchain55522.2022.00065

Furxhi, G. (2021). Employee's Resistance and Organizational Change Factors. *European Journal of Business and Management Research*, *6*(2), 30–32.

Gabel, S. (2013). Transformational leadership and healthcare. *Medical Science Educator*, *23*(1), 55–60. doi:10.1007/BF03341803

Gamble, C., Gowlett, J., & Dunbar, R. (2014). *Thinking big: How the evolution of social life shaped the human mind.* Thames & Hudson.

Gan, C., Guo, W., Chai, Y., & Wang, D. (2019). Unethical leader behavior and employee performance: A deontic justice perspec-tive. *Personnel Review, 49*(1), 188–201. doi:10.1108/PR-08-2018-0290

Ganin, A. A., Quach, P., Panwar, M., Collier, Z. A., Keisler, J. M., Marchese, D., & Linkov, I. (2020). Multicriteria Decision Framework for Cybersecurity Risk Assessment and Management. *Risk Analysis, 40*(1), 183–199. doi:10.1111/risa.12891 PMID:28873246

García de la Torre, C. (2007). Estudios sobre identidad y cultura en las organizaciones en América Latina. *Cuadernos de Administración, 38*, 21-51. Disponible en: http://bibliotecadigital.univalle.edu.co/ bitstream/10893/2151/1/ESTU-DIOS%20 SOBRE%20LA%20IDENTIDAD%20Y%20 LA%20CULTURA.pdf

Garcia-Retamero, R., & Lopez-Zafra, E. (2006). Prejudice against women in male-congenial environments: Perceptions of gender role congruity in leadership. *Sex Roles, 55*(1), 51–61. doi:10.100711199-006-9068-1

Gardner, T. (2017). *The value of sustainability to an organization.* Retrieved from https://hbr.org/2017/09/the-value-of-sustainability-to-an-organization

Gareth, J., Daniela, W., Trevor, H., & Robert, T. (2013). Springer texts in statistics. In G. Casella, S. Fienberg, & I. Olkin (Eds.), *An introduction to statistical learning* (1st ed., pp. 203–264).

Gartner. (2019). *The future of employee training and development relies on AI.* https://www.gartner.com/en/documents/3942674/the-future-of-employee-training-and-development-relies

Gartner. (2022). *Gartner top strategic predictions for 2022 and beyond.* https://www.gartner.com/en/documents/4009644/gartner-top-strategic-predictions-for-2022-and-beyond

Garvin, D. A. (2000). *Learning in action: A guide to putting the learning organization to work.* Harvard Business School Press.

Gast, B. (2011). *The 7 critical healthcare systems IT must protect.* Healthcare IT News. Retrieved April 22, 2023, from https://www.healthcareitnews.com/news/7-critical-healthcare-systems-it-must-protect

Gauthey, F., Ratiu, I., Rodgers, I., & Xardel, D. (1988). *Leaders sans frontières: Le défi des différences.* McGraw-Hill.

Gazzola, N., De Stefano, J., Theriault, A., & Audet, C. (2013). Learning to be supervisors: A qualitative investigation of difficulties experienced by supervisors-in-training. *The Clinical Supervisor, 32*(1), 15–39. doi:10.1080/07325223.2013.778678

Geertz, C. (1992). *La interpretación de las culturas.* Gedisa.

Geertz, C. (1996). Anti-antirrelativismo. In C. Geertz (Ed.), *Los usos de la diversidad* (pp. 93–127). Paidós.

Geiger, B., & Schaffhauser-Linzatti, M. M. (2020). The influence of team diversity and conflict on team creativity and innovation: A meta-analytic review. *Journal of Business and Psychology, 35*(2), 123–139.

Gélinas-Proulx, A., & Shields, C. M. (2022). *Leading for equity and social justice: Systemic transformation in Canadian education.* University of Toronto Press.

General Directorate of Public Hospitals. (2022). *City hospitals* [Şehir hastaneleri]. Retrieved 07.09.2022 from https://khgmsehirhastaneleridb.saglik.gov.tr/TR-43796/sehir-hastanelerimiz.html

Georgiadou, A., Mouzakitis, S., & Askounis, D. (2021). Assessing mitre att&ck risk using a cyber-security culture framework. *Sensors (Basel)*, *21*(9), 3267. doi:10.339021093267 PMID:34065086

Georgiadou, A., Mouzakitis, S., Bounas, K., & Askounis, D. (2022). A cyber-security culture framework for assessing organization readiness. *Journal of Computer Information Systems*, *62*(3), 452–462. doi:10.1080/08874417.2020.1845583

Gerea, C., & Herskovic, V. (2022). Transitioning from multichannel to Omnichannel customer experience in service-based companies: Challenges and coping strategies. *Journal of Theoretical and Applied Electronic Commerce Research*, *17*(2), 394–413. doi:10.3390/jtaer17020021

Gerlach, K., Spreng, N., Madore, K., & Schacter, D. (2014). Future planning: Default network activity couples with frontoparietal control network and reward-processing regions during process and outcome simulations. *Social Cognitive and Affective Neuroscience*, *9*(12), 1942–1951. doi:10.1093can/nsu001 PMID:24493844

Géron, A. (2019). *Hands-on machine learning with Scikit-Learn, Keras, and TensorFlow: Concepts, tools, and techniques to build intelligent systems* (2nd ed.). O'Reilly Media, Inc.

Gessaghi, V. (2011) La experiencia etnográfica y la clase alta. ¿Nuevos desafíos para la antropología? *Boletín de Antropología y Educación*, *2*, 17-26. Disponible en: https://es.scribd.com/document/423538599/Laexperiencia-etnografica-y-la-clase-alta-nuevos-desafios-para-la-antropolog

Ghani, B., Memon, K. R., Han, H., Ariza-Montes, A., & Arjona-Fuentes, J. M. (2022). Work stress, technological changes, and job insecurity in the retail organization context. *Frontiers in Psychology*, *13*(1), 1–14. doi:10.3389/fpsyg.2022.918065 PMID:36483719

Ghasabeh, M. S. (2021). Transformational Leadership: Implementing a Cultural Approach in Organizations. *The Journal of Values Based Leadership*, *14*(1), 101–118. doi:10.22543/0733.141.1340

Ghasabeh, M. S., Soosay, C., & Reaiche, C. (2015). The emerging role of transformational leadership. *Journal of Developing Areas*, *49*(6), 459–467. doi:10.1353/jda.2015.0090

Gibbons, J., & Barton, M. S. (2016). The association of minority self-rated health with Black versus white gentrification. *Journal of Urban Health*, *93*(6), 909–922. doi:10.100711524-016-0087-0 PMID:27761683

Gibson, D. M., Dollarhide, C. T., & McCallum, L. J. (2010). Nontenured assistant professors as American counseling association division presidents: The new look of leadership in counseling. *Journal of Counseling and Development*, *88*(3), 285–292. doi:10.1002/j.1556-6678.2010.tb00024.x

Giela, M. (2022). Cognitive Technologies in Smart City Services as the Future in Strategic Management of Cities. *Management Systems in Production Engineering*, *30*(3), 276–281. doi:10.2478/mspe-2022-0035

Giorgi, A. (1985). Introduction. In A. Giorgi (Ed.), *Phenomenology and psychological research* (pp. 1–7). Duquesne University Press.

Giorgi, A. (1997). The theory, practice, and evaluation of the phenomenological method as a qualitative research procedure. *Journal of Phenomenological Psychology*, *28*(2), 235–260. doi:10.1163/156916297X00103

Giorgi, A., & Giorgi, B. (2008). Phenomenological psychology. In C. Willig & W. Stainton-Rogers (Eds.), *The sage handbook of qualitative research in psychology* (pp. 165–178). Sage Publications. doi:10.4135/9781848607927.n10

Giorgi, A., Giorgi, B., & Morley, J. (2017). The descriptive phenomenological psychological method. In C. Willig & W. Stainton-Rogers (Eds.), *The sage handbook of qualitative research in psychology* (2nd ed., pp. 176–192). Sage Publications. doi:10.4135/9781526405555.n11

Gipolla, C. (2003). *Historia económica de la Europa preindustrial*. Crítica.

Glazer-Ramo, J. (2001). *Shattering the myths: Women in academe*. Johns Hopkins University Press.

Global Reporting Initiative. (2000). *Sustainability reporting guidelines (Amsterdam)*. U.S. Government Printing Office.

Glomb, T., & Richman, W. (2019). The effect of sexual harassment on employee outcomes: A meta-analysis. *The Journal of Applied Psychology*, *104*(6), 858–879.

Glosoff, H. L., Durham, J. C., & Whittaker, J. E. (2011). Supervision to prepare counselors as leaders and social justice advocates. In C. Y. Chang, C. A. Barrio Minton, A. Dixon, J. E. Myers, & T. J. Sweeney (Eds.), *Professional counseling excellence through leadership and advocacy* (pp. 185–205). Routledge.

Gokcumen, Ö., Gultekin, T., Alakoc, Y., Tug, A., Gulec, E., & Schurr, T. (2011). Biological ancestries, kinship connections, and projected identities in four central Anatolian settlements: Insights from culturally contextualized genetic anthropology. *American Anthropologist*, *113*(1), 116–131. doi:10.1111/j.1548-1433.2010.01310.x PMID:21560269

Golash-Boza, T., Duenas, M. D., & Xiong, C. (2019). White Supremacy, Patriarchy, and Global Capitalism in Migration Studies. *The American Behavioral Scientist*, *63*(13), 1741–1759. doi:10.1177/0002764219842624

Goldberg, Y. (2017). Neural network methods for natural language processing. *Synthesis Lectures on Human Language Technologies, 10*(1), 1-309.

Goldfarb-Tarrant, S., Robertson, A., Lazic, J., Tsouloufi, T., Donnison, L., & Smyth, K. (2020). Scaling Systematic Literature Reviews with Machine Learning Pipelines. *Proceedings of the First Workshop on Scholarly Document Processing*, 184–195. 10.18653/v1/2020.sdp-1.21

Goldratt, E. M. (1990). *What is this Thing Called Theory of Constraints and how Should it be Implemented?* Gower Publishing Company, Limited.

Gond, J. P., Lahiri, S., Reddy, P. R., & Suman, D. (2018). Sustainable strategies for competitive advantage: Role of corporate social responsibility (CSR). *International Journal of Business and Management*, *13*(3), 66–74.

Gong, B., Wang, J., & Cheng, J. (2019). Market Demand for Electric Vehicles under Technology Improvements and Tax Relief. *Emerging Markets Finance & Trade*, *56*(8), 1715–1729. doi:10.1080/1540496X.2019.1656606

Gonnet, J. P. (2012). Cultura, organizaciones y antropología. Una revisión crítica. Avá (Posadas), *Revista de Antropología*, *21*, 1-20. Disponible en: http:// www.scielo.org.ar/pdf/ava/n21/n21a07. pdf, https://www.redalyc.org/articulo.oa?id=169030268008

González, C., & Basaldúa, M. (2007) La formación de redes sociales en el estudio de actores y familias. Perspectiva de estudio en historia y antropología. *Redes. Revista Hispana para el Análisis de Redes Sociales, 12*, 1-27. Disponible en: https://revistes.uab.cat/redes/article/view/v12-n1-gonzalez-basaldua

Gonzalez, C. (2004). *Learning to Make Decisions in Dynamic Environments: Effects of Time Constraints and Cognitive Abilities*. Carnegie Mellon University, Department of Social and Decision Sciences. Retrieved from https://pdfs.semanticscholar.org/2ef4/2ab2c0d9fc49c0e5baeef3019979c512d217.pdf

Good, B. (1992). Culture and psychopathology: Directions for psychiatric anthropology. In T. Schwartz, G. White, & C. Lutz (Eds.), *New directions in psychological anthropology* (pp. 181–205). Cambridge University Press.

Goodenough, W. (1971). *Culture, Language, and Society*. Addison Wesley.

Goodland, R., & Daly, H. (1996). Environmental sustainability: Universal and non-negotiable. *Ecological Applications, 6*(4), 1002-1017. Retrieved from http://links.jstor.org/sici=1051-0761%281996611%

Gope, P., & Hwang, T. (2016). A Realistic Lightweight Anonymous Authentication Protocol for Securing Real-Time Application Data Access in Wireless Sensor Networks. *IEEE Transactions on Industrial Electronics, 63*(11).

Gorman, E. (2018). Sexual Harassment in the Restaurant Industry. *Harvard Business Review*. Retrieved from https://hbr.org/2018/11/sexual-harassment-in-the-restaurant-industry

Gourevitch, V., & Rousseau, J. J. (2018). *Rousseau: the Social Contract and other later political writings*. Cambridge University Press. doi:10.1017/9781316584606

GOV.UK. (2022, May 10). *Civil Service Diversity and Inclusion Dashboard*. https://www.gov.uk/government/publications/civil-service-diversity-inclusion-dashboard/civil-service-diversity-and-inclusion-dashboard

Govender, P., & Sivakumar, V. (2020). Application of k-means and hierarchical clustering techniques for analysis of air pollution: A review (1980–2019). *Atmospheric Pollution Research, 11*(1), 40–56. doi:10.1016/j.apr.2019.09.009

Gover, A. R., Harper, S. B., & Langton, L. (2020). Anti-Asian Hate Crime During the COVID-19 Pandemic: Exploring the Reproduction of Inequality. *American Journal of Criminal Justice, 45*(4), 647–667. doi:10.100712103-020-09545-1 PMID:32837171

Graham, C. (2018, August 29). Hypervisible, invisible: How to navigate White workplaces as a Black woman. *Career Contessa*. https://www.careercontessa.com/advice/black-woman-white-workplace/

Grandini, M., Bagli, E., & Visani, G. (2020). *Metrics for multi-class classification: an overview*. arXiv preprint arXiv:2008.05756.

Gravano, A. (1992). Antropología Práctica, muestra y posibilidades de la Antropología Organizacional. Publicar en Antropología y Ciencias Sociales, 1, 95-126.

Gravano, A. (1995). La imaginación antropológica; interpelaciones a la otredad construida y al método antropológico. Publicar en Antropología y Ciencias Sociales, 4, 71-91.

Gravano, A. (2008a). *¿Vecinos o ciudadanos? el fenómeno NIMBY (Not In My Back Yard) o SPAN (Sí, Pero No Aquí) del imaginario urbano en un proceso de participación social y su tratamiento desde la facilitación organizacional antropológica*. Trabajo presentado en II Congreso de la Asociación Latinoamericana de Antropología (ALA), Universidad de Costa Rica, Simposio "Imaginarios urbanos y participación social".

Gravano, A. (2008b). La cultura como concepto central de la Antropología. In Apertura a la Antropología, alteridad, cultura, naturaleza humana (3rd ed.). Proyecto Editorial.

Gravano, A. (Ed.). (2005). *Imaginarios de la ciudad media: emblemas, fragmentaciones yotredades urbanas, estudios de Antropología Urbana*. FACSO y SCYT de la UNICEN: Consejo Editor de la UNICEN.

Gravano, A. (1997). La cultura organizacional como herramienta de mejoramiento. In *El marco del trabajo humano, distintas corrientes en el análisis institucional y organizacional* (pp. 71–76). Area de Estudios e Investigación en Ciencia, Cultura y Sociedad, Cultura de la Ciudad de Buenos Aires.

Gravano, A. (2000). *Plan urbano ambiental: el proceso participativo del plan*. GCBA.

Gravano, A. (2005). *El barrio en la teoría social*. Espacio Editorial.

Graves, J. L., & Goodman, A. H. (2021). Chapter Four. Why Do Races Differ In Disease Incidence? In Racism, Not Race (pp. 82-101). Columbia University Press.

Greene, S., MacDonald, G., Arena, O., Srini, T., Ruth, G., Ezike, R., & Stern, A. (2019). *Technology and equity in cities: Emerging challenges and opportunities*. Academic Press.

Greenlee, T., Horn, G., Smith, D., Fahey, G., Goldstein, E., & Petruzzello, S. (2018). The influence of short-term fire-fighting activity on information processing performance. *Ergonomics*, *57*(5), 764–773. doi:10.1080/00140139.2014.897375 PMID:24670047

Greer, M. (2004). Overcoming invisibility. *American Psychological Association, 35*(8). http://www.apa.org/monitor/sep04/overcoming.aspx

Greer, T. M. (2010). A structural validation of the schedule of racist events. *Measurement & Evaluation in Counseling & Development*, *43*(2), 91–107. doi:10.1177/0272989X10373455

Grenz, S. (2017). *Sustainability measurement: A toolkit for assessing corporate sustainability performance*. Routledge.

Gressin, S. (2017). The equifax data breach: What to do. Federal Trade Commission.

Griffin, K. A. (2019). Institutional barriers, strategies, and benefits to increasing the representation of women and men of color in the professoriate: looking beyond the pipeline. In *Higher Education: Handbook of Theory and Research* (Vol. 35, pp. 1-73). https://diversity.ucdavis.edu/sites/g/files/dgvnsk731/files/inline-files/InstitutionalBarriersStrategies2020.pdf

Griffith, A. (2020, October 21). *What new disaggregated data tells us about federal public service diversity*. Policy Options. https://policyoptions.irpp.org/magazines/october-2020/what-new-disaggregated-data-tells-us-about-federal-public-service-diversity/

Grinnell, R. (2018, July 8). The persistence of memory: Are negative events easier to recall? *PsychCentral*. https://psychcentral.com/blog/the-persistence-of-memory-are-negative-events-easier-to-recall/

Gross, P. (2012). *A Q methodology Analysis of Individual Perspectives of Public Decision-Making Influences of Collaborative Processes*. Scholar Works. Retrieved from https://scholarworks.waldenu.edu/dissertations/975/

Grubbs-West, L. (2005). *Lessons in loyalty*. Cornerstone Leadership Institute.

Grudniewicz, A., Moher, D., Cobey, K. D., Bryson, G. L., Cukier, S., Allen, K., Ardern, C., Balcom, L., Barros, T., Berger, M., Ciro, J. B., Cugusi, L., Donaldson, M. R., Egger, M., Graham, I. D., Hodgkinson, M., Khan, K. M., Mabizela, M., Manca, A., ... Lalu, M. M. (2019). Predatory journals: No definition, no defence. *Nature*, *576*(7786), 210–212. doi:10.1038/d41586-019-03759-y PMID:31827288

Grzanka, P. R., & Cole, E. R. (2021). An argument for bad psychology: Disciplinary disruption, public engagement, and social transformation. *The American Psychologist*, *76*(8), 1334–1345. doi:10.1037/amp0000853 PMID:35113597

Guba, K., & Tsivinskaya, A. (2023). Expert judgments versus publication-based metrics: Do the two methods produce identical results in measuring academic reputation? *The Journal of Documentation*, *79*(1), 127–143. doi:10.1108/JD-02-2022-0039

Guest, P. M. (2016). Executive mobility and minority status. *Industrial Relations*, *55*(4), 604–631. doi:10.1111/irel.12153

Gumbs, A. (2018, November 26). New study proves Black women executives can't catch a break at work. *Black Enterprise*. https://www.blackenterprise.com/study-black-women-executives/

Gundel, B. E., Bartholomew, T. T., & Scheel, M. J. (2020). Culture and care: An illustration of multicultural processes in a counseling dyad. *Practice Innovations (Washington, D.C.)*, *5*(1), 19–31. doi:10.1037/pri0000104

Gupta, K., & Arora, N. (2019). Investigating consumer intention to accept mobile payment systems through unified theory of acceptance model: An Indian perspective November 2019. *South Asian Journal of Business Studies*. doi:10.1108/SAJBS-03-2019-0037

Gupta, A., Bhardwaj, A., Kanda, A., & Sachdeva, A. (2010). Theory of Constraints Based Approach to Effective Change Management. *International Journal of Research*, *1*(7), 40–48.

Haac. (2017, March). The IceCube Neutrino Observatory: Instrumentation and online systems. *Journal of Instrumentation : An IOP and SISSA Journal*, *12*.

Hadjichristidis, C., Summers, B., & Thomas, K. (2014). Unpacking estimates of task duration: The role of typicality and temporality. *Journal of Experimental Social Psychology*, *51*, 45-50. http://dx.DOI.org/10.1016/j.jesp.2013.10.009

Hadlington, L. (2018). The "Human Factor" in Cybersecurity. In Advances in digital crime, forensics, and cyber terrorism book series (pp. 46–63). IGI Global. doi:10.4018/978-1-5225-4053-3.ch003

Hajian, M., & Kashani, S. J. (2021). Evolution of the concept of sustainability. From Brundtland Report to sustainable development goals. In *Sustainable Resource Management* (pp. 1–24). Elsevier. doi:10.1016/B978-0-12-824342-8.00018-3

Haldorai, A., Ramu, A., & Chow, C. O. (2019). Big data innovation for sustainable cognitive computing. *Mobile Networks and Applications*, *24*(1), 221–223. doi:10.100711036-018-1198-5

Halimu, C., Kasem, A., & Newaz, S. S. (2019). Empirical comparison of area under ROC curve (AUC) and Mathew correlation coefficient (MCC) for evaluating machine learning algorithms on imbalanced datasets for binary classification. *Proceedings of the 3rd international conference on machine learning and soft computing*, 1-6. 10.1145/3310986.3311023

Hall-Ellis, S. D. (2015). Nudges and decision making: a winning combination. *The Bottom Line: Managing Library Finances*. doi:10.1108/BL-07-2015-0015

Hall, J. C. (2018). It is tough being a Black woman: Intergenerational stress and coping. *Journal of Black Studies*, *49*(5), 481–501. doi:10.1177/0021934718766817

Hall, J. C., Everett, J. E., & Hamilton-Mason, J. (2012). Black women talk about workplace stress and how they cope. *Journal of Black Studies*, *43*(2), 207–226. doi:10.1177/0021934711413272 PMID:22457894

Halme, M., Anttonen, M., Hrauda, G., & Kortman, J. (2006). Sustainability evaluation of European household services. *Journal of Cleaner Production*, *14*(17), 1529–1540. doi:10.1016/j.jclepro.2006.01.021

Halme, M., & Väänänen, K. (2018). Benefits of sustainability: An empirical assessment of the impact of sustainability on firm performance. *Business Strategy and the Environment*, *27*(3), 658–670.

Hamari, J., & Sjöklint, M. (2021). The sharing economy gamified: An analysis of gamification features in peer-to-peer rental services. *Journal of Business Research*, *122*, 624–634.

Hamdo, S. S. (2021). *Change Management Models: A Comparative Review* [Academic Paper]. Istanbul Okan University.

Hamill, J. (1990). *Ethno-logic: The anthropology of human reasoning*. University of Illinois.

Hammami, A., Hammami, S., Naffrechoux, E., & Lecompte, J. F. (2017). Measuring corporate sustainability performance: State of the art and directions for future research. *Sustainability*, *9*(11), 2091.

Han, Y., Liu, J., Lei, Y., Liu, L., & Ye, S. (2021). The Analysis and Application of Decentralized Cyber Layer and Distributed Security Control for Interconnected Conurbation Grids under Catastrophic Cascading Failures. *2021 3rd Asia Energy and Electrical Engineering Symposium (AEEES)*, 794-799, 10.1109/AEEES51875.2021.9402955

Haney, J., & Lutters, W. (2020). Security awareness training for the workforce: Moving beyond "check-the-box" compliance. *Computer*, *53*(10), 1–11. doi:10.1109/MC.2020.3001959 PMID:34131349

Hannafey, T., & Vitulano, L. A. (2013). Ethics and Executive Coaching: An Agency Theory Approach. *Journal of Business Ethics*, *115*(3), 599–603. doi:10.100710551-012-1442-z

Hannah, A., Baekkeskov, E., & Tubakovic, T. (2022). Ideas and crisis in policy and administration: Existing links and research frontiers. *Public Administration*, *100*(3), 571–584. doi:10.1111/padm.12862

Hao, J., & Ho, T. K. (2019). Machine learning made easy: A review of *scikit-learn* package in python programming language. *Journal of Educational and Behavioral Statistics*, *44*(3), 348–361. doi:10.3102/1076998619832248

Hardman, S., Fleming, K., Khare, E., & Ramadan, M. M. (2021). A perspective on equity in the transition to electric vehicle. *MIT Science Policy Review*, *2*, 46–54. doi:10.38105pr.e10rdoaoup

Hargett, C.W., Doty, J.P., Hauck, J.N., Webb, A.M.B., Cook, S.H., Tsipis, N.E., Neumann, J.A., , Andolsek, K. M., & Taylor, D. C. (2017). Developing a model for effective leadership in healthcare: A concept mapping approach. *Journal of Healthcare Leadership*, *9*, 69–78. doi:10.2147/JHL.S141664 PMID:29355249

Harnois, C. E., Bastos, J. L., Campbell, M. E., & Keith, V. M. (2019). Measuring perceived mistreatment across diverse social groups: An evaluation of the Everyday Discrimination Scale. *Social Science & Medicine*, *232*, 298–306. doi:10.1016/j.socscimed.2019.05.011 PMID:31121440

Harrell, J., Hall, S., & Taliaferro, J. (2003). Physiological responses to racism and discrimination: An assessment of the evidence. *American Journal of Public Health*, *93*(2), 243–248. doi:10.2105/AJPH.93.2.243 PMID:12554577

Harris, M., Consorte, J., Lang, J., & Byrne, B. (1993). Who are the whites? Imposed census categories and the racial demography of Brazil. *Social Forces*, *72*(2), 451–462. doi:10.2307/2579856

Harrison-Conwill, G. (2014). Informal ethnography in the corporate workplace: Applying foundational research methods in professional life. *Practical Anthropology*, *36*(2), 17–21. doi:10.17730/praa.36.2.4g331p0142864nl6

Hart, C., Crossley, A. D., & Correll, S. (2018). Study: When leaders take sexual harassment seriously, so do employees. *Harvard Business Review Digital Articles*, 1–5. Retrieved from https://hbr.org/2018/12/study-when-leaders-take-sexual-harassment-seriously-so-do-employees

Hart, S. L. (2005). *Capitalism at the crossroads: The unlimited business opportunities in solving the world's most difficult problems*. Wharton School Publishing.

Harvey, J. (2006). Understanding goal alignment models. *Chief Learning Officer*, *5*(5), 24–63.

Hassan, J., Shehzad, D., Habib, U., Aftab, M. U., Ahmad, M., Kuleev, R., & Mazzara, M. (2022). The rise of cloud computing: Data protection, privacy, and open research challenges—a systematic literature review (SLR). *Computational Intelligence and Neuroscience*, *2022*, 2022. doi:10.1155/2022/8303504 PMID:35712069

Hassan, R. (2019). Understanding the influence of technology on society. *Journal of Technology and Society*, *1*(1), 1–10.

Hassan, S., Puneet, P., Muchiri, M., & Ogbonnaya, C. (2022). Unethical Leadership: Review, Synthesis and Directions for Future Research. *Journal of Business Ethics*, *183*(2), 511–550. Advance online publication. doi:10.100710551-022-05081-6

Hastwell, C. (2020, January 7). What Are employee resource groups (ERGs)? *Great Place to Work*. https://www.greatplacetowork.com/resources/blog/what-are-employee-resource-groups-ergs

Haugh, H. M., & Talwar, A. (2010). How do corporations embed sustainability across the organization? *Academy of Management Learning & Education*, *9*(3), 384–396. doi:10.5465/amle.9.3.zqr384

Hay, I. (2006). Transformational leadership: characteristics and criticisms. *E Journal of Organizational Learning and Leadership*, *5*(2).

Hayes, J. A., McAleavey, A. A., Castonguay, L. G., & Locke, B. D. (2016). Psychotherapists' outcomes with White and racial/ethnic minority clients: First, the good news. *Journal of Counseling Psychology, 63*(3), 261–268. doi:10.1037/cou0000098 PMID:27078197

Hay, R. (2010). The relevance of ecocentrism, personal development, and transformational leadership to sustainability and identity. *Sustainable Development (Bradford), 18*(3), 163–171. doi:10.1002d.456

Health Services Planning Department. (2017). *Health service area* [Sağlık hizmet bölgesi]. Retrieved 01.09.2022 from https://planlamadb.saglik.gov.tr/TR,5708/saglik-hizmet-bolgesi.html

Heger, T., & Rohrbeck, R. (2012). Strategic foresight for collaborative exploration of new business fields. *Technological Forecasting and Social Change, 79*(5), 819–831. doi:10.1016/j.techfore.2011.11.003

Heggebø, K., Tøge, A. G., Dahl, E., & Berg, J. E. (2019). Socioeconomic inequalities in health during the Great Recession: A scoping review of the research literature. *Scandinavian Journal of Public Health, 47*(6), 635–654. doi:10.1177/1403494818801637 PMID:30301437

Heidegger, M. (1971). *The origin of the work of art.* Harper Books.

Heifetz, R. A. (1994). *Leadership without easy answers.* Belknap Press. doi:10.4159/9780674038479

Heinz, K. (2020, August 17). What does DEI mean in the workplace? *Built In.* https://builtin.com/diversity-inclusion/what-does-dei-mean-in-the-workplace#2

Heller, M. (2009). *Systems theory: An introduction.* Sage.

Hemel, D., & Lund, D. S. (2018). Sexual harassment and corporate law. *Columbia Law Review, 118*(6), 1583–1680. https://search.ebscohost.com/login.aspx?direct=true&AuthType=shib&db=buh&AN=132610149&site=ehost-live&custid=s8501869

Hemmatjo, R., Hajaghazadeh, M., Allahyari, T., Zare, S., & Kazemi, R. (2020). The effects of live-fire drills on visual and auditory cognitive performance among firefighters. *Annals of Global Health, 86*(1), 144. Advance online publication. doi:10.5334/aogh.2626 PMID:33262933

Hemmatjo, R., Motamedzade, M., Aliabadi, M., Kalatpour, O., & Farhadian, M. (2017). The effect of artificial smoke compound on physiological responses, cognitive functions and work performance during firefighting activities in a smoke-diving room: An intervention study. *International Journal of Occupational Safety and Ergonomics, 24*(3), 358–365. doi:10.1080/10803548.2017.1299995 PMID:28278005

Henderson, C. (2015). *How sustainability improves brand loyalty.* Retrieved from https://www.forbes.com/sites/christopherhenderson/2015/07/15/how-sustainability-improves-brand-loyalty/#1f2f7c3d3d14

Henderson, P. (1994). *Administrative skills in counseling supervision.* ERIC Digest. ERIC database. (ED372356)

Henderson, S. E., Henricksen, R. C., Jr., Liang, Y.-W. M., & Marks, D. F. (2016). *Counselor licensure supervision across the United States: A comparative look.* https://www.counseling.org/docs/defaultsource/vistas/article_09ccbf24f16116603abcacff0000bee5e7.pdf?sfvrsn=52a9442c_4

Henrich, J. (2016). *The secret of our success: How culture is driving human evolution, domesticating our species, and making us smarter.* Princeton University Press. doi:10.1515/9781400873296

Henrich, J., Boyd, R., Bowles, S., Camerer, C., Fehr, E., Gintis, H., McElreath, R., Alvard, M., Barr, A., Ensminger, J., Henrich, N., Hill, K., Gil-White, F., Gurven, M., Marlowe, F., Patton, J., & Tracer, D. (2005). "Economic man" in cross-cultural perspective: Behavioral experiments in 15 small-scale societies. *Behavioral and Brain Sciences*, *28*(6), 795–855. doi:10.1017/S0140525X05000142 PMID:16372952

Henrich, J., & Gil-White, F. (2001). The evolution of prestige: Freely conferred deference as a mechanism for enhancing the benefits of cultural transmission. *Evolution and Human Behavior*, *22*(3), 165–196. doi:10.1016/S1090-5138(00)00071-4 PMID:11384884

Henry, H. L., & Li, C.-S. (2022). Religious identity development and multicultural competence: A correlational study of counseling students. *Counseling and Values*, *67*(1), 116–137.

Herath, T. C., & Rao, H. R. (2009). Protection motivation and deterrence: A framework for security policy compliance in organisations. *European Journal of Information Systems*, *18*(2), 106–125. doi:10.1057/ejis.2009.6

Hernández, V. (2013). Genealogía de una elite rural: elucidación antropológica de una práctica de poder. *Mundo Agrario*, *13*(26). Disponible en: https://www.redalyc.org/pdf/845/84527468004.pdf

Hernández, B. (2012). La selección de personal, algunas consideraciones frente a sus prácticas. *Semestre Económico*, *15*(31), 173–186. doi:10.22395eec.v15n31a7

Hewlett, S. A., & Green, T. (2015). Black women ready to lead. *Center for Talent Innovation*. https://www.talentinnovation.org/_private/assets/BlackWomenReadyToLead_ExecSumm-CTI.pdf

Hewlett, S. A., & Wingfield, T. (2015, June 11). Qualified Black women are being held back from management. *Harvard Business Review*. https://hbr.org/2015/06/qualified-black-women-are-being-held-back-from-management

Heydari, P., Babamiri, M., Tapak, L., Golmohammadi, R., & Kalatpour, O. (2022). Weighing and prioritization of individual factors affecting the performance of industries firefighters. *Fire Safety Journal*, *127*, 103512. doi:10.1016/j.firesaf.2021.103512

Hibbard, D., Hibbard, M., & Stockman, J. W. (2006). *The canoe theory: A business success strategy for leaders and associates*. iUniverse.

Higginbotham, E. (2004). Invited reaction: Black and White women managers: Access to opportunity. *Human Resource Development Quarterly*, *15*(2), 147–152. doi:10.1002/hrdq.1095

High Availability Solutions ⎸ Imperva. (2022). *Learning Center*. https://www.imperva.com/learn/availability/high-availability/

Hilal, A. H., & Alibri, S. S. (2013). Using NVivo for data analysis in qualitative research. *International Interdisciplinary Journal of Education*, *2*(2), 181–186. doi:10.12816/0002914

Hilbert, M. (2012). Toward a Synthesis of Cognitive Biases: How Noisy Information Processing Can Bias Human Decision Making. *Psychological Bulletin*, *138*(2), 211–237. doi:10.1037/a0025940 PMID:22122235

Hill, J. (2020). Defining and measuring ESG performance. *Environmental, Social, and Governance (ESG) Investing*, 167-183. doi:10.1016/B978-0-12-818692-3.00009-8

Hill, L., & Hoggard, L. (2018). Active coping moderates associations among race-related stress, rumination, and depressive symptoms in emerging adult African American women. *Development and Psychopathology*, *30*(5), 1817–1835. doi:10.1017/S0954579418001268 PMID:30451137

Hill, R. P., Ainscough, T., Shank, T., & Manullang, D. (2007). Corporate social responsibility and socially responsible investing: A global perspective. *Journal of Business Ethics*, *70*(2), 165–174. doi:10.100710551-006-9103-8

Hilton, S. K., Madilo, W., Awaah, F., & Arkorful, H. (2023). Dimensions of transformational leadership and organizational performance: The mediating effect of job satisfaction. *Management Research Review*, *46*(1), 1–19. doi:10.1108/MRR-02-2021-0152

Hinterhuber, A. (2022). Digital transformation, the Holy Grail, and the disruption of business models: An interview with Michael Nilles. *Business Horizons*, *65*(3), 261–265. doi:10.1016/j.bushor.2021.02.042

Hite, R. L., & Milbourne, J. D. (2022). Divining the professional development experiences of K-12 stem master teacher leaders in the united states. *Professional Development in Education*, *48*(3), 476–492. doi:10.1080/19415257.2021.1955733

Hofbauer, J., & Podsiadlowski, A. (2014). Envisioning "inclusive organizations" - Guest Editorial. In J. Hofbauer & A. Podsiadlowski (Eds.), *Envisioning inclusive organizations: theory-building and corporate practice, Special issue. Equality, Diversity and Inclusion: An International Journal, 33(3), 214–219*. doi:10.1108/EDI-01-2014-0008

Hoffmann, V. (2018). How to reduce your company's carbon emissions. *Harvard Business Review*.

Holck, L. (2018). Unequal by structure: Exploring the structural embeddedness of organizational diversity. *Organization*, *25*(2), 242–259. doi:10.1177/1350508417721337

Holck, L., & Muhr, S. L. (2017). Unequal solidarity? Towards a norm-critical approach to welfare logics. *Scandinavian Journal of Management*, *33*(1), 1–11. doi:10.1016/j.scaman.2016.11.001

Holder, A., Jackson, M., & Ponterotto, J. (2015). Racial microaggression experiences and coping strategies of Black women in corporate leadership. *Qualitative Psychology*, *2*(2), 164–180. doi:10.1037/qup0000024

Holland, B. (2020). Capabilities, well-being, and environmental justice 1. In *Environmental Justice* (pp. 64–77). Routledge. doi:10.4324/9780429029585-7

Holm, M. (2018). 5 strategies to reduce water use in your business. *Harvard Business Review*.

Holt, H., Beutler, L. E., Kimpara, S., Macias, S., Haug, N. A., Shiloff, N., & Stein, M. (2015). Evidence-based supervision: Tracking outcome and teaching principles of change in clinical supervision to bring science to integrative practice. *Psychotherapy (Chicago, Ill.)*, *52*(2), 185–189. doi:10.1037/a0038732 PMID:25985042

Horn, G. P., Stewart, J. W., Kesler, R. M., DeBlois, J. P., Kerber, S., Fent, K. W., Scott, W. S., Fernhall, B., & Smith, D. L. (2019). Firefighter and fire instructor's physiological responses and safety in various training fire environments. *Safety Science*, *116*, 287–294. doi:10.1016/j.ssci.2019.03.017

Horowitz, M., Yaworsky, W., & Kickham, K. (2019). Anthropology's science wars: Insights from a new survey. *Current Anthropology*, *60*(5), 674–698. doi:10.1086/705409

Hosmer, D. T., & Morin, J. (2018). *Organizational development consulting: A guide to internal and external consulting*. Sage.

Houston, C. (2022). Why social scientists still need phenomenology. *Thesis Eleven*, *168*(1), 37–54. doi:10.1177/07255136211064326

Hsu, C., & Fingerman, K. (2021). Public electric vehicle charger access disparities across race and income in California. *Transport Policy*, *100*, 59–67. doi:10.1016/j.tranpol.2020.10.003

Huang, D. Z. (2021). Environmental, social and governance (ESG) activity and firm performance: A review and consolidation. *Accounting and Finance*, *61*(1), 335–360. doi:10.1111/acfi.12569

Huang, D. Z. (2021). Environmental, social and governance factors and assessing firm value: Valuation, signalling and stakeholder perspectives. *Accounting and Finance*, *62*(S1), 1983–2010. doi:10.1111/acfi.12849

Huang, Q., Zhang, Q., An, Y., & Xu, W. (2019). The relationship between dispositional mindfulness and PTSD/PTG among firefighters: The mediating role of emotion regulation. *Personality and Individual Differences*, *151*, 109492. doi:10.1016/j.paid.2019.07.002

Huang, X., Xia, Y., & Da-Wei, D. (2023). Distributed Event-Triggered Synchronization for Complex Cyber–Physical Networks under DoS Attacks. *Applied Sciences (Basel, Switzerland)*, *13*(3), 1716. doi:10.3390/app13031716

Hudson, A. N., Van Dongen, H., & Honn, K. A. (2020). Sleep deprivation, vigilant attention, and brain function: A review. *Neuropsychopharmacology*, *45*(1), 21–30. doi:10.103841386-019-0432-6 PMID:31176308

Hu, M. K., & Kee, D. M. H. (2022). Global institutions and ESG integration to accelerate SME development and sustainability. In *Handbook of Research on Global Institutional Roles for Inclusive Development* (pp. 139–156). IGI Global. doi:10.4018/978-1-6684-2448-3.ch008

HuminuikK.O'ConnorM.DockettK.KallivayalilD. J.McFarlandS. G.WyndhamJ.

Hunt, V., Prince, S., Dixon-Fyle, S., & Yee, L. (2018). *Delivering through diversity*. McKinsey & Company. https://www.mckinsey.com/business-functions/organization/our-insights/delivering-through-diversity

Hunter-Gadsen, L. (2018). The troubling news about Black women in the workplace. *Forbes*. https://www.forbes.com/sites/nextavenue/2018/11/06/the-troubling-news-about-black-women-in-the-workplace/?sh=37f0896f6053

Hussain, W. (2018). The Common Good. *The Stanford Encyclopedia of Philosophy*. https://plato.stanford.edu/archives/spr2018/entries/common-good

Husserl, E. (1970). *Logical investigations* (J. Findlay, Trans.). Humanities Press. (Original publication 1900)

Hu, W., Wang, Y., Ren, Y., & Cui, G. (2022). Designing and implementing a constructionist learning environment: Integrating social constructivism, instructional design principles, and educational technologies. *Journal of Educational Technology Development and Exchange*, *15*(1), 1–16. doi:10.18785/jetde.1501.01

Iftekhar, M., & Pannell, D. (2015). "Biases" in Adaptive Natural Resource Management. *Conservation Letters*, *8*(6), 388–396. doi:10.1111/conl.12189

Igboanugo, S., Bigelow, P. L., & Mielke, J. G. (2021). Health outcomes of psychosocial stress within firefighters: A systematic review of the research landscape. *Journal of Occupational Health*, *63*(1), e12219. doi:10.1002/1348-9585.12219 PMID:33780075

Ika, C., Novieastari, E., & Nuraini, T. (2019). The role of a head nurses in preventing interdisciplinary conflicts. *Enfermeria Clinica*, *29*, 123–127. doi:10.1016/j.enfcli.2019.04.019

Ikeziri, L. M., Souza, F. G., Gupta, M. P., & De Camargo Fiorini, P. (2019). Theory of constraints: Review and bibliometric analysis. *International Journal of Production Research*, *57*(15–16), 5068–5102. doi:10.1080/00207543.2018.1518602

Ilic, V., & Frăsineanu, E. (2019). Theoretical Approaches. Revisited and New Perspectives: Ethical Fundamentals in Scientific Research. *Annals of the University of Craiova, Psychology - Pedagogy, 18*(40).

Imel, Z. E., Baldwin, S., Atkins, D. C., Owen, J., Baardseth, T., & Wampold, B. E. (2011). Racial/ethnic disparities in therapist effectiveness: A conceptualization and initial study of cultural competence. *Journal of Counseling Psychology*, *58*(3), 290–298. doi:10.1037/a0023284 PMID:21534654

Imogen, F., Orr, C., & Thielking, M. (2022). Apply the framework method to qualitative psychological research: Methodological overview and worked example. *Qualitative Psychology*. Advance online publication. doi:10.1037/qup0000238

Inder, S., Sood, K., & Grima, S. (2022). Antecedents of behavioral intention to adopt Internet banking using structural equation modeling. *Journal of Risk and Financial Management*, *15*(4), 157. doi:10.3390/jrfm15040157

Information Security Policy Templates. (n.d.). SANS Institute. Retrieved April 22, 2023, from https://www.sans.org/information-security-policy/

Inga, S. M. (2021). The Seven epistemological myths of anthropology *Rev. Epistemol. Psychol. Science. Soc. (Arequipa)*, *4*, 89-103.

Innes, J. (2016). Collaborative rationality for planning practice. *The Town Planning Review*, *84*(1), 1–4. doi:10.3828/tpr.2016.1

Innes, J., & Booher, D. (2010). *Planning with complexity: An introduction to collaborative rationality for public policy*. Routledge.

InStride. (2021, February 19). *Diversity in the workplace statistics you need to know in 2023*. https://www.instride.com/insights/workplace-diversity-and-inclusion-statistics/

International Labor Organization. (2021). *Global survey on AI and the future of work*. https://www.ilo.org/global/topics/future-of-work/publications/global-survey-on-ai/lang--en/index.htm

INTERNATIONAL STANDARD ISO 9001: Quality management systems — Requirements (ISO 9001: 2015). (2015). International Organization for Standardization.

INTERNATIONAL STANDARD ISO/IEC 27001: Information technology — Security techniques — Information security management systems — Requirements (ISO/IEC 27001: 2022). (2022). International Organization for Standardization.

Introduction to Management: Management Types and Levels. (n.d.). *Lumens: Boundless Management*. https://courses.lumenlearning.com/boundless-management/chapter/management-levels-and-types/

Invensis Learning. (2022, October 11). *Risk Mitigation Strategies | The 5 Best Approaches of Risk Management | Invensis Learning* [Video]. YouTube. https://www.youtube.com/watch?v=pMKtWoec37c

Islam, M. M., Iqbal, H., Haque, M. R., & Hasan, M. K. (2017). *Prediction of breast cancer using support vector machine and K-Nearest neighbors. In 2017 IEEE Region 10 Humanitarian Technology Conference (R10-HTC)*. IEEE.

ISO 9241 is a multi-part standard from the International Organization for Standardization (ISO) covering ergonomics of human-computer interaction.

Izonin, I., Tkachenko, R., Shakhovska, N., Ilchyshyn, B., & Singh, K. K. (2022). A two-step data normalization approach for improving classification accuracy in the medical diagnosis domain. *Mathematics*, *10*(11), 1942. doi:10.3390/math10111942

Jacob, C. J., Stoler, J., & Roth, G. (2017). A pilot study of transformational leadership and college counseling outcomes. *Journal of Creativity in Mental Health*, *12*(2), 180–191. doi:10.1080/15401383.2016.1201033

Jameson, J. J., Thornton, G. C., & Byars-Winston, A. (2016). The role of organizational development in improving communication and feedback. *Human Resource Development Quarterly*, *27*(4), 377–396.

Jaros, S. (2010). Commitment to organizational change: A critical review. *Journal of Change Management*, *10*(1), 79–108. doi:10.1080/14697010903549457

Jean-Marie, G., Williams, V., & Sherman, S. (2009). Black women's leadership experiences: Examining the intersectionality of race and gender. *Advances in Developing Human Resources*, *11*(5), 562–581. doi:10.1177/1523422309351836

Jefferies, K., Goldberg, L., Aston, M., & Tomblin Murphy, G. (2018). Understanding the invisibility of black nurse leaders using a black feminist poststructuralist framework. *Journal of Clinical Nursing*, *27*(15-16), 3225–3234. doi:10.1111/jocn.14505 PMID:29752837

Jennings, C. (2006). Quality and value: The true purpose of peer review. *Nature*. Advance online publication. doi:10.1038/nature05032

Jeong, J., Mihelcic, J., Oliver, G., & Rudolph, C. (2019). Towards an Improved Understanding of Human Factors in Cybersecurity. *Color Imaging Conference*. 10.1109/CIC48465.2019.00047

Jeon, S. G., Han, J., Jo, Y., & Han, K. (2019, November). Being more focused and engaged in firefighting training: Applying user-centered design to VR system development. In *25th ACM Symposium on Virtual Reality Software and Technology* (pp. 1-11). 10.1145/3359996.3364268

Jimo, S., Abdullah, T., & Jamal, A. (2023, January). IoE Security Risk Analysis in a Modern Hospital Ecosystem. In *Cybersecurity in the Age of Smart Societies: Proceedings of the 14th International Conference on Global Security, Safety and Sustainability, London, September 2022* (pp. 451-467). Cham: Springer International Publishing. 10.1007/978-3-031-20160-8_26

Jinha, A. E. (2010). Article 50 million: An estimate of the number of scholarly articles in existence. *Learned Publishing*, *23*(3), 258–263. doi:10.1087/20100308

Jo, H., & Harjoto, M. (2011). Corporate governance and firm value: The impact of corporate social responsibility. *Journal of Business Ethics*, *103*(3), 351–383. doi:10.100710551-011-0869-y

Johns, F., & Riles, A. (2016). Beyond Bunker and Vaccine: The DNC Hack as a Conflict of Laws Issue. *The American Journal of International Law*, *110*, 347–351.

Johnson, D., Blumstein, D., & Fowler, J. H. (2013). The evolution of error: error management, cognitive constraints, and adaptive decision-making biases. *Trends in Ecology & Evolution, 28*(8), 474-481. http://dx.DOI.org/10.1016/j.tree.2013.05.014

Johnson, A. (1978). *Quantification in cultural anthropology*. Stanford University Press.

Johnson, C. C., Vega, L., Kohalmi, A. L., Roth, J. C., Howell, B. R., & Van Hasselt, V. B. (2020). Enhancing mental health treatment for the firefighter population: Understanding fire culture, treatment barriers, practice implications, and research directions. *Professional Psychology, Research and Practice*, *51*(3), 304–311. doi:10.1037/pro0000266

Johnson, T. J. (2020). Intersection of bias, structural racism, and social determinants with health care inequities. *Pediatrics*, *146*(2), e2020003657. doi:10.1542/peds.2020-003657 PMID:32690807

Jolliffe, I. T., & Philipp, A. (2010). Some recent developments in cluster analysis. *Physics and Chemistry of the Earth Parts A/B/C*, *35*(9-12), 309–315. doi:10.1016/j.pce.2009.07.014

Jolly, V. (2016). The Influence of Internet Banking on the Efficiency and Cost Savings for Banks' Customers. *International Journal of Social Sciences and Management*, *3*(3), 163–170. doi:10.3126/ijssm.v3i3.15257

Jones, K., Sabat, I., King, E., Ahmad, A., McCausland, T., & Chen, T. (2017). Isms and schisms: A meta-analysis of the prejudice-discrimination relationship across racism, sexism, and ageism. *Journal of Organizational Behavior*, *38*(7), 1076–1110. doi:10.1002/job.2187

Jones, P. W., & Smith, T. S. (2021). A guide to writing a literature review. *Journal of Transportation Safety & Security*, *13*(1), 28–43.

Jones, R. E., & Rainey, S. A. (2006). Examining linkages between race, environmental concern, health, and justice in a highly polluted community of color. *Journal of Black Studies*, *36*(4), 473–496. doi:10.1177/0021934705280411

Jordan, K. (2021). Initial trends in enrolment and dropout of massive open online courses. *Distance Education*, *42*(1), 14–28.

Jørgensen, S., & Pedersen, L. J. (2018). *Restart sustainable business model innovation*. Springer., doi:10.1007/978-3-319-91971-3

Jo, S., Han, H., Leem, Y., & Lee, S. (2021). Sustainable smart cities and industrial ecosystem: Structural and relational changes of the smart city industries in Korea. *Sustainability (Basel)*, *13*(17), 9917. doi:10.3390u13179917

Juliana, J., Stella, B., Austine, C. V., Budiono, E. D., & Klarissa, K. (2021). Antecedents on Customer Satisfaction Tuku Coffee Shop: A Perspective Expectation-Confirmation Theory and Kano's Model. *International Journal of Social, Policy, and Law*, *2*(3), 1–11.

Juma'h, A. H., & Alnsour, Y. (2020). The effect of data breaches on company performance. *International Journal of Accounting & Information Management*, *1*(1), 1–26. doi:10.1108/IJAIM-01-2019-0006

Jung, Y., Lee, J., & Shin, W. (2017). Sustained attention performance during sleep deprivation and following nap: Associated with trait-like vulnerability. *Sleep Medicine*, *40*, e151. doi:10.1016/j.sleep.2017.11.442

Kaase, M., & Newton, K. (1995). *Theories of Crisis and Catastrophe, Change and Transformation*. Academic. doi:10.1093/0198294727.003.0002

Kabir, U. Y., Ezekekwu, E., Bhuyan, S. S., Mahmood, A., & Dobalian, A. (2020). Trends and best practices in health care cybersecurity insurance policy. *Journal of Healthcare Risk Management*, *40*(2), 10–14. doi:10.1002/jhrm.21414 PMID:32441812

Kafle Ved, P. (2016). Internet of things standardization in ITU and prospective networking technologies. *IEEE Communications Magazine*, *54*(9), 43–49. doi:10.1109/MCOM.2016.7565271

Kahneman, D. (2011). *Thinking Fast and Slow*. FSG.

Kaiser, L. (2020). ESG integration: Value, growth and momentum. *Journal of Asset Management*, *21*(1), 32–51. doi:10.105741260-019-00148-y

Kalnicky, E. (2022, December 8). *Race, gender and public service leadership: Major findings from 360 assessment data*. Partner for Public Service. https://ourpublicservice.org/publications/race-gender-and-public-service-leadership-major-findings-from-our-360-data/

Kamei, F., Wiese, I., Lima, C., Polato, I., Nepomuceno, V., Ferreira, W., Ribeiro, M., Pena, C., Cartaxo, B., Pinto, G., & Soares, S. (2021). Grey Literature in Software Engineering: A critical review. *Information and Software Technology*, *138*, 106609. doi:10.1016/j.infsof.2021.106609

Kampa-Kokesh, S., & Anderson, M. Z. (2005). Executive Coaching: A comprehensive Review of the Literature. *Consulting Psychology Journal: Practice and Research, 53*(4), 205-228.

Kang, H. (2013). The prevention and handling of the missing data. *Korean Journal of Anesthesiology*, *64*(5), 402. doi:10.4097/kjae.2013.64.5.402 PMID:23741561

Kanitz, R., & Gonzalez, K. (2021). Are we stuck in the predigital age? embracing technology-mediated change management in organizational change research. *The Journal of Applied Behavioral Science, 57*(4), 447–458. doi:10.1177/00218863211042896

Kankane, S., DiRusso, C., & Buckley, C. (2018). *Can We Nudge Users Toward Better Password Management?* Human Factors in Computing Systems. doi:10.1145/3170427.3188689

Kaplan, R. S., & Norton, D. P. (2005). *The balanced scorecard: Measures that drive performance.* Academic Press.

Kaplan, R., & Mikes, A. (2012, June 1). Managing risks: A new framework. *Harvard Business Review.* https://hbr.org/2012/06/managing-risks-a-new-framework

Kar, A., Ilavarasan, V., Gupta, M., Janssen, M., & Kothari, R. (2019). Moving beyond Smart Cities: Digital Nations for Social Innovation & Sustainability. *Information Systems Frontiers, 21*(3), 495–501. doi:10.100710796-019-09930-0

Karhapää, S. J., Savolainen, T., & Malkamäki, K. (2022). Trust and performance: A contextual study of management change in private and public organisation. *Baltic Journal of Management, 17*(6), 35–51. doi:10.1108/BJM-06-2022-0212

Karlsson, M., Karlsson, F., Åström, J., & Denk, T. (2021). The effect of perceived organizational culture on employees' information security compliance. *Information & Computer Security.* doi:10.1108/ICS-06-2021-0073

Karthika, P., Murugeswari, R., & Manoranjithem, R. (2019). *Sentiment analysis of social media network using random forest algorithm. In 2019 IEEE international conference on intelligent techniques in control, optimization and signal processing (INCOS).* IEEE.

Kasdan, D. O. (2018). The ostrich paradox: why we underprepare for disasters. *Disaster Prevention and Management: An International Journal.*

Kasinathan, P., Pugazhendhi, R., Elavarasan, R. M., Ramachandaramurthy, V. K., Ramanathan, V., Subramanian, S., Kumar, S., Nandhagopal, K., Raghavan, R. R. V., Rangasamy, S., Devendiran, R., & Alsharif, M. H. (2022). Realization of Sustainable Development Goals with Disruptive Technologies by Integrating Industry 5.0, Society 5.0, Smart Cities and Villages. *Sustainability (Basel), 14*(22), 15258. doi:10.3390u142215258

Kasznar, A. P. P., Hammad, A. W., Najjar, M., Linhares Qualharini, E., Figueiredo, K., Soares, C. A. P., & Haddad, A. N. (2021). Multiple dimensions of smart cities' infrastructure: A review. *Buildings, 11*(2), 73. doi:10.3390/buildings11020073

Katsinas, S. G. (2019). Understanding the costs and benefits of distance education. In *The Handbook of Distance Education* (pp. 147–166). Routledge.

Kaufman, J. D., & Hajat, A. (2021). Confronting environmental racism. *Environmental Health Perspectives, 129*(5), 051001. doi:10.1289/EHP9511 PMID:34014764

Kayode, Ehiwe, & Olawale. (2016). *Secured Models for Online Bank Vulnerabilities in Nigeria.* https://www.semanticscholar.org/paper/Secured-Models-for-Online-Bank-Vulnerabilities-in-Kayode-Ehiwe/c7c9d6c3487003b-d7bc791a72985978d53ef6d10.SemanticScholar

Kayral, İ. H. (2019). Can the theory of broken windows be used for patient safety in city hospitals management model? [Kırık pencereler teorisi, şehir hastaneleri yönetim modelinde hasta güvenliği için kullanılabilir mi?]. *Hacettepe Journal of Health Administration, 22*(3), 677–694.

Kearney, E., & Gebert, D. (2009). Managing diversity and enhancing team outcomes: The promise of transformational leadership. *The Journal of Applied Psychology, 94*(1), 77–89. doi:10.1037/a0013077 PMID:19186897

Keeble, A. (2021). From Trauma Theory to Systemic Violence. *The City in American Literature and Culture, 276.*

Kemer, G., Li, C., Attia, M., Chan, C. D., Chung, M., Li, D., Colburn, A. N., Peters, H. C., Ramaswamy, A., & Sunal, Z. (2021). Multicultural supervision in counseling: A content analysis of peer-reviewed literature. *Counselor Education and Supervision, 61*(1), 2–14. doi:10.1002/ceas.12220

Kemfert, C. (2014). Energy efficiency and renewable energy – key to sustainability. *DIW Economic Bulletin*, (4), 24-29.

Kemp, R. (2018). How to Measure Corporate Sustainability. *Harvard Business Review.* Retrieved from https://hbr.org/2018/06/how-to-measure-corporate-sustainability

Kerr, M. (2003). Multigenerational family systems: Theory of bowen and its application. In G. G. Sholevar & L. D. Schwoeri (Eds.), *Textbook of family and couples therapy: Clinical applications* (pp. 103–126). American Psychiatric Publishing.

Kessler, R., Mickelson, K., & Williams, D. (1999). The prevalence, distribution, and mental health correlates of perceived discrimination in the United States. *Journal of Health and Social Behavior, 40*(3), 208–230. doi:10.2307/2676349 PMID:10513145

Ketola, T. (2009, December 11). Five leaps to corporate sustainability through a corporate responsibility portfolio matrix. *Corporate Social Responsibility and Environmental Management, 17*(6), 320–336. doi:10.1002/csr.219

Khan, V., Hafeez, M. H., Rizfi, S. M., Hasanain, A., & Maria, A. (2012). the relationship of leadership styles, employee's commitment, and organization Performance. *European Journal of Economics, Finance, and Administration.*

Khando, K., Gao, S., Islam, M. S., & Salman, A. (2021). Enhancing employees information security awareness in private and public organisations: A systematic literature review. *Computers & Security, 106*, 102267. doi:10.1016/j.cose.2021.102267

Khan, H. F. (2017). E-banking: Benefits and issues. *American Research Journal of Business and Management, 3*(1), 1–7.

Khuen, W. W., & Heng, T. B. (2022). Revisiting external stakeholders' role in environmental, social and governance (ESG) disclosure: A systematic literature review and research agenda. *ACBPP Official Conference Proceedings.* 10.22492/issn.2189-1001.2022.3

Kilovaty, I. (2021). Psychological data breach harms. *North Carolina Journal of Law & Technology, 23*(1), 1–66.

Kimberly, J. R., & McLellan, A. T. (2006). The business of addiction treatment: A research agenda. *Journal of Substance Abuse Treatment, 31*(3), 213–219. doi:10.1016/j.jsat.2006.06.018 PMID:16996384

Kim, H., Kim, M., & Lee, H. (2021). The effects of artificial intelligence on employee performance and organizational performance. *Journal of Business Research, 123*, 583–590. doi:10.1016/j.jbusres.2020.09.014

Kim, K., & Shin, D.-H. (2015). An acceptance model for smart watches: Implications for the adoption of future wearable technology. *Internet Research, 25*(4), 527–541. Advance online publication. doi:10.1108/IntR-05-2014-0126

Kim, S., & Hwang, H. (2022). How transformational leadership facilitates knowledge sharing and innovation: The mediating role of inter-unit collaboration. *Journal of Business Research, 145*, 63–74.

Kim, S., & Yook, S. (2018). The Influence of Posttraumatic Stress on Suicidal Ideation in Firefighters: Cognitive Emotion Regulation as a Moderator. *Fire Science and Engineering, 32*(2), 92–101. doi:10.7731/KIFSE.2018.32.2.092

Kim, Y., Kim, W., Bae, M., Choi, J., Kim, M., Oh, S., Park, K. S., Park, S., Lee, S.-K., Koh, S.-B., & Kim, C. (2022). The effect of polycyclic aromatic hydrocarbons on changes in the brain structure of firefighters: An analysis using data from the Firefighters Research on Enhancement of Safety & Health study. *The Science of the Total Environment, 816*, 151655. doi:10.1016/j.scitotenv.2021.151655 PMID:34785224

King, M. C. (2008, April). What sustainability should mean. *Challenge, 51*(2), 27–39. doi:10.2753/0577-5132510204

Kirkpatrick, D. L. (1959). Techniques for evaluating training programs. *The Journal of the American Society of Training Directors, 13*(11), 3–9.

Kite, V. (2020, February 28). *Urbanization and the evolution of cities across 10,000 years.* Academic Press.

Kiviliene, J., & Blazeviciene, A. (2019). Review of complex adaptive systems in nursing practice. *Journal of Complexity in Health Sciences, 2*(2), 46–50. doi:10.21595/chs.2019.21169

Kizilcec, R. F., & Halawa, S. A. (2020). Attrition and achievement gaps in online learning. *Proceedings of the sixth ACM conference on Learning @ Scale*, 215-218.

Kleiner, K. (2012). What you need to know about sexual harassment: Understanding sexual harassment is crucial to assure a productive workplace and avoid lawsuits. *Nonprofit World, 30*, 12–13. Retrieved from https://search.proquest.com/docview/1115474277?accountid=10378

Klenke, K. (2008). *Qualitative research in the study of leadership.* Emerald Group Publishing Limited.

Klimley, K. E., Van Hasselt, V. B., & Stripling, A. M. (2018). Posttraumatic stress disorder in police, firefighters, and emergency dispatchers. *Aggression and Violent Behavior, 43*, 33–44. doi:10.1016/j.avb.2018.08.005

Kluza, K., Ziolo, M., & Spoz, A. (2021). Innovation and environmental, social, and governance factors influencing sustainable business models - meta-analysis. *Journal of Cleaner Production, 303*, 127015. doi:10.1016/j.jclepro.2021.127015

Kneale, M. G. M., Young, A. A., & Dollarhide, C. T. (2018). Cultivating counseling leaders through district leadership cohorts. *Professional School Counseling, 21*(1b), 1–9.

Knittel, B., Coile, A., Zou, A., Saxena, S., Brenzel, L., Orobaton, N., Bartel, D., Williams, C. A., Kambarami, R., Tiwari, D. P., Husain, I., Sikipa, G., Achan, J., Ajiwohwodoma, J. O., Banerjee, B., & Kasungami, D. (2022). Critical barriers to sustainable capacity strengthening in global health: A systems perspective on development assistance. *Gates Open Research, 6*(116), 116. doi:10.12688/gatesopenres.13632.1 PMID:36415884

Kocyigit, M. (2022). Challenges and ethical issues in counseling supervision from faculty supervisors' perspectives. *Participatory Educational Research, 9*(5), 305–329. doi:10.17275/per.22.116.9.5

Kojola, E., & Pellow, D. N. (2021). New directions in environmental justice studies: Examining the state and violence. *Environmental Politics, 30*(1-2), 100–118. doi:10.1080/09644016.2020.1836898

Komninos, N., Kakderi, C., Mora, L., Panori, A., & Sefertzi, E. (2022). Towards high impact smart cities: A universal architecture based on connected intelligence spaces. *Journal of the Knowledge Economy, 13*(2), 1169–1197. doi:10.100713132-021-00767-0

Kondrasuk, J., Bailey, D., & Sheeks, M. (2005). Leadership in the 21st century: Understanding global terrorism. *Employee Responsibilities and Rights Journal, 17*(4), 263–279. doi:10.100710672-005-9054-8

Kosseff, J. (2022). *Cybersecurity law.* John Wiley & Sons.

Kotsantonis, S., & Serafeim, G. (2019). Four things no one will tell you about ESG data. *The Bank of America Journal of Applied Corporate Finance, 31*(2), 50–58. doi:10.1111/jacf.12346

Kouzes, J. M., & Posner, B. Z. (2017). *The leadership challenge: How to make extraordinary things happen in organizations.* Jossey-Bass.

Kovanis, M., Porcher, R., Ravaud, P., & Trinquart, L. (2016). The global burden of journal peer review in the biomedical literature: Strong imbalance in the collective enterprise. *PLoS One*, *11*(11), e0166387. doi:10.1371/journal.pone.0166387 PMID:27832157

Kowalski, K., & Kelley, K. (2021). Developing Effective Training Programs. *Harvard Business Review*. https://hbr.org/2021/03/developing-effective-training-programs

Kowalski, R., & Kelley, R. (2021). The Challenge of Training Needs Assessment. *Journal of Management Development*, *40*(2), 224–238.

Kowalski, S., & Kelley, M. (2013). Strategic planning for distance education in higher education. *Online Journal of Distance Learning Administration*, *16*(4).

Kowitt, B., & Zillman, C. (2021, January 26). New Walgreens CEO Rosalind Brewer will be the only Black woman chief executive in Fortune 500. *Fortune*. https://fortune.com/2021/01/26/walgreens-new-ceo-rosalind-roz-brewer-starbucks/

Kraemer, S., Carayon, P., & Clem, J. R. (2009). Human and organizational factors in computer and information security: Pathways to vulnerabilities. *Computers & Security*, *28*(7), 509–520. doi:10.1016/j.cose.2009.04.006

Krieg, L., Berning, M., & Hardon, A. (2017). Anthropology with algorithms? An exploration of online drug knowledge using digital methods. *Medicine Anthropology Theory*, *4*(3), 21–52.

Kronenfeld, D. (2018). *Culture as a system*. Routledge.

Kronenfeld, D., Bennardo, G., De Munck, V., & Fischer, M. (Eds.). (2011). *A companion to cognitive anthropology*. Wiley-Blackwell. doi:10.1002/9781444394931

Kruse, C., & Lundbergh, S. (2010). The governance of corporate sustainability. *Rotman International Journal of Pension Management*, *3*(2), 46–51.

Kubala, J. (2018). *5 ways to make your company more sustainable*. Retrieved from https://www.businessnewsdaily.com/7813-sustainable-business-practices.html

Kubik, A. (2022). Impact of the Use of Electric Scooters from Shared Mobility Systems on the Users. *Smart Cities*, *5*(3), 1079–1091. doi:10.3390martcities5030054

Kuhn, T. R. (2010). The advancement of technology. *Electric Perspectives*, *35*(3), 6.

Kuiper, J. A., Wu, X., Zhou, Y., & Rood, M. A. (2022). Modeling Electric Vehicle Charging Station Siting Suitability with a Focus on Equity (No. ANL-22/33). Argonne National Lab.

Kujawski, S., Słomko, J., Tafil-Klawe, M., Zawadka-Kunikowska, M., Szrajda, J., Newton, J. L., Zalewski, P., & Klawe, J. J. (2018). The Impact of total sleep deprivation upon cognitive functioning in firefighters. *Neuropsychiatric Disease and Treatment*, *14*, 1171–1181. doi:10.2147/NDT.S156501 PMID:29773948

Kumar, P., & Firoz, M. (2022). Does accounting-based financial performance value environmental, social and governance (ESG) disclosures? A detailed note on a corporate sustainability perspective. *Australasian Business. Accounting and Finance Journal*, *16*(1), 41–72. doi:10.14453/aabfj.v16i1.4

Kumar, P., Nikolovski, S., Ali, I., Thomas, M., & Ahuja, H. (2022). Impact of Electric Vehicles on Energy Efficiency with Energy Boosters in Coordination for Sustainable Energy in Smart Cities. *Processes (Basel, Switzerland)*, *10*(8), 1593. doi:10.3390/pr10081593

Kumar, S., Xiao, J. J., Pattnaik, D., Lim, W. M., & Rasul, T. (2022). Past, present and future of bank marketing: A bibliometric analysis of International Journal of Bank Marketing (1983–2020). *International Journal of Bank Marketing*, *40*(2), 341–383. doi:10.1108/IJBM-07-2021-0351

Kunda, G. (1986). *Engineering culture: Control and commitment in a high-tech corporation.* Temple University Press.

Kuper, A., & Marks, J. (2011). Anthropologists unite! *Nature*, *470*(7333), 166–168. doi:10.1038/470166a PMID:21307914

La Guardia, A. C. (2020). Counselor education and supervision: 2019 Annual Review. *Counselor Education and Supervision*, *60*(1), 2–21. doi:10.1002/ceas.12192

Laine, M. (2010). Towards sustaining the status quo: Business talk of sustainability in Finnish corporate disclosures 1987-2005. *European Accounting Review*, *19*(2), 247–274. doi:10.1080/09638180903136258

Lamba, M., Altan, Y., Aktel, M., & Kerman, U. (2014). Reconstruction in the Ministry of Health: An evaluation in terms of the new public management [Sağlık Bakanlığı'nda yeniden yapılanma: yeni kamu yönetimi açısından bir değerlendirme]. *Amme Idaresi Dergisi*, *47*(1), 53–78.

Lamb, W. F., Wiedmann, T., Pongratz, J., Andrew, R., Crippa, M., Olivier, J. G., Wiedenhofer, D., Mattioli, G., Khourdajie, A. A., House, J., Pachauri, S., Figueroa, M., Saheb, Y., Slade, R., Hubacek, K., Sun, L., Ribeiro, S. K., Khennas, S., de la Rue du Can, S., ... Minx, J. (2021). A review of trends and drivers of greenhouse gas emissions by sector from 1990 to 2018. *Environmental Research Letters*, *16*(7), 1–32. doi:10.1088/1748-9326/abee4e

Lam, M. L., & Wong, K. (2021). Shared Cybersecurity Risk Management in the Industry of Medical Devices. *International Journal of Cyber-Physical Systems*, *3*(1), 37–56. doi:10.4018/IJCPS.2021010103

Lancefield, D., & Rangen, C. (2021, May 5). 4 actions transformational leaders take. *Harvard Business Review*. Retrieved from https://hbr.org/2021/05/4-actions-transformational-leaders-take

Landau, E. (2010). *Putting 'science' back in anthropology.* CNN. http://news.blogs.cnn.com/2010/12/03/putting-science-back-inanthropology

Lane, S. (2019). *1 in 4 U.S. women report workplace sexual harassment, study finds.* Retrieved from https://www.cnn.com/2019/01/17/health/workplace-sexual-harassment-study-bn/index.html

Langner, R., & Eickhoff, S. B. (2017). Sustaining attention to simple tasks: A meta-analytic review of the neural mechanisms of vigilant attention. *Psychological Bulletin*, *139*(4), 870–900. doi:10.1037/a0030694 PMID:23163491

Lanier, M. (2020). Leadership development in law enforcement. *International Journal of Law Enforcement*, *21*(4), 36–40.

Lansing, S. (2002). 'Artificial societies' and the social sciences. *Artificial Life*, *8*(3), 279–292. doi:10.1162/106454602320991864 PMID:12537687

Lansing, S. (2003). Complex adaptive systems. *Annual Review of Anthropology*, *32*(1), 183–204. doi:10.1146/annurev.anthro.32.061002.093440

Larsen, C. (Ed.). (2010). *A companion to biological anthropology.* Wiley-Blackwell. doi:10.1002/9781444320039

Lašáková, A., & Remišová, A. (2015). *Unethical Leadership: Current Theoretical Trends and Conceptualization.* . doi:10.1016/S2212-5671(15)01636-6

Lash, J., & Wellington, F. (2007). Competitive advantage on a warming climate. *Harvard Business Review*, *85*(3), 94–103. PMID:17348173

Laufer, A. (2012). *Mastering the leadership role in project management: Practices that deliver remarkable results.* FT Press.

Laut, J. (2019). The value of executive leadership coaching in law enforcement. *Police Chief Magazine*, *86*(12), 16–19.

Lawton, R. (1998). Not working to rule: Understanding procedural violations at work. *Safety Science*, *28*(2), 77–95. doi:10.1016/S0925-7535(97)00073-8

Lea, B.-R., & Min, H. (2003). Selection of management accounting systems in Just-In-Time and Theory of Constraints-based manufacturing. *International Journal of Production Research*, *41*(13), 2879–2910. doi:10.1080/0020754031000109134

Lebihan, R. (2011). Business schools tap coaching trend. *Australian Financial Review*.

Lee, C. (2011). Bounded Rationality and the emergence of simplicity amidst complexity. *Journal of Economic Surveys*, *25*(3), 507–526. doi:10.1111/j.1467-6419.2010.00670.x

Lee, C. (2019). Toxic waste and race in the United States. In *Race and the Incidence of Environmental Hazards* (pp. 10–27). Routledge. doi:10.4324/9780429303661-2

Lee, C.-W., & Li, C. (2019). The process of constructing a health tourism destination index. *International Journal of Environmental Research and Public Health*, *16*(22), 4579. doi:10.3390/ijerph16224579 PMID:31752340

Lee, D., Peckins, M., Heinze, J., Miller, A., Assari, S., & Zimmerman, M. (2018). Psychological pathways from racial discrimination to cortisol in African American males and females. *Journal of Behavioral Medicine*, *41*(2), 208–220. doi:10.100710865-017-9887-2 PMID:28942527

Lee, I. (2021). Cybersecurity: Risk management framework and investment cost analysis. *Business Horizons*, *64*(5), 659–671. doi:10.1016/j.bushor.2021.02.022

Lee, J., & Choi, S. (2020). A systematic review of online learning definitions, concepts, and theories. *Educational Research Review*, *30*, 100326. doi:10.1016/j.edurev.2020.100326

Lee, J., & Choi, S. J. (2021). Hospital Productivity After Data Breaches: Difference-in-Differences Analysis. *Journal of Medical Internet Research*, *23*(7), 1–8. doi:10.2196/26157 PMID:34255672

Lee, R. D., & Greenlaw, P. S. (1995). The legal evolution of sexual harassment. *Public Administration Review*, *55*(4), 34–36, 33578. doi:10.2307/977127

Lehto, M., & Neittaanmäki, P. (2018). *Cyber security: Power and technology*. Springer. doi:10.1007/978-3-319-75307-2

Leigh, A. (2013). *Ethical leadership: creating and sustaining an ethical business culture*. Kogan Page Publishers.

Leigh, A., & Melwani, S. (2019). #BlackEmployeesMatter: Mega-Threats, Identity Fusion, and Enacting Positive Deviance in Organizations. *Academy of Management Review*, *44*(3), 564–591. doi:10.5465/amr.2017.0127

Lende, D., & Downey, G. (Eds.). (2012). *The encultured brain: An introduction to neuroanthropology*. Massachusetts Institute of Technology. doi:10.7551/mitpress/9219.001.0001

Lennartz, C., Proost, K., & Brebels, L. (2019). Decreasing overt discrimination increases covert discrimination: Adverse effects of equal opportunities policies. *International Journal of Selection and Assessment*, *27*(2), 129–138. doi:10.1111/ijsa.12244

Lennon, E., Hopkins, L., Einboden, R., McCloughen, A., Dawson, L., & Buus, N. (2022). Organizational Change in Complex Systems: Organizational and Leadership Factors in the Introduction of Open Dialogue to Mental Health Care Services. *Community Mental Health Journal*, •••, 1–10. PMID:35585467

Levasseur, R. E. (2001). People Skills: Change Management Tools—Lewin's Change Model. *Interfaces*, *31*(4), 71–73. doi:10.1287/inte.31.4.71.9674

Lewin, K. (1997). *Resolving social conflicts and field theory in social science.* American Psychological Association eBooks. doi:10.1037/10269-000

Lewis, R. (2018). The role of organizational development in developing and implementing policies and procedures. *Human Resource Development International, 21*(2), 191–203.

Liao, Y., Chen, C., Chen, H., & Chen, G. (2019). The effects of augmented reality on learning outcomes and motivation in a flipped classroom environment. *Journal of Educational Technology & Society, 22*(3), 214–226.

Li, C., Yan, X., & Wang, J. (2022). Business unit boundary spanning and knowledge sharing in multinational corporations. *Journal of Knowledge Management, 26*(1), 139–159.

Lievrouw, L. A. (2019). Technology and social change: The role of communication networks. *Journal of Communication, 69*(2), 266–276.

Li, J., & Liang, H. (2022). Employees' attitudes toward AI-powered training: The role of perceived usefulness, ease of use, and resistance to change. *International Journal of Human Resource Management,* ●●●, 1–24. doi:10.1080/09585 192.2022.2021389

Lin, C.-S. (2013). Revealing the 'Essence" of things: Using phenomenology in LIS research. *Qualitative and Quantitative Methods in Libraries, 4*, 469–478.

Lincoln, Y. S. (1995). Emerging criteria for quality in qualitative and interpretive research. *Qualitative Inquiry, 1*(3), 275–289. doi:10.1177/107780049500100301

Lindholm, H., Punakallio, A., Lusa, S., Sainio, M., Ponocny, E., & Winker, R. (2018). Association of cardio-ankle vascular index with physical fitness and cognitive symptoms in aging Finnish firefighters. *International Archives of Occupational and Environmental Health, 85*(4), 397–403. doi:10.100700420-011-0681-0 PMID:21789686

Lindström, J., & Försth, M. (2018). Fire test of profile plank for transformer pit fire protection. *Fire Technology, 52*(2), 309–319. doi:10.100710694-014-0409-2

Linnenluecke, M. K., Russell, S. V., & Griffiths, A. (2007). Subcultures and sustainability practices: The impact on understanding corporate sustainability. *Business Strategy and the Environment, 18*(7), 432–452. doi:10.1002/bse.609

Lin, W., Wu, Z., Lin, L., Wen, A., & Li, J. (2017). An ensemble random forest algorithm for insurance big data analysis. *IEEE Access : Practical Innovations, Open Solutions, 5*, 16568–16575. doi:10.1109/ACCESS.2017.2738069

Li, P., & Wei, C. (2019). An emergency decision-making method based on DS evidence theory for probabilistic linguistic term sets. *International Journal of Disaster Risk Reduction, 37*, 101178. doi:10.1016/j.ijdrr.2019.101178

Liu, G. (2018). 5 ways to reduce toxic chemicals in your business. *Harvard Business Review.*

Li, Y., Li, H., & Liang, J. (2019). Design and implementation of an online learning platform based on social constructivism. *International Journal of Emerging Technologies in Learning, 14*(16), 4–18. doi:10.3991/ijet.v14i16.11106

Llanque Ferrufino, R. J. (2002). Redes sociales y cultura organizacional en entidades públicas. *Revista de Antropología Experimental,* 2. http://www.ujaen. es/huesped/rae/rae-02.pdf

Locatis, C., Williamson, D., Gould-Kabler, C., Zone-Smith, L., Detzler, I., Roberson, J., Maisiak, R., & Ackerman, M. (2010). Comparing in-person, video, and telephonic medical interpretation. *Journal of General Internal Medicine, 25*(4), 345–350. doi:10.100711606-009-1236-x PMID:20107916

Lockard, F. W. III, Laux, J. M., Ritchie, M., Piazza, N., & Haefner, J. (2014). Perceived leadership preparation in counselor education doctoral students who are members of the American counseling association in cacrep-accredited programs. *The Clinical Supervisor*, *33*(2), 228–242. doi:10.1080/07325223.2014.992270

Loi, M., & Christen, M. (2020). *Ethical frameworks for cybersecurity.* Springer International Publishing. doi:10.1007/978-3-030-29053-5_4

Lomborg, B. (2020). Welfare in the 21st century: Increasing development, reducing inequality, the impact of climate change, and the cost of climate policies. *Technological Forecasting and Social Change*, *156*, 119981. doi:10.1016/j.techfore.2020.119981

Lomnitz, L., & Pérez-Lizaur, M. (1993). *Una familia de la élite mexicana, parentesco, clase y cultura 1820-1890.* Alianza Editorial.

Lopez, E., Minkel, A., & Vergara, R. (2020). 2020 HACR Corporate Inclusion Index Index™(CII) Report. *HACR.* https://hacr.org/2020-hacr-cii-report/

Lourau, R. (1979). *El análisis institucional.* Amorrortu.

Lüdeke-Freund, F. (2019). Business and sustainability: Understanding the scope and nature of the field. *Journal of Cleaner Production*, *208*, 463–479.

Lu, E. P., Fischer, B. G., Plesac, M. A., & Olson, A. P. J. (2022). Research Methods: How to Perform an Effective Peer Review. *Hospital Pediatrics*, *12*(11), e409–e413. doi:10.1542/hpeds.2022-006764 PMID:36214067

Luh, F., & Yen, Y. (2020). Cybersecurity in science and medicine: Threats and challenges. *Trends in Biotechnology*, *38*(8), 825–828. doi:10.1016/j.tibtech.2020.02.010 PMID:32441258

Lunenburg, F. C., & Ometein, A. O. (2010). *Educational administration: Concepts and practices.* Wadsworth/Cengage Learning.

Luntz, F. (2011). Win: The key principles to take your business from ordinary to extraordinary. Hachette UK.

Luxton, E. (2016). Why workplace anxiety costs us more than you think. *World Economic Forum.* https://www.weforum.org/agenda/2016/08/workplace-anxiety-costs-more-than-you-think/

Luzinski, C. (2014). Identifying Leadership Competencies of the Future: Introducing the Use of Strategic Foresight. *Nurse Leader*, *12*(4), 37–39. doi:10.1016/j.mnl.2014.05.009

Lynn, S. (2019, May 24). Meet the CEO of Bed, Bath and Beyond, she is the first Black woman to head a Fortune 500 company since Ursula Burns. *Black Enterprise.* https://www.blackenterprise.com/appointed-interim-ceo-of-bed-bath-beyond-she-is-the-first-black-woman-to-head-a-fortune-500-company-since-ursula-burns/

Lyons-Padilla, S., Markus, H. R., Monk, A., Radhakrishna, S., Shah, R., Dodson, N. A. D. IV, & Eberhardt, J. L. (2019). Race influences professional investors' financial judgments. *Proceedings of the National Academy of Sciences of the United States of America*, *116*(35), 17225–17230. doi:10.1073/pnas.1822052116 PMID:31405967

M. (2022). Moving human rights to the forefront of psychology: Summary of the final report of the APA task force on human rights. *American Psychologist, 77*(4), 589.

Mabin, V. J., Forgeson, S., & Green, L. W. (2001). Harnessing resistance: using the theory of constraints to assist change management. *Journal of European Industrial Training*, *25*(2/3/4), 168–191. doi:10.1108/EUM0000000005446

Machin, J., & Solanas, A. (2018, July). A review on the meaning of cognitive cities. In *2018 9th International Conference on Information, Intelligence, Systems and Applications (IISA)* (pp. 1-5). IEEE. 10.1109/IISA.2018.8633654

Mach, M., Ferreira, A. I., & Abrantes, A. C. (2022). Transformational leadership and team performance in sports teams: A conditional indirect model. *Applied Psychology*, *71*(2), 662–694. doi:10.1111/apps.12342

Maddikunta, P. K., Pham, Q. B. P., Deepa, N., Dev, K., Gadekallu, T. R., Ruby, R., & Liyanage, M. (2022). Industry 5.0: A survey on enabling technologies and potential applications. *Journal of Industrial Information Integration*, *26*, 100257. doi:10.1016/j.jii.2021.100257

Maddox, T. (2013). Professional women's well-being: The role of discrimination and occupational characteristics. *Women & Health*, *53*(7), 706–729. doi:10.1080/03630242.2013.822455 PMID:24093451

Madera, J. M., Guchait, P., & Dawson, M. (2018). Managers' reactions to customer vs. coworker sexual harassment. *International Journal of Contemporary Hospitality Management*, *30*(2), 1211–1227. doi:10.1108/IJCHM-02-2017-0081

Madgavkar, A., Krishnan, M., White, O., Mahajan, D., & Azcue, X. (2020, July 15). *COVID-19 and gender equality: Countering the regressive effects*. McKinsey. https://www.mckinsey.com/featured-insights/future-of-work/covid-19-and-gender-equality-countering-the-regressive-effects

Madhavan, S., & Balasubramanian, J. A. (2016). Planning Fallacy: A Case of Task Planning in IT Project Support Services. *Purushartha*, *9*(1), 57–67.

Madimenos, F. C., Gildner, T. E., Eick, G. N., Sugiyama, L. S., & Snodgrass, J. J. (2022). Bringing the lab bench to the field: Point-of-care testing for enhancing health research and stakeholder engagement in rural/remote, indigenous, and resource-limited contexts. *American Journal of Human Biology*, *34*(11), e23808. doi:10.1002/ajhb.23808 PMID:36166487

Madrigal, L. (2012). *Statistics for anthropology*. Cambridge University Press. doi:10.1017/CBO9781139022699

Maese, E., & Lloyd, C. (2021, May 26). *Understanding the Effects of Discrimination in the Workplace*. https://www.gallup.com/workplace/349865/understanding-effects-discrimination-workplace.aspx

Magee, W., & Upenieks, L. (2017). 'Stuck in the middle with you?' Supervisory level and anger about work. *Canadian Review of Sociology*, *54*(3), 309–330. doi:10.1111/cars.12152 PMID:28796459

Mahesh, B. (2020). Machine learning algorithms-a review. *International Journal of Science and Research*, *9*, 381-386.

Makipere, K., & Yip, G. S. (2008). Sustainable leadership. *Business Strategy Review*, *19*(1), 64–67. doi:10.1111/j.1467-8616.2008.00521.x

Males, J. R., Hudson, J., & Kerr, J. H. (2018). Application of an innovative performance demand model with canoe slalom athletes and their coach. *Journal of Sport Psychology in Action*, *9*(1), 63–71. doi:10.1080/21520704.2017.1326429

Malinka, K., Hujňák, O., Hanáček, P., & Hellebrandt, L. (2022). E-Banking Security Study—10 Years Later. *IEEE Access : Practical Innovations, Open Solutions*, *10*, 16681–16699. doi:10.1109/ACCESS.2022.3149475

Malinowski, B. (1944). *A scientific theory of culture and other essays*. University of North Carolina Press.

Malin, S. A., & Ryder, S. S. (2018). Developing deeply intersectional environmental justice scholarship. *Environmental Sociology*, *4*(1), 1–7. doi:10.1080/23251042.2018.1446711

Malygin, I., Komashinskiy, V., & Korolev, O. (2018). Cognitive technologies for providing road traffic safety in intelligent transport systems. *Transportation Research Procedia*, *36*, 487–492. doi:10.1016/j.trpro.2018.12.134

Management Daily. (n.d.). Retrieved from https://www.businessmanagementdaily.com

Mani & & Chou. (2017). Drivers of consumers' resistance to smart products. *Journal of Marketing Management, 33*(1-2).

Manis, M., Shedler, J., Jonides, J., & Nelson, T. E. (1993, September). Availability heuristic in judgments of set size and frequency of occurrence. *Journal of Personality and Social Psychology, 65*(3), 448–457. doi:10.1037/0022-3514.65.3.448

Manjikian, M. (2022). *Cybersecurity ethics: An introduction*. Taylor & Francis. doi:10.4324/9781003248828

Mann, S. T., & Merced, M. (2018). Preparing for entry-level practice in supervision. *Professional Psychology, Research and Practice, 49*(1), 98–106. doi:10.1037/pro0000171

Maritsa, E., Goula, A., Psychogios, A., & Pierrakos, G. (2022). Leadership development: Exploring relational leadership implications in healthcare organizations. *International Journal of Environmental Research and Public Health, 19*(23), 1–14. doi:10.3390/ijerph192315971 PMID:36498040

Markets and Markets. (2019). Augmented Reality in Training and Education Market by Component (Hardware and Software), Device Type (AR Headsets, AR Glasses, and AR Cards), and Geography (North America, Europe, APAC, and RoW). *Global Forecast to 2023*. https://www.marketsandmarkets.com/Market-Reports/augmented-reality-training-education-market-222455352.html

Markets and Markets. (2021). *Augmented Reality (AR) market by offering, device type, application, and geography - global forecast to 2025*. https://www.marketsandmarkets.com/Market-Reports/augmented-reality-virtual-reality-market-1185.html

Markopoulos, E., Aggarwal, V., & Vanharanta, H. (2019). Democratization of intrapreneurship and corporate entrepreneurship within the McKinsey's three horizons innovation space. *Human Systems Engineering and Design, II*, 1007–1017. doi:10.1007/978-3-030-27928-8_150

Marks, N. (2020). *Auditing that matters: Case studies discussion guide*. Independently Published.

Martell, K., & Sullivan, G. (1994). Strategies for managers to recognize and remedy sexual harassment. *Industrial Management (Des Plaines), 36*(3), 5. https://search.proquest.com/docview/211593867?accountid=10378

Martin, C. E., Tran, J. K., & Buser, S. J. (2017). Correlates of suicidality in firefighter/EMS personnel. *Journal of Affective Disorders, 208*, 177–183. doi:10.1016/j.jad.2016.08.078 PMID:27788381

Martin, M. M., & Caruso, C. (2019). *Leading academic change: Essential roles for senior leaders*. Stylus Publishing, LLC.

Mason, M. (2022). *What is sustainability and why is it important?* Retrieved 12.09.2022 from https://www.environmentalscience.org/sustainability

MasterClass. (2022, May 19). *What is lmx theory? The leader-member exchange at work - 2023 - MasterClass*. Retrieved from https://www.masterclass.com/articles/lmx

Mastro, O. S. (2022). Deterrence in the Indo-Pacific. *Asia Policy, 17*(4), 8-18. https://www.proquest.com/scholarly-journals/deterrence-indo-pacific/docview/2731215788/se-2

Mathewson, P. D., Evans, S., Byrnes, T., Joos, A., & Naidenko, O. V. (2020). Health and economic impact of nitrate pollution in drinking water: A Wisconsin case study. *Environmental Monitoring and Assessment, 192*(11), 1–18. doi:10.100710661-020-08652-0 PMID:33095309

Mauksch, S. (2017). Managing the dance of enchantment: An *ethnography* of social entrepreneurship events. *Organization, 24*(2), 133–153. doi:10.1177/1350508416644511

Mauss, M. (1925). *The gift: Forms and functions of exchange in archaic societies*. Norton Library.

Mavridis, P., & Giannakos, M. (2020). Using AI-based personalized learning to enhance student engagement and performance. *Journal of Educational Computing Research, 58*(6), 1366–1388. doi:10.1177/0735633120905959

Maximini, D. (2018). Organizational culture models. In *The Scrum Culture: Introducing agile methods in organizations* (pp. 187–204). Springer. doi:10.1007/978-3-319-73842-0_18

Mayfield, J., & Mayfield, M. (2012). the leadership relation between leader Motivating language and employee self-efficacy. A partial least squares model analysis. *Journal of Business Communication*. Advance online publication. doi:10.1177/0021943612456036

McCabe, B. J. (2018). Why buy a home? Race, ethnicity, and homeownership preferences in the United States. *Sociology of Race and Ethnicity (Thousand Oaks, Calif.)*, *4*(4), 452–472. doi:10.1177/2332649217753648

McCabe, M. P., & Hardman, L. (2005). Attitudes and perceptions of workers to sexual harassment. *The Journal of Social Psychology*, *145*(6), 719–740. doi:10.3200/SOCP.145.6.719-740 PMID:16334516

McCarthy, G., & Milner, J. (2012). Managerial coaching: challenges, opportunities and Training. Journal of Management Development, 32(7), 768-779. doi:10.1108/JMD-11-2011-0113

McCleskey, J. A. (2020). Forty years and still evolving: The theory of constraints. *American Journal of Management*, *20*(3), 65–74.

McCluney, C. L., Bryant, C. M., King, D. D., & Ali, A. A. (2017). Calling in Black: A dynamic model of racially traumatic events, resourcing, and safety. *Equality, Diversity and Inclusion*, *36*(8), 767–786. doi:10.1108/EDI-01-2017-0012

McCluney, C., & Rabelo, V. (2018). Conditions of visibility: An intersectional examination of Black women's belongingness and distinctiveness at work. *Journal of Vocational Behavior*. Advance online publication. doi:10.1016/j.jvb.2018.09.008

McConnell, A., & t Hart, P. (2019). Inaction and public policy: Understanding why policymakers 'do nothing'. *Policy Sciences*, *52*(4), 645–661. doi:10.100711077-019-09362-2

McDowell, J., & Carter-Francique, A. (2017). An intersectional analysis of the workplace experiences of African American female athletic directors. *Sex Roles*, *77*(5–6), 393–408. doi:10.100711199-016-0730-y

McFillen, J. M., O'Neil, D. A., Balzer, W. K., & Varney, G. H. (2013). Organizational diagnosis: An evidence-based approach. *Journal of Change Management*, *13*(2), 223–246. doi:10.1080/14697017.2012.679290

McGinn, J. M. (2022). Engaging and Leading Future Counseling Leaders. *MSJCC 10 Building Mindful Community 12 Peer Support in Times of COVID and Beyond 14 Navigating Trauma Utilizing*, *17*(2), 1–24.

McGirt, E. (2017, September 27). The Black ceiling: Why African American women aren't making it to the top in corporate America. *Fortune*. https://www.yahoo.com/news/black-ceiling-why-african-american-103035458.html

McGlowan-Fellows, B., & Thomas, C. S. (2005). Changing roles: Corporate mentoring of Black women. *International Journal of Mental Health*, *33*(4), 3–18. doi:10.1080/00207411.2004.11043387

McKeon, J. (2023, January 3). Scripps Health Reaches $3.5M Settlement After Ransomware Attack. *HealthITSecurity*. https://healthitsecurity.com/news/scripps-health-reaches-3.5m-settlement-after-ransomware-attack

McKibben, W. B., Umstead, L. K., & Borders, L. D. (2017). Identifying dynamics of counseling leadership: A content analysis study. *Journal of Counseling and Development*, *95*(2), 192–202. doi:10.1002/jcad.12131

McKinsey & Company. (2019). *How artificial intelligence will impact the future of workforce learning*. https://www.mckinsey.com/business-functions/mckinsey-digital/our-insights/how-artificial-intelligence-will-impact-the-future-of-workforce-learning

McKinsey & Company. (2021). *The impact of AI in the learning organization*. https://www.mckinsey.com/business-functions/mckinsey-digital/our-insights/the-impact-of-ai-in-the-learning-organization

Meany-Walen, K. K., Carnes-Holt, K., Barrio-Minton, C. A., Purswell, K., & Pronchenko-Jain, Y. (2013). An exploration of counselors' professional leadership development. *Journal of Counseling and Development, 91*(2), 206–215. doi:10.1002/j.1556-6676.2013.00087.x

Melas, D., Nagy, Z., & Kulkarni, P. (2017). Factor investing and ESG integration. *Factor Investing*, 389-413. doi:10.1016/B978-1-78548-201-4.50015-5

Méndez, P. F., Clement, F., Palau-Salvador, G., Diaz-Delgado, R., & Villamayor-Tomas, S. (2022). Understanding the governance of sustainability pathways: Hydraulic megaprojects, social–ecological traps, and power in networks of action situations. *Sustainability Science*. Advance online publication. doi:10.100711625-022-01258-0

Menéndez, E. (2006). Participación social en salud: las representaciones y las prácticas. In E. Menéndez (Ed.), *Spinelli, H.: Participación social ¿para qué?* (pp. 81–115). Lugar Editorial.

Merviö, M. (2020). *Global issues and innovative solutions in healthcare, culture, and the environment.* IGI Global. doi:10.4018/978-1-7998-3576-9

Metalidou, E., Marinagi, C., Trivellas, P., Eberhagen, N., Skourlas, C., & Giannakopoulos, G. (2014). The Human Factor of Information Security: Unintentional Damage Perspective. *Procedia: Social and Behavioral Sciences, 147*, 424–428. doi:10.1016/j.sbspro.2014.07.133

Meyer, I., Schwartz, S., & Frost, D. (2008). Social patterning of stress and coping: Does disadvantaged social status confer more stress and fewer coping resources? *Social Science & Medicine, 67*(3), 368–379. doi:10.1016/j.socscimed.2008.03.012 PMID:18433961

Meyer, J. P., Allen, N. J., & Smith, C. A. (1993). Commitment to organizations and occupation: Extensions and test of a three-component conceptualization. *The Journal of Applied Psychology, 78*(4), 538–551. doi:10.1037/0021-9010.78.4.538

Meznar, M. B., Carroll, A. B., & Chrisman, J. J. (1991). Social responsibility and strategic management: Towards an enterprise strategy classification. *Business and Professional Ethics Journal, 10*(1), 47-67. Retrieved from http://www.pdcnet.org

Micewski, E. R., & Troy, C. (2007). Business Ethics – Deontologically Revisited. *Journal of Business Ethics, 72*(1), 17–25. doi:10.100710551-006-9152-z

Michelon, G. (2011). Sustainability disclosure and reputation: A comparative study. *Corporate Reputation Review, 14*(2), 79–96. doi:10.1057/crr.2011.10

Miller, M. T. (2021). Competency-Based Education and Training: A Review of the Literature. *Journal of Vocational Education Research, 46*(1), 1–16.

Ministry of Development. (2018). *Developments in public-private partnership practices in the world and in Turkey 2017.* Retrieved from 18.01.2023 from https://www.sbb.gov.tr/wp-content/uploads/2019/05/Kamu-Ozel_Isbirligi_Raporu-2018.pdf

Ministry of Health. (2021). *Health statistics yearbook 2019.* Retrieved 09.09.2022 from https://sbsgm.saglik.gov.tr/eklenti/40566/0/health-statistics-yearbook-2019pdf.pdf

Ministry of Health. (2022). *2019-2023 strategic plan updated version* [2019-2023 stratejik planı güncellenmiş versiyonu]. Retrieved 10.09.2022 from https://sgb.saglik.gov.tr/TR-61668/tc-saglik-bakanligi-2019-2023--stratejik-plani-guncellenmis-versiyonu.html

Min, K., & Arkes, H. R. (2012). When Is Difficult Planning Good Planning? The Effects of Scenario-Based Planning on Optimistic Prediction Bias. *Journal of Applied Social Psychology*, *42*(11), 2701–2729. doi:10.1111/j.1559-1816.2012.00958.x

Mirchandani, D., & Ikerd, J. (2008). Building and maintaining sustainable organizations. *Organizational Management Journal*, *5*(1), 40–51. doi:10.1057/omj.2008.6

Mishra, P., & Mishra, R. (2011). *Strategic organizational development: Practices and processes*. Sage Publications.

Mishra, S., & Sahoo, C. K. (2020). Impact of training and development on employee performance: Evidence from Indian manufacturing firms. *Journal of Advances in Management Research*, *17*(3), 365–382.

Mitchell, T., & Krulicky, T. (2021). Big data-driven urban geopolitics, interconnected sensor networks, and spatial cognition algorithms in smart city software systems. *Geopolitics, History, and International Relations*, *13*(2), 9–22. doi:10.22381/GHIR13220211

Mittal, S., & Singh, T. (2020). Gender-based violence during COVID-19 pandemic: A mini-review. *Frontiers in Global Women's Health*, *1*, 4. doi:10.3389/fgwh.2020.00004 PMID:34816149

Miz, V., & Hahanov, V. (2014, September). Smart traffic light in terms of the cognitive road traffic management system (CTMS) based on the Internet of Things. In *Proceedings of IEEE east-west design & test symposium (EWDTS 2014)* (pp. 1-5). IEEE. 10.1109/EWDTS.2014.7027102

Mocatta, G., & Hawley, E. (2020). covid19? The coronavirus crisis as tipping point: Communicating the environment in a time of pandemic. *Media International Australia, Incorporating Culture & Policy*, *177*(1), 119–124. doi:10.1177/1329878X20950030

Mohajan, H. (2019). *The second industrial revolution has brought modern social and economic developments*. Academic Press.

Mohamad, N. E. (2020). Environmental, social and governance (Esg) disclosure and financial performance. *European Proceedings of Social and Behavioural Sciences*. doi:10.15405/epsbs.2020.12.05.57

Mohammadi, M., & Al-Fuqaha, A. (2018). Enabling cognitive smart cities using big data and machine learning: Approaches and challenges. *IEEE Communications Magazine*, *56*(2), 94–101. doi:10.1109/MCOM.2018.1700298

Mohr, R., & Purdie-Vaughns, V. (2015). Diversity within women of color: Why experiences change felt stigma. *Sex Roles*, *73*(9-10), 391–398. doi:10.100711199-015-0511-z

Mollen, D., & Ridley, C. R. (2021). Rethinking multicultural counseling competence: An introduction to the major contribution. *The Counseling Psychologist*, *49*(4), 490–503. doi:10.1177/0011000020986543

Momeni, E., & Antipova, A. (2022). A micro-level analysis of commuting and urban land using the Simpson's index and socio-demographic factors. *Applied Geography (Sevenoaks, England)*, *145*, 102755. doi:10.1016/j.apgeog.2022.102755

Morales, S. (2020). El problema de la inducción y la formulación de teorías científicas en antropología. *Revista Peruana de Antropología*, *5*(7), 128–142.

Mora-Rivera, J., & García-Mora, F. (2021). Internet access and poverty reduction: Evidence from rural and urban Mexico. *Telecommunications Policy*, *45*(2), 102076. doi:10.1016/j.telpol.2020.102076

Morden, T. (1999). Models of National Culture – Management Review. *Cross Cultural Management*, *6*(1), 19–44. doi:10.1108/13527609910796915

Morrison, G. R., Ross, S. M., & Kemp, J. E. (2013). *Designing effective instruction* (7th ed.). Wiley.

Morrison, P., Spofford, J., & Carswell, M. (2022). Supervision of cognitive behavioral therapy for substance use disorders. In E. A. Storch, J. S. Abramowitz, & D. McKay (Eds.), *Training and supervision in specialized cognitive behavior therapy: Methods, settings, and populations* (pp. 319–336). American Psychological Association. doi:10.1037/0000314-022

Morrisson-Saunders, A., & Therivel, R. (2006). Sustainability integration and assessment. *Journal of Environmental Assessment Policy and Management, 8*(3), 281–298. doi:10.1142/S1464333206002529

Morse, J. M. (2015). Critical Analysis of strategies for determining rigor in qualitative inquiry. *Qualitative Health Research, 25*(9), 1212–1222. doi:10.1177/1049732315588501 PMID:26184336

Moslehi, F., & Haeri, A. (2021). A novel feature selection approach based on clustering algorithm. *Journal of Statistical Computation and Simulation, 91*(3), 581–604. doi:10.1080/00949655.2020.1822358

Mostafa, S.G. (2020). Transformational Leadership, Information Technology, Knowledge management, firm performance: How are they linked? *The Journal of Value-Based Leadership, 13*(2).

Motairek, I., Chen, Z., Makhlouf, M. H., Rajagopalan, S., & Al-Kindi, S. (2022). Historical neighbourhood redlining and contemporary environmental racism. *Local Environment*, 1–11. doi:10.1080/13549839.2022.2155942 PMID:37588138

Moustakas, C. (1994). *Phenomenological research methods.* Sage Publications. doi:10.4135/9781412995658

Mulcahy, R. (2003). *Risk Management: Tricks of the Trade® for Project Managers : a Course in a Book.* RMC Publications.

Muñoz-Torres, M. J., Fernández-Izquierdo, M. Á., Rivera-Lirio, J. M., & Escrig-Olmedo, E. (2018). Can environmental, social, and governance rating agencies favor business models that promote a more sustainable development? *Corporate Social Responsibility and Environmental Management, 26*(2), 439–452. doi:10.1002/csr.1695

Murdock, G. (1967). *Ethnographic Atlas.* University of Pittsburgh Press.

Mustafa, M., Martin, L., & Hughes, M. (2016). Psychological ownership, job satisfaction and middle manager entrepreneurial behavior. *Journal of Leadership & Organizational Studies, 23*(3), 272–287. doi:10.1177/1548051815627360

Muthukrishna, M., Doebeli, M., Chudek, M., & Henrich, J. (2018). The cultural brain hypothesis: How culture drives brain expansion, sociality, and life history. *PLoS Computational Biology, 14*(11), e1006504. doi:10.1371/journal.pcbi.1006504 PMID:30408028

Nadel, S. (1953). Social control and self-regulation. *Social Forces, 31*(3), 265–273. doi:10.2307/2574226

Nadel, S. (1957). *The theory of social structure. The Free Press of Glencoe* (L. Nader, Ed.).

Nader, L. (Ed.). (2013). *Naked science: Anthropological inquiry into boundaries, power, and knowledge.* Routledge.

Naik, M. (2021). Recent advancements and key challenges with energy storage technologies for electric vehicles. *International Journal Of Electric And Hybrid Vehicles, 13*(3/4), 256–269. doi:10.1504/IJEHV.2021.123480

Nam, C., Kim, H., & Kwon, S. (2018). Effects of a Stress Management Program Providing Cognitive Behavior Therapy on Problem-focused Coping, Job Stress, and Depression in Firefighters. *Journal of Korean Academy of Psychiatric and Mental Health Nursing, 22*(1), 12. doi:10.12934/jkpmhn.2013.22.1.12

Nardone, A., Rudolph, K., Morello-Frosch, R., & Casey, J. (2020). Redlines and greenspace: The relationship between historical redlining and 2010 greenspace across the United States. *ISEE Conference Abstracts,* 2020(1). 10.1289/isee.2020.virtual.P-0061

Narkhede, S. (2018). Understanding auc-roc curve. *Towards Data Science, 26*(1), 220–227.

Nash, K. (Ed.). (2023, April 21). WSJ PRO Cybersecurity Newsletter. *Wall Street Journal*. Retrieved April 21, 2023, from http://createsend.com/t/d-035EE1F53B8C66232540EF23F30FEDED

Nasir, U. (2020). *Impact factor of top 1000 journals* (Version 2) [Csv]. Kaggle. https://www.kaggle.com/datasets/umair-nasir14/impact-factor-of-top-1000-journals

National Bureau of Statistics. (2020). *Telecoms Data: Active Voice and Internet per State, Porting and Tariff Information*. Author.

National Police Misconduct Reporting Project. (2020). *Police misconduct statistics*. Retrieved from https://www.policecrimes.com/misconduct.html

Nazari-Heris, M., Loni, A., Asadi, S., & Mohammadi-ivatloo, B. (2022). Toward social equity access and mobile charging stations for electric vehicles: A case study in Los Angeles. *Applied Energy*, *311*, 118704. doi:10.1016/j.apenergy.2022.118704

NCES. (2019, February). *Educational Attainment*. https://nces.ed.gov/programs/raceindicators/indicator_RFA.asp

Nemoto, E., Issaoui, R., Korbee, D., Jaroudi, I., & Fournier, G. (2021). How to measure the impacts of shared automated electric vehicles on urban mobility. *Transportation Research Part D, Transport and Environment*, *93*, 102766. doi:10.1016/j.trd.2021.102766

Neville, H. A., Ruedas-Gracia, N., Lee, B. A., Ogunfemi, N., Maghsoodi, A. H., Mosley, D. V., LaFromboise, T. D., & Fine, M. (2021). The public psychology for liberation training model: A call to transform the discipline. *The American Psychologist*, *76*(8), 1248–1265. doi:10.1037/amp0000887 PMID:35113591

Newsom & Dent. (2011). A Work Behavior Analysis of Executive Coaches. *International Journal of Evidence Based Coaching and Mentoring*, *9*(2), 1.

Ng, L. T. (2018). *Exploring transformational leadership and fellowship in a cultural context: The case of the Philippines*. Academic Press.

Nguyen, T. (2020). Return on investment (ROI). In K. L. Kreitner & C. Kinicki (Eds.), *Organizational behavior* (13th ed., pp. 654–656). McGraw-Hill Education.

Niazi, K. A. K., Akhtar, W., Khan, H. A., Yang, Y., & Athar, S. (2019). Hotspot diagnosis for solar photovoltaic modules using a Naive Bayes classifier. *Solar Energy*, *190*, 34–43. doi:10.1016/j.solener.2019.07.063

Nicholls, E., Ely, A., Birkin, L., Basu, P., & Goulson, D. (2020). The contribution of small-scale food production in urban areas to the sustainable development goals: A review and case study. *Sustainability Science*, *15*(6), 1585–1599. doi:10.100711625-020-00792-z

Nidumolu, R., Prahalad, C. K., & Rangaswami, M. R. (2009). Why sustainability is now the key driver of innovation. *Harvard Business Review*, *87*(9), 56–64.

Nielsen, F. (2016). *Introduction to HPC with MPI for Data Science*. Springer. doi:10.1007/978-3-319-21903-5

NIST Risk Management Framework. (2023, February 23). Computer Security Division, Information Technology Laboratory, National Institute of Standards and Technology, U.S. Department of Commerce. https://csrc.nist.gov/Projects/risk-management

Nobanee, H., Alhajjar, M., Abushairah, G., & Al Harbi, S. (2021). Reputational risk and sustainability: A bibliometric analysis of relevant literature. *Risks*, *9*(7), 1–13. doi:10.3390/risks9070134

Noble, H., & Smith, J. (2015). Issues of validity and reliability in qualitative research. *Evidence-Based Nursing*, *18*(2), 34–35. doi:10.1136/eb-2015-102054 PMID:25653237

Nobles, C. (2018). Botching Human Factors in Cybersecurity in Business Organizations. *Holistica*, *9*(3), 71–88. doi:10.2478/hjbpa-2018-0024

Noguchi, Y. (2018, November 20). *Work after #MeToo: A restaurant company tries to change its culture.* Retrieved from https://www.npr.org/sections/thesalt/2018/11/20/668211164/work-after-metoo-a-restaurant-company-tries-to-change-its-culture

Nooteboom, B. (2009). *A Cognitive Theory of the Firm.* Edward Elgar Publishing Limited. doi:10.4337/9781848447424

Norris, C., & Mitchell, F. D. (2014). Exploring the stress-support-distress process among Black women. *Journal of Black Studies*, *45*(1), 3–18. doi:10.1177/0021934713517898

Northouse, P. G. (2013). *Leadership Theory and Practice* (6th ed.). Western Michigan University.

Northouse, P. G. (2015). *Leadership: Theory and practice* (7th ed.). Sage.

Norton, R. D. (2022). *Structural Inequality: Origins and Quests for Solutions in Old Worlds and New.* Springer Nature. doi:10.1007/978-3-031-08633-5

Nowak, K., & Łukomska, B. (2021). The Impact of shift work on the well-being and subjective levels of alertness and sleepiness in firefighters and rescue service workers. *International Journal of Occupational Safety and Ergonomics*, *27*(4), 1056–1063. doi:10.1080/10803548.2021.1933320 PMID:34082652

O'Brien, K. (2021). Why higher education must help bridge the AI skills gap. *eCampus News*. https://www.ecampusnews.com/2021/01/26/why-higher-education-must-help-bridge-the-ai-skills-gap/

O'Rourke, D. (2004). *Opportunities and obstacles for corporate social responsibility reporting in developing countries.* World Bank Group.

OECD. (2021). Diversity and inclusion in the public service. In Government at a Glance 2021. doi:10.1787/1c258f55-en

Offermann, L. R., Basford, T. E., Graebner, R., Jaffer, S., De Graaf, S. B., & Kaminsky, S. E. (2014). See no evil: Color blindness and perceptions of subtle racial discrimination in the workplace. *Cultural Diversity and Ethnic Minority Psychology*, *20*(4), 499-507. doi:http://dx.doi.org.tcsedsystem.idm.oclc.org/10.1037/a0037237

Ogbanufe, O., & Kim, D. J. (2018). Comparing fingerprint-based biometrics authentication versus traditional authentication methods for e-payment. *Decision Support Systems*, *106*, 1–14. doi:10.1016/j.dss.2017.11.003

Oguz, A. B. (2020). Turkish health policies: Past, present, and future. *Social Work in Public Health*, *35*(6), 456–472. doi:10.1080/19371918.2020.1806167 PMID:32811368

Okai, E., Feng, X., & Sant, P. (2018, June). Smart cities survey. In *2018 IEEE 20th international conference on high performance computing and communications; IEEE 16th international conference on smart city; IEEE 4th international conference on data science and systems (HPCC/SmartCity/DSS)* (pp. 1726-1730). IEEE. 10.1109/HPCC/SmartCity/DSS.2018.00282

Okoh, A. E., Akinrolie, O., Bell-Gam, H. I., Adandom, I., Ibekaku, M. C., & Kalu, M. E. (2020). Nigerian healthcare workers' perception of transdisciplinary approach to older adults' care: A qualitative case study. *International Journal of Care Coordination*, *23*(2-3), 92–106. doi:10.1177/2053434520954362

Okoye. (2019). Customer service delivery in the Nigerian banking sector through engineering and technology-based channels. *International Journal of Civil Engineering and Technology*, *10*(1), 2156–2169.

Okpa, J. T., Ajah, B. O., Nzeakor, O. F., Eshiotse, E., & Abang, T. A. (2022). Business e-mail compromise scam, cyber victimization, and economic sustainability of corporate organizations in Nigeria. *Security Journal*, 1–23.

Oleksa-Marewska, K., & Tokar, J. (2022). Facing the post-pandemic challenges: The role of leadership effectiveness in shaping the affective well-being of healthcare providers working in a hybrid work mode. *International Journal of Environmental Research and Public Health*, 19(21), 1–19. doi:10.3390/ijerph192114388 PMID:36361264

Olowookere. (2021). *Nigerian Banks' e-banking Income Drops 27.3% Despite high Transactions*. Academic Press.

Onwuachi-Willig, A. (2021). The Trauma of Awakening to Racism: Did the Tragic Killing of George Floyd Result in Cultural Trauma for Whites? *Houston Law Review*, 58(4), 22269.

Opiyo, R. A. (2019). Inclusive practice and transformative leadership are entwined: Lessons for professional development of school leaders in Kenya. *Global Journal of Transformative Education*, 1(1), 52–67. doi:10.14434/gjte.v1i1.25981

Orji, U. J. (2019). Protecting Consumers from Cybercrime in the Banking and Financial Sector: An Analysis of the Legal Response in Nigeria. *Tilburg Law Review*, 24(1).

Orlowski, A., & Romanowska, P. (2019). Smart cities concept: Smart mobility indicator. *Cybernetics and Systems*, 50(2), 118–131. doi:10.1080/01969722.2019.1565120

Ortega, R. (2012). *Antropología Organizacional* (L. O. Vargas, Entrevistador). Academic Press.

Ortlieb, R., & Sieben, B. (2014). The making of inclusion as structuration: Empirical evidence of a multinational company. *Equality, Diversity and Inclusion*, 33(3), 235–248. doi:10.1108/EDI-06-2012-0052

Osei, M. B., Papadopoulos, T., Acquaye, A., & Stamati, T. (2023). Improving sustainable supply chain performance through organizational culture: A competing values framework approach. *Journal of Purchasing and Supply Management*, 29(2), 100821. doi:10.1016/j.pursup.2023.100821

OWASP Application Security Verification Standard 4.0.3. (2021, October). OWASP Foundation. https://owasp.org/www-project-application-security-verification-standard/

Ozer, M. A. (2016). A New Service Delivery Model in Health Sector: Public Private Partnership [Sağlık Sektöründe Yeni Bir Hizmet Sunum Modeli: Kamu Özel Ortaklığı]. *Journal of Social Security*, 6(1), 9–38.

Paarlberg, L. E., & Lavigna, B. (2010). Transformational leadership and public service motivation: Driving individual and organizational performance. *Public Administration Review*, 70(5), 710–718. doi:10.1111/j.1540-6210.2010.02199.x

Pace, C. (2018, August 31). How women of color get to senior management. *Harvard Business Review*. www.hbr.org/2018/08/how-women-of-color-get-to-senior-management

Pandas User Guide. (2023). Pydata.Org. https://pandas.pydata.org/docs/user_guide/index.html

Pang, B., Nijkamp, E., & Wu, Y. N. (2020). Deep Learning With TensorFlow: A Review. *Journal of Educational and Behavioral Statistics*, 45(2), 227–248. doi:10.3102/1076998619872761

Pappas, P., Vlachopoulou, M., & Chrissikopoulos, V. (2020). Measuring the impact of IT investments on financial and non-financial performance: A literature review. *Information & Management*, 57(2), 103168. doi:10.1016/j.im.2019.103168

Park, J. (2019). The adverse Impact of personal protective equipment on firefighters' cognitive functioning. *The Research Journal of The Costume Culture*, 27(1), 1–10. doi:10.29049/rjcc.2019.27.1.001

Park, J. J. (2020). Do We Really Know What We See? The Role of Cognitive Bias in How We View Race in Higher Education. *Change*, 52(2), 46–49. doi:10.1080/00091383.2020.1732776

Park, Y. M., & Kwan, M. P. (2020). Understanding racial disparities in exposure to traffic-related air pollution: Considering the spatiotemporal dynamics of population distribution. *International Journal of Environmental Research and Public Health*, *17*(3), 908. doi:10.3390/ijerph17030908 PMID:32024171

Parra, C. M. (2008). Quality of life market. *Journal of Human Development*, *9*(2), 207–227. doi:10.1080/14649880802078751

Parris, C. L., Hegtvedt, K. A., & Johnson, C. (2020). Assessments of environmental injustice among Black Americans. *Social Currents*, *8*(1), 45–63. doi:10.1177/2329496520950808

Parrott, L., & Stewart, W. (2012). Future landscapes: Managing within complexity. *Frontiers in Ecology and the Environment*, *10*(7), 382–389. doi:10.1890/110082

Partala, T., & Saari, T. (2015). Understanding the most influential user experiences in successful and unsuccessful technology adoptions. *Computers in Human Behavior*, *53*, 381–395. doi:10.1016/j.chb.2015.07.012

Pascual-Ezama, D., Dunfield, D., Gil-Gómez de Liaño, B., & Prelec, D. (2015). Peer Effects in Unethical Behavior: Standing or Reputation? *PLoS One*, *10*(4), e0122305. doi:10.1371/journal.pone.0122305 PMID:25853716

Pastor, M. (2007). Environmental justice: Reflections from the United States. *Reclaiming Nature*, 351-378. doi:10.7135/UPO9781843313465.015

Patil, P. P., Dwivedi, Y. K., & Rana, N. P. (2017). Digital Payments Adoption: An Analysis of Literature. In *Conference on e-Business, e-Services and e-Society* (pp. 61-70). Springer.

Paul, G. W., & Berry, D. M. (2013). *The Importance of Executive Leadership in Creating a Post-Merged Organizational Culture Conducive to Effective Performance Management*. S.A. Journal of Human Resources Management.

Payne-Sturges, D. C., Gee, G. C., & Cory-Slechta, D. A. (2021). Confronting racism in environmental health sciences: Moving the science forward for eliminating racial inequities. *Environmental Health Perspectives*, *129*(5), 055002. Advance online publication. doi:10.1289/EHP8186 PMID:33945300

Peltier, B. (2001). *The psychology of executive coaching: Theory and Application*. Sheridan Books.

Peña, W. (2008) La etnografía, una metodología apropiada al diagnóstico de la responsabilidad social empresarial. *Univ. Empresa*, *7*(15), 177-183. https://www.redalyc.org/pdf/1872/187214457008.pdf

Peng, J., Li, M., Wang, Z., & Yuying, L. (2021). Transformational Leadership and Employees' Reactions to Organizational Change: Evidence From a Meta-Analysis. *The Journal of Applied Behavioral Science*, *57*(3), 369–397. doi:10.1177/0021886320920366

PennLive. (2016, November 25). *Former Greensburg police chief pleads guilty to felony charges*. Retrieved from https://www.pennlive.com/news/2016/11/former_greensburg_police_chie.html

Perna, M. C. (2021). *Workplace Discrimination And Abuse Far More Common Than We Might Think*. Forbes. https://www.forbes.com/sites/markcperna/2021/05/26/workplace-discrimination-and-abuse-far-more-common-than-we-might-think/

Perry, L. & Gartner, Inc. (2023, April 19). *Top Strategic Cybersecurity Trends for 2023*. Gartner. https://www.gartner.com/en/articles/top-strategic-cybersecurity-trends-for-2023

Perry, B., Harp, K., & Oser, C. (2013). Racial and gender discrimination in the stress process: Implications for African American women's health and well-Being. *Sociological Perspectives*, *56*(1), 25–48. doi:10.1525op.2012.56.1.25 PMID:24077024

Perry, M. J., Arrington, S., Freisthler, M. S., Ibe, I. N., McCray, N. L., Neumann, L. M., Tajanlangit, P., & Trejo Rosas, B. M. (2021). Pervasive structural racism in environmental epidemiology. *Environmental Health*, *20*(1), 119. Advance online publication. doi:10.118612940-021-00801-3 PMID:34784917

Peteet, B.J., Brown, C.M., Lige, Q.M., & Lanaway, D. A. (2015). Impostorism is associated with greater psychological distress and lower self-esteem for African American students. *Current Psychology: Research and Reviews, 34*(1), 154-163.

Peterson, D. B., & Hicks, M. D. (1995). *The leader as coach: Strategies for coaching and Developing others*. Personnel Decisions.

Pew Research Center. (2020). *Trust in police is down among all Americans, but especially among black people*. Retrieved from https://www.pewresearch.org/fact- tank/2020/08/17/trust-in-police-is-down-among-all-americans-but-especially-among- black-people/

Pfiffner, M. (2022). *The Neurology of Business: Implementing the Viable System Model*. Springer Nature. doi:10.1007/978-3-031-14260-4

Pfleeger, S. L., & Caputo, D. D. (2012). Leveraging behavioral science to mitigate cyber security risk. *Computers & Security*, *31*(4), 597–611. doi:10.1016/j.cose.2011.12.010

Pham, T. (2021). *The Role of External Mechanisms and Transformational Leadership in Information Security Policy Effectiveness: A Managerial Perspective of Financial Industry in Vietnam* [Doctoral dissertation]. Auckland University of Technology.

Pham, B. T., Tien Bui, D., Pourghasemi, H. R., Indra, P., & Dholakia, M. (2017). Landslide susceptibility assesssment in the Uttarakhand area (India) using GIS: A comparison study of prediction capability of naïve bayes, multilayer perceptron neural networks, and functional trees methods. *Theoretical and Applied Climatology*, *128*(1), 255–273. doi:10.100700704-015-1702-9

Phillips, J. C., Hargons, C., Chung, Y. B., Forrest, L., Oh, K. H., & Westefeld, J. (2017). Society of counseling psychology leadership academy: Cultivating leadership competence and community. *The Counseling Psychologist*, *45*(7), 965–991. doi:10.1177/0011000017736141

Phillips, J. J., & Phillips, P. P. (2019). *Measuring the success of employee training: ROI and the value of learning*. Routledge.

Pieterse, A., Carter, R., & Ray, K. (2013). Racism-related stress, general life stress, and psychological functioning among Black American women. *Journal of Multicultural Counseling and Development*, *41*(1), 36–46. doi:10.1002/j.2161-1912.2013.00025.x

Piper, M. (2022, June 3). *Why the public sector needs a more diverse tech workforce*. Capgemini. https://www.capgemini.com/insights/expert-perspectives/why-the-public-sector-needs-a-more-diverse-tech-workforce/

Polasky, S., Kling, C. L., Levin, S. A., Carpenter, S. R., Daily, G. C., Ehrlich, P. R., Heal, G. M., & Lubchenco, J. (2019). Role of economics in analyzing the environment and sustainable development. *Proceedings of the National Academy of Sciences of the United States of America*, *116*(12), 5233–5238. doi:10.1073/pnas.1901616116 PMID:30890656

Pope-Davis, D. B., Toporek, R. L., Ortega-Villalobos, L., Ligiéru, D. P., Brittan-Powell, C. S., Liu, W. M., Bashshur, M. R., Codrington, J. N., & Liang, C. T. H. (2002). Client perspectives of multicultural counseling competence: A qualitative examination. *The Counseling Psychologist*, *30*(3), 355–393. doi:10.1177/0011000002303001

Porter, M., & Kramer, R. M. (2006). Strategy and society: The link between competitive advantage and corporate social responsibility. *Harvard Business Review*, *82*(12), 78–92. PMID:17183795

Poulsen, S. (n.d.). *Innovation and diversity in the public sector.* THNK. https://www.thnk.org/blog/innovation-and-diversity-in-the-public-sector/

Pozdniakova, A. M. (2018). Smart city strategies "London-Stockholm-Vienna-Kyiv": In search of common ground and best practices. *Acta Innovations.*

Prakash, O. (2020). History, Policy Making, and Sustainability. In *Interdisciplinary Approaches to Public Policy and Sustainability* (pp. 1-17). IGI Global Publisher. https://www.igi-global.com/book/interdisciplinary-approaches-public-policy-sustainability/227626

Price, D. (2000, Nov. 20). Anthropologists as Spies. *The Nation*, 24.

Proctor, R. W., & Chen, J. M. (2015). The Role of Human Factors/Ergonomics in the Science of Security. *Human Factors*, *57*(5), 721–727. doi:10.1177/0018720815585906 PMID:25994927

Project Management Institute. (2021). *The Standard for Project Management and a Guide to the Project Management Body of Knowledge.* PMBOK Guide.

Pulido, L. (2017). Rethinking environmental racism: White privilege and urban development in Southern California. In *Environment* (pp. 379–407). Routledge.

Pullen, A., Lewis, P., & Ozkazanc-Pan, B. (2019). A critical moment: 25 years of gender, work and organization. *Gender, Work and Organization*, *26*(1), 1–8. doi:10.1111/gwao.12335

Purdie-Vaughns, V. (2015, April 22). Why so few black women are senior managers in 2015? *Fortune.* https://fortune.com/2015/04/22/black-women-leadership-study/

Purdie-Vaughns, V., & Eibach, R. (2008). Intersectional invisibility: The ideological sources and social consequences of non-prototypicality. *Sex Roles*, *59*, 377–391. doi:10.100711199-008-9424-4

Puta, B. (2022). Does phenomenology (still) matter? Three phenomenological traditions and sociological theory. *International Journal of Politics Culture and Society*, *35*(3), 41–431.

Puyo, J. G. B. (2022). Ethical Leadership in Education: A Uniting View Through Ethics of Care, Justice, Critique, and Heartful Education. *Journal of Culture and Values in Education*, *5*(2), 140–151. doi:10.46303/jcve.2022.24

PwC Belgium. (2017). *Information Security Breaches Survey 2017 – Key takeaways.* Retrieved April 22, 2023, from https://www.pwc.be/en/documents/20170315-Information-security-breaches-survey.pdf

Pyrczak, F., & Tcherni-Buzzeo, M. (2018). *Evaluating Research in Academic Journals: A Practical Guide to Realistic Evaluation* (7th ed.). Routledge. doi:10.4324/9781351260961

Qi, X., Chen, G., Li, Y., Cheng, X., & Li, C. (2019). Applying neural-network-based machine learning to additive manufacturing: Current applications, challenges, and future perspectives. *Engineering (Beijing)*, *5*(4), 721–729. doi:10.1016/j.eng.2019.04.012

Qosha, N. (2019, November 20). Inclusive leadership: The role of psychological safety. *Training Industry.* https://trainingindustry.com/articles/leadership/inclusive-leadership-the-role-of-psychological-safety/

Quick Take: Women of Color in the United States. (2018, November 7). *Catalyst.* https://www.catalyst.org/research/women-of-color-in-the-united-states/

Rabenu, E., Yaniv, E., & Elizur, D. (2017). The relationship between psychological capital, coping with stress, well-being, and performance: Research and reviews research and reviews. *Current Psychology, 36*(4), 875-887. http://dx.doi.org.tcsedsystem.idm.oclc.org/10.1007/s12144-016-9477-4

Racial Trauma. (n.d.). *Mental Health America.* https://mhanational.org/racial-trauma

Raelin, J. (2012). The manager as facilitator of dialogue. *Organization, 20*(6), 818–839. doi:10.1177/1350508412455085

Rafiq, M., Zhang, X., Yuan, J., Naz, S., & Maqbool, S. (2020). Impact of a balanced scorecard as a strategic management system tool to improve sustainable development: Measuring the mediation of organizational performance through PLS-smart. *Sustainability (Basel), 12*(4), 1365. doi:10.3390u12041365

Raghupathi, W., Raghupathi, V., & Saharia, A. (2023). Analyzing Health Data Breaches: A Visual Analytics Approach. *AppliedMath, 3*(1), 175–199. doi:10.3390/appliedmath3010011

Raines, A. M., Capron, D. W., Stentz, L. A., Walton, J. L., Allan, N. P., McManus, E. S., Uddo, M., True, G., & Franklin, C. L. (2017). Posttraumatic stress disorder and suicidal ideation, plans, and impulses: The mediating role of anxiety sensitivity cognitive concerns among veterans. *Journal of Affective Disorders, 222*, 57–62. doi:10.1016/j.jad.2017.06.035 PMID:28672180

Ramjit, D. (2021). Stemoh Leadership: A Multicultural Christian Approach to Contemporary Leadership. *International Journal of Responsible Leadership and Ethical Decision-Making, 3*(2), 17–37. doi:10.4018/IJRLEDM.2021070102

Ramluckan, T., Van Niekerk, B., & Martins, I. (n.d.). A change management perspective to implementing a cybersecurity culture. *ECCWS 2020 20th European Conference on Cyber Warfare and Security,* 442-448.

Ranchordás, S. (2020). Nudging citizens through technology in smart cities. *International Review of Law Computers & Technology, 34*(3), 254–276. doi:10.1080/13600869.2019.1590928

Ranney, M. (2020). Leadership in law enforcement organizations. *International Journal of Police Science & Management, 22*(3), 21–25.

Ransom, J. (2020, July 6). Amy Cooper faces charges after calling police on black bird-watcher. *The New York Times.* https://www.nytimes.com/2020/07/06/nyregion/amy-cooper-false-report-charge.html

Rappaport, R. (1984). *Pigs for ancestors: Ritual in the ecology of a New Guinea people.* Yale University Press.

Rappaport, R. (1999). *Ritual and religion in the making of humanity.* Cambridge University Press. doi:10.1017/CBO9780511814686

Ray, B., & Shaw, R. (2019). Defining urban water insecurity: concepts and relevance. *Urban Drought: Emerging Water Challenges in Asia,* 1-15. doi:10.1007/978-981-10-8947-3_1

Raziq, M. M., Borini, F. M., Malik, O. F., Ahmad, M., & Shabaz, M. (2018). Leadership styles, goal clarity, and project success: Evidence from project-based organizations in Pakistan. *Leadership and Organization Development Journal, 39*(2), 309–323. doi:10.1108/LODJ-07-2017-0212

Razmjoo, A., Gandomi, A. H., Pazhoohesh, M., Mirjalili, S., & Rezaei, M. (2022). The key role of clean energy and technology in smart cities development. *Energy Strategy Reviews, 44*, 100943. doi:10.1016/j.esr.2022.100943

Rebensky, S., Carroll, M., Nakushian, A., Chaparro, M., & Prior, T. (2021). Understanding the last line of defense: human response to cybersecurity events. In *HCI for Cybersecurity, Privacy and Trust: Third International Conference, HCI-CPT 2021, Held as Part of the 23rd HCI International Conference, HCII 2021, Virtual Event, July 24–29, 2021, Proceedings.* Springer International Publishing. 10.1007/978-3-030-77392-2_23

Reegård, K., Blackett, C., & Katta, V. (2019). The concept of cybersecurity culture. In *29th European Safety and Reliability Conference* (pp. 4036-4043). 10.3850/978-981-11-2724-3_0761-cd

Reese, K., & ... 2019). A usability study of five two-factor authentication methods. *Proceedings of the Fifteenth Symposium on Usable Privacy and Security*.

Reinhardt, A. C., Leon, T. G., & Summers, L. O. (2022). The Transformational Leader in Nursing Practice–an approach to retain nursing staff. *Administrative Issues Journal*, *12*(1), 2. doi:10.5929/2022.12.1.1

Remedios, J., & Snyder, S. (2015). How women of color detect and respond to multiple forms of prejudice. *Sex Roles*, *73*(9-10), 371–383. doi:10.100711199-015-0453-5

Remedios, J., & Snyder, S. (2018). Intersectional oppression: Multiple stigmatized identities and perceptions of invisibility, discrimination, and stereotyping. *Journal of Social Sciences*, *74*(2), 265–281.

Reynoso, C. (2006). *Complejidad y caos: Una exploración antropológica*. Editorial Sb.

Richerson, P., Baldini, R., Bell, A., Demps, K., Frost, K., Hillis, V., Mathew, S., Newton, E., Naar, N., Newson, L., Ross, C., Smaldino, P., Waring, T., & Zefferman, M. (2016). Cultural group selection plays an essential role in explaining human cooperation: A sketch of the evidence. *Behavioral and Brain Sciences*, *39*, e3. doi:10.1017/S0140525X1400106X PMID:25347943

Ritchie, H., & Roser, M. (2018). Urbanization. *Our World in Data*.

Rivera, L. (2012). Hiring as cultural matching: The case of elite professional service firms. *American Sociological Review*, *77*(6), 999–1022. doi:10.1177/0003122412463213

Robbins, S. P., & Judge, T. A. (2017). *Essentials of Organizational Behavior: Student value edition. Place of publication not identified*. Prentice Hall.

Roberson, Q. M. (2019). Diversity in the Workplace: A Review, Synthesis, and Future Research Agenda. *Annual Review of Organizational Psychology and Organizational Behavior*, *6*(1), 69–88. doi:10.1146/annurev-orgpsych-012218-015243

Roberts, K., & Grabowski, M. (1996). Organizations, Technology and Structuring. In S. Clegg, C. Hardy & W. Nord (Eds.), Handbook of Organization Studies (pp. 409-423). Sage.

Robinson, S., Leach, J., Owen-Lynch, P., & Sünram-Lea, S. (2017). Stress Reactivity and Cognitive Performance in a Simulated Firefighting Emergency. *Aviation, Space, and Environmental Medicine*, *84*(6), 592–599. doi:10.3357/ASEM.3391.2013 PMID:23745287

Rodon, C., & Meyer, T. (2012). *Searching information on the Web and Planning Fallacy: A pilot investigation of pessimistic forecasts*. doi:10.1016/j.erap.2011.12.004

Rodrigo, Malaquiasa, & Hwangb. (2019). Mobile banking use: A comparative study with Brazilian and U.S. participants. *International Journal of Information Management*. www.elsevier.com/locate/ijinfomgt

Rodriguez-Rivero, R., Ortiz-Marcos, I., & Patino-Arenas, V. E. (2022). Exploring the influence of culture in the present and future of multicultural organizations: Comparing the case of spain and latin america. *Sustainability (Basel)*, *14*(4), 1–15. doi:10.3390u14042327

Rojalin, T., Antonio, D., Kulkarni, A., & Carney, R. P. (2022). Machine Learning-Assisted Sampling of Surface-Enhanced Raman Scattering (SERS) Substrates Improve Data Collection Efficiency. *Applied Spectroscopy*, *76*(4), 485–495. doi:10.1177/00037028211034543 PMID:34342493

Rollock, N. (2012). The invisibility of race: Intersectional reflections on the liminal space of alterity. *Race, Ethnicity and Education*, *15*(1), 65–84. doi:10.1080/13613324.2012.638864

Rosaldo, R. (1991). *Cultura y verdad, nueva propuesta de análisis social*. Grijalbo.

Rosa, M., Shirley, L., Gavarrete, M., & Alangui, W. (Eds.). (2017). *Ethnomathematics and its diverse approaches for mathematics*. Springer. doi:10.1007/978-3-319-59220-6

Rosemann, M., Becker, J., & Chasin, F. (2020). City 5.0. *Business & Information Systems Engineering, 63*(1), 71–77. doi:10.100712599-020-00674-9

Rosenfeld, P. (2011). Organizational systems theory: A framework for organizational development. *Consulting Psychology Journal, 63*(4), 289–301. doi:10.1037/a0023512

Rosenzweig, E., & Critcher, C. R. (2014). Decomposing Forecasting: The Salience-Assessment-Weighting (SAW) Model. *Current Directions in Psychological Science, 23*(5), 368–373. doi:10.1177/0963721414540300

Rosette, A. S., Phillips, K. W., & Leonardelli, G. J. (2006). The White Standard in Leadership Evaluations: Attributional Benefits of a White Corporate Leader. *Academy of Management Annual Meeting Proceedings*, F1–F6. 10.5465/ambpp.2006.22898280

Rosette, A., & Livingston, R. (2012). Failure is not an option for Black women: Effects of organizational performance on leaders with single versus dual-subordinate identities. *Journal of Experimental Social Psychology, 48*(5), 1162–1167. doi:10.1016/j.jesp.2012.05.002

Ross, N., & Bookchin, S. (2020). Perils of conversation: #MeToo and opportunities for peacebuilding. *Gender in Management, 35*(4), 391–404. doi:10.1108/GM-12-2019-0237

Rouse, M. (2011). *Memorandum of understanding (MOU or MoU)*. Retrieved from Whatis.com: https://whatis.techtarget.com/definition/memorandum-of-understanding-MOU-or-MoU

Rousseau, D. M. (1995). *Psychological contracts in organizations: Understanding written and unwritten agreements*. Sage. doi:10.4135/9781452231594

Rovetta, A., & Bhagavathula, A.S. (2020). COVID-19-Related Web Search Behaviors and infodemic Attitudes in Italy: Infodemiological Study. *JMIR Public Health Surveill, 6*(2) doi: :32338613PMCID:7202310 doi:10.2196/19374PMID

Rowe, A. K., Rowe, S. Y., Peters, D. H., Holloway, K. A., Chalker, J., & Ross-Degnan, D. (2018). Effectiveness of strategies to improve health-care provider practices in low-income and middle-income countries: A systematic review. *The Lancet. Global Health, 6*(11), e1163–e1175. doi:10.1016/S2214-109X(18)30398-X PMID:30309799

Ruggieri, R., Ruggeri, M., Vinci, G., & Poponi, S. (2021). Electric Mobility in a Smart City: European Overview. *Energies, 14*(2), 315–331. doi:10.3390/en14020315

Rutting, L., Vervoort, J., & Mees, H. (2022). Disruptive seeds: a scenario approach to explore power shifts in sustainability transformations. In *Sustainability Science*. Springer. https://link.springer.com/article/10.1007/s11625-022-01251-7#citeas

Ryttare, E. (2019). *Change management: A key in achieving successful cyber security: A multiple case study of organizations in Sweden*. Academic Press.

Saari, L., & Judge, T. (2004). Employee attitudes and job satisfaction. *Human Resource Management, 43*(4), 395–407. doi:10.1002/hrm.20032

Safa, N. S., Sookhak, M., Von Solms, R., Furnell, S., Ghani, N. A., & Herawan, T. (2015). Information security conscious care behaviour formation in organizations. *Computers & Security, 53*, 65–78. doi:10.1016/j.cose.2015.05.012

Saha, S., Saint, S., & Christakis, D. A. (2003). Impact factor: A valid measure of journal quality? *Journal of the Medical Library Association: JMLA, 91*(1), 42–46. PMID:12572533

Salali, G., Whitehouse, H., & Hochberg, M. (2015). A life-cycle model of human social groups produces a U-shaped distribution in group size. *PLoS One, 10*(9), e0138496. doi:10.1371/journal.pone.0138496 PMID:26381745

Saldana, J. (2021). *The coding manual for qualitative researchers* (4th ed.). Sage.

Salmi, N., & Rustam, Z. (2019). Naïve Bayes classifier models for predicting the colon cancer. *IOP Conference Series. Materials Science and Engineering, 546*(5), 052068. doi:10.1088/1757-899X/546/5/052068

Samans, R., & Nelson, J. (2022). *Sustainable enterprise value creation: Implementing stakeholder capitalism through full ESG integration.* Palgrave Macmillan. doi:10.1007/978-3-030-93560-3

Sample, J. (2015). Mitigating the Planning Fallacy in Project Forecasting: An OD Perspective. *Organization Development Journal, 33*(2), 51–66.

SánchezE. (1997). http://uam. academia.edu

Sanchez-Hucles, J., & Davis, D. D. (2010). Women and women of color in leadership: Complexity, identity, and intersectionality. *The American Psychologist, 65*(3), 171–181. doi:10.1037/a0017459 PMID:20350016

Sanguesa, J., Torres-Sanz, V., Garrido, P., Martinez, F., & Marquez-Barja, J. (2021). A Review on Electric Vehicles: Technologies and Challenges. *Smart Cities, 4*(1), 372–404. doi:10.3390martcities4010022

Sangwan, S. R., & Bhatia, M. P. S. (2020). Sustainable development in industry 4.0. In *A Roadmap to Industry 4.0: Smart Production, Sharp Business and Sustainable Development* (pp. 39–56). Springer. doi:10.1007/978-3-030-14544-6_3

Santos, M. J., & de Gortari, R. (2021). Familia y empresas un análisis desde la antropología social. *Telos: Revista de Estudios Interdisciplinarios en Ciencias Sociales, 23*(3), 728–746. doi:10.36390/telos233.14

Saowalux, P. & Peng, C. (2007). *Impact of Leadership Style on Performance: A Study of Six Sigma Professionals in Thailand.* International DSI/Asia and Pacific DSI.

Saravanan, S. (2018). 6 tips to reduce waste output in your business. *Harvard Business Review.*

Sarica, A., Cerasa, A., & Quattrone, A. (2017). Random forest algorithm for the classification of neuroimaging data in Alzheimer's disease: A systematic review. *Frontiers in Aging Neuroscience, 9*, 329. doi:10.3389/fnagi.2017.00329 PMID:29056906

Saunders, B., Sim, J., Kingstone, T., Baker, S., Waterfield, J., Bartlam, B., Burroughs, H., & Jinks, C. (2018). Saturation in qualitative research: Exploring its conceptualization and operationalization. *Quality & Quantity, 52*(4), 1893–1907. doi:10.100711135-017-0574-8 PMID:29937585

Savas, T., Keles, R., & Goktas, B. (2020). Public private partnership model: Ankara city hospital example [Kamu özel işbirliği modeli Ankara şehir hastanesi örneği]. *Journal of Health Sciences, 9*(2), 22-31.

Sawyer, J. E. (2017). *Organizational development: A process of learning and changing.* Jossey-Bass.

Schein, E. H. (2010). *Organizational Culture and Leadership.* Jossey-Bass.

Scherer, M. (2022, July 12). Understanding the adkar change management model. *Business (Atlanta, Ga.).*

Schlienger, T., & Teufel, S. (2002). Information Security Culture: The Socio-Cultural Dimension in Information Security Management. In *Information Security* (pp. 191–202). https://dblp.uni-trier.de/db/conf/sec/sec2002.html#SchliengerT02

Schmid, A. (2018, January 23). *From Smart to Savvy: The transition to Cognitive Cities (Part 3 of 3).* Qognify: Safeguarding Your World. https://www.qognify.com/from-smart-to-savvy-the-transition-to-cognitive-cities-part-3-of-3/

Schmidt, M. T., Elezi, F., Tommelein, I. D., & Lindemann, U. (2014). *Towards recursive plan-do-check-act cycles for continuous improvement.* Industrial Engineering and Engineering Management., doi:10.1109/IEEM.2014.7058886

Schneider, J., & Schneider, P. (2008). The anthropology of crime and criminalization. *Annual Review of Anthropology, 37*(1), 351–373. doi:10.1146/annurev.anthro.36.081406.094316

Schot, E., Tummers, L., & Noordegraaf, M. (2020). Working on working together. A systematic review on how healthcare professionals contribute to interprofessional collaboration. *Journal of Interprofessional Care, 34*(3), 332–342. doi:10.1 080/13561820.2019.1636007 PMID:31329469

Schramade, W. (2016). Integrating ESG into valuation models and investment decisions: The value driver adjustment approach. SSRN *Electronic Journal.* doi:10.2139/ssrn.2749626

SchuslerT. M.EspedidoC. B.RiveraB. K.HernandezM.HowertonA. M.SeppK.EngelM. D.MarcosJ.ChaudharyB. (2020). Students of color speak on racial equity in environmental sustainability. https://doi.org/ doi:10.32942/OSF.IO/NTEZC

Schuurman, D., Croon, M. A., & Hooft, E. A. J. (2021a). The role of strategic alignment in HRD and its contribution to organizational performance. *Human Resource Development Review, 20*(3), 254–280. doi:10.1177/1534484321990326

Schuurman, D., Mulder, M., Veldkamp, B. P., Van Vianen, A. E., & De Lange, A. H. (2021). Learning climate, employee well-being, and performance: The mediating role of employees' self-regulation of learning. *Journal of Occupational and Organizational Psychology, 94*(1), 219–239.

Schuurman, D., Van Rijswijk, J., & Plak, P. (2021). The impact of technological changes on the training and development of human capital. *Journal of Organizational Change Management, 34*(2), 330–345.

Scott, D., Ratiliff, B., & English, C. (2022). Sounding the alarm: Firefighter behavioral health and suicide prevention. *International Journal of Integrated Care, 22*(S2), 16. Advance online publication. doi:10.5334/ijic.ICIC21290

Security Awareness Training. (2023, April 6). SANS Institute. https://www.sans.org/security-awareness-training/

Security, I. B. M. (2021). *Cost of a data breach report 2021.* Retrieved from https://www.ibm.com/security/data-breach

Seh, A. H., Zarour, M., Alenezi, M., Sarkar, A. K., Agrawal, A., Kumar, R., & Ahmad Khan, R. (2020, May). Healthcare data breaches: insights and implications. In *Healthcare* (vol. 8, no. 2, p. 133). MDPI. https://www.ncbi.nlm.nih.gov/pmc/articles/PMC7349636/

Seljemo, C., Viksveen, P., & Ree, E. (2020). The role of transformational leadership, job demands and job resources for patient safety culture in Norwegian nursing homes: A cross-sectional study. *BMC Health Services Research, 20*(1), 1–8. doi:10.118612913-020-05671-y PMID:32847598

Semmens, E., Domitrovich, J., Conway, K., & Noonan, C. (2016). A cross-sectional survey of occupational history as a wildland firefighter and health. *American Journal of Industrial Medicine, 59*(4), 330–335. doi:10.1002/ajim.22566 PMID:26792645

Senge, P. M. (2006). The Fifth Discipline: The Art and Practice of the Learning Organization. Academic Press.

Senge, P. M. (1990). *The fifth discipline: The art and practice of the learning organization.* Doubleday Currency.

Senge, P. M. (2006). *The fifth discipline: The art & practice of the learning organization.* Doubleday.

Sepczuk, M., & Kotulski, Z. (2018). A new risk-based authentication management model oriented on user's experience. *Computers & Security, 73,* 17–33. doi:10.1016/j.cose.2017.10.002

Sepehri, A. (2019). An application of DEMATEL for transaction authentication in online banking. *International Journal of Data and Network Science, 3*(2), 71-76. doi:10.5267/j.ijdns.2019.1.002

Seppala, E., & Cameron, K. (2015, December 1). Proof that positive work cultures are more productive. *Harvard Business Review.* https://hbr.org/2015/12/proof-that-positive-work-cultures-are-more-productive

Serenko, A., & Dohan, M. (2011). Comparing the expert survey and citation impact journal ranking methods: Example from the field of Artificial Intelligence. *Journal of Informetrics, 5*(4), 629–648. doi:10.1016/j.joi.2011.06.002

Settles, I. H., Buchanan, N. T., & Dotson, K. (2019). Scrutinized but not recognized: (In)visibility and hypervisibility experiences of faculty of color. *Journal of Vocational Behavior, 113*, 62–74. doi:10.1016/j.jvb.2018.06.003

Shabbir, M. S., & Wisdom, O. (2020). The relationship between corporate social responsibility, environmental investments and financial performance: Evidence from manufacturing companies. *Environmental Science and Pollution Research International, 27*(32), 39946–39957. doi:10.100711356-020-10217-0 PMID:32797400

Shadows and light: Diversity management as phantasmagoria—Christina Schwabenland, Frances Tomlinson, 2015. (n.d.). Retrieved August 8, 2023, from https://journals-sagepub-com.proxymu.wrlc.org/doi/10.1177/0018726715574587

Shaheen, S., & Bouzaghrane, M. (2019). Mobility and Energy Impacts of Shared Automated Vehicles: A Review of Recent Literature. Current Sustainable/Renewable. *Energy Reports, 6*(4), 193–200. doi:10.100740518-019-00135-2

Shankar, A., & Jebarajakirthy, C. (2019). The influence of e-banking service quality on customer loyalty: A moderated mediation approach. *International Journal of Bank Marketing, 37*(1), 1119–1142. Advance online publication. doi:10.1108/IJBM-03-2018-0063

Sharma, I., Garg, I., & Kiran, D. (2020). Industry 5.0 and smart cities: A futuristic approach. *European Journal of Molecular and Clinical Medicine, 7*(08), 2515–8260.

Sharma, P., & Srinivasan, S. (2021). Adaptive Learning: Improving Student Performance and Engagement. *Journal of Educational Technology & Society, 24*(1), 86–98.

Sharma, S., & Aparicio, E. (2022). Organizational and team culture as antecedents of protection motivation among IT employees. *Computers & Security, 120*, 102774. doi:10.1016/j.cose.2022.102774

Shepperd, J., Waters, E., Weinstein, N., & Klein, W. (2015). A Primer on Unrealistic Optimism. *Current Directions in Psychological Science, 24*(3), 232–237. doi:10.1177/0963721414568341 PMID:26089606

Sherwin, B. (2014, January 24). Why women are more effective leaders than men. *Business Insider.* https://www.businessinsider.com/study-women-are-better-leaders-2014-1

Shetty, P., & Singh, S. (2021). Hierarchical clustering: A survey. *International Journal of Applied Research, 7*(4), 178–181. doi:10.22271/allresearch.2021.v7.i4c.8484

Shields, C. M. (2010). Transformative leadership: Working for equity in diverse contexts. *Educational Administration Quarterly, 46*(4), 558–589. doi:10.1177/0013161X10375609

Shields, C. M., & Hesbol, K. A. (2020). Transformative leadership approaches to inclusion, equity, and social justice. *Journal of School Leadership, 30*(1), 3–22. doi:10.1177/1052684619873343

Shin, D. H. (2006). VOLP: A debate over information service or telephone application in US. *Telematics and Informatics, 23*(2), 57–73. doi:10.1016/j.tele.2005.04.001

Shirey, M. R. (2013). Lewin's Theory of Planned Change as a Strategic Resource. *The Journal of Nursing Administration, 43*(2), 69–72. doi:10.1097/NNA.0b013e31827f20a9 PMID:23343723

Shirzadi, A., Bui, D. T., Pham, B. T., Solaimani, K., Chapi, K., Kavian, A., Shahabi, H., & Revhaug, I. (2017). Shallow landslide susceptibility assessment using a novel hybrid intelligence approach. *Environmental Earth Sciences*, *76*(2), 1–18. doi:10.100712665-016-6374-y

Shrikant, N., & Sambaraju, R. (2021). 'A police officer shot a black man': Racial categorization, racism, and mundane culpability in news reports of police shootings of black people in the United States of America. *British Journal of Social Psychology*, *60*(4), 1196–1217. doi:10.1111/bjso.12490 PMID:34350606

Siakwah, P. (2018). Tourism geographies and spatial distribution of tourist sites in Ghana. *African Journal of Hospitality, Tourism and Leisure*, *7*(1), 1–19.

Sijabat, R. (2022). The association of economic growth, foreign aid, foreign direct investment and gross capital formation in Indonesia: Evidence from the Toda–Yamamoto approach. *Economies*, *10*(4), 93. doi:10.3390/economies10040093

Silva Santisteban, F. (2018). *Antropología*. Biblioteca de la Universidad de Lima.

Şimşit, Z. T., Günay, N. S., & Vayvay, O. (2014). Theory of Constraints: A Literature Review. *Procedia: Social and Behavioral Sciences*, *150*, 930–936. doi:10.1016/j.sbspro.2014.09.104

Sinclair, A. (1993). Approaches to organisational culture and ethics. *Journal of Business Ethics*, *12*(1), 63–73. doi:10.1007/BF01845788

Singh, I. & Srivastava, R.K. (2020). Understanding the intention to use mobile banking by existing online banking customers: an empirical study. *Journal of Financial Services Marketing, 3*, 86-96.

SiscoM. R.ConstantinoS. M.GaoY.TavoniM.CoopermanA. D.BosettiV.WeberE. U. (2020). A finite pool of worry or a finite pool of attention? evidence and qualifications. *Preprint]. , 3*. doi:10.21203/rs.3.rs-98481/v1

Sitzmann, T., Ely, K., & Brown, K. G. (2019). A multilevel review of diversity, conflict, and synergy in teams: Challenges and opportunities for future research. *Annual Review of Organizational Psychology and Organizational Behavior*, *6*, 457–482.

Skaggs, S. (2012). Review of 'Race gender and the labor market: Inequalities at work'. *Gender & Society*, *26*(1), 123–125. doi:10.1177/0891243211423657

Sliter, M., Kale, A., & Yuan, Z. (2018). Is humor the best medicine? The buffering effect of coping humor on traumatic stressors in firefighters. *Journal of Organizational Behavior*, *35*(2), 257–272. doi:10.1002/job.1868

Smith, A., Watkins, M., Ladge, J., & Carlton, P. (2018, May 10). Interviews with 59 Black female executives explore intersectional invisibility and the strategies to overcome it. *Harvard Business Review*. https://hbr.org/2018/05/interviews-with-59-black-female-executives-explore-intersectional-invisibility-and-strategies-to-overcome-it

Smith, C. (2021, December 9). *Has the Public Sector Done Enough to Create a Diverse Workforce?* Governing. https://www.governing.com/work/has-the-public-sector-done-enough-to-create-a-diverse-workforce

Smith, A. N., Watkins, M. B., Ladge, J. J., & Carlton, P. (2019). Making the invisible visible: Paradoxical effects of intersectional invisibility on the career experiences of executive Black women. *Academy of Management Journal*, *62*(6), 1705–1734. doi:10.5465/amj.2017.1513

Smith, D. (1986). Institutional ethnography: A feminist method. *Resources for Feminist Research*, *15*(1), 6–13.

Smith, D. (2022). *Fraud and corruption: Cases and materials*. Springer Nature. doi:10.1007/978-3-031-10063-5

Smith, D., Manning, T., & Petruzzello, S. (2017). Effect of strenuous live-fire drills on cardiovascular and psychological responses of recruit firefighters. *Ergonomics*, *44*(3), 244–254. doi:10.1080/00140130121115 PMID:11219758

Smith, P. C. (1998). Sexual harassment and the psychological contract: Implications for organizational behavior. *Academy of Management Journal*, *41*(4), 403–416.

Smith, T. D., Hughes, K., DeJoy, D. M., & Dyal, M. A. (2018). Assessment of relationships between work stress, work-family conflict, burnout and firefighter safety behavior outcomes. *Safety Science*, *103*, 287–292. doi:10.1016/j. ssci.2017.12.005

Sobers, R. (2022). *166 Cybersecurity Statistics and Trends*. Varonis. Inside Out Security. https://www.varonis.com/blog/cybersecurity-statistics

Society for Human Resource Management. (2021a). *Assessing the Skills Gap and Workforce Readiness*. https://www.shrm.org/hr-today/trends-and-forecasting/research-and-surveys/Documents/Assessing-the-Skills-Gap-and-Workforce-Readiness.pdf

Society for Human Resource Management. (2021b). *Technology Skills Gap and Future of Work*. https://www.shrm.org/hr-today/trends-and-forecasting/research-and-surveys/pages/technology-skills-gap-future-of-work.aspx

Soderberg, G., Bechara, M. M., Bossu, W., Che, M. N. X., Davidovic, S., Kiff, M. J., ... Yoshinaga, A. (2022). *Behind the scenes of central bank digital currency: Emerging trends, insights, and policy lessons*. Academic Press.

Solove, D. J., & Citron, D. K. (2017). Risk and anxiety: A theory of data-breach harms. *Texas Law Review*, *96*(2), 1–38.

Song, Y., Ha, J., & Jue, J. (2020). Examining the Relative Influences of the Risk Factors and Protective Factors That Affect Firefighter Resilience. *SAGE Open*, *10*(4), 215824402098261. doi:10.1177/2158244020982610

Sosis, R. (2003). Why aren't we all hutterites? Costly signaling theory and religious behavior. *Human Nature (Hawthorne, N.Y.)*, *14*(2), 91–127. doi:10.100712110-003-1000-6 PMID:26190055

Spaur, M. (2008). Smart meter infrastructure is keystone of smart grid. *Natural Gas & Electricity*, *25*(3), 23–27.

Spector, B. (2011). *Implementing organizational change: Theory into practice-international edition*. Prentice Hall.

Spoz, A. (2021). Sustainable business models of companies. *Advances in Business Information Systems and Analytics*, 44–60. doi:10.4018/978-1-7998-6788-3.ch003

Stanley, I. H., Boffa, J. W., Hom, M. A., Kimbrel, N. A., & Joiner, T. E. (2017). Differences in psychiatric symptoms and barriers to mental health care between volunteer and career firefighters. *Psychiatry Research*, *247*, 236–242. doi:10.1016/j.psychres.2016.11.037 PMID:27930964

Stanley, I. H., Smith, L. J., Boffa, J. W., Tran, J. K., Schmidt, N. B., Joiner, T. E., & Vujanovic, A. A. (2018). Anxiety sensitivity and suicide risk among firefighters: A test of the depression-distress amplification model. *Comprehensive Psychiatry*, *84*, 39–46. doi:10.1016/j.comppsych.2018.03.014 PMID:29684659

Stanley, I., Hom, M., Spencer-Thomas, S., & Joiner, T. (2017). Examining anxiety sensitivity as a mediator of the association between PTSD symptoms and suicide risk among women firefighters. *Journal of Anxiety Disorders*, *50*, 94–102. doi:10.1016/j.janxdis.2017.06.003 PMID:28645017

Starner, T. (2016). Why 'middle managers' are an employer's most important leaders. *HRDive*. https://www.hrdive.com/news/why-middle-managers-are-an-employers-most-important-leaders/425140/#:~:text=The%20impact%20of%20a%20good%20middle%20manager%20goes%20beyond%20employee%20engagement.&text=In%20fact%2C%20a%20Wharton%20School,focus%20groups%2C%E2%80%9D%20she%20says

Steinhoff, R. L. (2015). Natural born leaders: Use of a self-assessment tool and benefits to coaching and development. *Journal of Practical Consulting*, *5*(2), 19–28.

Stenholm, D., Corin Stig, D., Ivansen, L., & Bergsjö, D. (2019). A framework of practices supporting the reuse of technological knowledge. *Environment Systems & Decisions, 39*(2), 128–145. https://DOI.org/10.1007/s10669-019-09732-4. doi:10.100710669-019-09732-4

Stevens-Watkins, D., Perry, B., Pullen, E., Jewell, J., & Oser, C. B. (2014). Examining the associations of racism, sexism, and stressful life events on psychological distress among African American women. *Cultural Diversity and Ethnic Minority Psychology, 20*(4), 561-569. http://dx.doi.org.tcsedsystem.idm.oclc.org/10.1037/a003700

Stinson, P., & Ross, R. (2017). Inadequate training and supervision of police officers as a cause of police misconduct. *Journal of Criminal Law and Criminology, 107*, 885–922. doi:10.2139/ssrn.2596304

Stoneking, M. (2017). *An introduction to molecular anthropology.* Wiley.

Storlie, C. A., & Herlihy, B. E. (2022). *Counseling leaders & advocates: Strengthening the future of the profession.* American Counseling Association.

Storlie, C. A., Parker-Wright, M., & Woo, H. (2015). Multicultural leadership development: A phenomenological exploration of emerging leaders in counselor education. *Journal of Counselor Leadership & Advocacy, 2*, 154–169. doi:10.1080/2326716X.2015.1054078

Storlie, C. A., & Wood, S. M. (2014). Developing social justice leaders through Chi Sigma Iota: A phenomenological exploration of chapter leader experiences, Part 1. *Journal of Counselor Leadership & Advocacy, 1*(2), 160–180. doi:10.1080/2326716X.2014.935984

Stout, J., Beidel, D., Brush, D., & Bowers, C. (2020). Sleep disturbance and cognitive functioning among firefighters. *Journal of Health Psychology, 26*(12), 2248–2259. doi:10.1177/1359105320909861 PMID:32126834

Strada. (2020, June 10). *Public Viewpoint: COVID-19 Work and Education Survey.* http://stradaeducation.org/wp-content/uploads/2020/06/Public-Viewpoint-Report-Week-9.pdf

Strang, K. D. (2011). Leadership substitute and personality impact on time and quality in virtual new product development project. *Project Management Journal, 42*(1), 73–90. doi:10.1002/pmj.20208

Strategy: Create and implement the best strategy for your business. (2005). Harvard Business School Publishing Corporation.

Sue, D. W., Lin, A. I., & Rivera, D. P. (2009). Racial microaggressions in the workplace: Manifestation and impact. In J. L. Chin (Ed.), Diversity in mind and in action, Vol. 2: Disparities and competence (pp. 157–172). Santa Barbara, CA: Praeger.

Sue, D. W., Arredondo, P., & McDavis, R. J. (1992). Multicultural counseling competencies and standards: A call to the profession. *Journal of Multicultural Counseling and Development, 20*(2), 64–88. doi:10.1002/j.2161-1912.1992.tb00563.x

Sue, D. W., & Sue, D. (2008). *Counseling the culturally diverse: Theory and practice.* Wiley.

Su, L., Hsu, M. K., & Boostrom, R. E. Jr. (2020). From recreation to responsibility: Increasing environmentally responsible behavior in tourism. *Journal of Business Research, 109*, 557–573. doi:10.1016/j.jbusres.2018.12.055

Sullivan, P. (2016). Leadership in social work: Where are we? *Journal of Social Work Education, 52*(51), 551–561. doi:10.1080/10437797.2016.1174644

Sumińska, S., Nowak, K., Łukomska, B., & Cygan, H. (2020). Cognitive functions of shift workers: Paramedics and firefighters – an electroencephalography study. *International Journal of Occupational Safety and Ergonomics, 27*(3), 686–697. doi:10.1080/10803548.2020.1773117 PMID:32436781

Sumner, A., Hoy, C., & Ortiz-Juarez, E. (2020). *Estimates of the impact of COVID-19 on global poverty* (No. 2020/43). WIDER Working Paper.

Sung, S. Y., Cho, Y. J., & Kim, H. (2019). Exploring the Role of Return on Investment (ROI) in Human Resource Development. *Sustainability*, *11*(12), 3324. doi:10.3390u11123324

Sutton, J., & Austin, Z. (2015, May-June). Qualitative Research: Data Collection, Analysis, and Management. *The Canadian Journal of Hospital Pharmacy*, *68*(3), 226–231. doi:10.4212/cjhp.v68i3.1456 PMID:26157184

Szymanski, D., & Stewart, D. (2010). Racism and sexism as correlates of African American women's psychological distress. *Sex Roles*, *63*(3-4), 226–238. doi:10.100711199-010-9788-0 PMID:20352053

Tagulao, T. C. S., & Marques, J. L. (2022). The Application of Nudge Theory in Ensuring Change Acceptance in the Hospitality-Gaming Industry – A Case Analysis from Macau SAR, China. *2022 13th International Conference on E-business, Management and Economics*. 10.1145/3556089.3556121

Tams, C. (2018, February 22). *Small Is Beautiful: Using gentle nudges to change organizations*. Forbes. Retrieved from https://www.forbes.com/sites/carstentams/

Tamunomiebi, M. D., & Ehior, I. E. (2019). Diversity and ethical issues in the organizations. *International Journal of Academic Research in Business & Social Sciences*, *9*(2), 839–864. doi:10.6007/IJARBSS/v9-i2/5620

Tan, J. (2017, December 6). For women of color, the glass ceiling is actually made of concrete. *HuffPost*. https://www.huffpost.com/entry/for-women-of-color-the-gl_b_9728056

Tan, A. B. C., van Dun, D. H., & Wilderom, C. (2023). Lean innovation training and transformational leadership for employee creative role identity and innovative work behavior in a public service organization. *International Journal of Lean Six Sigma*. Advance online publication. doi:10.1108/IJLSS-06-2022-0126

Tanzil, D., & Beloff, B. R. (2006). Assessing impacts: Overview on sustainability indicators and metrics. *Environmental Quality Management*, *15*(4), 41–56. doi:10.1002/tqem.20101

Tarbouriech, S., Navarro, B., Fraisse, P., Crosnier, A., Cherubini, A., & Sallé, D. (2022). An admittance-based hierarchical control framework for dual-arm robots. *Mechatronics*, *86*(1), 1–10.

Tardi, C. (2022, June 26). *Utilitarianism: What it is, founders, and main principles*. https://www.investopedia.com/terms/u/utilitarianism.asp

Tarhini, El-Masri, Ali, & Serrano. (2016). Extending the UTAUT model to understand the customers' acceptance and use of internet banking in Lebanon: A structural equation modeling approach. *Information Technology & People*.

Tatar, U., Gheorghe, A. V., & Keskin, O. F. (2020). *Space Infrastructures: from Risk to Resilience Governance*. IOS Press.

Taticchi, P., & Demartini, M. (2020). *Corporate sustainability in practice: A guide for strategy development and implementation*. Springer. https://link.springer.com/book/10.1007/978-3-030-56344-8

Taylor, D. E. (2020). Mobilizing for environmental justice in communities of color: An emerging profile of people of color environmental groups. In *Ecosystem management: Adaptive strategies for natural resources organizations in the twenty-first century* (pp. 33–67). CRC Press.

TED Institute [tedinstitute]. (2014, December 22). *Dario Gil: Cognitive systems and the future of expertise*. Youtube. https://www.youtube.com/watch?v=0heqP8d6vtQ

Teetzen, F., Bürkner, P.-C., Gregersen, S., & Vincent-Höper, S. (2022). The mediating effects of work characteristics on the relationship between transformational leadership and employee well-being: A meta-analytic investigation. *International Journal of Environmental Research and Public Health, 19*(5), 3133. doi:10.3390/ijerph19053133 PMID:35270825

Temples, A., Simons, D., & Atkinson, M. (2019b). Training and development in the workplace. In R. Burke & C. Cooper (Eds.), *The Oxford Handbook of Training and Development* (pp. 377–394). Oxford University Press.

Temples, A., Simons, D., & Atkinson, M. (2019c). Strategic employee training and development in a changing world. *International Journal of Training and Development, 23*(1), 1–10.

Temples, C., Simons, R., & Atkinson, L. (2019a). Using a needs assessment model to drive information-driven training for small business owners. *Journal of Workplace Learning, 31*(5), 315–326. doi:10.1108/JWL-01-2019-0011

Thaler, R. H., & Sunstein, C. R. (2008). *Nudge: Improving Decisions about Health, Wealth, and Happiness.* Yale University Press.

The Association for Executives in Healthcare Applications, Data & Analytics (AEHADA) Reveals Bold New Plan for Uniting Digital Health Tech Leadership - Healthcare IT - CHIME. (2023, April 25). *Healthcare IT - CHIME.* https://chimecentral.org/the-association-for-executives-in-healthcare-applications-data-analytics-aehada-reveals-bold-new-plan-for-uniting-digital-health-tech-leadership/

The Atlanta Journal-Constitution. (2016, October 16). *Georgia police chief jailed for stealing from city.* Retrieved from https://www.ajc.com/news/state--regional-govt--politics/georgia-police-chief-jailed-for-stealing-from-city/b5cX9ZJ5K-5CYhGw8dzJP2H/

The Health Sector Cybersecurity Coordination Center (HC3). (2019, April 12). *A Cost Analysis of Healthcare Sector Data Breaches.* https://www.hhs.gov/sites/default/files/cost-analysis-of-healthcare-sector-data-breaches.pdf

The Miami Herald. (2018, June 25). *Biscayne Park police chief pleads guilty in federal false arrest case.* Retrieved from https://www.miamiherald.com/news/local/community/miami-dade/biscayne-park/article213682024.html

The State of Women-Owned Businesses. (2017). *American Express.* www.ventureneer.com/wp-content/uploads/2017/11/2017-AMEX-SWOB-FINAL

Theory of Constraints Institute. (n.d.). *Theory of Constraints of Eliyahu M. Goldratt.* https://www.tocinstitute.org/theory-of-constraints.html

Thibault, T., Gulseren, D. B., & Kelloway, E. K. (2019). The benefits of transformational leadership and transformational leadership training on health and safety outcomes. In *Increasing occupational health and safety in workplaces* (pp. 334–348). Edward Elgar Publishing. doi:10.4337/9781788118095.00027

Thomas, A., Hacker, J., & Hoxha, D. (2011). Gendered racial identity of Black young women. *Sex Roles, 64*(7-8), 30–42. doi:10.100711199-011-9939-y

Thomas, A., Witherspoon, K., & Speight, S. (2008). Gendered racism, psychological distress and coping styles of African American women. *Cultural Diversity & Ethnic Minority Psychology, 14*(3), 307–314. doi:10.1037/1099-9809.14.4.307 PMID:18954166

Thomas, E. M., & Grafsky, E. L. (2021). Appalachian church leaders: An interpretive phenomenological analysis study to understand how substance use impacts their communities. *Pastoral Psychology, 70*(4), 379–397. doi:10.100711089-021-00956-3

Thomas, F. N., Waits, R. A., & Hartsfield, G. L. (2007). The influence of Gregory Bateson: Legacy or vestige? *Kybernetes, 36*(7/8), 871–883. doi:10.1108/03684920710777397

Thorkildsen, A., & Ekman, M. (2013). The complexity of becoming collaborative planning and cultural heritage. *Journal of Cultural Heritage Management and Sustainable Development*, *3*(2), 148–162. doi:10.1108/JCHMSD-10-2012-0053

Thorpe, J., Gray, E., & Cartwright-Smith, L. (2016). Show Us the Data: The Critical Role Health Information Plays in Health System Transformation. *The Journal of Law, Medicine & Ethics*, *44*(4), 592–597. doi:10.1177/1073110516684800 PMID:28661247

Tichy, N. M., & Devanna, M. A. (1986). The transformational leader. *Training and Development Journal*.

Tijani, J. A., & Ilugbemi, A. O. (2015). Electronic Payment Channels in the Nigeria Banking Sector and Its Impacts on National Development. *Asian Economic and Financial Review*, *5*(3), 521–531. doi:10.18488/journal.aefr/2015.5.3/102.3.521.531

Toepoel, V. (2012). Effects of incentives in surveys. In L. Gideon (Ed.), *Handbook of survey methodology for the social sciences* (pp. 209–223). Springer. doi:10.1007/978-1-4614-3876-2_13

Toolis, E. E. (2021). Restoring the balance between people, places, and profits: A psychosocial analysis of uneven community development and the case for placemaking processes. *Sustainability (Basel)*, *13*(13), 7256. doi:10.3390u13137256

Towards Data Science. (2021). *How AI is Transforming Employee Training and Development*. https://towardsdatascience.com/how-ai-is-transforming-employee-training-and-development-4f36c7e55d4e

Training Industry, Inc. (2017). *Measuring the business impact of learning: Key findings from training industry's survey*. https://trainingindustry.com/research/measuring-the-business-impact-of-learning-key-findings-from-training-industrys-survey/

Travis, D. J., & Thorpe-Moscon, J. (2018) Day-to-day experiences of emotional tax among women and men of color in the workplace. *Catalyst*. https://www.catalyst.org/research/day-to-day-experiences-of-emotional-tax-among-women-and-men-of-color-in-the-workplace/

Tribune, T. (2014, April 6). *Payne Springs police chief pleads guilty to theft charges*. Retrieved from https://www.texastribune.org/2014/04/06/payne-springs-police-chief- pleads-guilty-theft/

Triguero, I., García-Gil, D., Maillo, J., Luengo, J., García, S., & Herrera, F. (2019). Transforming big data into smart data: An insight on the use of the k-nearest neighbors algorithm to obtain quality data. *Wiley Interdisciplinary Reviews. Data Mining and Knowledge Discovery*, *9*(2), e1289. doi:10.1002/widm.1289

Trujillo, J. T. E. (2010). Anthropology in Mexico and Spain: Industry, work and organizations. *Journal of Anthropology and Sociology: Turns*, *12*, 197–226.

Tu, J. C., & Yang, C. (2019). Key factors influencing consumers' purchase of electric vehicles. *Sustainability (Basel)*, *11*(14), 3863. doi:10.3390u11143863

Tundys, B. (2022). Business models for sustainable value creation in companies and financial markets. *Fostering Sustainable Business Models through Financial Markets*, 125-152. doi:10.1007/978-3-031-07398-4_6

Turkish Medical Association. (2018). *Hidden privatization in treatment services: city hospitals workshop report* [Tedavi hizmetlerinde gizli özelleştirme: şehir hastaneleri çalıştay raporu]. https://ato.org.tr/files/documents/0673367001518504406.pdf

Turner, R., & Avison, W. (2003). Status variations in stress exposure: Implications for the interpretation of research on race, socioeconomic status, and gender. *Journal of Health and Social Behavior*, *44*(4), 488–505. doi:10.2307/1519795 PMID:15038145

Tversky, A., & Kahneman, D. (1992, October). Advances in prospect theory: Cumulative representation of uncertainty. *Journal of Risk and Uncertainty*, *5*(4), 297–323. doi:10.1007/BF00122574

Tynes, B. (2022). *Council Post: The Importance Of Diversity And Inclusion For Today's Companies*. Forbes. https://www.forbes.com/sites/forbescommunicationscouncil/2022/03/03/the-importance-of-diversity-and-inclusion-for-todays-companies/

Uchendu, B., Nurse, J. R., Bada, M., & Furnell, S. (2021). Developing a cyber security culture: Current practices and future needs. *Computers & Security*, *109*, 102387. doi:10.1016/j.cose.2021.102387

ul Amin, S., & Kamal, Y. (2016). Impact of natural born leader qualities on the project team performance: The influences of demographics (gender and age). *International Journal of Management, Accounting, and Economics, 3*(5), 306-318.

Ulven, J. B., & Wangen, G. (2021). A systematic review of cybersecurity risks in higher education. *Future Internet*, *13*(2), 39. doi:10.3390/fi13020039

United Nations CEPA. (2019, October). *CEPA Strategy Guidance Note: Promotion of public sector workforce diversity*. https://unpan.un.org/sites/unpan.un.org/files/Draft%20strategy%20note%20%20-%20public%20sector%20workforce%20diversity.pdf

Urban, G., & Koh, K. (2013). *Ethnographic research on modern business corporation. In Annual Review Anthropology* (Vol. 42). Estados Unidos.

Urrea, F., & Celis, J. (2016). Los estudios laborales en Colombia entre 1993 y 2014. In Los estudios laborales en América Latina. Orígenes, desarrollo y perspectivas. Universidad Autónoma Metropolitana – Iztapalapa y Anthropos Editorial.

US Legal. (n.d.). *African American law and legal definition*. https://definitions.uslegal.com/a/african-americans/

Uysal, Y. (2020). The private sector incentive factors in public-private partnership model: Case of city hospitals. *MANAS Journal of Social Studies*, *9*(1), 386–401.

Vaidya, B., & Mouftah, H. (2020). Smart electric vehicle charging management for smart cities. *IET Smart Cities*, *2*(1), 4–13. doi:10.1049/iet-smc.2019.0076

Valdiviezo-Diaz, P., Ortega, F., Cobos, E., & Lara-Cabrera, R. (2019). A collaborative filtering approach based on Naïve Bayes classifier. *IEEE Access : Practical Innovations, Open Solutions*, *7*, 108581–108592. doi:10.1109/ACCESS.2019.2933048

Valentí, S. (2009). *Ideólogos, teorizantes y videntes*. Edward Burnett Tylor. https://www.filosofia.org/aut/svc/index.htm

Valentine, S., & Godkin, L. (2019). Moral intensity, ethical decision making, and whistleblowing intention. *Journal of Business Research*, *98*, 277–288. doi:10.1016/j.jbusres.2019.01.009

Van Leeuwen, E., Cohen, E., Collier-Baker, E., Rapold, C., Schäfer, M., Schütte, S., & Haun, D. (2018). The development of human social learning across seven societies. *Nature Communications*, *9*(1), 2076. doi:10.103841467-018-04468-2 PMID:29802252

Vasileiou, I., & Furnell, S. (2019). *Cybersecurity education for awareness and compliance*. IGI Global. doi:10.4018/978-1-5225-7847-5

Vasilenko, S. A. (2015). Police Leadership Misconduct: An Examination of the Problem and Potential Solutions. *Law Enforcement Executive Forum*, *15*(1), 3–13.

Vázquez, F., Pena, A., Sánchez-González, P., García-Solano, M., & Burgos, D. (2021). Augmented reality in surgical training: A systematic review and meta-analysis. *Surgical Innovation*, *28*(1), 77–88.

Vázquez, J., Arrebola, R., Mirón, F. J., Rojas-Sola, J. I., & Jiménez, M. F. (2021). Augmented reality as a tool for surgical training: A systematic review. *Surgical Endoscopy*, 1–11.

Veeraraghavan. (2016, September 10). A hybrid computational strategy to address WGS variant analysis in >5000 samples. *BMC Bioinformatics*, *17*(1), 361. doi:10.118612859-016-1211-6 PMID:27612449

Venkatesh. (2003). User Acceptance of Information Technology: Toward a Unified View. *MIS Quarterly, 27*(3), 425-478.

Venkatesh. (2012). Consumer Acceptance and Use of Information Technology: Extending the Unified Theory of Acceptance and Use of Technology. *MIS Quarterly, 36*(1), 157-178.

Verstraete, M., & Zarsky, T. (2022). Cybersecurity Spillovers. *Brigham Young University Law Review*, *47*(3), 929–999. https://www.proquest.com/scholarly-journals/cybersecurity-spillovers/docview/2677676009/se-2

Vik, M. B., Finnestrand, H., & Flood, R. L. (2022). Systemic Problem Structuring in a Complex Hospital Environment using Viable System Diagnosis–Keeping the Blood Flowing. *Systemic Practice and Action Research*, *35*(2), 203–226. doi:10.100711213-021-09569-6 PMID:33935483

Villarosa, L. (2020). Pollution is killing Black Americans. This community fought back. *The New York Times Magazine*, 28.

Visser, M. (2010). System dynamics and group facilitation: Contributions from communication Theory. *System Dynamics Review*, *23*(4), 453–463. doi:10.1002dr.391

Viswanathan, L., & Varghese, G. (2018). Greening of business: A step towards sustainability. *Journal of Public Affairs*, *18*(2), e1705. doi:10.1002/pa.1705

Vugt, M. V., Hogan, R., & Kaiser, R. B. (2008). Leadership, Followership, and Evolution. American Psychologist Association, 63(3), 182-196. doi:10.1037/0003-066X.63.3.182

Wade, N. (2010). Anthropology a science? Statement deepens a rift. *The New York Times*. https://www.nytimes.com/2010/12/10/science/10anthropology.html

Wagaman, M. A., Odera, S. G., & Fraser, D. V. (2019). A pedagogical model for teaching racial justice in social work education. *Journal of Social Work Education*, *55*(2), 351–362. doi:10.1080/10437797.2018.1513878

Waldron, I. R. (2021). *There's something in the water: Environmental racism in Indigenous & Black communities.* Fernwood Publishing.

Walker, D., & Nauman, B. (2017). *Ethnic and Racial Diversity at Asset Management Firms.* https://www.mminst.org/sites/default/files/file_attach/MMI-FF%20Diversity_in_Asset_Mgmt_Full-Report-FINAL.pdf

Walker, A., Argus, C., Driller, M., & Rattray, B. (2017). Repeat work bouts increase thermal strain for Australian firefighters working in the heat. *International Journal of Occupational and Environmental Health*, *21*(4), 285–293. doi:10.1179/2049396715Y.0000000006 PMID:25849044

Walker-Fraser, A. (2011, August). An H.R. perspective on executive coaching for organizational Learning. *International Journal of Evidence Based Coaching and Mentoring*, *9*(2).

Wang, J., Cheng, G., Chen, T., & Leung, K. (2019). Team creativity/innovation in culturally diverse teams: A meta-analysis. *Journal of Organizational Behavior*, *40*(6), 693–708. doi:10.1002/job.2362

Wang, P., & Johnson, C. (2018). Cybersecurity incident handling: A case study of the equifax data breach. *Issues in Information Systems*, *19*(3). Advance online publication. doi:10.48009/3_iis_2018_150-159

Wang, S., & Guo, X. (2019). Analysis of training program evaluation model based on ROI. In *3rd International Conference on Education and Multimedia Technology (ICEMT)* (pp. 266-270). IEEE.

Wang, V., Nnaji, H., & Jung, J. (2020). Internet banking in Nigeria: Cyber security breaches, practices and capability. *International Journal of Law, Crime and Justice*, 62, 100415. doi:10.1016/j.ijlcj.2020.100415

Wang, W., Huang, H., Yin, Z., Gadekallu, T. R., Alazab, M., & Su, C. (2022). Smart contract token- based privacy-preserving access control system for industrial Internet of Things. *Digital Communications and Networks*.

Ward, J. H. Jr. (1963). Hierarchical grouping to optimize an objective function. *Journal of the American Statistical Association*, 58(301), 236–244. doi:10.1080/01621459.1963.10500845

Ware, L. (2021). Plessy's Legacy: The Government's Role in the Development and Perpetuation of Segregated Neighborhoods. *The Russell Sage Foundation Journal of the Social Sciences : RSF*, 7(1), 92–109. doi:10.7758/rsf.2021.7.1.06

Warner, J., & Corley, D. (2017, May). *The women's leadership gap*. Center for American Progress. https://www.americanprogress.org/issues/women/reports/2017/05/21/432758/womens-leadership-gap/

Wasylyshyn, K. M. (2003). Coaching and executive character: Core problems and basic approaches. *Consulting Psychology Journal*, 55(2), 94–106. doi:10.1037/1061-4087.55.2.94

Watkins, C. E. (1990). Development of the psychotherapy supervisor. *Psychotherapy (Chicago, Ill.)*, 27(4), 553–560. doi:10.1037/0033-3204.27.4.553

Watkins, C. E., Hook, J. N., DeBlaere, C., Davis, D. E., Wilcox, M. M., & Owen, J. (2022). Extending multicultural orientation to the group supervision of psychotherapy: Practical applications. *Practice Innovations (Washington, D.C.)*, 7(3), 255–267. doi:10.1037/pri0000185

Watson, M. (2011). Doing well by doing good: Ray C. Anderson as evangelist for corporate sustainability. *Business Communication Quarterly*, 74(1), 63–67. doi:10.1177/1080569910395567

Watters, A. (2023). *Top 50 Cybersecurity Statistics, Figures, and Facts. CompTIA. World Economic Forum.* Cybersecurity. After reading, writing, and arithmetic, the 4th 'r' of literacy is cyber-risk. https://www.weforum.org/agenda/2020/12/cyber-risk-cyber-security-education

Webb, R., & Buratini, J. (2018). Global challenges for the 21st century: The role and strategy of the agri-food sector. *Animal Reproduction*, 13(3), 133–142. doi:10.21451/1984-3143-AR882

Weeks, J. (2004). *Unpopular culture: The ritual of complaint in a British bank*. University of Chicago Press.

Wenson, E. (2010, November). After-coaching leadership skills and their impact on direct reports: Recommendations for organizations. *Human Resource Development International*, 13(5), 607–616. doi:10.1080/13678868.2010.520485

Wenzelburger, G., & Wolf, F. (2015). *Policy theories in the crisis?* Academic Press. doi:10.1108/02683940610684409

Wetsman, N., Dwyer, D., & Herndon, S. (2023, May 11). Cyberattacks on hospitals are growing threats to patient safety, experts say. *ABC News*. https://abcnews.go.com/Health/cyberattacks-hospitals-growing-threats-patient-safety-experts/story?id–99115898

What Is Ergonomics (HFE) ? (n.d.). The International Ergonomics Association. Retrieved April 22, 2023, from https://iea.cc/about/what-is-ergonomics/

What Is the Classification of Business Organization According to Size. (2020, April 9). *Reference.* https://www.reference.com/business-finance/classification-business-organization-according-size-f9a66b9751457c58#:~:text=With%20respect%20to%20size%2C%20business,employ%20250%20people%20or%20more

Whelan, S. (2023, August 23). *Tackling Cybersecurity Threats in the Biotechnology Industry.* Technology Networks. Retrieved from: https://www.technologynetworks.com/informatics/blog/tackling-cybersecurity-threats-in-the-biotechnology-industry-364979#:~:text=Pharmaceutical%20companies%20are%20now%20routinely,in%20the%20last%20year%20alone

Whisenant, W., Lee, D. L., & Dees, W. (2015). Role congruity theory: Perceptions of fairness and sexism in sport management. *Public Organization Review*, *15*(4), 475–485. doi:10.100711115-014-0281-z

Wiafe, I., Koranteng, F. N., Wiafe, A., Obeng, E. N., & Yaokumah, W. (2020). The role of norms in information security policy compliance. *Information and Computer Security*, *28*(5), 743–761. doi:10.1108/ICS-08-2019-0095

Widyawati, L. (2019). A systematic literature review of socially responsible investment and environmental social governance metrics. *Business Strategy and the Environment*, *29*(2), 619–637. doi:10.1002/bse.2393

Wilkie, D. (2018, February 2). Number of older Americans at work has grown 35 percent. *SHRM*. https://www.shrm.org/resourcesandtools/hr-topics/employee-relations/pages/older-workers-.aspx

Williams-BellF.McLellanT.MurphyB. (2018). The effects of exercise-induced heat stress on cognitive function in firefighters. doi:10.7287/peerj.preprints.2524v1

Williams, D. R. (2018). Stress and the Mental Health of Populations of Color: Advancing Our Understanding of Race-related Stressors. *Journal of Health and Social Behavior*, *59*(4), 466–485. doi:10.1177/0022146518814251 PMID:30484715

Williams, D. R., & Williams-Morris, R. (2000). Racism and mental health: The African American experience. *Ethnicity & Health*, *5*(3/4), 243–268. doi:10.1080/713667453 PMID:11105267

Williams, J. B. (2018). Accountability as a Debiasing Strategy: Testing the Effect of Racial Diversity in Employment Committees. *Iowa Law Review*, *103*(4), 1593–1638.

Williams, L., & Quave, K. (2019). *Quantitative anthropology.* Elsevier.

Willis, D. G., Sullivan-Bolyai, S., Knafl, K., & Zichi-Cohen, M. (2016). Distinguishing features and similarities between descriptive phenomenological and qualitative description research. *Western Journal of Nursing Research*, *38*(9), 1–20. doi:10.1177/0193945916645499 PMID:27106878

Wilmoth, M. J., Menozzi, M. C., & Bassarsky, M. L. (2022). *Why population growth matters for sustainable development.* Academic Press.

Wilson, J. R., & Rutherford, A. (1989, December). Mental Models: Theory and Application in Human Factors. *Human Factors*, *31*(6), 617–634. doi:10.1177/001872088903100601

Women of Color in the United States. (2013). *Catalyst.* https://www.catalyst.org/knowledge/African-American-women

Wong, B. K. M., & Hazley, S. A. S. A. (2020). The future of health tourism in the industrial revolution 4.0 era. *Journal of Tourism Futures*, *7*(2), 267–272. doi:10.1108/JTF-01-2020-0006

Woo, H., Storlie, C. A., & Balrinic, E. R. (2016). Perceptions of professional identity development from counselor educators in leadership positions. *Counselor Education and Supervision*, *55*(4), 278–293. doi:10.1002/ceas.12054

Worku, G., Tilahun, A., & Tafa, M. A. (2016). The impact of electronic banking on customers' satisfaction in Ethiopian banking industry (The Case of Customers of Dashen and Wogagen Banks in Gondar City). *Journal of Business & Financial Affairs*, *5*(2), 1–18.

World Bank. (2016). *Public-private partnerships in health: World Bank group engagement in health PPPs.* World Bank Washington.

World Business Council for Sustainable Development. (2020). *What is sustainability?* Retrieved from https://www. wbcsd.org/Topics/Sustainability/What-is-Sustainability

World Economic Forum. (2020). *The Future of Jobs Report 2020.* https://www.weforum.org/reports/the-future-of-jobs-report-2020

World Economic Forum. (2023). *Global Cybersecurity Outlook 2023.* https://www3.weforum.org/docs/WEF_Global_Security_Outlook_Report_2023.pdf

Wright, J. E. II, & Merritt, C. C. (2020). Social equity and COVID-19: The case of African Americans. *Public Administration Review*, *80*(5), 820–826. doi:10.1111/puar.13251 PMID:32836453

Wright, S. (Ed.). (2005). *Anthropology of organizations.* Routledge.

Wright, W. J. (2021). As above, so below: Anti-Black violence as environmental racism. *Antipode*, *53*(3), 791–809. doi:10.1111/anti.12425

Wu. (2019). *Behavior Regularized Offline Reinforcement Learning.* doi:https://doi.org/10.48550/arXiv.1911.11361

Wu, T., Yuan, K., Yen, D., & Xu, T. (2019). Building up resources in the relationship between work-family conflict and burnout among firefighters: Moderators of guanxi and emotion regulation strategies. *European Journal of Work and Organizational Psychology*, *28*(3), 430–441. doi:10.1080/1359432X.2019.1596081

Xu, M., David, J. M., & Kim, S. H. (2018). The fourth industrial revolution: Opportunities and challenges. *International Journal of Financial Research, 9*(2), 90-95.

Xu, Y., & Zhang, R. (2020). Key staff management in M & A based on Lmx Theory. In *International Conference on Social Science and Education Research* (pp. 608-617). Academic Press.

Xu, J., Cooke, F. L., Gen, M., & Ahmed, S. E. (2018). *Proceedings of the twelfth international conference on management science and engineering management.* Springer.

Xu, K., Tang, C., Liu, Y., Li, C., Wu, J., Zhu, J., & Dai, L. (2007). Improving selection methods for evolutionary algorithms by clustering. *Third International Conference on Natural Computation (ICNC 2007), 3*, 742–746. 10.1109/ICNC.2007.440

Xu, X., Lu, Y., Vogel-Heuser, B., & Wang, L. (2021). Industry 4.0 and Industry 5.0—Inception, conception and perception. *Journal of Manufacturing Systems*, *61*, 530–535. doi:10.1016/j.jmsy.2021.10.006

Xygalatas, D. (2014). The biosocial basis of collective effervescence: An experimental anthropological study of a firewalking ritual. *Fieldwork in Religion*, *9*(1), 53–67. doi:10.1558/fiel.v9i1.53

Yang, F.-J. (2018). An implementation of naive bayes classifier. In *2018 International conference on computational science and computational intelligence (CSCI).* IEEE.

Yang, X., Zhuge, C., Shao, C., Huang, Y., Hayse Chiwing, G., Tang, J., & Sun, M. (2022). Characterizing mobility patterns of private electric vehicle users with trajectory data. *Applied Energy*, *321*, 119417. doi:10.1016/j.apenergy.2022.119417

Yan, Z. (2018). *Analyzing Human Behavior in Cyberspace.* IGI Global.

Yeo, L. H., & Banfield, J. (2022). Human factors in electronic health records cybersecurity breach: An exploratory analysis. *Perspectives in Health Information Management*, *19*(1). https://www.ncbi.nlm.nih.gov/pmc/articles/PMC9123525/ PMID:35692854

Yesiltas, A. (2020). Public private partnership in the health sector: An evaluation on city hospitals [Sağlık sektöründe kamu özel ortaklığı: Şehir hastaneleri üzerine bir değerlendirme]. *International Journal of Health Management and Strategies Research*, 6(1), 15–28.

Ye, Y., Shi, Y., Xia, P., Kang, J., Tyagi, O., Mehta, R., & Du, J. (2022). Cognitive characteristics in firefighter wayfinding Tasks: An Eye-Tracking analysis. *Advanced Engineering Informatics*, 53, 101668. doi:10.1016/j.aei.2022.101668

Yigitcanlar, T., & Cugurullo, F. (2020). The Sustainability of Artificial Intelligence: An Urbanistic Viewpoint from the Lens of Smart and Sustainable Cities. *Sustainability (Basel)*, 12(20), 8548. doi:10.3390u12208548

Yigitcanlar, T., Kamruzzaman, M., Foth, M., Sabatini-Marques, J., da Costa, E., & Ioppolo, G. (2019). Can cities become smart without being sustainable? A systematic review of the literature. *Sustainable Cities and Society*, 45, 348–365. doi:10.1016/j.scs.2018.11.033

Yilmaz, G. (2014). Let's Peel the Onion Together: An Application of Schein's Model of Organizational Culture. *Communication Teacher*, 28(4), 224–228. Advance online publication. doi:10.1080/17404622.2014.939674

Yılmaz, V., & Aktas, P. (2021). The making of a global medical tourism destination: From state-supported privatisation to state entrepreneurialism in healthcare in Turkey. *Global Social Policy*, 21(2), 301–318. doi:10.1177/1468018120981423

Yoo, I. T. (2022). Cybersecurity Crisscrossing International Development Cooperation: Unraveling the Cyber Capacity Building of East Asian Middle Powers Amid Rising Great Power Conflicts. *Korea Observer*, 53(3), 447–470. doi:10.29152/KOIKS.2022.53.3.447

Yuchong, L., & Qinghui, L. (2021). A comprehensive review study of cyber-attacks and cyber security; Emerging trends and recent developments. *Energy Reports*, 7, 8176–8186. doi:10.1016/j.egyr.2021.08.126

Yu, E. P., Luu, B. V., & Chen, C. H. (2020). Greenwashing in environmental, social and governance disclosures. *Research in International Business and Finance*, 52, 101192. doi:10.1016/j.ribaf.2020.101192

Yukl, G. (2013). *Leadership in organizations* (8th ed.). Prentice Hall.

Zaccone, M. C., & Pedrini, M. (2020). ESG factor integration into private equity. *Sustainability (Basel)*, 12(14), 5725. doi:10.3390u12145725

Zakariazadeh, A. (2022). Smart meter data classification using optimized random forest algorithm. *ISA Transactions*, 126, 361–369. doi:10.1016/j.isatra.2021.07.051 PMID:34389178

Zambon, I., Colantoni, A., & Salvati, L. (2019). Horizontal vs vertical growth: Understanding latent patterns of urban expansion in large metropolitan regions. *The Science of the Total Environment*, 654, 778–785. doi:10.1016/j.scitotenv.2018.11.182 PMID:30448668

Zamora, D. (n.d.). Anxiety at work: A career-busting condition. *WebMD*. https://www.webmd.com/anxiety-panic/features/anxiety-at-work

Zarei, J. (2019). Augmented reality in education and training: A literature review. *Journal of Education and Practice*, 10(22), 136–147.

Zare, S., Hemmatjo, R., Allahyari, T., Hajaghazadeh, M., Hajivandi, A., Aghabeigi, M., & Kazemi, R. (2018). Comparison of the effect of typical firefighting activities, live-fire drills and rescue operations at height on firefighters' physiological responses and cognitive function. *Ergonomics*, 61(10), 1334–1344. doi:10.1080/00140139.2018.1484524 PMID:29862929

Zeidan, R. (2022). Why don't asset managers accelerate ESG investing? A sentiment analysis based on 13,000 messages from finance professionals. *Business Strategy and the Environment*, 31(7), 3028–3039. doi:10.1002/bse.3062

Zhang, K., Guo, H., Yao, G., Li, C., Zhang, Y., & Wang, W. (2018). Modeling Acceptance of Electric Vehicle Sharing Based on Theory of Planned Behavior. *Sustainability (Basel)*, *10*(12), 1–14. doi:10.3390u10124686

Zhang, T., Raza, S. A., Ahmad, S., & Afzal, H. (2019). Augmented Reality and Virtual Reality in Education: Concepts, Applications and Trends. *Journal of Educational Technology & Society*, *22*(2), 255–267.

Zhang, Y., Balilionis, G., Casaru, C., Geary, C., Schumacker, R., Neggers, Y., Curtner-Smith, M. D., Richardson, M. T., Bishop, P. A., & Green, J. M. (2014). Effects of caffeine and menthol on cognition and mood during simulated firefighting in the heat. *Applied Ergonomics*, *45*(3), 510–514. doi:10.1016/j.apergo.2013.07.005 PMID:23891504

Zhang, Y., & Bednall, T. (2016). Antecedents of Abusive Supervision: A Meta-analytic Review. *Journal of Business Ethics*, *139*(3), 455–471. doi:10.100710551-015-2657-6

Zhao, J., Xi, X., Na, Q., Wang, S., Kadry, S. N., & Kumar, P. M. (2021). The technological innovation of hybrid and plug-in electric vehicles for environment carbon pollution control. *Environmental Impact Assessment Review*, *86*, 106506. doi:10.1016/j.eiar.2020.106506

Zhao, L., & Malikopoulos, A. A. (2020). Enhanced mobility with connectivity and automation: A review of shared autonomous vehicle systems. *IEEE Intelligent Transportation Systems Magazine*, *14*(1), 87–102. doi:10.1109/MITS.2019.2953526

Zhao, S., Zhang, D., Duan, Z., Chen, J., Zhang, Y., & Tang, J. (2018). A novel classification method for paper-reviewer recommendation. *Scientometrics*, *115*(3), 1293–1313. doi:10.100711192-018-2726-6

Zhao, Z., Anand, R., & Wang, M. (2019). Maximum Relevance and Minimum Redundancy Feature Selection Methods for a Marketing Machine Learning Platform. *2019 IEEE International Conference on Data Science and Advanced Analytics (DSAA)*, 442–452. 10.1109/DSAA.2019.00059

Zhong, F. (2022). Security Control for Time-Varying Delay Systems Based on Random Switching Moving Defense Method in Cyber-Physical Environment. *Journal of Physics: Conference Series*, *2381*(1), 012068. doi:10.1088/1742-6596/2381/1/012068

Zhonghai, Z. (2023). The ritual process of the canoe dragon boat in the Qingshui river basin. *Traditions and Cultural Heritage: Genesis, Reproduction, and Preservation*, 116-125.

Zhou, Y., Gohlke, D., Sansone, M., Kuiper, J., & Smith, M. P. (2022). Using Mapping Tools to Prioritize Electric Vehicle Charger Benefits to Underserved Communities (No. ANL/ESD-22/10). Argonne National Lab.

Zhu, W., Yan, R., & Song, Y. (2022). Analysing the impact of smart city service quality on citizen engagement in a public emergency. *Cities (London, England)*, *120*, 103439. doi:10.1016/j.cities.2021.103439 PMID:34539020

Zimmermann, V., & Renaud, K. (2021). The Nudge Puzzle. *ACM Transactions on Computer-Human Interaction*, *28*(1), 1–45. doi:10.1145/3429888

Ziolo, M. (2021). *Adapting and mitigating environmental, social, and governance risk in business*. IGI Global. doi:10.4018/978-1-7998-6788-3

Ziolo, M. (2021). Business Models of Banks Toward Sustainability and ESG Risk. In *Sustainability in Bank and Corporate Business Models: The Link between ESG Risk Assessment and Corporate Sustainability* (pp. 185–209). Springer International Publishing. doi:10.1007/978-3-030-72098-8_7

Zvonkovic, J. N. (2015). *Development of the attitudes toward integrated health care scale* [Master's thesis]. Southern Illinois University.

About the Contributors

Darrell Norman Burrell is a visiting scholar at the Samuel DeWitt Proctor Institute for Leadership, Equity, and Justice at Rutgers University. Dr. Burrell has two doctorate degrees and five graduate degrees. Dr. Burrell received his first doctoral degree in Health Education from A.T. Still University in 2010. In 2021, Dr. Burrell completed his 2nd doctorate, a Doctor of Philosophy (Ph.D.) in Cybersecurity Leadership and Organizational Behavior at Capitol Technology University, Laurel, MD. Dr. Burrell completed a Master of Arts in Interfaith Action at Claremont Lincoln University as a Global Peacemaker Fellow in 2016. He has an EdS (Education Specialist Post Master's Terminal Degree) in Higher Education Administration from The George Washington. He has two graduate degrees, one in Human Resources Management/Development and another in Organizational Management from National Louis University. Dr. Burrell has a graduate degree in Sales and Marketing Management from Prescott College. He has over 20 years of management, teaching, and training experience in academia, government, and private industry.

* * *

Paula Anderson is the Founder, President, and CEO of PACE Consulting, an award-winning Behavioral Health Counseling and Organizational Consulting firm. She is an organizational psychologist, a licensed clinical professional counselor in the state of Maryland, and a nationally certified counselor. Dr. Anderson is also certified to provide clinical supervision to post-master's level professional counselors. Dr. Anderson provides organizational consulting services in workplace wellness, stress management, leadership and team development, diversity, equity, and inclusion to her clients.

Foluso Ayeni is a distinguished faculty member specializing in Information Systems and Decision Sciences at the Metro State University, located in Minneapolis/St. Paul, Minnesota, USA. He is also a Visiting Professor at Capitol Technology University in Laurel, Maryland, USA, Makerere University Business School, Kampala, Uganda and Nigerian University of Technology & Management in Lagos, Nigeria. He also holds the position of membership and publicity secretary, at the Midwest Association for Information Systems USA. Prof. Ayeni is recognized as a member of the Pan-African Scientific Research Council, contributing to advancements in scientific research and also a member of the Educational Testing Service (ETS) graduate network. Additionally, Prof. Ayeni serves as the Vice-President of the Board of Trustees, at ICT University which has its foundation based in Louisiana, USA, with multiple campuses in developing countries. He also holds the role of Executive Secretary for Initiative and Partnerships at the African Society for ICTs (ASICTs). With a bachelor's and master's degree in management information systems from Covenant University, as well as a Ph.D. from Southern University and A&M College in Louisiana, USA, Prof. Ayeni is highly educated in his field. Prof. Ayeni possesses extensive experience in higher education teaching and research, both in Sub-Saharan Africa and the USA. Notably, he received the Best Graduate Oral Presentation award at the Louisiana Academy of Sciences Conference in March 2018. His dedication to community development earned him the honorary title of Honorary Mayor-President in the City of Baton Rouge that same year. In 2014, he secured a Research/Internship Grant from the Association of African Universities, targeting underserved communities. With exceptional communication, time management, writing, and creativity skills, Prof. Ayeni's research interests span across various areas, including Educational Technologies, Cybersecurity Education, Knowledge Management, Public Health Informatics, Operations Research, Business Intelligence, and Big Data Technology. Currently, Prof. Ayeni serves as a Co-Principal Investigator for numerous Grant writing activities at ICITD, USA, and the ICT University Foundation, USA. He has been actively involved in pioneering and completing several developmental projects in Sub-Saharan Africa, such as the Louisiana Board of Regents' implementation of an Artifact and Theorizing E-Democracy and Citizen Participation in Sub-Saharan Africa, as well as the establishment of the Southern University Health Information Technology Laboratory. Prof. Ayeni is an alumnus of the World Bank Youth Summit from 2016 to 2018 and has participated in various international conferences. He has also published his research in reputable peer-reviewed journals and served as a resource person for the Harvard University Global Health Catalyst Conference in 2019. Prof. Ayeni's expertise and contributions extend beyond academia, as he has served as a chair, co-chair, and technical committee member for several international conferences and workshops. His research work has been published in respected journals such as the International Journal of Computing and Informatics, IEEE Xplore Digital Library, Science Journal of Public Health, American Journal of Applied Mathematics, and Springer Lecture Notes in Computer Science, with more publications currently under review in reputable peer-reviewed journals. As an active member of prestigious organizations including the Institute of Electrical and Electronics Engineers (IEEE), American Educational Research Association (AERA), Louisiana Academy of Sciences (LAS), and National Center for Science Education (NCSE), Prof. Ayeni remains at the forefront of his field.

Maria Baez is an organizational leadership psychologist, consultant, and coach. She is the founder-CEO of Baez Consulting LLC, an organization specializing in organizational diagnostic and change management. She also provides leadership development and growth training, such as mindful leadership applied to diversity, inclusion, equity, ethics, organizational readiness, and emotional intelligence. She has a Bachelor of Industrial Engineering, a Master of Operations Management, and a second Master of Business Administration with a concentration in Human Resources. Her work extends to being an esteemed author while providing training in areas of Diversity, Leadership, Technology, and Business.

De'Anjelo Bradley, MS CFO MIFireE, is a chief fire officer. Mr. Bradley is a staff member at Vance Air Force Base, Oklahoma, Mr. Bradley also founded a youth mentor organization (Planned Purpose Program). He received a Master of Science from Columbia Southern University. Mr. Bradley served in the U.S. Air Force and was honorably discharged. He graduated from Oklahoma State University with an advanced associate degree in Municipal Fire Protection and; a bachelor's degree in Technology in Emergency Response Administration (Magna Cum Laude). He completed his Graduate Degree from Columbia Southern University in Occupational Safety and Health (Suma Cum Laude) and is currently pursuing his doctorate in Occupational Safety and Health from Capitol Technology University. From 2004 to 2014, Chief Bradley completed tours in Ecuador, Afghanistan, Iraq, and Kuwait as a contract/combat Firefighter – becoming the first and youngest African American fire chief of Prevention/Operations Fire Chief for the country of Iraq in support of Operation Iraq Freedom and Operation New Dawn. Also, the youngest to hold the Regional Fire Chief Position for central Iraq. He is a credentialed Chief Fire Officer (Center for Public Safety Excellence-CPSE), Member grade for the Institute of Fire Engineers (MIFireE), International Association of Fire Chiefs-Member, Oklahoma State Fire Chiefs Association-Member, International Association of Black Professional Firefighters-Member, National Fire Protection Association-Member, Black Chief officers Committee-Member. He continues to excel in his field. In 2020 Chief Bradley was recognized by the National Fire Heritage Fire Center as a "Who's who?" in fire Protection for his contributions to the fire service both nationally and internationally.

Kim L. Brown-Jackson holds a Doctorate of Business Administration (DBA) in Quality Systems Management with specialization in Health Systems, a Master's in Biomedical Sciences in Pathology and Molecular Oncology with additional course work in Ph.D. in same areas, an Associates in Biotechnology and Forensic Science, an executive professional certificate in MBA, and Bachelor's in Biological Sciences with a cluster minor in Business Administration. She holds numerous professional certifications. Dr. Brown-Jackson has over 25 years of experience as a practitioner, academician, quality healthcare leader and performance and learning strategist guiding business process improvement through biomedical services, public health, advanced drug development, telemedicine/ telehealth initiatives, and leadership development. Specializes in regulatory compliant industries (biologics, medical device, pharmaceutical, financial, and aviation safety). She has taught at the collegiate, government, and corporate levels. She has contributed to over 6 book chapters, over 30 peer-reviewed journals, and delivered numerous presentations at conferences and on panels.

Leeshawn "Sarah" Buhr is a first-year doctoral candidate at Marymount University, studying business intelligence. She is an Army veteran whose hope is to bridge the gap between the military and civilian workforces with her research.

Sharon L. Burton is a multifaceted professional excelling as a dissertation chair, faculty member, facilitator, author, speaker, consultant, and TV co-host. With an extensive portfolio of over 100 scholarly publications and participation in 30+ professional conferences, Dr. Burton is an accomplished expert. Her proficiency extends to leadership, agile solutions, and fostering collaborations, rendering her a problem-to-solution value catalyst. She adeptly decodes technical intricacies for non-technical audiences and senior leadership while offering business process insights to technical teams. Dr. Burton's leadership spans cross-functional, virtual, and on-site teams. Dr. Burton's illustrious background encompasses roles such as Chief Learning & Compliance Officer-Administrator Representative for the Board of Trustees; Chief Learning Officer; Chief Learning Officer, Compliance, and Information Assurance Officer; Senior Change Management Officer; Senior Business Process Engineer; and Senior Program/Project Manager. Her influence even extends to cyber-security boards. As a mentor and coach, she champions learning advocacy. Dr. Burton's academic pursuits include a Ph.D. in Cybersecurity Leadership, a DBA in Quality Systems Management (focused on Business Process Improvement), and two MBA degrees in Human Resources Management and Management. Complemented by various certifications, Dr. Burton welcomes speaking engagements. Further insights can be found at .

Songul Cinaroglu is Associate Professor in the Department of Health Care Management at Hacettepe University, Turkey. She is a former visiting researcher at the Karlsruhe Institute of Technology (KIT)-Steinbuch Center for Computing (SCC)-Germany, University of Hamburg-Center for Health Economics (HCHE)-Germany, The University of Michigan-USA and of the University of Alabama-USA. Her main research interest is health economics, policy and outcomes research.

Jennifer Ferreras-Perez is a Doctor of Science in Cybersecurity student at Marymount University. She holds a Bachelor's degree in Forensic Pharmacology and two Master's degrees in Cybersecurity and IT. Her research focuses on the human factors of cybersecurity, particularly on how human cognitive limitations can impact cyber hygiene. Apart from her dissertation research, Jennifer has conducted studies on the benefits of implementing password managers in small and medium-sized enterprises, the impact of diversity in cybersecurity, and AI security risks in healthcare. Jennifer's academic journey began with her undergraduate studies in Forensic Pharmacology, which sparked her interest in the intersection of science and technology. She later pursued a career in cybersecurity and earned two master's degrees in the field. Her current research on human factors in cybersecurity is motivated by a desire to understand how individuals can be better equipped to protect themselves and their organizations from cyber threats. Jennifer's work has the potential to contribute significantly to the field of cybersecurity and promote safer digital practices for all.

Jesus Galvan graduated from school of physical and mathematical sciences (FCFM-UANL), CISSP, with technical experience in configuration and maintenance of network equipment and security as well as experience in compliance, vulnerability management and auditing. Knowledge in ethical hacking, volunteer in cyber security conferences and amateur astronomer.

John Grady is a Licensed Professional Counselor (LPC), Licensed Clinical Alcohol and Drug Counselor (LCADC), International Certified Clinical Supervisor (ICCS), Approved Clinical Supervisor (ACS), and National Certified Supervisor (NCC) who has earned a Doctor of Philosophy (PhD) in Organizational Leadership. A board-certified counselor and practitioner of Eye Movement Desensitization and Reprocessing (EMDR), Dr. Grady specializes in the treatment of trauma-related disorders and addiction disorders. He uses EMDR, along with other evidence-based treatments such as Cognitive Behavioral Therapy (CBT) and Rational Emotive Behavior Therapy (REBT), to help clients address a range of mental health challenges that include anxiety, mood, and obsessive-compulsive disorders. Dr. Grady's clinical experiences include working at nearly all levels of the Continuum of Care and with most mental health, substance abuse, and dual diagnosis client populations. In each of these levels of care, Dr. Grady has served as a counselor, clinical supervisor, and program director. Workplace settings include community agency, university, and medical organizations. Although he has worked with clients ranging from childhood to older adulthood, Dr. Grady currently works only with adults and older adults in individual, couples, family, and group counseling programs. Dr. Grady's academic journey includes earning an Associate in Arts degree in Liberal Arts/Education, a Bachelor of Science degree in Management Science, a Master of Arts degree in Counselor Education, and a Doctor of Philosophy in Organizational Leadership. His dissertation explored how clinical counseling supervisors developed their organizational leadership skills. Dr. Grady has taught in multiple graduate school programs (i.e. Counselor Education, Counseling for Mental Health and Wellness, and Human Services) at prestigious universities (e.g. New York University, Purdue University Global) since 2015 and has also taught undergraduate psychology courses. Additionally, Dr. Grady has co-authored the biography of boxing legend, Gerry Cooney ("Gentleman Gerry: A Contender in the Ring, a Champion in Recovery").

Jo Hall is a graduate of the United States Military Academy at West Point, the University of Maryland Global Campus and current DBA student at Marymount University in Arlington, Virginia.

Allison Huff, as an assistant professor in UArizona's Department of Family & Community Medicine, focuses on technology to address complex disorders, particularly focusing on how technology impacts SDOH. Previously, she was a behavioral health clinician working with individuals with serious mental illnesses and substance use disorders. Dr. Huff is PI and Co-I on several NSF, HRSA, and industry sponsored grants and leads clinical trials and research programs. She also is a mentor for several under-served pre-professional health and pre-med students each summer and through the academic year. Dr. Huff's Doctor of Health Education is from A.T. Still University, her Master of Education in Instructional Technology is from University of Oklahoma, and her Bachelor's in Psychology is from University of West Florida.

Chinyere Igwe is a recent Ph.D. graduate of the ICT University, Cameroon and a senior government official at the Nigerian Ministry of Information and Communications.

Angel J. Jones began his 24-year cybersecurity career as a service member with the U.S. Department of Homeland Security, Coast Guard, investigating cybercrime. His expertise has made him the go-to subject matter expert for complex cybersecurity and cyber investigation matters. Dr. Jones' experience includes serving as the Chief Information Security Officer for several global firms and senior executive roles in the federal government, proactively protecting organizations from adversarial dynamic cyber threats. Dr. Jones is an adjunct professor at the University of Virginia and an advisory board member for the Boston University Center for Cybercrime Investigation and Cybersecurity. Further, Dr. Jones holds several industry certifications, including the Certified Information Systems Security Professional (CISSP), Certified Information Security Manager (CISM), Certified Information Systems Auditor (CISA), Certified Chief Information Security Officer (CCISO), Certified in Risk and Information Systems Control (CRISC), Certified Data Privacy Solutions Engineer (CDPSE), Certified Information Privacy Manager (CIPM), Certified Ethical Hacker (CEH), EnCase Certified Examiner (EnCE), Digital Forensics Certified Practitioner (DFCP), AWS Certified Solutions Architect – Professional, AWS Certified Security - Specialty and Project Management Professional (PMP).

Eugene J. M. Lewis completed his Doctor of Philosophy (PhD) in Technology with an emphasis in Marketing in March of 2021 from Capitol Technology University. Dr. Lewis is the former Assistant Professor of Marketing at Oakwood University from 2005 to 2010. Furthermore, he serves as an Adjunct Professor teaching courses in the area Logistics/Supply Chain Management, Marketing, and Information Systems. He has worked in Academia for more than 15 years as a part-time and full-time professor. Currently, he serves as an Adjunct Professor for Edward Waters University, Lindsey Wilson University, and Alabama A&M University. Furthermore, he serves as a United States civil servant as the International Program Manager in the Aviation Industry in the Cargo CH-47 Program Office for the Department of the Army working in the Foreign Military Sales (FMS) arena. He has served the Department of Defense

(DOD) for more than 10 years. He has had the opportunity to work with many government officials and dignitaries in several countries all over the world.

Victor Mbarika is Stallings Distinguished International Scholar/MIS professor at East Carolina University(ECU) within the University of North Carolina System, in Greenville, North Carolina, USA. Prof. Mbarika is Founder and President, Board of Trustees, of The Information and Communication Technology University(ICT University), with multiple campuses in developing countries. Through his leadership as Board Chair, the ICT University was named Best University in Cameroon and also Best University in Central Africa, in terms of innovative use of ICTs in higher education. He is a philanthropist and has funded multiple ICT projects and scholarships worldwide. He is founder of the International Center for Information Technology and Development. Prof. Mbarika serves (or has served) as Visiting Professor at several Universities worldwide and is currently Visiting Leo Endowed Professor and Visiting Legacy Endowed Chair at Legacy University. He is an ICT consultant and holds a BSc in MIS from the U.S. International University, MSc in MIS from the University of Illinois at Chicago, and Ph.D. in MIS from Auburn University, USA. He completed his BSc, MSc, and Ph.D., all in five years. Prof. Mbarika is recipient of three Lifetime Achievement Awards in higher education. He has authored over 250 academic publications in the form of books, peer reviewed journals, conference proceedings and book chapters. Every year, he serves as Keynote Speaker at multiple conferences worldwide. Much of his research is on technology transfer in resource-poor settings. He was cited as being "in the forefront of academic research into ICT implementation in Africa, and has provided a theoretically-informed framework for understanding ICTs in less developed countries..." His scholarly publications have appeared in several of the "Basket of Top Eight" Information Systems journals. This includes *Journal of the Association for Information Systems (IS), European Journal of IS, IS Journal, Journal of Information Technology*, as well as in top ranked allied journals such as *IEEE Transactions on Engineering Mgmt, IEEE Spectrum and Communications of the ACM*. His work has also appeared in major media outlets such as Reuters, The Associated Press, and BBC. He has chaired (supervised) over 25 PhD students that have become University Presidents, Deans, Full Professors, Department Chairs and top government officials. He has received multiple grants (over $4 million) from the National Science Foundation, NASA, KPMG, Microsoft, African Development Bank, and other donors. The Voice Newspaper named Prof. Mbarika as Cameroon's Hero of the five years spanning 2016-2021; The Guardian Post newspaper named him as one of few "Cameroonians that moved mountains in 2021;" INSPIRE Magazine named Prof. Mbarika as one of the top 10 personalities in the diaspora influencing Cameroon and one of the top 100 overall. Prof. Mbarika received the prestigious U.S. State Department Fulbright grant five times to mentor scholars from developing nations. He is Founding Editor-in-Chief of The African Journal of Information Systems and senior board member of several journals. Prof. Mbarika is a Lifetime Member of the Beta Gamma Sigma Honor Society. He is a member of several academic associations, including Africa's first distinguished member of the Association of Information Systems. He holds over 30 academic excellence awards and has been featured on the cover page of several newspapers and magazines highlighting his research and consulting activities.

Stacey L. Morin is a Business Unit Chief Financial Officer in the Financial Services Industry working at the world's fifth-largest financial institution. Most of her career, 25+ years, has been in the Financial Services industry. She has a Bachelor's in Accounting from Eastern Michigan University – 1995 and MBA Finance from California State University Northridge – 2007. She holds several FINRA securities licenses that are required for her role. She is currently a Doctoral candidate with an expected graduation date of 2025. She writes and conducts research on diversity, equity, and inclusion in business sector.

Calvin Nobles is a Cybersecurity Professional and Human Factors Engineer with more than 25 years of experience. He is a Department Chair and Associate Professor at the Illinois Institute of Technology. He retired from the Navy and worked in the Financial and Services Industry for several years. He authored a book on the integration of technologically advanced aircraft in general aviation. He serves on the Cybersecurity Advisory Board at Stillman College and the Intelligence and National Security Alliance Cyber Council. He is a Cybersecurity Fellow at Harvard University.

Marwan Omar's academic career has consistently focused on applied, industry-relevant cyber security, Data Analytics, machine learning, application of AI to cyber security and digital forensics research and education that delivers real-world results. He brings a unique combination of industry experience as well as teaching experience gained from teaching across different cultures and parts of the world. He has an established self-supporting program in machine learning application to cyber security. He has established a respectable research record in AI and cyber security exemplified in the dozens of published papers and book chapters that have gained recognition among researchers and practitioners (more than 272 Google scholar citations thus far). He is actively involved in graduate as well as undergraduate machine learning education including curriculum development and assessment. Dr. Omar has recently published two books with Springer on Machine Learning and Cyber Security and has also published research with IEEE conference on Sematic Computing. Additionally, Dr. Omar holds numerous industry certifications including Comptia Sec+, ISACA CDPSE, EC-Council Certified Ethical Hacker, and SANS Advanced Smartphone Forensics Analyst. Dr. Omar has been very active and productive in both academia as well as the industry and he is currently serving as an associate professor of cyber security at Illinois Institute of Technology.

Jessica Parker is a student in the Doctor of Business Administration in Business Intelligence program at Marymount University, with an expected completion of December 2025. With over 25 years of Information Technology experience in executive leadership, financial management, project management, software quality assurance, business analysis, and data visualization, she has cultivated a diverse set of skills. From a global perspective, she has worked with Fortune 500 companies and multinational teams in countries including Australia, Brazil, China, England, France, Germany, India, Ireland, Italy, the Philippines, Switzerland, and Uruguay.

William L. Quisenberry is an Educator, Mentor, Coach, Researcher, and Consultant that seeks to use a servant approach to helping others achieve their goals. Dr. Quisenberry resides in Lexington, KY, and has a diverse background that includes studying and practicing within the field of business administration, coordinating implementation projects for Fortune 500 clients, managing and overseeing vendors/suppliers, operations management, project management, marketing, research analysis, consulting, and teaching at the collegiate level. Dr. Quisenberry has collaborated and worked on projects with a variety of major organizations in the marketplace that include: Lexmark International, Halliburton, Branch Banking and Trust, The U.S. Department of Veterans Affairs, Wal-Mart, The U.S. Army Corps of Engineers, Accenture, IBM, Best Buy, Lockheed Martin, John Hancock Financial, and the World Trade Center Association. Dr. Quisenberry holds a Bachelor of Business Administration (BBA) degree in Finance, a BBA in Marketing, as well as a Master of Business Administration degree from Sullivan University's Graduate School of Business, and a Post-Graduate Certification in Forensic Accounting from Davenport University. He also possesses a Doctor of Business Administration (DBA) degree with a specialization in Leadership from Walden University. Dr. Quisenberry's dissertation was titled, "Common Characteristics and Attributes of Self-Managed Virtual Teams." He was nominated for Walden University's Outstanding Research award, and his study was also nominated for the University's Doctoral Study of the Year award. Dr. Quisenberry strives to remain active in his local community. He currently serves on the Board of Directors for Fostering Goodwill, an agency based in Lexington, KY that seeks to provide resources, training, and mentorship to young adults who have aged out of the foster care system. He serves with multiple grassroots organizations that strive to build relationships, offer training, mentorship, programs, and services to various individuals or communities facing difficult challenges, such as at-risks youth, marginalized communities, and homeless populations. He also collaborates with several international organizations on similar outreach projects and initiatives. Dr. Quisenberry's background and current efforts help to shape his teaching approach, which emphasizes servitude and transformational leadership. He views his Learners as clients who all have something to contribute to the classroom, society, and life in general. With this in mind, he seeks to create an international community of servant, transformational leaders who are willing to leverage their experiences, training, education, and research to be positive social change agents.

Emad Rahim is an award-winning author, educator, entrepreneur, Fulbright Scholar and TEDx Speaker. He currently serves as the Kotouc Endowed Chair for the Project Management Center of Excellence at Bellevue University, Associate Professor at the College of Science and Technology, and Adjunct Faculty at Cornell University. He formerly served as the University Dean of Business at Colorado Tech and Director of Venture Connect at Morrisville State College, and Entrepreneur-in-Residence at Oklahoma State University, Visiting Scholar at Rutgers University and Syracuse University.

Dana-Marie Ramjit is a 2019 graduate of Walden University. She has been an educator for the past 14 years with several universities. Dr. Ramjit is currently a professor at Adler University, Vancouver Canada. In 2009 Dr. Ramjit completed a Master of Science degree in International Relations with the Institute for International Relations at the University of the West Indies. She engaged in research on globalization and the mass media. Dr. Ramjit has a Ph.D. in Public Policy and Administration with a specialization in international non-governmental organizations. Her dissertation research was on the relationship between the NGO-state relationship in a postinternational world. Dr. Ramjit's research interests are postinternationalism, contemporary governance, heterarchy, and leadership. Dr. Ramjit is the founder of the non-profit organization the Sapphire Project, aimed at poverty reduction, education, equality, and brining hope to poor and marginalized groups in society. Dr. Ramjit is a published author with the Public Administration Times, E-International Relations, and the International Affairs Forum.

Kevin Richardson occupies the role of Associate Professor of Business & Technology at Edward Waters University. His professional journey is marked by notable achievements, as he is a recognized Certified Diversity Professional and a Certified Trainer. With an impressive academic background, Dr. Richardson boasts two doctoral degrees and three graduate degrees. In 2016, he successfully attained his inaugural doctorate degree specializing in Operations and Quality Management Systems from The National Graduate School located in Washington, DC. Subsequently, in 2021, Dr. Richardson secured a distinguished Philosophy of Doctorate (Ph.D.) in Technology Management of Information Systems from Capitol Technology University situated in Laurel, MD. He also holds a Master of Science in Natural Resources Economics and Corporate Sustainability from Virginia Tech University in Blacksburg, VA. Dr. Richardson's academic pursuits extend to a Master's degree in Information Systems Engineering Management from Harrisburg Science & Technology University in Harrisburg, PA. He further diversified his knowledge with a third master's degree in Counseling Psychology obtained from Springfield College in Charleston, SC. Possessing a wealth of experience spanning over 25 years, Dr. Richardson has contributed significantly to the realms of management, teaching, and training across academia, government, and private industries. His tenure as an educator encompasses various institutions including Edward Waters University, Bethune Cookman University, Allen University, The National Graduate School of Quality Management, and Morris College.

Busra Saylan completed her master's degree from Hacettepe University, Faculty of Economics and Administrative Sciences, Department of Health Management. Her thesis is "Comparison of Health Professionals' Attitudes Towards Integrated Health Campuses (City Hospitals)" on city hospitals, which is one of the most up-to-date health policies in Turkey. She is currently continuing her education as a doctoral student at Hacettepe University. Her main research interests are big data, health informatics, and data analytics in integrated health campuses and health services.

Delores Springs served in healthcare, human services, and nonprofit leadership for over twenty years. Dr. Springs' compassion and drive for perfection are her strongest attributes. She specializes in designing competence building strategies and solutions in nonprofit, healthcare, government, academic, for-profit, and human service-oriented sectors. Dr. Springs has a doctorate in Strategic Leadership with a concentration in Strategic Foresight, a master's degree in Human Services and Executive leadership, and a bachelor's degree in Psychology. Along with her educational background, she holds specializations in Healthcare Organization Operations, Building Foundations in Global Health, and in other areas that include Lean Six Sigma, Diversity & Inclusion, Project Management, and other certifications in business and leadership.

Omar Vargas-González is Professor and Head of Systems and Computing Department at Tecnologico Nacional de Mexico Campus Ciudad Guzman, professor at Telematic Engineering at Centro Universitario del Sur Universidad de Guadalajara with a master degree in Computer Systems. Has been trained in Innovation and Multidisciplinary Entrepreneurship at Arizona State University (2018) and a Generation of Ecosystems of Innovation, Entrepreneurship and Sustainability for Jalisco course by Harvard University T.H. Chan School of Health. At present conduct research on diverse fields such as Entrepreneurship, Economy, Statistics, Mathematics and Information and Computer Sciences. Has colaborated in the publication of over 20 scientific articles and conducted diverse Innovation and Technological Development projects.

Yoshino W. White is a multi-talented professional with a diverse skill set. As an adjunct faculty professor and teacher, she demonstrates expertise in project management, technology, and agile solutions. As a facilitator and speaker, she helps to guide discussions or give presentations on various topics related to Industrial Engineering, and Quality and Regulatory Affairs. Her experience leading and transforming organizations confirms her strong business acumen and skill at identifying problems and implementing solutions. Her ability to communicate technical information to non-technical audiences and senior leadership also highlights her excellent communication skills. Overall, Professor White is a well-rounded individual with a range of skills and experiences that could be valuable in various contexts. Professor White has held the positions of Senior Manager, and Director of Quality – Product Development. She has also served as a head master of a learning program. She supports numerous others as mentor and coach. The following degrees are held: MSc. Industrial Engineering, and BS in Industrial Engineering. She holds the following certifications: Project Management Professional (PMP), Project Management Institute- Agile Certified Professional, and Certified SAFe® 4 Agilist. Professor White is available to speak at conferences, forums, and other initiatives.

Jorja Wright is a logistics manager for the Dept. of the Army. She focuses on maintaining optimal inventory stock posture, cultivating effective organizational processes, and fostering sustainable employee relationships. She received her doctorate degree in Executive Leadership from University of Charleston-West Virginia. She earned her MBA from the Nathan M. Bisk College of Business at Florida Institute of Technology, concentrating in healthcare management. Finally, she has a bachelor's degree in biology and a minor in chemistry from University of Alabama-Huntsville. During her graduate school tenure, Dr. Wright has published over 20 various peer-reviewed articles and conference proceedings on leadership and cybersecurity, to healthcare management and logistics. Dr. Wright is an innovative and talented professional with a diverse educational background focused on implementing policies that improve agile strategies, organizational sustainability and promoting scholarship within the business discipline.

Index

A

Adaptive Security Systems 28, 31

Affect 3, 13-14, 20-21, 23, 31-32, 34, 40-42, 49, 52, 54, 58, 75, 77, 81, 85, 95, 104, 110, 119, 129, 143, 146, 162, 201-203, 211, 217, 219, 246, 256, 258, 260, 262, 272, 296, 344

African American 15, 18, 20, 23-24, 55-60, 62, 65, 67-72, 159

Anthropology 267, 269-283, 285

Artificial Intelligence 32, 34, 96, 161, 206, 266, 271, 286, 289, 292-293, 296, 299-301, 303, 330-331, 347, 359

Audits 77, 206, 215-216, 218

Augmented Reality 286, 289, 294-296, 298-299, 301, 303

Authentication 9, 30, 76, 91, 140-146, 149-155, 208

Automation 74-75, 266

B

Business 11-13, 27-28, 32, 47, 49, 51, 63, 67, 69-77, 80, 82-86, 97, 100-102, 104-105, 121-130, 132, 134-139, 144, 154-156, 158, 161, 169, 171, 174-175, 178, 184-185, 187-191, 195, 197, 201-202, 205-207, 211-213, 215, 218, 220-221, 226, 233-234, 236-237, 240, 246, 250, 257, 261, 263, 265, 270-271, 273-274, 279, 285-288, 291-295, 297-298, 300-301, 303-304, 315-316, 319, 330, 332-342

Business Continuity 73-74, 76-77, 82-85, 134

Business Strategy 75, 136-138, 332, 340, 342

C

City Hospital 343, 346, 350, 357, 362

Clinical Supervision 171-172, 174, 188, 191-193, 195

Cognitive Cities 157-160, 164-165, 167-169

Community Psychology 13

Control Theory 28-31, 34, 36-37, 41-44

Corporate Community Relations 332

Corporate Social Responsibility (CSR) 47, 54, 136

Cost of Investment 304

Critical Diversity 46, 50

Critical Theory 46-52, 54

Culture 3, 5-12, 22, 25, 47, 49-50, 54, 58, 63, 80, 90-91, 93-98, 100-102, 117-118, 124-125, 127-129, 131-132, 134, 168, 172, 194, 197, 199-200, 203-205, 207, 209, 211-213, 215, 217-219, 223, 225-229, 231-233, 236-237, 244-247, 250, 271-274, 276-278, 280-285, 297, 306-309, 312-315, 317

Cyber Security 12, 28-37, 39-44, 77-78, 98, 101, 156, 199, 212

Cyber Security Warfare 28-34, 36-37, 39-43

Cyber-Biosecurity 1

Cybersecurity Risk Management 1-4, 10-11, 82-83, 98

D

Data Transformation 318, 322

Deal and Kennedy Culture 89-90, 96

Decision-Making 5-6, 21, 47, 73, 75-77, 79-80, 85-87, 89, 93-96, 98, 111-112, 131, 143-144, 167, 189, 199-200, 203-204, 219-220, 222-223, 226, 228, 231, 236, 238, 244, 246, 248-249, 262, 294, 304, 311, 323, 335-336

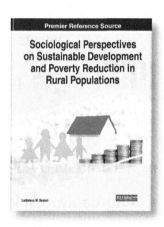

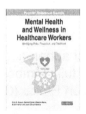

Printed in the United States
by Baker & Taylor Publisher Services